Sustainable Practices
Your Handbook for Effective Action
2025 Edition

Major Revision: 1
Minor Revision: 8

Written by **Fred Horch**

Edited by **Peggy Siegle**

Revision 25.1.8 — ISBN 979-8-9928169-0-7 — Last update: April 18, 2025

At a Glance

Where to start	Twenty Pivotal Practices, page 3
How to achieve sustainability goals	Pathways and Strategies, page 13
How to practice sustainability	Practice Guides, page 42
How to improve practices	Improving Practices, page 503
How to finance sustainability projects	Financing Projects, page 505
Mathematical definitions and formulas	Math, page 508
Scientific facts and theories	Science, page 510
Current and emerging sustainable technologies	Technology, page 541
Sustainability concepts and history	Sustainability Concepts, page 562
Definitions of sustainability terms	Glossary, page 565
Information by keyword	Index, page 570

© 2025 Sustainable Practice
Brunswick, Maine

www.suspra.com

About This Handbook

The more you know, the more power you have to make our world better for everyone. You now have at hand powerful knowledge. Use it well!

We're constantly revising this handbook
to keep up with the best thinking in sustainability.

Visit our companion website for the most up-to-date revision,
along with comprehensive resources and apps for practical sustainability.

www.suspra.com

Acknowledgments

Thank you to all the customers and staff of F.W. Horch Sustainable Goods & Supplies, who asked great questions and accomplished inspiring projects that really did make a positive difference–this handbook started out as notes and observations I kept over many years, talking to people who were out there saving our planet, not just worrying about it. There was never a dull day in the store thanks to the parade of colorful characters who challenged everything I thought I knew and gave me unvarnished, honest reviews of every product and service we sold.

I also want to thank my family, especially my wife Hadley for putting up with my decades-long obsession with all things sustainable. There is no one I would rather bike 75 miles with and then climb into a tent with in the pouring rain so we could volunteer to sort garbage and compost the next day at the Common Ground Country Fair.

Thank you to all the reviewers of various versions of this manuscript, especially my father-in-law, Ray Wilson, for many conversations and close readings of draft after draft. His book, *Process Mastering*, was especially influential in my thinking through how to accomplish all of the sustainability projects I've done in residential and commercial properties. And speaking of those projects, thank you to my business partners, Pat Coon and Keith Barkhau, at Spark Applied Efficiency, who have carried our electrical contracting business while I've been distracted getting this handbook over the finish line more than twenty years after first conceiving the idea for it.

Finally, I want to acknowledge the influence that the *Whole Earth Catalog* and *The Hitchhiker's Guide to the Galaxy* had on me growing up in the 1970s as I imagined what life could be in the far future–the year 1999. We really thought we'd have flying cars and moon bases and humanoid robots by then. What happened to our imagination and optimism? While few practices that really challenge conventional culture made it into this edition, I remain a big fan of accepting ideas that are a bit out there and keeping a sense of humor as we go about our lives on a tiny planet in a vast universe of possibilities.

Here's to all the crazy people, saving our planet every day even though everyone is telling us we can't!

Revision: 25.1.8

Foreword

If there's one handbook to own to know *how* to practice sustainability, this is it.

- Browse through it for ideas and inspiration.
- Study it on your own or as part of a class or team.
- Rely on it for real projects, for your own home or organization or for your clients.

Every practice in this handbook is science-based with measurable outcomes. Some practices apply to everyone, some apply only to homeowners or businesspeople. We attempt to provide everything you need to know to practice sustainability, no matter your stage of life or situation. The first section introduces practices and how to measure results. The bulk of this handbook are detailed guides explaining how to do each practice. Later sections help you understand concepts and history. Our aim is to provide you with a comprehensive and trustworthy source of sustainability knowledge so you can make wise decisions on matters important to you.

Visit our companion website at <www.suspra.com> for online tools, references, further reading, and resources. For each practice guide in this handbook, we have a page on that site where we keep an up-to-date list of relevant references and links.

This handbook is published by Sustainable Practice, a partnership between your humble author, Fred Horch, and my friend and editor, Peggy Siegle. As the former proprietor of a sustainable living retail store, I spent many years answering customer questions. My next venture, a mechanical contracting firm, provided a decade of insight installing LED lighting, heat pumps, solar arrays, batteries, electric vehicle chargers, and other high-performance equipment.

Our mission at Sustainable Practice is to use our knowledge to empower more people to make wiser decisions that better protect our planet's life support systems. These core values guide us:

Empathy	We believe that living a good life means leaving a legacy that shows concern for others. We imagine the world we want young people to inherit, then aim to make the best use of our own limited resources to help create that world.
Agency	We acknowledge that we have the ability to choose practices that have a more positive impact on our planet's ability to sustain human life.
Humility	We recognize that we have more to learn, and we admit when we're wrong. We forgive ourselves and others for being imperfect, letting go of guilt and resentment.
Democracy	We strive to lead by example to build broad support for sustainable public policies and laws.
Science	We make decisions based on verifiable evidence from scientific inquiry–rather than hearsay or wishful thinking.
Action	We use our knowledge to take action. We understand that our best intentions can't change our world, but our best actions can.
Honesty	We measure outcomes to keep ourselves honest. We acknowledge that Mother Nature doesn't give an A for effort; she grades on results.

Table of Contents

Introduction...1
    What Is Sustainable?... 1
    How Do You Practice Sustainability?.. 2
    How Affordable Are Sustainable Practices?.. 2

Twenty Pivotal Practices..3
    Practices Along Pathways...3
    Why These Twenty.. 4

Sustainability Indicators..10
    Measuring Suspra Indicators.. 10
    Community Indicators...10
    Food Indicators... 11
    Water Indicators... 11
    Movement Indicators... 11
    Energy Indicators..12
    Goods Indicators...12
    Habitat Indicators...12

Pathways and Strategies..13
    Implementation Levels.. 13
    Community Pathway..15
    Food Pathway..19
    Water Pathway... 23
    Movement (Transportation) Pathway... 26
    Energy Pathway..29
    Goods (Materials) Pathway.. 35
    Habitat (Buildings and Land) Pathway... 39

Practice Guides.. 42
    Community Practices.. 54
    Food Practices..127
    Water Practices... 216
    Movement (Transportation) Practices.. 260
    Energy Practices... 278
    Goods (Materials) Practices..380
    Habitat Practices.. 454

Improving Practices..503
    How to Measure Results.. 503
    How to Evaluate Practices... 503
    How to Plan... 503
    How to Aim (Set Goals)..504
    How to Commit... 504
    How to Do..504

Sustainable Practices Handbook — Table of Contents

Financing Projects **505**
- Project Financial Analysis 505
- Borrowing and Lending 507

Math **508**
- Numbers by Magnitude 508
- Notable Numbers 509
- Mathematical Symbols 509

Science **510**
- Units and Definitions 510
- Physics 514
- Chemistry 517
- Earth Sciences 522
- Biology 527
- Economics 536

Technology **541**
- Batteries 541
- Cleaning: Soaps, Solvents and Disinfectants 546
- Electric Motors 550
- Heat Pumps 552
- Insulation 555
- Solar Photovoltaics 557
- Windows 560

Sustainability Concepts **562**
- Planetary Boundaries 562
- United Nations Sustainable Development Goals 563
- Global Environmental Issues 563
- Sustainability Scoring Systems 564

Glossary **565**
Index **570**

Revision: 25.1.8   www.suspra.com

Introduction

By virtue of the size of our planet and the number of people sharing it, we've each got a finite environmental budget. It's our most profound duty to decide how to spend it.

The goal of this handbook is to empower you to *practice sustainability wisely*–so you can improve practices in households, organizations, and communities to help create a better future for everyone. Our theme is "think globally and act locally" to go from good intentions to effective action. Inside you'll find a "cookbook" of "recipes" breaking down projects into achievable steps on pathways to sustainability, plus a full complement of scientific, technical, engineering, and financial knowledge.

What Is Sustainable?

Earth's surface is the only habitat in the known universe that provides the air, water, food, goods, and everything else we require. Dividing Earth's 15.77 billion acres of habitable land by 8.2 billion human inhabitants equals less than *two acres* (about three quarters of a *hectare*, or 75 meters by 100 meters). A sustainable future is possible if we meet our needs using 0.75 hectares of habitable land per person.

Science shows that our planet's life-support systems naturally operate in a *global safety zone*. For instance, the Stockholm Resilience Centre has identified "a set of nine planetary boundaries within which humanity can continue to develop and thrive for generations to come." Although excessive pollution and unwise consumption are causing climate change *and **eight more*** global challenges, choosing sustainable practices will protect and restore Earth's ability to sustain human beings.

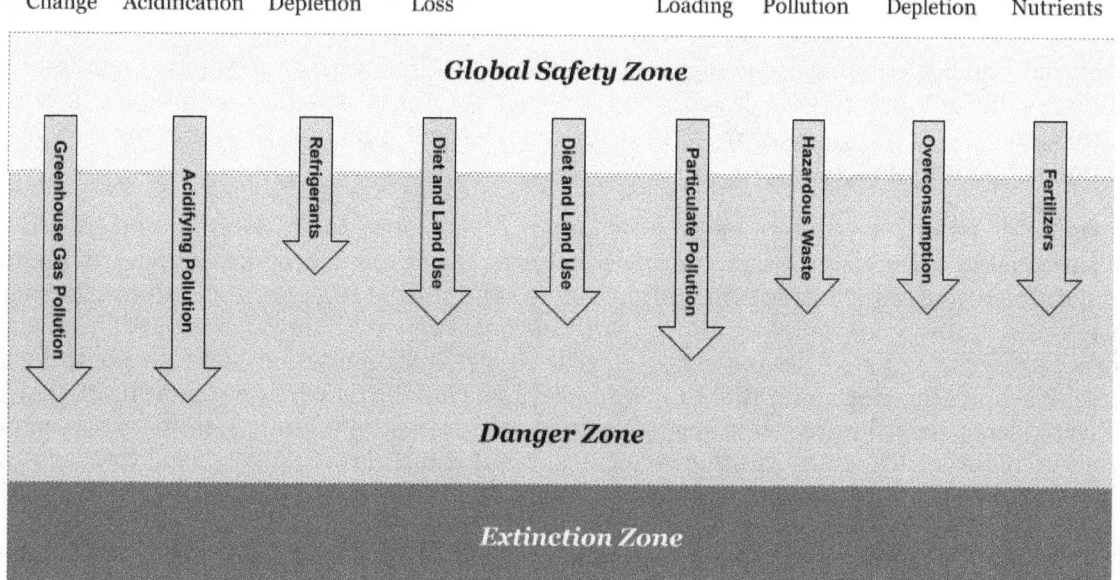

Figure adapted from the work of Johan Rockström et alia, as publicized by the Stockholm Resilience Centre

This handbook empowers you with practical, science-based strategies within your control that contribute to the collective shift needed to keep humanity's impacts within Earth's carrying capacity. Sustainable solutions to global challenges like deforestation are not political campaigns or corporate policies, but practices like eating more plant-based meals. Move beyond feeling helpless, hopeless, and isolated by improving measurable indicators of your own sustainability. Take purposeful action for the benefit of your inner sense of agency, your immediate environment, and far beyond.

How Do You Practice Sustainability?

The food you will eat, the air you will breathe, the fresh water you will drink, and all the goods you will enjoy are being made somewhere on Earth—mostly by a complex system of living organisms. By your practices, choose whether to save or degrade the small part of our planet's lifegiving ecosystem that sustains you. Choose not only *whether* to protect your planet, but *how*.

Much needs to be done to create a more sustainable future. Advocacy, protest, and lobbying to influence laws and regulations is important work that aims to create social change that enables sustainability. But it doesn't replace the need for people to step up with a direct approach, making immediate beneficial progress in their own spheres of influence without waiting for policy shifts. Be a sustainability *practitioner*; don't wait for politicians to act. Improve practices in households and organizations in your community to reduce negative environmental effects and increase positive impacts.

This handbook focuses on the practical "how-to" of sustainability—how to plan projects, implement improvements, and measure results. Whether you're already deeply engaged in advocacy work and want to see more tangible results or simply are ready to make positive changes in your everyday life, these practical skills will empower you to create environmental benefits immediately while building toward larger community transformation. We assume you want to be improving your own community step by step from the ground up—if so, you're reading the right book!

How Affordable Are Sustainable Practices?

The more modest your needs, the easier to meet them in sustainable ways. The cheapest strategy is conservation: practices like turning down the thermostat or taking shorter showers conserve resources but sacrifice some comfort or convenience for the common good. Everyone can financially afford that.

A much harder challenge is to raise your standard of living while lowering your environmental impacts. That requires a different strategy: *efficiency*. Invest time or money in better techniques or technology. For example, an LED light bulb costs more than an incandescent bulb but uses less power to provide the same amount of light for much longer.

Many sustainable practices save money over the long run, but some don't. Whether you should spend to be more sustainable depends on your values. For instance, if you're burning fossil fuel, you are turning a valuable natural resource into pollution and not paying the full price of your pollution. Your emissions only cost you a guilty conscience—and you can sidestep even that moral burden if you ignore the consequences of your actions, convince yourself that your pollution does no harm, or point the finger at someone else who is burning more fuel than you are. You can decide whether you want to take steps to stop polluting, keep polluting yourself but pay someone else to stop polluting, or just keep on polluting and devote your time and money to other priorities. What you choose to believe and how you choose to spend your own time and money shows what you truly value.

This comprehensive handbook helps you practice sustainability wisely whether you want to *save* money, live more simply, and conserve resources, or *invest* money, enjoy more creature comforts, and use resources more efficiently. You'll find out which sacrifices really make a difference and which just make life more difficult for insignificant environmental benefit. You'll discover a comprehensive system for measuring your environmental impacts, so you can avoid the trap of tunnel vision: rather than myopically obsessing over devilish details that do little to improve your sustainability score, you can turn your attention to easy opportunities for massive gains. You'll learn which investments earn a financial return over time, and which are charitable gifts for future generations, not resulting in pecuniary rewards but creating lasting positive change in the world.

Twenty Pivotal Practices

Twenty sustainable practices turn households and organizations into true leaders for positive change. Here they are, arranged in a logical order so you can start confidently on your journey to sustainability. If you are new to these practices, first work on them in your *own* home and organizations to get hands-on experience. Then as a sustainability coach or professional practitioner you can work to help improve these practices in *other* people's homes and organizations.

1. Grow a community that practices environmental sustainability.
2. Compost biodegradable solid waste.
3. Walk, cycle, or take public transit for local errands.
4. Eat more plants and little or no domesticated red meat (beef, lamb, etc.).
5. Plant a food garden or buy from local farmers who grow regeneratively.
6. Drink more water and fewer bottled beverages.
7. Clean with safe products in minimal packaging.
8. Recycle metal, clean cardboard, and glass; avoid plastic.
9. Seal and insulate attics, basements, and exterior walls.
10. Use LED lighting with motion sensors and daylight dimming.
11. Landscape with native plants using organic methods.
12. Wash clothes in cold water in an efficient machine.
13. Heat domestic water using electric heat pumps.
14. Dry clothes in a condensing dryer or on drying racks or lines.
15. Keep food cold in energy-efficient refrigerators and freezers.
16. Cook with induction ranges and circulating-fan convection ovens.
17. Drive electric vehicles when you can't walk, bike, or take transit.
18. Use electric heat pumps for space heating.
19. Generate solar electricity on-site or subscribe to a solar farm.
20. Flush water-efficient toilets.

Practices Along Pathways

These essential practices guide a household or organization along seven *pathways to sustainability*:

 Community Food Water Movement Energy Goods  Habitat

For each pathway, measure science-based sustainability indicators and score them against safe environmental limits according to the latest research. *Negative* scores show that practices are *unsustainable*—needs are being met in ways that drag Earth's life support systems down out of the safety zone, beyond planetary boundaries, into the danger or extinction zone. *Positive* scores mean that needs are being met in *sustainable* ways, keeping environmental impacts within the safety zone. On your sustainability journey, consider both the milestone scores you aim to achieve, and the next steps required to reach them.

Why These Twenty

In 1989, the Earth Works Group published *50 Simple Things You Can Do to Save the Earth*. In the decades since, thousands of people have made similar lists. (We just asked an AI how many such lists it can find on the Internet–it says 23,500.) What makes our list different is science. Of the myriad action steps you could take to save our planet, some really do make a huge positive difference, while others barely register an impact. Here are the twenty most important practices to do well in every household and organization on Earth.

1. **Grow a community that practices environmental sustainability.**
   Understand sustainability, demonstrate best practices, and interact in positive ways with other people.

   Start with the end in mind. The fact that sustainability is really a group effort is why growing a community that practices environmental sustainability is #1 on our list. We can keep global environmental impacts within safe limits when everyone is living in a sustainable home, interacting in sustainable organizations, and enjoying a sustainable community. Community indicators you can measure are how well people in your community understand sustainability (by testing knowledge), how many sustainable practices they demonstrate in their own households and organizations (by surveying practices), and how well they interact with other people (by evaluating interactions).

   On the community pathway, your starting point is your immediate family. The ultimate milestone is including everyone on Earth in your community, since your actions have larger ripple effects as you grow your community. The global total of everyone's environmental impacts is what matters in the end.

2. **Compost biodegradable solid waste.**
   Compost paper, cardboard, wood, food scraps, and yard trimmings to keep garbage trucks off the roads and organic material out of landfills.

   While the practice of "learning, doing, interacting" to grow community is very broad, the second practice on our list, composting biodegradable solid waste, is much more focused, at least in terms of action. But an interesting thing about composting is that it naturally encourages you to think more deeply about the goods you bring into your home and eventually must discard. Once you get into the habit of composting, you'll start carefully considering things like whether packaging can be composted and whether it contains toxic materials. Composting also affects sustainability indicators along the food pathway, being an essential practice to grow healthy farms and gardens.

3. **Walk, cycle, or take public transit for local errands.**
   Use your muscles to get around. Bicycles are best: you can go faster and farther and carry more weight riding a bike than walking.

   Active transportation–walking, cycling, or taking public transit–is another practice which is very focused in terms of your personal action, but has profound impacts on your community and our planet. In terms of how you move your body, the primary sustainability indicator is very simple: what is your average speed? If you keep track of the total distance you walk, cycle, drive, and fly in a year, you can easily calculate your average miles per hour. This single number packs in a tremendous amount of inferable data: how often you fly and how often you drive for travel, work, shopping, socializing, and other activities. A low-speed life indicates lower environmental impacts than a high-speed life.

Sustainable Practices Handbook Twenty Pivotal Practices

4. **Eat more plants and little or no domesticated red meat (beef, lamb, etc.).**
   Eat fruits, vegetables, and mushrooms; limit non-game red meat. A plant-based diet can feed four times as many people per square meter of land as a meat-based diet.

   Your diet is a daily choice with perhaps even more profound environmental impacts than how you move about the world. Of course, food is the primary pathway to consider here, and sustainability indicators include how much and which types of food you buy. As with the choices you make for movement, what you choose to eat not only has direct impacts on your own health, but also on the health of our shared environment.

5. **Plant a food garden or buy from local farmers who grow regeneratively.**
   Grow your own food or buy directly from local organic farms in season to protect our food supply and reduce processing, packaging, and shipping impacts.

   A practice closely related to what you eat is what you accept in terms of how your food is produced. Whether you choose to eat a meat-based or plant-based diet is only half the story. The other half is who grows the crops and raises the animals, and what impacts do their practices have on our environment? We're fortunate to have food labeling laws so we can determine the source of our food and know a little bit about the practices used to produce it. But you can have even more assurance about the provenance of your protein when you can talk directly with the farmers and growers yourself. Keeping a food journal that records what you choose to eat with details about the source and certifications (i.e., organic, fair trade, etc.) measures results along the food pathway.

6. **Drink more water and fewer bottled or brewed beverages.**
   Drink filtered tap water, rather than hot drinks or bottled beverages, to save money, conserve energy, and reduce plastic pollution.

   Drinking more tap water is probably the easiest way to save money and the planet at the same time. This is something everyone can do; the results are easy to quantify. How much less money are you spending, how much less garbage are you making, and how many delivery trucks are you keeping off the road? Bottle your own tap water at home in reusable bottles, for literally pennies on the dollar compared to buying bottled water in a store. Beyond infancy, healthy people can meet all of their hydration needs by eating good food and drinking water. All other beverages are luxuries–to be savored, for sure! Because this practice is about water for drinking, we note its connection to the food pathway, but it has implications for the goods pathway, by eliminating unnecessary plastic packaging, as well as the energy pathway, especially if you eliminate the energy demands of brewing a pot of coffee every morning.

7. **Clean with safe products in minimal packaging.**
   Choose biodegradable cleaning products free of perfumes, dyes, and synthetic antibacterial chemicals. Buy in bulk for less packaging.

   Our seventh pivotal practice, choosing safe, plant-based cleaning products in minimal packaging, has impacts measured by indicators on the goods pathway: how many goods and which types of materials are flowing through your home or organization? The goods pathway is about consuming goods in a sustainable way. When you really examine what you are doing when you are cleaning, you are moving material from inside a building to the outdoors. When you vacuum or sweep, all the detritus you collect, you put outside, either to compost or landfill. When you wipe off a counter or mop the floor, you pour the cleaning water down the drain, where it goes into a septic tank and then a leach field in your yard, or travels through a sewer system to a wastewater treatment plant and then is discharged into your local river, lake, or ocean.

Revision: 25.1.8   www.suspra.com

8. **Recycle metal, clean cardboard, and glass; avoid plastic.**
   Recycle paper, metal, clean cardboard, and glass if you can. Rather than filling your bin with "wish-cycling," buy less plastic.

Most of the goods you bring into your home you will eventually discard. Then you have five choices: reuse, compost, recycle, divert, or landfill. Unfortunately, reuse is not a practical option for most items, since it requires coordination among manufacturers, retailers, and consumers. We've already listed composting as #2 on our list of twenty pivotal practices. Recycling comes in here at #8.

The point of recycling is to put material back into productive use. Recycling companies do this very well for metal and clean cardboard, but glass is more of a challenge. It's actually helpful to add recycled glass to make new glass; however, shipping glass is expensive. Where crushed glass can't be recycled, it can be put in bags to mitigate beach erosion or used as an aggregate for construction projects. Turning a high-value product, like a glass bottle, into a lower-value product, such as sand, is called "downcycling."

Plastic recycling is almost impossible because there are thousands of ways to combine carbon, hydrogen, oxygen, nitrogen, chlorine, and sulfur into plastics, but each one of those plastic materials has a different melting point and requires a different process to recycle. For example, polyethylene terephthalate (PET) and polyethylene naphthalate (PEN) can't be recycled together. And you'll need completely different equipment to recycle high-density polyethylene (HDPE) versus low-density polyethylene (LDPE); both are often contaminated with per- and polyfluoroalkyl substances (PFAS).

Most "recycling" programs for plastic pick out one or two types of resin from the dozen you might have tossed together for recycling, and then burn or bury the rest. Although burning plastic does generate electricity, it also creates toxic air pollution and produces ash that contains dangerous compounds that must be managed carefully.

Reducing your use of plastic is the wiser course than trying to recycle it. In most situations, putting plastic waste in a recycling bin is really "wish-cycling," not recycling. Most plastic waste is buried, burned, or downcycled–no matter how much you wish it could all be recycled.

9. **Seal and insulate attics, basements, and exterior walls.**
   Use caulk, foam, and other methods to keep conditioned air from leaking out through walls, ceilings, floors, and around doors.

In homes that have heating or cooling systems to provide comfortable indoor conditions, keeping conditioned air from immediately leaking out is the single best way to get more value from your energy.

10. **Use LED lighting with motion sensors and daylight dimming.**
    Illuminate with light-emitting diodes (LEDs) for five times more light per joule compared to incandescents. Install and program motion sensors and automatic dimmers to save even more energy.

While stuffing insulation or squirting caulk into holes in your basement and attic is a low-tech practice to increase your energy efficiency, upgrading your lighting is an effective high-tech practice. For the same amount of energy, you can get ten times as much light from an LED as you can from a tungsten filament (incandescent lamp). And forget fluorescent lighting, which contains toxic mercury! You'll probably use less energy per day after you upgrade to LED lighting (unless you decide to install more lights or leave them on all the time). And you'll also notice an improvement along the goods pathway, as you no longer need to replace light bulbs every year or two. On average, LEDs last for ten years or more in a typical residential lighting fixture.

In addition to being inherently energy efficient and durable, LEDs are also easy to control—if you select dimmers and motion sensors that are designed to work with LEDs. Adding sensors to turn down or turn off lights when they are not needed saves even more energy, which will be reflected in your average power when you measure your sustainability indicators.

11. **Landscape with native plants using organic methods.**
Plant and cultivate species native to your area to conserve biodiversity; practice organic landscaping to protect our environment from synthetic hazards.

If you have a yard, you can make it a haven for wildlife. This is a case where thinking globally but acting locally really kicks in. What can you do about endangered species? You can protect your little piece of the biosphere, allowing the ecosystem that evolved in your area to persist and continue to evolve naturally. What can you do about deforestation? You can ensure that trees growing on your land reach maturity so they can produce and disperse seeds to sustain future forests. What can you do about aerosol loading? You can maintain deep-rooted vegetation that naturally keeps soil in place and produces clean air. What can you do about pollution from novel chemicals? You can avoid the use of synthetic pesticides. What can you do about excess nutrients in waterways? You can avoid using synthetic fertilizer.

The world is a big puzzle, but you can carefully consider how your little piece fits into the big picture. To mark your milestone on the habitat pathway, you can measure the amount of habitable land that you control, what you allow to live on your land, and what substances you spread on your land.

12. **Wash clothes in cold water in an efficient machine.**
Clean clothes in cold water, using biodegradable cold-water enzymes to remove stains and odors. Install a filter to trap microfibers to reduce microplastic pollution.

Washing in cold water works best if you use a detergent with biodegradable enzymes to remove stains and odors. Which types of detergents you use and what you do about microplastics—small pieces of synthetic fabrics that break off when you do your laundry—are two factors you can measure to indicate your environmental impacts on water systems. And washing in cold water consumes less energy and lowers your average power, indicating progress on the energy pathway.

13. **Heat domestic water using electric heat pumps.**
Heat water with an electric heat pump water heater to be up to four times more energy efficient than using conventional electric or gas water heaters.

Water for showers, sinks, and washing inside a home is called "domestic water." Heating this water is typically the second largest energy expense in a home after space heating and cooling. That's why choosing heat pump technology, which is much more energy efficient than burning fuel or sending current through a heating element, can lower your average power by a lot.

14. **Dry clothes in a condensing dryer or on drying racks or lines.**
    Wash and dry clothes efficiently without venting using an all-in-one washer-dryer. Hang clothes to air dry to save even more energy.

    You can burn fuel, use electricity, or wait for natural evaporation to dry your clothes. Choosing natural evaporation is the most energy efficient, but least time efficient. In general, whether you spend your time watching TV, writing a spy novel, or hanging clothes to dry does not have a measurable impact on the ability of our planet to support human life. But whether you choose to burn fossil fuel or use solar electricity to dry your clothes does have a measurable impact.

    In terms of energy, how you choose to dry your clothes will show up in your average power. Out of all your clothes-drying options, hanging your clothes to dry will have the biggest environmentally positive impact on your average power (i.e., lower it the most). Choosing a super-efficient condensing or heat pump dryer will help nudge you forward along the energy pathway compared to using a conventional vented dryer. An all-in-one washer / condensing dryer allows you to throw in a load of dirty laundry and take out a load of clean and dry laundry, using about half the energy as you'd need to put your dirty laundry in a conventional washing machine, and then transfer it to dry in a conventional vented dryer.

15. **Keep food cold in energy-efficient refrigerators and freezers.**
    Remove or replace older refrigerators and freezers. Refrigeration technology has become four times more energy-efficient since the 1970s.

    For decades, you probably have had a heat pump in your home: your refrigerator. The advances in technology that are making heat pumps popular for space heating and water heating have also helped make modern refrigerators much more energy efficient. Like the energy impacts of many other practices, your choice of refrigerator will be reflected in your average power score. Whatever portion of your average power that is due to keeping food and other things cold, you can cut it in half or more if you have an older refrigerator and upgrade to the newest, most efficient technology. And if you have an old refrigerator in a basement but don't really need it, that would be a great appliance to unplug to take an easy step forward on the energy pathway.

16. **Cook with induction ranges and circulating-fan convection ovens.**
    Upgrade to electric induction stoves and convection ovens to cook faster and more efficiently than gas or conventional electric stoves.

    If you prepare your own meals, you can choose a high-efficiency electric induction stove top and a convection oven to save time and energy. These technologies, along with microwave ovens, are safer and faster than old-fashioned electric coils or gas burners. After making the upgrade, you can check your average power to confirm that you have made a step forward along the energy pathway.

17. **Drive electric vehicles when you can't walk, bike, or take transit.**
    Drive (or hail) a battery-electric vehicle when you can't walk, ride a bike, or take transit.

    If you can't walk or cycle, you can drive an electric vehicle. Like cooking with induction, this leap to better technology will improve your average power sustainability indicator.

18. **Use electric heat pumps for space heating.**
    Use electric heat pumps rather than burning fuel for space heating. Heat pumps are much more efficient than combustion and can be powered by clean energy.

    Heat pumps are another technology to move you forward along the energy pathway, with your average power the key sustainability indicator to watch. If you're switching to electric heat pumps from a fuel-burning heating system, you'll also see your electricity energy percentage indicator improve.

19. **Generate solar electricity on-site or subscribe to a solar farm.**
    Generate electricity from sunlight on your own property or at a remote site. Solar power is becoming even more practical as batteries improve.

    Anywhere you've decided to maintain a building, a sidewalk, a driveway, or a road, you've cleared away plants that would be making productive use of the sunshine that reaches that part of our planet. It's just common courtesy to use modern technology to harness that free energy to meet your needs, rather than destroying more of our planet's ecosystem to meet your demand for electricity. The sustainability indicator to measure is the percent of your electricity that comes from solar power. The good news is that it is very easy to start on the pathway to 100% clean power–get a $10 solar charger for your cell phone, then work your way forward step by step from there until you're generating all your electricity from sunlight.

20. **Flush water-efficient toilets.**
    Install water-efficient sanitation. What uses the most water inside your home? Probably flushing toilets: North Americans flush toilets five times a day per person.

    Last and least, the lowly toilet is the single biggest water user in most homes. In North America, we treat and supply water clean enough to drink to almost every home, only to flush most of it down the drain in a toilet bowl. You can buy a flush toilet that uses less than a gallon per use, or really get serious about sustainability and try a composting or sawdust toilet that uses no water at all.

Sustainability Indicators

You matter. Your actions have consequences. Rise above negative people who say you don't make a difference—effective action is the best antidote to eco-anxiety.

Do the best you can with what you have. You can *manage* what you can *measure*. You can't directly measure all of your environmental impacts, but you can measure how much energy, water, and goods you consume—data that *indicate* how your practices affect natural systems—then decide how to keep your impacts within reasonable bounds. Carbon pollution is just one facet of a meaningful sustainability score—that's why many "carbon footprint calculators" do more than just count carbon dioxide emissions. If you're working to "reduce, reuse, and recycle," find out how much you buy, how much is second hand versus brand new, *and* how much you compost and recycle to gauge your success.

Measure a full range of science-based sustainability indicators to know how well you're handling your personal responsibility to respect planetary boundaries. As eight billion—and counting—people share one planet, we each decide how to use our individual share of Earth's global environmental budget. Track your sustainability indicators to reveal which collection of practices are within your environmental means, and which overstep your bounds, destroying Earth's resources that someone else needs to survive.

Measuring Suspra Indicators

Suspra Indicators are a set of indicators that factor into a single Suspra Score that will be *negative* if your practices, taken as a whole, are *unsustainable* and *positive* if your practices are *sustainable*. If you're not yet ready to set your sustainability goals, just quickly skim through this chapter. Keep these indicators in mind as you start improving practices. When you're ready to make a plan with attainable milestones, come back to this chapter. Measure Suspra Indicators before and after you take action to track your progress toward your next sustainability milestones.

Use the evaluation tools available on this handbook's free companion website at <www.suspra.com>. Besides calculating a Quick-Start, Regular, or Detailed Suspra Score, the tools on our website will also provide a personalized sustainability action plan to help you improve your Suspra Score.

Community Indicators

Sustainability Indicator	Measures
Scores on sustainability knowledge tests	How well you understand sustainability
Surveys of sustainable practices	Your community's level of sustainability
Number of people taking tests and surveys	How well you are interacting with others
Volunteer hours log	How well you are interacting with others

Take knowledge tests to measure your own knowledge and then invite other people in your community to take quizzes so you can better understand what your community knows about sustainability. Count and record the number of sustainable practices you are demonstrating in your own household and organizations. Survey other people in your community about their practices to better understand your community's level of sustainability. Keep a log of volunteer hours for yourself and other people in your community. High levels of volunteering indicate that people are interacting, which makes it easier to share knowledge and to implement best practices for sustainability across a community.

Food Indicators

Sustainability Indicator	Measures
Food budget	How much food and drink you buy
Tap water percentage	What you drink
Meal ingredients	What you eat
Certified organic percentage	How your food is produced
Food waste rate	How much food and drink you waste

Use your food budget (average dollars per day over the course of a year) as a quick way to indicate how much and what type of food you eat. Although a lower food budget generally indicates wasting less food and eating more plant-based meals, you can fine tune your Quick-Start Suspra Score by measuring additional indicators to calculate a Regular or Detailed Suspra Score. Keep a meal log to note specifically which types of food you are buying, and a garden log to report the food you are growing.

Water Indicators

Sustainability Indicator	Measures
Average flow rate	How much water you consume
Pollution rates	How well you are protecting water quality

Calculate your average flow rate based on all the water you buy per year, if you're on city water, or the amount of water you pump, if you're on a well. Evaluate your impact on water quality by keeping a log of your pollution prevention practices, such as picking up litter and pet waste.

Movement Indicators

Sustainability Indicator	Measures
Average speed	How fast you move
Travel modes	Which modes of transportation you use

Calculate your average speed based on the distance of all your trips (by passenger vehicle, public transit, or airplane) over a year. To measure your environmental impacts more precisely, keep a travel log.

Energy Indicators

Sustainability Indicator	Measures
Average power	How fast you consume energy
Electricity percentage	How much electricity versus fuel you use
Solar power percentage	How much clean energy you use

Calculate your average power and electricity percentage based on all the fuel and electricity you consume in one year. Calculate your solar power percentage based on how much solar electricity you buy or generate. The lower your average power, the easier it is to get to 100% solar power.

Goods Indicators

Sustainability Indicator	Measures
Goods budget	How many tangible goods you consume
Consumption rate	Which materials and substances you are buying
Reusing, composting & recycling rates	How well you are managing your waste

Use your goods budget (the money you spend to buy physical objects over the course of a year) to indicate how much and which types of goods you buy. Fine tune this indicator by keeping a log of the materials and substances passing through your home or organization, and noting how much you compost, recycle, landfill, or divert to a hazardous waste facility.

Habitat Indicators

Sustainability Indicator	Measures
Occupancy rate	How many people your land sustains
Building materials and certifications	How you are building and maintaining structures
Conservation budget	How much land you are helping to conserve
Land use	How much of your land is growing wild
Pesticide and fertilizer applications	How you are managing your landscape

Calculate your occupancy rate based on how many people have lived in your household or worked in your organization over the course of a year. Report the green building certifications your properties have obtained. Keep a construction log of the materials you've used to build or renovate structures. Use your conservation budget (the amount of money you donate for land conservation each year) and your own land use records to indicate how much land you are allowing to grow wild. Keep a log of pesticide and fertilizer applications to indicate your chemical impact on natural ecosystems.

Pathways and Strategies

Based on verifiable science, here are the sustainable best practices—selected from thousands of ideas published by environmental groups, government agencies, and other experts—that really make a positive difference for the future of our planet. We organize them by pathway, strategy, and implementation level to help you create effective plans to improve practices step by step to achieve meaningful and ultimately transformative sustainability milestones.

Which practices make sense for you depends on where you want to go next on your journey to sustainability and what you enjoy doing. You may prefer to invest in efficiency, or you may thrive on the challenge of frugally conserving resources. Familiarize yourself with every possible strategy so you can select the very best practices for your current situation. Read this chapter to find lists of practices by pathway and strategy; look up the details of each practice in the Practice Guides chapter.

Pathways	Strategies
Community	Understand sustainability Demonstrate sustainable practices Nurture good relationships
Food	Reduce food waste Choose wise ingredients Eat plant-based meals Cultivate healthy harvests
Water	Optimize water efficiency Conserve water Prevent water pollution
Movement	Reduce travel miles Get exercise Drive electric
Energy	Optimize energy efficiency Conserve energy Electrify Solarize
Goods	Buy less Choose green goods Maintain and reuse Manage waste wisely
Habitat	Shelter well Renovate wisely Protect nature

Sustainable Practices Handbook — Pathways and Strategies

Implementation Levels

Get a quick start with easy practices and work your way up to transformative practices.

Level 1. Quick Start

- **Focus:** Building awareness and taking first steps
- **Prerequisites:** None
- **Preparation:** You can start right away; no preparation required
- **Time / Cost:** < 1 hour per practice / Free or minimal cost (<$50)
- **Skills:** No special skills required
- **Equipment:** No specialized equipment needed
- **Scale:** Individual, household, or department

Level 2. Intermediate

- **Focus:** Building good habits and engaging others
- **Prerequisites:** Several Level 1 practices
- **Preparation:** Some preparation useful
- **Time / Cost:** Hours / Low to moderate cost ($50-2,500)
- **Skills:** Some skills may be required
- **Equipment:** Some special tools may be required
- **Scale:** Extended family or entire organization

Level 3. Advanced

- **Focus:** Creating structured programs and measuring impact
- **Prerequisites:** Multiple Level 2 practices
- **Preparation:** Significant preparation required
- **Time / Cost:** Days / Moderate to high cost ($2,500-25,000)
- **Skills:** Project management, leadership, technical expertise
- **Equipment:** Specialized tools or software may be required
- **Scale:** Up to neighborhood or campus

Level 4. Transformative

- **Focus:** Permanently changing habits and systems
- **Prerequisites:** Multiple Level 3 practices
- **Preparation:** Professional education or training required
- **Time / Cost:** Weeks or more / High cost ($25,000 or more)
- **Skills:** Strategic planning, system design, policy analysis
- **Equipment:** Extensive infrastructure may be required
- **Scale:** Up to whole community and region

Sustainable Practices Handbook
Pathways and Strategies

Community Pathway

Become an agent for positive change—share knowledge, demonstrate successful practices, and nurture good relationships among your community.

- Understand sustainability to build a solid foundation of knowledge to guide your practices.
- Demonstrate sustainability by implementing sustainable practices and leading by example.
- Interact with others in positive ways to nurture good relationships and strengthen connections, so community members can take meaningful steps together toward a sustainable future.

	Unsustainable	*Somewhat Sustainable*	*Positively Sustainable*
Understand Sustainability	Lacking an understanding of sustainability and believing falsehoods	Having a fact-based understanding of sustainability basics	Superbly understanding sustainability
Demonstrate Sustainability	Demonstrating few or no sustainable practices	Demonstrating several sustainable practices	Demonstrating many sustainable practices well
Nurture Good Relationships	Interacting rarely or never with others, or in negative ways	Interacting occasionally or neutrally with others	Interacting often and in positive ways with others

Understand Sustainability

Build a solid foundation of knowledge to inform and guide your practices

Quick-Start Practices to Understand Sustainability

Learn	Prompt AI to explain sustainability science. Read the best articles and books about sustainability science. Watch the best nature and technology documentaries. Take the best online courses about sustainability science.
Verify	Check credible sources to confirm facts and inferences. Take knowledge tests to verify your understanding of sustainability science.

Intermediate Practices to Understand Sustainability

Learn	Attend hands-on workshops to learn sustainable practices. Earn professional sustainability certifications.
Verify	Investigate the credibility of information sources. Conduct research to verify the environmental impacts of practices.

Advanced Practices to Understand Sustainability

Learn	Build a personal resource library for sustainable practices. Research sustainable practices in your community. Earn an undergraduate degree in an environmental field.

Revision: 25.1.8   www.suspra.com

Sustainable Practices Handbook Pathways and Strategies

| Verify | Develop procedures to measure sustainability indicators. |

Transformative Practices to Understand Sustainability

| Learn | Earn an advanced degree in an environmental field. |

Demonstrate Sustainability

Learn by doing and lead by example

Quick-Start Practices to Demonstrate Sustainability

Commit	Commit to improving sustainability indicators.
Act	Take action with quick-start sustainable practices.
Track Results	Keep a personal sustainability journal. Calculate a Quick-Start Suspra Score for your home or organization.

Intermediate Practices to Demonstrate Sustainability

Commit	Set achievable sustainability goals. Create simple plans to achieve sustainability goals.
Act	Take action with intermediate sustainable practices.
Track Results	Create and use checklists for sustainable practices. Calculate a regular Suspra Score for your home or organization.

Advanced Practices to Demonstrate Sustainability

Commit	Create a detailed sustainability plan for your household or organization.
Act	Take action with advanced sustainable practices.
Track Results	Calculate a detailed Suspra Score for your home or organization. Compare Suspra Scores to past periods to measure rates of change.

Transformative Practices to Demonstrate Sustainability

Act	Take action with transformative sustainable practices.
Track Results	Improve the Suspra scoring system.

Revision: 25.1.8

Nurture Good Relationships

Nurture a community of people who can take meaningful steps together toward a sustainable future

Quick-Start Practices to Nurture Good Relationships

Share	Forward verified articles and interesting opinion pieces to friends and family. Discuss environmental issues with friends and family.
Volunteer	Join volunteer environmental projects in your community.
Vote	Vote for pro-environment candidates and policies.

Intermediate Practices to Nurture Good Relationships

Share	Use social media to post photos and videos of your own sustainable practices. Blog about sustainability challenges you face and successes you achieve. Host parties to celebrate successes achieving sustainability goals. Offer tours of properties showcasing sustainable practices. Lead book clubs, discussion groups, and study circles on environmental topics.
Volunteer	Join a community service organization like Rotary, a church green team, or an environmental group. Become a sustainability coach. Organize and lead teams to accomplish sustainable projects.
Work	Suggest practical ways to reduce environmental impacts at work.

Advanced Practices to Nurture Good Relationships

Share	Build educational displays about sustainable practices. Publish infographics to explain environmental issues. Write articles or a newspaper column about sustainability. Give talks about sustainable practices. Teach classes and lead workshops about sustainable practices.
Volunteer	Serve on your local government's sustainability committee. Recruit and train sustainability coaches. Lead a local chapter of an environmental organization.
Work	Work in a job or for a company with an environmental mission.

Transformative Practices to Nurture Good Relationships

Share	Publish books and films about environmental sustainability. Host a sustainability podcast. Establish learning centers for sustainable practices. Build research programs for sustainable practices.
Volunteer	Start a sustainability coaching program in your community.

Work	Start a new organization or business with an environmental mission.
Govern	Develop certification systems for sustainability practitioners. Propose pro-environment ordinances and legislation. Run for public office.

 Food Pathway

Eliminate *food waste*, choose *eco-friendly ingredients*, eat *plant-based meals*, and buy or grow food from *healthy farms and gardens*.

- Food waste includes food that goes bad in storage and food that is prepared but not eaten. Reduce food waste by understanding expiration dates, buying only as much food as you can eat (including when dining out at restaurants), storing food properly, and eating leftovers rather than throwing them out.
- Eco-friendly ingredients have lower environmental impacts than close substitutes, such as ground turkey instead of ground beef, or aquafaba instead of eggs. When choosing seafood, in particular, eat from abundant stocks rather than overfished stocks.
- Eat plants more often than animals. Plant-based diets are more sustainable mostly due to the greater agricultural efficiency of growing crops compared to raising animals.
- Healthy farms and gardens produce food using regenerative practices, including certified organic methods, with beneficial environmental impacts that sustain agricultural productivity.

	Unsustainable	*Somewhat Sustainable*	*Positively Sustainable*
Reduce Food Waste	Often wasting food	Wasting food only occasionally	Very rarely wasting food
Choose Eco-Friendly Ingredients	Rarely choosing eco-friendly ingredients	Frequently choosing eco-friendly ingredients	Always choosing eco-friendly ingredients
Eat Plant-Based Meals	Rarely eating plant-based meals	Usually eating plant-based meals	Always eating vegan meals
Cultivate Healthy Harvests	Seldom supporting healthy farms or gardens	Often supporting healthy farms or gardens	Always getting food from healthy farms or gardens

Reduce Food Waste

Get more value from the money and time you spend on food

Quick-Start Practices to Reduce Food Waste

Understand	Understand food date labels. Understand food safety and signs of spoilage.
Buy	Buy "ugly" fruits and vegetables that have cosmetic blemishes. Buy dried, pickled, fermented, or frozen food that stores well. Buy root vegetables and fruit like blueberries that last longer than other types.
Store	Store bread and pastries in the freezer to prevent mold.
Eat	Prepare and order smaller portions so you have fewer leftovers.

Revision: 25.1.8

Sustainable Practices Handbook Pathways and Strategies

Intermediate Practices to Reduce Food Waste

Plan	Create a meal plan each week.
Buy	Buy perishable food in quantities no larger than you can eat before it spoils. Buy from local farms to reduce the risk of spoilage due to transportation.
Store	Wash and store produce well so it lasts longer. Organize your food storage system so you eat food before it spoils.
Eat	Save and eat leftovers rather than throwing them out. Bring a takeaway container when eating out so you can bring home leftovers.

Advanced Practices to Reduce Food Waste

Buy	Buy fruits and vegetables when they are in season and most affordable.
Store	Dry, freeze, can, or ferment what you can't eat fresh.
Eat	Make soup stock from vegetable scraps and leftover carcasses and bones.

Transformative Practices to Reduce Food Waste

Store	Create a community kitchen so people can preserve more home-grown food.
Share	Organize ways for local grocery stores to donate unsold food to people in need. Distribute preserved food from a community kitchen to people in need.

Choose Wise Ingredients

Improve the environmental impact of your diet

Quick-Start Practices to Choose Wise Ingredients

Select	Drink more tap water and less bottled water or bottled beverages. Select wild-caught venison instead of beef.
Avoid	Avoid eating all orange roughy, bluefin tuna fish, and Atlantic rock and Jonah crab.

Intermediate Practices to Choose Wise Ingredients

Select	Select Atlantic halibut or pike certified by the Marine Stewardship Council.
Avoid	Avoid meat from ranched ruminants that chew cud (beef, lamb, goat, deer, etc.)

Advanced Practices to Choose Wise Ingredients

Select	Select meat from wild-caught game instead of farmed meat from land animals. Select legumes (including aquafaba) instead of dairy or eggs. Only eat Giant Tiger Prawn (*Penaeus monodon*), Whiteleg shrimp (*Litopenaeus vannamei*), or eel if it is farmed in recirculating tanks. Only eat shark if it is blue, common thresher, or spiny dogfish from U.S. fisheries.
Avoid	Avoid eating meat from any mammal. Avoid eating codfish, except Atlantic cod caught with poles in the Gulf of Maine.

Eat Plant-Based Meals

Obtain more nutrition while consuming fewer agricultural resources

Quick-Start Practices to Eat Plant-Based Meals

Reduce	Reduce the amount of meat you add to pasta, rice, and tortilla meals.
Substitute	Drink water, fruit juice, or plant-based milk instead of mammal milk.

Intermediate Practices to Eat Plant-Based Meals

Plan	Find vegetarian recipes that taste good and are fun to make. Start eating plant-based meals at least once a week, then increase the frequency of plant-based meals so you're eating at least one plant-based meal per day.
Increase	Meet more nutritional needs by eating a wider variety of fruits and vegetables.
Substitute	Eat ice cream made from plant milk instead of mammal milk ice cream. Eat cheese made from plants instead of from mammal milk.

Advanced Practices to Eat Plant-Based Meals

Plan	Find vegan recipes that taste good and are fun to make. Begin observing meat-free Mondays, then increase meat-free days per week.
Increase	Try vegetarian and vegan meals from a wide variety of food traditions and cultures.
Substitute	Substitute plant-based products for all dairy products. Get your protein and fat from eggs, legumes, nuts, and other sources besides meat.

Transformative Practices to Eat Plant-Based Meals

Plan	Understand human nutrition and your own nutritional needs.
Increase	Eat an exclusively vegan diet.

Sustainable Practices Handbook   Pathways and Strategies

Serve	Change menus at public institutions, like schools, so they serve plant-based meals. Create a restaurant that serves plant-based meals.

Cultivate Healthy Harvests

Safeguard our food supply

Quick-Start Practices to Cultivate Healthy Harvests

Buy	Buy food that meets USDA organic standards. Buy palm oil certified by the Roundtable on Sustainable Palm Oil. Buy chocolate that scores "green" on the Chocolate Scorecard. Buy coffee that meets Rainforest Alliance standards.
Grow	Sprout seeds.

Intermediate Practices to Cultivate Healthy Harvests

Buy	Buy from local farmers who practice regenerative methods.
Grow	Grow microgreens. Grow a windowsill herb garden. Plant fruit bushes or vines and fruit or nut trees.

Advanced Practices to Cultivate Healthy Harvests

Grow	Grow a home garden that builds healthy soil and requires minimal pesticides. Raise chickens for eggs or meat using organic methods. Tap trees and boil down syrup using solar power.

Transformative Practices to Cultivate Healthy Harvests

Grow	Practice permaculture, landscaping and gardening in harmony with nature.

Sustainable Practices Handbook — Pathways and Strategies

Water Pathway

Use *one hundred liters of water or less per person per day* and *prevent water pollution.*

- Increasing water efficiency means investing in better techniques or technology so that you can use less water to meet all your needs without any inconvenience.
- Conserving water means accepting inconvenience or discomfort for the greater good of using less water.
- Preventing water pollution protects water quality.

	Unsustainable	*Somewhat Sustainable*	*Positively Sustainable*
Optimize Water Efficiency / **Conserve Water**	Using more than 200 liters of water per person per day	Using about 150 liters of water per person per day	Using 100 liters or less per person per day
Prevent Water Pollution	Doing nothing to prevent pollution	Preventing some pollution	Preventing almost all pollution

Optimize Water Efficiency

Decrease the amount of water you use to meet your needs, without discomfort or inconvenience

Quick-Start Practices to Optimize Water Efficiency

Maintain	Review water bills to check for leaks and fix them.
Streamline	Skip pre-rinsing dishes before putting them in a dishwasher. Scrape food waste into your compost bin, not down your garbage disposal.
Upgrade	Install showerheads and faucet aerators that meet WaterSense standards.

Intermediate Practices to Optimize Water Efficiency

Upgrade	Install toilets that meet WaterSense standards. Install sprinklers, and irrigation controllers that meet WaterSense standards. Install and use a more efficient automatic dishwasher. Install and use a more efficient washing machine.

Advanced Practices to Optimize Water Efficiency

Maintain	Install a leak detection system.
Upgrade	Install a hot water recirculation system so hot water arrives faster.

Revision: 25.1.8

Sustainable Practices Handbook   Pathways and Strategies

Transformative Practices to Optimize Water Efficiency

Maintain	Organize a "fix a leak" brigade for your neighborhood.

Conserve Water

Reduce your water use, accepting some inconvenience or discomfort for the greater good

Quick-Start Practices to Conserve Water

Economize	Flush toilets less frequently. Wait to run dishwashers and clothes washers until you have a full load. Take fewer or shorter showers. Wash clothes and vehicles less frequently. Take Navy showers: run water a few seconds to get wet, turn it off while you lather up with soap and shampoo, then turn the water back on to rinse off.
Substitute	Take short showers instead of baths. Sweep driveways and patios instead of hosing them down with water.

Intermediate Practices to Conserve Water

Displace	Put a brick or bottle in your toilet tank to displace some water.

Advanced Practices to Conserve Water

Substitute	Xeriscape: plant native drought-resistant species that improve the ability of your soil to hold moisture or install features such as rock gardens that require no water at all.

Transformative Practices to Conserve Water

Substitute	Install and use a waterless urinal. Install and use a composting toilet. Install and use an incinerating toilet.

Prevent Water Pollution

Protect water quality

Quick-Start Practices to Prevent Water Pollution

Cleaning	Choose non-polluting cleaning solutions. Choose soap free of antibacterial chemicals and without synthetic dyes or fragrances. Choose phosphate-free detergents.
Dispose	Pick up litter and pet waste and dispose of it safely. Dispose of medications and household hazardous waste safely, not down the drain.

Intermediate Practices to Prevent Water Pollution

Cleaning	Clean with steam rather than chemicals. Clean with electrolyzed water rather than chemicals.
Install	Install microfiber filters on washing machine drain lines. Install a rain barrel to retain precipitation and reduce runoff.

Advanced Practices to Prevent Water Pollution

Install	Install a rain garden to retain precipitation and reduce runoff. Install semi-permeable or permeable driveways and walkways to allow precipitation to soak into the ground rather than run off into storm drains. Install bridges or raised walkways across streams and wetlands.
Manage	Build fencing to prevent livestock and pets from wading in streams. Maintain an unmowed riparian strip of vegetation.

Transformative Practices to Protecting Water Quality

Install	Install green roofs to provide permeable areas over buildings.

 Movement (Transportation) Pathway

Travel 25 miles per day or less on average, get exercise by walking or cycling for short trips, and *drive fully electric vehicles* for longer trips.

- Traveling *more* than 25 miles per day on average indicates that your movement practices have significant *negative* environmental impacts. Very high average daily travel distance indicates that you often fly or drive long distances; it's infeasible to walk or bicycle more than 25 miles per day on average over the course of a year.
- Getting exercise while you move drastically reduces environmental impacts for several reasons. First, walking or bicycling places less wear and tear on machinery and roads. Second, these modes of movement use food, rather than fossil fuel, as the primary energy source, avoiding emissions of particulate matter, ozone, and other dangerous pollutants. Third, these low-speed modes of transportation are much less likely to kill or injure people or animals than high-speed modes such as driving a passenger vehicle.
- Fully electric vehicles (EVs) are typically four or five times more efficient than fuel-burning ones (achieving the equivalent of 130 miles per gallon compared to less than 30 miles per gallon). Hybrid vehicles combine a high-efficiency electric drivetrain with a low-efficiency fuel-burning engine to achieve fuel efficiency about half that of full EVs. Batteries in vehicles can be recharged with electricity generated from sunlight. When an EV reaches the end of its useful life, the materials in its motors and batteries are recycled to make new motors and batteries.

	Unsustainable	*Somewhat Sustainable*	*Positively Sustainable*
Reduce Travel Miles	Traveling more than 60 miles per day	Traveling around 40 miles per day	Traveling 25 miles or less per day
Get Exercise	Rarely using active transportation	Often using active transportation	Almost always using active transportation
Drive Electric	Driving non-hybrid fuel-burning vehicles	Driving hybrid vehicles	Driving fully electric vehicles

Reduce Travel Miles

Reduce the environmental impacts that high-speed movement causes

Quick-Start Practices to Reduce Travel Miles

Plan	Plan your use of fuel-burning vehicles to minimize both engine starts and mileage.
Shop	Shop online to purchase goods not available within walking or cycling distance.

Intermediate Practices to Reduce Travel Miles

Plan	Plan your work, family visits, and vacations to minimize air travel.

Advanced Practices to Reduce Travel Miles

Carpool	Share rides when traveling to a common destination.
Telecommute	Work from home.

Transformative Practices to Reduce Travel Miles

Telecommute	Encourage and empower employees to work from home.

Get Exercise

Improve your health, protect your planet, and get where you need to go

Quick-Start Practices to Get Exercise

Walk	Walk five minutes in nice weather so you can reduce engine starts and mileage.

Intermediate Practices to Get Exercise

Walk	Walk fifteen minutes in sunny or rainy weather.
Cycle	Ride a bicycle or a tricycle for fifteen minutes in nice weather.
Ride	Take micro-mobility (scooters) or public transit when convenient.

Advanced Practices to Get Exercise

Walk	Walk sixty minutes in all weather conditions.
Cycle	Ride a bicycle or a tricycle for sixty minutes in all weather conditions.
Ride	Travel by micro-mobility or public transit rather than renting a passenger vehicle.

Transformative Practices to Get Exercise

Live	Live without owning a passenger vehicle.

Drive Electric

Go faster and further than you can using muscle power, but still without any tailpipe emissions

Quick-Start Practices to Drive Electric

Choose	Choose an electric vehicle when ride sharing.

Intermediate Practices to Drive Electric

Borrow	Rent or borrow an electric vehicle.

Advanced Practices to Drive Electric

Buy	Buy a used plug-in hybrid vehicle.

Transformative Practices to Drive Electric

Buy	Buy or lease a new fully electric vehicle.
Cycle	Ride an electric bicycle or tricycle rather than drive a passenger vehicle.

Energy Pathway

Use *20 kilowatt hours or less* of energy per person per day, use *electricity* rather than fuel for energy, and generate electricity from *sunlight*.

- Energy flow charts published by the Lawrence Livermore National Laboratory show that the United States wastes two-thirds of its power due to the inefficiency of burning fuel. This means that if per person we're currently demanding 60 kWh per day, simply by electrifying and solarizing, we will reduce our energy demand to 20 kWh. Sufficient surface area on Earth is available to provide each person 20 kWh of solar electricity per day forever.
- Electrifying means replacing fuel-burning equipment, such as a gas stove or a diesel truck, with electric equipment, such as an induction stove or an electric truck. Fully electrifying every home and organization in North America will lower our total energy demand so that solar power, batteries, and pumped hydropower become a practical solution to our energy challenge.
- Fossil fuel and uranium are unsustainable diminishing resources; consuming these fuels today diminishes the amount available tomorrow. Wind, water, and sunlight are renewable resources; using these power resources today does *not* diminish the amount available tomorrow. Solar power is orders of magnitude more abundant than wind power, and much more evenly distributed. The ubiquity of sunlight, combined with the fact that photovoltaic modules convert light to electricity with no moving parts, makes solar by far the most practical renewable power supply on Earth (and in orbit). Batteries are the most practical way to store any amount of electricity (from millijoules to gigajoules); pumped hydropower is a cheap way to store huge amounts of energy for months. Natural gas turbines can provide temporary power while people build a sustainable energy system of solar arrays, batteries, and pumped hydropower facilities.

	Unsustainable	*Somewhat Sustainable*	*Positively Sustainable*
Optimize Energy Efficiency / **Conserve Energy**	Using more than 60 kWh per person per day	Using about 40 kWh per person per day	Using 20 kWh or less per person per day
Electrify	Burning fuel for most energy needs	Using electricity for most energy needs	Using electricity for all energy needs
Solarize	Generating no electricity from sunlight	Generating some electricity from sunlight	Generating all electricity from sunlight

Optimize Energy Efficiency

Decrease the energy you use to meet your needs, without discomfort or inconvenience

Quick-Start Practices to Optimize Energy Efficiency

Fenestration	Tightly close windows when outside air temperature or humidity is uncomfortable. In winter, open shades to let in direct sunshine; close them at night.

Heating & Cooling	Set back thermostats overnight and when you are away.
Lighting	Install energy-efficient light-emitting diode (LED) lighting.
Maintain	Clean coils, ducts, and filters to maintain efficiency of heating and cooling systems.
Refrigerating	Ensure your refrigerator has good air circulation around it to allow hot air to escape.
Sealing	Use caulk and foam to seal air gaps to reduce unwanted airflow.
Vehicles	Keep tires inflated to the proper pressure. Use cruise control to maximize fuel economy.
Washing	Wash clothes in cold water using detergents containing cold-water enzymes.

Intermediate Practices to Optimize Energy Efficiency

Appliances	Install smart power strips that automatically turn off devices. Replace inefficient televisions and computers with more efficient models.
Fenestration	Install storm windows or insulating inserts to reduce air and energy flows. Install and use window shades or awnings to keep the summer sun out. Fix cracked panes in windows.
Heating & Cooling	Install and program smart thermostats to control heating and cooling systems. Use wood stove fans to circulate warm air.
Lighting	Install motion sensors to turn off lighting automatically.
Maintain	Replace disposable filters per manufacturer recommendations. Maintain insulation around ducts that go through unconditioned spaces. Inspect and clean all fuel-burning equipment every year.
Plumbing	Insulate hot water and heating pipes.
Refrigerating	Shade refrigerators and freezers from sunlight.
Sealing	Maintain window and door weatherstripping to prevent unwanted airflow.
Vehicles	Use a trunk rack or hitch rack rather than a roof rack to improve fuel economy.
Washing	Install an energy-efficient washing machine with a high-speed spin cycle.

Advanced Practices to Optimize Energy Efficiency

Building	Check and upgrade insulation in the building envelope. Remove unused chimneys.

Sustainable Practices Handbook Pathways and Strategies

Cooking	Install an energy-efficient electric induction stove. Install an energy-efficient electric convection oven.
Fenestration	Repair or replace windows with broken seals. Install energy-efficient windows. Install energy-efficient doors.
Heating & Cooling	Locate and seal air leaks in ducting. Install an EPA-certified wood stove with dedicated makeup air. Install and use energy-efficient ceiling fans to circulate air. Install and use a whole-house fan. Install energy-efficient heat pumps for heating and cooling. Install a heat recovery or energy recovery ventilator.
Landscaping	Plant deciduous trees to provide noon and afternoon shade in summer. Plant evergreen trees and shrubs to provide windbreaks in winter.
Lighting	Install automatic dimmers to reduce energy use when daylight is available. Install light pipes to provide passive daylight in interior rooms.
Plumbing	Install an electric heat pump water heater.
Refrigerating	Install an energy-efficient refrigerator or freezer.
Vehicles	If you need a roof rack, choose an aerodynamic roof rack with a wind deflector.
Washing	Install a ventless electric clothes dryer.

Transformative Practices to Optimize Energy Efficiency

Building	Build a passive solar structure. Install a cool roof that reflects more sunlight than a conventional roof.
Heating & Cooling	Replace forced air with hydronic, electric, or advanced heat distribution.

Conserve Energy

Reduce your energy demand, accepting some inconvenience or discomfort for the greater good

Quick-Start Practices to Conserve Energy

Economizing	Unplug electronic devices so they don't draw power in standby mode. Drink more cold beverages and fewer hot beverages. Watch shows on your phone, tablet, or laptop rather than on a large television. Listen to music on headphones rather than speakers. Walk to your local library to check out and read printed books from their collection. Take colder showers to use less hot water.

Revision: 25.1.8   www.suspra.com

Sustainable Practices Handbook — Pathways and Strategies

Fenestration	Open windows in summer to catch cross breezes instead of running fans.
Heating & Cooling	Adjust thermostats lower all winter and higher all summer to save energy.
Lighting	Turn off lights when you leave a room if you'll be gone for more than a minute. Leave lights off when daylight is sufficient.
Driving	Drive slower. Drive gently. Drive with less weight; offload unnecessary items before driving. Keep windows rolled up at highway speeds to reduce drag.

Intermediate Practices to Conserve Energy

Economizing	Rake leaves instead of using a leaf blower. Shovel snow instead of using a snow blower.
Cooking	Cook in a microwave oven instead of a full-sized oven. Cook in a pressure cooker. Cook outside during the summer to reduce your indoor cooling load. Eat cold meals that don't require heat for cooking. Plan multi-meal cooking.
Heating & Cooling	Use fans instead of air conditioning to stay cool. Only heat and cool rooms that are in use.
Lighting	Install less powerful lighting. Use task lighting rather than ambient lighting that lights up an entire room.
Plumbing	Lower the temperature of domestic hot water for showers, sinks, and washing.
Refrigerating	Operate a single refrigerator instead of multiple refrigerators. Raise the temperature of your refrigerator without spoiling food too quickly.
Driving	Transport items inside your vehicle rather than on a rack.

Advanced Practices to Conserve Energy

Economizing	Choose flooring you can sweep instead of vacuum.
Cooking	Use a solar cooker.
Plumbing	Put your water heater on a timer and schedule your use of hot water.
Refrigerating	Move your refrigerator so that it isn't next to any heat sources, such as an oven. Install a smaller refrigerator that uses less power.
Driving	Remove roof racks or bike racks when not needed. If you drive an electric car in cold weather, minimize use of cabin heat.
Washing	Hang clothes to dry rather than use a gas or electric clothes dryer.

Sustainable Practices Handbook   Pathways and Strategies

Transformative Practices to Conserve Energy

Refrigerating	Dig a root cellar to store food.
Synchronizing	Synchronize electricity usage with solar power generation. Shift your schedule to get up before dawn to make maximum use of sunlight.

Electrify

Transition from burning fuel to using electricity for energy

Intermediate Practices to Electrify

Landscaping	Borrow or rent electric yard tools rather than fuel-burning ones. Buy electric outdoor power equipment.

Advanced Practices to Electrify

Cooking	Upgrade to a 100% electric cooking system.
Heating & Cooling	Upgrade to a 100% electric heating system.
Plumbing	Upgrade to a 100% electric water heating system.
Vehicles	Replace all fuel-burning vehicles with fully electric ones.

Transformative Practices to Electrify

Heating & Cooling	Organize a buying group in your neighborhood for heat pumps.
Lending	Create a library of things to lend out electric tools.

Solarize

Use clean solar power for energy

Quick-Start Practices to Solarize

Charge	Use solar chargers for cell phones and small devices.
Choose	Choose a "green" electricity supplier that generates electricity from sunlight. Subscribe to a community solar farm for electricity.

Revision: 25.1.8   33   www.suspra.com

Sustainable Practices Handbook — Pathways and Strategies

Intermediate Practices to Solarize

Install	Install a solar shed or greenhouse for storing and charging electric tools. Install solar-powered outdoor lighting. Install solar-powered water pumps. Install solar-powered attic fans.

Advanced Practices to Solarize

Install	Install solar thermal systems to heat water. Install a solar photovoltaic (PV) system to power your property.

Transformative Practices to Solarize

Install	Install batteries to store electricity.
Invest	Invest in a community solar farm.
Organize	Organize a group purchase of solar PV for your neighborhood. Build a direct current microgrid to distribute solar for a campus or neighborhood.

Goods (Materials) Pathway

Buy *25 kilograms of mass* or less per person per day on average, buy *eco-friendly materials*, *maintain and reuse* durable goods and packaging, and *compost or recycle* solid waste.

- The less mass of material goods purchased per day, the fewer the negative environmental impacts from mining, manufacturing, storing, shipping, and disposing. Lowering the amount of material flowing through your home to below 25 kilograms per person per day keeps these impacts well within safe planetary limits.
- Buying eco-friendly materials reduces the negative environmental impacts of the goods you buy. *Replenishing* materials (like wood) and fully *recyclable* materials (like glass and metal) are sustainable because we can use them over and over. With sustainable forestry practices, paper, cardboard, and wood are sustainable materials, especially if we return nutrients to the soil by composting. *Diminishing* materials (like plastic derived from fossil fuel) are not sustainable. Fossil-derived plastic is not a sustainable material because the feedstocks (fossil gas, oil, and coal) are not replenishing, and most plastic resins cannot be recycled.
- Maintaining and reusing goods and packaging reduces the environmental impacts associated with mining and manufacturing to produce new goods. Reusing is more sustainable than recycling because it is much more efficient; however, compared to recycling, reusing requires more careful coordination among manufacturers, retailers, and consumers for certain items, like packaging. The more expensive and durable the item, the more likely a reuse market exists.
- In a fully circular economy, eco-friendly materials enter a sustainable cycle in which they are fully reused, composted, or recycled rather than incinerated, landfilled, or dumped.

	Unsustainable	*Somewhat Sustainable*	*Positively Sustainable*
Buy Less	Buying 50 kg or more per day	Buying around 35 kg per day	Buying 25 kg or less per day
Choose Eco-Friendly Goods	Buying disposable goods, toxic substances, plastics, and fuels	Buying few disposable goods, and more non-toxic substances and durable goods	Buying only non-toxic substances and goods that can be fully reused, composted, or recycled
Maintain and Reuse	Never maintaining goods; always buying new	Doing essential maintenance; occasionally buying used	Carefully maintaining goods; frequently buying used goods
Manage Waste Well	Incinerating and landfilling waste	Recycling but not composting	Composting and recycling

Buy Less

Reduce the environmental impacts of your material consumption

Quick-Start Practices to Buy Less

Economize	Resist impulse purchases and cultivate intentional consumption. Track and adjust washing and cleaning frequency.
Choose	Give experiences or gift certificates rather than physical items.

	Buy quality items that are durable and repairable.

Intermediate Practices to Buy Less

Borrow	Borrow tools from a library of things or from family, friends, or neighbors. Rent rather than buy things you'll need only for a few days or weeks.
Economize	Buy concentrated solutions and in bulk to buy less unnecessary packaging. Use washable menstrual products.
Join	Join your local Buy Nothing group or use the Buy Nothing app. Participate in your local Freecycle Network.

Advanced Practices to Buy Less

Craft	Make household items from natural materials.
Lend	Lend your tools to family, friends, and neighbors so they don't have to buy.
Organize	Organize your possessions so you know what you already have.

Transformative Practices to Buy Less

Organize	Create a library of things
Volunteer	Lead your local Freecycle Network.

Choose Green Goods

Prevent pollution and close the loop on material flows

Quick-Start Practices to Choose Green Goods

Avoid	Avoid single-use plastic.
Cleaning	Use microfiber cloths to clean.

Intermediate Practices to Choose Green Goods

Avoid	Avoid products containing mercury, such as fluorescent lighting.
Cooking	Cook on stainless steel or cast iron; avoid non-stick coatings that contain PFAS (per- and polyfluoroalkyl substances).
Select	Buy products made from wood, glass, and metal–fully recyclable materials.

Advanced Practices to Choose Green Goods

Avoid	Avoid products with high amounts of volatile organic compounds. Avoid products made from plastic.
Clothing	Buy durable clothes made from natural fibers. Avoid clothing treated with PFAS for stain resistance or water repellency.
Furniture	Buy furniture made from wood or metal. Avoid furniture treated with PFAS for stain resistance or water repellency.
Select	Buy products that comply with RoHS (Restriction of Hazardous Substances).

Maintain and Reuse

Extend the useful life of products and reduce the need to manufacture new goods

Quick-Start Practices to Maintain and Reuse

Choose	Choose reusable goods, such as bagless vacuum cleaners with washable filters. Use rechargeable batteries rather than disposable ones.
Maintain	Read and keep maintenance manuals for reference. Inspect, clean, and replace components per operating instructions.
Reuse	Reuse containers and bags. Reuse glass jars for drinking glasses. Accept gifts of hand-me-down items from friends and family. Shop at second-hand stores and yard sales to buy used items.

Intermediate Practices to Maintain and Reuse

Repair	Repair torn clothing and broken zippers.

Advanced Practices to Maintain and Reuse

Repair	Repair efficient appliances; replace inefficient ones.

Transformative Practices to Maintain and Reuse

Organize	Organize a reuse program at your local school or community organization.
Repair	Lead a repair team for your local library of things.

Manage Waste Wisely

Return materials safely back into a circular economy

Quick-Start Practices to Manage Waste Wisely

Compost	Compost yard waste, such as leaves and grass clippings, in a simple outdoor pile. Bury organic waste to compost.
Discard	Landfill plastic and other synthetic waste materials.
Donate	Share hand-me-downs, such as children's clothing, with friends and family. Resell or donate useful items that are no longer needed.
Organize	Sort your waste into five streams: reuse, compost, recycle, landfill, and divert. Store household hazardous waste in a safe collection area.
Recycle	Recycle glass, metal, and clean cardboard.

Intermediate Practices to Manage Waste Wisely

Compost	Subscribe to a curbside composting program. Drop off kitchen and yard waste at a municipal composting facility. Compost in a three-bin outdoor system. Compost in a kitchen appliance.
Discard	Hire a junk removal company.
Recycle	Recycle electronic devices and batteries.

Advanced Practices to Manage Waste Wisely

Compost	Ferment first, then compost. Compost in an enclosed tumbler. Compost in a buried chamber. Compost in a worm bin. Compost in a fly house.

Transformative Practices to Manage Waste Wisely

Organize	Organize a neighborhood composting program. Organize a household hazardous waste collection event. Organize a neighborhood "green" yard sale and waste removal event.

Habitat (Buildings and Land) Pathway

Choose sustainable shelter and *build to green standards, renovate wisely* using non-toxic materials and green building techniques, and *protect natural systems.*

- Many green building certification and rating standards exist; meeting any of them improves sustainability indicators compared to building to conventional code minimums.
- Renovation projects (including both restorative and preventative maintenance as well as improvements) are chances to extend the useful life of buildings, abate hazards, and provide more people with shelter within the footprint of an existing building.
- Landscaping and land use decisions are opportunities to protect natural systems. For example, planting a garden instead of a lawn increases the amount of food available on Earth and provides more opportunities for native species to persist. Installing a permeable driveway instead of a hardscape increases your community's resilience against flooding and provides a path for precipitation to filter through sediment to recharge ground-water reservoirs.

	Unsustainable	*Somewhat Sustainable*	*Positively Sustainable*
Shelter Well	Building to code minimums	Implementing a few green building features	Achieving a green building certification
Renovate Wisely	Adding toxins, lowering occupancy	Fixing problems, maintaining occupancy	Abating hazards, increasing occupancy
Protect Nature	Destroying natural systems	Occasionally protecting natural systems	Consistently protecting natural systems

Shelter Well

Choose and build sustainable shelter for people

Quick-Start Practices to Shelter Well

Choose	Live in a walkable neighborhood. Live in an apartment building rather than a single-family house.
Share	Share housing with other people.

Intermediate Practices to Shelter Well

Choose	Select existing housing that meets high performance standards.
Inspect	Hire a professional rater to inspect and rate your home's performance.

Advanced Practices to Shelter Well

Choose	Choose to downsize into a smaller living space.
Share	Rent out rooms in your home to provide more housing in your community.

Revision: 25.1.8

Transformative Practices to Shelter Well

Build	Build a new "green" single family home. Build a new "green" commercial building. Build an apartment building.
Share	Build an accessory dwelling unit in your backyard to rent.
Develop	Develop a cohousing community with clustered homes and microgrid solar power.

Renovate Wisely

Maintain and renovate buildings in ways that have a more positive environmental impact

Quick-Start Practices to Renovate Wisely

Maintain	Clean kitchen and bathroom exhaust fans and ducting. Maintain indoor humidity below 60% to mitigate mold and mildew.

Intermediate Practices to Renovate Wisely

Abate	Replace fluorescent lighting that contains mercury. Replace thermostats that contain mercury. Remove or encapsulate surfaces covered in lead paint. Remove soil contaminated with lead paint chips. Install vapor barriers in basements.
Construct	Select lumber from locally available tree species. Use metal ground screws or helical posts rather than poured concrete footings. Choose fiberglass instead of vinyl windows.
Maintain	Fix roof leaks. Install gutters or roofline drainage to direct water away from buildings.
Paint	Paint with non-toxic, zero-VOC coatings.

Advanced Practices to Renovate Wisely

Abate	Abate asbestos.
Construct	Construct floors, walls, ceilings, and siding from reclaimed lumber. Construct fences and decking from rot-resistant recycled plastic composites. Construct siding from fiber cement that contains recycled content. Upgrade asphalt shingle roofing to metal roofing that simplifies adding solar.
Insulate	Insulate with cellulose, rock wool, or cotton, not fiberglass.
Maintain	Install battery backup to maintain power during grid outages.
Plumbing	Move plumbing runs to avoid frozen pipes.

Transformative Practices to Renovate Wisely

Construct	Construct walls from straw bales. Construct floors and walls from rammed earth. Construct walls from adobe.
Share	Convert rooms in your home to an in-law apartment to rent.

Protect Nature

Benefit from ecosystem services that nature provides for free

Quick-Start Practices to Protect Nature

Learn	Identify environmental hazards in and around your home and yard.
Manage	Keep cats indoors so birds and wild animals can live in your neighborhood. Keep dogs on leash when hiking in areas where sensitive species live.
Support	Donate money to land trusts and other organizations that conserve natural land. Vote for parks and wilderness areas.

Intermediate Practices to Protect Nature

Landscape	Plant native species in your yard. Manage pests with an integrated plan that minimizes synthetic pesticide use.
Support	Register your native plantings on the Homegrown National Park Biodiversity Map. Turn your yard or garden into a National Wildlife Federation Certified Wildlife Habitat.

Advanced Practices to Protect Nature

Landscape	Landscape with organic methods; avoid all synthetic fertilizers and pesticides.
Manage	Put your land under conservation easement.

Transformative Practices to Protect Nature

Remove	Remove roads on your land. Remove unnecessary buildings on your land.

Practice Guides

A
- Abating
  - Replacing Fluorescent Lighting, 463
  - Replacing Mercury Thermostats, 464
  - Encapsulating Lead Paint, 465
  - Removing Contaminated Soil, 466
  - Blocking Vapor, 467
  - Abating Asbestos, 469

- Acting
  - Taking Action, 73
  - Starting Quick-Start Practices, 73
  - Starting Intermediate Practices, 73
  - Starting Advanced Practices, 74
  - Starting Transformative Practices, 75

- Avoiding Materials
  - Deplastifying, 395
  - Avoiding Mercury, 396
  - Avoiding VOCs, 397
  - Avoiding All Plastic, 398

B
- Borrowing
  - Borrowing Tools, 381
  - Renting, 381
  - Renting Electric, 274

- Building
  - Insulating, 279
  - Removing Chimneys, 280
  - Going Passive Solar, 281
  - Cooling Roofs, 283
  - Building Homes, 455
  - Building Offices, 456
  - Building Apartments, 456

C
- Car-Free Living
  - Going Without a Car, 268

- Carpooling
  - Sharing Rides, 261

- Certifying
  - Certifying Your Sustainability, 76

- Charging
  - Using Solar Chargers, 363

- Choosing Electric
  - Ride Sharing, 276

- Choosing Goods
  - Choosing Reusables, 409
  - Choosing Rechargeables, 409

Choosing Less	Giving Experiences, 381
	Buying Quality, 381
Choosing Shelter	Living in a Walkable Neighborhood, 456
	Apartment Living, 457
	High-Performance Housing, 457
	Downsizing, 457
Cleaning	Choosing Safer Solutions, 245
	Choosing Soap, 246
	Avoiding Phosphate, 247
	Using Microfiber, 400
	Steaming, 247
	Electrolyzing, 249
Clothing	Choosing Natural Fibers, 401
	Avoiding PFAS, 402
Committing	Committing to Improve, 78
	Setting Achievable Goals, 79
	Creating Simple Plans, 79
	Creating Detailed Plans, 80
Composting	Safety, 419
	Collecting Kitchen Waste, 419
	Collecting Household Waste, 420
	Collecting Leaves, 421
	Using a Single Pile, 422
	Burying Organic Waste, 423
	Curbside Composting, 424
	Municipal Composting, 426
	Using Three Bins, 427
	Using a Kitchen Appliance, 430
	Fermenting First, 431
	Using a Tumbler, 433
	Using a Buried Chamber, 435
	Using Worms, 438
	Using Flies, 440
Constructing	Selecting Lumber, 470
	Screwing Foundations, 471
	Fenestrating with Fiberglass, 472
	Reclaiming Lumber, 472
	Recycling Plastic, 473

		Siding with Cement, 474
		Metal Roofing, 475
		Building with Straw, 476
		Building with Earth, 478
		Building with Adobe, 480
	Cooking	Avoiding PFAS, 404
		Microwaving, 333
		Pressure Cooking, 334
		Cooking Outside, 335
		Preparing Cold Meals, 336
		Preparing Multiple Meals, 337
		Induction Cooking, 285
		Convection Cooking, 286
		Solar Cooking, 339
		Cooking with Electricity, 354
	Crafting	Making Items, 382
	Cycling	Cycling Fifteen Minutes, 266
		Cycling Sixty Minutes, 266
		Riding E-Bikes, 276
D	Developing Shelter	Cohousing, 458
	Discarding	Landfilling, 443
		Removing Junk, 443
	Displacing	Displacing Tank Water, 234
	Donating	Sharing Used Items, 443
		Reselling or Donating, 444
	Drainscaping	Installing a Rain Garden, 250
		Permeable Paving, 252
		Building Bridges, 254
		Green Roofing, 254
	Driving	Driving Slower, 340
		Driving Gently, 340
		Offloading Weight, 340
		Rolling Up Windows, 340
		Transporting Items, 341
		Removing Racks, 341

		Minimizing Cabin Heat, 341
		Driving with Electricity, 355
E	Eating	Preparing Portions, 141
		Eating Leftovers, 143
		Bringing Containers, 146
		Making Soup Stock, 147
	Eating More Plants	Eating a Wider Variety, 182
		Sampling Food Traditions, 182
		Eating Vegan, 182
	Economizing	Flushing Toilets, 235
		Filling Loads, 235
		Cutting Short, 235
		Washing Less, 236
		Taking Navy Showers, 236
		Unplugging Appliances, 341
		Drinking Cold Beverages, 341
		Watching Shows on Small Screens, 342
		Listening on Headphones, 342
		Reading Printed Books, 342
		Resisting Impulses, 383
		Showering Colder, 342
		Adjusting Frequency, 384
		Using Elbow Grease, 342
		Buying in Bulk, 385
		Managing Menstruation, 387
		Sweeping, 342
F	Fenestration (Optimizing)	Closing Windows, 312
		Using Blinds, 313
		Opening Windows, 346
		Installing Inserts, 313
		Using Awnings, 314
		Fixing Panes, 315
		Repairing Windows, 317
		Installing Windows, 318
		Installing Doors, 320
	Food (Avoiding)	Avoiding Endangered Seafood, 176
		Avoiding Red Meat, 176
		Avoiding Mammals, 176
		Avoiding Cod, 176

	Food (Buying)	Buying Ugly, 128
		Buying Preserved, 130
		Buying Hardy, 133
		Buying USDA Organic, 189
		Buying Sustainable Palm Oil, 189
		Buying Chocolate, 189
		Buying Coffee, 190
		Buying Perishables, 135
		Supporting Local Farms, 137
		Supporting Organic Farmers, 190
		Buying In Season, 139
	Food (Selecting)	Drinking Tap Water, 176
		Eating Venison, 177
		Eating Certified Seafood, 177
		Eating Wild Game, 178
		Eating Legumes, 178
		Eating Farmed Seafood, 181
		Eating Shark, 181
	Food (Serving)	Changing Menus, 184
		Creating a Plant-based Restaurant, 185
	Food (Sharing)	Organizing Donations, 152
		Distributing Food, 155
	Food (Storing)	Storing Bread, 159
		Washing Produce, 161
		Organizing Food Storage, 164
		Preserving Food, 166
		Creating a Community Kitchen, 170
	Food (Understanding)	Learning Labels, 173
		Being Safe, 174
	Furnishing	Avoiding PFAS, 405
G	Governing	Developing Certification Systems, 123
		Proposing Legislation, 125
		Running for Office, 126
	Growing Food	Sprouting Seeds, 191
		Growing Microgreens, 194
		Growing Herbs, 197

			Growing Fruits and Nuts, 199
			Growing a Food Garden, 202
			Raising Chickens, 206
			Making Syrup, 209
			Practicing Permaculture, 212
H		Heating & Cooling	Setting Thermostats, 288
			Adjusting Thermostats, 343
			Programming Thermostats, 288
			Circulating Air, 289
			Sealing Ducts, 291
			Installing Wood Stoves, 292
			Fanning Rooms, 294
			Fanning Home, 296
			Pumping Heat, 298
			Ventilating, 299
			Heating Air with Electricity, 356
			Distributing Heat, 301
			Organizing a Buying Group, 358
I		Inspecting Shelter	Rating Performance, 459
		Insulating	Avoiding Fiberglass, 481
J		Joining	Joining Buy Nothing, 387
			Joining Your Freecycle Network, 388
L		Landscaping	Borrowing Electric Equipment, 359
			Buying Electric Equipment, 359
			Planting Natives, 490
			Managing Pests, 491
			Planting Shade Trees, 302
			Planting Windbreaks, 304
			Going Organic, 493
		Learning	Prompting AI, 55
			Reading to Understand Sustainability, 563
			Watching Documentaries, 56
			Taking Courses, 57
			Identifying Hazards, 495
			Attending Hands-On Workshops, 57
			Earning Certifications, 57
			Building a Resource Library, 59
			Researching Practices, 61

Earning an Undergraduate Degree, 63
Earning an Advanced Degree, 65

Lending
Lending Tools, 388
Lending Out Electric Tools, 360

Lighting
Installing LEDs, 305
Turning Off, 344
Leaving Off, 344
Controlling Lighting, 306
Reducing Power, 344
Task Lighting, 345
Dimming, 307
Piping Light, 309

M

Maintaining
Keeping Manuals, 410
Cleaning Fans and Ducts, 482
Controlling Humidity, 483
Fixing Roof Leaks, 484
Installing Gutters, 485
Installing Batteries, 487

Maintaining Efficiency
Cleaning Systems, 310
Replacing Filters, 310
Insulating Ducts, 310
Inspecting Burners, 312

Managing
Keeping Cats Indoors, 496
Keeping Dogs on Leash, 496
Fencing, 256
Growing Buffer Zones, 257
Placing an Easement, 496

Managing Waste
Picking Up Litter, 257
Handling Medical and Hazardous Waste, 257

O

Optimizing Appliances
Installing Smart Strips, 312
Upgrading Electronics, 312

Organizing
Organizing Possessions, 389
Creating a Library of Things, 390
Starting a Reuse Program, 411

Organizing Waste
Sorting Into Five Streams, 444
Storing Hazardous Waste, 445

		Neighborhood Composting, 447
		Collecting Hazardous Waste, 449
		Having a "Green" Neighborhood Yard Sale, 450
P	Painting	Avoiding Toxins, 488
	Planning Meals	Organizing Recipes, 150
		Creating a Meal Plan, 151
		Finding Vegetarian Recipes, 182
		Eating Plant-Based Meals, 183
		Finding Vegan Recipes, 183
		Scheduling Meat-Free Mondays, 184
		Understanding Nutrition, 184
	Planning Movement	Minimizing Engine Starts, 261
		Minimizing Air Travel, 261
	Plumbing	Insulating Pipes, 322
		Lowering Temperatures, 346
		Pumping Heat, 323
		Scheduling Hot Water, 346
		Heating Water with Electricity, 361
		Protecting Pipes, 488
	Plumbing (Maintaining)	Reviewing Bills to Check for Leaks, 217
		Detecting Leaks, 218
		Organizing a Leak Brigade, 219
	Plumbing (Upgrading)	Upgrading Showerheads and Aerators, 222
		Upgrading Toilets, 223
		Upgrading Irrigation, 226
		Upgrading Dishwashers, 228
		Upgrading Washing Machines, 230
		Installing Hot Water Recirculation, 233
R	Recycling	Recycling Metal, Cardboard, and Glass, 452
		Recycling Electronics and Batteries, 452
	Reducing Meat	Adjusting Recipes, 184
	Refrigerating	Circulating Air, 325
		Shading Refrigerators, 325
		Operating Just One, 348
		Raising Temperatures, 348
		Upgrading, 326

		Moving Refrigerators, 349
		Downsizing Refrigerators, 349
		Digging a Root Cellar, 350
	Removing	Removing Roads, 498
		Removing Buildings, 499
	Repairing	Fixing Clothing, 413
		Fixing Appliances, 415
		Leading a Team, 416
	Reusing	Reusing Containers, 412
		Reusing Jars, 413
		Accepting Used Items, 413
		Thrifting, 413
	Riding	Riding Convenient Transit, 269
		Riding All Transit, 270
	Sealing	Caulking, 326
		Weatherstripping, 328
S	Selecting Materials	Choosing Recyclables, 406
		Choosing RoHS, 408
	Sharing Knowledge	Forwarding Information, 87
		Discussing Issues, 87
		Using Social Media, 88
		Blogging, 88
		Hosting Parties, 89
		Offering Tours, 91
		Leading Discussions, 92
		Building Educational Displays, 93
		Publishing Infographics, 96
		Writing Articles, 98
		Giving Talks, 99
		Teaching Classes, 102
		Publishing Books and Films, 105
		Hosting a Podcast, 105
		Establishing Learning Centers, 106
		Building Research Programs, 106
	Sharing Habitat	Accessory Dwelling, 461
	Sharing Shelter	Living With Roommates, 460

	Renting Out Rooms, 460
	Creating an In-Law Apartment, 488
Shopping	Buying Online, 261
Solar (Choosing)	Choosing "Green" Electricity, 364
	Subscribing to Solar, 365
Solar (Installing)	Building a Solar Shed, 366
	Lighting, 367
	Pumping Water, 368
	Running Fans, 370
	Heating Water, 370
	Generating Electricity, 372
	Storing Electricity, 373
Solar (Investing)	Investing in Solar 401: Farming Electricity, 375
Solar (Organizing)	Purchasing Solar, 376
	Distributing Solar, 378
Streamlining Water Use	Skipping Pre-Rinsing, 221
	Composting Not Disposing, 221
Substituting	Replacing Mammal Milk, 187
	Taking Showers, 236
	Sweeping, 236
	Eating Plant-Based Ice Cream, 187
	Eating Plant-Based Cheese, 188
	Eating Plant-Based Dairy, 188
	Eliminating Meat, 188
	Xeriscaping, 236
	Using a Waterless Urinal, 238
	Using a Composting Toilet, 240
	Using an Incinerating Toilet, 242
Supporting	Conserving Land, 500
	Voting for Nature, 500
	Registering Your Biodiversity, 500
	Certifying Your Habitat, 501
Synchronizing	Using Solar Power, 352
	Getting Sleep, 352

T

Telecommuting	Working From Home, 262

		Employing Remote Workers, 263
	Tracking	Keeping a Journal, 80
		Calculating a Quick-Start Suspra Score, 81
		Using Checklists, 81
		Calculating a Regular Suspra Score, 82
		Calculating a Detailed Suspra Score, 83
		Comparing Suspra Scores, 83
		Improving the Suspra Scoring System, 85
V	Vehicles (Buying)	Buying a Plug-In Hybrid, 274
		Buying an EV, 274
	Vehicles (Optimizing)	Inflating Tires, 321
		Cruising, 322
		Using Racks, 322
		Improving Racks, 322
	Verifying Knowledge	Confirming Facts, 66
		Taking Knowledge Tests, 66
		Investigating Credibility, 67
		Researching Environmental Impacts, 68
		Measuring Sustainability Indicators, 68
	Volunteering	Joining Projects, 107
		Joining Organizations, 108
		Coaching Sustainability, 109
		Leading Teams, 111
		Serving on a Sustainability Committee, 112
		Recruiting Sustainability Coaches, 113
		Leading in an Environmental Organization, 115
		Starting a Sustainability Coaching Program, 115
		Leading Your Freecycle Network, 392
	Voting	Voting Pro-Environment, 118
W	Walking	Walking Five Minutes, 271
		Walking Fifteen Minutes, 271
		Walking Sixty Minutes, 272
	Washing	Using Cold Water, 330
		Upgrading Washing Machines, 330
		Drying Clothes, 331
		Hanging Laundry, 352

Working Making Practical Suggestions, 119
Working a Job with an Environmental Mission, 119
Starting an Organization or Business, 120

Community Practices

Understanding Sustainability, page 55	
Goals	**Indicators**
• Build knowledge to guide practices	• Scores on sustainability knowledge tests

Demonstrating Sustainability, page 73	
Goals	**Indicators**
• Learn by doing • Lead by example	• Number of sustainable practices being demonstrated well

Nurturing Good Relationships, page 87	
Goals	**Indicators**
• Strengthen connections so community members work together for a sustainable future	• Number of people taking tests and surveys • Volunteer hours logged

Understanding Sustainability

Learning 101: Prompting AI

Prompt artificial intelligence (AI) systems to explain sustainability science

Use AI as a starting point for understanding sustainability science, then verify knowledge through other sources such as articles or books. Ask AI chatbots to explain complex ideas in accessible ways, helping you understand concepts, relationships, and implications. AI is particularly useful for:

- Breaking down complex sustainability concepts into understandable pieces
- Explaining scientific terms in everyday language
- Connecting different aspects of sustainability science into a cohesive framework
- Providing personalized explanations based on your background and interests
- Answering follow-up questions as your understanding develops

However, AI may "hallucinate" (make up information) with no warning.

Learning 101: Equipment & Materials
- Computer, tablet, or smartphone with Internet access to an AI chatbot

Learning 101: Steps
1. Choose an AI that has a knowledge cutoff date within the past twelve months; newer models are generally more intelligent and less likely to hallucinate than older models.
2. Ask specific questions about sustainability concepts you want to learn.
3. Request explanations at the level of understanding you want: for example, "Explain planetary boundaries in simple terms a high school student would understand."
4. Ask for references to scientific journal articles and the names of the scientists who are experts in the subject to improve the quality of the AI responses to your prompts.
5. Request the AI to provide multiple perspectives: for example, "What are the different scientific viewpoints on how quickly we need to achieve net-zero emissions?"
6. Ask the AI how to improve the questions you are asking to get better answers.
7. Prompt for practical applications; for example, "Which everyday practices help keep environmental impacts within Earth's carrying capacity?"
8. Use follow-up questions to explore topics more deeply: for example, "Based on your response about sustainable agriculture, explain more about the beef industry and deforestation."
9. Verify AI responses against other AI, credible external sources like peer-reviewed articles, established scientific organizations, or this handbook.

Learning 101: Definitions
- **Artificial intelligence (AI)**: machines that can simulate human intelligence
- **Chatbots**: software applications powered by AI that converse with human users through text
- **Hallucinate**: when an AI generates information that seems factual but is actually false
- **Knowledge cutoff**: when an AI's pre-training stopped, limiting its awareness of recent events
- **Pre-training**: exposing an AI to data from books, articles, websites, and other sources, allowing it to learn patterns before the AI is refined for specific uses
- **Prompt**: input provided to an AI to elicit a response
- **Response**: information generated by an AI based on a prompt

Learning 101: Troubleshooting

Problem	Solutions
AI provides vague information	Ask more specific questions.
AI gives contradictory information	Normal behavior. Request clarification.
Information seems outdated	Check the AI's knowledge cutoff date. Verify with other sources.
Technical terms are confusing	Ask the AI to explain and define specific terms.
AI doesn't provide sources	Explicitly request references so you can verify information.

Learning 101: Limitations

- AI have knowledge cutoff dates and searches may not include all recent research
- AI may present incorrect information confidently
- AI may persuasively present false world views
- Local sustainability issues might not be accurately represented by AI models
- AI cannot replace in-depth study from primary scientific sources or hands-on experience

References and resources: <www.suspra.com/practice/community/learning-101.html>

Learning 102: Reading to Understand Sustainability

Find and read the best articles and books about sustainability science

Find and read high-quality sustainability literature to make informed decisions and improve sustainable practices. Start with accessible books or reports written for a general audience. As you build understanding, gradually incorporate more technical scientific papers. Look for the original source of facts or ideas to make sure you are getting an accurate understanding of them. Take structured notes to integrate knowledge across sources. Use methods like the three-column Cornell note-taking system or concept mapping to organize information. When reading scientific papers, pay particular attention to the methods section to evaluate the strength of evidence.

References and resources: <www.suspra.com/practice/community/learning-102.html>

Learning 103: Watching Documentaries

Find and watch the best nature and technology documentaries about sustainability

Select nature and technology documentaries that combine scientific accuracy with compelling storytelling. Problem-oriented documentaries explain environmental challenges; solution-oriented documentaries showcase innovations and success stories; and systems-thinking documentaries explore interconnections between human and natural systems.

Start with established documentary producers (BBC Earth, National Geographic, PBS, NOVA), explore documentaries on streaming services, check university and educational institution websites for free documentaries, consider film festival selections for cutting-edge sustainability documentaries, and ask librarians for recommendations.

References and resources: <www.suspra.com/practice/community/learning-103.html>

Learning 104: Taking Courses

Take the best online courses about sustainability science

Choose courses that combine scientific fundamentals with practical applications to help you understand planetary boundaries, systems thinking, and case studies. Quality courses are taught by recognized experts, include current research, and provide opportunities to apply theoretical concepts to real-world situations.

Begin with online courses that explain broad sustainability frameworks and concepts. As your knowledge grows, take specialized courses focusing on specific aspects of sustainability (renewable energy, sustainable agriculture, circular economy, etc.). Tailor assignments to your specific home, workplace, or community context. Establish a regular study schedule and create a dedicated learning environment to increase your odds of completion. Actively participate in discussion forums, peer review activities, and group projects.

References and resources: <www.suspra.com/practice/community/learning-104.html>

Learning 201: Attending Hands-On Workshops

Find and attend hands-on workshops to learn sustainable practices

Attend hands-on workshops for valuable experiential learning beyond what's possible to obtain from books, videos, or apps. Get direct instruction from experts, immediate feedback, and practical experience with tools and techniques. Connect with a community of like-minded individuals who share your sustainability interests. Offer to carpool with other participants if workshops are not within walking or cycling distance.

Identify the kind of workshops you want to attend by selecting specific skills you want to learn (gardening, solar, home energy efficiency, etc.) and determining your current skill level (beginner, intermediate, advanced). Look for high-quality workshops:

- Instructors with real-world experience, not just theoretical knowledge
- Group size below 16 to ensure individual attention
- Materials and methods that align with sustainable principles
- Content that can be directly applied in your local context

Communities often offer free or low-cost workshops funded by local governments or nonprofits, especially ones that focus on practices that save money over time (energy efficiency, food preservation, repair skills), making them both environmentally and economically beneficial. To find workshops, check community centers, cooperative extension offices, and public libraries, visit local sustainability organizations' websites and social media pages, search online platforms like Eventbrite, Meetup, or Facebook Events, contact local colleges and universities about continuing education programs, ask at garden centers, hardware stores, and tool libraries about upcoming demonstrations, or subscribe to newsletters from local environmental organizations and community groups.

References and resources: <www.suspra.com/practice/community/learning-201.html>

Learning 202: Earning Certifications

Earn professional sustainability certifications

Demonstrate your commitment to professional knowledge and standards in the field of sustainability by earning professional sustainability certifications. Online courses offer certificates of completion, but professional certifications require rigorous assessment of knowledge and skills, typically through examination or portfolio review. Professional sustainability certifications serve multiple purposes:

- Validate your expertise to employers, clients, and colleagues
- Provide structured learning paths to master important concepts
- Connect you with a community of similarly certified professionals
- Keep your knowledge current through continuing education requirements
- Demonstrate your commitment to sustainability standards and practices

Entry-level certifications like the International Society of Sustainability Professionals (ISSP) Sustainability Excellence Associate provide a strong foundation. Mid-career professionals may benefit from specialized certifications, such as LEED Green Associate for building professionals or the Association of Energy Engineers Certified Energy Manager for those focused on energy efficiency.

Consider the requirements for maintaining certification. Professional certifications typically require periodic renewal through continuing education, ensuring your knowledge remains current. These requirements ensure the certification maintains its value over time.

Learning 202: Equipment & Materials
- Budget for certification fees ($50-2,000 depending on certification)
- Time for study and examination preparation (10-100+ hours)

Learning 202: Steps
1. Identify your sustainability goals and interests
2. Research certification options
   - Look for certifications with industry recognition and accreditation
   - Verify the certification is current and valued in your region
   - Check certification prerequisites (education, experience, prior certifications)
   - Compare certification costs, time commitments, and renewal requirements
   - Assess the certification's credibility by researching the issuing organization
3. Evaluate certification quality using these criteria:
   - Requires demonstration of knowledge through testing or portfolio review
   - Maintained by established organizations with sustainability expertise
   - Includes continuing education requirements
   - Requires periodic renewal to maintain certification
   - Recognized by employers and professionals in the field
   - Available publicly (not limited to specific companies or private groups)
4. Select certifications to obtain: consider stackable certification pathways that build on each other
5. Complete certification requirements
6. Maintain and leverage your certification
   - List your certification in your email signature
   - Continue building expertise through practice and additional learning
   - Consider teaching or mentoring others in your certification area

Learning 202: Definitions
- **Accreditation**: Recognition that a certification meets standards for quality and integrity
- **Certificate**: Documentation of completion of a course or program (different from certification)
- **Certification**: Process that validates knowledge, skills, and competencies through assessment
- **Continuing Education Units (CEUs)**: Measurements for ongoing professional education requirements to maintain certification
- **Credential**: Official documentation of qualifications, which may include certifications
- **Portfolio review**: Assessment method requiring demonstration of completed work or projects

- **Recertification**: Process of renewing a certification, typically requiring continuing education
- **Stackable credentials**: Certifications designed to build upon each other in a career pathway

Learning 202: Troubleshooting

Problem	Solutions
High certification costs	Seek scholarships, employer training funds, or early registration discounts.
Difficulty finding study time	Break study sessions into 15-30 minutes. Use mobile apps to study during commutes. Schedule early morning or late evening study sessions.
Uncertainty about which certification to choose	Consult with professionals in your desired field, check job listings to see which certifications employers request, or take introductory courses before committing to full certification paths.
Overwhelming amount of study material	Create a structured study plan with specific goals, focus on official study guides first, use practice questions to identify knowledge gaps, and consider finding a mentor who already holds the certification.

Learning 202: Limitations

- Some certifications have geographic limitations in recognition or applicability
- A certification demonstrates knowledge but doesn't guarantee practical application skills
- The field of sustainability evolves rapidly, sometimes outpacing certification offerings
- Employer recognition of sustainability certifications varies widely by industry and region
- Some certifications emphasize theoretical knowledge over practical implementation
- Very specialized certifications may have limited applicability across different roles

References and resources: <www.suspra.com/practice/community/learning-202.html>

Learning 301: Building a Resource Library

Build a personal resource library for sustainable practices

Build a thoughtful, well-curated sustainability library to have access to reliable, context-specific information when you need it. Span the full spectrum from theoretical understanding to practical implementation. Foundational resources explain the "why" behind sustainability efforts, while practice guides and technical manuals address the "how." Include locally relevant resources that adapt general principles to your specific climate, ecosystem, and regulatory environment.

As you implement practices, document your experiences to create a personal knowledge base that reflects what works in your unique context. These records of personal implementation become some of the most valuable resources in your collection.

Learning 301: Equipment & Materials

- Bookshelf, filing cabinet, or digital storage system
- *Optional: Cloud storage account, external hard drive, reference management software (Zotero, Mendeley, EndNote), scanner (for digitizing printed materials)*

Learning 301: Steps

1. Plan your library structure
   - Create a categorization system based on pathways to sustainability (food, energy, water, etc.)
   - Establish a metadata system (author, publication date, topic tags, etc.)

Sustainable Practices Handbook — Community Practices: Understanding Sustainability

- o Decide on your balance of physical versus digital resources
2. Collect foundational resources
   - o Acquire basic references covering key sustainability principles
   - o Include at least one comprehensive sustainability handbook or textbook
   - o Gather practical guides relevant to your specific interests and local context
3. Develop a curation process
   - o Evaluate potential resources using criteria such as:
     - Scientific accuracy and currency of information
     - Practical applicability to your context
     - Authors' expertise and credibility
     - Balance of theoretical understanding and practical guidance
   - o Regularly audit existing resources to ensure they remain current and relevant
4. Organize your physical resources
   - o Use clearly labeled folders for loose papers and articles
5. Organize your digital resources
   - o Create a logical folder structure that mirrors your physical organization
   - o Use consistent file naming conventions
   - o Back up digital resources regularly onto a local hard drive
6. Supplement with dynamic resources (newsletters, journals, online forums)
7. Document your own experiences
   - o Keep journals or digital notes of your sustainability projects
   - o Take before-and-after photos of implementations
   - o Record measurements and outcomes of your practices
   - o Note adaptations you've made to standard practices for your specific context
8. Schedule periodic reviews to remove outdated or superseded materials
9. Share and collaborate
   - o Catalog your resources
   - o Invite others to contribute to and benefit from your library
   - o Create a community resource library
   - o Establish a system for lending materials to others
   - o Digitize key physical resources for backup and sharing
   - o Participate in resource exchanges with like-minded individuals

Learning 301: Definitions

- **Curation**: Selecting, organizing, and maintaining resources according to specific criteria
- **Digital repository**: An organized digital system for storing and retrieving electronic resources
- **Metadata**: Information about resources (author, date, topic) that enables storage and retrieval
- **Resource audit**: Systematic review of materials to evaluate their relevance and accuracy

Learning 301: Troubleshooting

Problem	Solutions
Information overload	Focus on your most immediate needs. Create a "to read" queue. Use a rating system to prioritize must-have versus nice-to-have resources.
Contradictory information	Check publication dates. Verify author credentials and source reliability. Consult multiple sources to establish consensus.
Storage limitations	Prioritize digital formats. Consider cloud storage solutions. For physical items, rotate seasonal resources to storage during off-seasons.

Revision: 25.1.8

Problem	Solutions
Difficulty finding specific information	Use better keywords and cross-references. Create a digital index even for physical resources. Digitize tables of contents from physical materials.

Learning 301: Limitations

- Quality resources may not be free, particularly academic publications
- Technical materials may require specialized knowledge to fully utilize
- Copyright restrictions may limit your ability to reproduce and share certain materials

References and resources: <www.suspra.com/practice/community/learning-301.html>

Learning 302: Researching Practices

Research sustainable practices in your community

Research sustainable practices in your community to gain crucial local context for implementing effective sustainability initiatives—considering your community's unique environmental conditions, cultural factors, economic realities, and existing infrastructure. Discover existing sustainability efforts that you can support, identify gaps where new initiatives are needed, recognize local experts and changemakers, understand the policies and regulations affecting sustainability in your area, and uncover the history of sustainability work in your community.

Community-based sustainability research connects academic knowledge with local wisdom. Long-time residents often possess invaluable knowledge about local environmental conditions, what conservation approaches have been tried in the past, and which community values will support or hinder sustainability initiatives. This "ground truth" perspective helps avoid implementing practices that might work theoretically but fail in your specific community context.

As you conduct your research, maintain respect for community members' time and knowledge. Approach the process with genuine curiosity rather than assumptions about what you'll find. Be prepared to discover unexpected sustainability innovations and challenges unique to your locality. Identify community-specific barriers to sustainability, whether they're regulatory obstacles, resource limitations, or social factors.

Learning 302: Steps

1. Define your research goals and establish boundaries for your research
2. Identify local knowledge sources
   - Contact your local sustainability office or environmental department
   - Reach out to community organizations focused on sustainability
   - Identify local businesses practicing sustainability innovations
   - Connect with academic institutions studying local sustainability
   - Find long-time community residents with historical knowledge
3. Gather existing documentation
   - Search local newspaper archives for sustainability initiatives
   - Review city council meeting minutes related to sustainability efforts
   - Examine local government sustainability plans and reports
   - Check library collections for local environmental publications
   - Review permits and public records for green building projects
   - Access local utility company reports on resource consumption
4. Conduct field research
5. Interview key stakeholders

- Prepare structured interview questions in advance
- Record interviews (with permission) or take detailed notes
6. Analyze local policies and incentives
    - Review zoning laws affecting sustainability implementation
    - Identify local incentives for sustainable practices
    - Examine building codes and their impact on green building
    - Assess transportation policies promoting sustainable mobility
    - Review waste management regulations and recycling programs
7. Compare practices across similar communities
    - Compare your community's progress with benchmark communities
    - Identify sustainability strategies that have worked elsewhere
    - Note innovative approaches that could be adapted locally
8. Organize and analyze your findings
9. Share your research
    - Create visual representations of your data
    - Share results with participants and community stakeholders
    - Present findings to local decision-makers

Learning 302: Definitions

- **Benchmark communities**: Similar communities used for comparison
- **Community assets**: Local resources, knowledge, skills, and institutions
- **Field research**: Direct observation and data collection about practices in context
- **Greenwashing**: Misleading claims about environmental benefits or practices
- **Local knowledge**: Information and understanding possessed by community members based on direct experience and observation
- **Participatory research**: Research that involves community members as active participants
- **Policy landscape**: Laws, regulations, incentives, and governance structures
- **Stakeholders**: Individuals, groups, and organizations with an interest in or influence on issues
- **Sustainability mapping**: Geographical representation of sustainability assets, practices, and challenges across a community

Learning 302: Troubleshooting

Problem	Solutions
Limited access to official documents	File public records requests. Attend public meetings where documents are discussed. Partner with local journalists. Use your local library.
Difficulty identifying local experts	Ask each contact for recommendations (snowball method). Post requests in community forums. Attend sustainability-related events.
Reluctance of stakeholders to share information	Explain how your research will benefit the community; offer to share your findings; be transparent about your goals; consider offering anonymity when appropriate; respect proprietary information.
Too much information	Develop a consistent organization system. Narrow your research scope.
Conflicting information from different sources	Cross-verify information with multiple sources. Note discrepancies in your findings.
No clear performance data	Document qualitative outcomes. Develop simple quantitative measurements. Ask practitioners about their evaluation methods.

Learning 302: Limitations

- Research quality depends heavily on the cooperation of community stakeholders
- Recent innovations may not have sufficient data to demonstrate effectiveness
- Technical or proprietary information may be inaccessible
- Your findings represent a snapshot in time and may become outdated as practices evolve
- Biases affect both your research approach and stakeholders' responses

References and resources: <www.suspra.com/practice/community/learning-302.html>

Learning 303: Earning an Undergraduate Degree

Earn an undergraduate degree in an environmental field

Earn an undergraduate degree in an environmental field to empower yourself to understand issues better, find meaningful work in line with your values, and build a network of mentors, friends and colleagues who share your interests. Programs combine natural and social sciences with policy, management, and technical skills. While the investment of time and money is significant, a degree positions you for careers in government agencies, non-profit organizations, consulting firms, research institutions, and corporations focused on sustainability.

Some environmental undergraduate programs focus on natural sciences (ecology, conservation biology, atmospheric science), while others emphasize policy, planning, management, or design. Many programs now offer interdisciplinary perspectives—a valuable approach given the complex nature of environmental problems. Environmental science and environmental studies programs have been joined by specialized programs in sustainable business, renewable energy technology, urban sustainability, food systems, climate science, and environmental justice.

When selecting a program, look for curricula that provide fundamental environmental knowledge while allowing specialization that matches your career interests. Employers value field experiences, laboratory work, internships, and independent research skills. Engage in extracurricular activities like environmental clubs, volunteer projects, and internships to build practical skills, demonstrate commitment, and develop the professional network needed for career advancement after graduation.

Learning 303: Equipment, Materials & Costs

- Application fees for colleges/universities ($50-100 per school)
- Standardized test fees (e.g., SAT, ACT) if required ($55-70)
- Tuition and educational expenses ($5,000-$70,000 per year depending on institution)
- Two years for an associate degree; four years for a bachelor's degree

Learning 303: Steps

1. Obtain a high school diploma or General Educational Development (GED)
2. Research environmental degree programs (6-12 months before applying)
   - Identify specific environmental fields that interest you
   - Research universities and colleges with strong programs in your chosen field
   - Consider factors such as program reputation, faculty expertise, research opportunities, internship connections, location, cost, and financial aid availability
   - Check accreditation status of institutions and programs
3. Prepare for standardized tests if required (4-6 months before application deadlines)
   - Check if your chosen programs have test-optional policies
   - Register for and take required standardized tests (SAT, ACT for undergraduate admission)
   - Schedule tests early enough to retake if necessary
4. Connect with admissions representatives and faculty (3-6 months before applying)
   - Attend college fairs and virtual information sessions; schedule campus tours when possible

- Talk to current students and alumni about their experiences
- Request information about specific environmental research or fieldwork opportunities
5. Prepare application materials (3-4 months before deadlines)
    - Draft personal statements focusing on your environmental interests and goals
    - Request letters of recommendation from teachers, mentors, or supervisors
    - Compile your academic records and transcripts
    - Create a curriculum vitae highlighting relevant experiences
6. Complete and submit applications (according to deadlines)
    - Apply for financial aid, scholarships, and grants
7. Evaluate admission offers (typically March-April for fall admission)
8. Accept an offer and prepare for enrollment
9. Complete degree requirements (typically 2 or 4 years)
    - Build relationships with faculty who can serve as mentors
    - Participate in environmental student organizations
    - Apply for research opportunities, field schools, and internships
    - Consider study abroad programs with environmental focuses
    - Create a portfolio of projects, research, and field experiences
10. Gain practical environmental experience
    - Secure internships or summer field experiences
    - Volunteer for local conservation projects
    - Participate in undergraduate research opportunities
    - Attend environmental conferences to build knowledge and network
11. Prepare for post-graduation (final year)
    - Update your resume with relevant coursework, projects, and experiences
    - Research graduate programs if continuing education is your goal
    - Connect with career services to prepare for job searches

Learning 303: Definitions

- **Accreditation**: Evaluation for quality and adherence to educational standards
- **Curriculum vitae (CV):** A summary of a person's education, qualifications, and experience
- **Environmental science**: Understanding natural systems using scientific methods
- **Environmental studies**: Interdisciplinary field examining environmental issues through multiple lenses including policy, economics, ethics, and science
- **Field experience**: Hands-on learning conducted in natural or community settings
- **Free Application for Federal Student Aid (FAFSA)**: Form used in the United States to determine student eligibility for federal financial aid
- **General Educational Development (GED):** A set of exams that shows you have a high school level of knowledge
- **Undergraduate degree:** a two-year associate degree or four-year bachelor's degree that is usually the first step in a college education, typically earned after high school

Learning 303: Troubleshooting

Problem	Solutions
Application fees are too expensive	Request application fee waivers based on financial need. Apply to schools offering free applications. Focus on fewer, better-matched schools.
Low standardized test scores	Research test-optional schools. Retake tests. Highlight environmental experience and passion in other application components.

Problem	Solutions
Limited environmental experience	Volunteer. Participate in citizen science projects. Take online environmental courses. Join environmental clubs or initiatives.
Cannot afford tuition	Apply for environmental scholarships and grants. Start at a community college and transfer. Explore schools offering cooperative education.
Program lacks desired specialization	Create a personalized concentration through electives. Pursue a minor in a complementary field. Seek independent study opportunities with faculty.
Limited internship opportunities	Apply early for competitive positions. Consider remote internships. Create your own internship.

Learning 303: Limitations

- Undergraduate environmental degrees require years of study
- Programs can be expensive, particularly at private institutions
- Some environmental careers require graduate education beyond a bachelor's degree

References and resources: <www.suspra.com/practice/community/learning-303.html>

Learning 401: Earning an Advanced Degree

Earn a post-undergraduate degree in an environmental field

Dramatically expand your capacity to create sustainable change through deeper expertise, professional credentials, and expanded networks by earning an advanced degree in an environmental field. Master's programs typically require one to three years to complete, while doctoral programs may require seven or more years. Professional degrees like the Juris Doctor (law) typically take three years.

- **Master of Science (MS)** programs emphasize research and technical skills in areas like ecology, environmental chemistry, or climate science.
- **Master of Arts (MA)** programs often focus on policy, communications, or education aspects of environmental issues.
- **Professional master's degrees** (MEM, MPH, MPA, MBA) emphasize practical skills for specific career paths in environmental management, public health, administration, or business.
- **Doctoral (PhD)** programs prepare students for research and academic careers, requiring significant original research.
- **Law degrees (JD)** prepare students for careers in environmental law and policy.

Funding opportunities (fellowships, scholarships, grants, and loans) vary widely between programs and degree types. PhD programs in the sciences often provide full funding through research and teaching assistantships, while professional master's programs typically offer less financial support. Balance multiple factors to choose the right program for you:

- **Fit with faculty research interests** is particularly crucial for research-based programs
- **Program culture and teaching approach** affect your daily experience and success
- **Geographic location** impacts networking opportunities and specific environmental contexts
- **Program reputation and connections** in your desired career field

Carefully prepare applications to competitive programs. Stand out with strong letters of recommendation, a compelling personal statement, relevant experience, and demonstrated knowledge of the program. Work in the field before applying to strengthen your application.

Throughout your graduate education, build skills and relationships that will serve your environmental career goals. Seek opportunities for applied projects, internships, and networking with professionals. Consider interdisciplinary training that combines technical understanding with policy, communication, or business skills, as environmental professionals increasingly work across traditional boundaries.

References and resources: <www.suspra.com/practice/community/learning-401.html>

Verifying 101: Confirming Facts

Confirm sustainability facts and inferences by checking credible sources

Verify facts and inferences to make wise decisions about sustainable practices. Checking original sources is important because information is often distorted as it passes through multiple channels. Distinguish credible information from misinformation, identify greenwashing, and understand the strength of evidence behind claims—before you share information or rely on it to change practices.

Scientific understanding of environmental issues advances continuously, so a fact considered accurate at one time may now be outdated. For example, a claim that "solar panels take more energy to produce than they generate" might be based on outdated studies from the 1970s, while current research shows modern solar panels typically generate many times more energy than required for their production.

Peer-reviewed scientific journals provide the most rigorous information but are technical and can be difficult to access. Government environmental agencies offer reliable regulatory information but are subject to partisan influence. Non-profit environmental organizations often translate scientific findings into actionable information but tend to emphasize advocacy perspectives. Industry sources can provide practical details but often minimize environmental concerns related to their products and services.

When evaluating sustainability claims, consider not just whether something is true in a narrow sense, but whether it represents the full picture. For example, a product might accurately claim to use "30% less packaging," but 30% less than what? Is the baseline comparison unusually wasteful? Does the reduced packaging use more environmentally harmful materials?

Match the verification process to the importance of the decision you're making. For minor choices, quick verification using trusted environmental resources may be sufficient. For major investments or community-wide sustainability initiatives, thorough verification involving multiple primary sources and expert consultation is warranted.

References and resources: <www.suspra.com/practice/community/verifying-101.html>

Verifying 102: Taking Knowledge Tests

Test your understanding of sustainability science

Get objective feedback about what you actually know versus what you think you know. Identify areas where deeper understanding can lead to better decisions and more effective actions. Test your knowledge to strengthen memory and comprehension more effectively than passive review. Each time you test yourself, you reinforce neural pathways, making your knowledge more accessible when you need to apply it in real-world situations. Effective sustainability knowledge tests assess understanding across multiple dimensions:

- **Factual knowledge**: Basic terminology, scientific principles, and established data
- **Conceptual understanding**: How sustainability systems and principles interconnect
- **Procedural knowledge**: How to implement specific sustainable practices
- **Applied knowledge**: How to adapt principles to specific contexts and situations
- **Critical thinking**: How to evaluate sustainability claims and make evidence-based decisions

Start with basic sustainability literacy tests that cover fundamental concepts across pathways (food, water, energy, waste, etc.). As your knowledge develops, take more specialized tests to assess deeper understanding in specific areas like renewable energy technologies, sustainable food systems, or circular economy principles. Analyze test results to determine why certain answers are correct and how concepts connect to practical applications. Fix knowledge gaps in foundational concepts that affect multiple areas of practice.

Remember that sustainability science continues to evolve. Retest regularly to stay current with emerging research and best practices while reinforcing and expanding your knowledge base. The goal isn't perfect scores, but continuous improvement that leads to more effective sustainability actions.

References and resources: <www.suspra.com/practice/community/verifying-102.html>

Verifying 201: Investigating Credibility

Investigate the credibility of sources for sustainability knowledge

Know how to investigate the credibility of your information sources to build a foundation of reliable knowledge to inform your sustainable practices. The sustainability field presents unique credibility challenges. Expertise comes from diverse fields—ecology, engineering, policy, economics, and more. Additionally, sustainability science is evolving rapidly, making currency of information particularly relevant. Finally, the political nature of environmental topics leads to deliberate misinformation campaigns. When evaluating sources, look for these hallmarks of credibility:

- **Transparency about authors and funding**: Credible sources clearly identify who created the content and how the work was funded, allowing you to assess potential biases.
- **Scientific methodology**: Reliable scientific information explains how conclusions were reached, acknowledges uncertainty, and considers alternative explanations.
- **Appropriate expertise**: The most credible information comes from individuals and organizations with relevant credentials and experience in their specific area of comment.
- **Institutional backing**: Content from established scientific, academic, governmental, and reputable non-governmental sources typically undergoes more rigorous review processes.
- **Citation of primary sources**: Trustworthy content references original research and primary sources that you can verify.

Understand the landscape of sustainability information sources to focus your evaluation efforts:

- **Highly Credible Sources**
    - Peer-reviewed scientific journals
        - Nature Climate Change, Environmental Science & Technology
    - Major scientific organizations
        - IPCC, National Academies of Sciences
    - Government research agencies
        - NOAA, EPA, NASA
    - Academic institutions with environmental expertise
    - Established environmental research organizations
        - Stockholm Resilience Centre, World Resources Institute

- **Generally Reliable Sources**
    - Science journalism from established outlets
    - Reports from major environmental NGOs
    - Industry sustainability reports (with careful bias consideration)
    - Well-researched books from experts in the field
    - Educational content from accredited institutions

- **Sources Requiring Investigation**
    - Corporate sustainability claims without third-party verification
    - Social media content about environmental issues
    - Political advocacy websites discussing sustainability
    - Personal blogs without clear expertise
    - News outlets with known partisan biases
    - Websites primarily selling "green" products

Evaluate with an ongoing process, as even highly credible sources can publish incorrect information (and may or may not retract it).

References and resources: <www.suspra.com/practice/community/verifying-201.html>

Verifying 202: Researching Environmental Impacts

Conduct research to verify the environmental impact of practices

Research environmental impacts to determine whether sustainability practices are achieving their intended environmental benefits. While scientific literature provides a foundation, get valuable insights from collecting real-world data that show how theoretical impacts manifest in your specific context.

For personal practices, take direct measurements for immediate, contextual data about environmental impacts. For example, track household water consumption before and after installing water-efficient fixtures for concrete evidence of impact. For organizational practices, get access to more extensive operational data for more comprehensive analysis across multiple impact categories.

Do life cycle assessment (LCA) to evaluate impacts from resource extraction through manufacturing, use, and disposal. Even simplified LCA approaches can reveal unexpected impacts in supply chains or end-of-life stages. Establish monitoring protocols that track changes over appropriate time frames—sometimes years or decades—for more meaningful data than one-time measurements. Many environmental impacts aren't immediate but accumulate over time.

Vigilantly maintain data quality. Apply statistical methods to identify significant trends amidst normal variations. Where direct measurement isn't feasible, measure proxy indicators correlated with your impact of interest. Remember that environmental systems are complex and interconnected. A practice that reduces impact in one category may increase it in another, which is why comprehensive impact assessment across multiple categories provides a better basis for decision making.

References and resources: <www.suspra.com/practice/community/verifying-202.html>

Verifying 301: Measuring Sustainability Indicators

Develop procedures to measure sustainability indicators

Measure sustainability indicators to transform abstract concepts into concrete, actionable data. Design simple protocols to provide objective feedback on whether your sustainability practices are making a difference. This practice guide helps you develop systematic procedures for collecting, analyzing, and reporting data about your environmental impact across all seven sustainability pathways.

The core principle behind effective measurement is consistency. Even simple measurements, if taken consistently over time, can reveal valuable insights about your progress toward sustainability. You don't need expensive monitoring equipment or complex protocols—start with utility bills, kitchen scales, and simple logs. Establish clear procedures and follow them regularly.

Balance comprehensiveness with practicality. Focus first on indicators most relevant to your specific sustainability goals and expand your measurement system as you build capacity. Integrate data collection into your routine. For example, weigh food waste while cleaning up after meals, check energy meters during your morning coffee, or log transportation data while planning your weekly schedule. Position measuring devices and logs where you'll naturally use them.

Connect measurements directly to practices you can change. For example, measure average shower length to decide whether to take shorter showers, measure distance driven per week to decide whether to do more trip planning, etc. Prioritize indicators that help you identify specific actions to reduce your environmental impact. Regularly review your data, identify patterns or problems, and adjust your practices accordingly. This cycle drives continuous improvement on your sustainability journey.

Adapt one of the following sample worksheets for your own use.

WORKSHEET 1: MONTHLY MEASUREMENT LOG

Date	Indicator	Measurement	Notes/Conditions

WORKSHEET 2: MEASUREMENT PROTOCOL TEMPLATE

Indicator Name:	
Definition:	
Purpose (why measure this):	
Unit of Measurement:	
Measurement Frequency:	
Responsibility (who measures):	
Equipment Needed:	
Step-by-Step Procedure:	1. 2. 3. 4.
Data Recording Method:	
Calculation Formula (if applicable):	
Baseline Value:	
Target Value:	
Related Practices:	
Notes:	

WORKSHEET 3: DATA ANALYSIS TEMPLATE

Indicator Name:	
Reporting Period:	
Baseline Value:	
Current Value:	
% Change from Baseline:	
Sustainability Trend:	Getting Better / Staying Stable / Getting Worse
Correlation with Practices:	Practice implemented: Date implemented: Observed effects:
Insights and Observations:	
External Factors Affecting Measurements:	
Action Items Based on This Data:	1. 2. 3. 4. 5. 6. 7.

WORKSHEET 4: SUSTAINABILITY INDICATOR SELECTION

Select Indicators to Measure	Measurement Methods	Frequency	Who Measures
Community ___ Sustainability knowledge test scores ___ Number of sustainable practices ___ Volunteer activities (h/yr)	___ Knowledge Tests ___ Practice Survey ___ Volunteer Log ___ Other:		
Food ___ Food budget ($/day) ___ Meal log (kg/day) ___ Food waste (kg/day)	___ Meals Log ___ Food Waste Log ___ Other		
Water ___ Average flow rate (L/s) ___ Pollution rate (L/s or kg/s)	___ Flow Calculator ___ Prevention Log ___ Other:		
Movement ___ Average speed (m/s) ___ Travel modes	___ Speed Calculator ___ Travel Log ___ Other		
Energy ___ Average power (W) ___ Electricity % of total ___ Solar % of electricity	___ Energy Calculator ___ Other		
Goods ___ Goods budget ($/day) ___ Consumption rate (kg/day) ___ Reusing rate (kg/day) ___ Composting rate (kg/day) ___ Recycling rate (kg/day)	___ Consumption Log ___ Solid Waste Log ___ Other		
Habitat ___ Occupancy rate ___ Building materials and certifications ___ Conservation budget ($/day) ___ Land use ___ Pesticide and fertilizer applications	___ Real Estate Report ___ Conservation Report ___ Land Care Log ___ Other		

References and resources: <www.suspra.com/practice/community/verifying-301.html>

Demonstrating Sustainability

Acting 001: Taking Action

Take action to practice sustainability

Acting 001: Equipment & Materials Common to All Practices

- Sustainability journal or app

Acting 001: Action Steps Common to All Implementation Levels

1. Study your chosen practices
   - Read relevant practice guides in this handbook
   - Search online for relevant resources; join online forums or relevant communities
   - Ask knowledgeable friends or family for advice
2. Set specific, clear goals for each practice
   - Document your starting point with notes or photos
   - Define how to measure success for each practice; set timeframes for implementation
3. Track your progress
   - Schedule regular reviews; note successes and challenges in your sustainability journal
   - Take progress photos; record quantifiable impacts
4. Adjust your approach based on results
   - Modify practices to better fit your situation; simplify steps that create friction or resistance
   - Add enhancements once basics are established
5. Integrate the practice into your routine; create systems that make the practice automatic
6. Share your experience to help others
   - Discuss your new practices with friends or family; encourage them to join you
   - Ask for tips from others practicing sustainability
   - Celebrate small wins to build momentum
   - Connect with local groups practicing similar activities
7. Build on your success
   - Evaluate which practices worked well; identify logical next steps
   - Once the current level of practices feels comfortable, try practices at the next level

References and resources: <www.suspra.com/practice/community/acting-001.html>

Acting 101: Starting Quick-Start Practices

Take action with quick-start practices

Quick-start sustainability practices are foundational building blocks that help you develop the mindset, habits, and confidence needed for more complex sustainability practices. Select practices that match your current living situation, daily routines, and personal interests. For instance, if you enjoy cooking, reducing food waste might be a natural first choice. If you're renting an apartment, focus on non-structural changes like adjusting thermostat settings rather than home renovations.

Understand the "why" behind each practice to increase motivation and adapt practices to your specific circumstances. While detailed research isn't necessary for quick-start practices, basic knowledge about environmental impacts helps you stay on task.

Progress is the goal, not perfection. Each quick-start practice you successfully implement builds confidence and creates momentum for further action. Practices become habits with consistent implementation. Once foundational practices feel automatic, you'll have the capacity to adopt more practices or upgrade to more advanced versions of practices you've already mastered.

References and resources: <www.suspra.com/practice/community/acting-101.html>

Acting 201: Starting Intermediate Practices

Take action with intermediate practices

Intermediate sustainability practices are the bridge between initial quick-start actions and more complex advanced practices. Compared to quick-start practices, intermediate practices:

- Require more preparation and planning
- Involve modest financial investments
- Need more time to implement fully
- Require some skill or knowledge
- May involve engaging others in your household or community

Success with intermediate practices requires some thought. Rather than just jumping in, research options, create plans, acquire resources, and develop new skills if necessary. While many quick-start practices can be done alone, intermediate practices tend to engage your family, roommates, neighbors, or coworkers. This social dimension brings both challenges and rewards—requiring communication and coordination but potentially multiplying your impact.

References and resources: <www.suspra.com/practice/community/acting-201.html>

Acting 301: Starting Advanced Practices

Take action with advanced practices

Advanced sustainability practices represent a significant step beyond intermediate practices in terms of complexity, resource requirements, and scale. They frequently involve hiring professionals, collaborating with neighbors, or forming a project team within your organization.

Shift from "doing what feels right" to "doing what really works." Achieve results to secure support for future initiatives and provide reliable guidance to others. Installing a home solar array is an example that requires careful planning, technical knowledge, resources, and often coordination across multiple stakeholders. Quantify outcomes to justify the greater investment practices like this require.

Bridge the gap between group efforts and systemic change. Inspire broader adoption and policy change. The documentation process becomes more formalized at this level. Communicate costs, benefits, and implementation steps for the benefit of others who might want to follow your lead. This documentation serves both to validate your own project and to accelerate adoption by providing a roadmap for others.

References and resources: <www.suspra.com/practice/community/acting-301.html>

Acting 401: Starting Transformative Practices

Take action with transformative practices

Transformative practices fundamentally alter the institutional structures that shape our world. Unlike practices that enhance existing systems, transformative practices reimagine and rebuild systems to operate within planetary boundaries while meeting human needs equitably.

Make significant investments to create lasting change at a community or regional scale. Examples include developing local renewable energy microgrids, creating circular economy industrial parks, establishing community land trusts, redesigning transportation systems, or transforming regional food systems. Successful transformative initiatives share several characteristics:

Systems thinking approach: Address root causes rather than symptoms. Map the system you aim to transform, identify feedback loops, and find leverage points where intervention can create ripple effects.

Multilevel engagement: Coordinate change at individual, organizational, and institutional levels. Engage diverse stakeholders including government entities, businesses, civic organizations, educational institutions, and community members, creating new relationships and power-sharing arrangements.

Paradigm shifts: Challenge dominant assumptions and values. Articulate alternative paradigms that align sustainability with community wellbeing while respecting diverse perspectives and creating space for meaningful dialogue about values and priorities.

Emergent strategy: Balance clear vision with adaptability, creating conditions for innovation and self-organization while maintaining focus on core sustainability goals.

Long time horizons: Over many years, move through phases of initiation, acceleration, and institutionalization. Sustain momentum through political cycles, leadership transitions, and changing economic conditions.

Co-learning processes: Apply scientific, traditional, and practical knowledge to inform new approaches. Create structured opportunities for reflection, integration of new information, and adaptation based on experience.

Beyond technical expertise in sustainability domains, cultivate:

- **Facilitative leadership** that builds collective capacity rather than centralized control
- **Systems intelligence** that sees patterns and relationships across domains
- **Political acumen** to navigate complex institutional landscapes
- **Personal resilience** to sustain effort through challenges and setbacks
- **Ethical clarity** about the values guiding transformation
- **Cultural sensitivity** to work effectively across diverse communities

Maintain awareness of power dynamics and ensure that transformation enhances equity rather than exacerbates disparities. Emphasize transparent governance, shared decision-making, and fair distribution of benefits. Aim to create ripple effects beyond your initial boundaries, inspiring similar efforts elsewhere and contributing to broader systemic shifts.

References and resources: <www.suspra.com/practice/community/acting-401.html>

Certifying 301: Certifying Your Sustainability

Certify your household, organization, or product to a sustainability standard

Clarify goals, improve performance to meet standards, increase credibility, reduce risks, join networks, and obtain access to opportunities and incentives by obtaining certification that your household or organization meets environmental and social standards. The certification landscape ranges from rigorous third-party verified systems to self-assessment tools. Third-party certifications typically require external verification and regular renewal, providing the highest level of credibility but also demanding more resources. Self-assessment frameworks offer guidance for improvement with lower costs and fewer formal requirements. When selecting a certification, consider one that both challenges your organization to improve and is recognized by your key stakeholders.

Building Certifications focus on the built environment's sustainability features.

BREEAM <breeam.com>
- **Focus:** Life cycle environmental performance of buildings
- **Organization:** BRE
- **Levels:** Acceptable, Pass, Good, Very Good, Excellent, Outstanding
- **Cost:** €2,000 to €20,000
- **Process:** Find an assessor, register, assess, check, certify
- **Timeframe:** 3-6 months
- **Renewal:** none (new construction), three years (existing buildings)
- **Best for:** Buildings in Europe

ENERGY STAR Certification <www.energystar.gov/buildings>
- **Focus:** Energy performance for buildings
- **Organization:** U.S. Environmental Protection Agency
- **Levels:** Single certification level (score of 75+ required)
- **Cost:** Free (but may require professional engineer verification)
- **Process:** Performance tracking, application, verification
- **Timeframe:** 3-6 months
- **Renewal:** Annual
- **Best for:** Organizations focusing specifically on energy efficiency improvement

Green Globes <thegbi.org/greenglobes/>
- **Focus:** Commercial buildings
- **Organization:** Green Building Initiative
- **Levels:** One to Four Globes
- **Cost:** $5,000-$25,000 (varies by project size)
- **Process:** Online assessment, third-party verification with on-site visit
- **Timeframe:** 3-12 months
- **Renewal:** Every three years
- **Best for:** Organizations seeking a flexible, less paperwork-intensive alternative to LEED

LEED (Leadership in Energy and Environmental Design) <www.usgbc.org/leed>
- **Focus:** Buildings and communities
- **Organization:** U.S. Green Building Council
- **Levels:** Certified, Silver, Gold, Platinum
- **Cost:** $1,500-$5,000+ (varies by project size and complexity)
- **Process:** Documentation submission, review, and verification
- **Timeframe:** 6-18 months
- **Renewal:** Every five years for existing buildings

- **Best for:** New construction, major renovations, and existing buildings seeking recognized environmental performance standards

Living Building Challenge <living-future.org/lbc>
- **Focus:** Buildings and communities
- **Organization:** International Living Future Institute
- **Levels:** Petal Certification, Living Certification
- **Cost:** $5,000-$20,000 (registration and certification)
- **Process:** Performance period verification, documentation review, and site visit
- **Timeframe:** Minimum 12-month performance period plus certification time
- **Renewal:** Annual reporting for some requirements
- **Best for:** Projects pursuing rigorous ecological standards and regenerative designs

WELL Building Standard <wellcertified.com>
- **Focus:** Indoor environment and occupant wellness
- **Organization:** International WELL Building Institute
- **Levels:** Silver, Gold, Platinum
- **Cost:** $4,000-$10,000+ (varies by size)
- **Process:** Documentation review and performance verification
- **Timeframe:** 6-12 months
- **Renewal:** Every three years
- **Best for:** Organizations prioritizing employee wellness

For homes, consider:

ENERGY STAR Certified Homes <www.energystar.gov/newhomes>
- **Focus:** Residential energy efficiency
- **Cost:** Depends on provider ($400-$1,000 typically)
- **Best for:** New home construction or complete renovations

LEED for Homes <www.usgbc.org/resources/leed-homes>
- **Focus:** Comprehensive residential sustainability
- **Cost:** $2,000-$5,000
- **Best for:** New homes or major renovations seeking comprehensive green certification

National Green Building Standard <www.ngbs.com/get-certified>
- **Focus:** Residential construction
- **Cost:** $500-$2,500
- **Best for:** Single-family and multifamily residential projects

Organization Certifications evaluate overall operations and management practices.

B Corporation <bcorporation.net>
- **Focus:** Overall business practices
- **Organization:** B Lab
- **Levels:** Single certification level (minimum score of 80 required)
- **Cost:** $1,000-$50,000+ annually (based on revenue)
- **Process:** B Impact Assessment, verification, legal requirements
- **Timeframe:** 6-10 months
- **Renewal:** Every three years
- **Best for:** For-profit companies formalizing social and environmental performance

Eco-Schools USA <www.nwf.org/eco-schools-usa>
- **Focus:** K-12 schools

- **Organization:** National Wildlife Federation
- **Levels:** Bronze, Silver, Green Flag
- **Cost:** Free
- **Process:** Seven-step framework, documentation, student leadership
- **Timeframe:** Varies (typically 1-3 years for Green Flag)
- **Renewal:** Green Flag renewed every two years
- **Best for:** Educational institutions seeking to integrate sustainability into curriculum and operations

Process or Product Certifications apply to specific activities or goods produced.

Green Seal Certification <greenseal.org/certification/>
- **Focus:** Products, services, and company operations
- **Organization:** Green Seal (independent non-profit)
- **Levels:** Single certification level with specific standards for different categories
- **Cost:** $2,500-$8,500+ for certification, plus annual fees based on product revenue
- **Process:** Application submission, documentation review, on-site audit/product testing, compliance monitoring
- **Timeframe:** 4-8 months from application to certification
- **Renewal:** Annual renewal with full reassessment every 3-5 years
- **Best for:** Consumer product manufacturers, hospitality businesses, and facility management services seeking third-party validation of environmental claims

For all certifications, costs typically include registration fees, documentation preparation (often requiring consultant support), verification expenses, and implementation costs to meet requirements. Factor in ongoing fees for maintenance and renewal.

References and resources: <www.suspra.com/practice/community/certifying-301.html>

Committing 101: Committing to Improve

Commit to improving sustainability indicators

Make explicit commitments to increase the likelihood of behavior change. A commitment that is specific, written, and shared with others leads to better performance than vague "try your best" goals. Define which sustainability indicators you'll improve, by how much, and by when. Double or triple the likelihood of follow through by specifying if-then plans for how you'll act in specific situations. Create mental shortcuts that bypass deliberation when situational triggers occur.

For organizations, commitments are most effective when they:

- Have strong leadership support
- Align with organizational values and strategic objectives
- Involve representative stakeholders during development
- Define roles and responsibilities clearly
- Establish regular reporting mechanisms

Balance ambition with realism. Start with modest but meaningful commitments to build confidence and momentum for more ambitious goals later.

References and resources: <www.suspra.com/practice/community/committing-101.html>

Committing 201: Setting Achievable Goals

Set achievable sustainability goals

Set achievable sustainability goals to transform vague aspirations into measurable results that reduce your environmental impact. Goals perceived as too difficult reduce motivation, while those perceived as too easy fail to inspire effort. "Meaningful" goals address real environmental issues and align with your values. "Achievable" goals recognize your real-world constraints and capabilities, setting you up for success rather than frustration or burnout. Consider both your values and your circumstances. For example, if you live in a water-stressed region, water conservation goals might be particularly meaningful. If you currently travel frequently by car, transportation-related goals might offer substantial impact opportunities.

Bring clarity to what can otherwise feel like an overwhelming challenge with the SMART framework (Specific, Measurable, Achievable, Relevant, Time-bound). Rather than a vague intention to "reduce waste," a SMART goal might be: "Reduce household landfill waste by 25% within six months by implementing a kitchen composting system and eliminating all single-use plastic items."

For your household, have family discussions to ensure everyone's perspectives are considered and all household members feel invested in the goals. For small organizations, involve representatives from different departments or functions to gain diverse insights and build broader commitment.

Sustainability is a journey with many milestones along the way. Your initial goals are starting points that will evolve as you learn, grow, and achieve.

References and resources: <www.suspra.com/practice/community/committing-201.html>

Committing 202: Creating Simple Plans

Create simple sustainability plans

Create a simple sustainability plan to transform goals into concrete actions. Unlike complex corporate sustainability strategies that might span decades and need extensive resources, a simple plan focuses on practices that can be implemented within weeks or months. This practical approach allows individuals, households, and small organizations to make steady progress without becoming overwhelmed.

Plan with all seven pathways to sustainability in mind rather than focusing only on the most visible or popular aspects. While you might not work on all pathways simultaneously, the pathway framework helps you identify which areas need attention that might otherwise be overlooked.

The power of a simple sustainability plan lies in its ability to break down potentially overwhelming environmental challenges into manageable steps. Each small action contributes to larger sustainability outcomes, creating momentum and visible progress. As you successfully implement practices in your plan, you'll likely find increased motivation to tackle more challenging sustainability goals.

Keep your plan visible and revisit it frequently. A simple sustainability plan should be a living document that guides daily decisions and actions. Regular check-ins help you celebrate successes, adjust approaches that aren't working, and maintain momentum toward your sustainability goals.

Your first simple plan will likely lead to additional plans as you make progress, encounter new challenges, and expand your sustainability aspirations. The planning skills you develop allow for increasingly sophisticated sustainability initiatives as you advance on your sustainability journey.

References and resources: <www.suspra.com/practice/community/committing-202.html>

Committing 301: Creating Detailed Plans

Create detailed sustainability plans to accomplish more ambitious projects

Creating a detailed sustainability plan moves beyond simple goal-setting to a comprehensive, strategic approach to achieving meaningful environmental impact. Detailed plans incorporate rigorous data analysis, comprehensive stakeholder engagement, and sophisticated implementation frameworks.

High-quality baseline data is the foundation of an effective detailed sustainability plan, allowing you to set meaningful targets and evaluate progress. Gather a full year of historical data to account for seasonal variations; supplement shorter baseline data series with industry benchmarks.

Detailed sustainability plans differ from simpler plans in several key ways:

Systems thinking approach: Examine the interconnections between systems and address root causes of unsustainability. For instance, instead of simply planning to install low-flow fixtures to reduce water consumption, analyze the entire plumbing system, addressing leaks, user behaviors, landscaping practices, and water reuse opportunities.

Multiple time horizons: Plan for immediate actions (within 6 months), short-term initiatives (6-12 months), and long-term transformative changes (one more more years). Allow for both quick wins to build momentum and fundamental shifts in operations and infrastructure.

Resource specificity: Provide comprehensive resource requirements including specific budget allocations, staffing needs, expertise requirements, and deployment timelines.

Adaptive management frameworks: Incorporate robust monitoring systems and decision frameworks for when and how to adapt strategies based on performance data and changing conditions.

Integration across sustainability pathways: Recognize that actions in one sustainability pathway affect others. For example, electrifying transportation affects both movement and energy pathways.

For a household, focus on coordinating major investments (like solar panels and heat pumps) with behavior changes and smaller upgrades to achieve comprehensive transformation. For an organization, align sustainability initiatives with strategic business objectives and include detailed implementation roadmaps for each department. At the community level, involve multiple stakeholders, address policy and infrastructure systems, and include governance mechanisms for collaborative implementation.

Balance comprehensiveness with clarity and flexibility. Provide enough detail to guide implementation while allowing for adaptation as circumstances change and new information becomes available.

References and resources: <www.suspra.com/practice/community/committing-301.html>

Tracking 101: Keeping a Journal

Keep a personal sustainability journal

A sustainability journal serves as both a record and a tool for improvement. Unlike a typical diary, it focuses on your sustainability journey, helping you identify patterns, measure progress, and maintain motivation. Combine quantitative tracking (numbers, measurements, data) with qualitative reflections (observations, feelings, insights). This dual approach helps you understand not just what happened, but why it happened and how it affected you. Choose a format depending on your preferences:

- **Chronological journal**: Daily or weekly entries recording all sustainability actions
- **Project-based journal**: Detailed tracking of specific sustainability initiatives
- **Data-focused journal**: Emphasis on metrics with supporting observations

- **Reflection-oriented journal**: Focus on your sustainability learning journey

Regardless of format, consistency matters more than perfection. Even brief, regular entries provide valuable insights over time. Keep a journal that works with your lifestyle and is enjoyable to maintain. Beyond personal benefit, your sustainability journal becomes a valuable reference for others who might want to implement similar practices. It provides realistic expectations about challenges, time investments, and results that aren't always captured in sustainability guides.

References and resources: <www.suspra.com/practice/community/tracking-101.html>

Tracking 102: Calculating a Quick-Start Suspra Score

Calculate a quick-start Suspra Score for your home or organization

Evaluate the environmental impacts of your practices by calculating a Suspra score. The Quick-Start version accepts estimated data and can be completed in about twenty minutes. Your overall Suspra Score will be either positive or negative. A negative score indicates that Earth cannot sustain all people living the way you do. A positive score indicates your practices are sustainable (i.e. Earth can sustain all people living the way you do). The further your score is from zero in either direction, the more unsustainable or sustainable your practices are.

Each pathway contributes to your overall score, so you can see which areas are having the most impact. For example, you might have positive scores in Food and Water, but a strongly negative score in Energy that pulls your overall score down. This granularity helps you prioritize which practices to improve next.

The Quick-Start Suspra Score is most valuable as:

- An initial assessment to identify sustainability strengths and weaknesses
- A baseline measurement before beginning sustainability improvements
- A motivational tool to engage household members or colleagues in sustainability efforts
- A simple way to track progress over time with minimal investment
- A gateway to more detailed sustainability assessment

When calculating your Quick-Start score, remember that estimates are acceptable—the goal is to get a general picture of your impacts, not perfect accuracy. As you become more committed to improving your sustainability, you can progress to the Regular or Detailed Suspra Score calculations, which require more precise measurements and verification of your practices.

References and resources: <www.suspra.com/practice/community/tracking-102.html>

Tracking 201: Using Checklists

Create and use checklists for sustainable practices

Use checklists to transform abstract goals into concrete, trackable actions and overcome common barriers to sustainable behavior. Unlike complex tracking systems, checklists are accessible to everyone, require minimal training, and provide immediate visual feedback on progress. First, they combat forgetfulness by providing consistent reminders of desired actions. Second, they reduce the mental effort required to remember multiple steps or practices. Third, they create accountability through visible records of completion. Finally, they help establish new habits by reinforcing regular action.

Food pathway checklists support meal planning, food inventory management, and food waste reduction. A weekly food checklist might include taking inventory before shopping, planning meals based on what needs to be used, and processing food items approaching expiration.

Water pathway checklists can help track irrigation schedules, water-saving practices, or leak inspections. For example, a monthly water maintenance checklist might include checking toilet flappers, faucet aerators, and outdoor hose connections for leaks.

Energy pathway checklists work well for regular audits of energy use (checking thermostats, equipment settings, or lighting). A seasonal energy checklist might include checking HVAC filters, adjusting thermostat programs, or inspecting weatherstripping before winter.

Goods pathway checklists excel at guiding proper sorting of recyclables, compostables, and landfill waste. Visual checklist posters near waste stations dramatically improve proper waste sorting.

Organizations can benefit from more structured checklist systems, including:

- **Procedural checklists** that standardize sustainable practices across different staff members
- **Audit checklists** for regular assessment of sustainability performance
- **Procurement checklists** to ensure purchasing decisions include sustainability criteria
- **Onboarding checklists** to train new staff on organizational sustainability practices

As you develop expertise with checklists, advance to more sophisticated systems like checklist hierarchies (overview checklists that point to more detailed sub-checklists) or integrated digital systems that can aggregate data from multiple checklists to identify patterns and opportunities.

References and resources: <www.suspra.com/practice/community/tracking-201.html>

Tracking 202: Calculating a Regular Suspra Score

Calculate a regular Suspra Score for your home or organization

Calculate a Regular Suspra Score for a comprehensive assessment of your sustainability practices across all seven pathways to sustainability. Unlike the Quick-Start assessment, which relies primarily on estimates, the Regular Score accepts precise actual measurements across all pathways, making it a more accurate reflection of your environmental impact. Your score is based on scientific understanding of planetary boundaries and sustainable resource use. A negative overall score indicates that your practices are unsustainable—if everyone lived as you do, we will exhaust Earth's capacity to support human life in the long term. A positive score indicates that your practices could be universally adopted without degrading Earth's capacity to support future generations.

Each pathway contributes to your overall sustainability score:

Community pathway evaluates your understanding of sustainability concepts, the practices you demonstrate, and how you interact with others to promote sustainability. This pathway recognizes that individual action alone is insufficient—successful sustainability requires collective effort.

Food pathway examines what you eat, how you source it, and how much you waste. Food choices, particularly regarding animal product consumption and food waste, have significant environmental impacts through land use, greenhouse gas emissions, and resource consumption.

Water pathway assesses direct water consumption and practices that affect water quality. The target of 100 liters (approximately 26 gallons) or less per person per day represents a level of water use that Earth can sustainably support for all people.

Movement pathway evaluates how you get around and how far you travel. Transportation options vary greatly in their environmental impact, with active transportation (walking, cycling) having minimal impact and air travel having a substantial impact per mile.

Energy pathway examines your energy consumption, sources, and efficiency. Converting all energy use (electricity, heating fuels, transportation fuels) into a common unit—kilowatt-hours (kWh) per person per day—allows comparison against a sustainable target of 20 kWh or less.

Goods pathway evaluates the flow of material goods through your life, including purchasing, maintenance, reuse, and waste management. The assessment considers both the volume of goods and the types of materials, with special attention to durable, repairable, and recyclable items.

Habitat pathway examines how you use and protect the land you control, whether as a homeowner, renter, or organization. This includes assessment of building efficiency, construction materials, land management practices, and biodiversity protection.

Your Regular Suspra Score provides both an overall assessment and individual pathway scores, helping you identify areas for improvement. A score is not a judgment but a tool for progress—highlighting successful practices while suggesting meaningful next steps on your sustainability journey.

References and resources: <www.suspra.com/practice/community/tracking-202.html>

Tracking 301: Calculating a Detailed Suspra Score

Calculate a detailed Suspra Score for your home or organization

Calculate a detailed Suspra Score for a comprehensive evaluation of your environmental impact across seven sustainability pathways. Enter precise measurements and extensive documentation for an in-depth picture of your sustainability performance that allows for more targeted improvements and better tracking of progress over time.

Each pathway contributes to your overall score, weighted according to scientific understanding of environmental impacts. The Suspra Score operates on a scale where zero represents the threshold between unsustainable and sustainable living. Negative scores indicate unsustainable practices that would exceed Earth's carrying capacity if everyone lived that way; positive scores indicate sustainable practices that would keep impacts within Earth's carrying capacity if everyone lived that way.

While requiring the most effort to complete, the detailed Suspra Score provides several advantages:

- **Higher precision**: Reduce uncertainty in your score with exact measurements
- **Comprehensive coverage**: Consider all aspects of your environmental impact
- **Actionable insights**: See exactly where improvements will have the greatest effect
- **Progress tracking**: Establish a reliable baseline for measuring future changes
- **Communication tool**: Provide credible documentation for sustainability claims
- **Decision support**: Prioritize sustainability investments based on quantified impacts

When interpreting your score, remember that sustainability is a process rather than a declaration. If your overall score is negative, you can identify ways to make significant positive changes. The detailed score shows not just where you stand, but how far you can go to reach sustainability milestones.

References and resources: <www.suspra.com/practice/community/tracking-301.html>

Tracking 302: Comparing Suspra Scores

Compare Suspra Scores to past periods to measure rates of change

Comparing Suspra Scores over time provides valuable insights into the effectiveness of your sustainability practices and helps maintain motivation by documenting progress. Unlike one-time assessments, tracking changes in scores shows the dynamic nature of sustainability improvements and helps identify which specific practices truly move the needle.

Tracking 302: Equipment & Materials
- Computer, tablet, or smartphone with Internet access
- Suspra Score reports

Tracking 302: Steps
1. Follow steps for calculating a Suspra Score (Tracking 102, Tracking 202, or Tracking 301)
2. Calculate scores for different time periods.
3. Prepare a report showing trends over time.
4. Reflect on your journey
   - Analyze what's working and what isn't
   - Consider how practices affect your quality of life, both benefits and challenges
5. Plan next steps
   - Identify practices to continue, modify, or discontinue
   - Research solutions to persistent challenges
   - Set specific goals for the next period

Tracking 302: Definitions
- **Trend line**: A line on a graph showing the general direction of scores over time

Tracking 302: Troubleshooting

Problem	Solutions
Scores fluctuate dramatically between periods	Ensure consistent measurement methodology. Check for seasonal factors affecting results. Look for major life events or changes that might explain variations. Using longer measurement periods to smooth out fluctuations.
No visible improvement despite new practices	Verify practices were implemented correctly. Check if the time period is sufficient to show results (some practices need longer to show impact). Check if external factors are offsetting improvements.
Difficulty determining cause of changes	Document all practices and external factors methodically.
Inconsistent data collection affects comparisons	Establish clear protocols for data collection. Use calendar reminders for regular data entry. Automate data collection (smart meters, apps). Note data gaps; avoid direct comparisons for those periods.
Scores improve but plateau over time	This is normal as "low-hanging fruit" is addressed first. Set new, more challenging goals. Change practices in pathways with less improvement. Work on transformative rather than incremental changes.
External factors overwhelm impacts	Focus on indicators less affected by external variables. Back out effect of external factors to reveal impact of practices.
Initial enthusiasm wanes with slow progress	Focus on pathways showing the most improvement to maintain motivation. Celebrate small wins and milestones. Share progress with others for accountability. Set interim goals that are achievable in shorter time frames.

Tracking 302: Limitations

- Some sustainability benefits may not be fully captured in quantitative scores
- Short-term comparisons miss seasonal variations or longer-term trends
- External factors beyond your control significantly influence many indicators
- Comparing between different households or organizations requires careful interpretation
- Improvement rates naturally slow as you address easier changes first
- Some sustainability practices have complex or indirect effects that are difficult to attribute
- The scoring system evolves as sustainability science advances

References and resources: <www.suspra.com/practice/community/tracking-302.html>

Tracking 401: Improving the Suspra Scoring System

Improve the Suspra Scoring System

The Suspra scoring system translates complex sustainability science into actionable insights for individuals and organizations. Improve this system not only to help yourself but also to help other users working toward sustainability goals. We're using GitHub to develop our open source software; that site provides extensive documentation for working on open source projects.

Tracking 401: Equipment & Materials

- Computer, tablet, or smartphone with Internet access
- *Optional: Integrated Development Environment (IDE)*

Tracking 401: Steps

1. Familiarize yourself with the current Suspra system
2. Identify improvement opportunities
3. Follow the GitHub link at <www.suspra.com>
4. Clone the repository ("repo") to get your own copy of the system to play with
5. Follow the instructions in the repo to make improvements

Tracking 401: Definitions

- **Bug**: An error, flaw, or fault in a computer program causing unexpected results
- **Clone**: A copy of a repository that allows developers to freely experiment
- **Integrated Development Environment:** software for writing software
- **Repository**: A storage location for software packages, often providing version control
- **Version control**: System that records changes to files over time to recall specific versions later

Tracking 401: Troubleshooting

Problem	Solutions
Proposed improvement rejected	Ask for clarification on why it wasn't accepted. Consider if there are technical constraints you weren't aware of. Refine your proposal based on feedback and resubmit if appropriate.
Conflicting ideas about scoring methods	Research scientific literature to support your position. Suggest implementing optional alternative calculation methods. Propose an A/B test to compare different approaches with users.

Problem	Solutions
Proposed feature seems too large to implement	Break the feature into smaller, independently valuable components. Develop a proof of concept showing the most critical functionality. Collaborate with other contributors to share the workload.

Tracking 401: Limitations
- Not all scientifically valid metrics are easy to collect from users
- Sustainability science continues to evolve, requiring ongoing updates
- System improvements rely on the resources of the development team

References and resources: <www.suspra.com/practice/community/tracking-401.html>

Nurturing Good Relationships

Sharing 101: Forwarding Information

Forward verified articles and interesting opinions to friends and family

Grow community understanding of sustainability by sharing valuable information with friends and family. Forward verified articles and interesting opinions to spread awareness about environmental issues and solutions without requiring the recipient to actively search for this information themselves.

If you receive a forwarded email, first verify that the information is true, then edit the message to remove extraneous details before forwarding it on. Not only does trimming messages save time, but it also reduces the amount of computer storage and energy required. Pay special attention to removing large images or attachments; a quick summary and a link to the full article is the most resource-efficient way to share information.

Send directly to specific people who would appreciate the content. Time your shares thoughtfully (avoid overwhelming recipients with multiple shares). Respect privacy by using BCC when emailing multiple recipients who don't know each other.

Not every sustainability article deserves forwarding, and not every contact will appreciate the same type of content. Prioritize truly valuable content over merely interesting pieces. Match the content to the recipient's interests and level of environmental awareness. Someone just beginning their sustainability journey might appreciate practical tips, while someone already knowledgeable might value in-depth analysis or emerging research. When forwarding information, briefly explain why you found the article valuable and how it connects to the recipient's interests or previous conversations.

Finally, approach information sharing as a conversation starter rather than a lecture. Be open to feedback and recognize that information sharing works best as a two-way exchange.

References and resources: <www.suspra.com/practice/community/sharing-101.html>

Sharing 102: Discussing Issues

Discuss environmental issues with friends and family

Discuss environmental issues with friends and family to create ripple effects of positive change as ideas spread through social networks. Conversations with friends are more effective than debates with strangers because people tend to be more receptive to information from trusted sources. The goal isn't to convert others to your viewpoint but to open a dialogue. Sharing your personal experience is more compelling than reciting statistics. When people hear how sustainability practices have benefited someone they know, they're more likely to consider those practices themselves.

Start with shared values to provide psychological safety for exploring potentially divisive topics. People are more receptive to discussing sustainability issues when they feel their values and identity aren't being threatened. Keep in mind that most people are motivated by immediate, visible benefits rather than abstract global impacts. Framing environmental actions in terms of health benefits, cost savings, or community well-being often resonates more than distant climate impacts.

A single conversation rarely transforms someone's perspective entirely, but plants seeds that grow over time as they encounter more information and observe your positive example.

References and resources: <www.suspra.com/practice/community/sharing-102.html>

Sharing 201: Using Social Media

Use social media to post photos and videos of your own sustainable practices

Social media provides powerful tools to normalize sustainable living and inspire practical action. Rather than lecturing about environmental problems, show your personal sustainable practices in action to demonstrate that these behaviors are accessible, beneficial, and rewarding. Effective content is

- **Practical and actionable**: People want solutions they can implement immediately
- **Visually compelling**: Clear, well-lit photos and videos that show processes and results
- **Educational but not preachy**: People are open to learning but don't want to be shamed
- **Authentic and relatable**: Show real efforts including setbacks, not just perfect outcomes
- **Specific and evidence-based**: Include measurements, data, and reliable information

Quick tips like energy-saving habits work well as short-form content, while project-based activities like building a rain barrel or starting a garden benefit from tutorials and time-lapse videos. Emphasize multiple benefits beyond environmental impact to reach people with various motivations. For example, line-drying clothes saves money, extends clothing lifespan, and gives laundry a fresh scent.

As you share your practices on social media, you'll likely connect with others on similar journeys who can provide encouragement, tips, and knowledge exchange. These connections can sustain your environmental commitment when challenges arise. Consistency matters more than perfection. Regular posts about modest sustainable practices you genuinely maintain are more impactful than occasional showcases of elaborate eco-projects that aren't part of your daily life. Your followers will appreciate your honesty about the manageable steps you're taking rather than an unrealistic portrayal of sustainability.

References and resources: <www.suspra.com/practice/community/sharing-201.html>

Sharing 202: Blogging

Blog about sustainability challenges you face and success you achieve

Blogging about sustainability differs fundamentally from social media posting. While social media platforms like Instagram or Twitter excel at quick updates and wide reach, blogs provide space for deeper reflection, detailed documentation, and comprehensive resource sharing. Social media posts are typically brief, ephemeral, and algorithm-dependent, whereas blogs allow you to build a searchable, organized repository of your sustainability journey that readers can explore at their own pace.

A sustainability blog serves multiple valuable purposes:

Personal documentation: Create a detailed record of your sustainability experiments, challenges, and successes. Track progress over time, remember key lessons, and see how your thinking evolves.

Knowledge sharing: Document both successes and failures to help others avoid common pitfalls and replicate effective practices. Your specific local context and personal experience offer unique insights that general sustainability resources might miss.

Community building: Connect with like-minded individuals facing similar challenges. Get emotional support, practical advice, and collaborative opportunities that strengthen your sustainability efforts.

Accountability: Share your sustainability goals and progress publicly to create gentle pressure to persist through challenges. Knowing that people are following your journey helps maintain motivation.

Balance honesty about challenges with celebration of successes. Readers learn most from your complete journey—including setbacks, unexpected obstacles, and failures. When sharing challenges, focus on problem-solving approaches and lessons learned rather than simply venting frustrations. Combine personal narrative with practical information. Share your emotional journey and values, but also include specific details like costs, time requirements, measurements, and technical specifics that help readers evaluate whether to try similar practices themselves.

As your blog grows, readers will turn to you for advice or inspiration. Embrace this community-building role while remaining honest about the limits of your expertise. Link to scientific sources, reference established resources, and connect readers with subject matter experts when appropriate.

References and resources: <www.suspra.com/practice/community/sharing-202.html>

Sharing 203: Hosting Parties

Host parties to celebrate successes achieving sustainability goals

Host parties to celebrate sustainability achievements, inspire others through demonstration, normalize sustainable practices, and build community around environmental values. Make the celebration itself a model of sustainability to show that sustainable living is enjoyable and accessible. Create an atmosphere where guests feel empowered rather than guilty. Successful sustainability celebrations balance practical demonstrations with fun. They clearly communicate the value and impact of the sustainable choices being celebrated, without being preachy.

Sharing 203: Equipment & Materials
- Invitations (digital or on recycled/plantable paper)
- Venue (your home, garden, office, or community space)
- Food and beverages (locally sourced, plant-based options)
- Reusable tableware (plates, cups, utensils, napkins)
- Activities and entertainment (aligned with sustainability themes)
- *Optional: Display materials highlighting your sustainability achievements*
- *Handouts on sustainable practices*
- *Party favors (plantable seeds, homemade preserves, etc.)*

Sharing 203: Steps
1. Plan your celebration
   - Celebrate an achievement (renovation completion, garden planting, EV transition, waste reduction milestone, etc.)
   - Set a date, time, and budget
   - Choose a venue that minimizes travel for most guests
   - Identify people who would appreciate your achievement or benefit from learning about it
2. Create and send sustainable invitations
   - Use digital invitations when possible (email, messaging apps, or event platforms)
   - If using physical invitations, choose recycled paper or plantable seed paper
   - Include details about carpooling, public transportation options, or bike routes
   - Mention that the party itself will demonstrate sustainable practices (give examples)
   - Request RSVPs to help reduce food waste through proper planning
3. Plan sustainable food and drinks
   - Choose locally sourced, seasonal, and plant-based options
   - For low-budget options, organize a potluck asking guests to bring plant-based dishes
   - Label foods clearly for dietary restrictions
   - Provide filtered tap water with natural flavors (cucumber, mint, citrus)
   - If serving alcohol, choose local or organic options in recyclable containers
   - Plan portion sizes based on RSVPs to minimize food waste
4. Prepare the venue

- Use natural light when possible, or energy-efficient lighting
- Set thermostats at reasonable temperatures
- Arrange furniture to create comfortable conversation areas for discussing sustainability
- Set up clearly labeled waste stations (compost, recycling, landfill)
- Use reusable tableware instead of disposables
- If reusable isn't available, choose compostable options over plastic disposables

5. Create sustainable decorations
    - Use potted plants, garden flowers, or natural items (pinecones, branches)
    - Repurpose existing decorations or borrow items
    - Use LED string lights if additional lighting is needed
    - Create signs or displays showcasing your sustainability achievements
    - Avoid balloons, glitter, and other single-use decorative items
6. Develop engaging activities
    - Plan a brief tour or demonstration of your sustainable achievement
    - Prepare a few conversation starters about your sustainability journey
    - Consider hands-on activities (seed planting for a garden celebration, test-driving EVs for a fleet conversion, etc.)
    - Offer a "positive action wall" where guests can write down an action they're inspired to take
7. Host the party
    - Welcome guests and thank them for coming
    - Briefly share the story of your sustainability achievement
    - Guide guests to food, activities, and waste stations as needed
    - Facilitate connections between guests who might learn from each other
8. Document and share your celebration
    - Collect testimonials and reactions to your sustainability initiatives
    - Take photos or videos to share with those who couldn't attend
    - Capture key moments of engagement with your sustainable achievement
    - Ask guests for permission before posting photos on social media
9. Manage end-of-party logistics sustainably
    - Encourage guests to take home leftovers in reusable containers
    - Properly sort remaining waste
    - Save and store reusable decorations for future events
    - Compost appropriate food waste
    - Clean with eco-friendly products
10. Follow up after the party
    - Send digital thank-you notes with photos from the event
    - Share resources for guests who expressed interest in adopting similar sustainable practices
    - Invite feedback for future sustainable gatherings

Sharing 203: Definitions

- **Locally sourced**: Food and materials produced within 100 to 250 miles
- **Plant-based**: Foods derived from plants with minimal or no animal products
- **Potluck**: A meal where each guest brings a dish to share
- **Seed paper**: Biodegradable paper embedded with plant seeds that can be planted after use
- **Sustainability milestone**: A measurable change in environmental impact
- **Zero waste**: Eliminating waste sent to landfills through reuse, recycling, and composting

Sharing 203: Troubleshooting

Problem	Solutions
Limited budget for the celebration	Host a potluck where guests contribute dishes. Use free digital invitations. Decorate with items from nature. Hold the event during daylight hours to save on lighting. Borrow serving dishes and tableware from friends or family.
Some guests are skeptical about sustainability	Focus on concrete benefits beyond environmental impact (e.g., cost savings, health improvements, increased comfort). Keep the tone celebratory rather than judgmental. Showcase easy-to-measure practical aspects.
Difficulty avoiding disposable items	Ask friends to loan tableware. Check if your local community has a "party kit" lending library. Consider compostable options made from plant fibers as a last resort. For very large gatherings, consider hiring a washing service.
Weather issues for outdoor celebrations	Have a backup indoor location. Rent or borrow canopies or tents. Schedule a rain date. Consider seasonal timing for outdoor events.
Guests want to bring conventional gifts	Have a "no gifts" policy. Suggest specific sustainable alternatives like donations to charity, plants, secondhand items, or experience gifts.
Mixed dietary preferences among guests	Offer primarily plant-based options; label all foods clearly. Focus on natural plant-based dishes like salads with nuts, rather than meat substitutes. Provide recipe cards for popular dishes.
Generating interest in the topic	Create interactive elements rather than lectures. Prepare specific stories about your journey. Focus on benefits that resonate with your audience.
Transportation emissions	Suggest carpooling options. Choose a central location accessible by public transit. Provide bike parking. Offer a virtual component for distant friends.

Sharing 203: Limitations

- Perfect sustainability is impossible; focus on being better rather than perfect
- Guest transportation may create unavoidable environmental impacts
- Sustainable options may cost more than conventional alternatives, creating budget challenges
- Weather can limit outdoor celebration options which are often more energy-efficient
- Digital invitations and communication exclude those without reliable internet access
- Local and seasonal food availability varies by region and season

References and resources: <www.suspra.com/practice/community/sharing-203.html>

Sharing 204: Offering Tours

Offer tours of properties showcasing sustainable practices

Tours offer a powerful, tangible way to demonstrate sustainable practices in action. Unlike reading or hearing about sustainability, tours provide direct observation of working systems, allowing visitors to see, touch, and sometimes taste the results of sustainable practices. This experiential learning creates stronger motivation and clearer understanding than abstract discussions.

Balance inspiration with practical education. Show visitors what's possible and teach them how to implement practices themselves. Make sustainable living feel accessible rather than overwhelming. While showcasing impressive features can inspire visitors, the most valuable tours also highlight simple, affordable changes with significant impact. Demonstrate a range of options from basic to advanced to reach visitors at different stages of their sustainability journeys.

Different property types lend themselves to showcasing different sustainable practices:

Homes and apartments are ideal for everyday practices like energy efficiency upgrades, water conservation, waste management systems, and sustainable food practices. These settings allow visitors to envision similar changes in their own living spaces.

Gardens and yards showcase native plantings, rain gardens, composting systems, food production, and wildlife habitat creation. Seasonal tours of the same property can demonstrate how sustainable landscapes evolve throughout the year.

Businesses and organizations can highlight larger-scale sustainability systems, employee engagement practices, sustainable supply chains, and how sustainability aligns with operational goals.

Farms demonstrate regenerative agriculture, soil building, water management, integrated pest management, and local food systems.

Community spaces show collaborative projects like community gardens, shared solar installations, or cooperative conservation efforts.

Theme tours by pathway (energy, water, food, etc.) or showcase integrated approaches across multiple sustainability domains. Help visitors understand both the specific practices and how they interconnect as a system. When visitors can see real people implementing sustainable practices in contexts similar to their own, these practices seem more achievable. Personal stories of challenges, mistakes, and successes humanize the sustainability journey and help visitors envision their own next steps.

References and resources: <www.suspra.com/practice/community/sharing-204.html>

Sharing 205: Leading Discussions

Lead book clubs, discussion groups, and study circles on environmental topics

Leading environmental discussion groups creates powerful opportunities for shared learning, community building, and collective action. Unlike lectures or presentations, discussions engage participants as active contributors rather than passive recipients. Through thoughtful conversation, people process information more deeply, challenge assumptions, connect concepts to their lives, and develop the confidence to act on environmental knowledge.

Balance intellectual exploration with emotional engagement. Many environmental topics—climate change, biodiversity loss, environmental justice—carry emotional weight. Acknowledge these feelings to keep the conversation constructive. Create a supportive atmosphere where participants can express concerns without becoming overwhelmed by eco-anxiety.

Different discussion formats serve different purposes:

- **Book clubs** work well for exploring comprehensive treatments of environmental topics.
- **Study circles** focus on analyzing specific environmental issues or developing particular skills, often with an action orientation. They typically involve a structured curriculum and may culminate in a project or community initiative.
- **Single-session discussion groups** can respond to current events, research findings, or local issues. They are more accessible to time-constrained participants.

Environmental discussions are most productive when participants engage with evidence-based information and connect it to their personal experiences and values. As facilitator, ensure factual accuracy but respect diverse perspectives. Not all viewpoints are equally valid when discussing scientific topics, but participants can process information through their own cultural and experiential lenses. The impact of environmental discussions extends beyond the meetings themselves. Successful groups foster deeper relationships and inspire changes in participant behavior.

References and resources: <www.suspra.com/practice/community/sharing-205.html>

Sharing 301: Building Educational Displays

Build educational displays about sustainable practices

Educational displays explain sustainability concepts visually, allowing viewers to engage at their own pace, returning to points of interest or skipping ahead as desired. Balance content with eye-catching design. Too much text overwhelms viewers, while too little fails to convey necessary information. Create an emotional connection through examples, storytelling, or interaction. Physical displays work well in community centers, libraries, schools, farmers markets, and public events. Digital displays can reach broader audiences online. Create versions in both formats to maximize reach and accessibility.

In your educational displays, include:

- **Solutions:** Acknowledge challenges; describe practical actions and positive outcomes
- **Local relevance:** Connect global concepts to local conditions, resources, and opportunities
- **Credible information:** Cite reliable sources and current science

Remember that sustainability displays themselves should model sustainable principles. Use recycled or renewable materials, design for reusability or recyclability, and minimize waste in production.

Sharing 301: Equipment & Materials

- Paper or recycled materials for visuals
- Display boards (trifold made from compostable or recyclable materials)
- Sustainable mounting materials (thumbtacks, eco-friendly tape, clips)
- Scissor, knife, or paper cutter
- *Optional: Computer with design software or simple word processing program*
- *Printer or print service access*
- *Easel, table, or wall space for display*
- *Projector, screen, or digital display*
- *Real objects, models, or samples related to your sustainability topic*
- *QR code generator for linking to additional resources*
- *Interactive elements (flip cards, sliders, movable parts)*
- *Lighting for physical displays*

Sharing 301: Steps

1. Define your educational goals
   - Identify the specific sustainable practice you want to explain
   - Determine your target audience (children, general public, specialists)
   - Establish 2-3 clear learning objectives for your display
   - Select sustainability messages that visitors should remember
   - Consider what actions you want viewers to take after seeing your display
2. Research your topic thoroughly
   - Gather accurate, up-to-date information from credible sources
   - Collect compelling statistics, facts, and success stories
   - Find or create visuals that support your key messages
   - Identify common misconceptions to address

- Consider local relevance to your community
3. Plan your display structure
    - Sketch a layout showing the flow of information
    - Create a hierarchy of information (primary, secondary, detailed)
    - Plan for different learning styles (visual, textual, interactive)
    - Design the display for your specific venue and audience
    - Ensure the display is accessible to people with different abilities
4. Develop engaging content
    - Write concise, jargon-free text that explains the sustainable practice
    - Create a compelling title that draws attention
    - Develop headings and subheadings to organize information
    - Keep text blocks under 50 words for readability
    - Include clear calls to action for viewers
5. Create visual elements
    - Design or select impactful images that illustrate key points
    - Create simple diagrams or infographics to explain complex concepts
    - Use a consistent color scheme related to your sustainability theme
    - Incorporate before and after visuals to show impact
    - Include real objects or models to create tactile interest
6. Add interactive components
    - Design simple interactive elements to engage viewers
    - Create QR codes linking to more detailed information online
    - Include questions that prompt reflection
    - Add movable parts that demonstrate sustainability principles
    - Create a feedback mechanism to gauge viewer understanding
7. Produce the display
    - Print materials using sustainable options (recycled paper, soy-based inks)
    - Assemble components in a logical flow
    - Ensure durability appropriate to the display's intended lifespan
    - Test interactive elements to ensure they function properly
    - Have someone unfamiliar with your topic review for clarity
8. Install the display
    - Select a visible location with appropriate lighting
    - Position at a height accessible to your target audience
    - Ensure stability and safety in the installation
    - Consider traffic flow around the display
    - Test visibility from different angles and distances
9. Evaluate effectiveness
    - Observe how people interact with your display
    - Collect formal or informal feedback from viewers
    - Note which aspects draw the most attention
    - Identify areas for improvement
    - Document the display's impact on awareness or behavior
10. Maintain and update
    - Check regularly for damage or wear
    - Update content as new information becomes available
    - Refresh elements that show signs of aging
    - Consider seasonal or periodic changes to maintain interest
    - Document lessons learned for future displays

Sharing 301: Definitions

- **Call to action**: A prompt that encourages viewers to take a specific action

- **Digital display**: A display that requires an electronic device and screen to show
- **Infographic**: Easy-to-understand visual representation of complex information
- **Interactive element**: Component that invites physical engagement or manipulation
- **Learning objective**: What viewers should know or be able to do after seeing the display
- **Physical display**: Tangible presentation using objects and printed materials
- **QR code**: Code that, when scanned with a smartphone, links to a web page
- **Sustainable materials**: Made from resources with minimal environmental impacts
- **Target audience**: Specific group of people for whom the display is primarily designed

Sharing 301: Troubleshooting

Problem	Solutions
Display attracts little attention	Place the display in a more prominent location. Add color or movement. Create a more compelling title. Add lighting to highlight key elements. Incorporate a surprising element or question.
Viewers don't stop long enough to engage	Reduce text density. Add more visuals. Create a clear entry point. Add an interactive element. Pose an intriguing question at the beginning.
Information seems overwhelming	Reduce content. Create clearer information hierarchy. Break complex topics into smaller pieces. Group related information visually.
Interactive elements break or malfunction	Redesign using more durable materials or with fewer moving parts. Create simple instructions. Add clear visual cues for proper use.
Display materials deteriorate quickly	Use more durable materials. Laminate paper elements. Position away from direct sunlight. Create replacement components in advance.
Content becomes outdated	Design so sections can be updated. Include creation date on display.
Text difficult to read	Increase font size. Add white space. Improve contrast between text and background. Use simpler fonts. Reduce the amount of text.
Display appears cluttered or disorganized	Remove some content. Add white space. Group related elements with consistent styling. Establish a clearer visual hierarchy.
Viewers miss the call to action	Make the action call more prominent. Use contrasting colors. Place at eye level. Reduce competing elements. Create take-away materials.

Sharing 301: Limitations

- Effectiveness depends heavily on placement and visibility
- Displays alone rarely change behavior without supporting programs
- Digital displays require technological access and skills
- Material choices present sustainability tradeoffs
- Physical displays have environmental impacts in production and disposal

References and resources: <www.suspra.com/practice/community/sharing-301.html>

Sharing 302: Publishing Infographics

Publish infographics to explain environmental issues

Help audiences grasp the scale of environmental challenges, understand cause-and-effect relationships, visualize trends over time, and see connections between seemingly unrelated factors. Infographics transform abstract concepts and statistical data into visual stories that audiences can quickly understand and remember. Effective environmental infographics simplify without oversimplifying, making scientific information digestible without sacrificing accuracy. When designed well, infographics combine the credibility of data-driven content with the emotional impact of visual storytelling.

Focus on one clear message rather than trying to explain everything about an issue. Guide viewers through a coherent narrative, using visual cues to direct attention to the most important elements. Use line charts for trends over time, bar charts for comparisons, pie charts for showing proportions, and maps for geographical data. Accurately represent data without distortion or exaggeration. Choose colors that create sufficient contrast for readability. Organize information through consistent coding: blues and greens for positive data, warning colors like red and orange for threats.

Decide your distribution strategy. For social media platforms, post simple, bold graphics with minimal text that can be understood quickly while scrolling. On websites, publish more detailed, vertically-oriented infographics that viewers can take time to explore. Include clear, specific calls to action to transform passive viewers into active participants helping to solve environmental issues.

Sharing 302: Equipment & Materials
- Computer with Internet access
- Apps for data management, graphic design, image editing, and data visualization
- Access to reliable environmental data sources
- Cloud storage account for file management
- *Optional: Budget for stock images or premium design tools*

Sharing 302: Steps
1. Define your purpose and audience
    - Identify the specific environmental issue you want to explain
    - Determine your target audience (general public, policymakers, students, etc.)
    - Establish clear goals for your infographic (educate, inspire action, change behavior)
2. Research and gather reliable data
    - Collect data from credible scientific sources and note sources for proper attribution
    - Verify all facts and statistics with multiple reliable sources
    - Look for unexpected patterns or relationships in the data that tell a compelling story
    - Organize your data in a spreadsheet for easy reference
3. Plan your infographic narrative
    - Decide which emotional response you want to evoke
    - Focus on one central message with supporting points
    - Structure information in a logical flow that guides the viewer
    - Identify key statistics or facts that will have the most impact
4. Design your infographic
    - Choose a format that suits your content (flowchart, timeline, comparison, map, etc.)
    - Create a rough sketch or wireframe of your layout
    - Prioritize visual elements over text
    - Select fonts, styles, and colors that enhance readability
5. Refine your content for clarity
    - Write concise, jargon-free text explanations
    - Create a clear visual hierarchy to guide the viewer's attention

- Include a brief introduction and conclusion
- Include a call to action if appropriate
6. Review and revise
   - Get feedback from subject matter experts
   - Verify that visualizations accurately represent the data
   - Test with members of your target audience for understanding
   - Revise based on feedback, focusing on clarity and impact
7. Prepare for publication
   - Create versions in different dimensions for various platforms
   - Provide proper attribution for data sources
   - Create text descriptions for accessibility
8. Publish and distribute
   - Post on your website or blog and share on social media platforms
   - Submit to environmental organizations and relevant publications with permission to share
   - Consider paid promotion for wider reach

Sharing 302: Definitions

- **Infographic**: Easy-to-understand visual representation of complex information
- **Resolution**: The amount of detail in an image, measured in pixels or dots per inch (DPI)
- **Stock images**: Pre-created images available for licensing and use in design projects
- **Visual narrative**: The story told through a sequence of visual elements
- **Wireframe**: A basic visual guide representing the skeletal framework of an infographic

Sharing 302: Troubleshooting

Problem	Solutions
Infographic is too text-heavy	Replace paragraphs with short lists. Convert text explanations to simple visuals. Focus on key statistics rather than detailed explanations.
Data is too complex to visualize simply	Break complex data into multiple simpler visualizations. Focus on the most relevant subset of data that supports your main message.
Design looks cluttered or disorganized	Increase white space between elements. Reduce the number of colors and fonts. Organize elements in a grid. Establish a clear visual hierarchy.
Feedback indicates the message is unclear	Clearly state your main point. Add directional cues to guide the viewer's eye. Test with audience members to identify specific points of confusion.
Low engagement on social media	Create platform-specific versions. Add motion or animation to static infographics. Time posts for maximum visibility. Test different versions.
Visualizations misrepresent the data	Review with a data expert. Start axes at zero when using bar charts. Use consistent scales. Add context to prevent misleading conclusions.
File size too large for web publishing	Compress images. Reduce resolution (dots per inch). Export in web-optimized formats like SVG for vector graphics.

Sharing 302: Limitations

- Even the best infographics cannot convey the full complexity of environmental systems
- Creating high-quality infographics requires time and design skills
- Data visualization software and professional design tools can be expensive
- Oversimplification risks misrepresenting nuanced environmental issues

- Infographics may quickly become outdated as new environmental data emerges

References and resources: <www.suspra.com/practice/community/sharing-302.html>

Sharing 303: Writing Articles

Write articles or a newspaper column about sustainable practices

Write articles about sustainable practices to share knowledge and inspire action. Translate complex environmental concepts into understandable, relevant, and actionable information for readers. Combine technical accuracy with engaging storytelling. Consider how sustainable practices fit into readers' lives, address their concerns, and offer realistic solutions. On controversial topics, present multiple perspectives fairly. Acknowledge uncertainties, but don't let them prevent you from making clear recommendations based on the best available evidence.

Adapt your writing style to match your publication. Newspaper columns need concise, straightforward language with the most important information first. Magazines allow for more narrative development and exploration of nuance. Online articles benefit from subheadings, short lists, and other formatting that facilitates scanning. Academic publications require rigorous citations.

A regular column offers opportunities to build audience trust and explore sustainability topics in depth over time. If writing a recurring column, develop a consistent voice and consider creating a series that builds readers' knowledge progressively. Incorporate reader questions and feedback. Focus on timely, relevant sustainability topics connected to current events, seasons, or local issues.

Sharing 303: Equipment & Materials
- Computer with Internet access

Sharing 303: Steps
1. Define your goal and audience
2. Research thoroughly, going to primary sources
3. Prompt AI to produce an outline organizing your notes and research
    - Explain that you are writing an article (500-800 words for newspapers, 800-1,500 for magazines, 1,500+ for in-depth features)
    - Ask AI to review your notes and research and then suggest an outline
    - Review and revise
4. Write the body of the article
    - Submit to AI for criticisms and suggestions for improvement
    - Critically evaluate all AI output
5. Write the introduction and conclusion
    - Summarize key points without simply repeating
    - End with a call to action, thought-provoking question, or forward-looking statement
    - Reinforce the significance of the topic
6. Edit rigorously
    - Set your draft aside before editing (ideally sleep on it)
    - Check for clarity, accuracy, and flow
    - Eliminate unnecessary jargon and simplify complex ideas
    - Ensure all claims are supported by credible sources
    - Verify that your article meets publication guidelines
7. Submit and promote your article

Sharing 303: Definitions
- **Call to action**: A prompt that encourages viewers to take a specific action

- **Credible sources**: Reliable information providers
- **Sidebars**: Supplementary information presented separately from the main article text

Sharing 303: Troubleshooting

Problem	Solutions
Topic feels too technical for general audience	Focus on practical applications rather than theory. Use analogies. Begin with relatable everyday situations. Break complex topics into pieces.
Difficulty finding local sources or examples	Contact local sustainability offices, environmental organizations, or university extension offices. Join community social media groups to find practitioners. Attend community events related to sustainability.
Editor rejects article as too advocacy-oriented	Revise with a more balanced presentation of facts. Include multiple perspectives. Let evidence lead to conclusions. Focus on objective benefits rather than moral imperatives.
Information becomes outdated quickly	Focus on foundational principles that remain relevant. Include timeless practices alongside trending topics. Update digital versions when new information emerges. Indicate when data is time sensitive.
Struggle to meet word count limits	Narrow focus. Eliminate redundancies. Save tangential information for future articles. Use concise language.
Feedback that article is too negative or overwhelming	Balance problems with solutions. Highlight success stories. Break actions into manageable steps. Emphasize progress already being made. End with a hopeful, action-oriented conclusion.
Unable to secure interviews with experts	Reach out to local practitioners. Contact university professors or extension offices. Quote publications when interviews aren't possible.

Sharing 303: Limitations

- Regular column writing requires significant time commitment
- AI is replacing human-written content
- Some publications may resist articles perceived as too political or advocacy-oriented
- Traditional publication channels have declining readership compared to social media

References and resources: <www.suspra.com/practice/community/sharing-303.html>

Sharing 304: Giving Talks

Give talks about sustainable practices

Give talks about sustainable practices to spread knowledge and inspire action in your community. In-person presentations create direct human connections. Your audience can see your passion, ask questions, and meet others in the audience who share their interests in sustainability. Balance scientific accuracy with accessibility and inspiration. Use scientific data to establish credibility; share personal stories and local examples to make abstract concepts relatable. Go beyond raising awareness to offering practical solutions that audience members can implement in their own lives.

When planning your talk, consider the key questions your audience will have: "Why should I care?", "How does this affect me?", and "What can I do about it?" Address these questions early to engage your audience and keep their attention. Rather than just talking, show compelling images, simple diagrams, and real objects if possible. Photos of local environmental conditions or sustainability projects in your community are particularly effective for establishing relevance. Incorporate simple demonstrations, polls, or hands-on activities to encourage audience members to process information actively.

Address controversial topics and respond to skepticism by acknowledging different viewpoints respectfully, focusing on shared values, and relying on credible scientific evidence. Try not to "win an argument" but to open minds and inspire positive action.

After your presentation, make it easy for inspired audience members to take next steps. Provide handouts with specific actions they can take and ways to connect with others working on sustainability in your community. Consider collecting contact information from those who want to learn more or get involved in future initiatives.

Sharing 304: Equipment & Materials

- Microphone and projector (if available at venue)
- *Optional: Computer with presentation software*
- *USB drive with backup copy of presentation*
- *Pointer and remote slide advancer*

Sharing 304: Steps

1. Identify your purpose and audience
   - Define your specific goals for the talk (educate, inspire action, build awareness)
   - Research your audience's knowledge level, interests, and values
   - Determine appropriate length and format based on the venue and occasion
   - Identify what sustainability topics will resonate most with this specific audience
2. Develop compelling content
   - Select a few main points to focus on rather than covering too many topics
   - Gather credible information from reputable sources
   - Include local examples and data whenever possible
   - Put scientific data in context with stories and real-world applications
   - Share solutions to problems
3. Create effective visual aids (optional)
   - Use a consistent, readable design
   - Select high-quality, meaningful images
   - Create simple graphs or charts that communicate one point each
   - Limit text on slides (aim for six lines or fewer per slide)
   - Consider using physical objects or samples when appropriate
4. Organize your presentation
   - Start with a compelling opening that establishes relevance
   - Clearly state your main message within the first minute
   - Present information in a logical sequence
   - Balance facts with stories, examples, and case studies
   - Plan interactive elements (polls, brief discussions, demonstrations)
   - Prepare a strong conclusion with clear calls to action
   - Allocate time for questions
5. Practice your delivery
   - Time your presentation to ensure it fits within the allotted time
   - Anticipate and prepare for potential questions
6. Prepare for the venue
   - Have a backup plan for technology failures
   - Visit the location beforehand if possible
   - Check technology compatibility and connections

- Arrive early to test equipment and address any issues
- Adjust your presentation for room size and lighting
- Arrange handouts or materials for easy distribution
7. Deliver your presentation effectively
    - Connect with your audience (eye contact, welcoming tone)
    - Speak clearly and at a moderate pace
    - Explain your visual aids
    - Monitor audience engagement; wrap up if everyone in audience is bored
    - End on time
8. Handle questions effectively
    - Prepare responses in advance for common concerns
    - Repeat questions to ensure everyone heard them
    - Answer concisely and honestly
    - Capture questions you can't answer to follow up later
    - Be willing to say "I don't know, but I'll find out"
    - Redirect hostile questions to constructive topics
9. Follow up after your talk
    - Share your presentation materials if appropriate
    - Provide additional resources for those interested in learning more
    - Follow up on any questions you couldn't answer during the talk
    - Request feedback to improve future presentations
    - Connect interested audience members with local resources

Sharing 304: Definitions

- **Call to action**: A prompt that encourages people to take a specific action

Sharing 304: Troubleshooting

Problem	Solutions
Technology fails during presentation	Have printed notes as backup. Be prepared to continue without slides. Bring handouts that contain key information or visuals.
Audience seems disengaged	Pause and ask a question to restart engagement. Move into a brief interactive activity. Wrap up quickly if you have lost your audience.
Hostile or challenging questions	Thank the person for their perspective. Seek common ground. Focus on scientific data. Offer to continue the discussion after the presentation.
Running out of time	Skip ahead if necessary. Prioritize your key messages and calls to action. Be prepared to summarize main points.
Too much technical information for audience	Use analogies to explain complex concepts. Break information into smaller chunks. Use visual aids to clarify. Offer simplified explanations.
Nervousness affecting your delivery	Practice deep breathing before starting. Focus on audience members who appear friendly. Refer to printed notes for security.
Questions you can't answer	Honestly acknowledge when you don't know something. Offer to research and follow up. Ask if others in the audience have insights to share.
Smaller audience turnout than expected	Give the best presentation you can. Adjust the room setup if possible. Use the opportunity for more personalized interaction.

Sustainable Practices Handbook Community Practices: Nurturing Good Relationships

Sharing 304: Limitations
- In-person talks reach only those who attend
- Complex sustainability topics are difficult to cover comprehensively in a single presentation
- Audience composition may limit how technical or specific you can be
- Some venues have technological limitations that restrict your visual presentation options
- Environmental topics can be politically charged in some communities, creating resistance
- Lack of scientific consensus on some sustainability solutions creates communication challenges
- Audience members may have widely varying knowledge, making it difficult to engage everyone

References and resources: <www.suspra.com/practice/community/sharing-304.html>

Sharing 305: Teaching Classes

Teach classes and give workshops about sustainable practices

Teaching classes and workshops about sustainable practices multiplies your environmental impact. Sharing your knowledge enables hundreds of others to make positive changes in their own lives. Sustainability topics particularly well-suited for teaching others include:

- Composting and waste reduction
- Plant-based cooking and food preservation
- Home energy and water auditing and conservation techniques
- Do-it-yourself natural cleaning products
- Basic mending and repair skills
- Native plant gardening

Approach your role with humility; teaching is a skill developed through practice. Even if you're not yet an expert teacher, your passion and practical knowledge can inspire others. Teach what you know well and have personally implemented. When designing your curriculum, consider the following principles:

Balance theory and practice: While understanding "why" sustainability matters motivates change, most participants usually want to learn "how" to implement practices. Aim for roughly 30% theory and 70% practical application in your teaching.

Meet participants where they are: Levels of knowledge, abilities, and resources differ; offer options and adaptations so everyone can implement sustainable practices in their unique context.

Use multiple teaching methods: Some people learn by hearing, others by seeing, and most by doing. Incorporate explanations, demonstrations, and hands-on practice.

Make it interactive: Engage participants through questions, discussions, problem-solving activities, and skills practice to build confidence and reinforce learning.

Address barriers honestly: Acknowledge time, cost and convenience challenges to sustainable practices and offer solutions. Honesty prepares participants for real-world implementation.

Connect to values: Link sustainable practices to values participants already hold, such as saving money, staying healthy, making friends, or being more independent from commercial pressures.

Your enthusiasm for sustainability is contagious. Teach the practices you model, share your personal experiences (including mistakes and lessons learned), and create a supportive learning environment.

Sharing 305: Equipment & Materials
- Lesson plan or course outline

- Visual aids (slides, posters, handouts)
- Demonstration materials relevant to your topic
- Sign-in sheet or registration system
- Evaluation forms for participant feedback
- Timer or clock
- *Optional: Platform for online classes*
- *Microphone and webcam for virtual teaching*
- *Projector and screen for slide shows*
- *Name tags for in-person workshops*
- *Digital or physical resource list for participants*

Sharing 305: Steps

1. Define your teaching goals and audience
   - Identify specific sustainable practices you can effectively teach
   - Determine your target audience (beginners, intermediates, families, etc.)
   - Establish learning objectives: what should students be able to do after your class
2. Plan your class structure and content
   - Choose between a one-time workshop or multi-session class
   - Decide whether to teach in person or virtually
3. Develop class materials
   - Prepare more content than you think you'll need
   - Create clear, visually appealing slides or posters
   - Limit text on visual aids (use the 6x6 rule: no more than 6 bullet points, 6 words each)
   - Prepare handouts that summarize key points and provide additional resources
   - Gather or create physical examples and demonstration materials
   - Develop hands-on activities that reinforce key concepts
4. Prepare and test your teaching environment
   - For in-person teaching:
     - Visit the venue in advance if possible
     - Check lighting, seating, acoustics, and available technology
     - Test any electronic equipment before participants arrive
   - For virtual teaching:
     - Test your Internet connection, camera, and microphone
     - Familiarize yourself with the virtual platform's features
     - Prepare digital materials in accessible formats
     - Have a backup plan for technical difficulties
5. Practice your delivery
   - Rehearse your complete presentation, especially demonstrations
   - Time each section to ensure you can cover all material
   - Practice explaining complex concepts in simple terms
   - Prepare responses to potential questions
6. Promote your class or workshop
   - Write a compelling description highlighting benefits for participants
   - Share details through community calendars, social media, and relevant organizations
   - Set up a registration system to track participants
   - Send reminders to registrants before the class
7. Facilitate the learning experience
   - Arrive early to set up and greet participants
   - Begin with a brief introduction of yourself and the topic
   - Establish ground rules for participation
   - Use a warm-up activity to engage participants immediately
   - Check for understanding throughout the session

- Demonstrate sustainable practices before asking participants to try them
- Address questions clearly and concisely
- Manage time carefully, adjusting as needed
8. Encourage practical application
    - Include hands-on components where participants practice the sustainable skills
    - Provide troubleshooting tips for common challenges
    - Share real-world examples and success stories
    - Offer specific next steps participants can take after the class
9. Gather feedback and evaluate
    - Distribute evaluation forms or digital surveys
    - Ask specific questions about content clarity, pace, and usefulness
    - Request suggestions for improvement
    - Collect ideas for future class topics
10. Follow up and refine
    - Send thank-you messages with additional resources
    - Review participant feedback and self-evaluate

Sharing 305: Definitions

- **Active learning**: Engaging students in the learning process through activities, not lectures
- **Curriculum**: The knowledge and lessons taught

Sharing 305: Troubleshooting

Problem	Solutions
Participants with varying knowledge	Start with a knowledge assessment. Prepare challenges for advanced participants. Pair knowledgeable participants with beginners.
Running out of time	Prioritize key points and hands-on activities. Have a "must cover" list identified in advance. Provide handouts for uncovered material.
Technical difficulties in virtual classes	Have a co-host to manage technical issues. Have a reliable backup plan (like a phone conference) for severe technical issues.
Low participant engagement	Ask more questions. Use small-group discussions. Have students get up and move around.
Difficult questions you can't answer	Acknowledge when you don't know an answer. Offer to research and follow up (and actually do so). Ask for answers from the group.
Dominating participants	Establish ground rules at the start. Go "round robin." Say, "Let's hear from someone who hasn't spoken yet." Ask dominant participants to help others.
Hands-on activities taking too long	Pivot to simplified versions that can be completed more quickly if needed. Prepare partially completed examples to save time.
Participants struggling to implement practices	Break processes into smaller steps. Provide additional guidance. Create handouts with step-by-step instructions. Share videos.

Sharing 305: Limitations

- You may have to create your own opportunities to teach sustainability classes or workshops
- Teaching requires preparation time
- One-time workshops rarely lead to mastery; sustainable practices often require ongoing support

- Some sustainable practices are difficult to teach
- Workshop spaces may not have all the facilities needed for certain demonstrations
- Learning depends on factors beyond the teacher (motivation, resources, support)
- Teaching is a skill; your first workshops may have areas for improvement

References and resources: <www.suspra.com/practice/community/sharing-305.html>

Sharing 401: Publishing Books and Films

Publish books and films about environmental sustainability

Publish books and films to reach diverse audiences, explain complex concepts, showcase solutions, and motivate systemic change. Help people take action by writing a practical guidebook. Explore the human stories behind environmental issues with narrative nonfiction. Introduce sustainability concepts to young audiences with children's books. Provide in-depth analysis for students with a textbook. Communicate sustainability messages in documentaries, or use your creativity for fictional, animated, or experimental films. Make short-form videos that are easy to share and use in educational contexts.

Artificial intelligence is transforming the publishing landscape, making it easier to write and publish books; independent filmmaking is becoming easier, too. However, traditional publishers and film distributors offer quality control and have marketing power that is difficult to replicate independently. If you are a first-time author or filmmaker, consider hiring a professional to help you prepare your manuscript or film concept and find a publisher or distributor. Take writing or film-making classes to learn how to hone the craft of becoming an author or filmmaker.

Consider the environmental impact of your publishing process. For books, promote digital formats; minimize the impact of hard copies using recycled paper, vegetable-based inks, and print-on-demand technology (which reduces waste). For films, consider sustainability practices during shooting.

Finally, think beyond publication. Connect your work to relevant organizations and campaigns. Ask experts to review your material; issue corrections or publish follow-up works as warranted.

References and resources: <www.suspra.com/practice/community/sharing-401.html>

Sharing 402: Hosting a Podcast

Host a sustainability podcast

Create a podcast to influence people seeking practical, accessible information about sustainable living. Establish a personal connection through your voice and storytelling, making sustainability more relatable. Find the intersection between your passion and expertise and your audience's needs.

Interview-based podcasts showcase experts who bring credibility and varied viewpoints. This format also helps build your network. Panel discussions are friends or colleagues who get together to talk about sustainability issues. Solo shows share your personal experiences and ideas; sharing both successes and challenges provides more value to your listeners. Remember that podcast listeners often want actionable information. Provide practical takeaways that listeners can implement in their own lives. Solicit stories about changes listeners have made after hearing your podcast. Follow a "learn, act, share" framework: educate listeners about an issue, provide specific actions they can take, and encourage them to share their experiences and knowledge with others.

Partner with sustainability organizations, businesses, and educational institutions. They can provide resources, expertise, and additional distribution for your podcast.

References and resources: <www.suspra.com/practice/community/sharing-402.html>

Sharing 403: Establishing Learning Centers

Establish a learning center for sustainable practices

A sustainability learning center is a physical hub where community members can gather to access resources, learn practical skills, and connect with others interested in sustainable living. Unlike temporary workshops or one-off events, a dedicated center provides ongoing, reliable access to sustainability education and builds community capacity for environmental action.

Learning centers can take many forms, from a few educational resources in a small area in an existing community space (such as a library), to a dedicated facility with demonstration areas for renewable energy, sustainable building techniques, organic gardening, and other practices. Funding typically comes from multiple sources including donations, membership fees, program revenue, and possibly public funding. Diversifying funding sources increases long-term stability.

Choose an organizational structure based on your vision and available resources:

- **Program within an existing organization**: Leverages established infrastructure but has less independence in decision-making
- **Independent non-profit organization**: Provides autonomy but requires establishing governance structures and securing independent funding
- **Social enterprise for-profit model**: Generates revenue through services while maintaining educational mission

Design your space and programs to facilitate relationship-building and collaborative learning among participants. Your center's physical environment should exemplify the sustainability principles you teach. Consider incorporating visible elements like solar panels, rainwater harvesting systems, or demonstration gardens that serve both educational and functional purposes. Make your building itself a teaching tool by displaying information about its sustainable features.

Start with core offerings that match both your expertise and community interests, then expand as capacity and demand grow. Consider incorporating elements like tool libraries, seed exchanges, repair cafés, or community gardens that give people practical ways to implement what they learn. Regularly assess your programs to ensure they remain relevant and impactful in your community.

References and resources: <www.suspra.com/practice/community/sharing-403.html>

Sharing 404: Building Research Programs

Build a research program for sustainable practices

You don't need a university position to build a valuable research program for sustainable practices. Community-based research efforts often start with a single passionate person who notices a problem, gets curious, and starts asking questions. The key is persistence.

Research is simply organized curiosity. Academic researchers use specialized language and techniques, but the core process—asking questions, gathering information systematically, analyzing patterns, and sharing findings—is accessible to everyone. Community-based research brings the added benefit of local knowledge, practical perspective, and direct connection to the people who can use the findings.

Effective community research programs for sustainability share common features:

Local relevance. Rather than studying abstract global issues, community researchers focus on specific local challenges: why native plants aren't thriving in neighborhood gardens, which household practices produce the least waste, or how to provide public transportation. This local focus makes the research more immediately useful than studies covering broader areas.

Diverse types of knowledge. Community research programs recognize that valuable knowledge comes from lived experience, traditional ecological knowledge, and practical expertise.

Affected communities as researchers, not just subjects. Community-based research invites community members to help shape research questions, collect information, analyze findings, and decide how to use the results. This participation helps the work have more real-world relevance.

Action, not just understanding. Community research programs typically aim to create change, not just knowledge. They intentionally link their findings to practical actions and evaluate the results—creating a continuous cycle of learning and improvement.

Accessible communications. Rather than writing academic papers, community researchers share findings as visual displays at community events, social media posts, short videos, hands-on workshops, and simple guides. This puts their research within reach of more people in the community.

Research programs can start small and grow naturally. You might begin as an individual investigator documenting observations about a local sustainability challenge, then form a small research circle with others who share your interest. As your work gains visibility and credibility, you might formalize into a community research collective, a citizen science hub, or eventually a nonprofit research organization. Each stage can produce valuable findings while building capacity for the next level.

Finding resources for community research requires creativity but is entirely possible. Foundations offer small grants for community projects. Businesses provide in-kind support like meeting spaces. Online crowdfunding can raise money for supplies. Partnerships with schools or community colleges yield student volunteers. Diversify your support to sustain your sustainable research.

References and resources: <www.suspra.com/practice/community/sharing-404.html>

Volunteering 101: Joining Projects

Join environmental projects in your community

Connect with like-minded people while volunteering to benefit your community and ecosystem. Most environmental organizations rely heavily on volunteers to accomplish their mission, making your contribution genuinely valuable. One-time events (like stream cleanups or tree plantings) are excellent starting points, while ongoing projects provide deeper engagement and skill development.

Identify your interests, skills, and availability, then find local environmental projects by searching online volunteer platforms, visiting websites of local environmental and community organizations, checking social media groups focused on community action, contacting your city's sustainability office, conservation district, or parks department, or looking for posters at community centers, libraries, and farmers markets.

References and resources: <www.suspra.com/practice/community/volunteering-101.html>

Volunteering 201: Joining Organizations

Join a community service organization or an environmental group

Environmental organizations and community service groups offer structured opportunities to volunteer, learn from experienced members, and build community connections. When choosing an organization to join, consider both alignment with your values and practical factors like cost of joining.

Sustainable Practices Handbook Community Practices: Nurturing Good Relationships

National organizations with local chapters offer the benefits of established structures and broader influence, while grassroots local groups may be more flexible. If you find the right fit, consider taking on leadership roles that further amplify your impact and influence in your community.

Volunteering 201: Equipment & Materials
- Budget for membership fees (if any)
- Transportation to meetings

Volunteering 201: Steps
1. Identify your environmental interests and values
2. Research organizations in your community
3. Attend an initial meeting or event
4. Complete the membership process
5. Integrate into the organization
6. Maintain active participation

Volunteering 201: Definitions
- **Chapter**: A local branch of a larger national or international organization
- **Grassroots organization**: Local groups formed by community members
- **Membership dues**: Regular financial contributions required to maintain membership
- **Mission statement**: A formal statement of an organization's core purpose and focus
- **Service organization**: Groups like Rotary, Lions Club, or Kiwanis that work on various community improvement projects

Volunteering 201: Troubleshooting

Problem	Solutions
Organization inactive	Look for another more active group or offer to help reinvigorate activities.
Membership fees are too expensive	Ask about sliding scale options, student/senior discounts, or fee waivers. Consider volunteering in lieu of fees if allowed.
Meeting times conflict with your schedule	Inquire about virtual attendance options, alternative meeting times, or project-based participation that fits your schedule.
You feel unwelcome	Connect with membership coordinators. Bring a friend.
Organization disorganized	Offer your organizational skills to help, or look for more established groups.
No meaningful ways to contribute	Speak with leaders about matching your skills to needs. Explore different committees within the organization.

Volunteering 201: Limitations
- Rural areas may have fewer established environmental organizations
- Membership commitments may not align with changing personal circumstances
- Virtual-only participation may limit relationship building and influence

References and resources: <www.suspra.com/practice/community/volunteering-201.html>

Volunteering 202: Coaching Sustainability

Become a volunteer sustainability coach

As a sustainability coach, you serve as both guide and accountability partner, helping individuals and households implement practical changes for a more sustainable future using a consistent process:

1. **Assessing**: Understanding the current practices, priorities, and constraints of the household
2. **Goal-setting**: Collaboratively identifying achievable and meaningful changes
3. **Action planning**: Breaking goals down into specific, manageable steps
4. **Implementing**: Providing knowledge, resources, and encouragement
5. **Progress tracking**: Measuring changes and celebrating successes
6. **Adapting**: Adjusting approaches based on what's working and what isn't

Recognize that behavior change is both technical and psychological. While providing practical knowledge is important, equally valuable is understanding the motivations, barriers, and values that shape household decisions. Some clients may be motivated by cost savings, others by environmental impact, and still others by health benefits or community connection.

Coaching typically requires ten hours per month, including preparation, sessions, follow-up, and your own continued learning. Many coaches find it most effective to work with two or three households at a time, allowing for personalized attention while still creating meaningful community impact.

Unlike paid professional coaching or consulting, volunteer sustainability coaching focuses on accessible, practical changes rather than technical assessments or specialized expertise. Your role is to help households navigate the journey toward sustainability by sharing knowledge, providing encouragement, and connecting them with resources—not to be an expert in every aspect of sustainability.

True coaching helps people move beyond dependency to empowerment. Build your client's capacity to continue making sustainable choices independently, long after your formal relationship has ended.

Volunteering 202: Equipment & Materials

- Demonstrated knowledge of sustainable practices (intermediate level or higher)
- Passed sustainability knowledge tests (e.g., Suspra Knowledge Test)
- Sustainability coaching kit

Volunteering 202: Steps

1. Prepare yourself with knowledge and experience
2. Find a coaching opportunity
3. Develop your coaching approach
4. Build coaching skills
5. Create a coaching toolkit
6. Establish clear boundaries
7. Conduct effective coaching sessions
8. Provide ongoing support
9. Document impact and results
10. Continue your own education

Volunteering 202: Definitions

- **Action plan**: A detailed roadmap that breaks larger sustainability goals into specific, achievable steps with timelines
- **Active listening**: Fully concentrating on what someone is saying rather than just passively hearing, including asking clarifying questions and summarizing understanding

- **Household assessment**: Evaluating current practices across sustainability pathways
- **Impact measurement**: Quantifying the environmental benefits of sustainable practices
- **Sustainability coaching**: The practice of guiding individuals or households to adopt more environmentally sustainable practices through education, goal-setting, and ongoing support

Volunteering 202: Troubleshooting

Problem	Solutions
Client loses motivation after initial enthusiasm	Break goals into smaller, more achievable steps. Connect actions to the client's personal values. Celebrate small wins.
Client faces unexpected barriers to changes	Help brainstorm creative alternatives. Connect them with community resources or support. Adjust goals.
You don't know the answer to a technical question	Be honest about knowledge limitations. Research the answer after the session. Connect the client with appropriate experts or resources. Use the opportunity to learn together.
Client expects you to do the work for them	Clarify your role as a coach, not a service provider. Focus on teaching skills. Reiterate their responsibility for implementation.
Difficulty measuring or seeing tangible results	Develop simple before-and-after metrics. Look for qualitative changes in habits and awareness. Track progress in multiple areas to show cumulative impact. Take photos to document visible changes.
Scheduling conflicts or frequent cancellations	Establish clear policies upfront. Offer flexible scheduling options. Consider virtual coaching. Assess whether commitment is the underlying issue.
Client has household members who are resistant	Ask to include all household members in at least one session. Focus on benefits that matter to resistant members. Find compromise practices everyone can support.
You feel burned out or overwhelmed	Reduce your client load. Set more boundaries on time and availability. Take breaks between coaching relationships.

Volunteering 202: Limitations

- Complex technical issues require professional expertise
- Limited time commitment means progress may be slower than with paid coaching services
- Coaching effectiveness depends heavily on client motivation and follow-through
- Some sustainable changes require financial investments that may be beyond client resources
- Results vary widely based on household circumstances

References and resources: <www.suspra.com/practice/community/volunteering-202.html>

Volunteering 203: Leading Teams

Organize and lead teams to accomplish sustainable projects

Successful sustainability team leaders combine project management skills with environmental knowledge and strong interpersonal abilities. Team members often bring varying levels of environmental knowledge and may have different motivations for participating—from building career skills to passionate environmental advocacy. As a leader, your role is to channel this diversity into a cohesive force while maintaining focus on measurable sustainability outcomes.

Begin by defining a project with clear environmental impact goals. Whether you're organizing a community garden, conducting energy audits, restoring habitat, or implementing a zero-waste program, your project should have measurable outcomes. This clarity helps team members understand the purpose of their work and stay motivated through challenges.

The composition of your team significantly influences project success. If you're able to recruit volunteers, choose ones with complementary skills and ensure they understand how their role contributes to sustainability goals. While technical skills are important, also look for volunteers with organizational abilities, communication skills, and genuine interest in environmental issues. Volunteers need clear direction but also want autonomy and space for creativity. Regular communication, transparent decision-making processes, and consistent recognition of contributions create an environment where volunteers feel valued.

Tracking and communicating impact is particularly important for sustainability projects. Collecting data on environmental metrics (emissions reduced, waste diverted, habitat restored) provides evidence of your team's effectiveness and helps team members see the tangible results of their work. These measurements also provide valuable information for future sustainability initiatives and can help secure additional support or funding.

Remember that your leadership role extends beyond project management to include sustainability education. Many volunteers join teams to learn more about environmental issues and solutions. By incorporating learning opportunities, you not only improve project execution but also build broader community capacity for sustainability action.

Volunteering 203: Equipment & Materials
- Team of employees or volunteers

Volunteering 203: Steps
1. Define your sustainability project
2. Recruit or train your team
3. Create team structure and processes
4. Build team cohesion and shared purpose
5. Develop a detailed project plan
6. Lead effective meetings
7. Manage project execution
8. Support volunteer engagement and growth
9. Measure and communicate impact
10. Conduct project reflection and closure

Volunteering 203: Definitions
- **Project scope**: The defined boundaries of a project, including what is and is not included
- **Stakeholders**: Individuals or groups affected by or interested in the project's outcomes
- **Team charter**: A team's purpose, values, goals, and operational guidelines

Volunteering 203: Troubleshooting

Problem	Solutions
Volunteers drop out mid-project	Build redundancy into roles. Document processes so new volunteers can step in. Develop a roster of backup volunteers. Conduct exit interviews.

Problem	Solutions
Different levels of knowledge on team	Create a resource library for self-guided learning. Pair knowledgeable volunteers with newcomers. Schedule brief learning sessions before meetings. Focus on concrete tasks while gradually building understanding.
Conflict between team members	Address issues promptly in private conversations. Focus on project goals rather than personalities. Use structured conflict resolution processes. Revisit team charter and shared values. Reassign roles if necessary.
Project falls behind schedule	Break tasks into smaller, more manageable chunks. Reassess timeline and adjust if needed. Identify bottlenecks and provide additional support. Consider scope reduction while preserving core sustainability impacts.
Volunteers becoming overwhelmed or burning out	Check in regularly about workload and stress levels. Encourage realistic commitments and boundary-setting. Rotate demanding tasks. Schedule breaks or reduced activity periods. Express genuine appreciation regularly.
Difficulty measuring sustainability impact	Simplify metrics. Focus on a few key indicators. Partner with local experts for measurement help. Use proxy measures when necessary. Document qualitative impacts alongside quantitative data.
Lack of resources for project completion	Identify the minimum resources needed for core impact. Explore creative alternatives to purchased materials. Develop partnerships with local businesses or organizations. Adjust project scope to match resources.
Uneven participation among team members	Clarify expectations during recruitment. Check in privately with less active members. Create various levels of involvement options. Ensure tasks match skills and interests. Recognize all forms of contribution.
Loss of team motivation	Connect work to visible impacts. Share success stories from similar projects. Break long projects into achievable phases with celebrations. Bring in guest speakers or new perspectives.

Volunteering 203: Limitations
- Volunteer teams have limited time availability compared to paid staff
- Team members may have varying levels of commitment and reliability
- Sustainability projects often require specialized knowledge that may be scarce
- Measurement of environmental impacts can be technically challenging
- Team performance depends on many factors, not just leadership

References and resources: <www.suspra.com/practice/community/volunteering-203.html>

Volunteering 301: Serving on a Sustainability Committee

Serve on your local government's sustainability committee

Be at the intersection of policy, community action, and environmental stewardship by serving on a local government sustainability committee. These committees vary widely in structure and authority—some are formal bodies that make policy recommendations, while others serve primarily in an advisory or community education capacity. They address a range of environmental issues, including energy efficiency, renewable energy, recycling, waste reduction, water conservation, transportation, land use, and climate resilience. Committees may broadly consider all these areas or have a more specific mandate, such as implementing a climate action plan or developing green building policies.

Balance advocacy to achieve environmental progress with collaboration to find common ground with diverse stakeholders. Be visionary in identifying potential initiatives while remaining realistic about implementation constraints. Serve as a bridge between community needs and government processes.

Approach your service with passion and patience. Local government sustainability work moves more slowly than many people expect. Change usually happens only incrementally through persistent effort over time. Budget constraints, competing priorities, and existing regulations create obstacles. However, committees can achieve significant impact through strategic focus, community engagement, and alignment with broader government goals. Recognize that building relationships, understanding systems, and developing politically feasible recommendations are as important as technical environmental knowledge. Hold fast to the idea that your committee will create lasting change by institutionalizing environmental considerations into government decision-making processes.

References and resources: <www.suspra.com/practice/community/volunteering-301.html>

Volunteering 302: Recruiting Sustainability Coaches

Recruit and train sustainability coaches

Recruiting effective volunteer sustainability coaches means finding individuals who combine passion for environmental sustainability with the interpersonal skills needed to guide others. Unlike direct action (like tree planting or cleanup events), coaching requires strong communication skills, patience, and the ability to meet people where they are in their sustainability journey. Look for people who demonstrate empathy, listening skills, and cultural competence, such as existing community leaders, educators, and retired professionals.

When recruiting, emphasize both the environmental impact and the personal benefits, including skill development, community connections, and the opportunity to create meaningful change. Be transparent about the time commitment required and the support your program will provide. Training in two areas is critical to coach success:

1. **Content knowledge** about pathways to sustainability and specific practices
2. **Coaching skills** including effective communication, needs assessment, goal setting, progress monitoring, and handling resistance to change

Include both theoretical knowledge and practical application in your training curriculum. Role-playing coaching scenarios, analyzing case studies, and practicing with feedback help volunteers develop confidence and competence. Consider a "shadowing" period where new coaches observe experienced ones before working independently. Plan to be continuously identifying and training new coaches to replace volunteers who move on. Creating a positive, supportive experience for your coaches will help with retention and make recruitment easier through word-of-mouth referrals.

Volunteering 302: Equipment & Materials
- Meeting space or video conferencing for interviews and training sessions
- Sign-up forms and volunteer agreements
- Screening and interview questions
- Training curriculum for coaches
- *Optional: Budget for background checks if working with vulnerable populations*

Volunteering 302: Steps
1. Define the role and requirements of sustainability coaches

2. Develop a recruitment strategy
3. Implement your recruitment campaign
4. Screen and select candidates
5. Design comprehensive training
6. Deliver initial training
7. Match coaches with opportunities
8. Provide ongoing support and development

Volunteering 302: Definitions
- **Pathways to sustainability**: The framework for organizing sustainable practices in this handbook: community, food, water, movement, energy, goods, and habitat
- **Sustainability coach**: A volunteer who helps individuals, households, or organizations implement sustainable practices through guidance, education, and support

Volunteering 302: Troubleshooting

Problem	Solutions
Too few applicants	Expand recruitment channels. Ask current volunteers to help recruit. Revise messaging to better communicate benefits. Partner with existing organizations. Reduce time commitment.
Applicants with insufficient knowledge	Create a tiered entry system where volunteers can start with less responsibility. Provide more initial training for volunteers. Pair knowledgeable coaches with those needing development.
Volunteer dropouts during training	Check if training is too demanding or scheduled inconveniently. Provide training in smaller modules. Improve clarity about expectations before recruitment. Survey dropouts to identify issues.
Misalignment between volunteer expectations and reality	Improve position descriptions. Include current coaches in information sessions. Provide more thorough orientation. Create opportunities to observe before committing.
Uneven coaching quality	Strengthen training, particularly around coaching skills. Implement a certification process. Provide templates and materials for coaches to use. Establish a mentoring system. Conduct periodic quality assessments.
Volunteers lacking confidence	Extend the shadowing period. Provide more practice opportunities with feedback. Create scripts or talking points for common situations. Establish a buddy system for mutual support.
Difficulty retaining coaches	Check workload and time expectations. Survey coaches about their experience. Improve recognition and appreciation efforts. Organize get togethers to create social connections among coaches.
Cultural barriers between coaches and community	Recruit more diverse coaches. Provide cultural competency training. Develop partnerships with cultural community organizations. Create culturally appropriate materials.

Volunteering 302: Limitations
- Volunteer coaching competes with many other demands for people's time
- Few volunteers will have both sustainability knowledge and coaching skills

- Training volunteers requires significant investment of time and resources
- Volunteer availability may not match community needs
- Volunteer turnover requires ongoing recruitment
- Volunteer coaching programs may not reach all segments of the community equally

References and resources: <www.suspra.com/practice/community/volunteering-302.html>

Volunteering 303: Leading in an Environmental Organization

Lead a local chapter of an environmental organization

As a leader in an environmental organization, you serve as both a champion of your environmental cause and a steward of the organization that supports it. Align your leadership style with your organization's values. Environmental organizations frequently emphasize democratic principles, inclusion, and participatory decision-making. However, your group may prefer a hierarchical leadership model, depending on its culture, size, and the urgency of issues you address.

Leading a chapter of an established organization provides access to resources, proven models, recognition, and support networks. However, it also requires navigating the parent organization's expectations, reporting requirements, and sometimes complex approval processes. Maintain a clear focus on advancing environmental sustainability through collective action; develop your organizational structures and processes with this mission in mind.

Work to make your organization representative of the communities you serve.

- Reach out to diverse stakeholders and community members
- Ensure leadership opportunities are accessible to people of different backgrounds
- Address barriers to participation
- Recognize and value different forms of environmental knowledge and expertise
- Consider environmental justice in your organization's work

Environmental work often involves long-term challenges that can take decades to address. Balance short-term achievements with steady progress toward longer-term goals. Celebrate small victories, recognize volunteer contributions, and regularly communicate impact to sustain engagement.

References and resources: <www.suspra.com/practice/community/volunteering-303.html>

Volunteering 401: Starting a Sustainability Coaching Program

Start a sustainability coaching program in your community

Sustainability coaching programs bridge the chasm between awareness and action by providing personalized guidance to individuals, households, and organizations. Volunteer coaches offer ongoing support to overcome the challenges of behavior change and practical implementation.

A well-designed coaching program creates a multiplier effect in your community. Each trained coach can support multiple clients, who in turn influence their own networks. This cascading impact accelerates sustainable practices across the community far beyond what you could accomplish alone.

Successful sustainability coaching programs typically include several key elements:

A structured approach: While coaching is personalized, having a consistent set of assessment tools, coaching protocols, and progress tracking methods ensures quality and allows for program evaluation.

Appropriate scope: Focusing your program on specific sustainability pathways (energy, water, food, etc.) or audience segments (households, small businesses, etc.) creates clarity and manageability.

Coach support systems: Volunteer coaches need ongoing support, continuing education, and a community of peers. Regular coach gatherings, advanced training, and access to expert resources maintain coach engagement and knowledge.

Measurable outcomes: Tracking both program outputs (number of coaches trained, coaching sessions conducted) and outcomes (actual sustainability improvements achieved) provides accountability and helps secure ongoing support.

Community integration: The most effective programs collaborate with existing community institutions like libraries, schools, faith communities, and local government. These partnerships provide credibility, resources, and participant referrals.

Aim to balance structure with flexibility. Coaches need clear frameworks and resources, but also the freedom to adapt to each client's unique situation. Similarly, your program needs established processes but must remain adaptable to community feedback and changing conditions. As you build your program, remember that sustainability coaching addresses both technical knowledge (what practices to implement) and change management (how to overcome barriers to implementation).

Volunteering 401: Equipment & Materials
- Computer with Internet access
- Website with project information
- Meeting space (physical or virtual)
- Curriculum and training materials for coaches
- Online document sharing system
- Budget for program expenses ($500-5,000 initial investment)
- *Optional: Printed materials for outreach*

Volunteering 401: Steps
1. Conduct a community assessment to identify needs and find potential partners
2. Develop your program structure
   - Define your coaching program's mission, vision, and goals
   - Establish the scope of sustainability practices you'll address
   - Determine your coaching approach (one-on-one, group workshops, etc.)
   - Create a program timeline with milestones
   - Develop a budget and funding strategy
   - Design a program governance structure (advisory board, steering committee)
3. Build your coaching framework
   - Develop or adapt a sustainability assessment tool
   - Create structured pathways for different sustainability topics
   - Design coach training curriculum and certification process
   - Create coaching session templates and resources
   - Develop data collection and evaluation methods
4. Establish program operations
   - Create policies and procedures
     - Volunteer recruitment and management
     - Client intake and matching
   - Establish communication channels for coaches and participants
5. Recruit and train your initial coach cohort
   - Identify recruitment channels for potential coaches
   - Create compelling coach recruitment materials

- Screen and interview coach candidates
- Conduct initial coach training sessions
6. Launch and promote your program
   - Create program branding and materials
   - Establish an online presence and engage with local media
   - Hold a launch event or information session
   - Present the program to community organizations
7. Run your program
   - Match trained coaches with participants
   - Provide ongoing support to coaches
   - Monitor initial coaching relationships
   - Collect early feedback and make adjustments
   - Document early successes and challenges
8. Grow and sustain your program
   - Secure ongoing funding
   - Conduct regular program evaluations
   - Recognize and celebrate volunteer contributions
   - Develop advanced training for experienced coaches
   - Build partnerships for program expansion
   - Document and share program impacts

Volunteering 401: Definitions

- **Assessment:** Process to measure impacts and identify opportunities for improvement
- **Coach certification:** Verifying that volunteer coaches have requisite knowledge and skills
- **Intake process:** Procedure for accepting new participants into the program
- **Matching:** Pairing coaches with participants based on needs, expertise, and compatibility
- **Peer mentoring:** Having experienced coaches support newer coaches
- **Program evaluation:** Systematic assessment of a program's processes, outputs, and outcomes

Volunteering 401: Troubleshooting

Problem	Solutions
Difficulty recruiting enough coaches	Broaden recruitment channels. Reduce time commitment required. Create entry-level roles. Partner with local colleges or universities. Offer incentives like professional development or certification.
Coach turnover	Improve coach screening. Recognize volunteers regularly. Provide ongoing learning opportunities. Reduce time commitment required.
Inconsistent coaching quality	Strengthen initial training. Implement a coach certification process. Create detailed coaching guides. Establish a mentoring system. Conduct periodic quality checks. Provide continuing education.
Low participant engagement	Improve program promotion. Clarify program benefits. Simplify the participation process. Gather and act on participant feedback. Target recruitment. Partner with trusted community organizations.
Insufficient program funding	Develop multiple funding streams. Apply for grants. Seek business sponsorships. Explore fee-for-service models. Partner with local government or utilities.

Revision: 25.1.8

Problem	Solutions
Difficulty measuring impact	Implement better baseline assessments. Develop simple, consistent metrics. Create user-friendly tracking tools. Focus on a few key indicators rather than trying to measure everything.
Volunteer coach burnout	Set realistic expectations for volunteer time. Create boundaries around coach responsibilities. Provide emotional support. Celebrate successes. Implement regular breaks. Encourage coaches to practice self-care.
Program scope creep	Revisit and reinforce program boundaries. Create clear criteria for program scope. Develop referral relationships with complementary programs.

Volunteering 401: Limitations

- Requires significant time investment to develop and manage
- Depends on a steady supply of volunteer coaches
- Funding sources are limited
- Coaching is more resource-intensive than mass education approaches
- Tends to attract already-motivated participants rather than those most resistant to change
- May require specialized expertise for certain sustainability pathways
- Program success depends heavily on the quality of the training materials and support systems

References and resources: <www.suspra.com/practice/community/volunteering-401.html>

Voting 101: Voting Pro-Environment

Vote for for pro-environment candidates and policies

Register to vote and participate in elections to support candidates and policies that protect natural resources, address climate change, reduce pollution, and promote sustainability. These decisions help ensure that our planet can continue to sustain human life within environmental boundaries. While environmental issues can be polarizing, the fundamental question is whether a candidate or policy will help keep Earth's life-support systems functioning within the safety zone. Look beyond partisan politics to assess specific environmental positions.

Local and regional elections often have the most immediate impact on environmental conditions in your community. School boards, city councils, county commissioners, and other local positions make decisions about land use, water management, waste handling, and other issues with direct environmental consequences. When researching candidates, examine their past actions, not just their promises. Officials with existing records can be evaluated on their voting history, introduced legislation, and public statements on environmental issues. For newcomers, look at their career background, organizational affiliations, and campaign funding sources.

Ballot measures often have significant environmental implications, especially those concerning land use, transportation infrastructure, energy policy, and natural resource management. Read the full text, as titles can sometimes be misleading about environmental impacts.

Environmental endorsements from reputable conservation organizations can provide valuable guidance. These groups typically perform detailed assessments of candidates' environmental positions and voting records. However, it's still important to do your own research, as these organizations may prioritize different environmental concerns than you do.

References and resources: <www.suspra.com/practice/community/voting-101.html>

Working 201: Making Practical Suggestions

Suggest practical ways to reduce environmental impacts at work

Business realities determine which suggestions for reducing environmental impacts at work will be effective. Start with ideas that create multiple benefits: a combination of cost savings, operational improvements, employee satisfaction boosts, and environmental protections. For example, energy efficiency reduces expenses and pollution; recycling bins reduce disposal costs, create a tidier and more organized workplace, and return materials to productive uses.

Observe before assuming. Take time to understand current practices and identify specific opportunities. Measure baseline usage to create a foundation for demonstrating success later. When possible, pilot your ideas in your own work area first—this proves your concept and demonstrates your commitment.

Frame your suggestions in economic terms to improve their reception. Calculate and highlight potential cost savings, productivity improvements, or competitive advantages. If your suggestion requires investment, calculate the return on investment or payback period. Connect your ideas to existing business goals or challenges whenever possible.

Building relationships and allies is equally important. Before making formal suggestions, discuss your ideas informally with colleagues to refine them and build support. Identify key decision-makers and understand their priorities. A "green team" with representatives from different departments can provide valuable perspectives and help advance initiatives across the organization.

When your suggestions are implemented, ensure the impacts are measured and communicated. Visible success creates momentum for further initiatives. If suggestions aren't adopted, use this as a learning opportunity to refine your approach for future recommendations.

References and resources: <www.suspra.com/practice/community/working-201.html>

Working 301: Working a Job with an Environmental Mission

Work in a job or for a company with an environmental mission

Working in a job with an environmental mission aligns your career with your values. Environmental jobs exist across the economy—from nonprofit advocacy to corporate sustainability, government regulation to clean tech startups. When searching for environmental jobs, consider organizations whose primary mission is environmental and those with environmental departments or initiatives.

- **Science and research roles** focus on understanding environmental systems and impacts
- **Policy and advocacy positions** work to influence environmental regulations and decisions
- **Planning and management jobs** develop and implement environmental programs
- **Education and communications roles** raise awareness and build environmental literacy
- **Engineering and technical positions** design and implement environmental solutions
- **Business and finance roles** advance sustainability through economic systems

Employers want to hire people who can learn quickly, communicate well, and take pride in their work. Most environmental roles require systems thinking—the ability to understand complex interconnections between environmental, social, and economic factors.

You can blaze your own trail to environmental work no matter your background. Common entry points are volunteering, internships, and starting sustainability initiatives as an entry-level worker in an organization. Building a successful environmental career requires resilience, continuous learning, and the ability to find opportunities for positive impact in every situation.

References and resources: <www.suspra.com/practice/community/working-301.html>

Working 401: Starting an Organization or Business

Start a new organization or business with an environmental mission

Start a new nonprofit organization or for-profit business with an environmental mission to achieve larger sustainability ambitions than you can achieve alone.

Nonprofit organizations reinvest all profits into programs rather than distribute them to owners. In many jurisdictions, nonprofit organizations can access grants, tax-deductible donations, and specialized funding not available to for-profit businesses. The nonprofit model works well when the environmental impact you seek doesn't naturally generate revenue, or when clients can't afford to pay for services.

For-profit businesses sell products or services and allow owners to keep profits or reinvest them in the business. They can access conventional business funding like loans and equity investments. For-profit business models work well when customers will pay directly for environmental solutions.

Hybrid models combine elements of both approaches:

- **Benefit corporations** consider environmental and social impacts alongside profits
- **Social enterprises** generate revenue through business activities but reinvest profits into environmental missions
- **For-profit with a nonprofit arm** allows for corporations to facilitate grant-funded programs
- **Cooperatives** are owned by members who share a commitment to environmental values

These environmental business and organization models have relatively low barriers to entry:

1. **Environmental consulting** provides expertise on sustainability to other organizations, requiring knowledge and experience rather than physical infrastructure.
2. **Educational services** offer workshops, courses, or training on environmental topics like composting, energy efficiency, or sustainable living practices.
3. **Repair and refurbishing** extends the life of products through repair services, reducing waste and resource consumption while generating revenue.
4. **Resale and upcycling** keeps usable items out of landfills while creating value through secondhand shops, online marketplaces, or creative repurposing.
5. **Community organizing** builds local capacity for environmental action through neighborhood initiatives, tool libraries, skill shares, and advocacy campaigns.
6. **Local food** initiatives address sustainability in food systems through community gardens, farmers markets, community supported agriculture, or food recovery programs.
7. **Environmental communication** services include writing, design, photography, or video production focused on sustainability topics.
8. **Green home and office services** provide energy auditing, waste collection and processing, or eco-friendly cleaning services.

Your environmental mission gives you distinctive advantages:

- Provides a clear purpose that attracts aligned team members, customers, and supporters
- Taps into growing market demand for environmentally responsible products and services
- Positions you to benefit from policies and incentives supporting environmental initiatives
- Connects you with communities of practice and support networks in the sustainability field

Implementing sustainable practices in your business or organization builds credibility with stakeholders and provides opportunities to test and demonstrate the practices you advocate. Consider

Sustainable Practices Handbook   Community Practices: Nurturing Good Relationships

environmental impacts in purchasing decisions, energy use, waste management, transportation, and all other aspects of your operations.

As your organization grows, regularly revisit your mission to ensure your activities remain focused on your environmental goals. Maintain clear metrics to track both organizational health and environmental impact, so you can continuously improve your practices.

Working 401: Equipment & Materials

- Depends on the business (start by creating a work space in your home)
- *Optional: business partners*

Working 401: Steps

1. Research the landscape and validate your idea
   - Identify the specific environmental challenges you want to address
   - Research how existing organizations are addressing similar challenges
   - Analyze gaps in current services or products
   - Identify your target audience and their needs
   - Outline the products or services you'll offer
   - Build prototypes of your products and conduct test runs of your services
   - Refine your concept based on feedback from potential customers or beneficiaries
2. Build your founding team
   - Recruit team members who complement your strengths
   - Develop a board of directors or advisors with relevant expertise
3. Establish your business model and organizational structure
   - Draft a concise statement of your mission, vision, and values
   - Map out key activities, resources, and partnerships
   - Create a financial forecast, including your revenue streams or funding sources
   - Research legal structures available in your jurisdiction
   - Select the structure that best supports your environmental mission
     - Non-profit organization, informal association, etc.
     - Sole proprietorship, partnership, limited liability company, etc.
   - Obtain required licenses and permits
4. Secure initial resources
   - Consider bootstrapping options that require minimal capital
   - Research grants specific to environmental initiatives
   - Explore crowdfunding platforms focused on sustainability
   - Investigate angel investors interested in environmental ventures
   - Apply for fiscal sponsorship (for nonprofits not yet established)
   - Seek in-kind donations of space, equipment, or expertise
5. Create a minimum viable product or pilot program
   - Develop the simplest version of your product or service
   - Test it with a small group of customers or beneficiaries
   - Gather feedback and make improvements
   - Document early successes and lessons learned
   - Collect case studies and testimonials
6. Develop operational systems
   - Establish operating procedures that reflect your environmental values
   - Set up basic accounting and financial management systems
   - Register a domain name
   - Set up your email and other communication channels
   - Begin using an online document sharing platform (Google Drive, etc.)
7. Launch and market your organization

Revision: 25.1.8

- Develop a simple marketing plan focused on your environmental mission
- Create a basic website that communicates your purpose
- Establish social media presence on platforms your audience uses
- Connect with networks and communities related to your mission
- Host a launch event
8. Evaluate, learn, and adapt
   - Establish metrics to track both organizational and environmental performance
   - Gather regular feedback from customers, beneficiaries, and stakeholders
   - Review operational efficiency and environmental practices
   - Identify strengths, weaknesses, and areas for improvement
   - Document and share lessons learned with your community

Working 401: Definitions

- **Benefit corporation**: A legal business structure that requires consideration of environmental and social impacts alongside financial returns
- **B Corp Certification**: A third-party certification for businesses meeting standards of environmental and social performance
- **Bootstrapping**: Building a business using personal resources and early revenue
- **Environmental, Social, and Governance (ESG)**: Criteria used to evaluate an organization's performance on sustainability and ethical practices
- **Fiscal sponsorship**: An arrangement where an established nonprofit provides legal and financial oversight for a new initiative
- **Greenwashing**: Making misleading claims about environmental benefits or practices
- **Impact investing**: Investments made with the intention of generating positive, measurable social and environmental impact alongside financial returns
- **Mission-driven**: Placing purpose and impact at the center of organizational decision-making
- **Minimum viable product**: The simplest version of a product or service that can be tested with customers
- **Social enterprise**: An organization that applies commercial strategies to maximize improvements in environmental and human well-being

Working 401: Troubleshooting

Problem	Solutions
Difficulty balancing environmental mission with financial sustainability	Start with a clear business model that generates revenue. Focus on products or services where environmental benefits create customer value. Consider a hybrid approach with both commercial and grant-funded activities. Develop multiple revenue streams.
Lack of credibility as a new environmental organization	Partner with established environmental organizations to build trust. Earn relevant certifications or credentials in your field. Document and share measurable impact data. Build an advisory board with recognized experts. Start small and demonstrate success before expanding.
Limited startup funding	Begin with low-cost pilot programs that demonstrate your concept. Apply for startup grant funding. Consider fiscal sponsorship to access nonprofit funding. Use crowdfunding targeted at environmentally conscious supporters. Start as a side project while maintaining other income.
Unclear differentiation from existing organizations	Conduct thorough research on similar organizations in your region. Identify specific unmet needs or underserved populations. Develop a

Problem	Solutions
	unique approach or technology. Focus on a particular geographic area or environmental issue. Collaborate rather than compete.
Burnout from trying to do too much	Start with a narrowly focused mission. Build systems and processes that reduce repetitive work. Delegate and distribute leadership. Set realistic timelines for growth and impact.
Difficulty measuring environmental impact	Start with simple, specific metrics related to your core mission. Use existing frameworks. Focus on outcomes you can directly observe.
Regulatory hurdles or compliance issues	Consult with legal experts. Join industry associations that provide regulatory guidance. Start in jurisdictions with favorable policies. Begin with less regulated aspects while building capacity for compliance.

Working 401: Limitations

- Requires time and resources to start a new business or organization
- Securing funding for environmental initiatives can be challenging
- Competition from established organizations or "greenwashed" alternatives can create confusion
- Some environmental challenges cannot be solved by individual businesses or organizations

References and resources: <www.suspra.com/practice/community/working-401.html>

Governing 401: Developing Certification Systems

Develop professional standards and certification systems for sustainability practitioners

Develop a certification system to transform aspirational sustainability principles into concrete, measurable practitioner standards. Establish credibility, promote consistent practice, protect consumers, and accelerate adoption of sustainable approaches across sectors by providing specific criteria. Create value for multiple stakeholders: practitioners gain recognition and market differentiation, consumers receive quality assurance, and the environment benefits from improved practices. Establish minimum performance standards while encouraging continuous improvement beyond those thresholds.

Credibility is the foundation of any successful certification system. Put in place governance structures that prevent conflicts of interest, transparent development processes, and rigorous, defensible assessment methods. Third-party accreditation from organizations like the American National Standards Institute (ANSI) or the International Accreditation Forum can provide additional credibility by confirming that the certification body meets established standards for certification programs.

A comprehensive certification system typically requires from 18 to 36 months to develop. The costs of development can be difficult to recover, so it may be a labor of love that will be part of your legacy for the world. Certifications typically undergo substantial revision after their first few years as real-world implementation reveals opportunities for improvement.

Governing 401: Equipment & Materials

- An organization to develop and administer your certification system

Governing 401: Steps

1. Establish the need for certification

2. Form a development committee
3. Define the scope and purpose of certification
4. Research existing systems and standards
5. Develop knowledge, skills, and performance criteria
6. Design assessment methods
7. Create governance and administrative structures
8. Develop certification requirements and processes
9. Build operational infrastructure
10. Pilot test the certification system
11. Obtain third-party accreditation (if applicable)
12. Launch and market the certification
13. Establish quality assurance systems
14. Plan for continuous improvement

Governing 401: Definitions

- **Accreditation**: Formal recognition that a certification body meets established standards for developing and administering certification programs
- **Assessment**: Structured evaluation of an individual's abilities against defined criteria
- **Certification**: Formal recognition that an individual has demonstrated specific competencies according to established standards
- **Competency**: Measurable abilities critical to successful job performance
- **Continuing education unit**: Standardized measurement used to recognize participation in qualified continuing professional education activities
- **Delphi method**: Reaching consensus through multiple rounds of anonymous questionnaires and controlled feedback
- **Job analysis**: Systematic process of determining the tasks, duties, responsibilities, and knowledge required for a specific job or role
- **Practice analysis**: Research process to identify and validate the knowledge and skills necessary for competent practice in a profession
- **Recertification**: Process by which certified individuals maintain their credentials through continuing education or re-examination
- **Subject matter expert**: Individual with specialized knowledge, skills, or experience in the field being certified
- **Validity**: Extent to which an assessment measures what it is intended to measure

Governing 401: Troubleshooting

Problem	Solutions
Difficulty recruiting diverse stakeholders	Offer multiple participation options (in-person, remote, asynchronous). Provide stipends for participation. Partner with other organizations. Conduct targeted outreach through professional networks.
Disagreement among stakeholders on standards	Use structured decision-making processes like the Delphi method. Focus on outcomes rather than prescriptive practices. Create tiered certification levels. Document dissenting viewpoints.
Certification too costly for practitioners	Develop scholarship programs. Create staged certification pathways. Partner with educational institutions. Seek employer sponsorships.
Low initial certification uptake	Create early adopter incentives. Partner with employers or large organizations. Develop complementary education programs. Consider geographic phasing to build momentum.

Problem	Solutions
Assessment methods not accurately measuring competency	Run additional pilot testing. Conduct validation studies with expert practitioners. Use multiple assessment methods. Analyze results for bias or inconsistency. Hire experts to redesign assessment.
Certification system too complex to administer	Automate administrative processes. Prioritize core competencies. Partner with established certification bodies for administrative functions.
Certification becoming outdated as field evolves	Establish regular review cycles. Create a technical advisory committee for emerging issues. Implement modular design that allows updating specific components. Include adaptability criteria in the certification itself.
Lack of sufficient funding for development	Seek grants. Develop partnerships with industry associations. Explore phased development approach. Consider licensing existing frameworks. Investigate hybrid volunteer and professional development models.

Governing 401: Limitations

- Standards development processes typically take 18 months at minimum
- Voluntary certifications have limited impact without regulatory recognition or market demand
- Rapid evolution in sustainability fields can quickly outdated fixed standards
- Certification alone doesn't ensure implementation of sustainable practices
- Some sustainability practices are difficult to assess through standardized methods

References and resources: <www.suspra.com/practice/community/governing-401.html>

Governing 402: Proposing Legislation

Propose ordinances and legislation to promote sustainability

Proposing legislation to advance sustainability is a powerful way to create systemic change beyond individual actions; however, resolutions that accomplish nothing are easier to pass than ordinances or laws that have real impact. Successful sustainability legislation shares several characteristics:

Clarity: The proposal clearly defines the problem and solution without ambiguity.
Feasibility: Implementation is practical within existing systems and available resources.
Measurability: The policy includes specific metrics to evaluate success.
Equity: Benefits and costs are distributed fairly across the community.
Economic viability: The proposal provides ways to compensate affected parties.

In a typical city or town, the ordinance process might involve:

1. Initial proposal to city council or relevant committee
2. Staff review and recommendations
3. Public hearings
4. Committee deliberation and recommendations
5. Full council vote
6. Implementation by city departments

At the state or federal level, the process becomes more complex, with multiple committees, readings, and opportunities for amendment.

Relationships are more important than the technical aspects of your proposal. Get to know decision-makers, understand their priorities and constraints, and frame sustainability initiatives in terms of their ambitions and priorities. This might mean emphasizing economic benefits, public health, or long-term security. Even if your first legislative attempt is unsuccessful, the process builds valuable capacity for future efforts. You'll develop coalition relationships, legislative expertise, and greater understanding of community perspectives that will strengthen subsequent initiatives.

References and resources: <www.suspra.com/practice/community/governing-402.html>

Governing 403: Running for Office

Run for public office to ensure sustainability is a priority in government

Run for public office as a sustainability advocate to shape environmental policy and raise community awareness, even if you don't win. When environmentally-minded candidates are on the ballot, they elevate sustainability in public discourse, educate voters about local environmental challenges, and push other candidates to address these issues. Model sustainable practices in your campaign itself. Consider digital communications over printed materials, use recycled materials for necessary printing, minimize single-use items at events, and utilize active transportation, public transit, or carpooling for campaign activities.

Local government is particularly important for sustainability initiatives. Municipal and county governments decide zoning, building codes, transportation infrastructure, water management, waste systems, and energy procurement—all of which have environmental impacts. As a local elected official, you can champion ordinances requiring energy efficiency in buildings, promote green infrastructure, advocate for public transit, implement robust recycling programs, or protect local natural resources.

Translate sustainable public policy into tangible local benefits: clean water for families, reduced energy costs, green spaces for recreation, improved public health, resilience against disasters, and new green job opportunities. This approach makes environmental policies more accessible and compelling to voters across the political spectrum.

Build broad coalitions to avoid being perceived as a single-issue candidate. Connect with diverse stakeholders—business owners concerned about energy costs, parents worried about children's health, older residents seeking walkable neighborhoods, and young voters passionate about climate action. Demonstrate how sustainability enhances economic development, public health, fiscal responsibility, and quality of life to win wider support.

The relationships built during campaigns, the research conducted, the coalitions formed, and the public awareness raised all contribute to positive long-term change. Many unsuccessful candidates later secure appointments to environmental committees, successfully advocate for specific initiatives, or win in subsequent elections. The knowledge and networks developed during a campaign remain valuable assets for ongoing environmental advocacy.

References and resources: <www.suspra.com/practice/community/governing-403.html>

Food Practices

Reduce Food Waste, page 128	
Goals	Indicators
• Eliminate food waste	• Amount of food purchased or grown but not eaten

Choosing Wise Ingredients, page 176	
Goals	Indicators
• Select ingredients with better environmental impacts • Avoid ingredients with worse environmental impacts	• Amount and types of food purchased

Eating Plant-based Meals, page 182	
Goals	Indicators
• Improve the environmental impact of your diet	• Percentage of plant-based meals

Cultivating Healthy Harvests, page 189	
Goals	Indicators
• Support farms that build healthy soil • Grow food in healthy ways	• How much food purchased or grown comes from healthy farms and gardens

Reducing Food Waste

Buying Food 101: Buying Ugly

Buy "ugly" fruits and vegetables that have cosmetic blemishes

Buy "ugly" produce to reduce food waste while saving money. Much farm-grown produce in the United States is rejected by retailers based solely on appearance, despite being perfectly nutritious and flavorful. By purchasing this cosmetically imperfect produce, you help create a market for food that might otherwise be discarded.

Appearance standards for produce are primarily marketing inventions rather than indicators of quality or nutrition. In fact, some studies suggest that produce with minor blemishes may produce more antioxidants as a natural defense mechanism. Many of the world's best chefs deliberately seek out imperfect produce, recognizing that irregular appearance often comes with superior flavor.

You can source ugly produce in several ways. Subscription services offer convenience but may have limited customization. Farmers markets provide the freshest options. Grocery store programs offer accessibility but sometimes provide less significant discounts.

Remember that the goal is to use the food efficiently once purchased. Having a plan before buying is crucial. For items with limited shelf life, consider batch-preparing meals for freezing or involving the whole family in processing sessions to make quick work of preserving your bounty.

Buying Food 101: Equipment & Materials
- Reusable shopping and produce bags
- Knife (for inspecting produce if permitted)
- *Optional: Cooler bag for transporting temperature-sensitive items*

Buying Food 101: Steps
1. Locate sources of "ugly" produce
   - Check local farmers markets where growers often sell imperfect produce at a discount
   - Look for "ugly produce" programs at conventional grocery stores
   - Search for dedicated "ugly produce" subscription services in your area
   - Ask at your local food co-ops about imperfect produce sections
   - Inquire at farm stands or U-pick farms about "seconds" (produce with cosmetic imperfections)
   - Check small, independent grocery stores which often have more flexible produce standards
2. Learn to recognize acceptable versus unacceptable imperfections
   - Acceptable cosmetic flaws include:
     - Unusual shapes or sizes
     - Minor bruising
     - Scarring on the skin
     - Discoloration that doesn't affect firmness
     - Misshapen or asymmetrical form
   - Avoid produce with:
     - Mold growth
     - Significant soft spots
     - Foul odors
     - Oozing or leaking
     - Deep cuts that expose the interior
3. Shop strategically

Sustainable Practices Handbook
Food Practices: Reducing Food Waste

- Shop early at farmers markets for best selection
- Ask vendors specifically about discounted "seconds" or end-of-day markdowns
- Buy ugly produce with specific meal plans in mind
- Purchase only what you can use within a reasonable timeframe
- Focus on items where appearance doesn't affect your intended use (soups, smoothies, etc.)

4. Inspect before purchasing
   - Check all sides of the produce
   - Gently press to test firmness
   - Smell items for freshness (when appropriate)
   - Inspect where stems connect to the produce (often the first place to show problems)
   - Ask questions about how recently the produce was harvested
5. Transport carefully
   - Pack imperfect produce separately from other groceries
   - Place softer items on top to prevent further bruising
   - Use caution with already-bruised produce as it may damage more easily
   - Keep temperature-sensitive items cool during transport
6. Process soon after purchase
   - Sort ugly produce by ripeness level
   - Plan to use the most damaged items first
   - Wash produce only when you're ready to use it (unless very dirty)
   - Cut away bruised or damaged portions before storage
   - Consider processing heavily blemished produce immediately by:
     - Cooking into soups, stews, or sauces
     - Freezing for later use
     - Making jams, pickles, or preserves
     - Adding to smoothies or juices

Buying Food 101: Definitions

- **Cosmetic blemishes**: Imperfections that don't affect edibility, nutrition, or taste
- **Food waste**: Edible food that is discarded rather than consumed
- **Gleaning**: The act of collecting leftover crops from farmers' fields after commercial harvest
- **Grade standards**: USDA classifications based on appearance, size, and quality
- **Imperfect produce**: Fruits and vegetables that don't meet aesthetic standards
- **Seconds**: Farmer terminology for produce with minor defects sold at a discount

Buying Food 101: Troubleshooting

Problem	Solutions
Ugly produce spoils faster than expected	Check for hidden damage that may accelerate spoilage. Process more vulnerable parts immediately. Store properly in appropriate containers. Review your refrigerator temperature settings.
Subscription box contains items you don't use	Customize your box when possible. Trade unwanted items with neighbors or friends. Learn new recipes to utilize unfamiliar produce. Contact the company to adjust preferences.
Can't find ugly produce programs locally	Ask produce managers to start a program. Connect with local farms directly about purchasing their "seconds." Join or start a CSA that accepts all produce grades. Find or create a food swap group in your community.

Revision: 25.1.8

Problem	Solutions
Difficulty determining if blemishes are safe	Follow the "when in doubt, throw it out" rule. Cut away questionable areas and check the rest of the produce.
Family resistance to ugly produce	Do taste tests comparing regular and ugly produce. Involve family in preparation (smoothies, soups). Process ugly produce into unrecognizable forms initially. Educate on the environmental benefits and cost savings.
Too much ugly produce at once	Preserve by freezing, canning, or dehydrating. Share with neighbors. Create a batch cooking day. Organize a community meal using the surplus.

Buying Food 101: Limitations

- Ugly produce may not be available in your area
- Limited selection compared to conventional produce
- Some cosmetic imperfections may hide actual quality issues
- Some blemished produce may require immediate processing
- Household members may resist eating visually imperfect foods

References and resources: <www.suspra.com/practice/food/buying-101.html>

Buying Food 102: Buying Preserved

Buy dried, pickled, fermented, or frozen food that stores well

Buying preserved food to reduce food waste, save money, and ensure you always have nutritious ingredients on hand. Avoid preserved products that contain unnecessary amounts of sodium or sugar. Prioritize options with minimal processing and additives.

Dried foods have exceptional shelf life (up to five years when properly stored) and concentrate nutrients and flavors while reducing weight and volume. They're economical, especially when purchased in bulk. Dried beans, grains, and fruits provide excellent nutritional value and versatility.

Fermented foods offer probiotic benefits that support gut health along with unique umami flavors. Traditional fermentation methods preserve vegetables, dairy, soy products, and beverages through beneficial bacteria that transform sugars into acids, producing foods like yogurt, kefir, sauerkraut, kimchi, miso, and tempeh. This process enhances the nutritional profiles of fermented foods.

Pickled foods are preserved using acidic solutions, typically vinegar. This method creates tangy flavor profiles while extending shelf life significantly. Pickles, olives, capers, and various vegetables maintain many of their original nutrients while developing new flavor dimensions.

Frozen foods lock in nutrients at their peak freshness. Modern flash-freezing techniques preserve texture and nutritional content, making frozen fruits and vegetables sometimes more nutritious than "fresh" produce that has spent days in transit and storage. Frozen foods offer exceptional convenience while minimizing waste through portion control.

By maintaining a well-stocked supply of diverse preserved foods, you create a sustainable food system in your home that can accommodate unexpected changes in schedule, weather disruptions, or other challenges that might otherwise lead to less sustainable restaurant meals or food delivery.

Buying Food 102: Equipment & Materials

- Reusable shopping bags or containers for bulk purchases

- Food storage containers for home use (glass jars, airtight containers)
- Insulated bags or coolers for transporting frozen foods
- *Optional: Smartphone or notepad for lists and research*
- *Kitchen scale for bulk foods*
- *Thermometer to verify freezer temperature*

Buying Food 102: Steps

1. Research preserved food options
   - Learn about different preservation methods (drying, pickling, fermenting, freezing)
   - Identify which preserved foods align with your dietary preferences
   - Research nutrition profiles of preserved foods compared to fresh alternatives
   - Learn about proper storage requirements for different preserved foods
2. Plan your preserved food shopping
   - Inventory your current preserved food stock
   - Create a list of preserved items to complement your meal plan
   - Balance your shopping list across preservation methods for dietary variety
3. Shop for dried foods
   - Look for dried beans, lentils, peas, and other legumes
   - Select whole grains like rice, quinoa, and oats
   - Choose dried fruits without added sugars when possible
   - Consider dried mushrooms, seaweed, and herbs for flavor enhancement
   - Inspect packaging for tears or signs of moisture
4. Shop for fermented foods
   - Select traditionally fermented products (sauerkraut, kimchi, miso, tempeh)
   - Look for "live," "raw," or "unpasteurized" on labels for probiotic benefits
   - Check for proper refrigeration of live fermented foods in the store
   - Examine packaging for bulging, excessive liquid, or unusual discoloration
5. Shop for pickled foods
   - Choose vinegar-preserved foods like pickled vegetables and fruits
   - Look for options without artificial preservatives or excessive sodium
   - Check that jars are properly sealed with no signs of spoilage
   - Consider refrigerated versus shelf-stable options based on your storage space
6. Shop for frozen foods
   - Select frozen fruits and vegetables harvested at peak ripeness
   - Choose frozen proteins (meat, fish, plant-based) with minimal additives
   - Check packages for freezer burn or signs of thawing and refreezing
   - Look for IQF (Individually Quick Frozen) items for easier portion control
   - Purchase frozen items last during your shopping trip so they don't thaw
7. Transport preserved foods safely
   - Use insulated bags for frozen foods
   - Keep fermented and refrigerated pickled foods cool during transport
   - Handle glass jars carefully to prevent breakage
   - Keep dried foods separated from wet or frozen items
8. Store preserved foods properly at home
   - Place frozen foods in freezer immediately
   - Store dried foods in cool, dry locations in airtight containers
   - Keep fermented foods refrigerated at proper temperatures
   - Follow specific storage instructions for each preservation method
9. Track and rotate your preserved food inventory
   - Create a simple inventory system for your preserved food supplies
   - Organize with oldest products in front to use first (FIFO: first in, first out)
   - Label containers with purchase dates if not already marked

- Periodically review stored items for quality and freshness

Buying Food 102: Definitions

- **Fermentation**: A metabolic process where microorganisms convert carbohydrates to acids, gases, or alcohol, preserving food and creating beneficial bacteria
- **FIFO (First In, First Out)**: Rotating older products to be used before newer ones
- **Flash freezing**: A rapid freezing method that creates smaller ice crystals, maintaining food quality and texture better than slow freezing
- **IQF (Individually Quick Frozen)**: A freezing process where items are frozen separately before packaging, preventing them from freezing together in clumps
- **Kahm yeast:** A harmless, white or creamy yeast biofilm that can form on the surface of fermenting liquids like kombucha, kefir, or lacto-fermented vegetables
- **Pickling**: Food preservation using an acidic solution that prevents microbial growth
- **Probiotic**: Live microorganisms that provide health benefits when consumed
- **SCOBY (symbiotic culture of bacteria and yeast):** A culinary fermentation culture of lactic acid bacteria, acetic acid bacteria, and yeast, found in kombucha and sourdough
- **Shelf life**: The length of time a food product remains safe and suitable for consumption
- **Umami**: One of the five basic tastes, described as savory or meaty, common in fermented foods

Buying Food 102: Troubleshooting

Problem	Solutions
Dried foods have moisture or signs of pests	Return product to the store if recently purchased. Transfer to airtight containers with oxygen absorbers. Consider freezing for 48 hours to eliminate potential pests in dry goods.
Frozen foods show freezer burn	Use affected portions for soups or stews where texture changes are less noticeable. Check your freezer temperature (should be 0°F/-18°C or below). Use better quality freezer bags or containers in the future.
Fermented foods taste or smell "off"	Trust your senses—if it smells or tastes unpleasant, discard it. Some color variation is normal, but sliminess, mold (except white kahm yeast on some products), or unusual smells indicate spoilage.
Pickled foods have cloudy brine	Some cloudiness is normal for naturally fermented pickles. For vinegar pickles, cloudiness may indicate spoilage—check for off smells or bulging lids and discard if present.
Jarred foods have bulging lids	Never taste—discard immediately. Bulging indicates possible botulism risk, especially in home-canned low-acid foods.
Difficulty managing inventory	Create a simple spreadsheet or use a pantry app to track preserved foods. Implement a clear organization system with labeled shelves or containers. Take periodic inventory to identify items nearing expiration.
Preserved foods are too expensive	Watch for sales and buy in bulk when prices are low. Compare unit prices between different preservation methods. Consider seasonal bulk buying followed by home freezing or dehydrating.
Family members reluctant to eat preserved foods	Start with familiar preserved options like frozen berries or pasta sauce. Incorporate preserved ingredients into favorite recipes. Educate your family about nutritional benefits and environmental impact.

Sustainable Practices Handbook   Food Practices: Reducing Food Waste

Buying Food 102: Limitations
- Some preservation methods alter food textures, which may affect recipe outcomes
- High-quality preserved foods can be more expensive than conventional options
- Many commercially preserved foods contain higher levels of sodium, sugar, or additives
- Some preservation methods reduce certain nutrients while concentrating others
- Frozen foods require reliable electricity and sufficient freezer space
- Glass jars for fermented and pickled items are heavy and breakable
- Dried foods require rehydration time, which requires meal planning
- Some preserved options have higher environmental impacts from packaging
- Limited variety of preserved foods may be available in some geographic regions

References and resources: <www.suspra.com/practice/food/buying-102.html>

Buying Food 103: Buying Hardy

Buy hardy root vegetables and fruits that last longer than perishable types

Hardy fruits and vegetables are those that naturally store well for extended periods without significant loss of quality or nutrition. Incorporating more hardy produce into your diet helps reduce food waste, lower your grocery budget, and decrease the environmental impact of your food choices.

Root vegetables store particularly well because they evolved to store energy in their underground parts. Their thick skins and dense flesh protect them from moisture loss and decay. Similarly, long-lasting fruits like winter apples and citrus have protective skins and natural preservative compounds that extend their usable life. Longer shelf life means fewer shopping trips, reducing transportation emissions. Additionally, hardy produce often requires less packaging than delicate fruits and vegetables.

Having hardy produce on hand creates a buffer against disruptions in food supply or personal circumstances that might limit shopping opportunities. Financially, hardy produce offers excellent value. Their longer shelf life means less waste due to spoilage. Many hardy vegetables are also among the most affordable produce options year-round; buying in season and in bulk can maximize savings.

Buying Food 103: Equipment & Materials
- Reusable shopping bags or mesh produce bags
- Storage containers for home use
- Cool, dark storage space at home (basement, pantry, or refrigerator)
- *Optional: Kitchen scale to track food usage*
- *Food storage reference guide*
- *Meal planning calendar*

Buying Food 103: Steps
1. Identify hardy produce varieties with long shelf lives
   - Root vegetables: potatoes, carrots, beets, turnips, rutabagas, parsnips, onions, garlic
   - Hardy fruits: apples (storage varieties), citrus fruits, winter squash, pears (storage varieties)
   - Hardy greens: cabbage, celery, kale
   - Other long-lasting produce: winter squash, pumpkins
2. Select the freshest specimens
   - Choose firm, heavy vegetables without soft spots, mold, or sprouting
   - Select produce with intact skins free from cuts, bruises, or punctures
   - For root vegetables, look for firm specimens with minimal rootlets or sprouts
   - For fruits like apples, select firm fruits without bruises or dents
3. Check for longevity indicators

- Choose newer harvests when available (ask store staff about harvest dates)
- Select thick-skinned varieties within each produce type
- Look for produce explicitly labeled as "storage variety" or "keeper"
- Choose slightly under ripe specimens for maximum storage life
4. Buy in appropriate quantities
    - Purchase according to your available storage space and consumption patterns
    - Start with smaller quantities until you learn your household's usage rate
5. Plan for rotation and use
    - Buy a mix of hardy produce with different storage lifespans
    - Develop a use plan that prioritizes eating less hardy items first
    - Check stored produce regularly and use items showing early signs of decline

Buying Food 103: Definitions

- **Cultivar:** A specific type of fruit or vegetable, bred for specific characteristics
- **Curing:** Drying and hardening the skin to extend storage life
- **Hardy:** Remaining edible for extended periods under proper storage conditions
- **Keeper:** Term used for varieties of produce specifically noted for their long storage life
- **Root vegetables:** Edible plant roots or tubers that store energy underground
- **Storage varieties:** Cultivars of fruits or vegetables developed for extended shelf life
- **Winter squash:** Hard-skinned squash varieties that can be stored for months

Buying Food 103: Troubleshooting

Problem	Solutions
Hardy produce spoiling prematurely	Check storage conditions—most root vegetables need cool, dark, slightly humid storage. Keep different produce types separated as some emit ethylene gas that speeds ripening. Ensure adequate air circulation.
Difficulty finding truly hardy varieties	Ask produce managers about storage varieties. Shop at farmers markets where vendors can recommend long-lasting varieties. Research specific variety names known for longevity.
Limited storage space for bulk purchases	Focus on highest-density nutritional options first. Utilize under-bed storage, closet floors, or other cool spots. Consider sharing bulk purchases with friends or neighbors.
Produce developing sprouting	Use sprouting items promptly. For potatoes and onions, cooler storage temperatures can delay sprouting. Some sprouted items remain edible; just remove sprouts before cooking.
Family tires of eating the same vegetables	Research diverse recipes for hardy vegetables. Try different cooking methods for variety. Combine hardy staples with perishable ingredients.
Uncertainty about how much to buy	Start with smaller quantities and track usage rates. Create a weekly meal plan before shopping.
Finding unexpected soft spots	Cut away small, affected areas; use the rest promptly. Check stored produce regularly. Store damaged items separately and use them first.

Buying Food 103: Limitations

- Hardy produce provides less variety than highly perishable items
- Some nutritional diversity may be sacrificed

- Storage conditions in many modern homes aren't ideal for long-term produce storage
- The longest-lasting varieties sometimes have less intense flavor than more perishable types
- Certain cooking techniques don't work as well with long-stored produce as with fresh
- Some hardy varieties may be less available in conventional grocery stores
- Storage life varies based on handling before purchase, which consumers can't control
- Climate and humidity in your region affect how well and how long produce can be stored

References and resources: <www.suspra.com/practice/food/buying-103.html>

Buying Food 201: Buying Perishables

Buy perishable food in quantities no larger than you can eat before it spoils

Perishable foods—which include fresh fruits and vegetables, dairy, eggs, meat, and seafood—generally last from a few days to two weeks, depending on the item and storage conditions.

- Highly perishable (2-3 days): Berries, ripe avocados, fresh herbs, lettuce, ripe stone fruits
- Moderately perishable (4-7 days): Broccoli, cucumbers, zucchini, grapes, fish, ground meat
- Less perishable (1-2 weeks): Apples, oranges, carrots, cabbage, hard cheese, eggs

Proper storage dramatically extends the usable life of perishables. Account for the specific conditions in your home. Factors like refrigerator temperature, humidity levels, and how frequently the refrigerator door is opened can significantly impact shelf life. Take the time to store items correctly immediately after purchase to add days to their freshness and expand your safe consumption window.

Meal planning creates the framework for precise purchasing. Start with a conservative approach—it's better to slightly underestimate and make an additional small purchase mid-week than to overbuy and waste food. Maintain flexibility by having some shelf-stable or frozen options available to supplement fresh foods when plans change.

Buying Food 201: Equipment & Materials
- Meal plan or list of planned recipes for the week
- Shopping list
- Reusable shopping and mesh produce bags
- Food storage containers
- *Optional: Small cooler or insulated bag for transport*
- *Kitchen scale for weighing food*
- *Refrigerator thermometer*
- *Food storage tracking app*

Buying Food 201: Steps
1. Assess your current food situation
   - Before shopping, take inventory of what food you already have
   - Note which perishables you consistently finish and which often spoil
2. Plan your meals strategically
   - Create a realistic meal plan for the next week
   - Plan to use the most perishable items earliest in your meal schedule
   - Include "flexible meals" that can use perishables that need to be consumed quickly
   - Schedule a "use it up" meal near the end of your planning period
3. Make a precise shopping list
   - List exact quantities needed for your planned meals
   - Specify units (two apples, not "some apples")
4. Shop with precision

- Buy only what's on your list unless you can adjust your meal plan immediately
- Purchase the smallest available package of perishables that meets your needs
- Choose items with the latest expiration dates when available
- Inspect produce carefully for signs it will spoil quickly (soft spots, bruising)
5. Store perishables properly after purchase
    - Transport perishables home quickly, using a cooler if needed
    - Clean and prep produce appropriately for storage
    - Store items at proper temperatures (refrigerator should be 35-38°F or 1.7-3.3°C)
    - Use proper storage containers to extend freshness
    - Place new purchases behind older items in your refrigerator
6. Monitor consumption and adjust future purchases
    - Keep track of what gets used completely and what spoils
    - Adjust quantities on future shopping lists based on consumption patterns
    - Note seasonal variations in how quickly produce ripens
    - Refine your purchasing habits based on household patterns

Buying Food 201: Definitions

- **First-in, first-out (FIFO)**: Use older items before newer ones to prevent spoilage
- **Flash-freezing**: Rapidly freezing foods to maintain quality for longer storage
- **Perishable foods**: Items that spoil relatively quickly and typically require refrigeration
- **Sell-by date**: Date for retailer inventory control, not a food safety date
- **Shelf life**: The period during which food remains safe to eat and maintains acceptable quality
- **Shrinkage**: Reduction in size, weight, or volume of produce as it loses moisture or deteriorates
- **Use-by date**: Recommended date for peak quality, not necessarily related to food safety

Buying Food 201: Troubleshooting

Problem	Solutions
Consistently having spoiled produce	Buy smaller quantities more frequently. Shop at stores that sell individual produce items. Adjust your meal plan to use highly perishable items sooner. Consider switching some fresh items to frozen alternatives.
Unexpected schedule changes that prevent cooking	Freeze perishable items before they spoil if you won't use them as planned. Create a list of quick "rescue recipes" that use perishables when time is limited. Share excess with neighbors or friends.
Limited access to stores for frequent shopping	Vary your purchases to include items with different shelf lives. Arrange your meal plan to use highly perishable items immediately, longer-lasting items later. Alternate between fresh and frozen or preserved options.
Buying perishables for single-person household	Look for bulk bins where you can purchase exact amounts. Ask at deli counters for half portions. Split larger packages with friends or neighbors. Choose loose produce rather than pre-packaged. Freeze portion-sized amounts of perishables you can't finish.
Family members not eating perishable items	Involve everyone in meal planning. Have contingency frozen or shelf-stable options. Create a designated "eat first" area in the refrigerator for items that need to be consumed quickly.
Perishables spoiling faster than expected	Check your refrigerator temperature with a thermometer; adjust if needed. Review storage methods for specific items. Purchase from vendors with faster turnover of fresh products. Buy some items less ripe.

Sustainable Practices Handbook
Food Practices: Reducing Food Waste

Buying Food 201: Limitations
- Buying in smaller quantities may increase per-unit cost compared to bulk purchases
- More frequent shopping trips require additional time and transportation
- Some areas have limited access to stores with fresh perishables
- Packaging waste may increase with smaller-quantity purchases
- Highly variable household schedules can make precise meal planning challenging
- Some perishable items are only sold in pre-packaged quantities
- Seasonal variations affect both availability and shelf life of perishable produce

References and resources: <www.suspra.com/practice/food/buying-201.html>

Buying Food 202: Supporting Local Farms

Buy from local farms to reduce the risk of spoilage due to transportation

When you purchase directly from a farmer, you're often buying produce harvested within the previous 24 hours. This freshness advantage compared to conventional grocery stores means:

- **Extended storage life at home**: Produce that hasn't spent days in transit has more of its shelf life remaining when you purchase it.
- **Better flavor and texture**: Local farmers can harvest at optimal ripeness.
- **Higher nutritional value**: Some nutrients, particularly vitamin C and certain B vitamins, begin degrading immediately after harvest. Fresher produce retains more of these nutrients.
- **Reduced physical damage**: Local food changes hands fewer times, reducing risks of physical damage that accelerates spoilage.

Beyond reducing spoilage, supporting local farms creates a more resilient food system in your community. Many local farmers employ sustainable growing practices that protect soil health and biodiversity. Learn exactly how your food was grown, meet the people who grew it, and keep food dollars circulating in your local economy. Farmers can advise you on the best storage methods for their specific varieties, which may differ from generic advice. They can also alert you to peak harvest times, so you can plan purchases when produce is at its freshest and most affordable.

Buying Food 202: Equipment & Materials
- Reusable bags and containers for transporting produce
- Cooler or insulated bags for temperature-sensitive items
- Food storage containers for home use
- *Optional: Calendar for tracking seasonal availability*

Buying Food 202: Steps
1. Locate local food sources
    - Search online directories like LocalHarvest.org, USDA's Local Food Directories, or your state's farm bureau website
    - Check social media groups focused on local food in your area
    - Visit your community farmers market
    - Look for roadside farm stands when driving through rural areas
    - Ask at local grocery stores which items are sourced locally
2. Research farms that use regenerative or sustainable practices
    - Look for farms with organic or regenerative agriculture certifications
    - Visit farm websites to learn about their growing practices
    - Contact farms directly to ask about their methods
    - Join local sustainable agriculture organization to get recommendations

3. Explore different purchasing options
   - Farmers markets: Regular markets where multiple farmers sell directly to consumers
   - Community Supported Agriculture (CSA): Subscribe for a share of a farm's harvest
   - Farm stands: Direct sales at the farm location
   - U-pick operations: Harvest your own produce at the farm
   - Food co-ops: Member-owned grocery stores that often source locally
   - Farm-to-door delivery services: Local farms that deliver to your home
4. Plan your purchases
   - Check what's currently in season in your region
   - Plan meals based on what's locally available rather than creating a shopping list first
   - Determine how much fresh produce your household can store and consume
5. Visit farms or farmers markets
   - Shop early for best selection
   - Bring your own bags and containers
   - Ask farmers about their harvest times, handling practices, and best storage methods
   - Build relationships with farmers for future purchasing
6. Evaluate produce freshness
   - Look for vibrancy of color and firmness in fruits and vegetables
   - Smell produce for freshness (ripe produce should smell fresh and flavorful)
7. Transport and store properly
   - Get produce home quickly, especially in warm weather
   - Keep produce cool during transport with insulated bags or coolers
   - Place delicate items on top to prevent crushing
   - Store according to the farmer's recommendations
   - Prioritize eating the most perishable items first
8. Track your results
   - Record food waste
   - Keep track of favorite farms and their seasonal offerings

Buying Food 202: Definitions

- **Food miles**: The distance food travels from where it is grown to where it is consumed
- **Locavore**: A person who primarily eats food grown or produced locally (within 100-250 miles)
- **Regenerative agriculture**: Farming practices that build soil health and restore ecosystems
- **Seasonal eating**: Consuming foods during their natural local harvest season

Buying Food 202: Troubleshooting

Problem	Solutions
Limited local farm options in your area	Expand your search radius. Look for food hubs that aggregate products from multiple small farms. Investigate food co-ops that source regionally. Consider starting a neighborhood buying club.
Locally grown food is more expensive	Focus on seasonal items when they're abundant and prices are lower. Buy in bulk when possible.
No transportation to reach farms	Look for farmers markets with public transit access. Investigate farm delivery services or pickup points. Organize carpools with neighbors.
Limited time to shop at farmers markets	Find a CSA with convenient pickup times. Look for farm stands with extended hours. Check for online ordering options from local farms. Coordinate with neighbors to take turns shopping.

Sustainable Practices Handbook   Food Practices: Reducing Food Waste

Problem	Solutions
Produce spoils before you can use it all	Purchase smaller quantities. Properly store produce. Learn preservation methods. Share purchases with friends or neighbors.
Unfamiliar with how to prepare seasonal items	Ask farmers for advice. Look for recipes provided at farmers markets. Join local food groups on social media.
Farms don't accept credit or debit cards	Bring cash. See if the farm accepts digital payment apps. Ask about pre-payment options for regular customers.
Unsure if a farm uses sustainable practices	Ask about pest management, soil building, and water conservation practices. Visit the farm. Check for certifications.

Buying Food 202: Limitations

- Seasonal availability means you won't find the same variety year-round
- Local doesn't automatically mean organic or sustainable
- Geographic limitations affect availability in different regions
- Winter options are limited in colder climates
- Higher upfront costs are possible (though often balanced by less waste)
- Requires more planning than conventional grocery shopping
- May require more frequent shopping trips
- CSA shares come with uncertainty about what you'll receive
- Transportation to farms may not be accessible
- Time constraints may make regular farmers market visits challenging

References and resources: <www.suspra.com/practice/food/buying-202.html>

Buying Food 301: Buying In Season

Buy fruits and vegetables when they are in season and most affordable

Buy fruits and vegetables in season for multiple benefits: lower costs, superior flavor, higher nutritional value, reduced environmental impact, and greater connection to local food systems. Seasonal produce can be grown in your specific climate during a particular time of year. Seasonal buying also creates opportunities for community connection. Pooling purchases with neighbors, participating in harvest events, and sharing preservation sessions strengthen social bonds while making seasonal eating more economical and enjoyable.

Develop food literacy—understand when specific crops naturally mature in your region. In temperate climates, asparagus briefly flourishes in spring, tomatoes peak in summer, apples dominate fall, and storage crops like winter squash carry through colder months. Patterns vary by location; seasonal eating in Maine differs dramatically from seasonal eating in Southern California or Florida.

Price signals provide reliable indicators of seasonality. When a particular fruit or vegetable suddenly becomes abundant and inexpensive, it's likely at peak season. Conversely, high prices often indicate out-of-season produce. Farmers markets, community supported agriculture, farm stands, and u-pick operations connect you directly with growers and naturally limit availability to what's currently in season. Conventional grocery stores may also offer local, seasonal options.

Seasonal eating requires flexibility and adaptability. Rather than starting with specific recipes that might require out-of-season ingredients, begin with what's currently available and abundant, then determine how to prepare it. Save money on ingredients by buying at the height of the season when prices typically reach their lowest point. For maximum benefit, purchase larger quantities of peak-season items and preserve the excess through freezing, canning, drying, or fermenting. This extends seasonal benefits throughout the year and provides insurance against price fluctuations.

Buying Food 301: Equipment & Materials
- Seasonal food chart for your region (printable or digital)
- Reusable shopping bags and produce mesh bags
- Calendar or note-taking app to track seasonal produce
- Food storage containers for proper storage at home
- *Optional: Insulated bags for transporting perishable items, kitchen scale to weigh food*

Buying Food 301: Steps
1. Learn your region's growing seasons
   - Build relationships with vendors who can alert you when special items become available
   - Obtain a seasonal produce chart specific to your climate region
   - Keep records of when specific items appear and disappear from local markets
   - Join community supported agriculture (CSA) email lists or social media groups
2. Plan your shopping around seasonal availability
   - Plan meals around seasonal ingredients rather than choosing recipes first
   - Be flexible and willing to substitute ingredients based on what's in season
   - Check what's currently in season before making your shopping list
3. Shop at sources that prioritize seasonal foods
   - Visit farmers markets during harvest seasons
   - Join a CSA (Community Supported Agriculture) program
   - Shop at food co-ops and natural food stores with local sourcing policies
   - Check farm stands and U-pick farms
   - Look for "local" sections in conventional grocery stores
4. Identify truly fresh, in-season produce by appearance, texture, and smell
   - Check for local origin labels and harvest dates
   - Look for abundance of specific items (abundance often indicates peak season)
   - Note significant price drops (typically indicates peak season supply)
   - Ask vendors directly when an item was harvested and where it was grown
   - Observe natural physical characteristics (larger size, more vibrant color, stronger aroma)
5. Buy at peak season for maximum savings
   - Consider pooling resources with friends or neighbors for bulk purchases
   - Purchase larger quantities when prices hit their seasonal low point
   - Track prices throughout the season to identify the optimal purchasing window
   - Be prepared to process excess harvest through freezing, canning, or drying

Buying Food 301: Definitions
- **Community Supported Agriculture (CSA)**: Consumers buy shares of a farm's harvest before the growing season, receiving seasonal produce throughout the harvest
- **Food literacy**: The ability to understand how food affects health, environment, and social systems, including knowledge of where food comes from and how it's produced
- **Food miles**: The distance food travels from production to consumption
- **Peak season**: The height of a crop's natural harvest period
- **Seasonality**: When crops mature and are harvested in a specific region
- **U-pick**: Farms that allow customers to harvest their own produce

Buying Food 301: Troubleshooting

Problem	Solutions
Can't identify whether produce is in season	Look for country of origin labels. Ask vendors directly about harvest timing. Check prices. Use seasonal food apps specific to your region.
Limited variety during certain seasons	Embrace preserved forms of seasonal produce (frozen, canned, dried). Buy storage crops that keep well (winter squash, root vegetables, apples).
Seasonal produce spoils before you can use it	Purchase smaller quantities. Learn proper storage techniques. Process immediately after purchasing. Split large purchases with friends or family.
Farmers market prices are too high	Look for "seconds" or "imperfect" produce. Shop near closing time when vendors may offer discounts. Buy in bulk to reduce per-unit costs.
Can't always shop at farmers markets due to schedule	Look for CSA programs with flexible pickup options. Check if your farmers market offers pre-orders or extended hours. Buy seasonal produce available at grocery stores. Share shopping duties with neighbors.
Preserving seasonal abundance is overwhelming	Start with simple freezing techniques. Process small batches regularly instead of large batches. Learn quick preservation methods like refrigerator pickling. Join community preservation events where work is shared.
Family resistance to seasonal eating patterns	Focus on familiar seasonal items first. Involve family in selecting and preparing seasonal foods. Highlight especially delicious peak-season items. Maintain some flexibility rather than strict seasonality rules.
Difficulty planning meals around availability	Develop a repertoire of flexible recipes that work with multiple types of produce. Learn to substitute similar items within recipe frameworks. Practice improvisational cooking rather than strict recipe adherence.

Buying Food 301: Limitations

- Climate and geography significantly restrict local growing seasons in many regions
- True seasonal eating may limit diversity of diet during certain times of year
- Seasonal patterns require continuous learning and adaptation
- Storage and preservation require additional time, skills, and equipment
- Farmers markets and local sources may be inaccessible in some areas
- Seasonal produce may be unavailable to those in food deserts or without transportation
- Initial investment in bulk seasonal purchases may be prohibitive for limited budgets
- Seasonal eating requires more planning and kitchen skills than convenience-focused shopping

References and resources: <www.suspra.com/practice/food/buying-301.html>

Eating 101: Preparing Portions

Prepare and order smaller portions so you have fewer leftovers

Reduce food waste by preparing and ordering portion sizes that you can finish during a meal. First, this directly reduces food waste by ensuring you prepare only what will be consumed. Second, it conserves the resources used to produce, transport, and store that food. Finally, it saves money that would otherwise be spent on food that ends up discarded.

Sustainable Practices Handbook — Food Practices: Reducing Food Waste

When cooking at home, measuring ingredients and using smaller plates creates both visual and practical barriers to overserving. In restaurants, portions are typically oversized. A restaurant steak may be 16 ounces when nutritional guidelines suggest 6 ounces is appropriate. Order strategically—choosing appetizers, splitting entrees, or requesting half portions—to enjoy dining out while reducing waste. For those who host gatherings, accurate portion planning prevents overcooking "just to be safe." Have a plan for leftovers before the meal begins so extra food doesn't go to waste.

Eating 101: Equipment & Materials
- Measuring cups and spoons
- Smaller plates and bowls
- Food storage containers
- *Optional: Kitchen scale, meal planning notebook or app*

Eating 101: Steps
1. Evaluate home meal preparation
   - Start by evaluating your typical food waste—note what regularly gets thrown away
   - Cook only what you need by measuring ingredients based on actual consumption patterns
   - Use measuring cups and smaller plates to help control portion sizes
   - Serve food from the stove or counter rather than placing serving dishes on the table
   - Wait 10-15 minutes before considering second helpings
   - If preparing recipes, adjust quantities downward if they typically yield too much food
2. Shop wisely
   - Create a meal plan before shopping to avoid excess purchases
   - Buy smaller quantities of perishable items even if the unit price is higher
   - Choose loose produce instead of pre-packaged when possible
   - For items you use infrequently, buy from bulk bins in exact amounts needed
   - Consider the shelf life of ingredients when determining quantities
3. Plan your restaurant dining
   - Review portion sizes on the menu or ask your server
   - Order appetizers or small plates instead of entrees
   - Split a main dish with your dining companion
   - Request a half portion (many restaurants will accommodate this)
   - Ask for sauces and dressings on the side to avoid over-sauced dishes
   - Decline complimentary items you don't plan to eat (breadbasket, etc.)
   - Order as you go rather than all at once
4. Plan gatherings and parties
   - Calculate portions based on 4-6 ounces of protein per person
   - Plan for one or two side dish servings per person
   - Use the "one less than you think" rule—prepare one fewer dish than you initially planned
   - Create a buffet with smaller serving utensils to encourage modest portions
   - Have containers ready so guests have a convenient way to take leftovers home
5. Adapt recipes
   - Reduce recipes that typically produce too much
   - Write down adjusted quantities before cooking to avoid mistakes
   - For recipes that don't divide easily, cook full amount but freeze half before cooking

Eating 101: Definitions
- **Bulk bins**: Self-serve containers where customers can take precisely the amount needed
- **Food waste**: Edible food that is discarded rather than consumed
- **Half portion**: A reduced-size restaurant meal, sometimes available at a reduced price
- **Portion**: The amount of a particular food served to eat at one time
- **Serving**: A standardized amount of food defined by dietary guidelines

Sustainable Practices Handbook

Food Practices: Reducing Food Waste

- **Unit price**: The cost of an item per unit of measure (per ounce, pound, etc.)

Eating 101: Troubleshooting

Problem	Solutions
Family members have different appetite levels	Serve a base portion to everyone, keep extras in serving dishes, and store uneaten food promptly.
Restaurant portions are too large	Order appetizers instead, request a half portion, or split a meal with a dining companion.
Recipes don't easily scale down	Use online recipe scaling calculators. For odd fractions (like 1/3 of an egg), beat the egg and measure out the proportion you need.
Bulk purchasing seems more economical	Calculate the true cost including waste. Consider sharing bulk purchases with friends or neighbors.
Unexpected guests arrive	Keep shelf-stable items on hand that can quickly supplement a meal. Have a list of simple additions you can prepare quickly.
Leftovers are too small to save	Maintain a "bits and pieces" container in the freezer for small amounts of vegetables or meats that can later be used in soups or stir-fries.
Cooking for one leads to waste	Seek out recipes designed for single servings. Freeze individual portions of larger recipes.

Eating 101: Limitations

- Some recipes are difficult to prepare in small quantities
- Buying smaller quantities may cost more per unit
- Cultural expectations of abundance may create social pressure to prepare more
- Not all restaurants are willing to accommodate half-portion requests

References and resources: <www.suspra.com/practice/food/eating-101.html>

Eating 201: Eating Leftovers

Save and eat leftovers rather than throwing them out

Eating leftovers reduces food waste and saves money, but food safety is paramount: the USDA identifies the "Danger Zone" as temperatures between 40°F and 140°F (4°C and 60°C), where bacteria multiply rapidly. Refrigerate perishable food within two hours to minimize risk.

Many restaurants serve oversized portions. When dining out, bring a take-away container or ask for one at the end of your meal if you can't finish your food. Bring an insulated bag or keep a small cooler in your car to transport cold items home.

Refrigerators are designed to cool warm foods, so you don't need to wait until leftovers are room temperature before refrigerating them. The sooner you refrigerate hot food, the safer it is. Use this storage timeline as a general guideline for refrigerated leftovers:

3-4 days:

- Casseroles

- Cooked seafood, meat or poultry
- Cooked vegetables (without sauces)
- Pies
- Pizza
- Sliced fruit
- Soup

5-7 days:

- Bacon, ham
- Hard-boiled eggs (in shell)
- Rice and quinoa
- Tofu

For freezer storage, leftovers remain safe indefinitely at 0°F (-18°C); however, quality deteriorates.

Glass containers with airtight lids are ideal for most refrigerated leftovers as they don't absorb odors or stains. Containers designed specifically for freezing or heavy-duty freezer bags work best for freezing.

Eating 102: Equipment & Materials

- Food storage containers in various sizes (glass or BPA-free plastic)
- Masking tape and permanent marker for labeling
- Refrigerator thermometer and digital food thermometer
- Freezer bags or containers; aluminum foil; airtight silicone or beeswax food covers
- Insulated bag or cooler for transporting cold leftovers from restaurants
- *Optional: Vacuum sealer and bags*
- *Smartphone with food inventory app*

Eating 102: Steps

1. Prepare leftovers for storage promptly
   - Cool hot foods within two hours of cooking (one hour if room temperature is > 90°F/32°C)
   - Divide large quantities into smaller, shallow containers for faster cooling
   - Leave some airspace in containers to allow for expansion when freezing
   - Use an insulated container to transport cold leftovers from restaurants
2. Label all leftover containers
   - Write the contents and date on masking tape or directly on container lids
   - For freezer items, add the quantity or number of servings
3. Store leftovers properly
   - Refrigerate most cooked leftovers at 40°F (4°C) or below
   - Store raw meat in dedicated area to prevent cross-contamination
   - Keep leftovers in airtight containers to preserve quality and prevent odors
   - Place highly perishable foods (seafood, poultry) in coldest part of refrigerator
4. Organize your refrigerator and freezer for visibility
   - Put new leftovers toward the back of the refrigerator
   - Move older items to the front so they're visible and get used first
   - Group similar types of leftovers together
5. Create a leftover inventory system
   - Keep a whiteboard or list on the refrigerator noting what leftovers are available
   - *Optional: Use a food inventory smartphone app to track leftovers with expiration alerts*
   - Check inventory before grocery shopping or ordering takeout
6. Reheat leftovers safely
   - Bring soups, sauces, and gravies to a rolling boil
   - Heat solid leftovers to an internal temperature of 165°F (74°C)

Sustainable Practices Handbook — Food Practices: Reducing Food Waste

- Stir food during reheating to ensure even heating
- Cover food to retain moisture when microwaving
- Let food stand for a few minutes after microwaving to allow heat to distribute evenly
7. When in doubt, throw it out
    - Discard any food that has developed an off odor, flavor, or appearance
    - Follow the storage timeline guidelines (see discussion section)
8. Incorporate leftover meals into your weekly routine
    - Designate specific "leftover nights" in your meal planning
    - Eat the most perishable leftovers first
    - Prioritize leftovers for lunch the next day

Eating 102: Definitions

- **Cross-contamination**: The transfer of pathogens or allergens from one food to another
- **Danger Zone**: Temperature range between 40°F and 140°F (4°C and 60°C) where bacteria multiply most rapidly
- **Food spoilage**: The process by which food deteriorates to the point it becomes unappetizing, potentially unsafe, or unsuitable for consumption
- **Freezer burn**: Surface dehydration that occurs when food is improperly stored in the freezer, resulting in dry spots
- **Pathogens**: Microorganisms (bacteria, viruses, parasites) that can cause foodborne illness
- **Perishable foods**: Foods that spoil quickly without refrigeration
- **Shelf-stable foods**: Foods that can safely remain at room temperature in a sealed container

Eating 102: Troubleshooting

Problem	Solutions
Leftovers dried out during storage	Store with tight-fitting lids. Add a tablespoon of water before reheating. Cover when reheating in a microwave.
Forgot when leftovers were made	When in doubt, throw it out. Establish a consistent labeling system for future leftovers. Use masking tape and a marker to date containers.
Leftovers have freezer burn	Cut away freezer-burned portions. Use vacuum sealing, removing air from storage bags, or wrapping tightly in freezer-safe materials.
Unpleasant smell in refrigerator	Clean your refrigerator regularly. Store pungent foods in airtight containers. Place an open box of baking soda in your refrigerator.
Family doesn't know about leftovers	Maintain a whiteboard inventory on the refrigerator. Group leftovers together on a dedicated shelf. Label clearly with contents and dates.
Forgetting to eat leftovers in time	Set reminders. Create a leftover rotation system. Schedule regular "leftover nights." Move older items forward.
Family reluctant to eat leftovers	Store in attractive, clean containers. Make eating leftovers a scheduled part of weekly meal planning. Lead by example by eating leftovers yourself.
Restaurant leftovers leak in transit	Carry a small kit with extra containers and plastic bags. Keep a small cooler in your car.

Eating 102: Limitations

- Some foods don't maintain good quality when stored as leftovers (fried foods, dressed salads)

- Food safety concerns limit how long leftovers can be kept
- Limited refrigerator and freezer space can restrict leftover storage capacity
- Restaurant leftovers may be difficult to transport safely
- Texture and flavor quality of certain foods diminishes significantly after storage
- Reheating certain foods (particularly seafood) may produce strong odors

References and resources: <www.suspra.com/practice/food/eating-201.html>

Eating 202: Bringing Containers

Bring a takeaway container when eating out so you can bring home leftovers

Restaurant portions are often much larger than a single recommended serving. Bring your own containers to restaurants to reduce food waste and avoid disposable packaging. This practice has become increasingly accepted, though cultural norms and restaurant policies vary. Some restaurants enthusiastically support the practice, while in others, it may be met with confusion or resistance. Health regulations may restrict restaurants from filling customer-provided containers, though this usually applies to meals being served into containers rather than customers packing their own leftovers.

Develop a "restaurant kit" ready to grab when dining out. A thoughtfully prepared kit makes the process smooth and stress-free, removing barriers to making this a consistent practice. Start with casual dining establishments, then extend to more formal settings as you become comfortable with the routine. Most servers and restaurant staff are happy to accommodate customers who are trying to reduce waste, especially if you're polite and explain your reasoning if asked.

Eating 202: Equipment & Materials
- Reusable food containers with secure, leak-proof lids
- Small cloth bag or tote to carry containers
- Small hand towel or napkin (to wrap containers or wipe spillage)
- *Optional: Insulated bag or cooler, utensils if you plan to eat leftovers away from home*

Eating 202: Steps
1. Select containers that are the right size, seal securely, and won't leak
2. Prepare your container kit
    - Clean and dry containers thoroughly before packing them
    - Place containers in a dedicated bag that's easy to carry
    - Include a cloth napkin or small towel for potential spills
    - If appropriate, add an ice pack for foods requiring refrigeration
3. Bring your containers to the restaurant
    - For buffet-style restaurants: check restaurant policy before bringing containers
    - Keep your container bag accessible but out of the way during your meal
    - In casual settings, you can place your bag on an empty chair or under the table
4. Time your container introduction appropriately
    - For casual restaurants, simply take out your container when you're ready to go
    - For upscale restaurants, ask your server if they would mind if you pack your own leftovers, or if they'd prefer to do it for you
5. Pack your leftovers
    - Pack similar foods together to maintain quality (avoid mixing hot and cold items)
    - Secure lids tightly and check for leaks before placing in your bag
    - Use your napkin or towel to clean any spills on the outside of containers
6. Transport leftovers safely
    - Keep sensitive foods (meat, dairy, etc.) cool, below the temperature danger zone
7. At home, handle leftovers appropriately

- Transfer food to proper storage containers
- Refrigerate perishables promptly
- Label with date (if that will help you remember to eat them)

Eating 202: Definitions

- **Food waste**: Edible food that is discarded rather than consumed
- **Leftovers**: Uneaten food remaining after a meal, suitable for later consumption
- **Portion size**: The amount of a food served in a single sitting
- **Single-use packaging**: Containers, wrappers, or bags designed to be used only once
- **Temperature danger zone**: 40°F to 140°F (4°C to 60°C), the temperature range in which bacteria multiply rapidly in food

Eating 202: Troubleshooting

Problem	Solutions
Restaurant staff seems uncomfortable	Politely explain you're reducing waste. Offer to have them check with a manager if they're unsure.
Food leaks inside your bag	Use containers with secure locking mechanisms. Test containers with water before using them for food. Put containers in plastic bags for transport.
Containers take up too much space	Look for collapsible silicone containers. Use containers that nest when empty. Choose appropriately sized containers.
Embarrassed about bringing containers	Start with casual restaurants where the practice is more common. Use stylish containers and bags that don't look out of place.
Forgot to bring containers	Use the containers the restaurant provides. Make a habit of keeping spare containers in your car or bag.
Containers develop stains or odors	Clean containers promptly after use. Choose glass or stainless steel containers that resist staining.
Food spoils before you can eat it	Label containers with the date. Plan to eat leftovers within four days. Freeze portions.

Eating 202: Limitations

- Some social situations may make bringing containers inappropriate
- Some restaurants may have policies against using customer-provided containers
- High-end restaurants may frown upon the practice as contrary to their dining experience
- Not all foods maintain their quality as leftovers
- Glass containers, while durable and non-staining, can be heavy to carry and may break
- Insulated carriers may be needed for safe transport of perishable foods

References and resources: <www.suspra.com/practice/food/eating-202.html>

Eating 301: Making Soup Stock

Make soup stock from vegetable scraps and leftover carcasses and bones

Make stock from vegetable scraps and leftover bones to transform what would otherwise be waste into a flavorful foundation for countless dishes. Homemade versions allow complete control over ingredients, sodium levels, and flavor profiles. They're also more economical when made from scraps that would otherwise be discarded. The nutritional value of homemade stock often exceeds commercial versions, with bone stocks providing collagen, minerals, and other nutrients that leach from bones.

Collect scraps systematically. Keep a container in your freezer; add stems, peels, and stalks to it each time you cook. Onions, carrots, celery, mushrooms, and herbs all contribute excellent flavor. Avoid cruciferous vegetables (broccoli, cabbage, cauliflower) as they can make stock bitter, and starchy vegetables like potatoes that can make stock cloudy. Different stocks serve different culinary purposes:

- **Vegetable stock** is light and versatile, excellent for vegetarian cooking and quick soups
- **Chicken stock** is versatil, with a balanced flavor that works in most recipes
- **Beef or pork stock** is heartier and richer, ideal for stews, gravies, and robust soups
- **Fish stock** is delicate and best used in seafood dishes, risottos, and chowders

The key to great stock is low, slow heat. A gentle simmer—not a rolling boil—extracts flavor without making the stock cloudy or greasy. The longer you simmer animal bones, the more collagen and minerals are extracted, creating a richer mouthfeel and potentially more nutritional benefits.

After straining, compost the spent vegetables. If you've made bone stock, softened bones can be crushed and added to garden soil or compost. Fat from meat stocks can be saved for cooking—schmaltz (chicken fat) and tallow (beef fat) are traditional cooking fats with high smoke points.

Eating 301: Equipment & Materials
- Container for collecting vegetable scraps
- Chef's knife and cutting board
- Strainer or colander
- Large stockpot (8-16 quart) or slow cooker
- Large spoon for skimming
- Storage containers (glass jars, freezer-safe containers, or ice cube trays)
- *Optional: Fine-mesh sieve and cheesecloth (for clearer stock), instant Pot or pressure cooker, funnel for filling storage containers, labels and marker, kitchen scale to measure scraps*

Eating 301: Steps
1. Collect and store vegetable scraps over time
    - Save vegetable trimmings (onion and carrot peels, celery leaves, herb stems, etc.)
    - Store vegetable scraps in a container in the freezer until you have four cups
    - Avoid vegetables that will overpower stock (broccoli, Brussels sprouts) or discolor it (beets)
2. For meat stock, save bones and carcasses
    - Save chicken carcasses, beef and pork bones, shrimp shells, and fish bones after meals
    - Store in a freezer-safe container until ready to use
    - *Optional: For brown stock, roast bones at 425°F (220°C) for 25-30 minutes*
3. Prepare your pot
    - Choose a pot large enough to hold all ingredients plus water
    - For vegetable stock: use 1 part vegetable scraps to 2 parts water
    - For meat stock: use 1 part bones and carcass to 3 parts water
4. Add aromatics for flavor (adjust quantities based on batch size)
    - 1-2 bay leaves
    - 5-10 peppercorns
    - Few sprigs of fresh herbs or 1-2 teaspoons dried herbs (thyme, parsley, rosemary)
    - *Optional: 1-2 tablespoons apple cider vinegar or lemon juice (extract minerals from bones)*
5. Simmer the stock
    - For vegetable stock: Bring to a boil, then reduce heat and simmer for 45-60 minutes
    - For chicken stock: Simmer for 3-4 hours

- For beef or pork stock: Simmer for 6-8 hours
- For fish stock: Simmer for 30-45 minutes
- *Pressure cooker: Vegetable (5-10 minutes), chicken (30-40 minutes), beef (60 minutes)*
- *Slow cooker: Vegetable (2-3 hours, high), chicken (8 hours, low), beef (12+ hours, low)*
6. Use a large spoon to skim surface foam to produce a clearer, cleaner-tasting stock
7. Strain the stock
    - Place a colander or strainer over a large bowl or pot
    - Pour stock through the strainer to remove solids
    - *For clearer stock, strain again through a fine-mesh sieve lined with cheesecloth*
8. Compost the solids
9. Cool the stock properly
    - Divide hot stock into smaller containers to cool faster
    - Refrigerate or freeze
10. Remove fat (optional)
    - Refrigerate stock overnight
    - Once chilled, solid fat can be easily removed from the top and composted
    - *Optional: Keep some fat for added flavor depending on intended use*
11. Store the stock
    - Refrigerate stock in sealed containers for up to five days
    - Freeze stock for longer storage
    - *Optional: For convenient use, freeze in ice cube trays or 1-cup portions*
    - Label containers with date and type of stock
12. Use your homemade stock
    - Use in soups, stews, risottos, gravies, and sauces
    - Use to cook grains like rice or quinoa for added flavor
    - Use as a base for braising vegetables or meats

Eating 301: Definitions

- **Aromatics**: Ingredients like herbs, spices, and vegetables that add fragrance and flavor
- **Bone broth**: Similar to stock but typically simmered even longer (12-24+ hours)
- **Brown stock**: Stock made from roasted bones, resulting in deeper color and flavor
- **Carcass**: The skeleton of an animal, especially poultry, after the meat has been removed
- **Court bouillon**: A quickly-made aromatic broth used primarily for poaching fish and seafood
- **Fond**: Browned bits stuck a pan after cooking meat; add to stock for deeper flavor
- **Mirepoix**: A flavor base made of 2 parts onion, 1 part carrot, and 1 part celery
- **Remouillage**: A weak stock made by resimmering bones that have already been used for stock
- **Stock**: Liquid made by simmering bones, vegetables, and aromatics in water
- **White stock**: Stock made from unroasted bones, resulting in a lighter color and flavor

Eating 301: Troubleshooting

Problem	Solutions
Stock is cloudy	Use slower, gentler heat. Don't stir the stock while simmering. Skim foam regularly. Strain stock through a fine-mesh sieve lined with cheesecloth.
Stock lacks flavor	Increase ratio of scraps and bones to water. Roast bones before making stock. Add more aromatics. Simmer longer to concentrate flavor.
Stock is greasy	Refrigerate and remove solidified fat from the top. For immediate use, use a fat separator or skim with paper towels.

Problem	Solutions
Stock didn't gel when cooled	Use more bones with connective tissue (chicken feet, wings, necks; beef knuckles). Ensure long enough cooking time. Use less water relative to bones. Add a tablespoon of vinegar to help extract collagen.
Vegetable stock tastes bitter	Avoid cruciferous (broccoli, cabbage) or spoiled vegetables. Simmer for only 45 to 60 minutes. Avoid vegetable skins that might be bitter.
No space to store stock	Reduce stock by simmering longer; dilute to use. Freeze in ice cube trays for small, convenient portions. Pressure can for shelf-stable storage.
Stock smells off	If it smells unpleasant, discard it. Ensure proper cooling (within two hours) and refrigeration. Use clean equipment.

Eating 301: Limitations
- Requires a long time to simmer
- Limited refrigerator or freezer space can constrain storage options
- Some bones (like large beef bones) may be difficult to work with in home kitchens
- Not all bones and scraps are suitable: quality matters for flavor and safety
- Stocks have limited refrigerator shelf life (5 days)
- Making large batches requires significant pot and container space
- Collecting enough scraps takes time and dedicated freezer space
- Without pressure canning equipment, long-term storage requires freezer space

References and resources: <www.suspra.com/practice/food/eating-301.html>

Planning Meals 200: Organizing Recipes

Organize recipes for meal planning

Planning Meals 200: Equipment & Materials
- System for saving and organizing recipes
- *Optional: Recipe app*

Planning Meals 200: Steps
1. Find recipes
   - Search online by ingredient, technique, or meal
   - Check your local library for recipe books
   - Download recipe apps
   - Ask friends and family for favorite recipes
   - Schedule regular time to find and try new recipes to prevent boredom
2. Organize recipes
   - Use physical or digital recipe cards for frequently used recipes
   - Tag recipes by key ingredients, preparation time, occasion, and appeal
   - Note which recipes were successful and any modifications you made
   - Sort recipes by category (quick meals, special occasions, kid-friendly, etc.)
3. Test and adapt recipes
   - Start with the recipe exactly as written the first time
   - Make notes about taste, texture, and satisfaction level
   - Adjust seasonings, cooking times, or ingredients in subsequent attempts

Sustainable Practices Handbook   Food Practices: Reducing Food Waste

- Experiment to find your preferences
- Create a "recipe development" section in your notes for tracking modifications

References and resources: <www.suspra.com/practice/food/planning-200.html>

Planning Meals 201: Creating a Meal Plan

Create a meal plan each week

Create a meal plan each week to reduce the number of shopping trips, saving time and transportation-related emissions. Plan complementary meals that use similar ingredients, so you eat perishable items before they spoil. For example, if cilantro is needed for Monday's meal, plan another dish using cilantro later in the week to avoid wasting the remainder of the bunch.

Incorporate plant-based meals into your plan. Beans, lentils, and tofu provide protein with less environmental harm than animal proteins, especially red meat. Reduce meat consumption by implementing "Meat-free Monday" or using meat as a flavoring. Choose seasonal produce that requires less energy for production (no heated greenhouses) and transportation (shorter distances), and which is often more affordable and flavorful.

"Eat what you have" rather than always starting with recipes and buying all new ingredients. "Flexibility day" is for using up odds and ends or creating meals from leftovers. Think of it as your "refrigerator clean-out" day, where creativity converts random ingredients into a cohesive meal.

Planning Meals 201: Equipment & Materials
- Calendar or planner
- Notebook or digital device for recording your plan
- Inventory checklist for pantry, refrigerator, and freezer
- Access to recipes (cookbooks, websites, or apps)

Planning Meals 201: Steps
1. Take inventory of what you already have
   - Create a "use first" section in your refrigerator for items that need quick consumption
   - Check your refrigerator, pantry, and freezer
   - Note items approaching their "use by" dates, especially perishables
   - Make a list of items that need to be used this week
2. Check your schedule for the week ahead
   - Note days when you'll need quick meals and when you'll be eating away from home
   - Plan for appropriate number of meals
   - Batch cook on less busy days
3. Structure your meal plan
   - Prioritize meals that incorporate perishable items already on hand
   - Include plans for using or preserving leftovers
   - Designate one day as "flexibility day" for using up odds and ends
4. Design your meals with sustainability in mind
   - Plan plant-based meals
   - Choose recipes that use similar ingredients to minimize waste
   - Incorporate seasonal and local produce
   - Plan to use the entire food item (e.g., stems, peels)
5. Review and improve
   - Note which meals worked well and which didn't
   - Track any food waste, identify patterns, and make adjustments as necessary
   - Maintain a collection of successful, low-waste recipes

Revision: 25.1.8

Planning Meals 201: Definitions

- **Batch cooking**: Preparing large quantities of food at once to be used for multiple meals
- **Complementary meals**: Different dishes that use the same perishable ingredients
- **Cook once, eat twice**: Prepare extra portions for leftovers or for making a second meal
- **Flexibility day**: A designated day in the meal plan for using up odds and ends or leftovers
- **Plant-based meals**: Vegetables, fruits, grains, and legumes, with minimal animal products

Planning Meals 201: Troubleshooting

Problem	Solutions
Plan is too ambitious; meals don't get made	Start planning just three days at a time. Include ultra-simple meals or "assembly only" options. Be realistic about your time and energy.
Produce spoils before you can use it	Buy smaller quantities. Store produce properly. Plan to use more delicate produce earlier in the week. Consider frozen options for backup.
Family members don't eat the planned meals	Involve everyone in the planning process. Keep a list of "family favorite" meals. Mix in new recipes alongside familiar ones.
Too much food waste despite planning	Measure portions accurately. Track waste to identify patterns. Reduce recipe sizes. Plan specific uses for leftovers. Add more "flexibility days."
Not enough time to cook planned meals	Prep ingredients in advance. Choose simpler meals. Use time-saving appliances. Try backup quick meal options that use shelf-stable ingredients.
Difficulty keeping track of what to use first	Implement a "first in, first out" system. Use a whiteboard on the fridge to list priority items. Create an "eat first" bin for items that need quick use.
Unexpected schedule changes	Prioritize cooking meals with the most perishable ingredients first. Freeze ingredients you won't be able to use this week.
Limited budget for quality ingredients	Focus on affordable whole foods like beans, grains, and seasonal produce. Stretch more expensive ingredients across multiple meals. Check local farmers' markets near closing time for discounts.

Planning Meals 201: Limitations

- Requires regular time commitment for planning, shopping, and preparation
- Challenging for households with very unpredictable schedules
- Fresh, local, and organic ingredients may be more expensive or inaccessible for some budgets
- Specific dietary restrictions may limit flexibility in using up certain ingredients
- Seasonal eating can be difficult in regions with limited growing seasons
- May require learning new cooking techniques and recipes for plant-based or whole food meals

References and resources: <www.suspra.com/practice/food/planning-201.html>

Sharing Food 401: Organizing Donations

Organize ways for local grocery stores to donate unsold food to people in need

Organize food donations from grocery stores to address food waste and food insecurity. Grocery stores benefit from reduced waste disposal costs, enhanced community relationships, and alignment with sustainability goals. Recipients gain affordable access to nutritious food. Your program serves as the

Sustainable Practices Handbook Food Practices: Reducing Food Waste

crucial link making these benefits possible. Start with food categories that are easier to handle safely and that grocery stores discard regularly:

- Bakery items approaching sell-by dates
- Produce with cosmetic imperfections
- Dairy nearing sell-by dates but still within safe consumption periods
- Dry goods with damaged packaging or approaching expiration

As your program develops expertise and capacity, expand to include prepared foods and meat products, which require more stringent temperature control and faster distribution.

Build strong relationships with store management and staff. Each grocery store has unique procedures, concerns, and capabilities. Understand their specific needs and constraints; design a donation process that integrates smoothly with their operations. Track all donations meticulously, maintain temperature logs for perishable items, and regularly compile impact reports. Show grocery store managers the tangible results of their participation.

Make food safety your top priority. The Bill Emerson Good Samaritan Food Donation Act provides liability protection for good-faith donors, but this isn't a substitute for proper food handling. Maintain strict food safety standards to protect recipients and maintain the confidence of grocery partners.

As your program grows, add value for grocery partners, such as detailed waste tracking that helps them improve their ordering patterns. Your program may evolve into a genuine partnership where grocers see it as an asset to their operations rather than simply a recipient of donations.

Sharing Food 401: Equipment & Materials

- Volunteers to pick up food and deliver to food pantries, homeless shelters, and other recipients
- Transportation for site visits and food collection
- *Optional: Digital camera or smartphone for documentation, printer for paper handouts, labels and marking pens, scale for weighing donations*

Sharing Food 401: Steps

1. Research local food insecurity and existing programs
   - Contact local food banks, soup kitchens, and shelters to understand current needs
   - Research existing food recovery programs to avoid duplication and identify gaps
   - Document specific needs (types of food, delivery times, storage capabilities)
2. Understand food donation regulations and protections
   - Research the Bill Emerson Good Samaritan Food Donation Act and local food donation laws
   - Contact your local health department for food safety regulations
   - Prepare simple one-page summaries of legal protections for potential donors
3. Build a team and establish your organization
   - Recruit volunteers with diverse skills (logistics, food handling, communication)
   - Create a simple organizational structure with clear roles
   - Develop a mission statement and operational protocols
   - Find an existing non-profit fiscal sponsor or establish a new non-profit organization
   - Ensure all team members receive food safety training
4. Identify and approach potential grocery partners
   - Research local grocery stores, focusing first on independent stores or regional chains
   - Prepare a concise, professional proposal outlining mutual benefits
   - Request in-person meetings with store managers
   - Present a clear, simple process that minimizes store staff workload
   - Address common concerns proactively (liability, staff time, reputation)
5. Develop food handling and safety protocols

- Create written food safety guidelines based on health department requirements
- Establish temperature monitoring procedures for perishable items
- Develop protocols for food transportation and storage
- Create a tracking system for donations (date, source, type, quantity, destination)
- Train all volunteers on proper food handling procedures
6. Create efficient logistics systems
    - Develop regular pickup schedules that accommodate store operations
    - Create routes that minimize transportation time for perishable items
    - Establish a system for unexpected or irregular donations
    - Prepare contingency plans for staffing shortages or transportation issues
    - Document all processes in simple, clear manuals for volunteers
7. Launch a pilot program
    - Start with one grocery store and one recipient organization
    - Focus initially on easiest-to-handle food categories (bakery, dry goods)
    - Implement tracking system from day one
    - Schedule regular check-ins with both donors and recipients
    - Document challenges and successes during the pilot phase
8. Establish feedback and improvement systems
    - Create feedback forms for grocery partners and recipient organizations
    - Hold regular team meetings to discuss challenges and improvements
    - Track key metrics (pounds recovered, people served, volunteer hours)
    - Adjust protocols based on experience
    - Document successful practices for future expansion
9. Expand the program
    - Approach additional grocery stores with documented success stories
    - Expand to handle more complex food categories
    - Recruit additional volunteers as needed
    - Develop resources for onboarding new partners efficiently
    - Collaborate with complementary organizations
10. Maintain relationships
    - Schedule regular check-ins with grocery partners
    - Recognize and appreciate grocery staff and management
    - Provide impact reports to partner stores (pounds donated, meals served)
    - Offer regular refresher training for volunteers
    - Develop strategies for volunteer retention and recognition

Sharing Food 401: Definitions

- **Bill Emerson Good Samaritan Food Donation Act**: Federal legislation that protects food donors from civil and criminal liability when donating to nonprofit organizations in good faith
- **Cold chain**: The temperature-controlled supply chain for safely handling perishable foods
- **Customer Relationship Management**: Software systems for managing relationships and interactions with partners and volunteers
- **Date labels**: "Sell-by, best-by, use-by" labels indicate quality but not necessarily safety
- **Food insecurity**: Limited or uncertain access to adequate food for an active, healthy life
- **Food recovery**: Collecting unsellable edible food and redistributing it to people in need
- **Liability waiver**: A legal release from responsibility
- **Perishable food**: Food requiring refrigeration or having a short shelf life
- **Shelf-stable food**: Food that can safely remain at room temperature in sealed containers
- **Temperature danger zone**: 40°F to 140°F (4°C to 60°C), the range in which harmful bacteria grow most rapidly

Sharing Food 401: Troubleshooting

Problem	Solutions
Grocery stores concerned about liability	Provide information about the Bill Emerson Good Samaritan Food Donation Act. Offer to handle all aspects of food safety after donation. Create simple liability release forms.
Irregular or unpredictable donation quantities	Develop flexible distribution networks that can handle fluctuating volumes. Create a notification system for large donations. Establish relationships with multiple recipient organizations. Freeze or preserve food.
Difficulty maintaining volunteer schedules	Recruit on-call volunteers. Develop clear, simple protocols so new volunteers can step in easily. Partner with local schools, colleges, or businesses for service days. Implement volunteer management software.
Food spoilage during transportation	Invest in proper transportation equipment (coolers, insulated bags). Optimize routes to minimize transportation time. Implement strict temperature monitoring. Train volunteers on proper food handling.
Recipient organizations with limited storage capacity	Schedule smaller deliveries. Help recipients acquire additional storage through grants or donations. Develop a network of many recipient organizations. Process highly perishable items into more stable forms.
Store employees unsure what can be donated	Create clear, visual guidelines for store staff. Offer training sessions for store employees. Assign a dedicated liaison for each store. Provide regular positive feedback when appropriate items are donated.
Donated food not meeting recipient needs	Survey recipient organizations about preferred food types. Develop relationships with multiple grocery stores. Create educational materials for recipients about using unfamiliar food items.
Communication breakdowns	Establish clear points of contact at all organizations. Create multiple communication channels (email, phone, text). Schedule regular check-in meetings. Document all agreements and procedures in writing.

Sharing Food 401: Limitations

- Reliance on volunteer labor makes scheduling and consistency challenging
- Transportation and proper storage of perishable foods require significant resources
- Donations are unpredictable in quantity, quality, and type
- Store-level management changes can disrupt established donation programs
- Recipient organizations may have limited capacity to receive, store, and distribute donations
- Legal and health regulations vary by location and can complicate operations
- Food recovery programs rarely recover costs through traditional funding models
- Some food (especially prepared food) has very short safe redistribution windows
- Seasonal fluctuations in surplus food can create planning challenges
- Corporate policies may override local store management decisions about donations

References and resources: <www.suspra.com/practice/food/sharing-401.html>

Sharing Food 402: Distributing Food

Distribute preserved food from a community kitchen to people in need

Organize volunteers in community kitchens to transform seasonal abundance into year-round food security. Distribute preserved food from a community kitchen to build a vital link between local food production, preservation efforts, and community members in need. Many local farms and gardens experience periods of excess harvest. Community kitchens with preservation and distribution programs solve this problem by creating a three-part system:

1. **Glean** - Harvest excess produce from farms and gardens
2. **Preserve** - Process this seasonal abundance into shelf-stable, frozen, or refrigerated foods
3. **Distribute** - Get these preserved foods to people who need them throughout the year

Align your distribution schedule in harmony with the natural rhythms of your local foodshed. Provide high-quality locally-grown preserved food to established food pantries, community centers, faith communities, and mutual aid networks who already have connections to people in need. Consider food safety requirements when planning your distribution:

- **Shelf-stable items** (canned goods, dehydrated foods, properly sealed jams): Flexible distribution options, including centralized pickup locations or inclusion in food pantry offerings
- **Refrigerated items** (fresh pickles, some preserves): Limited distribution window, best distributed directly to recipients who can use them promptly
- **Frozen items** (frozen fruits, vegetables, prepared meals): Require insulated transport and either immediate use or recipient freezer access

Match your distribution approach to your community's specific needs and resources. Urban neighborhoods benefit from pickup locations at community centers, while rural communities might need volunteer delivery routes. Prioritize recipient dignity by:

- Creating a welcoming environment free from judgment
- Offering choices rather than pre-selecting packages
- Providing clear information about food items and preparation
- Scheduling distribution times on evenings and weekends, rather than during work hours
- Minimizing visible identifiers of charity

Solicit and incorporate feedback about what foods are most valued by the people you serve; share this knowledge with your farmers and gardeners to inform future growing decisions. Distribution events can become opportunities for neighbors to connect, share recipes and preparation tips, and discover other community resources.

Sharing Food 402: Equipment & Materials

- Community kitchen that meets commercial kitchen codes
- Computer with Internet access
- Inventory of preserved foods from community kitchen (canned, dried, frozen, etc.)
- Food-safe transport containers (insulated bags, coolers, sturdy boxes)
- Temperature monitoring devices for cold and frozen items
- Handwashing supplies and food handler gloves
- Distribution record sheets and pens
- Labels and markers for food packages
- Informational materials about food contents (ingredients, nutrition, preparation)
- Calendar of local harvests and seasonal abundance
- Contact list of local farms and community gardens
- *Optional: Folding tables and chairs for distribution sites*
- *Pop-up canopy for outdoor distribution*
- *Digital or printed sign-up forms for recipients*
- *Smartphone or tablet for digital recordkeeping*

Sustainable Practices Handbook Food Practices: Reducing Food Waste

Sharing Food 402: Steps
1. Plan for seasonal preservation and distribution
    - Create an annual calendar based on local growing seasons
    - Coordinate with local farms and gardens about expected harvest surpluses
    - Plan preservation activities around seasonal abundance
    - Schedule volunteer capacity for high-volume preservation periods
    - Forecast distribution needs based on preservation volumes
2. Establish gleaning relationships and systems
    - Build relationships with local farmers, community gardens, and home gardeners
    - Create a simple system for farms and gardeners to notify you of available excess
    - Organize volunteer teams for gleaning (harvesting excess produce)
    - Arrange transportation from farms and gardens to your community kitchen
    - Track sources and quantities of gleaned produce
    - Store, wash, process, and preserve food in your community kitchen
3. Assess what you have to distribute
    - Inventory all preserved foods by type, quantity, and preservation method
    - Match distribution volume to your preservation capacity
    - Prioritize distribution of items nearing expiration
4. Identify distribution partners and methods
    - Connect with food pantries, community centers, and faith communities
    - Consider direct distribution methods such as neighborhood pickup sites or delivery routes
    - Evaluate which methods best reach your intended recipients with minimal barriers
5. Develop a distribution schedule
    - Create a realistic schedule based on volunteer availability and recipient needs
    - Align distribution schedule with your preservation calendar and seasonal availability
6. Prepare foods for distribution
    - Bundle complementary items into meal kits
    - Include preparation instructions for unfamiliar items
    - Label all packages with contents, production date, and basic storage information
    - Note all ingredients to alert of possible allergens (nuts, dairy, wheat, eggs, soy)
    - Provide information about the local farms that supplied the original produce
7. Set up distribution site
    - Choose a location that's accessible, dignified, and provides necessary infrastructure
    - Arrange food items in logical groupings for efficient distribution
    - Create clear signage about available items and any limits
8. Ensure food safety during transport and distribution
    - Handle all unpackaged food with clean hands or food-safe gloves
    - Maintain appropriate temperatures for different food types
        - Cold foods: Below 40°F (4°C)
        - Frozen foods: Below 0°F (-18°C)
    - Use insulated containers with ice packs for refrigerated items
    - Keep transport time as short as possible
9. Distribute food to recipients
    - Greet recipients warmly and treat all with dignity and respect
    - Offer choices rather than pre-selecting items
    - Provide information about proper storage and preparation
10. Keep basic records
    - Document distribution date, types and quantities of food distributed
    - Record number of households or individuals served
    - Note any feedback about food preferences or needs
    - Track which items are the most and least popular
11. Collect feedback from recipients

- Ask what preserved foods are most useful and enjoyed
- Inquire about preparation challenges or successes
- Learn about additional food needs not being met
- Use feedback to inform future gleaning and preservation efforts
12. Follow up and improve
    - Thank and recognize contributing farms and gardens
    - Share results and lessons learned with community kitchen volunteers
    - Communicate impact to stakeholders and supporters
    - Expand successful distribution channels

Sharing Food 402: Definitions

- **Community kitchen**: A shared kitchen facility where people can prepare food together, often used for food preservation, education, and community building
- **Food pantry**: An organization that distributes food directly to those in need
- **Foodshed**: The geographic region that produces food for a particular population
- **Gleaning**: Collecting excess or leftover crops after the primary harvest
- **Preservation methods**: Canning, dehydrating, freezing, pickling, and fermenting
- **Seasonal abundance**: Periods when specific crops are harvested in large quantities
- **Shelf-stable**: Foods that can safely remain at room temperature for extended periods
- **Temperature danger zone**: 40-140°F (4-60°C), the temperature range where harmful bacteria multiply rapidly

Sharing Food 402: Troubleshooting

Problem	Solutions
Unpredictable volume from gleaning	Develop flexible preservation plans that can scale up. Build a network of on-call volunteers for high-volume periods. Have backup preservation methods for when kitchen capacity is overwhelmed.
Mismatch between gleaned produce and community preferences	Survey recipients about preferences before the growing season. Share this information with farm and garden partners. Process less popular produce into more accepted forms (e.g., tomato sauce vs. whole tomatoes).
Low turnout at distribution events	Partner with established organizations that already reach your target population. Adjust timing or location to better meet community needs. Improve outreach through multiple communication channels.
Not enough volunteers for distribution	Create clear, manageable volunteer shifts. Partner with service groups or faith communities. Consider distribution methods that require fewer volunteers, such as integration with existing food pantries.
Food safety concerns during transport	Invest in quality insulated containers. Monitor temperatures during transport. Keep transport times as short as possible. Distribute foods that match your capacity to maintain safe temperatures.
Recipients unfamiliar with preserved foods	Include simple recipe cards with unfamiliar items. Offer cooking demonstrations. Create a social media group or website with preparation videos. Partner with nutrition education programs.
Excess of certain preserved foods	Survey recipients about preferences before preserving large quantities. Create variety packs to introduce new items alongside favorites. Partner with multiple distribution channels to reach more diverse audiences.

Sustainable Practices Handbook — Food Practices: Reducing Food Waste

Problem	Solutions
Transportation limitations	Organize volunteer delivery routes. Partner with organizations that have transportation capacity. Establish multiple small distribution points within walking distance of recipients.
Cultural mismatches in food preferences	Survey the community about preferred foods before planning preservation projects. Include community members in planning. Provide culturally appropriate preparation suggestions.
Maintaining recipient privacy and dignity	Distribute discreetly. Avoid public identification as charity. Use a farmers' market-style setup to normalize the experience.

Sharing Food 402: Limitations

- Gleaning and preservation activities are tied to seasonal availability
- High-volume harvest periods may overwhelm kitchen capacity and volunteer availability
- Community kitchens produce limited quantities
- Home-preserved foods may have shorter shelf life than commercially produced equivalents
- Distribution capacity is constrained by volunteer availability and transportation resources
- Some recipients may lack storage capabilities, especially for refrigerated or frozen items
- Volunteer-based distribution systems may struggle with consistency and sustainability
- Food distribution alone doesn't address systemic causes of food insecurity
- Preserving and distributing culturally appropriate foods requires specific knowledge
- Gleaning, preservation, and distribution require coordination among multiple stakeholders

References and resources: <www.suspra.com/practice/food/sharing-402.html>

Storing Food 101: Storing Bread

Store bread and pastries in the freezer to prevent mold

Bread molds quickly at room temperature, especially in warm, humid environments. Freeze bread to extend its shelf life and prevent mold. This practice is particularly valuable for households that don't consume bread quickly or for preserving special homemade loaves and pastries. While refrigeration above freezing temperatures can delay mold, it actually accelerates retrogradation (starch molecules recrystallizing), causing bread to go stale. Freezing stops both mold growth and retrogradation.

- Lean breads (made primarily with flour, water, yeast, and salt) freeze exceptionally well
- Enriched breads with higher fat content (brioche, challah) may undergo texture changes but remain good for two months
- Sourdough bread maintains its distinctive flavor and keeps well frozen
- Crusty artisanal breads may lose some crispness but can be refreshed in a hot oven

For pastries, freezing works best before adding icings, fillings, or decorations. Croissants, scones, and unfrosted muffins freeze quite well, though their optimal storage time is shorter than for simple breads.

Minimize bread's exposure to air, which causes freezer burn and affects taste and texture. Package airtightly—either through careful wrapping or using specialized containers. Pre-slice bread before freezing so you can take only what you need while keeping the rest frozen.

When thawing bread, control moisture. Thawing in wrapping can trap condensation, resulting in soggy bread. For crusty breads, unwrap, thaw at room temperature, then warm briefly in an oven

Storing Food 101: Equipment & Materials

- Freezer with temperature at or below 0°F (-18°C)
- Freezer-safe storage containers or bag
- Cutting board and bread knife (for pre-slicing)
- *Optional: Vacuum sealer and compatible bags*
- *Labels and marker for dating*

Storing Food 101: Steps

1. Prepare your bread for freezing
   - For store-bought sliced bread: Keep in original packaging if it's intact and sealable
   - For whole loaves: Slice bread before freezing for easier use (unless you plan to use the entire loaf at once)
   - For pastries: If possible, freeze before adding frosting or decoration
2. Package bread properly
   - Wrap bread tightly to prevent air exposure:
     - Option 1: Double wrap in plastic wrap then foil
     - Option 2: Place in a freezer bag and remove as much air as possible
     - Option 3: Use a vacuum sealer for longest preservation
   - For sliced bread: Place parchment or wax paper between slices if they tend to stick
3. *Optional: Label and date your bread*
4. Place bread in the freezer
   - Avoid placing heavy items on top of soft breads or pastries
   - Position newer items behind or below older items to use oldest first
5. Thaw bread as needed
   - Individual slices: Thaw at room temperature (10-15 minutes) or toast directly from frozen
   - Whole loaves: Unwrap, thaw at room temperature (2-3 hours) or in refrigerator (overnight)
   - To refresh texture: Sprinkle with water and heat in oven at 350°F (175°C) for 5 minutes
   - For pastries: Thaw uncovered at room temperature to prevent sogginess

Storing Food 101: Definitions

- **Enriched bread**: Bread containing ingredients like eggs, butter, milk, or sugar that add fat, protein, or sugar beyond basic flour, water, yeast, and salt
- **Freezer burn**: Dehydration that occurs when food is exposed to air in the freezer
- **Lean bread**: Bread made primarily with flour, water, yeast, and salt, without enrichment
- **Retrogradation**: The process where starch molecules realign and recrystallize, causing bread to become stale
- **Room temperature**: Typically 68-72°F (20-22°C)

Storing Food 101: Troubleshooting

Problem	Solutions
Bread develops freezer burn	Ensure bread is wrapped tightly with minimal air exposure. Double wrap for longer storage. Consider using a vacuum sealer for extended storage.
Bread becomes soggy when thawed	Thaw bread unwrapped at room temperature. For crusty breads, refresh in a 350°F (175°C) oven for 5 minutes after thawing.
Slices stick together when frozen	Place parchment paper or wax paper between slices before freezing. Partially freeze slices on a baking sheet before packaging together.

Problem	Solutions
Bread has strange odor after freezing	Ensure your freezer is clean and doesn't contain strong-smelling foods. Use double wrapping or airtight containers. Check for mold before freezing.
Bread texture changes after freezing	Some texture change is normal. Refresh bread in the oven after thawing. Use bread within recommended timeframes.
Bread thaws with condensation	Remove bread from freezer packaging before thawing to allow moisture to escape.

Storing Food 101: Limitations

- Some artisanal crusty breads will never fully regain their original texture after freezing
- Frosted or filled pastries may not freeze well due to texture changes
- Requires freezer space, which may be limited in some households
- Requires planning ahead for thawing whole loaves
- Not suitable for bread already showing signs of mold or spoilage
- May slightly alter taste or texture, particularly in enriched breads
- Requires plastic or silicone freezer bags

References and resources: <www.suspra.com/practice/food/storing-101.html>

Storing Food 201: Washing Produce

Wash and store produce well so it lasts longer

Wash produce to remove surface dirt, pesticide residues, and potential pathogens, but also extend shelf life by removing spoilage-causing organisms. The ideal time to wash most produce is just before use, as added moisture can speed spoilage. However, washing certain items ahead of time can be beneficial:

- Leafy greens can be washed, thoroughly dried, and stored with a dry paper towel
- Root vegetables and thick-skinned fruits can be washed and stored for several days

Refrigerate these items:

- Leafy greens: Store in a container lined with paper towels to absorb moisture. Replace paper towel if it becomes saturated.
- Herbs (except basil): Trim stems and place in a glass with 1 inch of water, cover loosely with a plastic bag, and refrigerate. Change water every three days.
- Berries: Store in a container lined with paper towels, loosely covered. Do not wash until just before eating.
- Cruciferous vegetables: Store in perforated plastic bags or containers that allow some airflow.
- Root vegetables: Store in perforated plastic bags in the crisper drawer.
- Cut vegetables: Store in airtight containers with a damp paper towel.

Do not refrigerate these items (store at room temperature):

- Tomatoes: Store stem-side down on a counter away from direct sunlight.
- Potatoes, onions, and garlic: Store in a cool, dark, well-ventilated place (not refrigerated).
- Stone fruits: Keep at room temperature until ripe, then refrigerate.
- Bananas: Hang on a banana hook or place on a countertop away from other fruits.
- Winter squash: Store in a cool, dark place with good ventilation.

Some fruits produce ethylene gas, which speeds ripening and can cause premature spoilage in ethylene-sensitive produce. Keep these separated:

- Ethylene producers: Apples, avocados, bananas, melons, peaches, pears, tomatoes
- Ethylene-sensitive: Broccoli, Brussels sprouts, cabbage, carrots, cucumbers, eggplant, leafy greens, peppers, squash, sweet potatoes

The key principles are removing surface contaminants, controlling moisture, providing appropriate airflow, and storing at the optimal temperature.

Storing Food 201: Equipment & Materials

- Kitchen sink
- Colander or strainer
- Clean kitchen towels or paper towels
- Vegetable brush (for firm produce)
- Salad spinner (for leafy greens)
- White vinegar or food-grade hydrogen peroxide
- Cutting board and knife
- Storage containers (glass or plastic with lids)
- Perforated produce bags or containers
- Airtight containers
- *Optional: Food-grade produce wash, spray bottle, baking soda, mesh produce bags*

Storing Food 201: Steps

1. Prepare your workspace
   - Clean your sink, countertops, and cutting board
   - Assemble necessary equipment and materials
   - Wash your hands thoroughly with soap and water
2. Sort your produce
   - Separate produce by type and ripeness
   - Set aside very ripe items to use first
3. Prepare produce for washing
   - Remove any rubber bands, twist ties, or packaging
   - Cut off damaged or wilted parts
   - For leafy greens, separate leaves from stems if needed
4. For leafy greens (lettuce, spinach, kale, etc.)
   - Fill a large bowl with cold water
   - *Add 1 tablespoon white vinegar per gallon of water (optional)*
   - Submerge greens and swish gently for one minute
   - For particularly dirty greens, change water and repeat
   - Lift greens out (don't pour through a strainer, as dirt settles at bottom)
5. For berries and delicate fruits
   - Place in a colander and rinse gently under cool running water
   - For a deeper clean, mix 1 part vinegar to 3 parts water in a bowl
   - Soak briefly (30 seconds), then rinse with plain water
   - Do not wash berries until just before use if possible
6. For firm fruits and vegetables (apples, pears, potatoes, carrots)
   - Rinse under cool running water
   - Scrub firmly with a clean vegetable brush
   - For waxed produce, create a solution of 1 tablespoon baking soda per 2 cups of water
   - Soak for 12 minutes, then scrub and rinse thoroughly
7. For cruciferous vegetables (broccoli, cauliflower)

- o Soak in cold, salted water (2 tablespoons salt per gallon) for 15 minutes to kill insects
- o Rinse thoroughly under cold running water, getting into all crevices
- o Shake off excess water
8. Dry all produce thoroughly
   - o Air dry on clean kitchen towels or pat dry with paper towels or clean cloth
   - o Use a salad spinner for leafy greens
   - o Ensure produce is completely dry before storage to prevent mold growth
9. Prepare produce for storage
   - o For items that need to be trimmed, do so now
   - o For herbs, trim stems and place in water like fresh flowers
   - o For vegetables like carrots or celery, consider cutting into sticks and storing in water
10. Store properly based on produce type
    - o Use the appropriate storage method for each type of produce (see Discussion section)
    - o Label containers with the date of washing
    - o Place in the appropriate location (refrigerator, countertop, pantry)
11. Check stored produce regularly
    - o Inspect every three days for signs of spoilage
    - o Remove any pieces that have begun to decay
    - o Use the "first in, first out" method, using older produce first

Storing Food 201: Definitions

- **Crisper drawer**: A compartment in a refrigerator designed to maintain higher humidity, ideal for storing fresh produce
- **Cross-contamination**: Transfer of pathogens from one food item to another
- **Ethylene gas**: A natural plant hormone that speeds ripening and can cause premature spoilage
- **Food-grade hydrogen peroxide**: 3% hydrogen peroxide that is safe for food contact
- **Perforated bags**: Storage bags with small holes that allow for appropriate airflow while maintaining humidity
- **Produce wash**: Commercial products specifically designed to clean fruits and vegetables
- **Respiration rate**: The rate at which produce "breathes," consuming oxygen and releasing carbon dioxide, affecting how quickly it deteriorates after harvest
- **Transpiration**: The process by which moisture is released from harvested fruits and vegetables, affecting texture and quality over time

Storing Food 201: Troubleshooting

Problem	Solutions
Leafy greens wilting quickly after washing	Ensure greens are thoroughly dried before storage. Store on a dry paper towel to absorb excess moisture. Make sure the container has some ventilation. Check that refrigerator temperature is below 40°F or 4°C.
Mold developing on berries	Wait to wash berries until just before use. Add a dry paper towel to the storage container to absorb moisture. Inspect and remove any berries showing early signs of decay.
Root vegetables becoming soft or sprouting	Store away from ethylene-producing fruits. Ensure proper ventilation in storage containers. Store in a cool location but not too cold. For potatoes and onions, ensure that the storage area is dark to prevent sprouting.

Problem	Solutions
Herbs turning black or slimy	Dry herbs thoroughly after washing. Treat herbs like flowers: trim stems, place in water, change water every few days. For delicate herbs, lay them on a damp paper towel, roll up, and place in a plastic bag.
Fuzzy white or gray growth on vegetables	Discard affected portions. Lower the humidity in the storage container. Check refrigerator temperature. Ensure produce is completely dry before storage. Clean storage containers thoroughly.
Carrots and celery becoming limp	Store root-down in a container with an inch of water; change water every few days. Or wrap in a damp paper towel inside a container or bag.
Apples or pears developing brown spots	Store in perforated plastic bags in the refrigerator. Keep away from ethylene-sensitive produce. Check for bruised areas before storage.
Cut produce turning brown	Dip cut surfaces in lemon juice or ascorbic acid solution before storing. Store in an airtight container with minimal air space. Use within a day.

Storing Food 201: Limitations
- Delicate produce (like raspberries) may deteriorate faster when washed, even if dried thoroughly
- Cannot indefinitely extend the life of highly perishable items

References and resources: <www.suspra.com/practice/food/storing-201.html>

Storing Food 202: Organizing Food Storage

Organize your food storage system so you eat food before it spoils

Organize your food storage by creating visibility and access to items in the order they should be used. The "first in, first out" (FIFO) method ensures older items get used before newer ones.

Keep refrigerators below 40°F (4°C). Doors are the warmest area, bottom shelves the coolest. Different foods require different storage approaches: most fruits and vegetables need refrigeration, except tomatoes, potatoes, onions, garlic, and bananas. Review food storage weekly to catch items before they spoil and incorporate them into meal planning.

Storing Food 202: Equipment & Materials
- Clear storage containers (glass or plastic)
- Labels and marker
- Refrigerator and pantry thermometers
- Stackable bins or baskets
- Whiteboard or clipboard for inventory
- *Optional: Shelf liner*
- *Rotating can rack*
- *Lazy Susan/turntable*
- *Food storage app*

Storing Food 202: Steps
1. Assess storage areas
    - Check refrigerator temperature (40°F/4°C or below)
    - Check freezer temperature (0°F/-18°C or below)

- Measure pantry spaces for appropriate containers
    - Identify problem areas where food often spoils
2. Clean and prepare storage areas
    - Empty one area at a time
    - Clean surfaces with mild soap and water
    - Install shelf liners if desired
3. Establish storage zones by food type
    - Refrigerator:
        - Top: Ready-to-eat foods, leftovers, drinks
        - Middle: Dairy, eggs, packaged foods
        - Bottom: Raw meat, poultry, seafood
        - Crisper drawers: Separate fruits and vegetables
        - Door: Condiments, butter, soft cheeses
    - Pantry:
        - Eye-level: Frequently used items and nearest expiration dates
        - Upper shelves: Backup supplies, less frequently used items
        - Lower shelves: Heavier items, bulk goods
4. Implement "first in, first out" (FIFO) system
    - Place new items behind older ones
    - Use rotating can racks or manually rotate canned goods
5. Label everything clearly
    - Contents and date
    - For leftovers, include name of dish and "use by" date
    - For frozen foods, include date frozen and quantity
    - For bulk pantry items, include purchase date and expiration
6. Use containers strategically
    - Transfer dry goods to airtight containers
    - Use clear containers to see contents easily
    - Choose appropriately sized containers
    - Store ingredients used together in the same area
7. Create an inventory system
    - List pantry staples and their locations
    - Track frozen items with a simple list
    - Update when adding or using items
    - Take photos before shopping (optional)
8. Implement weekly food review routine
    - Schedule before grocery shopping
    - Check for items approaching expiration
    - Move foods that need to be used soon to a designated area
    - Plan meals around ingredients that need to be used
9. Adjust purchasing habits
    - Buy only what you can use before spoilage
    - Purchase highly perishable items in smaller quantities
    - Match purchasing volume to available storage space
10. Maintain your system
    - Clean refrigerator shelves monthly
    - Wipe pantry shelves quarterly
    - Reassess and adjust system as needed

Storing Food 202: Definitions

- **Airtight container**: Vessel that prevents air exchange
- **Cross-contamination**: Transfer of harmful bacteria from one food to another

- **FIFO (First In, First Out)**: Storage method where older items are used before newer ones
- **Humidity-controlled drawer**: Refrigerator compartment that maintains moisture levels
- **Use-by date**: Last date recommended for product use at peak quality

Storing Food 202: Troubleshooting

Problem	Solutions
Food still spoiling	Check refrigerator temperature. Examine door seals. Move perishables to colder areas. Schedule more frequent reviews.
Running out of space	Remove duplicates. Use stackable containers. Buy smaller quantities more frequently.
Family not following system	Simplify system. Label shelves clearly. Create visual guides. Include family in setup.
Tracking expiration dates	Create a centralized list. Use a whiteboard. Try an inventory app with expiration tracking. Use color-coded labels.
Forget freezer contents	Maintain a freezer inventory list. Organize with clear bins by food type.
Produce wilting quickly	Check humidity settings. Store fruit and vegetables separately. Use produce storage bags.

Storing Food 202: Limitations
- No system can indefinitely extend the life of highly perishable foods
- Initial setup requires time and possibly money for containers
- Requires cooperation from household members

References and resources: <www.suspra.com/practice/food/storing-202.html>

Storing Food 301: Preserving Food

Dry, freeze, can, or ferment what you can't eat fresh

Inhibit spoilage to extend the time available to eat food:

- **Drying** removes moisture microorganisms need to grow. It concentrates flavors and creates lightweight, compact food.
- **Freezing** slows enzymatic activity and microbial growth by lowering temperatures. It best maintains original texture, flavor, and nutrition.
- **Canning** creates a vacuum seal and kills pathogens through heat processing. Water bath canning works for high-acid foods (pH below 4.6), while low-acid foods require pressure canning.
- **Fermenting** uses beneficial bacteria to convert sugars to acid, creating conditions hostile to harmful bacteria. This enhances nutritional value by creating probiotics and increasing vitamins.

Choose methods based on food type, available equipment, storage space, and desired texture and flavor.

Sustainable Practices Handbook
Food Practices: Reducing Food Waste

Storing Food 301: Equipment & Materials

General

- Fresh produce or other foods
- Cutting board, knives, measuring tools
- Kitchen timer and food thermometer
- Storage containers and labels

For Drying

- Food dehydrator or oven with low temperature
- Baking sheets and parchment paper

For Freezing

- Freezer (0°F/-18°C or colder)
- Freezer-safe containers or bags
- Blanching pot, strainer, and ice bath setup

For Canning

- Water bath canner or pressure canner
- Canning jars, new lids, and bands
- Jar lifter, funnel, bubble remover
- pH test strips for low-acid foods

For Fermenting

- Fermentation vessels (crocks, glass jars)
- Weights and airlock lids
- Non-iodized salt

Storing Food 301: Steps

Planning and Preparation

1. Choose appropriate preservation method:
   - **Drying**: Fruits, herbs, some vegetables, meat jerky
   - **Freezing**: Most fruits, vegetables, meats, prepared dishes
   - **Water bath canning**: High-acid foods (fruits, properly acidified tomatoes)
   - **Pressure canning**: Low-acid foods (vegetables, meats, soups)
   - **Fermenting**: Vegetables, dairy (yogurt, kefir), some fruits
2. Clean workspace, equipment, and hands thoroughly
3. Select high-quality, unblemished produce at peak ripeness

Method: Drying Food

1. Prepare food:
   - Slice uniformly (1/4 to 1/2 inch thick)
   - Blanch vegetables briefly
   - Pretreat fruits prone to browning with lemon juice solution
2. Arrange in single layer in dehydrator or low-temperature oven (140-150°F)
3. Dry until:
   - Herbs: crisp and crumbly (2-4 hours)
   - Fruits: leathery with no moisture when cut (6-16 hours)
   - Vegetables: brittle or leathery (4-12 hours)
   - Meat jerky: firm but pliable (4-6 hours)

4. Cool completely before packaging in airtight containers
5. Label with contents and date

Method: Freezing Food

1. Prepare food:
   - Wash and trim
   - Blanch vegetables for recommended time
   - Drain thoroughly and pat dry
2. Package properly:
   - Use freezer-safe containers or bags
   - Remove as much air as possible
   - Leave 1/2 inch headspace in rigid containers
   - Flash freeze berries or individual items on a tray first, then put in a container
3. Label and date all packages
4. Freeze quickly and maintain 0°F (-18°C) or below

Method: Water Bath Canning

1. Prepare equipment:
   - Inspect and wash jars, lids, and bands
   - Keep jars hot until filling
   - Prepare canner with hot water
2. Follow tested recipe precisely for safe acidity levels
3. Fill jars:
   - Leave proper headspace (typically 1/4 to 1/2 inch)
   - Remove air bubbles
   - Wipe jar rims clean
   - Apply lids and bands finger-tight
4. Process in boiling water:
   - Ensure water covers jars by 1-2 inches
   - Start timing when water returns to rolling boil
   - Process for recommended time
   - Adjust for altitude if necessary
5. Cool jars undisturbed for 12 hours, then check seals

Method: Pressure Canning

1. Follow water bath canning steps 1-3
2. Use pressure canner according to manufacturer's instructions:
   - Add specified water amount
   - Vent steam for 10 minutes before applying weight
   - Process at correct pressure; adjust for altitude
   - Maintain steady pressure throughout processing
3. Allow your canner to depressurize naturally
4. Remove jars and cool as with water bath canning

Method: Fermenting

1. Prepare vegetables or fruits:
   - Shred, slice, or chop
   - For cabbage, massage with salt to release juices
   - For other vegetables, prepare brine (2-3% salt solution)
2. Pack into fermentation vessel:
   - Ensure vegetables are submerged

Sustainable Practices Handbook   *Food Practices: Reducing Food Waste*

- - Leave two inches headspace
    - Place weight on top
    - Cover with airlock lid or cloth
3. Ferment at room temperature (65-75°F):
    - Sauerkraut: 1-4 weeks
    - Pickles: 1-2 weeks
    - Kimchi: 3 days to 3 weeks
4. Check daily for first week, remove any surface mold
5. Transfer to refrigerator when desired flavor is reached

Storing Food 301: Definitions

- **Blanching**: Briefly immersing foods in boiling water followed by ice water to deactivate enzymes
- **Botulism**: Foodborne illness from toxins produced by *Clostridium botulinum* bacteria
- **Brine**: Salt and water solution used in pickling and fermentation
- **Flash freezing**: Freezing individual pieces on a tray before packaging
- **Headspace**: Unfilled space between food and container rim
- **pH**: Measure of acidity; critical for determining appropriate canning methods
- **Vacuum seal**: Removal of air to prevent oxidation and microbial growth

Storing Food 301: Troubleshooting

Problem	Solutions
Dried foods moldy	Food wasn't dried completely; redry if caught early. Use airtight containers. Add a desiccant packet.
Freezer burn	Use better packaging that removes more air. Double-wrap foods. Use within recommended timeframes.
Canning jars don't seal	Wipe rims thoroughly. Use new lids. Process for full recommended time. Check for jar defects.
Mold on ferments	Remove carefully without disturbing lower layers. Ensure food stays submerged. Use an airlock system.
Discoloration	Ensure proper blanching time. Use ascorbic acid for fruits. Pretreat dried fruits with lemon juice.
Loss of texture	Choose an appropriate preservation method for each food. Don't overcook when blanching.

Storing Food 301: Limitations

- Requires significant time investment, especially during harvest season
- Each method needs specific equipment and storage conditions
- Improper techniques can lead to foodborne illness
- Energy costs for freezing are ongoing
- Canning requires continuing investment in new lids
- Some nutrients are lost, especially with heat methods
- Pressure canning has a learning curve and safety considerations
- Fermenting produces strong odors in small spaces

References and resources: <www.suspra.com/practice/food/storing-301.html>

Revision: 25.1.8

Sustainable Practices Handbook   Food Practices: Reducing Food Waste

Storing Food 401: Creating a Community Kitchen

Create a community kitchen so people can preserve more home-grown food

Create a community kitchen for food preservation to offer many advantages over home preservation:

- **Efficiency of Scale:** Commercial equipment processes larger quantities faster. Multiple pressure canners, industrial dehydrators, and flash freezers make preserving substantial harvests practical.
- **Knowledge Exchange:** Community kitchens facilitate intergenerational knowledge transfer, with experienced preservers sharing techniques while newcomers bring fresh perspectives.
- **Resource Sharing:** Members share access to high-quality tools rather than each household purchasing rarely-used equipment.
- **Food Waste Reduction:** Community kitchens can quickly process unexpected harvests or gleaning opportunities.
- **Community Resilience:** The kitchen builds food security and emergency preparedness by preserving excess during abundant seasons.

Balance accessibility with sustainability, using sliding-scale fees, work-exchange options, or membership models that include some free access.

Storing Food 401: Equipment & Materials

- Community organizing materials (meeting space, communication tools)
- Business planning resources
- Suitable physical space
- Commercial-grade kitchen equipment:
    - Multiple high-BTU stoves/cooktops
    - Large-capacity sinks
    - Food processors, mixers, and blenders
    - Water-bath and pressure canners
    - Commercial dehydrators
    - Flash freezers and storage freezers
    - Vacuum sealers
- Food preparation equipment
- Storage systems
- Sanitizing equipment
- Recordkeeping system

Storing Food 401: Steps

1. Form a planning committee
    - Gather community members with diverse skills and knowledge, including food preservation knowledge, business experience, legal expertise
    - Establish roles and decision-making processes
    - Create vision and mission statement
2. Assess community needs and resources
    - Survey about food preservation interests and needs
    - Identify existing skills and equipment
    - Map seasonal food surpluses
    - Determine scale needed
3. Research regulatory requirements
    - Investigate zoning laws for commercial kitchens
    - Learn health department and food safety regulations
    - Research permits and licenses needed

Sustainable Practices Handbook — Food Practices: Reducing Food Waste

- - Determine insurance requirements
  - Consider legal structures (nonprofit, cooperative)
4. Develop a sustainable business model
   - Create startup and operating budgets
   - Explore funding options
   - Design membership or fee structures
   - Plan for long-term financial sustainability
5. Secure a suitable location
   - Look for existing commercial kitchens available for use
   - Or identify locations for building new or renovating
   - Ensure accessibility
   - Consider proximity to gardens and farms
   - Verify utilities can support commercial equipment
6. Design the kitchen for preservation activities
   - Create zones for different preservation methods
   - Include adequate ventilation
   - Plan for sufficient electrical capacity
   - Ensure ample counter space and storage
   - Design with food safety and workflow in mind
7. Equip the kitchen appropriately
   - Prioritize equipment based on community needs
   - Consider used equipment from restaurant supply stores
   - Seek donations from businesses updating kitchens
   - Ensure all equipment meets health code requirements
8. Establish operating procedures
   - Create reservation systems
   - Develop cleaning and sanitizing protocols
   - Establish food safety guidelines
   - Create equipment training procedures
   - Design storage systems
   - Develop conflict resolution procedures
9. Train community members
   - Offer food safety certification courses
   - Provide equipment training
   - Organize skill-sharing workshops
   - Create accessible instructional materials
10. Launch and manage the kitchen
    - Hold community open house
    - Schedule dedicated times for different preservation activities
    - Implement maintenance routines
    - Collect feedback for improvements
    - Track usage patterns
11. Build community around food preservation
    - Organize group preservation events during harvest peaks
    - Create system for sharing excess produce
    - Facilitate knowledge exchange
    - Document local preservation wisdom
    - Celebrate community achievements
12. Ensure long-term sustainability
    - Develop volunteer management program
    - Create leadership succession plans
    - Implement regular financial reviews

Sustainable Practices Handbook

Food Practices: Reducing Food Waste

- o Establish equipment replacement funds
- o Build relationships with local farms and gardens

Storing Food 401: Definitions

- **Commercial-grade equipment:** Kitchen equipment designed for high-volume use meeting regulatory requirements
- **Flash freezing:** Rapidly freezing food at extremely low temperatures to maintain quality
- **Food safety certification:** Training in proper food handling procedures required for commercial kitchens
- **Food sovereignty:** The right of peoples to healthy, culturally appropriate food produced through sustainable methods
- **Gleaning:** Collecting leftover crops from farmers' fields or urban fruit trees
- **Sliding scale:** Fee structure that adjusts based on users' ability to pay

Storing Food 401: Troubleshooting

Problem	Solutions
Finding suitable space	Use existing commercial kitchens during off-hours. Partner with churches, schools, or community centers. Consider mobile kitchen options.
High startup costs	Phase equipment purchases by priority. Apply for community grants. Share equipment with existing kitchens. Organize fundraising events.
Low participation	Schedule around seasonal harvests when motivation is highest. Offer introductory workshops. Partner with community gardens.
Conflicts over kitchen use	Implement a clear reservation system. Create standard operating procedures. Establish a mediation committee. Schedule dedicated times for different methods.
Regulatory hurdles	Consult with health inspectors during planning. Learn from established community kitchens. Start with less regulated activities.
Volunteer burnout	Establish a rotation system for responsibilities. Celebrate volunteers regularly. Create limited time commitments. Build a leadership pipeline.

Storing Food 401: Limitations

- Regulatory requirements vary widely and may present significant challenges
- Start-up costs can be substantial
- Finding appropriate space with necessary utilities is difficult
- Success depends on sustained community participation
- Governance becomes complex as the kitchen grows
- Insurance costs can be significant
- Some preservation methods require consistent supervision

References and resources: <www.suspra.com/practice/food/storing-401.html>

Understanding Food 101: Learning Labels

Understand food date labels

Date labels primarily indicate quality, not safety, for most foods. Only infant formula has federally regulated expiration dates in the United States. "Best if Used By" dates indicate peak quality, not when food becomes unsafe. "Sell By" dates are for retailers' inventory management. Fresh produce may not have explicit date labels, requiring visual inspection instead.

Understanding Food 101: Equipment & Materials
- Food packages with date labels
- Smartphone with Internet access (to look up unfamiliar terms)

Understanding Food 101: Steps
1. Collect various food packages with different date labels
2. Identify the type of date label on each product:
    - "Best if Used By/Before" indicates best flavor or quality
    - "Use By" is the last date recommended for peak quality
    - "Sell By" tells stores how long to display the product
    - "Freeze By" indicates when to freeze for peak quality
    - "Expiration Date" is mainly used for infant formula and baby foods
3. Record and categorize the labels
4. Research manufacturer-specific terms if needed
5. Learn how date labeling differs by country
6. Create a personal reference system for interpreting labels

Understanding Food 101: Definitions
- **Best if Used By/Before**: Date indicating best flavor or quality; not a safety date
- **Closed Dating**: Code of letters/numbers identifying production date and time
- **Expiration Date**: Last date a food should be eaten (mainly for infant formula)
- **Food Safety**: Protection from harm caused by contaminated food
- **Food Quality**: Characteristics that make food acceptable to consumers
- **Open Dating**: Calendar dates on food products
- **Sell By**: Date for store inventory management
- **Use By**: Last date recommended for peak quality (not safety for most foods)

Understanding Food 101: Troubleshooting

Problem	Solutions
Can't find date information	Look all over the package including bottom and crimped ends. Contact manufacturer if needed.
Unclear date format	The US typically uses Month / Day / Year. European countries use Day / Month / Year. Look for a spelled-out month.
Product has date code	Check the manufacturer's website or call customer service.
Product past its date but looks fine	For most foods, if properly stored, it's likely still safe. Use sensory evaluation.
No date; fresh produce	Use visual cues, firmness, smell, and proper storage knowledge.

Sustainable Practices Handbook
Food Practices: Reducing Food Waste

Problem	Solutions
Multiple dates on same package	Earlier dates are typically "Sell By" for retailers. Consumer guidance is the later date.

Understanding Food 101: Limitations
- Date labeling doesn't account for improper storage after purchase
- Sensory evaluation is still required regardless of date labels
- Date label interpretation varies by country and region
- Freezing can extend shelf life beyond printed date
- Small producers may use different systems than large manufacturers

References and resources: <www.suspra.com/practice/food/understanding-101.html>

Understanding Food 102: Being Safe

Understand food safety and signs of spoilage

Different foods spoil in different ways. Proteins develop sliminess and off-odors; fruits and vegetables show mold and softening; grains may develop insects or rancidity. Spoilage rate depends on temperature, moisture, acidity, preservatives, and processing methods.

Understanding Food 102: Equipment & Materials
- Your senses (sight, smell, touch, and sometimes taste)
- Thermometer for refrigerator temperature (32-40°F or 0-4°C)
- Thermometer for food internal temperature
- Good lighting for visual inspection
- Clean cutting boards and knives
- Airtight food storage containers

Understanding Food 102: Steps
1. Set up your kitchen for food safety:
   - Keep refrigerator between 32-40°F (0-4°C)
   - Keep freezer at or below 0°F (-18°C)
   - Store raw meat on bottom shelf to prevent drips
   - Use separate cutting boards for meat and produce; clean surfaces and tools thoroughly
2. Look for general signs of spoilage:
   - **Visual**: Mold, slime, unusual color changes, freezer burn
   - **Smell**: Sour, rotten, fermented, or "off" odors
   - **Texture**: Slimy, sticky, unusually soft, dried out, or mushy
   - **Taste**: Only if other signs aren't present - check for sour, bitter, fizzy, or off-flavors
3. Check specific spoilage signs by food type:
   - **Meat/poultry**: Sticky film, discoloration, sour smell, sliminess
   - **Fish/seafood**: Strong fishy/ammonia smell, milky film, sunken eyes, soft flesh
   - **Dairy**: Separation, unwanted mold, curdling, sour smell
   - **Produce**: Soft spots, discoloration, mold, fermented smell
   - **Eggs**: Sulfur smell, floating in water, cloudy/pink whites, discolored yolk
   - **Dry goods**: Insects, webs, rancid smell, mold, clumping
4. Discard food when:
   - Visible mold appears (except certain hard cheeses)
   - Strong off-odors develop

- Canned goods are bulging, leaking, or severely dented
- Meat/poultry/seafood was left at room temperature over two hours
- Soft produce has extensive mushy areas
- Food was cross-contaminated by raw meat juices
- Leftovers have been refrigerated over four days
5. Use judgment with borderline cases:
    - Trim affected areas on hard fruits and vegetables
    - Cut away mold on hard cheeses with 1-inch margin
    - Discard soft foods with any mold
    - When in doubt, throw it out

Understanding Food 102: Definitions

- **Cross-contamination**: Transfer of harmful bacteria from one food to another
- **Foodborne illness**: Sickness from consuming contaminated foods
- **Freezer burn**: Dehydration causing grayish-brown dry spots on frozen food
- **Mold**: Fungal growth appearing as fuzzy spots on food
- **Pathogens**: Microorganisms that can cause disease
- **Rancidity**: Breakdown of fats resulting in unpleasant smell and taste
- **Spoilage**: Food deterioration making it unsuitable for consumption

Understanding Food 102: Troubleshooting

Problem	Solutions
Uncertain if meat is spoiled	Check for sliminess, off-colors, strong odors. Cook to the proper temperature or discard.
Unsure about moldy cheese	Hard cheeses: Cut away mold with 1-inch margin. Soft cheeses: Discard entirely.
Produce with small, spoiled areas	Firm produce: Cut away affected areas with 1-inch margin. Discard soft produce with mold.
Canned goods with minor dents	Small side dents are usually fine. Discard cans with seam dents or deep dents. Always discard bulging cans.
Floating eggs	Floating indicates age but not necessarily spoilage. Crack into a separate bowl and check the smell first.
Leftovers getting old	Label leftovers with dates. Discard refrigerated leftovers after four days.
Freezer-burned food	Cut away affected portions or use in recipes where texture matters less.
Conflicting signs	Trust your instincts. When in doubt, discard the food.

Understanding Food 102: Limitations

- Not all harmful bacteria cause detectable changes in food
- Those with compromised sense of smell may miss odor changes
- Some spoilage cues require experience to recognize
- High-risk individuals should be more cautious with borderline foods
- Some fermented foods naturally have odors that seem like spoilage

References and resources: <www.suspra.com/practice/food/understanding-102.html>

Choosing Wise Ingredients

Avoiding Food 101: Avoiding Endangered Seafood

Avoid eating orange roughy, bluefin tuna fish, and Atlantic rock and Jonah crab

Orange roughy (*Hoplostethus atlanticus*) are slow-growing and late to mature, making them highly vulnerable to overfishing. Bluefin tuna (*Thunnus thynnus*) populations have been severely depleted due to high demand. Atlantic rock (*Cancer irroratus*) and Jonah crabs (*Cancer borealis*) are also facing overfishing in certain regions.

References and resources: <www.suspra.com/practice/food/avoiding-101.html>

Avoiding Food 201: Avoiding Red Meat

Eat protein from sources other than ranched ruminant animals that chew their cud

Ranched ruminant animals include cows, sheep, and goats; their flesh is considered "red meat." Raising these animals contributes to deforestation and habitat loss. Protein sources like poultry, pork, fish, legumes (beans, lentils, chickpeas), tofu, tempeh, or nuts and seeds require less land and water.

References and resources: <www.suspra.com/practice/food/avoiding-201.html>

Avoiding Food 301: Avoiding Mammals

Eat protein from sources other than mammalian animals

Mammals are animals that produce milk to nourish their young. Raising cattle, sheep, pigs, goats and other mammals for meat contributes to deforestation and habitat loss. Protein sources like poultry, fish, legumes, and plant-based alternatives such as tofu and tempeh require less land and water.

References and resources: <www.suspra.com/practice/food/avoiding-301.html>

Avoiding Food 302: Avoiding Cod

Avoid eating cod that is not caught sustainably

When purchasing cod, look for certifications like the Marine Stewardship Council (MSC) blue fish label, which indicates sustainably sourced seafood. Consult sustainable seafood guides like the Monterey Bay Aquarium's Seafood Watch or the Marine Conservation Society's Good Fish Guide to identify cod fisheries that assess fisheries based on fish population health and fishing methods.

References and resources: <www.suspra.com/practice/food/avoiding-302.html>

Selecting Food 101: Drinking Tap Water

Drink more tap water and fewer bottled beverages

Save money and energy, eliminate the production of unnecessary sweeteners, artificial colors, and artificial flavors, and reduce bottling, packaging, and transportation impacts. Prioritize drinking tap water and consciously reduce your consumption of bottled water, sodas, juices, and other drinks packaged in single-use containers. Fill a reusable water bottle from a faucet to make tap water easily accessible on the go. Encourage your workplace or community center to install attractive, well-maintained water dispensers.

Enhance the taste of tap water by adding slices of fresh fruit, vegetables, or herbs. If you're concerned about water quality, use a filter containing activated charcoal. In most countries, tap water quality is strictly regulated, meaning it meets rigorous safety standards that bottled water—often subject to fewer controls—may not. Share local water quality reports to build trust in tap water.

References and resources: <www.suspra.com/practice/food/selecting-101.html>

Selecting Food 102: Eating Venison

Eat wild-caught venison instead of beef

Venison is deer meat, which can be obtained by hunting wild, free-ranging animals. This contrasts sharply with beef production, which typically involves intensive farming practices that contribute to deforestation, artificially high greenhouse gas emissions, and significant water and land usage. Wild game requires minimal intervention and results from natural ecosystems. Sourcing venison locally reduces food miles, but availability varies depending on location and season.

References and resources: <www.suspra.com/practice/food/selecting-102.html>

Selecting Food 201: Eating Certified Seafood

Eat seafood certified as better for our planet

Seafood certification provides third-party verification that products meet sustainability standards such as population health, fishing or farming methods, habitat impacts, and management practices. The most widely recognized wild-capture seafood certification is the **Marine Stewardship Council (MSC)**, which uses a blue label and assesses fisheries based on sustainable fish stocks, minimizing environmental impact, and effective management. For farmed seafood, the **Aquaculture Stewardship Council (ASC)** is the leading global certification, evaluating farms on environmental impacts, animal welfare, and social responsibility.

Other important certifications include **Best Aquaculture Practices (BAP)**, which uses a star system to indicate how many steps in the supply chain are certified; **Friend of the Sea**, which certifies both wild and farmed products; and **Naturland**, which applies organic standards to aquaculture. Regional programs like **NOAA Fisheries' FishWatch** (US), **Ocean Wise** (Canada), and **Responsibly Sourced Seafood** (UK retailers) provide additional guidance for specific markets.

Certification complements but differs from seafood recommendation programs like Seafood Watch, which categorize seafood into "Best Choices," "Good Alternatives," and "Avoid" based on sustainability criteria. While Seafood Watch evaluates all seafood regardless of certification, certification programs only label seafood that meets their specific standards. Using both resources provides the most comprehensive guidance.

When selecting between certified options, consider additional factors:

- **Species diversity**: Choosing less popular species reduces pressure on heavily fished stocks
- **Local vs. imported**: Local seafood isn't automatically more sustainable
- **Fresh vs. frozen**: Properly frozen seafood preserves quality while reducing waste
- **Processing method**: Minimally processed seafood often has less environmental impact

Selecting Food 201: Definitions

- **Aquaculture**: Farming of aquatic organisms including fish, mollusks, crustaceans, and algae
- **Aquaculture Stewardship Council**: Certifies farmed seafood
- **Best Aquaculture Practices**: Certification program that addresses environmental and social responsibility, animal welfare, food safety, and traceability
- **Bycatch**: Unintentional capture of non-target species during fishing operations
- **Chain of Custody**: Documentation that tracks certified seafood from harvest to point of sale
- **Marine Stewardship Council**: Certifies wild-capture fisheries
- **Overfishing**: Harvesting fish at a rate faster than they can reproduce
- **Seafood Watch**: Program run by the Monterey Bay Aquarium that provides science-based recommendations about seafood sustainability
- **Stock**: A population of a species in a defined geographical area
- **Traceability**: The ability to track seafood from harvest to consumer

References and resources: <www.suspra.com/practice/food/selecting-201.html>

Selecting Food 301: Eating Wild Game

Eat wild-caught game instead of farmed meat from land animals

Wild game, such as deer, elk, or wild boar, naturally forages, requiring no dedicated land for pasture or feed production. Furthermore, wild game populations, when managed responsibly through regulated hunting, help maintain ecological balance, preventing overgrazing and promoting biodiversity. Source wild game from local hunters to foster a more resilient food system and economy.

References and resources: <www.suspra.com/practice/food/selecting-301.html>

Selecting Food 302: Eating Legumes

Eat legumes instead of dairy or eggs

Legumes are the seeds from plants in the family *Fabaceae*, which includes beans, lentils, peas, peanuts, and soybeans. They are nutritional powerhouses that can effectively replace animal products like dairy and eggs in your diet, offering comparable and in some aspects superior nutrition.

Aquafaba (Latin for "bean water") is the viscous liquid that results from cooking chickpeas or other legumes. The proteins and starches in aquafaba give it unique properties that allow it to:

- Foam when whipped (like egg whites)
- Emulsify oils and other ingredients
- Bind ingredients together in baking
- Provide structure and leavening

Aquafaba is particularly valuable for creating vegan versions of traditionally egg-heavy foods like meringues, macarons, mousses, and mayonnaise. While chickpea aquafaba is most common due to its neutral flavor and color, the cooking liquid from other legumes like white beans and black beans can also function as egg replacers. In addition to aquafaba, other legume-based egg substitutes include:

- Tofu (for scrambles, quiches, and creamy desserts)

- Chickpea flour (for omelets and frittatas)
- Mashed beans (for binding in baked goods)

Selecting Food 302: Equipment & Materials
- Blender or food processor, strainer or colander
  Basic legumes to keep on hand: chickpeas (garbanzo beans), black beans, lentils (red, green, or brown), soybeans or edamame, split peas
- *Optional equipment: Pressure cooker or Instant Pot, immersion blender, hand mixer, fine mesh strainer or nut milk bag, tofu press*

Selecting Food 302: Steps
1. Replace mammal milk with legume-based milk alternatives
   - Purchase ready-made soy milk (the most nutritionally similar to mammal milk)
   - Make homemade legume milk:
     - Soak one cup dry soybeans overnight
     - Drain, rinse, and blend with 3-4 cups water
     - Strain through a nut milk bag or fine mesh strainer
     - Optional: add vanilla, sweetener, or salt to taste
2. Replace mammal milk yogurt with legume-based yogurt
   - Purchase ready-made soy yogurt
   - Make homemade soy yogurt:
     - Warm four cups of soy milk to 180°F (82°C)
     - Cool to 115°F (46°C)
     - Add two tablespoons of store-bought soy yogurt as starter
     - Incubate for 8-12 hours until set
3. Replace mammal cheese with legume-based alternatives
   - For ricotta-style cheese, blend:
     - 1.5 cups firm tofu
     - 2 tablespoons nutritional yeast
     - 1 tablespoon lemon juice
     - 1/2 teaspoon salt
   - For spreadable cheese, blend soaked cashews with cooked white beans
   - For melty cheese sauce, blend:
     - 1 cup cooked white beans or chickpeas
     - 1/4 cup nutritional yeast
     - 1 tablespoon lemon juice
     - 1 tablespoon tapioca starch
     - Seasonings (salt, garlic powder, onion powder)
     - 1/2 cup water (adjust for desired consistency)
4. Collect and prepare aquafaba
   - Method 1: Drain liquid from canned chickpeas into a bowl
   - Method 2: Cook dried chickpeas and reserve cooking water
   - If too thin, reduce liquid by simmering
   - *Optional: Refrigerate for up to 1 week or freeze in ice cube trays*
5. Use aquafaba to replace egg whites
   - Basic ratio: 3 tablespoons aquafaba = 1 egg white
   - Whip for meringues and mousses:
     - Whip with a hand or stand mixer until soft peaks form (5-10 minutes)
     - Add 1/4 teaspoon cream of tartar for stability (optional)
     - Gradually add sugar while continuing to whip until stiff peaks form
   - For baked goods:
     - Use unwhipped aquafaba to replace eggs in cookies, brownies, and cakes

Sustainable Practices Handbook   Food Practices: Choosing Wise Ingredients

- Basic ratio: 3 tablespoons aquafaba = 1 whole egg
6. Use other legume-based egg replacers
   - For binding in baked goods:
     - 1/4 cup mashed or pureed white beans = 1 egg
     - 3 tablespoons chickpea flour mixed with 3 tablespoons water = 1 egg
   - For scrambles and omelets:
     - Crumble firm tofu and season with nutritional yeast, turmeric, salt, and pepper

Selecting Food 302: Definitions

- **Aquafaba**: The viscous liquid resulting from cooking beans, particularly chickpeas
- **Complete protein**: Containing all nine essential amino acids in sufficient amounts
- **Legumes**: Plants in the family *Fabaceae*, including beans, lentils, peas, and soybeans
- **Nutritional yeast**: Deactivated yeast with a cheesy flavor, often fortified with B vitamins
- **Plant-based**: Foods derived from plants with minimal processing and no animal products
- **Tofu**: A food made by coagulating soy milk and pressing the resulting curds into blocks

Selecting Food 302: Troubleshooting

Problem	Solutions
Aquafaba won't whip to stiff peaks	Reduce aquafaba by simmering to concentrate proteins. Add 1/4 teaspoon cream of tartar for stability. Ensure all equipment is completely free of oil or fat. Try chilling the aquafaba and mixing bowl before whipping.
Digestive discomfort after eating legumes	Start with smaller portions. Try lentils and split peas. Soak dried beans thoroughly; discard soaking water. Cook with kombu, bay leaf, or digestion-friendly spices like cumin and ginger. Thoroughly cook beans.
Homemade soy milk has strong beany flavor	Blanch soaked soybeans in boiling water for 1 minute, then drain and rinse before blending. Add vanilla extract and a small amount of sweetener.
Baked goods have different texture	Adjust leavening agents (add 1/4 teaspoon additional baking powder when using legume-based egg replacers). Reduce liquid slightly in recipes using aquafaba. Allow batter to rest for 10-15 minutes before baking.
Legume-based cheese doesn't melt	Add 1-2 tablespoons of tapioca starch to cheese recipes. Heat slowly over low heat. For stretchy texture, add 1 tablespoon of refined coconut oil.
Family members resistant to legumes	Add legumes to familiar dishes (blend white beans into pasta sauce, add lentils to soups). Use legumes in strongly flavored dishes like chili or curry. Try commercial products (like soy milk or tofu) before homemade versions.

Selecting Food 302: Limitations

- Legume-based alternatives do not perfectly replicate the taste and texture of dairy and eggs
- Some people have allergies to specific legumes (particularly soy and peanuts)
- Homemade legume-based alternatives are time-consuming to prepare
- Aquafaba can be inconsistent in thickness and protein content
- Not all legume-based substitutions work in all recipes; some experimentation may be needed
- Gut microbiomes may take time to adjust to legume consumption
- Legumes do not contain vitamin B12

References and resources: <www.suspra.com/practice/food/selecting-302.html>

Selecting Food 303: Eating Farmed Seafood

Select farmed seafood grown in recirculating tanks

Look for certification from Aquaculture Stewardship Council (ASC), Best Aquaculture Practices (BAP), and GlobalG.A.P., which have developed standards specific to recirculating systems (RAS) that address water quality, energy use, feed sourcing, and animal welfare. Unlike traditional aquaculture that uses open nets in oceans or ponds, RAS operations circulate water through tanks and filtration systems that maintain optimal conditions for fish health. The controlled environment allows for harvest throughout the year, providing reliable access to seafood regardless of season. Sustainability benefits include:

- **Water conservation**: 95-99% less water consumption than conventional aquaculture
- **Pollution prevention**: Waste is captured and often converted to fertilizer
- **Escape elimination**: RAS completely contains farmed species
- **Disease control**: Reduced pathogen exposure, decreasing the need for antibiotics
- **Land efficiency**: Can be located on non-agricultural land, reducing habitat conversion
- **Solar power**: Can be powered completely by solar electricity

The best RAS systems employ multiple stages of filtration, including mechanical, biological, and sometimes ultraviolet or ozone treatments to maintain water quality.

References and resources: <www.suspra.com/practice/food/selecting-303.html>

Selecting Food 304: Eating Shark

Select shark from U.S. waters that are fished sustainably

Shark consumption raises concerns due to overfishing of many species globally, but fisheries management organizations consider certain shark species in United States waters, like spiny dogfish (*Squalus acanthias*), to be fished at sustainable levels. Look for eco-labels or consult sustainable seafood guides to identify shark options from U.S. fisheries certified as sustainable.

References and resources: <www.suspra.com/practice/food/selecting-304.html>

Eating Plant-Based Meals

Eating More Plants 203: Eating a Wider Variety

Meet more nutritional needs by eating a wider variety of fruits and vegetables

Broaden the types of fruits and vegetables you consume. Actively seek out new and different items each week to ensure a comprehensive intake of vitamins, minerals, and phytonutrients, as different plants offer unique nutritional profiles. By diversifying your plant intake, you not only boost your personal health but also support a more resilient and biodiverse food system.

References and resources: <www.suspra.com/practice/food/eating-203.html>

Eating More Plants 302: Sampling Food Traditions

Try vegetarian and vegan meals from a wide variety of food traditions and cultures

Expand your plant-based repertoire by exploring vegetarian and vegan dishes from diverse culinary traditions around the world. Many traditional plant-based diets are inherently sustainable, relying on locally available, seasonal ingredients and minimizing reliance on resource-intensive animal agriculture. Actively seek out and try meals from cultures known for their rich vegetarian or vegan cuisine. For example, explore Indian lentil dals and vegetable curries, Ethiopian stews with injera bread, Mediterranean mezze platters, or East Asian tofu and noodle dishes. This practice makes plant-based eating more exciting and flavorful.

References and resources: <www.suspra.com/practice/food/eating-302.html>

Eating More Plants 401: Eating Vegan

Eat an exclusively vegan diet

Eating a vegan diet moves beyond vegetarian and plant-based diets to eliminate all animal products, including meat, dairy, eggs, and honey. Explore the wide variety of plant-based foods available: legumes, grains, vegetables, fruits, nuts, and seeds. Learn about plant-based protein combinations and experiment with vegan recipes to discover new favorite meals. Be mindful of vitamin B12, which is typically supplemented in vegan diets.

References and resources: <www.suspra.com/practice/food/eating-401.html>

Planning Meals 202: Finding Vegetarian Recipes

Find vegetarian recipes that taste good and are fun to make

The most exciting vegetarian cooking embraces vegetables, grains, and legumes for their inherent flavors and textures rather than replacing meat. Cultures with centuries-long traditions of vegetarian cooking—such as those in parts of India, the Mediterranean, Ethiopia, and East Asia—offer rich resources for dishes that highlight plant ingredients. Think in terms of expanding your repertoire rather than restricting it. Embrace the opportunity to discover new ingredients and techniques and broaden your culinary skills and experiences.

When evaluating vegetarian recipes, pay particular attention to the balance of flavors and textures. The most satisfying vegetarian meals often combine multiple elements: something creamy, something crunchy, something protein-rich, something fresh, and something with umami flavor. This variety creates dishes with complexity and satisfaction.

Making vegetarian cooking fun often comes down to the approach. Cooking with others, participating in challenges like "cook every recipe in a vegetarian cookbook," or hosting themed dinner parties can transform vegetarian cooking from a dietary restriction into a creative pursuit.

References and resources: <www.suspra.com/practice/food/planning-202.html>

Planning Meals 203: Eating Plant-Based Meals

Start eating plant-based meals once a week, and then increase frequency

Embrace the sustainable food pathway by intentionally planning meals around plant-based ingredients. Start by committing to one plant-based meal per week; increase the frequency as you become comfortable and discover new recipes. Plant-based meals prioritize vegetables, fruits, legumes, grains, nuts, and seeds, minimizing or eliminating animal products like meat, dairy, and eggs. Plant-based agriculture requires less land, water, and energy than animal agriculture. By thoughtfully planning these meals, you can ensure balanced nutrition. Explore online resources and cookbooks for inspiration and recipes to make plant-based eating a delicious and regular part of your diet.

References and resources: <www.suspra.com/practice/food/planning-203.html>

Planning Meals 301: Finding Vegan Recipes

Find vegan recipes that taste good and are fun to make

Moving from vegetarian to vegan cooking is a significant step toward more sustainable eating. While vegetarian cooking eliminates meat, poultry, and fish, vegan cooking goes further by removing dairy, eggs, honey, and other less obvious animal-derived ingredients like gelatin and whey. Vegan cooking is an opportunity to explore the vast world of plant-based ingredients. Rather than trying to replicate meat, celebrate plants and mushrooms for their own flavors, textures, and nutritional benefits.

Vegan cooking has evolved tremendously in recent years. What was once a niche diet has exploded into a diverse, creative culinary movement. Modern vegan recipes range from simple whole-food meals to sophisticated gourmet creations. Cashews or sunflower seeds can transform into creamy sauces, jackfruit can mimic pulled pork, aquafaba (the liquid from canned chickpeas) can replace egg whites in meringue, and nutritional yeast can add cheesy flavor to countless dishes. These discoveries make eating vegan feel like an adventure rather than a sacrifice.

A balanced vegan diet should include a variety of protein sources, healthy fats, complex carbohydrates, and micronutrient-rich fruits and vegetables. Look for recipes that incorporate a diverse range of ingredients to ensure you're meeting your nutritional needs.

Becoming proficient at vegan cooking is a journey. You'll likely encounter some less successful meals along the way, but each attempt builds your skills and intuition. Over time, you'll develop a repertoire of reliable recipes and techniques that make vegan cooking not just sustainable but genuinely enjoyable.

References and resources: <www.suspra.com/practice/food/planning-301.html>

Planning Meals 302: Scheduling Meat-Free Mondays

Begin observing meat-free Mondays, and then increase meat-free days per week

The Meat-Free Mondays concept is simple: once a week, commit to a whole day without eating meat. Start by designating Mondays as your meat-free day. As you become more comfortable, expand to additional days. To get started, plan your Monday meals in advance. Explore vegetarian or vegan recipes online or in cookbooks, focusing on dishes that excite you. Think about hearty vegetable curries, flavorful pasta dishes, or satisfying bean-based meals. As you progress, involve your household or team in choosing recipes and preparing meals, making it a collaborative and enjoyable experience.

References and resources: <www.suspra.com/practice/food/planning-302.html>

Planning Meals 401: Understanding Nutrition

Understand human nutrition and your own nutritional needs

Human nutrition is the study of the food and drink your body needs to function well–including the vitamins, minerals, carbohydrates, proteins, fats, and fiber in what you eat and drink. Knowing your nutritional needs means understanding the right balance of these nutrients for your age, activity level, and specific health conditions.

Learn to read food labels and understand serving sizes. Guidelines from national health organizations offer a starting point for recommended daily intakes of various nutrients. Consult a registered dietitian or nutritionist for personalized advice, especially if you have specific dietary needs or health concerns.

Prioritize obtaining your nutrition from whole, unprocessed foods that are sustainably produced and packaged. By focusing on nutrient-dense foods, you can reduce reliance on resource-intensive processed foods and ensure your diet supports both your well-being and a healthy environment.

References and resources: <www.suspra.com/practice/food/planning-401.html>

Reducing Meat 101: Adjusting Recipes

Reduce the amount of meat you add to pasta, rice, and tortilla meals

Make a meaningful step towards a more sustainable diet, without drastically changing your eating habits, by reducing the meat consumption in your favorite recipes for pasta, rice, and tortillas. Consider meat to be a supporting ingredient. Introduce new flavors and textures. For pasta sauces, halve the amount of ground beef or sausage and double up on vegetables like mushrooms, zucchini, or lentils. In rice-based meals like stir-fries or paella, reduce the chicken or shrimp and increase the tofu, beans, or mixed vegetables. For tacos, burritos, and quesadillas, try using half the usual amount of beef or chicken and add black beans, pinto beans, or seasoned vegetables like bell peppers and onions.

References and resources: <www.suspra.com/practice/food/reducing-meat-101.html>

Serving Food 401: Changing Menus

Change menus at public institutions to serve more plant-based meals

Transform institutional menus to incorporate more eco-friendly, plant-based options to reduce environmental impact while potentially improving health outcomes and managing costs. Public institutions—including schools, hospitals, prisons, and government facilities—have enormous potential for positive environmental impact through menu changes. However, these institutions have established procurement contracts and diverse constituencies with varying receptiveness to change.

Lasting change requires more than just new recipes—it demands strategic engagement with stakeholders at all levels. Kitchen staff need proper training and motivation to prepare unfamiliar items. Administrators need compelling evidence that changes align with institutional priorities. And diners need convincing to eat less meat. Replacing meat with plant proteins should reduce costs, creating a compelling financial argument alongside environmental benefits. If plant-based options cost more, budget constraints are likely to trump sustainability goals. Recognize that many people want to eat meat, and dairy and meat producers will lose money if institutions adopt plant-based menus.

Decide whether to try a gradual, phased approach or attempt wholesale menu overhauls. Starting with one day per week (like Meat-free Monday) or focusing on one meal period can prove the concept and build momentum. Consider whether modifying familiar dishes to reduce animal products while maintaining familiar flavors (like bean-beef blended burgers) will be more palatable than introducing entirely unfamiliar plant-based dishes. If you are completely changing menus, rather than offering plant-based versions of heavily meat-centered dishes, draw inspiration from traditionally plant-forward Mediterranean, Indian, or East Asian cuisines.

Nutrition requirements play a crucial role in menu planning, particularly in schools and healthcare settings. Work with registered dietitians to ensure that new plant-based options meet all regulatory requirements and provide adequate nutrients, especially protein, iron, calcium, and vitamin B12.

Measure and communicate success to build support for expanding initiatives. Track metrics including ingredients purchased, total costs, and diner satisfaction to demonstrate the full value of menu changes.

References and resources: <www.suspra.com/practice/food/serving-401.html>

Serving Food 402: Creating a Plant-based Restaurant

Create a restaurant that serves plant-based meals

Restaurants are an easy business to imagine, but a hard business to run. Nonetheless, thousands of people open new ones every year. Develop a compelling menu and source fresh ingredients to serve delicious eco-friendly plant-based meals. Build strong relationships with local farmers. Direct connections with growers not only ensure ingredient quality but also create a genuine story for diners about their food's origins. If you can convince farmers to plant specific varieties for your restaurant, you can create unique menu offerings.

Plant-forward cooking—where plants take center stage with animal products used sparingly or as flavor accents—has become a defining characteristic of eco-friendly restaurants. Even restaurants that aren't exclusively vegetarian or vegan are offering substantial plant-based options and reducing conventional meat portions. To differentiate your restaurant, tell the story of your ingredients through menu descriptions, server knowledge, visual displays, and digital content. Educating customers about sustainable food helps to create demand for eco-friendly ingredients beyond your restaurant.

Serving Food 402: Equipment, Materials and Costs
- Location with a commercial kitchen and public restrooms or a food truck
- Connections with local farmers and sustainable food suppliers
- Budget $175,000 to $700,000 and from six months to 2 years to open a new restaurant

Serving Food 402: Steps
1. Define your sustainable food philosophy
   - Identify which aspects of food sustainability matter most to you
   - Decide on your non-negotiable standards (organic, local, etc.)
   - Create a mission statement that communicates your values
2. Develop your ingredient sourcing strategy

- Create standards for your ingredients
- Research seasonal availability of fresh ingredients
- Compile a database of sustainable suppliers with contact information
- Investigate food hubs and farmer cooperatives in your region
- Visit local farms within your defined radius to establish relationships and verify practices
- Determine which third-party certifications you'll require
- Develop a questionnaire for potential suppliers
- Communicate sourcing strategy to customers
3. Design a seasonally adaptive menu
    - Build a core menu framework that accommodates seasonal changes
    - Create versatile, adaptable signature dishes
    - Design menu descriptions that highlight sustainability features
4. Implement whole-ingredient utilization strategies
    - Design dishes that use multiple parts of the same ingredient
    - Create secondary products from trimmings and byproducts
    - Develop preservation techniques for surplus seasonal ingredients
    - Train staff in creative whole-ingredient cooking
5. Build your brand
    - Develop educational materials about your sourcing practices
    - Train staff to communicate ingredient stories and sustainability practices
    - Create visual displays showing farm partnerships and ingredient sources
    - Establish a regular schedule for menu updates based on seasonality
    - Consider obtaining relevant sustainability certifications for your restaurant
6. Continuously evaluate and improve
    - Establish metrics to measure your environmental impact
    - Regularly review supplier practices and certifications
    - Collect customer feedback on sustainable menu items
    - Stay informed about emerging sustainable food trends and research
    - Join restaurant sustainability networks to share best practices

Serving Food 402: Definitions

- **Farm-to-table**: Restaurant philosophy emphasizing short supply chains and direct relationships with local producers
- **Food hubs**: Organizations that aggregate and distribute food from multiple local farms
- **Plant-forward**: Emphasizes plant ingredients without necessarily being vegetarian or vegan
- **Regenerative agriculture**: Farming practices that restore soil health and sequester carbon
- **Seasonal eating**: Consumption patterns aligned with local growing seasons
- **Whole-ingredient utilization**: Using all edible parts of ingredients to minimize waste

Serving Food 402: Troubleshooting

Problem	Solutions
Higher costs of sustainable ingredients	Include less expensive sustainable ingredients (legumes, grains). Use premium ingredients as accents rather than main components. Position your restaurant as an elegant dining experience.
Inconsistent supply of local ingredients	Develop flexible menu items that can accommodate substitutions. Build relationships with multiple producers. Preserve seasonal abundance through fermenting, canning, freezing, or drying. Create a core menu of reliable items supplemented by specials.

Problem	Solutions
Staff lacks knowledge about eco-friendly practices	Implement regular staff training about ingredient sources and sustainability practices. Schedule farm visits for key team members. Create reference materials with ingredient details and talking points.
Customers resistant to higher prices	Enhance your menu descriptions and décor. Improve staff training. Offer affordable menu options alongside premium items.
Seasonal limitations in harsh climates	Develop preservation techniques for extending seasonal ingredients. Build relationships with greenhouse growers. Supplement local products with imports during off-seasons.
Suppliers making unverified eco-claims	Conduct site visits to verify practices. Request specific certifications. Ask detailed questions about production methods. Create a supplier questionnaire to standardize evaluation.
Balancing sustainability with customer expectations	Start with familiar dishes made with better ingredients. Offer both traditional and more adventurous sustainable choices. Use detailed menu descriptions that highlight the quality and story behind ingredients.

Serving Food 402: Limitations

- Availability of sustainable ingredients varies greatly by geographic location and season
- Higher ingredient costs require higher menu prices or creative menu engineering
- Small-scale sustainable farms may struggle with consistent volume and delivery requirements
- Consumer education remains an ongoing challenge requiring constant reinforcement
- Demand for plant-based restaurant meals may not be sufficient to keep you in business

References and resources: <www.suspra.com/practice/food/serving-402.html>

Substituting 101: Replacing Mammal Milk

Drink water, fruit juice, or plant-based milk instead of mammal milk

Instead of cow, goat, or other mammal milks, drink water, fruit juice, or plant-based milks like almond, soy, oat, or rice milk. Plain water is the most sustainable choice for hydration, but plant-based milks generally require fewer resources and emit less pollution than animal dairy production.

References and resources: <www.suspra.com/practice/food/substituting-101.html>

Substituting 201: Eating Plant-Based Ice Cream

Eat plant-based ice cream instead of mammal milk ice cream

Explore the delicious world of plant-based ice creams. Made from bases like coconut, almond, soy, oat, or cashew milk, these frozen desserts offer a creamy alternative to animal dairy products. Chocolate flavors tend to mask the underlying plant taste better than vanilla, helping to make this practice work for those accustomed to the taste of cow milk ice cream.

References and resources: <www.suspra.com/practice/food/substituting-201.html>

Substituting 202: Eating Plant-Based Cheese

Eat plant-based cheese instead of mammal milk cheese

Swap out cheese made from mammal milk (cow, goat, etc.) for plant-based cheese in your meals and snacks. Plant-based cheeses are now widely available in most grocery stores, crafted from ingredients like cashews, soy, almonds, and even root vegetables. Experiment with different types–from slices and shreds for sandwiches and pizzas to creamy blocks for cheese boards–to discover your preferred substitutes.

References and resources: <www.suspra.com/practice/food/substituting-202.html>

Substituting 301: Eating Plant-Based Dairy

Substitute plant-based ingredients for all mammal-milk dairy products

Replace all mammal-milk dairy–such as milk, cheese, yogurt, butter, and ice cream–with options derived from plants like soy, almonds, oats, coconuts, and cashews. Experiment with different plant-based milks in your coffee and cereal, try vegan cheeses on pizzas and sandwiches, explore coconut yogurt for breakfast, and discover plant-based butters for baking and cooking.

References and resources: <www.suspra.com/practice/food/substituting-301.html>

Substituting 302: Eliminating Meat

Get all your protein and fat from other sources besides meat

Incorporate legumes like lentils, beans, and chickpeas into your meals–they are packed with protein and fiber. Tofu and tempeh, made from soybeans, can be seasoned to mimic meat in many dishes. Nuts and seeds provide healthy fats and protein. Explore plant-based meat alternatives, to ease the transition.

References and resources: <www.suspra.com/practice/food/substituting-302.html>

Cultivating Healthy Harvests

Buying Food 104: Buying USDA Organic

Buy food certified to USDA organic standards

Buying food certified to the United States Department of Agriculture (USDA) organic standards means choosing products that are produced using methods that promote ecological balance and conserve biodiversity. For crops, this means no synthetic fertilizers, pesticides, or herbicides are used. For livestock, it means animals are raised in living conditions accommodating their natural behaviors (like grazing on pasture) and fed organic feed. Look for the USDA organic seal on food packaging to ensure your choices meet these standards.

References and resources: <www.suspra.com/practice/food/buying-104.html>

Buying Food 105: Buying Sustainable Palm Oil

Buy palm oil certified by the Roundtable on Sustainable Palm Oil

When you shop for products containing palm oil, look for certification by the Roundtable on Sustainable Palm Oil (RSPO). Palm oil is a common ingredient in many foods, cosmetics, and household goods. Conventional palm oil production is linked to deforestation, habitat loss for endangered species like orangutans, and social issues. RSPO-certified palm oil has been produced according to a set of environmental and social criteria, aiming to minimize the negative impacts of palm oil production. Look for the RSPO trademark on packaging.

References and resources: <www.suspra.com/practice/food/buying-105.html>

Buying Food 106: Buying Chocolate

Buy chocolate that scores "green" on the Chocolate Scorecard

The Chocolate Scorecard evaluates chocolate brands based on criteria like child labor, deforestation, and climate impact, assigning color-coded scores ranging from red (worst) to green (best). By selecting "green" rated chocolate, you support companies committed to ethical sourcing, fair labor practices, and environmentally sound cocoa production.

References and resources: <www.suspra.com/practice/food/buying-106.html>

Buying Food 107: Buying Coffee

Buy coffee that meets Rainforest Alliance standards

The Rainforest Alliance is an international non-profit organization working to conserve biodiversity and promote the rights and well-being of workers, their families and communities. Coffee bearing the Rainforest Alliance Certified seal has been produced using environmentally and socially responsible methods. By purchasing Rainforest Alliance certified coffee, you are directly contributing to a more sustainable coffee industry.

References and resources: <www.suspra.com/practice/food/buying-107.html>

Buying Food 203: Supporting Organic Farmers

Buy from local farmers who practice regenerative methods

Regenerative agriculture focuses on building soil health, increasing biodiversity, improving water cycles, and sequestering carbon. Buy food directly from farmers who practice regenerative agriculture to enable them to compete with farmers who do not.

Buying Food 203: Equipment & Materials
- Section featuring local farmers in a conventional grocery store, farmers market, farmstand, or community supported agriculture subscription

Buying Food 203: Steps
1. Find regenerative farmers in your area:
    - Search for farmers markets, CSA programs, and farm stands
    - Look for farms labeled "regenerative," "beyond organic," or "biodynamic"
    - Ask vendors about their soil-building practices and pest management
    - Check for signs of certification like Regenerative Organic Certified
2. Ask key questions to identify regenerative practices:
    - "How do you build soil health?"
    - "What cover crops do you use?"
    - "How do you manage pests without synthetic chemicals?"
    - "How do you rotate crops and livestock?"
    - "What water conservation methods do you use?"
3. Join a CSA (Community Supported Agriculture):
    - Pay upfront for a season of produce
    - Pick up weekly share of harvested items
    - Be prepared to try new vegetables and adapt meal plans
4. Shop at farmers markets:
    - Bring your own bags and small bills
    - Shop early for best selection or late for possible discounts
    - Buy in bulk during peak season for preservation
5. Visit farms that offer direct sales:
    - Call ahead to confirm hours and availability
    - Respect farm boundaries and follow biosecurity measures
    - Pick-your-own can offer lower prices for seasonal items

| Sustainable Practices Handbook | Food Practices: Cultivating Healthy Harvests |

6. Develop relationships with farmers:
   - Ask about their challenges and successes
   - Provide feedback on products
   - Consistently support the same farms when possible

Buying Food 203: Definitions

- **CSA (Community Supported Agriculture)**: Subscription model where consumers buy shares of a farm's harvest in advance
- **Regenerative agriculture**: Farming practices that restore soil health and biodiversity while producing food
- **Cover crops**: Plants grown to protect and improve soil between production periods
- **Food hub**: Regional center that aggregates, distributes, and markets food from local producers
- **SNAP/EBT**: Supplemental Nutrition Assistance Program/Electronic Benefits Transfer; government food assistance some farmers markets accept

Buying Food 203: Troubleshooting

Problem	Solutions
Can't find regenerative farms locally	Look for "sustainable," "conservation," or "organic" farms that also focus on soil health. Join online local food groups to find recommendations. Check with extension offices.
Limited seasonal selection	Embrace seasonal cooking. Learn food preservation methods. Supplement with grocery store items as needed.
Higher prices than conventional	Buy "seconds" (imperfect produce) when available. Purchase in bulk during peak season. Join work-trade programs if farms offer them.
Inconvenient pickup locations/times	Coordinate pickups with neighbors. Ask about alternative arrangements. Look for multiple outlets where farmers sell their products.
Unfamiliar vegetables in CSA	Ask farmers for recipes. Use online resources to identify and cook with unfamiliar items. Swap with other CSA members.

Buying Food 203: Limitations

- Availability varies by region and season
- May require more time for shopping and food preparation
- Can cost more than conventional grocery store options
- Limited options during winter in cold climates
- May require adjusting meals based on what's available

References and resources: <www.suspra.com/practice/food/buying-203.html>

Growing Food 101: Sprouting Seeds

Sprout seeds

Sprouting is one of the simplest ways to grow fresh, nutrient-dense food at home. This practice requires minimal space, equipment, and time, making it ideal for beginners, apartment dwellers, or those without garden space. Different seeds offer unique flavors, textures, and nutritional benefits:

- **Alfalfa sprouts** provide a mild, slightly nutty flavor and crisp texture. They're rich in vitamins A, C, and K, as well as folate and various minerals.
- **Broccoli sprouts** have a high concentration of sulforaphane, a compound with potential health benefits. They have a mild, slightly spicy flavor similar to radish.
- **Mung bean sprouts**, commonly used in Asian cuisine, offer a crisp, bean-like flavor and are excellent sources of protein, fiber, and vitamins.
- **Lentil sprouts** are earthy, nutty, and slightly sweet, providing protein, iron, and folate.
- **Radish sprouts** add a spicy kick to dishes and contain beneficial antioxidants.

Create the ideal conditions for germination—moisture, air, and appropriate temperature—while regularly rinsing to prevent mold and bacterial growth. Each rinse supplies fresh water and oxygen while removing potential pathogens and metabolic waste products from the developing sprouts. Experiment with different varieties, sprouting methods, and culinary uses for your homegrown sprouts.

Proper hygiene is crucial for safe sprouting. Start with clean equipment and seeds labeled for sprouting. Rinse and thoroughly drain to prevent the conditions that could allow harmful bacteria to multiply. Keeping sprouts between 65-75°F also supports healthy sprouting while discouraging pathogen growth.

Growing Food 101: Equipment & Materials
- Seeds for sprouting (organic, untreated, specifically labeled for sprouting)
- Glass jar (quart or half-gallon size)
- Sprouting lid or fine mesh screen with rubber band
- Measuring spoons
- Clean water
- Colander or strainer
- Small bowl or dish rack for draining
- Clean kitchen towel
- *Optional: Dedicated sprouting kit or tray system, food-grade hydrogen peroxide (3%) for sanitizing seeds, small spray bottle for rinsing*

Growing Food 101: Steps
1. Select appropriate seeds
   - Choose fresh seeds specifically labeled for sprouting
   - Popular beginner options include alfalfa, broccoli, mung beans, lentils, and radish
2. Measure seeds
   - Start with 1-2 tablespoons of small seeds (alfalfa, broccoli, radish)
   - For larger seeds (mung beans, lentils, chickpeas), use 1/4 cup
   - Note that seeds expand 5-10 times their dry volume when sprouted
3. Clean jar and equipment
   - Wash glass jar and sprouting lid with hot, soapy water
   - Rinse thoroughly to remove any soap residue
   - *Optional: Boil jar for 10 minutes or run through dishwasher*
4. Prepare seeds for sprouting
   - Inspect seeds and remove any debris or damaged seeds
   - *Optional: Sanitize seeds by soaking in a solution of 3% food-grade hydrogen peroxide and water (1:1 ratio) for 5 minutes, then rinse thoroughly*
5. Soak seeds
   - Place measured seeds in your jar
   - Fill jar 3/4 full with cool, clean water
   - Secure sprouting lid or mesh screen (with screw band or rubber band)
   - Let seeds soak according to type:
     - Small seeds (alfalfa, broccoli, radish): 4-8 hours

- Medium seeds (clover, mustard): 6-8 hours
- Large seeds (mung beans, lentils, chickpeas): 8-12 hours
  - After initial soaking, drain water completely through sprouting lid
  - Rinse seeds again with more cool water, swirling to ensure all seeds are rinsed
  - Drain rinse water thoroughly
6. Continue to rinse seeds
   - Rinse seeds twice a day (morning and evening)
   - Use cool water and drain thoroughly after each rinse
   - Maintain regular rinsing schedule until sprouts appear, depending on seed type:
     - Alfalfa: 4-6 days
     - Broccoli: 3-5 days
     - Radish: 3-5 days
     - Mung beans: 2-4 days
     - Lentils: 2-3 days
     - Chickpeas: 2-3 days
   - Seeds are ready when they have sprouted tails about 1/4" to 2" long (varies by type)
   - Some sprouts (alfalfa, broccoli) benefit from a few hours of indirect sunlight on the final day to develop chlorophyll
7. Harvest sprouts
   - *Optional: Gently spread sprouts on a clean kitchen towel to remove additional moisture*
   - Transfer to a clean container with lid for storage
8. Store properly
   - Keep sprouts refrigerated in a container that allows some airflow
   - Consume within one week for optimal freshness and nutrition
   - Continue to rinse and drain every day or two while storing to maintain freshness

Growing Food 101: Definitions

- **Chlorophyll**: The green pigment in plants that allows them to convert sunlight into energy
- **Germination**: The process of a seed beginning to grow and develop into a plant
- **Hypocotyl**: The stem portion of a sprouting seed
- **Mucilage**: A gelatinous substance some seeds produce when soaked (especially common with chia and flax)
- **Pathogen**: Microorganisms like bacteria or fungi that can cause disease
- **Sprouting lid**: A specialized lid for jars that allows water drainage while containing seeds
- **Sulforaphane**: A beneficial compound found in high concentration in broccoli sprouts

Growing Food 101: Troubleshooting

Problem	Solutions
Seeds not sprouting	Verify seed freshness and quality. Ensure seeds are meant for sprouting. Check water quality (chlorinated water can inhibit sprouting). Verify that the temperature is not below 65° F.
Mold or unpleasant smell	Increase rinsing frequency to 3-4 times daily. Ensure thorough draining after each rinse. Improve air circulation around sprouts. Reduce humidity in the sprouting area. Discard the batch if mold is visible or smell is foul.
Sprouts turning brown	Increase rinsing frequency. Move to a cooler location.
Slow growth	Check temperature (too cold slows growth). Verify seed quality. Some seeds simply take longer than others to sprout.

Problem	Solutions
Seeds clumping together	Use fewer seeds next time. Rinse more gently to avoid matting. Break up clumps gently during rinsing.
Hulls not separating from sprouts	For seeds with persistent hulls, try filling the jar with water after sprouts are mature, agitate gently, and remove hulls that float to top. Or place sprouts in a bowl of water and gently stir; hulls will float to the surface.
Sprouts spoil quickly	Ensure sprouts are thoroughly drained before refrigerating. Dry sprouts before refrigerating. Store in a container that allows some airflow. Rinse every 1-2 days while storing. Keep refrigerated at all times.
Sprouts taste bitter	Harvest earlier or rinse more frequently. Some varieties naturally have stronger flavors that mellow with a final rinse before serving.

Growing Food 101: Limitations
- Risk of foodborne illness if proper hygiene practices aren't followed
- Not all seeds are suitable for sprouting
- Some common garden seeds are treated with chemicals not safe for consumption
- Some individuals are advised to avoid raw sprouts due to pathogen risk
- Limited growing space in jar systems can result in dense, tangled sprouts
- Regular attention is required (2-3 times daily) to maintain proper moisture and prevent spoilage
- Some seeds like chia and flax form a gel-like mucilage when wet, making them difficult to sprout in jar systems
- Seasonal temperature variations can affect sprouting times and success rates

References and resources: <www.suspra.com/practice/food/growing-101.html>

Growing Food 201: Growing Microgreens

Grow microgreens

Microgreens are young vegetable greens harvested just after the first true leaves have developed, typically 1-3 inches tall, renowned for their concentrated nutrients and intense flavors. They differ from sprouts (germinated seeds eaten whole, including roots) and baby greens (slightly older than microgreens with more developed leaves).

Microgreens grow quickly (1-3 weeks), require minimal space, are ideal for urban dwellers with limited gardening space, and make an excellent entry point for beginning gardeners. Their short growth cycle means rapid feedback and learning opportunities, while requiring minimal investment. Nearly any edible plant can be grown as a microgreen, but some varieties perform better than others.

- **Mild flavors**: Sunflower, peas, broccoli, kale, cabbage
- **Spicy/peppery options**: Radish, arugula, mustard
- **Herbal varieties**: Basil, cilantro, dill
- **Colorful selections**: Red amaranth, purple kohlrabi, red cabbage

Each variety has specific growing requirements and flavor profiles. Start with fast-growing, resilient varieties like broccoli, radish, or sunflower before experimenting with more delicate herbs. Common challenges in microgreen cultivation are mold and damping-off disease, typically resulting from overwatering, poor air circulation, or contaminated seeds. Reduce these risks by bottom watering and providing good ventilation; a small fan is particularly helpful in humid environments. Microgreens can

Sustainable Practices Handbook   **Food Practices: Cultivating Healthy Harvests**

be grown hydroponically in growing mats, but soil-based growing is most common for home growers. Consider coconut coir as a growing medium—it's more sustainable than peat.

Growing Food 201: Equipment & Materials
- Seeds specifically labeled for microgreens (or organic vegetable/herb seeds)
- Growing medium (potting soil, coconut coir, or soilless mix)
- Shallow trays or containers (1-2 inches deep) with drainage holes
- Spray bottle
- Scissors or sharp knife for harvesting
- *Optional: Hydrogen peroxide for sanitizing, clear plastic wrap or humidity dome, small fan for air circulation, grow lights, small scale for weighing yield, seed soaking container, pH testing strips, thermometer*

Growing Food 201: Steps
1. Select your growing containers
   - Choose shallow trays with drainage holes
   - Clean containers thoroughly with mild soap and water
   - If repurposing containers, poke several small drainage holes in the bottom
2. Prepare your growing medium
   - Fill containers with 1-1.5 inches of moistened growing medium
   - Level the surface while keeping it loose, not compacted
   - Pre-moisten soil by mixing with water until it feels like a wrung-out sponge
3. Measure and prepare your seeds
   - Calculate seed quantity (typically 1-2 tablespoons per 10" x 10" tray, depending on seed type)
   - *Optional: Soak larger seeds (sunflower, peas, beans) for 8-12 hours to speed germination*
   - *Optional: Sanitize seeds with food-grade hydrogen peroxide solution to prevent mold*
4. Sow the seeds
   - Sprinkle seeds evenly across the growing medium surface
     - Small seeds: approximately 10-12 seeds per square inch
     - Larger seeds: 4-6 seeds per square inch
   - Aim for seeds to be close but not piled on top of each other
5. Cover the seeds
   - For most varieties, cover with a thin layer (⅛ inch) of growing medium
   - For seeds that don't need covering, gently press them into contact with the growing medium
   - Mist the surface with water using a spray bottle
6. Create a germination environment
   - *Optional: Cover with clear plastic wrap or humidity dome to retain moisture*
   - For seeds that benefit from a "blackout period," cover the tray to block light
   - Place in a location with suitable germination temperature, between 65-75°F (18-24°C)
7. Water during germination phase
   - Keep growing medium consistently moist but not soggy
     - Bottom water: Place growing tray in a pan of water for 10 minutes, then remove
     - Top water: Use a spray bottle or small watering can with a gentle stream
8. Expose to light
   - When most seeds have sprouted, expose growing tray to light
     - Place in a location with bright, indirect natural light
     - Or position a grow light 4-6 inches above plants for 12-16 hours daily
9. Care for growing microgreens
   - Water daily, preferably from the bottom
   - Ensure good air circulation to prevent mold (use a small fan if needed)
   - Rotate trays if growing near a window to prevent leaning
10. Harvest at optimal time

Revision: 25.1.8

- Harvest when first true leaves appear after cotyledons (seed leaves)
- Don't water them six hours before you harvest, to reduce risk of mold
- Use clean, sharp scissors to cut just above the soil line
11. Store properly
    - Refrigerate unwashed microgreens on a dry paper towel in an airtight container
    - Wash just before using
    - Most varieties will keep for 5-7 days when stored properly
12. Begin next crop
    - Start new trays every week for continuous harvest
    - Compost used growing medium or allow it to rest for three weeks before reusing

Growing Food 201: Definitions

- **Bottom watering**: Watering plants by placing the growing tray in a shallow pan of water and allowing the growing medium to absorb moisture from below.
- **Coconut coir**: A growing medium made from the fibrous material found between the hard, internal shell and outer coat of a coconut, used as a sustainable alternative to peat.
- **Cotyledons**: The first leaves to appear after germination, often called "seed leaves." These emerge from the seed itself and don't resemble the plant's true leaves.
- **Damping-off**: A disease caused by fungi that causes seedlings to collapse at the soil line.
- **Growing medium**: The substrate in which plants grow, providing physical support, water retention, and sometimes nutrients.
- **Microgreens**: Young vegetable greens harvested just after cotyledon development, typically when they are 1-3 inches tall and have produced their first true leaves.
- **True leaves**: The second set of leaves to develop after the cotyledons. "True leaves" display the characteristic appearance of the mature plant.

Growing Food 201: Troubleshooting

Problem	Solutions
Seeds not germinating	Check seed quality and expiration date. Ensure growing medium is moist but not waterlogged. Verify temperature is between 65-75°F (18-24°C). Some varieties may need pre-soaking.
Mold growth	Reduce watering frequency. Improve air circulation with a small fan. Ensure proper spacing between seeds. Try bottom watering instead of top watering. Wash seeds with hydrogen peroxide before planting.
Leggy, stretched seedlings	Increase light intensity or move closer to light source. Ensure 12-16 hours of light daily. Rotate trays to prevent leaning toward light sources.
Yellowing leaves	Likely ready to harvest—don't wait too long. If premature, check for overwatering or nutrient deficiency in the growing medium.
Microgreens falling over	Likely ready to harvest. If premature, check for overwatering or insufficient light causing weak stems.
Slow growth	Check temperature (too cold slows growth). Verify adequate light. Some varieties naturally grow slower than others.
Uneven germination	Ensure even seed distribution when sowing. Check for consistent moisture across the tray. Pre-soak larger seeds for more uniform germination.

Revision: 25.1.8

Problem	Solutions
Root rot	Reduce watering frequency. Ensure containers have adequate drainage. Allow the soil surface to dry slightly between waterings.

Growing Food 201: Limitations

- Yields smaller quantities of food compared to full-sized vegetable gardens
- Requires continuous replanting for steady harvests
- Some varieties can be expensive if using specialized microgreen seeds
- Delicate nature means they must be used quickly after harvest
- Not all vegetables perform well as microgreens
- Growing medium must be replaced or regenerated between crops
- Regular attention needed for watering, especially in warm or dry environments
- Limited caloric value despite high nutrient density

References and resources: <www.suspra.com/practice/food/growing-201.html>

Growing Food 202: Growing Herbs

Grow a windowsill herb garden

Grow culinary herbs, either annuals (completing their lifecycle in one season) or perennials (returning year after year). Annual herbs like basil, cilantro, and dill tend to grow and die quickly, requiring reseeding to provide a continual supply. Perennial herbs like rosemary, thyme, mint, and oregano grow more slowly but a single plant can provide harvests for years with proper care. Mediterranean herbs like rosemary, thyme, oregano, and sage prefer drier conditions and more sun, while soft herbs like basil, cilantro, and parsley typically need more consistent moisture and may tolerate a bit less light.

The key to success with a windowsill herb garden is observation. Daily attention allows you to catch potential problems early and develop an intuitive understanding of each plant's needs. This close relationship with your plants builds essential skills that transfer to larger growing projects and deepens your connection to the food you consume.

Growing Food 202: Equipment & Materials

- Window with 4-6 hours of daily sunlight (or grow light system)
- Herb seeds or starter plants
- Potting soil
- Containers with drainage holes (4-6 inches deep)
  - Recycled containers (yogurt cups, food containers)
  - Terracotta pots
  - Plastic nursery pots
- Saucers or trays to catch water
- Small watering can or spray bottle
- *Optional: Organic fertilizer (diluted fish emulsion, compost tea, or seaweed extract), scissors or pruning shears, plant markers or labels, small trowel, pebbles or broken pottery pieces for drainage*

Growing Food 202: Steps

1. Select your herbs based on growing conditions
   - For sunny windows (6+ hours direct sun): basil, rosemary, thyme, sage, oregano
   - For partial sun windows (4-6 hours): mint, parsley, chives, cilantro, dill

- For low light windows (less than 4 hours): mint, parsley, chives
- Start with 3-5 varieties to avoid overcrowding
2. Prepare your containers
    - Clean containers thoroughly if reusing
    - Ensure each container has drainage holes (drill or puncture if needed)
    - Place a layer of pebbles or broken pottery at the bottom for improved drainage
    - Position saucers under each container to catch excess water
3. Fill containers with potting soil
    - Use organic potting soil specifically formulated for containers
    - Fill containers to about 1/2 inch below the rim
    - Lightly tamp down soil but don't compact it heavily
4. Plant your herbs
    - For seed starting:
        - Follow seed packet instructions for planting depth (generally 1/4 inch deep)
        - Sow seeds more densely than recommended, then thin seedlings later
        - Mist the soil surface gently to avoid displacing seeds
    - For starter plants:
        - Dig a hole slightly larger than the root ball
        - Gently remove plant from nursery container
        - Place in hole and fill in around roots, firming soil gently
        - Water thoroughly after planting
5. Position your herb garden
    - Place containers in your sunniest window
    - Rotate containers every few days for even growth
    - Keep herbs away from cold drafts and heat sources
    - Group plants with similar water needs together
6. Water properly
    - Test moisture by inserting finger 1 inch into soil - water when it feels dry
    - Water at soil level, avoiding wetting leaves
    - Allow water to drain completely, emptying saucers after 30 minutes
    - Water in the morning to allow any wet leaves to dry during the day
7. Care for your herbs
    - Observe plants daily for signs of stress, pests, or disease
    - Rotate containers for even growth
    - Pinch growing tips regularly to encourage bushier growth
    - Remove any yellowing or damaged leaves promptly
8. Harvest sustainably
    - Wait until plants are 6-8 inches tall before first harvest
    - Cut no more than 1/3 of the plant at one time
    - Harvest in the morning when essential oil content is highest
    - Use sharp scissors to make clean cuts
    - Harvest outer leaves first, allowing inner growth to continue
9. Maintain for longevity
    - Feed monthly with diluted organic fertilizer during growing season
    - Repot when roots become visible through drainage holes
    - Prune regularly to prevent flowering (except when collecting seeds)
    - Replace fast-growing annual herbs (basil, cilantro, dill) as needed

Growing Food 202: Definitions

- **Annual**: Plants that germinate, grow, and produce seeds in one growing season
- **Bolting**: When herbs rapidly produce flowers and seeds, often caused by heat or stress, usually making leaves less flavorful

- **Drainage**: The ability of water to flow through soil and out of a container, preventing root rot
- **Neem oil**: A naturally occurring pesticide found in seeds from the neem tree
- **Perennial**: Plants that live for multiple years, such as rosemary, thyme, mint, and oregano
- **Pinching**: Removing the growing tips to encourage bushier growth and prevent flowering
- **Potting soil**: Specialized growing medium formulated for container plants

Growing Food 202: Troubleshooting

Problem	Solutions
Leggy, sparse growth	Increase light exposure. Rotate plants regularly. Pinch tips to encourage branching. Move to a sunnier window or add supplemental lighting.
Yellowing leaves	Check watering: could indicate over or under-watering. Ensure proper drainage. Check for pests under leaves. Add fertilizer.
Wilting despite moist soil	Inspect roots. Remove from the pot, trim damaged roots, and repot in fresh soil. Ensure container drains properly.
Herbs flowering too quickly	Harvest more frequently. Pinch flower buds as they appear. Check that the temperature isn't too warm. Replace plants if they're determined to flower.
Pest infestations	Isolate affected plants. Spray with a mild soap solution (1 teaspoon liquid soap to 1 quart water). Wipe leaves with damp cloth. Apply neem oil.
White crust on soil or pot	Mineral buildup from tap water or fertilizer. Scrape off surface crust. Switch to rainwater or filtered water. Reduce fertilizer concentration.
Mold on soil surface	Reduce watering frequency. Improve air circulation. Remove the affected soil layer and replace. Water in the morning so the soil surface dries daily.
Herbs not very flavorful	Increase light exposure. Reduce watering (slight stress can increase flavor). Harvest at optimal time (morning). Check that you're not overfertilizing.

Growing Food 202: Limitations

- Window space limits the number and size of herbs you can grow
- Indoor light conditions may not be sufficient for all herbs, especially in winter
- Some herbs (dill, cilantro, etc.) are challenging to maintain indoors long-term
- Limited root space in containers can restrict growth and longevity
- Herbs with extensive root systems (mint, lemongrass) quickly outgrow windowsill containers
- Disease and pest problems can spread quickly between closely spaced plants
- Herbs require regular attention; not suitable for frequent travelers without a care system

References and resources: <www.suspra.com/practice/food/growing-202.html>

Growing Food 203: Growing Fruits and Nuts

Plant and tend fruit bushes or vines, and fruit or nut trees

Grow your own fruits and nuts to establish perennial food systems that can produce for decades. The key to success with fruits and nuts is proper site selection and preparation. Most fruit plants require full sun (at least 6-8 hours daily) and well-drained soil. Consider the mature size of trees and shrubs when planning—a standard apple tree grows about 25 feet tall and wide, while dwarf varieties might get only to 10 feet. Select plants that are well-adapted to your climate zone. Cooperative extension offices and nurseries can recommend varieties suited to your region's chill hours, disease resistance needs, and soil conditions. Native fruits often require less maintenance and are better adapted to local conditions.

Build healthy soil through regular additions of organic matter and maintaining biodiversity in and around your fruit garden. Create habitat for beneficial insects, birds, and other wildlife to maintain a balanced ecosystem that naturally controls many pest problems.

Start with easier fruits like strawberries, raspberries, or blueberries before tackling more demanding tree fruits. Bushes and vines typically produce more quickly than trees—you might wait five years for significant tree fruit harvests, while berries may produce in their first year. Some plants can pollinate themselves, while others require a second compatible pollinator variety planted nearby.

Each year, you'll learn more about your plants' specific needs and behavior. Take notes on flowering times, harvest periods, yield, and pests. Use this information to improve your yields.

Growing Food 203: Equipment & Materials
- Bushes, vines, or trees appropriate for your climate
- Sunny location to plant (if growing new plants)
- Shovel, spade, or garden fork
- Water source (hose, watering can, or irrigation system)
- Pruning shears and loppers
- Garden gloves
- Compost or aged manure
- Mulch (wood chips, straw, or leaf litter)
- Stakes, trellis, or support system (for vines and young trees)
- Garden twine or plant ties
- *Optional: Organic fertilizer specific to fruit and nut plants*
- *pH testing kit*
- *Wheelbarrow or garden cart*
- *Drip irrigation supplies*
- *Protective netting or row cover (for bird and pest protection)*
- *Soil amendments based on soil test results*

Growing Food 203: Steps
1. Plan your fruit and nut garden (3-6 months before planting)
   - Assess your growing zone and climate conditions
   - Choose fruit and nut varieties that thrive in your region
   - Select planting sites with appropriate sun exposure (minimum 6-8 hours for most fruits)
   - Test soil pH and amend as needed (most fruits prefer 6.0-7.0 pH)
   - Plan for pollination needs (many fruit trees require cross-pollination)
   - Map locations, allowing adequate spacing between plants at maturity
   - Buy plants from reputable nurseries
   - Put down cardboard to kill grass and weeds in area where you will be planting
2. Prepare planting sites (1-2 weeks before planting)
   - Mark planting locations according to spacing requirements
   - For trees: dig holes 2-3 times wider than root balls and as deep as root height
   - For bushes: dig holes twice as wide as root balls and as deep as root height
   - For vines: prepare trellises or support structures
   - Add compost to planting holes (roughly 25% compost to 75% native soil)
   - If soil is heavy clay, add additional organic matter to improve drainage
3. Plant your fruit and nut varieties (during late fall, winter, or early spring when possible)

- Sustainable Practices Handbook — Food Practices: Cultivating Healthy Harvests

  - Water plants thoroughly before removing from containers
  - Gently remove plants from containers, taking care to minimize damage to roots
  - For bare-root plants, soak roots in water for an hour before planting
  - Place plant in hole at proper depth (crown of roots should be at soil level)
  - Backfill with soil/compost mixture, pressing firmly around roots to remove air pockets
  - Create a watering basin around each plant, so water doesn't run off but soaks in
  - Water deeply immediately after planting
  - Apply three inches of mulch around base, keeping it three inches away from trunks/stems
4. Provide initial care (first 6 months)
    - Water consistently and deeply, especially during establishment
    - Install stakes or supports for young trees and vines to keep them upright despite wind
    - Prune at planting time only to remove damaged branches
    - Remove any fruit that forms in first year to encourage root establishment
    - Protect young plants from animal damage with guards or fencing
    - Monitor for pests and diseases weekly
5. Establish a maintenance routine
    - Water (ongoing)
        - Provide deep, infrequent watering rather than frequent shallow watering
        - Adjust watering based on season, rainfall, and plant maturity
        - Install drip irrigation for efficient watering (optional)
    - Prune (ongoing)
        - Learn specific pruning requirements for each plant
        - Remove dead, diseased, or crossing branches
        - Thin fruiting branches to improve air circulation and fruit quality
        - Train vines regularly to support systems
    - Fertilize (annually)
        - Apply compost around drip line annually in spring
        - Use specific organic fertilizers based on plant needs
        - Avoid fertilizing in late summer or fall to prevent tender new growth before winter
    - Manage pests and diseases (as needed)
        - Inspect plants regularly for signs of problems
        - Identify issues early and treat with least-toxic methods first
        - Consider row covers or netting to prevent bird damage to fruit
    - Harvest fruits or nuts annually

Growing Food 203: Definitions

- **Bare-root**: Plants sold without soil around their roots, available during dormant seasons
- **Chill hours**: The number of hours below 45°F (7°C) that certain fruit trees require during winter to break dormancy and produce fruit properly
- **Cross-pollination**: Transfer of pollen between different varieties of the same species, required by many fruit trees to produce fruit
- **Drip line**: The outer edge of a tree's branch spread, where water drips to the ground, and where most feeder roots are found
- **Pollinate:** Deposit pollen so that fertilization occurs, and fruits or nuts can develop
- **Root stock**: The root portion of a grafted tree that determines characteristics like size, disease resistance, and hardiness
- **Self-fertile**: Plants able to pollinate themselves without requiring another variety nearby
- **Scion**: The upper portion of a grafted tree that determines the fruit variety

Growing Food 203: Troubleshooting

Problem	Solutions
Plants fail to establish after planting	Check watering frequency (too much or too little). Ensure planting depth is correct (not too deep). Protect from harsh sun or wind during establishment. Verify plants are appropriate for your climate zone.
Trees or bushes don't produce fruit	Verify pollination requirements; add a second pollinizer plant if needed. Wait until plants are old enough to bear fruit. Ensure plants receive adequate sunlight. Confirm plants have received sufficient chill hours. Avoid over-fertilizing with nitrogen.
Fruit drops before ripening	Look for insect pests. Thin fruit early in the season to prevent overbearing. Ensure consistent watering, especially during fruit development. Check for nutrient deficiencies with a soil test.
Diseases on leaves or fruit	Improve air circulation through proper pruning. Remove fallen leaves and fruit that may harbor disease. Apply organic fungicides preventatively for known regional problems. Plant disease-resistant varieties in the future.
Animal damage to plants	Install tree guards around trunks to prevent rodent damage. Use fencing to keep out deer and larger animals. Use netting to deter birds.
Poor fruit quality or size	Thin fruit properly to improve remaining fruit size and quality. Ensure adequate nutrients with compost or fertilizer. Water consistently as fruit develops. Verify varieties are well-suited to your growing conditions.
Winter damage to trees	Plant varieties appropriate for your hardiness zone. Avoid fertilizing late in the growing season. Protect young trees with wraps or guards for the first few winters. Gradually acclimate plants in fall by reducing water slightly.

Growing Food 203: Limitations

- Fruit and nut plants require several years to mature and produce significant harvests
- Many fruits and nuts require substantial space, especially at mature size
- Specific pollination requirements can complicate planning and plant selection
- Climate limitations restrict which varieties will thrive in your area
- Some fruits and nuts have specific soil requirements that may require significant amendments
- Fruits and nuts are susceptible to a variety of pests and diseases that require monitoring
- Harvests may come all at once, requiring time for processing or preservation
- Wildlife pressure on fruit and nuts can be significant and difficult to manage

References and resources: <www.suspra.com/practice/food/growing-203.html>

Growing Food 301: Growing a Food Garden

Grow a home garden that builds healthy soil and requires minimal pesticides

Grow a home garden in healthy soil, a living ecosystem containing billions of microorganisms that support plant health. Healthy soil grows healthy plants, which naturally resist pests and diseases, reducing the need for chemical interventions, which protects soil biology, which builds even healthier soil. Conventional gardening attempts to replace healthy soil with synthetic fertilizers; ecological gardening nurtures a soil ecosystem to create the conditions for plants to thrive naturally.

Add compost, grow cover crops, and use mulch to build organic matter, which provides nutrients, improves soil structure, and feeds beneficial soil organisms. Over time, these practices create soil that:

- Retains moisture while still draining well
- Contains balanced nutrients for steady plant growth
- Hosts diverse microorganisms that protect plants from pathogens
- Develops stable structure that allows air and water flow
- Stores carbon, contributing to climate stability

Healthy plants growing in biologically active soil naturally resist many pests and diseases. Give your plants even more help by growing a diverse garden with habitat for beneficial insects that eat pest insects. Flowers interplanted with vegetables attract pollinators and predatory insects that keep pest populations in check. When disease and pest problems do occur, use integrated pest management:

1. Create and maintain optimal growing conditions
2. Monitor regularly to catch problems early
3. Accurately identify diseases and pests before taking action
4. Use the least toxic, most targeted intervention first
5. Apply stronger measures only when necessary

Manage pests at acceptable levels; recognize that every insect is a part of a functioning ecosystem. Over time, an ecological food garden becomes increasingly resilient. Soil improves year after year. Beneficial insect populations establish themselves and become an army of helpers in your organic garden.

Discover which plant varieties thrive in your specific conditions, so you can get higher yields with less toil. Work with natural processes to co-create productive, beautiful spaces that provide nutritious food.

Growing Food 301: Equipment & Materials

- Seeds or seedlings appropriate for your climate
- Sunny space for planting (in containers or in ground)
- Garden tools
  - Shovel or spade, garden fork, rake, trowel
  - Pruners or scissors
  - Watering can or hose with adjustable nozzle
  - Wheelbarrow or garden cart
- Soil building materials
  - Compost, aged manure
  - Mulch materials (straw, leaves, wood chips)
- Garden planning supplies
  - Garden journal or notebook
  - Plant markers or labels
  - Calendar for scheduling plantings
- *Optional: Soil test kit*
- *Cover crop seeds (clover, buckwheat, winter rye)*
- *Floating row covers or insect netting*
- *Trellises, stakes, or cages for climbing plants*
- *Rainwater collection system*
- *Compost bin or pile*

Growing Food 301: Steps

1. Plan your garden location, layout, and schedule
   - Choose a site that receives at least six hours of sun daily
   - Observe drainage patterns; avoid or build raised beds in areas where water pools

- Create a garden map with planned locations for different crops
- Determine your USDA hardiness zone and average frost dates
- Create a calendar of what to plant when, based on your climate
2. Test and prepare your soil
    - Conduct a soil test to determine pH and nutrient levels
    - Avoid excessive tilling which disturbs soil structure and biology
    - For new gardens, use a no-dig method:
        - Layer cardboard over grass, overlapping edges by 6 inches
        - Add four inches of garden soil mix, including compost or aged manure, on top
    - For established gardens, add two inches of compost each fall
3. Select appropriate plants
    - Choose disease-resistant varieties adapted to your region and climate
    - Group plants by families to facilitate crop rotation
    - Include companion plants that deter pests or enhance growth
        - Hosts for beneficial insects (e.g., marigolds, zinnias, and cosmos)
        - Aromatic plants that repel pests (e.g., basil, dill, mint)
4. Establish your garden
    - For direct seeding:
        - Follow seed packet instructions for planting depth and spacing
        - Keep soil consistently moist until germination
    - For transplants:
        - Harden off seedlings by gradually introducing them to outdoor conditions
        - Plant on a cloudy day or in the evening to reduce transplant shock
        - Water thoroughly after planting
    - Apply three inches of mulch around plants, keeping it away from stems
    - Install supports for climbing plants early to avoid disturbing roots later
5. Implement water-wise practices
    - Install soaker hoses or drip irrigation for efficient watering
    - Water in the early morning to reduce evaporation
    - Water deeply to encourage deep root growth; allow soil surface to dry between waterings
    - Water at the base of plants to keep foliage dry
    - Use mulch to retain soil moisture and suppress weeds
6. Maintain soil health throughout the growing season
    - Add compost or compost tea regularly during the growing season
    - Cut weeds off at soil surface without disturbing subsoil structure
    - Keep garden beds covered with cover crops or mulch at all times to reduce weed pressure
7. Monitor and manage pests using integrated approaches
    - Install physical barriers like row covers for susceptible crops
    - Inspect plants regularly for signs of pests or disease
    - Promptly remove leaves or entire plants showing signs of fungal or bacterial infection
    - Identify pests correctly, then take least invasive action:
        - Handpick larger pests like caterpillars and beetles
        - Use soapy water sprays for aphids and mites
        - Introduce beneficial insects like ladybugs or predatory mites
    - Apply insecticides as a last resort:
        - Insecticidal soaps for soft-bodied insects
        - Neem oil for multiple pest types
        - *Bacillus thuringiensis* (Bt) for caterpillars
8. Harvest properly
    - Harvest in the morning when plants are well-hydrated
    - Pick vegetables at their peak; remove all overripe produce quickly
    - Use clean, sharp tools to avoid damaging plants

9. Prepare your garden for seasonal transitions
    - Remove and bury (at least 12" deep) crop residues from plants that showed disease
    - Leave healthy plant material to decompose and build soil
    - Plant cover crops to prevent weeds from establishing
    - Add a layer of compost before winter
    - Protect perennial plants with mulch in cold climates

Growing Food 301: Definitions

- **Beneficial insects**: Insects that pollinate plants or prey on pest insects
- **Compost**: Decomposed organic matter used to build soil fertility and structure
- **Compost tea**: Liquid fertilizer made by steeping compost in water to extract nutrients and beneficial microorganisms
- **Companion planting**: Growing different plants together that benefit each other
- **Cover crop**: Plants grown primarily to build soil, prevent erosion, and suppress weeds
- **Crop rotation**: Change what is planted in an area to interrupt pest and disease cycles and balance soil nutrients
- **Hardiness zone**: Regions defined by average annual minimum winter temperatures
- **Hügelkultur**: Constructing raised beds from a base layer of decaying wood covered by soil
- **Integrated Pest Management (IPM)**: A systematic approach to pest management that uses a combination of techniques to control pests while minimizing environmental impact
- **Mulch**: Surface material to conserve moisture, suppress weeds, and regulate soil temperature
- **No-till gardening**: Minimizing digging or tilling to protect soil structure
- **Sheet mulching**: Adding mulch on top to convert areas to garden beds without digging
- **Soil food web**: The community of organisms living all or part of their lives in the soil
- **Succession planting**: Planting crops in time intervals to provide continuous harvests

Growing Food 301: Troubleshooting

Problem	Solutions
Poor germination	Check soil temperature. Ensure consistent moisture during germination. Consider pre-sprouting seeds indoors. Check seed age and quality.
Stunted plant growth	Test soil pH and nutrient levels. Ensure plants are receiving adequate sunlight. Check for root-bound plants or compacted soil. Verify proper plant spacing. Apply compost tea to boost microbiological activity.
Nutrient deficiency symptoms	Identify specific deficiency through visual symptoms. Add appropriate organic amendments (compost, kelp meal, bone meal). Adjust soil pH if necessary. Ensure adequate soil moisture for nutrient uptake.
Pest infestations	Identify pests correctly before treatment. Introduce or attract appropriate beneficial insects. Use physical barriers like row covers. Apply insecticides.
Disease issues	Improve air circulation between plants. Water at soil level rather than on foliage. Remove and dispose of infected plant material. Practice crop rotation. Select disease-resistant varieties for future plantings.
Excessive weeds	Apply organic mulch three inches thick. Use deep mulch in pathways. Cut weeds more frequently. Burn weeds before planting. Use cover crops.

Problem	Solutions
Poor pollination	Plant flowers to attract pollinators. Hand pollinate certain crops (squash, tomatoes). Avoid applying any pesticides during flowering. Ensure your garden is pesticide-free to protect pollinator health.
Clay soil or poor drainage	Build raised beds. Add more compost and organic matter. Use cover crops with deep roots, such as daikon radish. Avoid working soil when wet.
Sandy soil that dries quickly	Add more compost and organic matter. Use thicker mulch layers. Try *hügelkultur* beds (wood holds moisture). Water more frequently.

Growing Food 301: Limitations

- Building healthy soil takes time—significant improvements often take 2-3 years
- Pest and disease pressure varies by region and can be severe in some areas despite best practices
- Weather extremes can damage crops regardless of soil health or gardening methods
- Soil contamination may require testing and remediation before food growing
- Zoning restrictions or homeowner association rules may limit garden size or location

References and resources: <www.suspra.com/practice/food/growing-301.html>

Growing Food 302: Raising Chickens

Raise backyard chickens for eggs or meat using organic methods

Before starting your flock, consider the full lifecycle commitment. Laying hens typically produce well for two years, though they can live for ten. Have a plan for aging hens: keep them as pets, eat them, or find them new homes. If you intend to breed your own replacement birds, you'll need a rooster, which will crow and tend to be aggressive. Heritage breeds can reproduce naturally and make excellent broody hens (hens that sit on and hatch eggs). Most urban areas prohibit keeping roosters in backyard flocks.

Hens (female chickens) integrate well into home gardens and small-scale agriculture. They eat insects and weed seeds, provide nutrient-rich manure for compost, and convert food scraps into eggs—an almost perfect closed-loop system. Six hens can produce 24 eggs weekly during their prime laying years while producing nitrogen-rich manure that, when properly composted, becomes excellent garden fertilizer. Without roosters, hens lay unfertilized eggs which do not develop into chicks.

Organic chicken keeping focuses on prevention rather than treatment. Provide appropriate space, nutrition, and housing while using natural methods to maintain health. Chickens evolved as woodland edge creatures that forage and dig in dirt for seeds, insects, and plants. Mimic these natural conditions while protecting your flock from predators. The deep litter method exemplifies this approach: provide six inches of carbon-rich bedding (straw, wood shavings) in the coop; rarely completely remove it. Beneficial microorganisms and insects colonize this material, breaking down chicken droppings and creating valuable compost. This system closely resembles a forest floor, providing chickens with natural foraging opportunities even when confined in their coop.

Growing Food 302: Equipment & Materials

- Chicks, pullets or grown chickens
- Chicken coop with perch and nesting boxes
- Predator-proof metal "hardware cloth" (not chicken wire)
- Secure outdoor run (10 square feet per bird)
- Feeder and waterer

Sustainable Practices Handbook
Food Practices: Cultivating Healthy Harvests

- Organic chicken feed
- Bedding material (straw, pine shavings, or hemp)
- Grit and calcium supplements
- Compost system for coop waste
- *Optional: Heat source for chicks (if starting with day-old chicks), brooder box for raising chicks, automatic coop door opener*

Growing Food 302: Steps

1. Check local regulations and prepare your site
   - Research local zoning laws and homeowners association rules regarding backyard chickens
   - Determine maximum flock size allowed in your area
   - Choose a level, well-drained location for your coop and run
   - Select a site that receives partial shade during hot weather
2. Design and build or purchase your chicken housing
   - Ensure enclosed coop has three square feet of space per bird
   - Include one nesting box for every four hens
   - Install perches 18-24 inches off the ground (allow nine inches per bird)
   - Ensure proper ventilation while preventing drafts
   - Create easy access for egg collection and cleaning
   - Surround run with predator-proof fencing (metal "hardware cloth") buried 12 inches deep
   - Cover run with chicken wire or netting to prevent aerial predators
3. Choose an appropriate chicken breed
   - For egg production: consider Leghorns, Rhode Island Reds, Plymouth Rocks, or Australorps
   - For dual-purpose (eggs and meat): consider Orpingtons, Wyandottes, or Sussex
   - For cold climates: choose cold-hardy breeds with small combs (Plymouth Rock, Wyandotte)
   - For hot climates: select heat-tolerant breeds (Leghorns, Minorcas)
   - For families with children: consider docile breeds (Orpingtons, Sussex)
4. Acquire your chickens
   - Purchase day-old chicks
     - Set up a brooder with heat lamp (95°F for first week, reduce 5°F weekly)
     - Provide chick starter feed and shallow water container
     - Use paper towels or newspaper for first few days before switching to regular bedding
     - Handle chicks gently daily to socialize them
     - Move to coop when fully feathered (around 6 weeks)
   - Purchase started pullets (young hens, 16-20 weeks old)
     - Introduce directly to coop
     - Keep confined to coop for first week to establish "home"
   - Adopt rescue hens
     - Contact local animal shelters or chicken rescue organizations
     - Be prepared for possible health or behavioral issues
5. Feed them organic food
   - Ensure constant access to clean, fresh water
   - Feed organic feed appropriate for your birds' age and purpose
   - Provide free-choice calcium supplement (crushed oyster shell) for laying hens
   - Offer free-choice grit if birds don't have access to soil
   - Supplement with kitchen scraps (vegetables, fruits, grains)
   - Allow foraging time for insects, seeds, and plants
6. Manage your flock using natural methods
   - Establish a deep litter system in the coop (six inches of bedding regularly topped up)
   - Provide dust bathing areas with diatomaceous earth to control external parasites
   - Rotate run areas to prevent parasite buildup
7. Monitor health using preventative measures

Revision: 25.1.8

- Observe birds daily for normal behavior and physical condition
- Provide adequate space to prevent stress and disease
- Regularly clean and refresh water containers
- Quarantine new birds for 30 days before introducing to flock
- Add 1 tablespoon organic apple cider vinegar per gallon of water to boost immune function
- Provide nutritional supplements during stressful periods (molt, extreme weather)
8. Collect eggs promptly
    - Gather eggs at least once daily (twice in extreme temperatures)
    - Gently clean eggs only if necessary (dry brushing preferred); use or refrigerate after washing
    - Keep track of laying patterns to monitor flock health
9. Manage waste sustainably
    - Use deep litter method in coop to create usable compost (carbon:nitrogen ratio of 30:1)
    - Age compost at least six months before using in food gardens
    - Apply fresh chicken manure only to areas where food won't be grown for 120 days
10. Prepare for seasonal challenges
    - Ensure adequate ventilation and water in summer
    - Apply petroleum jelly to combs and wattles to prevent frostbite in cold weather
    - Provide extra light in winter if egg production is desired (14-16 hours total)
    - Plan for molting (natural feather replacement) with protein-rich diet
11. For meat production
    - Raise specific meat breeds (Cornish Cross, Freedom Rangers) or dual-purpose breeds
    - Kill birds at appropriate age (8-12 weeks for Cornish Cross, 16-20 weeks for heritage breeds)

Growing Food 302: Definitions

- **Brooder**: A heated enclosure for raising young chicks until they develop feathers
- **Broody hen**: A hen exhibiting nesting behavior, willing to sit on and hatch eggs
- **Chick**: A very young chicken which will grow into a hen or a rooster
- **Deep litter method**: Providing a deep layer of coop bedding that is seldom completely removed, creating a foraging and composting floor under the perch
- **Dual-purpose breed**: Chicken breed suitable for both egg laying and meat production
- **Free-range**: Production system where birds have access to outdoor areas
- **Hen**: A female chicken which will lay eggs; only fertilized eggs will develop into chicks
- **Heritage breed**: Breeds raised before industrial agriculture, capable of natural reproduction
- **Molt**: Annual process of losing and replacing feathers, reducing or stopping egg production
- **Nesting box**: Enclosed space where hens lay eggs
- **Perch**: Elevated bar where chickens sleep (roost)
- **Pullet**: Young female chicken less than one year old
- **Rooster**: A male chicken which will not lay eggs, but will mate with hens to fertilize their eggs
- **Vent**: The cloaca from which chickens poop and lay eggs

Growing Food 302: Troubleshooting

Problem	Solutions
Reduced egg production	Check daylight hours (supplement light in winter if desired). Assess for parasites. Evaluate nutrition. Consider the age of birds. Check for hidden egg caches. Evaluate stress factors like predator presence or overcrowding.
Chickens destroying garden	Create barriers around garden beds. Provide alternative scratching areas. Use mobile chicken tractors to control where chickens forage. Create designated dust bathing areas with sand or dry dirt.

Problem	Solutions
Predator problems	Identify predator type by tracks or attack patterns. Reinforce coop with hardware cloth (not chicken wire). Add motion-activated lights. Use secure locks that raccoons can't open. Consider livestock guardian animals.
Neighbor complaints	Address concerns promptly. Maintain a clean coop to prevent odors. Keep appropriate rooster-to-hen ratios or eliminate roosters. Share eggs with neighbors. Create visual barriers with attractive plantings.
Aggressive hens	Evaluate flock size and space. Introduce new birds carefully using quarantine. Address broody behavior by collecting eggs frequently. Separate injured birds until healed.
External parasites (mites, lice)	Provide dust bathing areas with food-grade diatomaceous earth. Use organic treatments like diluted neem oil for serious infestations.
Internal parasites (worms)	Practice pasture rotation. Keep the coop clean and dry. Add food-grade diatomaceous earth to feed (2% of mix). Mix in herbs like garlic, oregano, and thyme in feed. Consult with poultry veterinarian for severe cases.
Winter egg slowdown	Provide 14 hours of light daily (artificial light on timer if necessary). Increase protein in diet (20% protein feed; offer nuts or mealworms). Ensure unfrozen water access. Provide extra calories during cold weather.

Growing Food 302: Limitations

- Local regulations may restrict or prohibit keeping backyard chickens
- Roosters are prohibited in many urban areas due to noise concerns
- Chicken keeping requires upfront investment in housing and equipment
- Egg production naturally declines after 2-3 years while chickens can live 8-10 years
- Potential for zoonotic disease transmission (e.g., Salmonella or bird flu)
- Time commitment for daily care, cleaning, and management
- Daily care requirements make travel challenging without a knowledgeable caretaker

References and resources: <www.suspra.com/practice/food/growing-302.html>

Growing Food 303: Making Syrup

Tap trees and boil down syrup using solar power

Make syrup with solar power by using an electric induction hot plate instead of a wood-fired evaporator for a more sustainable approach to this time-honored practice. Sap flows when temperatures fluctuate between freezing nights and thawing days. This cycle typically occurs for 4-6 weeks in late winter to early spring, depending on your climate zone.

Approximately forty to fifty gallons of maple sap produce one gallon of syrup; this ratio varies by tree species and growing conditions. Birch sap has a much lower sugar content (0.5-1.5%) requiring a ratio closer to 100:1, while black walnut (2%) and boxelder maple (1.5-2%) fall somewhere in between.

- Birch syrup has a distinctive spicy-sweet flavor with mineral notes
- Black walnut produces a distinctive earthy, nutty syrup
- Boxelder (a maple species) creates a syrup similar to maple but with its own character

Using induction plates for boiling offers several advantages over traditional methods:

- Faster and more convenient; no need to tend a fire
- Portable induction cooktops and pots are more affordable than evaporators
- Precise temperature control reduces the risk of scorching
- More energy efficient than burning any type of fuel
- No air pollution from combustion
- Clean electricity can be generated forever by solar modules

The process requires close attention. Learn to judge the subtle changes in boiling patterns, color, and consistency that indicate perfect doneness. As water evaporates and the sugar concentration increases, the boiling point rises and the risk of scorching increases. Transfer to smaller pots and reduce heat as you approach the final stages. For those with access to many trees, reverse osmosis can remove up to 75% of the water before boiling begins, dramatically reducing energy requirements and processing time.

Growing Food 303: Equipment & Materials

- Maple, birch, walnut, or boxelder trees
- Spiles (metal or plastic taps)
- Hand drill with 7/16" or 5/16" drill bit (depending on spile size)
- Collection containers (food-grade buckets with lids or specialized sap bags)
- Food-grade tubing (if using a bucket collection system)
- Hammer or rubber mallet
- Induction hot plate (1800W recommended)
- Large, wide stainless steel pots or pans
- Fine mesh strainer or cheesecloth
- Coffee filters or special-purpose maple syrup filters
- Funnel
- Glass bottles or mason jars for storage
- *Optional: Tree identification guide*
- *Candy thermometer*
- *Reverse osmosis system for larger batches*
- *Refractometer to measure sugar content (brix) of syrup*
- *Hydrometer to measure density*

Growing Food 303: Steps

1. Identify suitable trees for tapping:
   - Sugar maple (*Acer saccharum*) is ideal with 2-3% sugar content
   - Other maple varieties work but produce less sweet sap
   - Birch, walnut, and boxelder trees are alternatives with different flavor profiles
2. Select healthy trees with a minimum diameter of 10 inches (25 cm) at chest height
3. Plan to tap when daytime temperatures rise above freezing but nighttime temperatures still drop below freezing (typically February to March in the northern hemisphere)
4. Choose a spot at a height of about 3-4 feet (90-120 cm) from the ground
5. Drill a hole two inches (5 cm) deep at a very slight upward angle
6. Clear wood shavings from the hole
7. Gently tap the spile into the hole with a hammer or rubber mallet until secure but not forced
8. Hang your collection container from the spile or connect tubing into a ground-level container
9. For larger trees (18+ inches diameter), you can add a second tap on the opposite side
10. Check collection containers daily during sap flow season
11. Transfer sap to refrigerated storage if not processing immediately
12. Process sap within 7 days, ideally within 24 hours
13. Keep collected sap cold (below 38°F/3°C) to prevent spoilage

14. Filter the raw sap through cheesecloth to remove debris before processing
15. Set up your induction hot plate in a well-ventilated outdoor area with access to electricity from your solar array
16. Pour filtered sap into a metal pot (greater surface area increases evaporation rate)
17. Set the induction hot plate to high power to bring sap to a strong boil
18. As sap reduces, add more sap while maintaining the boil
19. Monitor carefully to prevent scorching or boiling over
20. Use a spoon to skim off foam that develops during boiling
21. Continue boiling until sap reaches approximately 7°F (4°C) above the boiling point of water at your elevation (typically around 219°F/104°C at sea level)
22. Reduce heat as syrup thickens to prevent scorching
23. Test consistency by:
    - Using a refractometer to reach 66-67% sugar content
    - Watching how syrup "sheets" or drips off a spoon
    - Using a hydrometer designed for syrup
24. While still hot (above 180°F/82°C), filter the finished syrup through a coffee filter
25. Pour hot syrup into clean glass containers, leaving minimal headspace
26. Seal immediately; invert bottles briefly to sterilize tops
27. Store syrup in a cool, dark place
28. Refrigerate after opening
29. At the end of the season, remove taps gently from trees
30. Trees will heal the tap holes naturally; do not plug or seal them
31. Clean all equipment thoroughly with hot water (avoid soap with equipment that contacts syrup)
32. Store equipment in a clean, dry place for next season

Growing Food 303: Definitions

- **Brix**: Measurement of sugar content; maple syrup should be 66-67° Brix
- **Hydrometer**: A tool that measures the density of liquids
- **Induction cooking**: Using electromagnetic energy to directly heat cookware
- **Refractometer**: An instrument that measures the sugar content of liquids
- **Reverse osmosis**: A filtration process that removes water from sap
- **Sap**: The nutrient-rich liquid that flows through a tree's vascular system
- **Sheeting**: When hot syrup runs off a spoon in a sheet rather than in drops
- **Spile**: A specialized tap inserted into a drilled hole in a tree to direct sap flow
- **Syrup**: Sap that has been boiled down to a high sugar content; a shelf stable sweetener
- **Tapping**: The process of drilling into a tree and inserting a spile to collect sap

Growing Food 303: Troubleshooting

Problem	Solutions
Little or no sap flow	Check weather conditions; sap flows best with freezing nights and thawing days. Verify tap depth and angle. Try a different tree.
Sap appears cloudy or has an off smell	Discard and clean equipment thoroughly. Sap spoils quickly at temperatures above 40°F (4°C).
Syrup boils over	Use a larger pot. Reduce heat slightly. Monitor constantly.
Final syrup is too thin	Boil until temperature reaches 7°F/4°C above the boiling point of water at your elevation. Use a refractometer or hydrometer to confirm density.
Final syrup is too thick	Add a small amount of filtered sap or pure water, reheat, and stir in.

Revision: 25.1.8

Problem	Solutions
Syrup has a bitter or "off" taste	May be caused by scorching, bacterial growth in stored sap, or contamination from unclean equipment. Check all equipment for cleanliness. Monitor temperature carefully during boiling.
Crystallization in stored syrup	Syrup was likely boiled too long or has become supersaturated with sugar. Reheat gently with a small amount of water to dissolve crystals.
Hot plate too weak	Look for models rated at least 1800W. Process in smaller batches.

Growing Food 303: Limitations

- Off-grid solar systems require large batteries to power induction hot plates
- Processing capacity is limited by the power of available induction hot plates
- Weather-dependent both for sap collection and solar power generation
- Smaller scale than traditional wood-fired operations
- Significant time commitment during sap flow season, which lasts only a few weeks
- Trees can only be tapped during specific temperature conditions
- Need outdoor or well-ventilated space due to significant steam production
- Energy intensive process even with renewable energy sources

References and resources: <www.suspra.com/practice/food/growing-303.html>

Growing Food 401: Practicing Permaculture

Landscape and garden in harmony with nature

Practice permaculture ("permanent agriculture") to create sustainable human habitats that work with nature rather than against it. Rather than focusing on annual crops in isolated beds, create integrated systems where each element serves multiple functions; support important functions (like food production or water management) by multiple elements. Aim for resilience and stability similar to natural ecosystems.

In arid regions, emphasize water harvesting and drought-tolerant plantings. In wet temperate climates, focus on managing excess water and extending growing seasons. In tropical areas, work with the abundant growth potential and multiple canopy layers. For suburban or urban yards, maximize productive use of small spaces through vertical growing, multi-purpose social areas, clever water management, and connecting with neighbors for resource sharing and expanded impact. Stack functions to yield abundance. Embrace community building and skill sharing.

Food forests exemplify permaculture. Mimic forest structures with multiple layers—canopy trees, understory trees, shrubs, herbaceous plants, ground covers, root crops, and vines—to create productive ecosystems that require minimal intervention once established. Select each plant not just for its harvest but also for how it fixes nitrogen, attracts pollinators, repels pests, creates mulch, or provides shade.

View problems differently to find solutions. Excess water becomes a resource when directed to swales or ponds. Fast-growing "weeds" become valuable biomass for mulch or compost. Steep slopes become productive terraced gardens. Transitioning an existing yard to permaculture doesn't require removing everything and starting over. Observe what's already working, gradually replace resource-intensive elements (like lawns) with productive ones, and strategically add plants and structures that serve multiple functions. The transition can happen in phases over many years.

Sustainable Practices Handbook   Food Practices: Cultivating Healthy Harvests

Growing Food 401: Equipment & Materials

- Land
- Notebook and pen or tablet or computer for observations and design planning
- Measuring tape and stakes for mapping
- Soil testing kit to assess soil conditions
- Permeable landscaping materials for paths and water management
- Diverse plants suited to your climate zone
  - Perennial vegetables, herbs, and fruits
  - Nitrogen-fixing plants
  - Native flowering plants
  - Tree and shrub seedlings
- Compost or composting materials
- Mulch materials (straw, wood chips, leaves)
- *Optional: Rainwater harvesting equipment, software or large sheets of paper for detailed mapping, camera or smartphone for documentation, reference books specific to your region*

Growing Food 401: Steps

1. Study the core principles of permaculture
   - Care for the Earth and for people
   - Fair share (return surplus to Earth and people)
   - Work with nature, not against it
   - Every element performs multiple functions
   - Every important function is supported by multiple elements
   - Use and value renewable resources
   - Produce no waste
   - Integrate rather than segregate
   - Use small and slow solutions
   - Use and value diversity
   - Respond to change creatively
2. Conduct a thorough site assessment over multiple seasons if possible
   - Note sun patterns throughout the day and year
   - Observe water flow during heavy rainfalls and spring thaws
   - Identify existing plants and wildlife
   - Map structures, utilities, and access points
   - Determine wind patterns and microclimates
   - Test soil quality and composition
   - Note neighbor relationships and boundaries
3. Document your observations in a site map or journal
4. Research your local climate patterns, native ecosystems, and traditional food growing practices
5. Define your goals and needs (food production, wildlife habitat, beauty, etc.)
6. Apply zone planning (organizing elements by frequency of use):
   - Zone 0: House and daily living space
   - Zone 1: Intensively managed areas visited daily (herbs, salad greens)
   - Zone 2: Areas visited regularly (main vegetable gardens, small animals)
   - Zone 3: Occasional visits (main crops, orchards, larger animals)
   - Zone 4: Semi-wild areas (food forests, timber)
   - Zone 5: Wild areas (observation and harvesting only)
7. Analyze sectors (external influences):
   - Sun, wind, and water flows (including potential flooding)
   - Fire risks
   - Views (desirable and undesirable)
   - Noise or pollution sources

Revision: 25.1.8

8. Design for efficient energy patterns:
   - Place elements that need daily attention nearest to the house
   - Connect elements that can benefit each other
   - Plan for efficient paths that follow natural movement patterns
9. Manage water:
   - Swales (shallow ditches) on contour to slow and infiltrate water
   - Rainwater harvesting systems and rain gardens to capture runoff
   - Pond or small water features as appropriate
10. Identify and plan for key permaculture elements based on your climate and goals:
    - Water features
    - Food forest or guild plantings, annual vegetable beds, and perennial plantings
    - Habitat areas and social spaces
    - Compost systems
11. Begin with water management and irrigation systems
12. Establish access paths and boundaries
13. Build soil fertility:
    - Create compost systems
    - Sheet mulch to suppress grass and build soil
    - Plant nitrogen-fixing cover crops in areas for future planting
14. Plant trees and larger perennials:
    - Consider mature size and spacing
    - Plant largest elements first (trees, then shrubs, then smaller plants)
    - First establish hardy pioneer species that improve conditions for later plantings
15. Add understory plantings in successive layers:
    - Shrubs and smaller trees
    - Herbaceous perennials
    - Ground covers
    - Root crops
    - Vines and climbers
16. Create beneficial plant groupings (guilds) around trees and throughout the landscape.
17. Keep a garden journal, note plant interactions, and document yields and challenges
18. Incorporate annual vegetables in appropriate zones, using sustainable growing methods.
19. Maintain compost systems, chop and drop mulching from appropriate plants
20. Integrate animals if appropriate for manure and pest management
21. Practice minimal disturbance techniques:
    - No-till methods for annual gardens
    - Strategic pruning rather than removal
    - Selective weeding, recognizing beneficial volunteers
22. Save seeds and propagate the most successful plants to increase resilience
23. Harvest appropriately and process abundance (preserve, share, sell)
24. Make incremental changes based on observations
25. Increase diversity over time by adding complementary species
26. Share knowledge, plants, and harvests with your community

Growing Food 401: Definitions

- **Chop and drop mulching**: Pruning plants and leaving the material on the ground as mulch
- **Contour**: A line of equal elevation across a landscape
- **Food forest**: A multi-layered, diverse group of edible plants that mimics forest structure
- **Guild**: A harmonious assembly of plants (and sometimes animals) that benefit each other
- **Microclimate**: A small area with climate conditions different from the surrounding area
- **No-till**: Gardening methods that avoid disturbing soil structure through digging or tilling
- **Perennial**: A plant that lives for more than two years

- **Pioneer species**: Hardy plants that improve conditions to allow other species to establish
- **Sheet mulching**: A layered mulching technique to suppress grass and build soil
- **Stacking functions**: Designing elements to serve multiple purposes
- **Succession**: The process of change in an ecosystem's structure over time
- **Swale**: A shallow ditch dug on contour to slow, spread, and sink water

Growing Food 401: Troubleshooting

Problem	Solutions
Overwhelming complexity when starting	Start with small, manageable projects like an herb spiral or keyhole garden bed. Focus on one permaculture principle at a time. Join local permaculture groups for support and guidance.
Poor plant establishment	Ensure proper soil preparation before planting. Use pioneer species to improve conditions. Create microclimate protection for sensitive plants. Water well until plants are established. Use mulch.
Excessive pest damage	Increase plant diversity to attract beneficial insects. Incorporate pest-confusing companion plants. Create habitat for insect-eating birds and beneficial wildlife. Use physical barriers such as fences and row covers.
Too much water	Reassess your contour lines and swale placement. Add more organic matter to improve soil water absorption. Consider additional water-harvesting features. Adjust plant selection to better match your water reality.
Overgrowth and system chaos	Prune more frequently. Use succession planning to replace overly vigorous plants. Harvest more aggressively.
Insufficient yields for effort	Plant new varieties. Incorporate more perennials that produce with less maintenance. Streamline maintenance routines. Wait for plants to mature.
Neighbors or code compliance concerns	Create attractive borders. Share harvests with neighbors. Learn local regulations before implementing conspicuous elements. Join or form community groups advocating for sustainable landscaping rights.
Soil fertility not improving	Increase your compost inputs. Add more nitrogen-fixing plants. Keep chickens. Test soil regularly; address specific deficiencies. Harvest less.

Growing Food 401: Limitations

- Permaculture requires ongoing observation and a significant learning curve
- Full system maturity and peak production can take years, particularly for tree systems
- Space constraints may limit the implementation of all permaculture elements in urban settings
- Local regulations may restrict certain practices (water harvesting, livestock, structures)
- Climate extremes may require additional infrastructure or modified approaches
- Some permaculture techniques may not align with conventional aesthetic expectations
- Finding appropriate plant material may be challenging in some regions
- Economic returns on investment may be delayed compared to conventional gardening

References and resources: <www.suspra.com/practice/food/growing-401.html>

Water Practices

Optimizing Water Efficiency, page 217	
Goals	**Indicators**
• Consume less water per person per day	• Average water flow rate per person

Conserving Water, page 234	
Goals	**Indicators**
• Consume less water per person per day	• Average water flow rate per person

Preventing Water Pollution, page 245	
Goals	**Indicators**
• Prevent water pollution	• How many pollution prevention practices are being done

Optimizing Water Efficiency

Maintaining Plumbing 101: Reviewing Bills to Check for Leaks

Review water bills to check for leaks

Regular review of water bills is an effective way to detect hidden leaks. Average households lose about 10,000 gallons annually due to leaks. A single toilet leak can waste 200-400 gallons daily, while a dripping faucet might waste 20 gallons. These leaks can increase water bills by 10-30% each month.

Maintaining Plumbing 101: Equipment & Materials
- Water bills (ideally 12 months)

Maintaining Plumbing 101: Steps
1. Collect your water bills from the past 12 months.
2. Locate water consumption data on your bill (gallons, cubic feet, or cubic meters).
3. Calculate your average daily water usage:
   - Divide total water used by days in billing period.
   - Example: 6,000 gallons ÷ 30 days = 200 gallons per day.
4. Compare your current usage with historical baseline.
5. Look for unexplained increases of 10% or more.
6. Account for seasonal variations and unusual water usage events.
7. Verify that the meter on your utility bill matches your actual meter.
8. Perform a meter test if you suspect a leak:
   - Ensure all water is turned off.
   - Read your water meter and note numbers.
   - Wait two hours without using any water.
   - Re-read meter; if changed, you likely have a leak.

Maintaining Plumbing 101: Definitions
- **Baseline water usage**: Normal water consumption pattern based on historical bills
- **Billing period**: Specific time frame covered by a utility bill
- **CCF/HCF**: 100 cubic feet of water (748 gallons), a common billing unit
- **Cubic foot**: Volume measurement equal to 7.48 gallons of water
- **Estimated reading**: Bill based on estimated rather than actual meter readings

Maintaining Plumbing 101: Troubleshooting

Problem	Solutions
No access to past bills	Contact utility for billing history. Use your town's average household consumption as a temporary baseline.
Significant but explainable increase	Calculate expected impact of known changes. If the actual increase exceeds expected amount, investigate for leaks.
Meter reading doesn't match bill	Contact utility to report discrepancy. Take photos of your meter. Request a meter re-read.

Problem	Solutions
Consumption increasing but no visible leaks	Check irrigation systems. Listen for running water in walls. Look for damp areas. Consider hiring a plumber.
Irregular billing	Calculate daily average use to normalize different billing period lengths.

Maintaining Plumbing 101: Limitations
- Cannot detect very small leaks
- Doesn't pinpoint leak locations
- Requires several months of data for reliable baseline
- Cannot distinguish between wasteful usage and actual leaks

References and resources: <www.suspra.com/practice/water/maintaining-plumbing-101.html>

Maintaining Plumbing 301: Detecting Leaks

Install a leak detection system

Leak detection systems provide early warning against leaks and water damage. Flow-based systems monitor water patterns through your main line, while sensor-based systems use moisture sensors in high-risk areas. Advanced systems can learn household usage patterns and alert when abnormal activity occurs. Many include automatic shut-off capabilities to prevent catastrophic damage.

Maintaining Plumbing 301: Equipment & Materials
- Water leak detection system (smart system or flow-based system)
- Smartphone or tablet and WiFi network (for smart systems)
- Plumbing tools

Maintaining Plumbing 301: Steps
1. Select an appropriate leak detection system:
   - Choose between flow-based or sensor-based systems
   - Consider smart systems with smartphone alerts
2. *Hire a plumber if you aren't comfortable doing the work yourself*
3. Prepare for installation:
   - Read manufacturer's instructions thoroughly
   - Identify main water supply line for flow sensor
   - Map locations for moisture sensors near high-risk areas
4. Turn off your water supply (if necessary)
5. Install the flow-based detection system per manufacturer's instructions (if applicable)
6. Install moisture sensors per manufacturer's instructions (if applicable)
7. Install the automatic shut-off valve (if included)
8. Connect the control unit
9. Restore water and test for leaks
10. Set up system software (if applicable)
11. Test the system:
    - Create controlled "leak" situations
    - Confirm notifications work
    - Test automatic shut-off valve if included

Maintaining Plumbing 301: Definitions

- **Automatic shut-off valve:** Motorized valve closing automatically when leak is detected
- **Control unit:** Central hub receiving information from sensors
- **Flow-based detector:** Device monitoring water flow rate to detect unusual patterns
- **Moisture sensor:** Device detecting water or high humidity levels
- **Smart system:** Leak detection system connecting to WiFi for remote monitoring
- **Threshold settings:** Parameters determining when system triggers alerts

Maintaining Plumbing 301: Troubleshooting

Problem	Solutions
False alarms	Adjust sensitivity settings. Move sensors from high-humidity areas.
Sensors won't connect to hub	Check battery levels. Ensure sensors are within range (30-150 feet). Remove obstacles between sensors and hub.
Flow sensor shows no water flow	Verify water supply is on. Check for clogs. Ensure correct installation direction.
Smart system won't connect to WiFi	Place the hub closer to the router. Verify connection to 2.4GHz network (not 5GHz). Reset hub.
App notifications not received	Enable notifications in phone settings. Verify account information. Test internet connection.

Maintaining Plumbing 301: Limitations

- Flow-based systems may not detect very slow leaks
- Smart systems rely on consistent WiFi and power
- Some systems require professional installation
- Not all systems detect leaks in outdoor pipes

References and resources: <www.suspra.com/practice/water/maintaining-plumbing-301.html>

Maintaining Plumbing 401: Organizing a Leak Brigade

Organize a "fix a leak" brigade for your neighborhood

Mobilize a neighborhood leak brigade of community members to help homeowners identify and fix water leaks, saving water while building connections. Recruit and train volunteers to hand out educational materials, or (if you have the institutional capacity to vet, train, and insure volunteers) look for leaks and fix simple ones. Provide support from professional plumbers. Maintain clear boundaries on what volunteers can do.

Maintaining Plumbing 401: Equipment & Materials

- Meeting space for training
- Materials explaining to how to identify leaks and fix simple ones
- *Optional: Water conservation kits, website explaining program*

Maintaining Plumbing 401: Steps

1. Research and plan (three months before launch).
   - Determine scope of services: educational only or direct service component

- Create project plan with timeline
  - Contact municipality and water utility about partnership
  - Identify plumbing professionals for training and referrals
  - Approach hardware stores for donations
  - Contact neighborhood associations
2. Develop legal framework (two months before launch)
   - Check local regulations
   - Create homeowner consent forms (if applicable)
   - Develop volunteer agreements
   - Establish referral policies for professional help
3. Recruit volunteers (two months before launch)
   - Create recruitment materials
   - Present at community meetings
   - Reach out to trade schools or retired plumbers
   - Screen volunteers appropriately
4. Train volunteers (one month before launch)
   - Organize sessions led by professional plumbers
   - Focus on common household leaks, detection, basic fixes
   - Create procedure handbook
   - Conduct role-playing exercises
5. Create operations system (three weeks before launch)
   - Establish scheduling system
   - Develop assessment forms
   - Set up data collection
   - Create emergency protocols
6. Launch and promote
   - Create sign-up process
   - Hold kick-off event
   - Distribute announcements
   - Target high-usage homes
   - Table at community events
7. Implement service protocol (if applicable)
   - Send volunteers in pairs
   - Follow standard procedure:
     - Initial assessment
     - Documentation
     - Simple fixes when appropriate
     - Professional recommendations when needed
   - Keep written records of each visit
8. Monitor and Support
   - Hold regular volunteer meetings
   - Provide ongoing training
   - Replenish supplies
   - Rotate assignments to prevent burnout
9. Evaluate and Expand (six months after launch)
   - Analyze water savings data
   - Collect feedback and identify improvements

Maintaining Plumbing 401: Definitions

- **Aerator**: Device attached to faucet end that introduces air, reducing water flow
- **Flapper**: Rubber valve in toilet tank controlling water release
- **GPM**: Gallons Per Minute, unit for water flow measurement

- **Leak detection tablets**: Dye tablets revealing toilet leaks
- **Silent leak**: Water leak occurring without obvious signs
- **Water audit**: Systematic examination to identify water waste

Maintaining Plumbing 401: Troubleshooting

Problem	Solutions
Low volunteer turnout	Partner with service organizations. Offer skill-building incentives. Create flexible commitments.
Difficulty finding participants	Partner with utility to identify high-usage homes. Offer free conservation kits.
Liability concerns	Secure insurance coverage. Use clear waivers. Establish strict protocols on volunteer limitations.
Lack of technical expertise	Recruit retired plumbers. Create a tiered volunteer system. Develop step-by-step guides.
Volunteer burnout	Limit to specific campaign periods. Rotate responsibilities. Celebrate accomplishments.
Limited funding	Seek hardware store donations. Apply for conservation grants. Partner with utilities.

Maintaining Plumbing 401: Limitations
- Volunteers can only address simple plumbing issues
- Liability concerns limit work scope
- Local regulations may restrict who can perform certain work
- Homeowners may be reluctant to allow volunteers into homes

References and resources: <www.suspra.com/practice/water/maintaining-plumbing-401.html>

Streamlining Water Use 101: Skipping Pre-Rinsing

Skip pre-rinsing dishes by scraping off food into your compost pail

Set up a system to compost your kitchen scraps. Then, instead of using water to rinse uneaten food off dishes, use a spoon or spatula to scrape off food scraps into a sink strainer basket or directly into a kitchen compost pail.

References and resources: <www.suspra.com/practice/water/streamlining-use-101.html>

Streamlining Water Use 102: Composting Not Disposing

Put food into your compost pail rather than down your garbage disposal

Instead of using your garbage disposal to dispose of food scraps, collect food waste like vegetable peels, coffee grounds, and fruit cores in a designated compost pail in your kitchen. Garbage disposals consume water and electricity to send food waste to wastewater treatment plants or septic fields. Excess food waste can overwhelm treatment processes, potentially leading to the release of untreated sewage during heavy rains. Composting transforms food waste into a valuable amendment for your garden or community green spaces, promoting a circular economy while conserving resources.

Sustainable Practices Handbook
Water Practices: Optimizing Water Efficiency

References and resources: <www.suspra.com/practice/water/streamlining-use-102.html>

Upgrading Plumbing 101: Upgrading Showerheads and Aerators

Install showerheads and faucet aerators that meet WaterSense standards

WaterSense-labeled showerheads use no more than 2.0 gallons per minute (GPM) compared to standard shower heads that use 2.5 GPM or more. WaterSense bathroom faucet aerators use a maximum of 1.5 GPM compared to standard aerators that use 2.2 GPM. Modern water-efficient fixtures achieve water savings through aerators that mix air with water, flow regulators, flow-compensating devices, and atomizing technology.

Upgrading Plumbing 101: Equipment & Materials

- WaterSense-certified shower head
- WaterSense-certified faucet aerators
- Adjustable wrench or pliers with jaw protectors
- Teflon or plumber's tape
- Needle-nose pliers (for removing old aerator if stuck)
- Rags or towels to protect fixtures
- *Optional: Small brush for cleaning threads, white vinegar for mineral deposit removal, penetrating oil for stuck fixtures, bucket and timer for measuring flow rate*

Upgrading Plumbing 101: Steps

1. Measure current water flow (optional but recommended)
   - Place a bucket under your showerhead or faucet
   - Turn on water fully for exactly 15 seconds
   - Measure the collected water in gallons
   - Multiply by 4 to determine gallons per minute (GPM)
2. Select appropriate WaterSense products
   - Choose showerheads rated at 2.0 GPM or less
   - Choose bathroom faucet aerators rated at 1.5 GPM or less
   - Choose kitchen faucet aerators rated at 1.8 GPM or less
3. Turn off water supply
   - For faucets, turn off water valves under the sink
   - For showers, turn off main water supply if there's no dedicated shower valve
4. Remove old shower head
   - Place a rag over the shower arm to protect the finish
   - Using an adjustable wrench, carefully turn the old shower head counterclockwise
   - If stuck, apply penetrating oil to the connection, wait 10 minutes, and try again
5. Prepare the shower arm
   - Clean threads with a small brush to remove old tape, debris, or mineral deposits
   - For stubborn mineral buildup, wrap a cloth soaked in white vinegar around the threads for 15 minutes
   - Dry thoroughly
6. Install new shower head
   - Wrap Teflon tape clockwise around the shower arm threads (4 wraps)
   - Hand-tighten the new showerhead clockwise
   - Use the wrench with a protective cloth to give a final quarter-turn
7. Remove old faucet aerator
   - Unscrew the aerator counterclockwise from the tip of the faucet
   - Use needle-nose pliers with a cloth if the aerator is stuck
   - For extremely stuck aerators, apply vinegar to dissolve mineral deposits

Revision: 25.1.8

8. Install new faucet aerator
   - Ensure rubber washer is properly seated inside the new aerator
   - Hand-tighten the aerator clockwise onto the faucet
   - Avoid using tools which could damage the aerator or the faucet finish
9. Test installation
   - Turn on water supply
   - Check for leaks at connection points
   - If leaking, turn off water, tighten slightly more, and retest
10. *Check flow rate (optional)*
    - *Repeat the flow measurement from Step 1*
    - *Confirm the flow now meets WaterSense standards*

Upgrading Plumbing 101: Definitions

- **Aerator:** A device on a faucet that mixes air with water to reduce flow but maintain pressure
- **Flow rate:** Water volume per time, typically measured in gallons per minute (GPM)
- **GPM (Gallons Per Minute):** Standard measurement of water flow in plumbing fixtures
- **Penetrating oil:** Lubricant designed to loosen rusted or mineral-stuck parts
- **Shower arm:** The pipe extending from the wall that connects to the showerhead
- **Teflon/plumber's tape:** Thread-sealing tape that prevents leaks at threaded connections
- **WaterSense:** EPA program that certifies water-efficient products meeting specific performance and efficiency standards

Upgrading Plumbing 101: Troubleshooting

Problem	Solutions
Leaks at connection points	Ensure proper Teflon tape application. Check for cross-threading. Tighten connection slightly more. Inspect washer and gasket for damage.
Poor water pressure after installation	Check if the flow restrictor can be removed. Ensure the aerator isn't clogged with debris. Clean mineral deposits from fixtures.
Cannot remove old fixture	Apply penetrating oil and wait 15 minutes. Use a rubber strap wrench for better grip. Apply heat with hairdryer to expand metal.
Irregular spray pattern	Clean mineral deposits from spray holes using vinegar. Check for debris in internal channels. Ensure the washer is properly seated.
Fixture swivels or feels loose	Check for missing or damaged washers. Ensure proper thread engagement. Use Teflon tape correctly. Tighten appropriately.

Upgrading Plumbing 101: Limitations

- Very low water pressure systems may not work well with some water-saving fixtures
- Homes with older plumbing may have incompatible thread sizes or corroded connections
- Some multi-function shower heads use more water in certain settings
- Extremely hard water areas may experience faster clogging of efficient fixtures

References and resources: <www.suspra.com/practice/water/upgrading-101.html>

Upgrading Plumbing 201: Upgrading Toilets

Install toilets that meet WaterSense standards

Revision: 25.1.8

WaterSense labeled toilets use no more than 1.28 gallons per flush (gpf)—a savings of at least 60% per flush compared to older toilets that use 3.5 or 7 gpf. Choose from gravity-fed toilets (most common, quieter), pressure-assisted toilets (more flushing power, noisier), dual-flush toilets (different volumes for liquid vs. solid waste), or vacuum-assisted toilets (combine good performance with efficiency).

Upgrading Plumbing 201: Equipment & Materials

- WaterSense toilet or components (replacement flapper, fill valve, or dual-flush converter kit)
- Wax ring with sleeve
- New toilet supply line
- Toilet shims (if needed)
- Caulk and caulk gun
- Toilet bolt caps
- Plumbing tools
- *Optional: Toilet flange repair kit, socket wrench set*

Upgrading Plumbing 201: Steps

Hire a professional plumber if you're not comfortable doing the work yourself

A. Replacing an Entire Toilet

1. Prepare for installation
   - Turn off the water supply valve located behind the toilet
   - Flush the toilet to empty the tank and bowl
   - Disconnect the water supply line from the toilet
   - Sponge out remaining water from the tank and bowl
   - Measure the rough-in distance (from wall to center of toilet flange)
2. Remove the old toilet
   - Remove the caps covering the toilet mounting bolts at the base
   - Unscrew the nuts from the mounting bolts
   - Gently rock the toilet to break the wax seal
   - Lift the toilet straight up and away from the flange
   - Remove the old wax ring and clean the flange area
   - Stuff a rag in the flange opening to prevent sewer gases from escaping
3. Inspect the flange
   - Check for cracks or damage to the toilet flange
   - If damaged, install a repair kit before proceeding
   - Ensure mounting bolts are in good condition; replace if necessary
4. Prepare the new toilet
   - Install any included components (like the fill valve or flapper) if not pre-installed
   - If separate, attach the tank to the bowl following manufacturer's instructions
   - Turn the toilet upside down on a towel or padding
   - Install the new wax ring on the toilet's outlet horn
5. Install the new toilet
   - Remove the rag from the flange
   - Position the new toilet by aligning the holes with the mounting bolts
   - Carefully lower the toilet straight down onto the flange
   - Apply even pressure to compress the wax ring and create a seal
   - Install washers and nuts on the mounting bolts
   - Tighten nuts alternately until the toilet is secure (do not overtighten)
   - Use level to ensure toilet sits evenly (use shims if necessary)
6. Connect water supply and finish installation
   - Connect the new flexible water supply line to the fill valve and supply valve
   - Turn on the water supply slowly and check for leaks

Sustainable Practices Handbook
Water Practices: Optimizing Water Efficiency

- Adjust the water level in the tank according to manufacturer's instructions
- Install bolt caps and caulk around the base of the toilet (leaving the back uncaulked)
- Test flush several times to ensure proper operation

B. Upgrading Toilet Components

1. Upgrading a flapper
   - Turn off water supply and flush toilet
   - Remove tank lid and disconnect the chain from the flush lever
   - Remove old flapper by sliding it off the overflow tube pegs
   - Install new water-efficient flapper following package instructions
   - Reattach chain to flush lever, ensuring proper slack
   - Turn water back on and test flush
2. Installing a high-efficiency fill valve
   - Turn off water supply and flush toilet
   - Disconnect supply line from the fill valve
   - Remove old fill valve by unscrewing the locknut under the tank
   - Install new high-efficiency fill valve according to package instructions
   - Reconnect water supply and adjust water level
   - Test for proper operation
3. Installing a dual-flush converter
   - Turn off water supply and flush toilet
   - Remove tank lid
   - Follow the specific instructions included with your converter kit
   - Turn water back on and test both flush options

Upgrading Plumbing 201: Definitions

- **Dual-flush**: Toilet system offering two flush options: reduced volume for liquid waste and full volume for solid waste
- **Fill valve**: The mechanism that refills the toilet tank after flushing
- **Flapper**: The rubber valve that controls water flow from the tank to the bowl during flushing
- **Flush valve**: The opening at the bottom of the tank that allows water to rush into the bowl
- **Gallons per flush (gpf)**: Measurement of water volume used during a flush
- **Rough-in distance**: Measurement from the finished wall to the center of the toilet flange
- **Toilet flange**: The pipe fitting that connects the toilet to the drainpipe and anchors the toilet to the floor
- **Wax ring**: Sealing component that creates a watertight connection between the toilet and flange
- **WaterSense**: EPA program that certifies water-efficient products that perform as well as or better than standard models

Upgrading Plumbing 201: Troubleshooting

Problem	Solutions
Toilet rocks or is unsteady	Use plastic shims to level the toilet. Trim excess shim material and caulk around the base to secure.
Leaking between tank and bowl	Check tank-to-bowl gasket. Ensure bolts connecting the tank to the bowl are tight but not overtightened. Replace gasket if damaged.
Leaking at the base	Remove the toilet and replace the wax ring. Check flange for damage. Ensure the toilet is properly seated and bolts are evenly tightened.

Revision: 25.1.8

Problem	Solutions
Running toilet after installation	Adjust the valve to the proper water level. Check flapper for proper seating. Ensure the chain has the correct slack.
Weak flush with new toilet	Check for partial clog in trapway or drain. Verify nothing is caught under the flapper. Adjust water level in the tank.
Incomplete emptying of bowl	Verify the toilet is level. Check the vent stack for blockage. Ensure no wax ring material is obstructing the outlet passage.
Dual-flush mechanism not working properly	Verify installation according to manufacturer's instructions. Adjust water level if necessary.
Ghost flushing (toilet runs at random times)	Replace flapper which may be allowing water to seep past. Check the fill valve for proper operation.

Upgrading Plumbing 201: Limitations

- Upgrading toilets requires moderate plumbing skills
- Older homes may have non-standard rough-in measurements requiring special toilet models
- Toilet removal can be physically demanding due to weight
- Damaged flanges may require additional repairs beyond simple toilet replacement
- Water pressure issues in the home may affect the performance of some water-efficient models

References and resources: <www.suspra.com/practice/water/upgrading-201.html>

Upgrading Plumbing 202: Upgrading Irrigation

Install sprinklers and irrigation controllers that meet WaterSense standards

WaterSense-labeled controllers automatically adjust watering schedules based on local conditions (saving an average home nearly 7,600 gallons annually). High-efficiency rotary nozzles apply water more slowly in larger droplets, increasing absorption and reducing runoff. Drip irrigation delivers water directly to plant roots with up to 90% efficiency compared to 65-75% for sprinkler systems. For optimal water efficiency, irrigate in the early morning (before 7 AM) when evaporation rates are lowest.

Upgrading Plumbing 202: Equipment, Materials and Cost

- $1,500-$4,000 for typical residential systems
- WaterSense labeled irrigation controller or timer
- WaterSense labeled sprinkler heads and nozzles
- Backflow preventer
- Polyethylene tubing or metal pipe (appropriate for your climate)
- Rain sensor or soil moisture sensor
- Valve boxes
- Drip irrigation components (if installing)
- Junction box and waterproof wire connectors (for controller wiring)
- Gardening and plumbing tools
- *Optional: Landscape design plan, valve manifold assembly, electrical wire for valves, pipe fittings (tees, elbows, adapters), sprinkler head risers*

Upgrading Plumbing 202: Steps

1. *Hire a professional if you are not comfortable doing the work yourself*

2. Plan your system
   - Create a diagram showing lawn areas, garden beds, trees, and hardscape
   - Identify water source location and available water pressure and flow rate
   - Mark zones based on plant types and sun exposure
   - Determine the location for your controller, valves, and pipe routes
3. Select WaterSense certified components
4. Gather permits and locate utilities
5. Install the irrigation controller
6. Install the valve manifold
7. Lay irrigation pipes
8. Install sprinkler heads
9. Install drip irrigation in appropriate zones
10. *Optional: Program your WaterSense controller*
11. Test and adjust the system
12. Complete the installation
13. Educate yourself and household members

Upgrading Plumbing 202: Definitions

- **Backflow preventer**: Prevents irrigation water from flowing into the potable water supply
- **Drip irrigation**: Delivering water directly to plant root zones at low pressure
- **Emitter**: A small device in drip irrigation systems that regulates water flow to individual plants
- **Evapotranspiration (ET)**: Combined evaporation from soil and transpiration from plants
- **Hydrozoning**: Grouping plants with similar water requirements together in irrigation zones
- **Lateral line**: Smaller pipes that branch off from the main line
- **Matched precipitation rate**: Sprinklers that apply water at the same rate across a zone
- **Pressure regulator**: Keeps water pressure at the optimal level for irrigation components
- **Rotary nozzle**: A high-efficiency nozzle that delivers rotating streams rather than mist
- **Smart controller**: An irrigation controller that automatically adjusts watering schedules based on environmental conditions
- **Valve**: A device that controls water flow to a specific zone in an irrigation system

Upgrading Plumbing 202: Troubleshooting

Problem	Solutions
Controller won't power on	Check electrical connections and fuses. Verify the transformer is plugged in. Test outlet with another device.
Sprinkler head doesn't pop up	Clear debris around the head. Check for adequate water pressure. Inspect for damage or clogs in the riser.
Uneven watering or dry spots	Check for proper head-to-head coverage. Verify matched precipitation rates. Look for clogged nozzles.
Water leaking from fittings	Turn off the system and allow it to dry. Apply pipe thread sealant or replace fittings. Check for cracked pipes.
Drip emitters not dispensing water	Check for clogged filters. Verify the pressure regulator is functioning. Examine emitters for clogs.
Controller not connecting to Wi-Fi	Check Wi-Fi signal strength. Verify network credentials. Update controller firmware.

Problem	Solutions
Sensor not communicating	Check sensor wiring connections. Verify that the sensor is properly installed. Replace batteries if applicable.
Irrigation runs during or after rain	Verify rain sensors are properly installed and functioning. Check controller settings for a rain delay feature.

Upgrading Plumbing 202: Limitations
- Installation requires moderate to advanced plumbing and basic electrical skills
- Weather-based controllers may not respond quickly enough to sudden weather changes
- Some smart controllers require stable Wi-Fi connections and regular firmware updates
- Underground installation makes future modifications more challenging
- Complete system replacement may require significant landscape disruption

References and resources: <www.suspra.com/practice/water/upgrading-202.html>

Upgrading Plumbing 203: Upgrading Dishwashers

Install a more efficient automatic dishwasher

Modern ENERGY STAR certified dishwashers use roughly 3.5 gallons of water per cycle, compared to older models that used up to 10 gallons. With proper installation, modern dishwashers are designed to work effectively without pre-rinsing dishes. Portable dishwashers offer an excellent alternative for renters or homes where permanent installation isn't possible, connecting to standard kitchen faucets and draining directly into the sink.

Upgrading Plumbing 203: Equipment & Materials
- Measuring tape
- Plumbing hand tools (level, adjustable wrench, screwdriver set, pliers, Teflon tape, etc.)
- Bucket and towels
- New dishwasher with ENERGY STAR and WaterSense certification
- 3/8" compression fitting or braided stainless steel supply line
- Junction box, wire nuts, and electrical tape (for hardwired models)
- Dishwasher drain hose
- Hose clamps
- *Optional: Dishwasher installation kit*
- *Pipe cutter (if modifying plumbing)*
- *Voltage tester*
- *Air gap device (if required by local code)*

Upgrading Plumbing 203: Steps
1. *Hire a licensed plumber if you are not confident in your own plumbing abilities*
2. Select an efficient dishwasher
   - ENERGY STAR certified model
   - WaterSense labeled model
   - Models with soil sensors that adjust cycle length and water use
3. Prepare for installation
   - Measure the installation space (standard dishwashers are typically 24" wide, 24" deep, and 35" high)
   - Confirm your existing water, electrical, and drain connections are compatible

- Purchase any needed adapters or installation kits
- Read the manufacturer's installation instructions thoroughly
4. Remove the old dishwasher (for built-in models)
    - Turn off power to the dishwasher at the circuit breaker
    - Shut off the water supply valve (typically under the sink or in the basement)
    - Place a bucket and towels under the water connection
    - Disconnect the water supply line from the dishwasher inlet valve
    - Remove the screws securing the dishwasher to the countertop or cabinet frame
    - Disconnect the drain hose from the sink drain or garbage disposal
    - For hardwired models: Remove the access panel and disconnect wires
    - For plug-in models: Unplug the power cord
    - Slide the dishwasher out from the cabinet space
5. Dispose of the old dishwasher responsibly
    - If dishwasher still works: sell used or donate to charitable organizations
    - Check with your local appliance retailer about recycling programs
    - Contact your municipal waste management for large appliance disposal guidelines
6. Prepare the installation area
    - Clean the floor and surrounding area; check for and repair any water damage
    - Ensure water supply and drain connections are accessible
    - Verify the electrical connection meets current code requirements
7. Install the new dishwasher (built-in models)
    - Attach the water inlet and drain hoses to the dishwasher if not pre-installed
    - Apply Teflon tape to the water supply connection threads
    - Carefully slide the dishwasher into the cabinet opening, routing hoses and electrical through appropriate access holes
    - Level the dishwasher by adjusting the legs
    - Connect the drain hose to the sink drain or garbage disposal using a high loop or air gap as required by local code
    - Connect the water supply line to the dishwasher inlet valve and tighten with a wrench
    - For hardwired models: Connect electrical wires using wire nuts
    - For plug-in models: Plug into appropriate outlet
    - Secure the dishwasher to countertop or cabinet with mounting brackets and screws
    - Replace the access panel and toe kick
8. Install the new dishwasher (portable models)
    - Place the unit near your kitchen sink
    - When ready to use, attach the unicouple adapter to your kitchen faucet
    - Ensure the drain hose is positioned to drain into the sink
    - Plug into a grounded electrical outlet
9. Test the installation
    - Turn on the water supply valve and check for leaks at all connections
    - Restore power at the circuit breaker
    - Run a test cycle without dishes
    - Check again for leaks during operation
    - Verify proper draining
10. Optimize dishwasher settings
    - Program the efficiency or eco mode as the default setting
    - Set the water temperature to 120°F (49°C) for optimal cleaning and efficiency

Upgrading Plumbing 203: Definitions

- **Air gap**: A device that prevents backflow of wastewater into the dishwasher
- **ENERGY STAR**: A government-backed symbol for energy efficiency
- **High loop**: A section of the drain hose that's elevated to prevent backflow

- **Junction box**: An enclosure housing electrical connections
- **Soil sensors**: Technology that detects how dirty dishes are and adjusts the cycle accordingly
- **Unicouple adapter**: The connector used to attach portable dishwashers to a kitchen faucet

Upgrading Plumbing 203: Troubleshooting

Problem	Solutions
Dishwasher doesn't fit in the cabinet opening	Confirm exact measurements before purchasing. Check for obstructions in the cabinet space. Consider a smaller (18") dishwasher if space is limited.
Water leaking from connections	Ensure all connections are tight. Check for damaged washers or gaskets. Verify Teflon tape is properly applied to threaded connections.
Dishwasher not draining properly	Ensure the drain hose has a proper high loop or air gap. Check for kinks in the drain hose. Remove the knockout plug from the garbage disposal.
Electrical issues (no power)	Verify the circuit breaker is on. Check for loose wire connections. Test the outlet with a voltage tester. Ensure the door latch is fully engaged.
Dishwasher not level	Adjust the leveling legs until the unit is even. An unlevel dishwasher can cause performance issues and potential leaks.
Water supply issues	Make sure the water supply valve is fully open. Check for kinks in the supply line. Verify water pressure is adequate (20-120 psi is typical).

Upgrading Plumbing 203: Limitations
- Built-in dishwashers require a dedicated electrical circuit, water supply, and drainage system
- Portable dishwashers require storage space and counter space during operation
- Older homes may need electrical or plumbing upgrades to support modern dishwashers
- Rental properties may restrict permanent appliance installation
- DIY installation may void warranty if not done according to manufacturer specifications

References and resources: <www.suspra.com/practice/water/upgrading-203.html>

Upgrading Plumbing 204: Upgrading Washing Machines

Install a more efficient washing machine

Front-loading washing machines are typically more efficient than top-loading models, using a horizontal axis design that requires less water since clothes are tumbled through a small pool of water rather than fully submerged. This design also extracts more water during the spin cycle, reducing drying time. Using stainless steel-braided hoses rather than standard rubber hoses provides important protection against leaks and flooding.

Upgrading Plumbing 204: Equipment & Materials
- New ENERGY STAR certified washing machine
- Appliance dolly or hand truck
- Plumbing hand tools (level, adjustable wrench, screwdriver set, pliers, Teflon tape, etc.)
- Tape measure
- Bucket and towels
- Washing machine hoses (preferably stainless steel-braided)
- Drain hose clamp

- Flashlight
- *Optional: Drain pan to place under washer*
- *Washing machine hose shut-off valve*

Upgrading Plumbing 204: Steps

1. Prepare the installation space
   - Measure the installation space to ensure your new machine will fit
   - Verify power supply requirements (typically 120V outlet with a dedicated 15 or 20-amp circuit)
   - Confirm water supply connections (hot and cold)
   - Check that drainpipe is accessible and at proper height (typically 30"-48" above floor)
   - Ensure floor is level, clean, and structurally sound
2. Remove the old washing machine (if replacing)
   - Turn off water supply valves to the washer
   - Unplug the power cord
   - Disconnect the hot and cold water hoses (have bucket and towels ready for water spillage)
   - Disconnect the drain hose from the standpipe or utility sink
   - Use an appliance dolly to move the old machine out
3. Inspect and prepare water connections
   - Check water supply valves for leaks or corrosion
   - Consider replacing old valves or installing shutoff valves if not present
   - Apply Teflon tape to the threads of both hot and cold water connections
4. Position the new washing machine
   - Remove all shipping materials, including bolts, straps, and packing
   - Use an appliance dolly to move the machine to its location
   - Set the washing machine in place, leaving a few inches of clearance to work behind it
5. Level the washing machine
   - Place a level on top of the machine
   - Adjust the leveling feet (usually by turning clockwise to raise, counterclockwise to lower)
   - Check level front-to-back and side-to-side
   - Tighten lock nuts on the leveling feet once level
6. Connect water supply hoses
   - Identify hot and cold water connections (usually red for hot, blue for cold)
   - Hand-tighten the hoses to the corresponding water supply valves
   - Hand-tighten the opposite ends to the proper inlet ports on the washer
   - Using an adjustable wrench, give each connection an additional quarter turn
7. Install the drain hose
   - Connect the drain hose to the washing machine if not already attached
   - Insert the other end into the standpipe, utility sink, or dedicated drain
   - Ensure the drain hose height follows manufacturer recommendations
   - Secure with a clamp if needed
   - Form a U-shaped high loop in the drain hose to prevent siphoning
8. Final connections and testing
   - Plug the power cord into the electrical outlet
   - Slowly turn on both water supply valves and check for leaks
   - If leaks occur, tighten connections slightly or reapply Teflon tape
   - Run the washing machine through a quick test cycle
   - Check again for leaks, vibration, or unusual noises
   - Ensure proper drainage during and after the cycle
9. Finalize the installation
   - Push the washing machine into its final position (if needed)
   - Ensure there's sufficient space for ventilation according to manufacturer specifications

- Keep the manual and installation instructions for future reference

Upgrading Plumbing 204: Definitions
- **Appliance dolly**: A specialized hand truck designed to move large appliances safely
- **Drain pan**: A shallow container placed under the washing machine to catch minor leaks before they damage flooring
- **ENERGY STAR**: A U.S. government-backed symbol for energy efficiency
- **Leveling feet**: Adjustable supports at the bottom of the washing machine
- **Shipping bolts**: Special bolts that secure the drum during shipping; must be removed before operation
- **Standpipe**: A vertical pipe connected to the home's drainage system where the washing machine's drain hose empties
- **Water Factor (WF)**: How many gallons per cycle per cubic foot the washer uses; lower numbers indicate more efficient use of water

Upgrading Plumbing 204: Troubleshooting

Problem	Solutions
Washing machine vibrates excessively	Ensure the machine is properly leveled. Check that all shipping materials have been removed. Consider installing anti-vibration pads under the feet.
Water leaks from hose connections	Tighten connections slightly with a wrench. Ensure rubber washers are properly seated. Apply Teflon tape to threaded connections.
Washing machine won't fill with water	Verify water supply valves are fully open. Check for kinks in inlet hoses. Inspect inlet screens for debris and clean if necessary.
Drain issues or water backup	Ensure drain hose is properly positioned at recommended height. Check for clogs in the drain hose or standpipe.
Machine won't power on	Check that the unit is plugged in. Verify the outlet has power. Ensure the power cord isn't damaged.
Unusual noises during operation	Verify the machine is level. Check for loose items in the drum. Ensure all shipping materials have been removed.

Upgrading Plumbing 204: Limitations
- Installing a new washing machine requires adequate space, proper water connections, electrical supply, and drainage
- Older homes may need electrical or plumbing upgrades to accommodate washing machines
- Front-loading machines typically require a minimum of 21" front clearance for the door to open properly
- Installation on upper floors may require additional floor reinforcement to support the weight
- Smart washing machines may require Wi-Fi connectivity and smartphone compatibility for full functionality

References and resources: <www.suspra.com/practice/water/upgrading-204.html>

Upgrading Plumbing 301: Installing Hot Water Recirculation

Install a hot water recirculation system to deliver hot water faster

Install a hot water recirculation system to reduce water waste and waiting time for hot water at your fixtures. These systems work by continuously circulating hot water through your pipes, eliminating the need to run water while waiting for it to heat up. Most systems consist of a small pump installed at your water heater or under a remote sink, plus a return line back to your water heater. Some advanced models include timers or on-demand activation to maximize energy efficiency. Installation complexity varies depending on your home's plumbing configuration—retrofit options are available for existing homes, while full dedicated-line systems work best in new construction or renovations. For maximum sustainability impact, pair your recirculation system with an energy-efficient water heater.

References and resources: <www.suspra.com/practice/water/upgrading-301.html>

Conserving Water

Displacing 201: Displacing Tank Water

Install a brick or bottle in your toilet tank to displace water

If your toilet uses more than 2 gallons per flush, displace water in your toilet tank to reduce water consumption, ideally without affecting flushing performance. Plastic bottles are preferred over bricks as they don't deteriorate or release sediment. Each 1-liter bottle saves approximately 1 liter (0.26 gallons) per flush, while a standard brick displaces about 0.5 gallons (1.9 liters).

Displacing 201: Equipment & Materials

- Plastic bottles (16-20 oz) or brick
- Sand or pebbles (optional for weighting bottles)
- Scissors or utility knife
- Water-resistant tape
- Ruler or measuring tape
- *Optional: Toilet tank dye tablets*

Displacing 201: Steps

1. Check if your toilet is suitable for displacement
   - High-efficiency toilets (1.6 gallons/6 liters or less) not suitable; already water efficient
   - Older toilets (3.5-7 gallons/13-26 liters) are ideal candidates
   - Check your toilet's gallons per flush (GPF) rating
2. Prepare your displacement device
   - **For plastic bottles:** Remove label and cap, rinse thoroughly, fill 2/3 with water, add sand if needed for weight, replace cap, seal with tape
   - **For bricks:** Choose one that fits without interfering with mechanisms, rinse thoroughly, consider sealing or wrapping in plastic
3. Turn off the water supply valve behind the toilet
4. Flush to drain most water from the tank
5. Remove the tank lid carefully
6. Identify mechanisms inside the tank (flush valve, fill valve, flapper, flush handle chain)
7. Position displacement device away from moving parts, typically in corners
8. Turn the water back on and let tank fill completely
9. Test flush the toilet
   - If flush is insufficient, remove displacement or use smaller device
   - If flush works well but you want more savings, add more displacement
10. Check periodically for deterioration or interference with mechanisms

Displacing 201: Definitions

- **Displacement device**: Object placed in a toilet tank to reduce water used per flush
- **Flapper**: Rubber seal at tank bottom that lifts during flushing
- **Fill valve**: Mechanism controlling water flow into the tank
- **Flush valve**: Mechanism releasing water from tank to bowl
- **GPF**: Gallons Per Flush

Displacing 201: Troubleshooting

Problem	Solutions
Toilet doesn't flush completely	Remove or reduce displacement device size. Check for interference with mechanisms.
Water level too low	Adjust float height or use a smaller displacement device.
Device floating	Add sand or pebbles to bottles. Secure with waterproof tape if needed.
Brick deteriorating	Remove immediately. Replace with sealed brick or plastic bottles.
Leaking	Check that the device isn't interfering with the flapper seal.
Multiple flushes needed	Reduce displacement device size to ensure effective single flushes.

Displacing 201: Limitations

- Not suitable for efficient toilets (1.6 GPF/6 liters or less)
- May decrease flush effectiveness if too much water is displaced
- Bricks can deteriorate and potentially damage components
- Does not fix underlying issues like leaks
- Less effective than replacing with a high-efficiency toilet

References and resources: <www.suspra.com/practice/water/displacing-201.html>

Economizing 101: Flushing Toilets

Flush toilets less frequently

Observe the advice, "If it's yellow let it mellow," to save many gallons of water every day. In most homes in North America, more potable water is used to flush toilets than for anything else.

References and resources: <www.suspra.com/practice/water/economizing-101.html>

Economizing 102: Filling Loads

Wait to run dishwashers and clothes washers until you have a full load

Fuller loads mean fewer wash cycles and fewer gallons of water used per week. If you have very few possessions, a full load may mean running the wash when you no longer have any clean dishware or clothes, even if there is still room in your appliance. Machine washing generally uses less water than hand washing, depending on the design of the appliance and your handwashing technique.

References and resources: <www.suspra.com/practice/water/economizing-102.html>

Economizing 103: Cutting Short

Take fewer or shorter showers

Modern shower heads use between 1.25 and 2.5 gallons (5 and 10 liters) of water per minute. Older shower heads use up to 3.5 gallons (13 liters) of water per minute.

References and resources: <www.suspra.com/practice/water/economizing-103.html>

Economizing 104: Washing Less

Wash clothes and vehicles less frequently

Wear clothes more than once before washing. Spot wash vehicles to remove salt or debris. Or allow rain to naturally clean off dirt.

References and resources: <www.suspra.com/practice/water/economizing-104.html>

Economizing 105: Taking Navy Showers

Take Navy showers

Take "Navy showers": get wet, turn off the water to soap up, and then turn it back on to rinse. This practice drastically reduces water usage by eliminating water flow while soaping and shampooing. An easy step for individuals and households to conserve water, this practice requires no special skills or equipment, adds negligible time to your routine, and is completely free.

References and resources: <www.suspra.com/practice/water/economizing-105.html>

Substituting 102: Taking Showers

Take short showers instead of baths

Showers are generally more water-efficient than baths. A standard bath can require approximately 70 gallons of water, while a five-minute shower uses significantly less, between 10 to 25 gallons, depending on the showerhead's flow rate. To make your showers even more sustainable, aim for showers under 5 minutes. You can use a timer, a shower playlist of a few songs, or simply be mindful of your water usage to keep your showers brief. Beyond water conservation, shorter, cooler showers can also reduce energy consumption by decreasing the amount of hot water used.

References and resources: <www.suspra.com/practice/water/substituting-102.html>

Substituting 103: Sweeping

Sweep driveways and patios instead of hosing them down with water

Instead of reaching for the hose to clean your driveway or patio, grab a broom instead. Hosing down paved surfaces is a waste of potable water and may carry pollutants into storm drains and local waterways. By switching to sweeping, you conserve water and reduce potential water pollution.

References and resources: <www.suspra.com/practice/water/substituting-103.html>

Substituting 303: Xeriscaping

Landscape with drought-resistant species or features that require no water

Xeriscaping is a water-efficient landscaping approach that works with your local climate to create landscapes that thrive with minimal water. It's applicable in all climate zones, not just desert regions.

Key Principles
- Group plants with similar water needs (hydrozoning)
- Focus on native and drought-tolerant plants
- Understand your specific site conditions (soil, sun, wind, drainage)
- o-Plan for a two-year establishment period when plants need regular watering

- Can be implemented gradually in phases

Key Benefits
- Conserves water
- Reduces mowing, fertilizers, and pesticides
- Supports local pollinators and wildlife
- Helps manage stormwater runoff
- Reduces soil erosion
- Can have diverse aesthetic options (not just rocks and cacti)
- Requires less maintenance once established

Start by analyzing your site conditions, selecting appropriate plants for your climate zone, and creating zones based on water needs. New plants will require regular watering during their establishment period before becoming more self-sufficient.

Substituting 303: Equipment & Materials
- Garden gloves and basic hand tools (trowel, pruners, rake)
- Drought-resistant native plants appropriate for your region
- Organic mulch (bark, wood chips, straw, or compost)
- Inorganic mulch (gravel, river rock, or decomposed granite)
- Newspaper or cardboard for sheet mulching
- *Optional: Soil testing kit, shovel, wheelbarrow, pickaxe, soil amendments*
- *Drip irrigation components for establishment phase*

Substituting 303: Steps
1. Research and plan your xeriscape
   - Determine your climate zone and identify native drought-resistant plants
   - Observe your yard's sun exposure, drainage patterns, and microclimates
   - Create a design dividing your yard into hydrozones (areas with similar water needs)
   - Check local regulations and association rules
2. Analyze and prepare your soil
   - Test soil pH, nutrient levels, and composition
   - Improve soil structure with targeted amendments to increase water retention
   - Use compost to improve water-holding capacity
3. Remove or reduce existing lawn
   - Option 1: Sheet mulching - cover grass with cardboard, add 6 inches of mulch
   - Option 2: Cover with black plastic for 8 weeks to kill grass
   - Option 3: Manually remove sod with shovel or sod cutter
4. Establish minimal irrigation
   - Install simple drip irrigation for the establishment period (first two years)
   - Group plants with similar water needs together
   - Consider installing a rain barrel to collect roof runoff
5. Select and plant strategically
   - Choose native and adapted plants suited to your local climate
   - Plant in appropriate hydrozones based on water needs
   - Leave appropriate spacing for mature size
6. Install hardscaping elements
   - Create permeable pathways using gravel or spaced pavers
   - Consider dry creek beds to direct water flow during rain events
   - Use boulders and decorative rocks as focal points
7. Apply appropriate mulch
   - Cover all bare soil with 2-4 inches of organic mulch for planting beds

Sustainable Practices Handbook — Water Practices: Conserving Water

- Use inorganic mulch for pathways and non-planted areas
- Keep mulch a few inches away from plant stems and tree trunks
8. Establish maintenance routines
    - Water deeply but infrequently during the establishment period
    - Gradually reduce watering as plants establish root systems
    - Destroy weeds before they seed

Substituting 303: Definitions

- **Hydrozone**: Area where plants with similar water requirements are grouped together
- **Microclimate**: Small area where climate differs from surrounding area
- **Mulch**: Protective layer on soil surface to reduce evaporation and suppress weeds
- **Native plants**: Species that occur naturally in a region without human introduction
- **Xeriscape**: Landscaping method that reduces or eliminates supplemental water needs

Substituting 303: Troubleshooting

Problem	Solutions
Plants dying	Ensure plants are appropriate for your specific climate zone. Water more frequently during the establishment phase. Check soil drainage.
Soil too compacted for planting	Add organic matter. Consider sheet mulching or raised beds. Use plants with strong roots that can penetrate compacted soil.
Erosion on slopes	Plant deep-rooted native grasses. Install terraces for steeper slopes. Use erosion control blankets while plants establish.
Weeds taking over	Ensure mulch is thick enough (3 inches). Address weeds promptly. Consider landscape fabric under inorganic mulch in problem areas.

Substituting 303: Limitations

- Initial transformation requires time and effort
- Full establishment typically takes three years
- Some municipalities or associations may restrict landscape choices
- Xeriscaping knowledge is regional—what works in one climate may fail in another

References and resources: <www.suspra.com/practice/water/substituting-303.html>

Substituting 401: Using a Waterless Urinal

Install and use a waterless urinal

Conserve water by installing waterless urinals. They allow urine to flow down into a trap system that prevents sewer gases from escaping while allowing liquid to pass through.

1. **Cartridge systems:** Use replaceable cartridges with sealant liquid; require replacement every 3-6 months (e.g., Falcon Waterfree, Sloan Waterfree)
2. **Liquid seal systems:** Use plant-based oil poured directly into drain; require periodic replenishment (e.g., EcoTrap)
3. **Membrane trap systems:** Use flexible silicone membranes or valves; don't require chemical sealants and have fewer replacement parts (e.g., Uridan, Urimat)

Benefits

- Eliminates water consumption
- Reduces maintenance (no flush valves) and improve hygiene (no flush handles)
- Reduces energy consumption for water pumping and treatment

Implementation Tips
- Train cleaning staff on specific maintenance procedures (don't pour water in)
- For residential use, consider membrane systems (lower maintenance)
- For commercial use, high-traffic locations may benefit from cartridge systems

Most failures result from improper installation or inadequate maintenance.

Substituting 401: Equipment & Materials
- Waterless urinal fixture
- Mounting hardware
- Appropriate trap or cartridge system (specific to urinal model)
- *Optional: Basic hand tools required for plumbing projects*

Substituting 401: Steps

A. Planning and Preparation
1. Check local building codes and obtain necessary permits
2. Select an appropriate waterless urinal system:
   - Cartridge, liquid seal, membrane trap, or integrated trap systems
3. **Hire a licensed plumber if you are not confident in your DIY skills**

B. Installation
1. Remove existing urinal (for retrofits)
2. Prepare the drain
   - Clean existing drain opening and pipe
   - Install adapter if needed
3. Install the urinal and trap system per manufacturer instructions

C. Maintenance
1. Daily cleaning
   - Spray recommended cleaner on surfaces and wipe with microfiber cloth
   - Never pour water down waterless urinals
2. Weekly maintenance: check for odors and add sealant liquid if needed
3. Replace cartridges according to schedule (typically every 3-6 months)

Substituting 401: Definitions
- **Cartridge**: Replaceable component containing odor-blocking mechanism
- **Liquid sealant**: Special fluid creating barrier between urine and air to prevent odors
- **Membrane trap**: Flexible component allowing urine to pass while preventing odors
- **Trap insert**: Removable component creating odor barrier in drain

Substituting 401: Troubleshooting

Problem	Solutions
Odors	Check trap and cartridge installation. Ensure proper sealant liquid level. Clean with manufacturer-recommended cleaner.

Problem	Solutions
Slow drainage	Clear debris from trap. Check for sediment buildup. Inspect drain line for blockage.
Leaking at drain	Tighten connections. Apply new plumber's putty. Check for damaged gaskets.
Urine "pooling" in bowl	Clean bowl with manufacturer-recommended cleaner. Check fixture level. Verify drain isn't blocked.
Mineral buildup	Perform periodic maintenance with descaling solution. Increase frequency of cartridge changes.

Substituting 401: Limitations
- Some building codes may not permit waterless urinals
- Initial cost is higher than conventional urinals
- Retrofitting existing plumbing can be challenging
- Regular maintenance essential to prevent odor problems
- Mineral buildup in drain lines can occur if maintenance is neglected
- Some models require ongoing purchases of proprietary cartridges

References and resources: <www.suspra.com/practice/water/substituting-401.html>

Substituting 402: Using a Composting Toilet

Install and use a composting toilet

Conserve water by using composting toilets rather than conventional flush toilets. Composting toilets use aerobic decomposition (requiring very little water) to break down human waste, converting urine, feces, and toilet tissue into a valuable soil amendment.

Core Principles
- **Separation:** Separate urine from feces controls moisture and optimizes decomposition
- **Aeration:** Provide ventilation and occasional turning of compost; oxygen is essential
- **Carbon-Nitrogen Balance:** Add carbon-rich material (sawdust, wood chips) to balance nitrogen-rich human waste
- **Moisture Control:** Maintain 40-60% moisture levels (like a wrung-out sponge)
- **Temperature:** Keep temperatures between 90-140°F (32-60°C) to speed decomposition

System Types
- **Self-Contained Commercial Units:** All-in-one fixtures (e.g., Nature's Head, Sun-Mar, Separett); ideal for small spaces
- **Centralized Systems:** Separate toilet from composting chamber below (e.g., Clivus Multrum, Phoenix); higher capacity
- **Do-It-Yourself Bucket Systems:** Simple, low-cost option requiring frequent emptying; often called "humanure" systems

Benefits
- Save 25,000-35,000 gallons of water annually for a family of four
- Reduce demand on municipal infrastructure
- Transform waste into a resource

Sustainable Practices Handbook
Water Practices: Conserving Water

Implementation Considerations
- Check local regulations—many jurisdictions now permit them, especially in rural areas
- Costs range from under $100 (DIY) to $2,000+ (commercial units)
- Greywater (sink/shower water) must be addressed separately
- Properly finished compost (after two years) is recommended for ornamental plants, not food crops
- Final compost volume reduces by 70-90% from original waste

Maintain proper carbon-nitrogen ratio, aeration, and moisture levels.

Substituting 402: Equipment & Materials
- Manufactured composting toilet unit or DIY materials
- Carbon-rich material (sawdust, coconut coir, peat moss, or wood shavings)
- Scooper for carbon material
- Toilet paper (preferably recycled)
- Dedicated cleaning supplies
- Gloves (rubber or nitrile)
- Hand sanitizer and soap
- Spray bottle with vinegar solution
- Compost thermometer
- Ventilation components

Substituting 402: Steps
1. **Plan and prepare**
   - Research local regulations and permit requirements
   - Select appropriate system type based on space, users, and emptying capabilities
   - Plan ventilation route (ideally straight up through roof)
2. **Install your chosen system**
   - **Self-contained units**:
     - Follow manufacturer's instructions
     - Install vent pipe through wall or roof with weatherproof seal
     - Connect power for fan if electric
     - Secure toilet to floor
   - **Centralized systems**:
     - Construct composting chamber below toilet area
     - Install toilet fixture connected to drop chute
     - Ensure proper ventilation with fan
     - Test for leaks and odors
   - **Do-It-Yourself bucket system**:
     - Construct wooden box to hold bucket at toilet height
     - Install toilet seat on top
     - Line bucket with compostable bag if desired
     - Add 2" of carbon material to bottom
3. **Prepare for first use**
   - Add starter layer of finished compost or garden soil
   - Add 4" of carbon material
   - Moisten chamber material slightly if completely dry
4. **Use the toilet**
   - After each use, add enough carbon material to cover waste completely
   - Close lid after use
5. **Maintain the system**
   - Weekly: Check moisture level and stir if system design allows

- Monthly: Inspect ventilation and check temperature
- Empty finished compost according to system design (typically every 12 months)
- Use finished compost only on ornamental plants following local regulations

Substituting 402: Definitions

- **Aerobic decomposition**: Biological breakdown of organic matter with oxygen
- **Carbon-nitrogen ratio**: Balance between carbon and nitrogen materials (optimal range 25:1 to 30:1)
- **Humanure**: Human waste that has been properly composted
- **Thermophilic composting**: High-temperature process that accelerates decomposition
- **Urine diversion**: System that separates urine from solid waste

Substituting 402: Troubleshooting

Problem	Solutions
Foul odors	Check ventilation for blockages. Add more carbon material. Stir compost to improve aeration. Clean urine diversion components.
Too wet compost	Add more carbon material. Improve urine diversion. Increase ventilation.
Insects (flies, gnats)	Ensure all waste is completely covered with carbon material. Repair insect screens on ventilation.
Slow decomposition	Check temperature - add insulation in cold environments. Ensure proper moisture (like a wrung-out sponge).
Urine diversion blockage	Clean with vinegar solution to dissolve mineral buildup. Increase slope of diversion components.

Substituting 402: Limitations

- Requires more user involvement than conventional toilets
- May require behavior change for household members and guests
- Some systems require electricity for fans or heaters
- Regular maintenance essential for proper operation
- Limited or prohibited by building codes in some areas
- Most jurisdictions prohibit using end product on food crops

References and resources: <www.suspra.com/practice/water/substituting-402.html>

Substituting 403: Using an Incinerating Toilet

Install and use an incinerating toilet

Choose an electric incinerating toilet as a waterless sanitation solution to burn human waste to ash at temperatures between 900-1,400°F (480-760°C).

Key Features
- Zero water consumption (compared to 1.6-5 gallons per flush for traditional toilets)
- Reduces waste and tissue paper to sterile ash (only two cups per month for a household)
- Ash can be safely disposed of with regular household waste or used for non-food plants
- Multiple safety mechanisms including temperature monitors and automatic shutdown features

Ideal Applications
- Water-scarce areas
- Locations without sewage system access
- Sites where septic systems aren't feasible
- Places where traditional plumbing installation is challenging
- Areas with freezing conditions

Implementation Considerations
- Higher initial installation cost than conventional toilets
- Energy requirements: 1.5-2.0 kWh per cycle
- Power requirements: 1,800 to 3,500 watts
- A single unit can serve a family of six people
- Requires proper ventilation
- Commercial models available for higher-usage settings

Substituting 403: Equipment & Materials
- Incinerating toilet unit
- Electricity supply (120V or 240V depending on model)
- Venting materials (stainless steel pipe, roof flashing)
- Non-combustible floor material (if installing on combustible flooring)
- Toilet seat liner papers/bags
- Grounding wire and electrical connections
- Basic tools (screwdriver set, drill, measuring tape, level, pipe cutter)
- Vent pipe sealant/high-temperature silicone
- *Optional: Propane connection, carbon monoxide detector, surge protector*

Substituting 403: Steps
1. Research and select an appropriate unit
   - Verify local building codes permit installation
   - Calculate electrical requirements (most require a 15-20 amp dedicated circuit)
   - Select model sized for your household
2. Prepare for installation
   - Apply for necessary permits
   - Ensure adequate ventilation
   - Confirm adequate electrical service or sufficient battery capacity
   - Create non-combustible floor area if needed
3. Install the toilet unit
   - Position according to manufacturer specifications
   - Ensure level placement with recommended clearances
   - Secure to floor if required
4. Install the venting system
   - Cut appropriate opening in roof or wall
   - Install vent pipe maintaining proper clearances from combustibles
   - Seal all connections with high-temperature silicone
   - Install proper flashing and vent cap
5. Complete electrical connections
   - Connect to dedicated circuit or battery
   - Install ground wire according to code
6. Test the system
   - Test electrical connections before operation

- Follow manufacturer's startup procedures
- Run a complete cycle to ensure proper operation
- Verify proper venting with no smoke or odors
7. Operate and maintain
    - Line bowl with manufacturer-approved liner or toilet paper
    - Close lid after use
    - Activate incineration cycle (typically 30-60 minutes)
    - Allow full cycle to complete
    - Remove ash regularly (typically every four weeks)
    - Clean bowl with non-abrasive cleaners
    - Inspect venting system quarterly

Substituting 403: Definitions

- **Ash pan**: Container that collects incinerated waste residue
- **Catalytic converter**: Component that helps reduce emissions and odors
- **Cycle time**: Duration for complete incineration (typically 30-60 minutes)
- **Vent stack**: Pipe system directing exhaust gases outside

Substituting 403: Troubleshooting

Problem	Solutions
Smoke or odors	Check the vent pipe for obstructions. Verify pipe connections are sealed. Ensure vent cap functions correctly.
Incomplete incineration	Verify power supply. Check the heating element. Ensure the lid is properly closed during the cycle.
Unit won't start	Check power connection and circuit breaker. Verify lid safety switch is engaged. Ensure the ash pan is properly seated.
Unexpected shutdowns	Check the vent system for proper flow. Verify temperature sensors function correctly. Ensure stable power supply.

Substituting 403: Limitations

- Requires electricity, vulnerable to power outages unless you have battery storage
- High initial cost ($1,500-$4,000 plus installation)
- Energy consumption for each cycle (1.5-2.0 kWh)
- Limited capacity per cycle (typically six uses before incineration)
- Cannot accept non-organic materials or hygiene products
- Requires proper ventilation system
- Some jurisdictions have special permitting requirements

References and resources: <www.suspra.com/practice/water/substituting-403.html>

Preventing Water Pollution

Cleaning 101: Choosing Safer Solutions

Clean with non-polluting solutions

Homemade cleaning solutions provide more sustainable alternatives to conventional products. White vinegar dissolves mineral deposits. Baking soda works as a gentle abrasive and deodorizer. Liquid castile soap breaks down grease. Lemon juice brightens and removes hard water deposits. Hydrogen peroxide serves as a less-toxic alternative to bleach.

Cleaning 101: Equipment & Materials

- White vinegar (5% acetic acid)
- Baking soda (sodium bicarbonate)
- Liquid castile soap (unscented)
- Lemon juice (fresh or bottled)
- Spray bottles
- Measuring cups and spoons
- Mixing bowls
- Clean cloths or rags
- Scrub brushes
- Microfiber cloths
- Hydrogen peroxide (3% solution)
- *Optional: Essential oils for fragrance*
- *Borax for tougher cleaning*
- *Washing soda for stronger cleaning*
- *Olive oil for wood polish*
- *Citric acid powder for hard water stains*

Cleaning 101: Steps

1. Understand your cleaning needs
   - Identify surfaces and areas to clean
   - Determine type of cleaning required
   - Consider special circumstances (allergies, children, pets)
2. Prepare basic all-purpose cleaner
   - Mix 1 part white vinegar with 1 part water in a spray bottle
   - Add 10-20 drops of essential oil for scent (optional)
   - Label the bottle clearly
3. Create specialized cleaners
   - **Bathroom surfaces:** Sprinkle baking soda, spray with water, wait 10 minutes, spray with vinegar, scrub and rinse
   - **Glass and mirrors:** Mix 1 part vinegar with 4 parts water
   - **Wood surfaces:** Mix 1/4 cup vinegar, 2 cups water, and 2 tablespoons olive oil
   - **Tile and grout:** Make a paste with baking soda and water, apply to grout lines, wait 10 minutes, scrub, rinse
4. Make a gentle scrubbing cleaner
   - Combine 1/4 cup baking soda with 1 tablespoon liquid castile soap
   - Add just enough water to make a paste
   - Use for sinks, tubs, and stovetops
5. Use hydrogen peroxide as a disinfectant
   - Keep hydrogen peroxide in a dark spray bottle

- Spray surfaces after cleaning with vinegar solution (use separately)
- Allow to air dry
6. Use lemon juice for specific tasks
    - Apply directly to cutting boards to disinfect
    - Use on copper or brass to remove tarnish
    - Mix with salt for wooden cutting boards
7. Store solutions properly
    - Keep in labeled containers out of reach of children
    - Store vinegar solutions for up to 1 month
    - Make fresh batches of other cleaners as needed

Cleaning 101: Definitions

- **Acetic acid:** The active component in vinegar
- **Alkaline:** Having a pH greater than 7; breaks down grease
- **Biodegradable:** Capable of being decomposed by organisms
- **Castile soap:** A vegetable oil-based soap
- **Disinfectant:** A substance that kills microorganisms
- **Microfiber:** Synthetic cloths with very fine fibers

Cleaning 101: Troubleshooting

Problem	Solutions
Vinegar solution leaves streaks	Use distilled water. Add 1 tablespoon cornstarch per cup. Use lint-free cloth. Polish until dry.
Baking soda residue remains	Rinse thoroughly. Spray with vinegar to dissolve residue. Wipe with damp microfiber cloth.
Not effective on tough grease	Pre-treat with undiluted castile soap. Add washing soda to the mixture. Allow the solution to sit longer.
Natural cleaners not disinfecting	Clean surfaces before disinfecting. Allow hydrogen peroxide to remain wet for 10 minutes. Use undiluted vinegar for stronger effect.
Vinegar smell lingers	Add citrus peels to vinegar before using. Add essential oils. Ventilate.

Cleaning 101: Limitations

- Requires more time and effort than chemical products
- Vinegar and acidic cleaners shouldn't be used on marble, granite, stone, or hardwood floors
- Homemade solutions have shorter shelf life (4 weeks)
- Natural disinfectants are less powerful than bleach

References and resources: <www.suspra.com/practice/water/cleaning-101.html>

Cleaning 102: Choosing Soap

Choose soap free of antibacterial chemicals without synthetic dyes or fragrances

Some soaps contain ingredients like triclosan or triclocarban, which are antibacterial agents that can disrupt aquatic ecosystems and contribute to antibiotic resistance. Synthetic dyes and fragrances, often derived from petrochemicals, can also pollute water and air, and may cause skin irritation or allergic reactions in some individuals. Reduce the introduction of harmful chemicals into the environment by looking for labels that explicitly state "antibacterial-free," "dye-free," and "fragrance-free," or choose brands that prioritize natural ingredients and transparent labeling.

References and resources: <www.suspra.com/practice/water/cleaning-102.html>

Cleaning 103: Avoiding Phosphate

Choose phosphate-free detergents

Phosphates in detergents contribute to water pollution, specifically a process called eutrophication. When phosphate-rich wastewater enters lakes and rivers, it acts like a fertilizer, causing excessive growth of algae and aquatic plants. This algal bloom depletes oxygen in the water when it decomposes, harming fish and other aquatic life. Choosing phosphate-free detergents reduces your contribution to this type of water pollution. Look for "phosphate-free" labels on detergent packaging.

References and resources: <www.suspra.com/practice/water/cleaning-103.html>

Cleaning 201: Steaming

Clean with steam rather than chemicals

Clean with water heated to approximately 245°F (118°C) to break down dirt and kill pathogens without chemicals. The high temperature causes dirt to expand and loosen while the moisture captures particles. Steam cleaning is especially valuable for households with children, pets, or people with chemical sensitivities or respiratory conditions.

Cleaning 201: Equipment & Materials

- Steam cleaner (handheld, canister, or steam mop)
- Distilled or demineralized water
- Microfiber cloths
- Heat-resistant gloves
- Towels for drying
- *Optional: Extension wand or specialized attachments*
- *Bucket for catching runoff*
- *Soft bristle brush for stubborn dirt*

Cleaning 201: Steps

1. Choose the right steam cleaner
   - Handheld units for small areas and detail cleaning
   - Canister models for larger jobs
   - Steam mops specifically for floors
2. Prepare the area
   - Remove loose debris by sweeping or vacuuming
   - Move or cover items that shouldn't get wet
   - Test on an inconspicuous area first
   - Ensure good ventilation
3. Prepare your steam cleaner
   - Fill with distilled or demineralized water to prevent mineral buildup
   - Attach appropriate cleaning head
   - Allow unit to fully heat up
   - Wear heat-resistant gloves
4. Steam clean methodically
   - Hold nozzle 2 inches from surface

- Move slowly to allow steam to penetrate
- Work in small sections from top to bottom
- Apply steam for 15 seconds on stubborn stains
- Wipe away loosened dirt with microfiber cloth
5. Adjust technique for different surfaces
    - **Floors:** Use slow, overlapping passes; change pads when dirty
    - **Grout:** Apply steam directly with concentrated nozzle
    - **Countertops:** Use short bursts and wipe immediately
    - **Appliances:** Use detail attachments for crevices
    - **Upholstery:** Hold steamer 8 inches away, use quick passes
6. Dry and finish
    - Wipe excess moisture with clean microfiber cloths
    - Allow surfaces to air dry completely
    - Use a squeegee for windows and glass
7. Maintain your steam cleaner
    - Empty and rinse water tank after each use
    - Allow to cool completely before storage
    - Descale regularly according to manufacturer instructions
    - Clean or replace attachments as needed

Cleaning 201: Definitions

- **Descaling:** Removing mineral buildup from inside a steam cleaner
- **Distilled water:** Water with impurities and minerals removed
- **Dry steam:** Steam containing very little moisture, better for fabrics
- **Wet steam:** Steam with higher moisture content, better for hard surfaces
- **Pressure rating:** Measurement indicating how forcefully steam is expelled
- **Sanitizing:** Reducing bacteria to safe levels

Cleaning 201: Troubleshooting

Problem	Solutions
Surface still dirty after steaming	Hold the steamer longer (15 seconds). Move slower. Use a brush attachment. Check if the unit is fully heated.
Streaking on glass	Use less steam. Wipe immediately with clean cloth. Finish with a squeegee.
Steam cleaner not producing steam	Check the water level. Ensure the unit is heated. Verify power. Check for mineral buildup.
Water spots left behind	Use distilled water. Wipe surfaces immediately. Buff dry with clean cloth.
Excessive moisture on surfaces	Hold the steamer farther away. Use shorter bursts. Use more absorbent cloth.
Damage to sealed wood floors	Reduce steam level. Move more quickly. Ensure floor sealing is intact. Use a steam mop designed for wood.

Cleaning 201: Limitations

- Can damage heat-sensitive surfaces including unsealed wood, cork, delicate fabrics
- May damage adhesives
- Cannot remove certain stains, especially set-in oil-based stains

- Requires electricity
- Initial cost is higher than basic cleaning supplies
- Steam can cause burns if used improperly
- Not effective for cleaning large amounts of loose debris
- May not be practical for quick tasks due to setup and heating time

References and resources: <www.suspra.com/practice/water/cleaning-201.html>

Cleaning 202: Electrolyzing

Clean with electrolyzed water rather than chemicals

Electrolyzed water creates a cleaning and disinfecting solution using salt, water, and electricity. The process produces acidic water (pH 2.5-3.5) effective for disinfection, and alkaline water (pH 11-12) effective for breaking down oils. The active component, hypochlorous acid, is the same compound your immune system produces to fight infection.

Cleaning 202: Equipment & Materials

- Commercial electrolyzed water system
- Non-metallic container (glass or plastic)
- Spray bottles for storing solution
- pH test strips
- Safety gloves
- Safety glasses
- *Optional: TDS meter to measure salt concentration*

Cleaning 202: Steps

Making electrolyzed water:

1. Purchase an electrolyzed water generator
2. Follow manufacturer's instructions for setup
3. Add specified amount of water and salt
4. Run the electrolysis cycle
5. Collect solution in spray bottles
6. Label containers with contents and date
7. Use solution within two weeks

Using electrolyzed water:

1. Spray solution directly onto surfaces
2. Allow to sit for 30 seconds for disinfection
3. Wipe with clean microfiber cloth
4. For stubborn stains, let sit 3 minutes
5. No rinsing required

Cleaning 202: Definitions

- **Electrolysis:** Chemical process using electrical current to drive a chemical reaction
- **Hypochlorous acid (HOCl):** Weak acid effective as a disinfectant
- **pH:** Scale specifying acidity or basicity
- **Sodium hydroxide:** Base formed during electrolysis that breaks down oils
- **Electrolyzed water:** Water transformed into a cleaning solution through electrolysis

Cleaning 202: Troubleshooting

Problem	Solutions
Not disinfecting effectively	Ensure proper salt concentration. Increase electrolysis time. Verify pH range.
Solution losing effectiveness	Store in opaque bottles away from light and heat. Make smaller batches. Use within two weeks.
Unpleasant smell	Reduce salt concentration. Ensure proper ventilation.
Electrolyzer stops working	Clean to remove mineral buildup. Check salt levels. Contact manufacturer if under warranty.

Cleaning 202: Limitations

- Limited shelf life (two weeks)
- Less effective for heavy-duty cleaning like baked-on grease
- Commercial units can be costly initially
- Not recommended for sterling silver, aluminum, or delicate surfaces
- May cause discoloration of fabrics
- Water quality and salt purity affect effectiveness

References and resources: <www.suspra.com/practice/water/cleaning-202.html>

Drainscaping 301: Installing a Rain Garden

Install a rain garden to retain precipitation and reduce runoff

Reduce stormwater flows and recharge groundwater by planting a basin as a rain garden to capture, absorb, and filter runoff from impervious surfaces. Choose a naturally low area to which you can direct water from a downspout, patio, driveway, or other hard surface that doesn't allow water through. A three-zone planting approach accommodates the moisture gradient: bottom zone plants tolerate temporary flooding, middle zone plants prefer consistent moisture, and outer zone plants prefer well-drained soil. Native plants are best due to their deep root systems that enhance infiltration.

Do a percolation test in the area you're planning to use as a rain garden to determine whether you'll need to amend your soil to increase the percolation rate. Here's how:

1. Dig a hole 12" in diameter by 12" deep.
2. Fill with water and let sit overnight to saturate the soil.
3. Refill with water to measure drainage.
4. Lay a stick, pipe, or other straight edge across the top of the hole.
5. Use a tape measure or yardstick to measure the distance between the top of the water and the straight edge.
6. Measure the distance every hour until the hole is empty.
7. Note how many inches per hour the water level drops.

A percolation rate of 1 inch or more per hour is ideal for rain gardens. Sandy soils drain faster; clay soils drain slower. Adding sand or compost to clay soil can increase the percolation rate.

Drainscaping 301: Equipment & Materials

- Shovel, spade, or excavation equipment

- Rake
- Measuring tape
- Garden hose or string (for marking garden outline)
- Level
- Soil testing kit
- Wheelbarrow
- Compost or organic matter
- Sand (for poorly draining soils)
- Native plants appropriate for rain garden conditions
- Mulch (shredded hardwood or pine straw)
- Stones or river rock (for inflow areas)
- *Optional: Drain tile or perforated pipe for overflow management*
- *Water source for establishing plants*

Drainscaping 301: Steps

1. Select an appropriate location
   - Choose a site at least 10 feet from building foundations
   - Position downslope from downspouts, driveways, or other runoff sources
   - Verify the area is not above utility lines (call 811 before digging)
   - Ensure the site receives at least partial sun (4 hours daily)
   - Avoid areas with existing drainage problems or standing water
2. Size your rain garden appropriately
   - Make the rain garden about 25% of the drainage area
   - Design for 200 square feet for average homes
   - Make a depression 4-8 inches deep based on soil type where rainwater will puddle
3. Test your soil
   - Perform a percolation test
   - Identify soil type (sandy, loamy, or clay) to determine amendments
4. Design your rain garden as a slight depression in your landscape
   - Create a kidney or crescent shape that follows land contours
   - Design with a flat bottom and gently sloping sides (no steeper than 3:1 ratio)
   - Plan for three moisture zones: center (wettest), middle (moist), and outer edge (driest)
5. Prepare the site
   - Mark the outline using a garden hose or string
   - Remove grass and weeds from the area
   - Excavate soil to create a depression with a flat bottom
   - Create a berm on the downhill side to retain water and allow it to soak in
6. Amend the soil
   - For clay soils: Mix in sand and compost (50% native soil, 25% sand, 25% compost)
   - For sandy soils: Add compost (70% native soil, 30% compost)
   - Ensure soil mix is 12-18 inches deep
7. Create inflow and overflow areas
   - Line entry point with stones to prevent erosion
   - Create a defined overflow area on the downslope side to handle excess water
8. Plant appropriate vegetation
   - Select native plants adapted to both wet and dry conditions
   - Plant according to moisture zones
   - Add 2-3 inches of mulch
   - Water deeply when first planted
9. Periodically clean debris from inflow and overflow areas

Drainscaping 301: Definitions

- **Berm**: A raised earth barrier that helps contain water within the rain garden
- **Infiltration**: The process by which water enters and moves through soil
- **Impervious surface**: Any surface that doesn't allow water to penetrate
- **Percolation test**: A test to determine how quickly water drains through soil

Drainscaping 301: Troubleshooting

Problem	Solutions
Standing water persists more than 48 hours	Improve drainage with more sand and organic matter. Install an underdrain. Increase garden size.
Plants dying in center	Select more water-tolerant species. Check soil composition. Adjust depression depth.
Erosion at entry point	Add more stones at inflow. Create a wider, gentler slope at entry point.
Water bypasses the garden	Check grading. Create small berms to guide water flow.
Excessive weed growth	Apply thicker mulch. Increase planting density to shade out weeds.

Drainscaping 301: Limitations

- Requires adequate space with appropriate runoff
- Not suitable for areas with high water tables (less than 2 feet below surface)
- Challenging in very dense clay soils without significant amendments
- Intense downpours will overflow the rain garden

References and resources: <www.suspra.com/practice/water/drainscaping-301.html>

Drainscaping 302: Permeable Paving

Install semi-permeable or permeable driveways and walkways

Install permeable paving to allow water to pass through the surface and infiltrate into the ground, reducing runoff and recharging groundwater. The key to success is proper subgrade preparation and appropriate base layers. The base must support expected loads while providing water storage capacity. Most failures result from inadequate base preparation, improper material selection, or over-compaction that reduces permeability.

Drainscaping 302: Equipment & Materials

Equipment

- Tape measure and stakes for layout
- String line and level
- Square-edged shovel and flat spade
- Rake
- Wheelbarrow
- Tamper (hand or powered)
- Chalk line or marking paint
- *Optional: Plate compactor (can be rented)*

Materials

- Base materials: Crushed, angular, open-graded aggregate (¾-1" stone)
- Bedding material (varies by system)
- Edge restraints
- Permeable paving material (choose one):
  - Permeable concrete pavers or brick
  - Porous concrete mix
  - Porous asphalt mix
  - Plastic grid systems with aggregate fill
  - Resin-bound gravel

Drainscaping 302: Steps

1. Plan and design your permeable surface
   - Check local regulations and permitting requirements
   - Perform a percolation test to determine soil infiltration rate
   - Calculate materials needed based on area and depth requirements
2. Prepare the site
   - Mark the installation area with stakes and string
   - Remove existing surface materials
   - Excavate to required depth (8-12" for walkways, 12-18" for driveways)
   - Grade for slight slope (1-2%) away from buildings
3. Install edge restraints
   - Position edge restraints around perimeter
   - Ensure they are level or follow designed grade
4. Create the sub-base and base layers
   - Add 6-12" layer of open-graded crushed stone for sub-base
   - Level and lightly compact each 3-4" layer
   - Do not over-compact as this reduces permeability
5. Install the permeable surface
   - For Permeable Pavers:
     - Spread 1.5-2" of bedding material
     - Set pavers with proper spacing (1/8" - 1/4")
     - Fill joints with specified aggregate
   - For Porous Concrete:
     - Mix according to supplier specifications
     - Pour and level to 4-6" thickness
     - Allow to cure per specifications
   - For Plastic Grid Systems:
     - Lay grid sections with proper connections
     - Fill cells with specified material
6. Create overflow drainage
   - Install overflow channels at low points
   - Connect to existing drainage or appropriate outlet
7. Test the system
   - Spray with garden hose to verify water infiltrates properly

Drainscaping 302: Definitions

- **Bedding layer**: Material directly beneath the permeable surface
- **Open-graded aggregate**: Stone with minimal fine particles allowing water flow through
- **Percolation test**: Method to determine drainage rate, measured in inches per hour
- **Permeability**: Ability of material to allow water flow through it

- **Void ratio**: Volume of void spaces divided by volume of solids in a material

Drainscaping 302: Troubleshooting

Problem	Solutions
Surface ponding or slow drainage	Clean surface with pressure washer or vacuum. Check for clogged materials. Ensure overflow drains function properly.
Pavers become uneven	Check edge restraints. Verify base preparation. Reset affected pavers.
Weed growth	Remove weeds promptly. Apply corn gluten meal as natural pre-emergent.
Reduced permeability	Perform regular maintenance with vacuum sweeping or pressure washing.

Drainscaping 302: Limitations
- Not suitable for contaminated soils or high water tables
- Requires more extensive base preparation than conventional paving
- May not support heavy vehicle loads without professional engineering
- Requires regular maintenance to maintain permeability
- Not all systems suitable for all climate zones

References and resources: <www.suspra.com/practice/water/drainscaping-302.html>

Drainscaping 303: Building Bridges

Install bridges or walkways across streams and wetlands

Install bridges over streams and wetlands to prevent soil compaction, protect sensitive vegetation, maintain natural water flow, and reduce erosion from foot traffic. Minimize environmental impact by choosing appropriate materials, designing for minimal footprint, building during dry seasons, and ensuring the structure allows for natural water flow and wildlife movement.

References and resources: <www.suspra.com/practice/water/drainscaping-303.html>

Drainscaping 401: Green Roofing

Install green roofs to provide permeable areas over buildings

Green roofs capture precipitation and release it slowly through evapotranspiration or controlled drainage. Extensive systems use a shallow growing medium and drought-tolerant plants like sedums, require minimal maintenance, and add 15-30 pounds per square foot. Intensive systems have a deeper growing medium to support more plant diversity, but need regular maintenance and add significant weight (80 or more pounds per square foot). Select plants based on your climate zone, rainfall patterns, and expected maintenance frequency.

Drainscaping 401: Equipment & Materials
- Structural engineering report (confirming roof can support added weight)
- Waterproofing membrane
- Root barrier layer
- Drainage layer
- Filter fabric/geotextile
- Growing medium/engineered soil

- Plants suitable for green roofs (sedums, grasses, perennials)
- Roof edge protection/retention system
- Irrigation system components (if needed)
- Safety equipment (harnesses, non-slip footwear, guardrails)
- Landscaping tools
- Access equipment (ladders, scaffolding, or lifts)
- *Optional: Leak detection system*

Drainscaping 401: Steps

1. Assess and prepare the building structure
   - Obtain structural engineering assessment to verify load-bearing capacity
   - Ensure roof is appropriately sloped (minimum 2% for drainage)
   - Address any existing roof issues before proceeding
2. Plan your green roof system
   - Choose between extensive (lightweight, low-maintenance) or intensive (deeper soil, wider plant variety) systems
   - Plan vegetation-free zones around roof penetrations, edges, and equipment
3. Prepare safety protocols
   - Install fall protection
   - Establish safe access routes for people and materials
   - Schedule work during appropriate weather
4. Install waterproofing membrane
   - Clean and prepare existing roof surface
   - Apply waterproofing according to manufacturer specifications
   - Conduct water testing before proceeding
5. Install root barrier
   - Apply barrier over waterproofing membrane
   - Ensure seams are properly overlapped and sealed
   - Pay special attention to areas around drains and penetrations
6. Install drainage layer
   - Place drainage layer over root barrier
   - Integrate with existing drainage systems
7. Apply filter fabric
   - Cover drainage layer with filter fabric or geotextile
   - Overlap seams by at least 6 inches
8. Install growing medium
   - Spread growing medium to specified depth
   - Avoid compacting the medium
   - Keep medium away from drains and vegetation-free zones
9. Install edge protection and retention systems
   - Secure edge treatments around roof perimeter
   - Establish vegetation-free zones around drains and equipment
10. Install irrigation system (if required)
    - Test system before planting
    - Include moisture sensors to prevent overwatering
11. Plant vegetation
    - Install plants according to design plan
    - For extensive roofs, use pre-grown mats, plugs, or cuttings
    - Water thoroughly after planting
12. Establish maintenance protocol
    - Document as-built conditions with photographs
    - Create a maintenance schedule

Drainscaping 401: Definitions

- **Extensive green roof**: Lightweight system with shallow growing medium (3-6 inches) and drought-tolerant plants
- **Evapotranspiration**: Water transfer from land to air through soil evaporation and plant transpiration
- **Growing medium**: Engineered lightweight soil mix designed for green roofs
- **Intensive green roof**: System with deeper growing medium (8+ inches) supporting wider plant variety
- **Root barrier**: Layer preventing plant roots from damaging waterproofing
- **Semi-Intensive green roof**: System with growing medium deep enough (8 inches) to support a garden
- **Vegetation-free zone**: Areas kept plant-free around roof edges, penetrations, and equipment

Drainscaping 401: Troubleshooting

Problem	Solutions
Plants fail to establish	Check moisture levels. Change plant species. Install in spring.
Drainage issues/ponding water	Inspect drainage paths for blockages. Check that filter fabric hasn't clogged. Verify growing medium hasn't compacted.
Leaks appearing after installation	Locate the exact position. Remove affected green roof components. Repair waterproofing membrane.
Growing medium erosion	Install additional erosion control materials. Check irrigation pressure. Add temporary stabilizing netting.
Weeds	Remove weeds before they set seed. Reduce watering.

Drainscaping 401: Limitations

- Requires significant upfront investment (three times higher than conventional roofing)
- Not all existing buildings have adequate structural capacity for retrofits
- Maintenance requirements higher than conventional roofing
- Potential for leaks requires careful installation and quality control
- Steep slopes present significant installation challenges

References and resources: <www.suspra.com/practice/water/drainscaping-401.html>

Managing 301: Fencing

Build fencing to prevent livestock and pets from wading in streams

Fence off streams to prevent livestock and pets from causing bank erosion, sediment pollution, and habitat destruction. The fence creates a buffer zone that filters runoff, stabilizes banks, and provides wildlife habitat. Different animals require different fence types: cattle need 3-5 strand barbed or high-tensile wire; horses need more visible fencing; sheep and goats require smaller openings. Install the fence far enough from the stream to protect the riparian zone and allow vegetation to establish.

References and resources: <www.suspra.com/practice/water/managing-301.html>

Sustainable Practices Handbook
Water Practices: Preventing Water Pollution

Managing 302: Growing Buffer Zones

Maintain riparian vegetation as buffer zones

Use native plants to establish riparian (areas next to water) buffer zones that serve as the transition between water and land. Create three zones for comprehensive protection: Zone 1 (streamside) stabilizes banks and shades water, Zone 2 (middle) absorbs nutrients and slows floodwaters, and Zone 3 (outer) filters surface runoff. Width requirements increase with steeper slopes and sensitive waterways, but generally start at 15 feet / 4.5 meters. Native plants usually require less maintenance and provide better habitat and soil stabilization than non-natives.

References and resources: <www.suspra.com/practice/water/managing-302.html>

Disposing of Waste 101: Picking Up Litter

Pick up litter and pet waste and dispose of it safely

Whenever you are out for a walk, whether in your neighborhood, a park, or along a trail, bring along an empty plastic bag and take a moment to look around and collect any visible litter. This includes everything from plastic bottles and wrappers to discarded food containers and cigarette butts. Dispose of collected litter and pet waste properly in designated trash receptacles or bring it home for appropriate disposal. Litter-free environments are safer for wildlife and more enjoyable for everyone. Furthermore, picking up litter demonstrates sustainable practices and encourages others to do the same, fostering a culture of environmental responsibility.

References and resources: <www.suspra.com/practice/water/disposing-waste-101.html>

Disposing of Waste 102: Handling Medical and Hazardous Waste

Dispose of medications and household hazardous waste safely

Properly dispose of hazardous waste and medications to protect water supplies, wildlife, and sanitation workers. Most communities offer collection facilities or events for hazardous waste disposal. For medications, take-back programs are increasingly available at pharmacies and law enforcement facilities. When these options aren't available, put household hazardous waste in a sealed container before placing it in household trash.

Some especially dangerous medicines, such as fentanyl patches, come with instructions to flush used items or leftover amounts down a toilet. The FDA has determined that the 15 active pharmaceutical ingredients on its "flush list" present negligible eco-toxicological risk when diluted in wastewater effluent.

Managing Waste 102: Equipment & Materials
- Sturdy containers with tight-fitting lids (glass or plastic)
- Original packaging for hazardous products (if still available)
- Cardboard boxes for transportation
- Newspaper or cat litter for containing spills
- Heavy-duty trash bags
- Disposable gloves
- Permanent marker
- Duct tape
- Plastic zipper bags

Managing Waste 102: Steps

1. Identify household hazardous waste
    - Look for signal words: CAUTION, WARNING, DANGER, or POISON
    - Common household hazardous wastes include automotive fluids, batteries, cleaning products, electronics, fluorescent bulbs, paints, and pesticides
2. Identify medical waste requiring special disposal
    - Prescription and over-the-counter medications
    - Sharps (needles, lancets, syringes)
    - Medical equipment with batteries or electronics
3. Store hazardous waste safely until disposal
    - Keep products in original containers with labels intact
    - Never mix different hazardous products
    - Store in cool, dry location away from children and pets
    - Keep flammables away from heat sources
4. Properly dispose of medications
    - Use medication take-back programs if available
    - If no take-back options exist and the drug is not on the FDA flush list:
        - Mix medications with undesirable substance (coffee grounds, cat litter, or dirt)
        - Place in a sealed container and dispose in household trash
        - Scratch out personal information on prescription bottles and recycle or landfill them
    - For sharps, use FDA-cleared containers or puncture-resistant containers
5. Dispose of household hazardous waste
    - Find local disposal options: permanent facilities, collection events, or retail take-back programs
    - Transport in original containers when possible
    - Pack in boxes with absorbent material
    - Keep incompatible materials separate
    - Transport in vehicle trunk, not in passenger compartment
6. Handle spills and leaks properly
    - Wear protective gear (gloves, eye protection)
    - Contain small spills with absorbent material
    - For large spills, evacuate the area and call local authorities
7. Reduce future hazardous waste generation
    - Buy only what you need and will use completely
    - Choose less-toxic alternatives when available
    - Use up products completely before disposal when safe

Managing Waste 102: Definitions

- **Corrosive**: Substance that can damage materials or skin on contact
- **Flammable**: Substance that can easily ignite and burn
- **Hazardous waste**: Material potentially harmful to human health or environment
- **Reactive**: Substance that can react with air, water, or other substances
- **Sharps**: Needles, syringes, or other medical items that can pierce skin
- **Signal words**: Words on product labels indicating severity of hazard

Managing Waste 102: Troubleshooting

Problem	Solutions
No collection facility	Check for periodic collection events or mail-back programs.

Problem	Solutions
Unknown substances or unlabeled containers	Don't open; contact the local hazardous waste authority.
Leaking containers	Place in a larger container with absorbent material; keep upright.
Not sure if something is hazardous	Check product label; when in doubt, treat it as hazardous.
Disposal facility won't accept certain items	Ask staff for alternatives or contact the manufacturer.

Managing Waste 102: Limitations
- Local disposal options vary by location
- Transportation requires a vehicle and physical ability
- Some disposal may require fees
- Take-back programs may have quantity limits
- Storage space while awaiting disposal may be limited

References and resources: <www.suspra.com/practice/water/disposing-waste-102.html>

Movement (Transportation) Practices

Reducing Travel Miles, page 261	
Goals	**Indicators**
• Travel less distance per person per year • Reduce vehicle mileage per year	• Average personal speed • Transportation modes

Getting Exercise, page 266	
Goals	**Indicators**
• Increase active transportation trips • Decrease vehicular trips	• Average personal speed • Transportation modes

Driving Electric, page 274	
Goals	**Indicators**
• Eliminate fuel consumption • Reduce air, water, and noise pollution • Increase energy efficiency	• Transportation modes

Reducing Travel Miles

Carpooling 301: Sharing Rides

Share rides when traveling to a common destination

Make ride-sharing a regular and reliable part of your routine, extending beyond occasional lifts to family or friends. Initiate or join carpool programs at work, or explore community ride-sharing initiatives facilitated through online platforms and apps designed for carpooling. These digital tools can help you connect with individuals traveling similar routes, manage schedules efficiently, and even split costs fairly. Establish clear communication protocols within your carpool group, including agreed-upon schedules, pick-up locations, and communication channels for delays or changes. Consider a rotating driver schedule to share the driving burden and vehicle costs equitably amongst participants. Fewer cars on the road directly translates to less air pollution and decreased traffic congestion, contributing to healthier and more livable communities. Carpooling also fosters social connections and frees up money for better uses.

References and resources: <www.suspra.com/practice/movement/carpooling-301.html>

Planning Movement 101: Minimizing Engine Starts

Plan vehicle use to minimize both engine starts and mileage

Reduce both cold starts and total miles driven by combining trips geographically rather than by purpose. Cold engine starts produce significantly higher emissions and cause more engine wear than warm operation. Keep a journal of your trips for one month, then analyze to determine which trips you could combine next month.

References and resources: <www.suspra.com/practice/movement/planning-101.html>

Planning Movement 201: Minimizing Air Travel

Minimize air travel

While sometimes necessary, air travel is more polluting than other types of transportation. Before booking a flight, consider whether you could achieve your goals through virtual meetings, or by traveling closer to home. For shorter distances, explore alternatives like train travel, bus, or even cycling. If flying is unavoidable, choose direct flights as they are generally more fuel-efficient than those with layovers. Pack light to reduce the plane's weight.

References and resources: <www.suspra.com/practice/movement/planning-201.html>

Shopping 101: Buying Online

Shop online for items you can't get within walking or cycling distance

When you need to purchase items not available within walking or cycling distance, shop online. Instead of individual shoppers driving multiple vehicles to stores, online platforms allow one delivery van to make multiple stops to deliver packages to consumers. Online shopping allows you to find what you need from home rather than visiting stores to shop. Furthermore, online marketplaces offer a wider selection of eco-friendly and ethically sourced goods compared to local stores, empowering you to make more sustainable purchasing decisions. To maximize the sustainability benefits of online shopping, plan ahead and combine your purchases into fewer, larger orders to minimize packaging and delivery trips. Consider also choosing slower shipping options, which can be more energy-efficient.

References and resources: <www.suspra.com/practice/movement/shopping-101.html>

Telecommuting 301: Working From Home

Work from home

Work from home to save energy and prevent pollution. Set up a dedicated workspace with ergonomic considerations and take frequent breaks to prevent physical injuries. Keep up to date with software updates to minimize security risks from hackers and malicious software. Be intentional about staying connected with colleagues. Regularly assess and adjust your remote work setup and habits.

Telecommuting 301: Equipment & Materials
- Computer with reliable Internet connection
- Webcam and headset with microphone
- External monitor, keyboard, and mouse
- Dedicated workspace
- Ergonomic chair
- Adequate lighting
- *Optional: Backup Internet provider, standing desk, noise-canceling headphones, printer/scanner, battery power supply*

Telecommuting 301: Steps
1. Assess your remote work potential
   - Evaluate your current job for remote possibilities
   - Identify which job functions can be performed remotely
2. Create a plan to work remotely
   - For existing employment:
     - Research company's remote work policies
     - Consider your employer's needs; prepare a proposal explaining how you'll meet them
     - Suggest a trial period with performance metrics
   - For job seekers:
     - Research companies with strong remote cultures
     - Create a resume or portfolio demonstrating remote work capability
3. Set up your home workspace
   - Choose a dedicated location with minimal distractions
   - Set up ergonomic workstation:
     - Ensure adequate lighting
     - Adjust chair height so feet rest flat on floor
     - Position monitor at eye level, about arm's length away
     - Place keyboard and mouse to maintain straight wrists
4. Install technology infrastructure
   - Get a laptop or desktop computer with a webcam and a microphone
   - Get fast Internet (25 Mbps download/5 Mbps upload)
   - *Optional: Secure a backup internet solution (such as a cell phone data plan)*
   - Install necessary software and set up cloud storage and file synchronization
5. Build communication skills
   - Establish communication expectations, including availability for phone calls and video conferences, and response times to emails and texts
   - Learn effective video conference practices, including taking and sharing notes

6. Build and maintain professional connections
   - Schedule regular check-ins with colleagues and supervisors
   - Participate actively in virtual team meetings
   - Join online professional communities
   - Attend virtual conferences and webinars

Telecommuting 301: Definitions

- **Asynchronous communication**: Communication that doesn't happen in real-time
- **Ergonomics**: The science of designing the workplace to fit the worker
- **Hybrid work**: A model combining some remote work with some in-office time
- **Pomodoro Technique**: Time management method using focused work intervals

Telecommuting 301: Troubleshooting

Problem	Solutions
Employer reluctant to allow remote work	Focus on business benefits. Suggest trial period. Offer a hybrid schedule.
Unreliable Internet	Upgrade plan. Set up mobile hotspot backup. Change Internet providers.
Distractions at home	Establish a dedicated workspace. Use noise-canceling headphones.
Feeling isolated	Join professional communities. Work occasionally from public spaces.
Difficulty maintaining boundaries	Establish firm work hours. Create physical separation for workspace from living space. Develop transition rituals.
Technology failures	Test and maintain equipment. Have a backup option such as a cell phone.
Ergonomic discomfort	Buy better furniture. Take movement breaks. Exercise daily.

Telecommuting 301: Limitations

- Not all jobs can be performed remotely
- Home environments may lack adequate space
- Reliable high-speed Internet access is not universally available
- May lead to overworking due to blurred boundaries
- Career advancement may require more face-to-face interactions
- Initial home office setup requires investment

References and resources: <www.suspra.com/practice/movement/telecommuting-301.html>

Telecommuting 401: Employing Remote Workers

Encourage and empower employees to work from home

Provide remote work opportunities to prevent pollution and conserve energy while expanding talent pools and shedding real estate costs. Reimagine workflows rather than simply replicating in-office practices remotely. Evolve from oversight based on observation to leadership based on clear expectations and outcome measurement. While technology enables remote work, human elements like culture, communication, and trust determine success. Consider hybrid approaches that combine remote work flexibility with occasional in-person interactions to maintain social bonds.

Telecommuting 401: Equipment & Materials
- Computer with video conferencing capabilities for each employee
- Reliable high-speed Internet service
- Digital collaboration tools (communication platforms, video conferencing, project management, document collaboration)
- Remote work policies, procedures, and training material
- *Optional: Remote desktop software, monitoring tools, ergonomic assessment resources*
- *Secure virtual private network*

Telecommuting 401: Steps
1. Assess telecommuting feasibility
    - Audit job roles to determine remote-compatible positions
    - Evaluate technology infrastructure and identify gaps
    - Survey employees about preferences
    - Review security requirements and compliance considerations
2. Develop a remote work policy
    - Define eligibility criteria
    - Establish expectations for availability and productivity
    - Create guidelines for company equipment use
    - Outline security protocols
    - Address tax and legal implications
3. Prepare technical infrastructure
    - Upgrade network capacity
    - Implement secure remote access solutions
    - Deploy collaborative platforms
    - Establish technical support systems for remote employees
4. Create an equipment and workspace program
    - Develop standardized setup checklist
    - Create equipment loan agreements
    - Provide ergonomic assessment resources
5. Train managers on remote leadership
    - Coach on outcome-based management
    - Develop protocols for virtual team building
    - Train on effective remote communication
    - Establish performance evaluation frameworks
6. Train employees for remote success
    - Conduct security awareness training
    - Provide instruction on collaboration tools
7. Implement a pilot program
    - Select participants
    - Set clear success metrics
    - Gather feedback and document challenges and solutions
8. Scale the program organization-wide
    - Refine policies based on pilot feedback
    - Develop rollout schedule
9. Redesign organizational processes
    - Convert paper-based workflows to digital systems
    - Establish asynchronous work guidelines
    - Update human resources processes for remote operations
10. Monitor, evaluate, and improve
    - Develop key performance indicators and track productivity metrics
    - Conduct regular employee satisfaction surveys

- Update policies based on feedback

Telecommuting 401: Definitions

- **Asynchronous work**: Tasks that don't require simultaneous participation
- **Distributed team**: Workforce spread across multiple locations without a central office
- **Hybrid work**: Approach combining remote work with regular office attendance
- **Remote-first**: Organizational approach designing all processes for remote work by default

Telecommuting 401: Troubleshooting

Problem	Solutions
Employee isolation	Schedule periodic in-person gatherings.
Evaluating performance	Shift to outcome-based metrics. Implement clear goal frameworks. Provide remote leadership training.
Communication breakdowns	Establish clear protocols. Document decisions. Do more synchronous, rather than asynchronous remote work. Meet in person more frequently.
Security concerns	Implement multi-factor authentication. Conduct security audits. Provide security training.
Technology access	Provide technology stipends. Offer equipment lending programs.
Culture dissipates	Document values. Recognize achievements. Schedule social events.

Telecommuting 401: Limitations

- Not all roles can be performed remotely
- Organizations with sensitive data face security challenges
- Remote work can make spontaneous collaboration more challenging
- Internet infrastructure varies by location, creating inequities
- Initial technology costs can be significant
- Complex tax implications may arise for cross-jurisdictional work

References and resources: <www.suspra.com/practice/movement/telecommuting-401.html>

Getting Exercise

Cycling 201: Cycling Fifteen Minutes

Cycle fifteen minutes in nice weather to complete short trips

Learn how to ride a bicycle or acquire a tricycle so you can cycle for fifteen minutes to replace car trips for errands, commuting, or social visits within three miles. At a comfortable pace of 10 mph (16 kph), this distance is manageable for most people without specialized equipment or high fitness levels. Keep your bicycle or tricycle and gear ready for spontaneous trips. For carrying items, backpacks work for light loads while panniers shift weight to the bicycle frame.

References and resources: <www.suspra.com/practice/movement/cycling-201.html>

Cycling 301: Cycling Sixty Minutes

Cycle sixty minutes in all weather to complete longer trips

Sixty-minute cycling trips typically cover 8-15 miles (13-25 km) depending on fitness, terrain, and conditions. This makes cycling viable for many urban and suburban commutes. Compared to shorter rides, longer all-weather cycling requires more preparation, better route planning, and higher quality gear. Physical demands adapt over time; most cyclists find their trips become significantly easier after two weeks of regular riding. Reassess routes, gear, and timing seasonally.

Cycling 301: Equipment & Materials

- Reliable bicycle or tricycle with appropriate maintenance
- Helmet
- Weather-appropriate cycling clothing:
    - Rain gear (waterproof jacket, pants, shoe covers)
    - Cold weather layers (thermal base layers, gloves, headwear)
    - Hot weather gear (moisture-wicking, sun-protective clothing)
- Visibility equipment (lights, reflective clothing, high-visibility vest)
- Portable bicycle repair kit (spare tube, tire levers, multi-tool, pump)
- Backpack or pannier bags
- Water bottle
- Smartphone with navigation
- *Optional: Fenders, bike computer, change of clothes, sunscreen, winter-specific gear*

Cycling 301: Steps

1. Become proficient with shorter cycling trips
2. Prepare your bicycle for longer trips
    - Perform regular maintenance checks
    - Install appropriate accessories (fenders, lights, racks)
    - Consider upgrading tires for typical weather conditions
    - Position your bike for maximum comfort
3. Plan appropriate routes for 60-minute trips
    - Research bike-friendly routes (8-15 miles [13-25 km])
    - Identify safe roads with bike lanes or low traffic
    - Plan for restroom access and water refill points
    - Consider alternative routes for weather changes
4. Develop a weather assessment system
    - Check forecasts before your ride

Sustainable Practices Handbook — Movement Practices: Getting Exercise

- Learn to recognize dangerous conditions
- Establish personal safety thresholds
- Prepare contingency plans
5. Dress appropriately for weather conditions
    - Wet weather: Wear waterproof gear, install fenders
    - Cold weather (32-50°F): Layer clothing, protect extremities
    - Very cold weather (below 32°F): Add extra insulation, protect all exposed skin
    - Hot weather (above 80°F): Lightweight clothing, sunscreen, extra water
6. Develop a cycling strategy for longer rides
    - Start at a sustainable pace
    - Use appropriate gearing for terrain
    - Practice efficient pedaling (70-90 rpm cadence)
    - Adjust pace according to weather
7. Enhance riding skills for varying conditions
    - Wet conditions: Reduce speed, avoid slick surfaces, brake earlier
    - Snowy conditions: Lower tire pressure slightly, maintain straight line
    - Hot conditions: Adjust pace, use shaded routes, hydrate regularly
8. Implement visibility strategies
    - Use lights in low-light conditions
    - Wear reflective and high-visibility clothing
    - Signal turns well in advance
9. Prepare for arrival
    - Cool down during final minutes
    - Plan for changing clothes if necessary
    - Know where to secure your bicycle
10. Have an emergency plan
    - Carry photo identification and emergency contacts
    - Know basic roadside repairs
    - Research backup transportation options
    - Share your route with an emergency contact for extreme conditions
11. Track and plan your rides
    - Record routes, times, and conditions
    - Note challenging sections

Cycling 301: Definitions

- **Base layer**: Moisture-wicking clothing worn against skin
- **Cadence**: Pedaling rate measured in revolutions per minute (rpm)
- **Fenders/Mudguards**: Shields over wheels to prevent water and debris spray
- **Handlebar mitts**: Insulated covers that protect hands but allow brake and shifter operation
- **Layering system**: Multiple thin layers that can be added or removed as needed
- **Studded tires**: Winter bicycle tires with metal studs for ice traction

Cycling 301: Troubleshooting

Problem	Solutions
Cold hands and feet	Use handlebar mitts. Wear winter boots. Use chemical warming packs.
Glasses fogging	Apply anti-fog treatment. Use ventilated glasses or a breath deflector.
Overheating in gear	Choose breathable gear with vents. Reduce pace. Partially unzip when safe.

Problem	Solutions
Chain problems	Clean and lubricate. Consider belt-drive or internal gear hub.
Arriving sweaty	Slow your pace. Bring a change of clothes. Use wet wipes.
Navigation	Preload routes. Use a waterproof phone case or dedicated GPS computer.
Mechanical issues	Carry a repair kit & know how to use it. Call your emergency contact.

Cycling 301: Limitations
- Not all routes are safely cyclable in extreme conditions
- Some workplaces lack adequate facilities for bike storage or changing
- Carrying large items becomes more challenging
- Quality all-weather gear requires initial investment
- Extreme weather (blizzards, severe heat) may make cycling unsafe regardless of preparation
- Time commitment includes changing clothes and additional maintenance

References and resources: <www.suspra.com/practice/movement/cycling-301.html>

Living Car Free 401: Going Without a Car

Live without owning a passenger vehicle

Create a reliable multi-modal transportation system using walking, cycling, public transit, and occasional shared vehicles. Most car-free individuals discover improved health, reduced stress, and significant financial savings. Modern technology with navigation apps, ride-hailing services, and delivery options makes suburban car-free living more accessible now than in recent past decades.

Living Car Free 401: Equipment & Materials
- Smartphone with map and transportation apps
- Weather-appropriate clothing and footwear
- Bicycle and maintenance equipment (if cycling)
- Public transit pass
- Cargo bags for carrying items
- Budget for alternative transportation
- *Optional: E-bike, folding cart, car-sharing memberships*

Living Car Free 401: Steps
1. Assess your transportation needs
   - Locate essential services within walking distance (if any)
   - Consider daily trips and travel plans for the next year
2. Research available transportation alternatives
   - Map public transportation routes relative to your needs
   - Identify bike-friendly routes to common destinations
   - Research car-sharing, ride-hailing, and rental services
3. Build your transportation toolkit
   - Obtain necessary equipment (bicycle, transit pass) and gear
   - Set up accounts with car-sharing or ride-hailing services; download apps
4. Create storage space for transportation equipment (bicycle, etc.)
5. Adapt your lifestyle
   - Consolidate trips and errands

- Sustainable Practices Handbook — Movement Practices: Getting Exercise

     - Shift to local shopping or online shopping
     - Carry cargo by bicycle, or a borrowed or rented vehicle
  6. Develop contingency plans
     - Create backup transportation plans for emergencies
     - Keep a fund for unexpected transportation needs
  7. Reduce car dependency systematically
     - Begin with a "car-light" transition period
     - Replace more and more car trips
  8. Sell your passenger vehicle (if applicable)
  9. *Optional: Join or create a car-free community group for support*

Living Car Free 401: Definitions

- **Active transportation**: Human-powered movement (walking, cycling)
- **Car-free**: Lifestyle without personal vehicle ownership
- **Car-light**: Reduced but not eliminated car usage
- **Car-sharing**: Services providing short-term vehicle access
- **Ride-hailing**: On-demand transportation services like Uber or Lyft

Living Car Free 401: Troubleshooting

Problem	Solutions
Grocery shopping	Use a backpack or panniers for cycling; a folding cart for walking. Use grocery delivery services. Shop more frequently for smaller loads.
Bad weather	Invest in quality gear and equipment, such as bicycles with studded tires. Use transit as backup. Plan around severe weather using forecast apps.
Unreliable transit	Allow buffer time. Use real-time tracking apps. Hail rides.
Emergency situations	Hail rides. Establish emergency contacts. Keep an emergency fund.
Transporting large items	Rent or borrow a truck or a trailer. Use a delivery service.
Managing with children	Invest in child-carrying equipment. Practice transit use during non-peak times. Connect with other car-free families.

Living Car Free 401: Limitations

- Viability depends on location, urban design, and available infrastructure
- More challenging with mobility limitations
- Difficult in areas with extreme weather
- May require more transportation time
- Complicates emergency situations and large purchases
- More challenging for families with children

Resources and references: <www.suspra.com/practice/movement/car-free-401.html>

Riding 201: Riding Convenient Transit

Take public micro-mobility, buses, or trains when convenient

Convenient transit might mean a quick scooter ride to a nearby meeting, hopping on a bus for your commute, or taking the train for longer distances when doing so isn't vastly less convenient than driving a private vehicle. By opting for these public modes of transport, you directly contribute to less traffic congestion and reduced air pollution. Taking public transit is an opportunity to act for the greater good.

References and resources: <www.suspra.com/practice/movement/riding-201.html>

Riding 301: Riding All Transit

Take public micro-mobility, buses, or trains rather than renting a passenger vehicle

Use public transit and micro-mobility services when traveling or commuting. Transit works best in cities with well-developed transportation networks, but technology has improved access everywhere through trip planning apps and contactless payments. Wear a facemask and gloves if you are concerned about catching a communicable disease when riding on public transit.

Riding 301: Equipment & Materials
- Smartphone with transit and mobility apps
- Digital payment methods or physical transit cards
- Weather-appropriate clothing and comfortable shoes
- Backpack or messenger bag
- Water bottle
- *Optional: Portable power bank, rain poncho, small first aid kit*

Riding 301: Steps
1. Plan your transit strategy before your trip
    - Research transit options at your destination
    - Download relevant apps
    - Identify needed transit passes
    - Map major transit hubs near accommodations
2. Pack light and transit-friendly
    - Use wheeled luggage and backpacks for daily use
3. Select accommodations near transit
    - Choose lodging near major transit hubs
4. Navigate from airports or terminals
    - Research dedicated transit links before arrival
    - Download offline maps
    - Purchase transit cards if required
5. Use multimodal trip planning
    - Use apps to plan trips combining multiple transit types
    - Check real-time arrivals
    - Plan alternatives for service disruptions
6. Use micro-mobility options
    - Locate bike share stations or scooters
    - Follow local regulations
    - Check battery levels before starting
7. Understand the local payment system
    - Learn fare zones and transfer policies
8. Optimize daily routes
    - Plan itineraries around transit accessibility and service times
    - Group destinations by transit lines
9. Prepare for service disruptions
    - Check transit alerts before journeys
    - Know alternative routes

10. When traveling to new cities, ask locals for insights

Riding 301: Definitions

- **Fare zone**: Geographic areas that determine journey cost
- **Micro-mobility**: Transportation using lightweight rental vehicles like bikes or scooters
- **Multi-modal transportation**: Using multiple methods in a single journey
- **Transit hub**: Central location where multiple transit routes converge

Riding 301: Troubleshooting

Problem	Solutions
Service canceled	Check for alternative routes. Use micro-mobility for shorter trips.
Device battery dies	Carry a power bank. Keep physical maps and transit cards.
Micro-mobility malfunction	Force-close and reopen apps. Have backup transit options.
Missing last service	Know night bus routes. Have rideshare apps installed.

Riding 301: Limitations

- Generally less convenient and less comfortable than driving passenger vehicles
- Risk of contracting communicable diseases from other passengers
- Longer travel times than rental cars for destinations outside urban centers
- Weather significantly impacts comfort and feasibility
- Limited early morning or late night options
- Restricted carrying capacity
- Some tourist destinations poorly served by public transit

References and resources: <www.suspra.com/practice/movement/riding-301.html>

Walking 101: Walking Five Minutes

Walk five minutes in nice weather to reduce engine starts and mileage

Instead of hopping in your car for that quick errand to the corner store or that short trip to a nearby colleague's office, choose to walk instead. Short car trips are often the least efficient in a fuel-burning vehicle, as engines are cold and catalytic converters are not yet working optimally, leading to higher emissions per mile. Walking is a zero-emission mode of transport, contributing to cleaner air in your community. It's also a chance to enjoy a bit of fresh air and gentle exercise, making it a win-win for both your health and the planet.

References and resources: <www.suspra.com/practice/movement/walking-101.html>

Walking 201: Walking Fifteen Minutes

Walk fifteen minutes in sunny or rainy weather to complete more trips on foot

Being prepared with the proper clothes to walk fifteen minutes, whether it's sunny or rainy, allows you to complete trips on foot to a nearby store, post office, or friend's house, or to take public transportation. By choosing to walk for these shorter distances, you'll reduce your reliance on cars, decrease traffic congestion, and prevent pollution, contributing to cleaner air and quieter streets in your community.

Walking also offers numerous personal health benefits. Regular short walks improve cardiovascular health, boost mental acuity, and improve feelings of well-being. Embrace the opportunity to experience your neighborhood at a slower pace, noticing details you might miss when driving, and connect with your surroundings in a more meaningful way.

References and resources: <www.suspra.com/practice/movement/walking-201.html>

Walking 301: Walking Sixty Minutes

Walk sixty minutes in all weather to complete long trips on foot

Walk for up to an hour to complete trips up to 4 miles (6.5 km). Use the layering principle (base layer for moisture, mid-layer for insulation, outer layer for protection) across seasons. Consider sidewalk locations, neighborhood conditions, shade, traffic volume, lighting, and amenities like water fountains when planning routes.

Walking 301: Equipment & Materials
- Comfortable, supportive footwear with good traction
- Weather-appropriate clothing (layers, rain gear, sun protection)
- Small backpack for essentials
- Water bottle
- Mobile phone with navigation app or paper map
- Small first aid kit
- Reflective gear or light for low visibility
- Identification and emergency contact information
- *Optional: Trekking poles, umbrella, hat, sunglasses, sunscreen, portable charger, snack*

Walking 301: Steps
1. **Prepare your body**
   - Build walking endurance gradually
   - Limber up and stretch lightly before starting
   - Bring a water bottle
   - Wear proper footwear and weather-appropriate clothing
2. **Plan your route**
   - Map a route of appropriate distance (3-4 miles [5-6.5 km] for 60 minutes)
   - Consider loop routes or straight routes with public transportation returns
   - Identify rest areas, water fountains, and public restrooms
   - Check weather forecast
   - If walking in remote areas, share your route with an emergency contact
3. **Dress for weather conditions**
   - Hot weather: Light clothing, sunscreen, extra water
   - Cold weather: Layers, hat, gloves, thermal socks
   - Rain: Waterproof footwear and jacket
   - Snow or ice: Insulated waterproof boots with traction
   - Wind: Wind-resistant outer layer
4. **Maintain comfortable pace**
   - Use the "talk test"–you should be able to carry on conversation
   - Start moderate rather than fast
5. **Navigate safely in urban environments**
   - Use pedestrian crossings

- Make eye contact with drivers
- Be aware of surroundings
- Walk facing traffic where no sidewalks exist
6. **Cool down at end of walk**
    - Reduce pace in final five minutes
    - Stretch after walking

Walking 301: Definitions

- **Base layer**: Clothing worn next to skin that wicks moisture away
- **Hot spots**: Areas of irritation that may develop into blisters
- **Ice grippers**: Removable traction devices for footwear in icy conditions
- **Talk test**: Ability to carry on conversation while exercising, indicating moderate intensity
- **Trekking poles**: Adjustable walking sticks for stability and reduced joint impact

Walking 301: Troubleshooting

Problem	Solutions
Foot pain or blisters	Wear moisture-wicking socks and shoes that fit well. Apply moleskin.
Leg or joint fatigue	Check walking mechanics at a shoe store that offers this evaluation. Build distance gradually. Use trekking poles. Talk to a doctor.
Overheating	Dress in removable layers. Walk during cooler hours. Bring water to drink.
Unexpected weather	Carry emergency poncho. Know sheltered locations. Have bail-out options.
Safety concerns	Research routes ahead. Walk during daylight. Carry a cell phone.

Walking 301: Limitations

- Severe weather or poor pedestrian infrastructure may make walking unsafe
- Limited carrying capacity
- Personal safety concerns in some areas
- Time constraints for longer trips

References and resources: <www.suspra.com/practice/movement/walking-301.html>

Driving Electric

Borrowing 201: Renting Electric

Rent or borrow an electric vehicle

Reduce or eliminate the amount of fuel you burn by choosing a plug-in hybrid or a fully electric vehicle when you need to borrow or rent one. Find out its electric range, especially if it is a plug-in model, and learn how to charge it.

References and resources: <www.suspra.com/practice/movement/borrowing-201.html>

Buying Vehicles 301: Buying a Plug-In Hybrid

Buy a used plug-in hybrid passenger vehicle

Rather than buying a mild hybrid or non-hybrid fuel-burning vehicle, buy a used *plug-in* hybrid vehicle. Hybrid vehicles have a battery and an electric traction motor that provides some or all of the power to move the vehicle. Mild hybrid vehicles burn fuel to charge their batteries; plug-in hybrid vehicles can charge their batteries from an electrical outlet or dedicated electric vehicle charging equipment.

References and resources: <www.suspra.com/practice/movement/buying-301.html>

Buying Vehicles 401: Buying an EV

Buy or lease a new fully electric passenger vehicle

Drive an electric vehicle to prevent pollution and save energy. Instead of visiting gas stations, plug in where you park to charge your car's battery. EVs available as of 2025 offer 200-300 miles of range, sufficient for most drivers' weekly needs on a single charge, and require less maintenance than fuel-burning vehicles with no oil changes, fewer brake repairs, and fewer moving parts overall.

Driving 401: Equipment, Materials and Cost
- Monthly lease or car payment ($129-$500+)
- *Optional: Electrical outlet or dedicated electric vehicle charger*

Driving 401: Steps
1. Assess your passenger vehicle needs
    - Know how far you need to drive per year
    - Consider passenger and cargo requirements
    - Determine charging access (at home, work or school)
2. Research EV models
    - Get a list of all models available; filter to those within your budget
    - Compare range, efficiency, and charging speeds
    - Check reliability ratings and warranty coverage
3. Understand EV charging basics
    - Level 1 (120 volt alternating current): 3-5 miles (5-8 km) per hour
    - Level 2 (240 volt alternating current): 25-35 miles (40-55 km) per hour
    - Level 3 (direct current): hundreds of miles or kms per hour
    - Map charging stations along your routes
    - Identify your vehicle's charging port type
4. Plan home charging

- Verify electrical panel capacity
- Get installation quotes for:
  - 240V outlet ($300-$600)
  - Level 2 charging unit ($500-$1,000 plus installation)
5. Test drive multiple EVs
6. Compare financing options
   - Evaluate buying versus leasing
   - Get pre-approved financing if buying
7. Prepare for delivery
   - Install home charging or identify charging locations
   - Download essential apps (manufacturer, charging networks)
   - Review insurance coverage
8. Adapt to EV ownership
   - Learn efficient driving techniques
   - Plan longer trips around charging stops

Driving 401: Definitions

- **Battery electric vehicle (BEV)**: Vehicle powered exclusively by electricity stored in batteries
- **CCS**: Older direct current fast charging standard (prior to 2022 in North America)
- **DC fast charging**: High-power charging adding 100-200+ miles in 20-30 minutes
- **EVSE**: Electric Vehicle Supply Equipment (charging station)
- **Level 1/2 charging**: Using 120 volt or 240 volt, respectively, alternating current
- **NACS**: Newer direct current fast charging standard (since 2022 in North America)
- **One-pedal driving**: Using mainly accelerator pedal for both acceleration and braking
- **Preconditioning**: Warming or cooling the battery and cabin while plugged in
- **Regenerative braking**: System recapturing energy during deceleration

Driving 401: Troubleshooting

Problem	Solutions
Limited home charging	Use workplace or public charging.
Range anxiety	Plan trips with charging stops. Set display to percentage rather than miles.
Unaffordable	Buy a used EV.
Cold weather range loss	Precondition while plugged in. Use seat heaters instead of cabin heat. Plan more frequent charging stops.
Apartment charging challenges	Ask building management to install charging. Use workplace or public charging.
Battery longevity concerns	Review warranty details. Follow recommended charging practices. Avoid charging above 80%; avoid discharging below 20%.

Driving 401: Limitations

- Home charging installation difficult for renters or apartment dwellers
- Charging infrastructure still being installed in some regions
- Cold weather reduces range
- Higher initial purchase price than comparable fuel-burning vehicles
- Public charging stations sometimes unreliable or occupied

- Charging EVs takes longer than refueling fuel-burning vehicles
- Limited model availability in some vehicle categories
- Local service expertise may be limited in some areas

References and resources: <www.suspra.com/practice/movement/driving-401.html>

Choosing Electric 101: Ride-Sharing

Choose an electric vehicle when ride-sharing

When you use ride-sharing services, make a conscious choice to select electric vehicles (EVs) if available. Many ride-sharing platforms now offer options to specifically request or prioritize EVs. Some platforms may also offer incentives for choosing greener rides. Encourage ride-sharing companies to further invest in electric fleets and accelerate the transition to sustainable transportation.

References and resources: <www.suspra.com/practice/movement/choosing-electric-101.html>

Cycling 401: Riding E-Bikes

Ride an e-bike rather than drive a passenger vehicle

Ride e-bikes to replace passenger vehicle trips. An electric motor provides assistance when pedaling, making hills, headwinds, longer distances, and heavier payloads more manageable. Add a bike trailer to carry heavy or bulky loads. Modern e-bikes provide up to 80 miles (130 km) of range depending on battery size, rider weight, terrain, assistance level, and weather. Manage your battery and do regular maintenance for reliable performance.

Cycling 401: Equipment, Materials and Cost

- Purchase price ($500-$2,000+)
- Bicycle helmet
- Bicycle lock (U-lock with cable recommended)
- Rain gear and reflective clothing
- Bicycle lights (front and rear)
- Bike repair kit, including tire pump with pressure gauge
- E-bike battery charger
- *Optional: Storage bags or panniers, Fenders, smartphone mount, extra battery*

Cycling 401: Steps

1. Choose the right e-bike for your needs
   - Consider typical trips (commuting, errands, recreation)
   - Select appropriate class (1, 2, or 3), style, and battery range
   - Test ride before purchasing
2. Learn your e-bike's features
   - Read owner's manual thoroughly
   - Practice in a traffic-free area to understand power levels and controls
3. Set up charging routine
   - Establish safe charging location at home where battery fire won't spread
   - Follow manufacturer's charging guidelines
   - Track battery range in different conditions
4. Replace car trips systematically
   - Set specific car-replacement goals
   - Plan bike-friendly routes
5. Add practical accessories

- Install weather protection (fenders, etc.)
- Add cargo capacity (panniers, baskets)
- Ensure visibility with lights and reflectors
6. Develop all-weather riding strategies
    - Acquire appropriate clothing
    - Plan alternative routes when needed
7. Maintain your e-bike
    - Check tire pressure frequently
    - Keep drive components clean
    - Follow maintenance schedule
8. Ride safely and legally
    - Follow traffic laws; signal turns and lane changes
    - Wear appropriate safety gear (helmet, gloves)

Cycling 401: Definitions

- **Class 1, 2, 3 e-bikes**: Legal classifications based on assistance type and maximum speed
- **Controller**: Electronic component regulating power from battery to motor
- **Panniers**: Bags that attach to bicycle racks
- **Pedal-assist**: System providing motor assistance only when pedaling
- **Range**: Maximum distance on a single battery charge
- **Throttle**: Control delivering motor power without pedaling
- **Watt-hours or Amp-hours**: Battery energy capacity measurement

Cycling 401: Troubleshooting

Problem	Solutions
Battery depletes fast	Check tire pressure and drivetrain. Use lower assistance levels; pedal more.
Motor cuts out	Check battery connection. Inspect wiring. Verify speed sensor alignment.
Rain	Install fenders. Use waterproof clothing. Use anti-fog treatment on glasses.
E-bike feels too heavy	Practice handling in safe areas. Increase tire pressure. Clean chain.
Carrying cargo	Add baskets, panniers, or racks. Get a cargo e-bike. Pull a bike trailer.
Battery won't charge	Verify outlet works. Check connections. Inspect charger indicator lights.
Range too short	Carry spare battery. Stop to recharge. Use less assistance. Pedal more.

Cycling 401: Limitations

- Limited range and less carrying capacity compared to passenger vehicles
- Weather impacts comfort and practicality
- Higher initial cost than conventional bicycles
- Security concerns (e-bikes are valuable theft targets)
- Battery performance degrades in cold weather

References and resources: <www.suspra.com/practice/movement/cycling-401.html>

Energy Practices

Optimizing Energy Efficiency, page 279	
Goals	**Indicators**
• Consume less energy per person per day	• Power demand per person

Conserving Energy, page 333	
Goals	**Indicators**
• Consume less energy per person per day	• Power demand per person

Electrifying, page 354	
Goals	**Indicators**
• Eliminate fuel consumption • Reduce air, water, and noise pollution • Increase energy efficiency	• Electricity percentage of energy consumption

Solarizing, page 363	
Goals	**Indicators**
• Eliminate fuel consumption • Reduce air, water, and noise pollution	• Solar percentage of energy consumption

Optimizing Energy Efficiency

Building 301: Insulating

Check and upgrade insulation in your building envelope

Insulate to reduce the amount of energy necessary to maintain comfortable and safe indoor temperatures. Cellulose insulation is made from recycled paper treated with fire retardants and has lower environmental impact than fiberglass. It provides about R-3.5 to R-3.8 per inch. Air sealing before insulating is crucial: think of insulation as a sweater and air sealing as a windbreaker. Attic insulation is typically the most cost-effective improvement, followed by basements and walls.

Building 301: Equipment & Materials

- Cellulose insulation (loose-fill or dense-pack) and insulation blower (can be rented)
- Weatherstripping and air sealing materials (caulk and caulk gun, expanding foam, etc.)
- Dust mask or respirator, safety goggles, and work gloves
- Measuring tape, utility knife, and basic tools for home improvement projects

Building 301: Steps

1. Assess current insulation
   - Check energy bills for seasonal spikes
   - Rent or borrow a thermal (infrared) camera to see heat loss in a building
   - Measure existing insulation depth
   - Note moisture, pest, or structural issues
2. Research requirements
   - Determine R-value goal that makes sense for your climate zone
   - Calculate how much insulation material you'll need
3. ***Hire a professional or get training in how to seal and insulate***
4. Air seal before insulating
   - Seal gaps around penetrations (pipes, wires, vents)
   - Caulk around windows, doors, fixtures, and outlets
   - Allow sealants to cure before installing insulation
5. Install attic insulation
   - Install rafter vents to maintain ventilation
   - For loose-fill cellulose:
     - Set up insulation blower per manufacturer's instructions
     - Fill to desired depth with even coverage
     - Install depth markers
   - For mineral wool batts, lay perpendicular to joists for second layer
   - Insulate and air seal the attic access
6. Insulate basement or crawlspace
   - For basement walls, apply rigid foam or spray foam
   - For basement ceiling, install insulation between joists
   - Address moisture issues first in crawl spaces
7. Insulate walls (if applicable)
   - For existing walls: use dense-pack technique through access holes
   - For open walls: install insulation between studs with no gaps
8. Record type and R-value of insulation installed; take pictures

Building 301: Definitions

- **Air sealing:** Closing gaps and holes in the building envelope

- **R-value**: Measure of thermal resistance; higher values indicate better insulation
- **Dense-pack cellulose**: Cellulose installed at higher density (3.5-4.5 lbs/cf [56-72 g/L])
- **Thermal bridging**: Heat transfer that occurs across more conductive components

Building 301: Troubleshooting

Problem	Solutions
Difficult areas	Use rigid tube extension on blower hose. Consider rigid foam for tight spots
Uneven coverage	Use depth markers. Check frequently. Rake gently to even out loose-fill.
Existing insulation wet	Fix moisture source. Remove and replace damaged sections.
Recessed lighting	Use only IC-rated fixtures with insulation; create a dam for non-IC fixtures.

Building 301: Limitations

- Dense-packing walls requires experience and specialized equipment
- Homes with knob-and-tube wiring require electrical upgrades first
- Cellulose can be damaged by prolonged moisture exposure
- Existing moisture problems must be addressed before insulating

References and resources: <www.suspra.com/practice/energy/insulating-301.html>

Building 302: Removing Chimneys

Remove unused chimneys

If you no longer use a chimney, remove it to improve energy efficiency by eliminating a major air shaft that creates thermal bridges through your building envelope. Metal chimneys (flue pipes) are relatively easy to remove; masonry chimneys require more effort. Partial removal (taking down the chimney to below the roofline) eliminates the most problematic portion while leaving interior sections intact. Complete removal eliminates all energy losses and adds more usable interior space to your building.

Building 302: Equipment & Materials

- Safety equipment: respirator, goggles, hard hat, gloves, steel-toed boots
- Demolition tools: sledgehammer, hammer and chisel, reciprocating saw
- Structural materials: lumber for supports, roofing materials
- Cleanup equipment: contractor bags, tarps, shop vacuum with HEPA filter

Building 302: Steps

1. Assess and prepare
   - Confirm chimney is no longer in use
   - Look for asbestos in older chimneys; hire a home inspector if you're not sure
   - Obtain necessary permits
2. *Hire professionals*
   - *Hire a structural engineer to check for structural issues*
   - *Hire an asbestos remediation company if asbestos is present*
3. Contain dust (masonry chimneys)
   - Cover floors and furniture with tarps; create dust barriers with plastic sheeting
   - Turn off nearby HVAC systems; ensure proper ventilation (open windows, etc.)
4. Remove top portion (masonry chimneys)

Sustainable Practices Handbook
Energy Practices: Optimizing Energy Efficiency

- Work from roof to remove crown and top courses
- For partial removal, stop two feet below roofline
- For complete removal, continue through house
5. Repair the roof
6. Remove interior portions (for complete removal)
    - Work from top to bottom, one floor at a time
    - Install temporary supports if needed
    - Break chimney into manageable sections; remove debris regularly
7. Repair openings in ceilings and walls
8. Address foundation (for complete removal)
    - Remove chimney base and hearth
    - Patch foundation opening according to code

Building 302: Definitions

- **Chimney crown**: The top concrete portion that covers and seals the chimney
- **Flashing**: Metal sheets installed where chimney meets the roof to prevent water infiltration
- **Load-bearing**: A structural element that supports weight of the building above it

Building 302: Troubleshooting

Problem	Solutions
Asbestos	Stop work immediately. Hire a licensed asbestos abatement contractor.
Load-bearing chimney	Hire professionals to remove.
Roof leaks	Check flashing installation. Ensure proper overlapping of materials.
Excessive dust.	Improve barriers. Use an air scrubber. Spray water on demolition.

Building 302: Limitations

- Do-it-yourself removal is not appropriate for load-bearing masonry chimneys
- Special permits may be required in historic districts
- Older chimneys may contain hazardous materials requiring professional abatement
- Improper removal can compromise structural integrity

References and resources: <www.suspra.com/practice/energy/building-302.html>

Building 401: Going Passive Solar

Build a passive solar structure

Collect and use solar energy through properly oriented windows (aperture), absorbing heat in dark surfaces (absorber), storing heat in dense materials (thermal mass), moving heat throughout the space (distribution), and preventing overheating with properly sized overhangs (control). Direct gain is simplest, with sunlight directly entering living spaces. Indirect gain collects heat in a thermal mass wall for later release. Isolated gain collects heat in a separate space like a sunroom.

Building 401: Equipment & Materials

- Site assessment tools: compass, solar path calculator, tape measure
- Design materials: grid paper, design software (optional)
- High-performance windows (low-e, double or triple-glazed)

- Thermal mass materials (concrete, stone, brick, tile, water containers)
- Shading devices (overhangs, awnings, trellises)
- Insulation materials
- Air sealing materials

Building 401: Steps

1. Assess site's solar potential
   - Determine true south (northern hemisphere) or true north (southern hemisphere)
   - Document sun path throughout seasons
   - Identify features that block solar gain
   - Measure solar access using a solar path calculator
2. Research passive solar principles for your climate
   - Identify your climate zone
   - Determine optimal glazing area (typically 7-12% of floor area)
   - Calculate appropriate thermal mass quantities (6-10 times area of south-facing glass)
   - Research recommended overhang dimensions for your latitude
3. Plan your design
   - For new construction, incorporate:
     - Sun-facing orientation (south in northern hemisphere)
     - Appropriate window placement and sizing
     - Properly sized thermal mass
     - Seasonal solar control (overhangs)
     - Superinsulation and air-sealing
   - For retrofits, identify feasible modifications:
     - Adding south-facing windows or seasonal solar control
     - Adding thermal mass
     - Improving insulation and air sealing
4. Obtain necessary approvals and permits
5. Implement direct gain components
   - Install high-performance windows on sun-facing walls
   - Size overhangs to block summer sun but allow winter sun
   - Add thermal mass in direct sunlight or within radiative reach:
     - Concrete or tile floors (4 inches [10 cm] thick)
     - Masonry walls (6 inches [15 cm] thick)
     - Water containers
6. Implement indirect gain strategies (if applicable)
   - For Trombe walls:
     - Build masonry wall 16 inches (40 cm) thick
     - Place glazing 1-6 inches (2-15 cm) from surface
     - Include vents for heat distribution
   - For water walls:
     - Install water containers behind sun-facing glazing
7. **Implement superinsulation and air-sealing**
   - Install high R-value insulation in all exterior surfaces
   - Thoroughly air-seal the building envelope
8. **Add natural cooling strategies**
   - Design for cross-ventilation with operable windows
   - Use thermal mass for night-flush cooling in appropriate climates
9. **Create operational procedures**
   - Develop routines for seasonal adjustments
   - Document system operation for future reference

Building 401: Definitions

- **Direct gain**: Passive solar approach where sunlight directly enters living spaces
- **Indirect gain**: System where heat is collected in thermal mass before being released
- **Isolated gain**: Collection of solar energy in a space separate from main living area
- **Thermal mass**: Materials with high heat capacity that store thermal energy
- **Trombe wall**: Dark-colored high thermal mass wall behind glazing

Building 401: Troubleshooting

Problem	Solutions
Winter overheating	Add adjustable interior shading. Incorporate ventilation to distribute heat.
Insufficient heating	Remove anything blocking winter sun. Add thermal mass to store heat.
Summer overheating	Add exterior shade screens. Improve night ventilation to flush stored heat.
Temperature swings	Add thermal mass (determined by the area of south-facing glass).
Glare	Install light shelves. Use shades. Position seating away from direct sun.

Building 401: Limitations

- Requires suitable solar access, often limited by site constraints
- Performance depends on local climate and weather patterns
- Initial costs higher than conventional construction
- Limited improvements possible when retrofitting existing buildings
- Requires proper occupant behavior for optimal performance
- Less effective at extreme northern or southern latitudes

References and resources: <www.suspra.com/practice/energy/buliding-401.html>

Building 402: Cooling Roofs

Install a cool roof that reflects more sunlight than a conventional roof

Reflect more sunlight and absorb less heat than a standard roof by installing a cool roof. Traditional roofs absorb 85-95% of solar energy and reach 150-185°F (65-85°C) on hot days; cool roofs stay 50-60°F (28-33°C) cooler under the same conditions. The two key properties of cool roof materials are the ability to reflect sunlight and the ability to radiate absorbed heat.

Building 402: Equipment & Materials

- Infrared thermometer
- Protective clothing (gloves, safety glasses, boots, hard hat)
- Roofing materials (white/light-colored shingles, reflective metal, or cooling membrane)
- Reflective roof coating (acrylic, silicone, or elastomeric)
- Pressure washer or roof cleaner
- Brushes, rollers, or sprayers for coating application
- Roof patching materials

Building 402: Steps

1. Assess your current roof
    - Measure the square footage

- Determine condition and remaining lifespan
- Check for damage or weak spots
- Measure roof temperature on a sunny day
2. Choose an approach
   - For existing roofs in good condition: reflective coating
   - For roofs needing replacement: light-colored or reflective materials
3. Research local codes, rules, and incentives
4. For coating an existing roof:
   - Clean thoroughly with pressure washer, allow to dry completely
   - Repair any damage
   - Apply primer, first, and second coat per manufacturer's instructions
5. For installing new cool roof materials:
   - Remove existing roofing (if necessary)
   - Install appropriate underlayment
   - Install cool roof materials according to specifications:
     - Reflective shingles or tiles
     - Reflective membranes
     - Metal roofing with reflective finish
6. Document the installation
   - Record product information and warranties
   - Save receipts for rebate applications

Building 402: Definitions

- **Albedo**: Measure of surface reflectivity; 0 = complete absorption, 1 = complete reflection
- **Emissivity**: Ability of material to emit absorbed heat (1 = perfect emitter)
- **Solar Reflectance Index**: Measure of a material's ability to reject solar heat (0-100%)

Building 402: Troubleshooting

Problem	Solutions
Peeling or blistering	Ensure proper surface preparation. Use primer if recommended.
Reduced reflectivity	Clean annually with gentle detergent. Reapply coating every 5-10 years.
Poor adhesion	Ensure the roof is completely clean and dry. Use an appropriate primer.
Condensation in attic	Improve attic ventilation. Check for air leaks to the attic.

Building 402: Limitations

- Maximum benefit in hot, sunny climates; less benefit in cold regions
- Potential for slight increases in winter heating costs in mixed climate zones
- Neighborhood or homeowner association restrictions may limit roof appearance or colors
- Reflectivity decreases over time; requires ongoing maintenance
- Not all existing roof types can be effectively coated

References and resources: <www.suspra.com/practice/energy/building-402.html>

Sustainable Practices Handbook
Energy Practices: Optimizing Energy Efficiency

Cooking 301: Induction Cooking

Install an energy-efficient electric induction stove

Use electricity efficiently to cook by installing induction appliances that use electromagnetic fields to heat magnetic (cast iron, carbon steel, most stainless steel) cookware directly. Test cookware with a magnet; if a magnet does not stick to the cookware, it will not heat up on an induction burner. To provide sufficient electrical power, homes may need electrical upgrades, possibly including a utility service upgrade from 100 amps to 200 amps or even 400 amps. Offgrid homes need battery systems that can provide at least 5 kW of dedicated power for a 30-inch induction cooktop. Modern induction ranges include safety features like automatic shut-off, child locks, and precise temperature control.

Cooking 301: Equipment, Materials and Cost

- Induction range ($1,000-$4,000+) or portable cooktop ($100-200)
- Induction-compatible cookware (cast iron, carbon steel, most stainless steel)

Cooking 301: Steps

1. Assess your cooking needs and kitchen space
   - Measure available space, including width, depth, and height
   - Consider cooking habits and needed number of burners
   - Decide between built-in cooktop or freestanding range
   - Determine size (standard 30-inch or larger 36-inch)
2. Select an appropriate induction unit
   - Compare energy efficiency ratings and power output
   - Check number and size of cooking zones and controls
   - Look for features like automatic pot detection and power boost
   - Consider ENERGY STAR certification
3. ***Hire an electrician unless you have the necessary electrical knowledge and skills***
4. Evaluate your home's electrical capacity
   - Check capacity of electrical service; hire an electrician to upgrade service if necessary
   - Check electrical panel for available capacity
   - Verify or add a 240 volt 50 amp dedicated circuit
5. Prepare for installation
   - Turn off power at circuit breaker; verify power is off using circuit tester
   - Remove existing appliance (if necessary)
   - Clean installation area
6. For built-in cooktop installation:
   - Ensure countertop cut-out matches specifications
   - Install required brackets
   - Feed power cord through cabinet opening
   - Apply sealing strip if required
   - Lower cooktop into place and secure
7. For freestanding range installation:
   - Ensure proper opening width between cabinets
   - Install anti-tip bracket to floor
   - Connect power cord to range if not pre-installed
   - Slide range into position and adjust leveling legs
8. Complete electrical connections
   - For direct-wiring: connect ground, neutral, and hot wires
   - For cord and plug: ensure secure connections
9. Test the installation
   - Restore power at circuit breaker

Revision: 25.1.8

- Test all cooking zones with compatible cookware
- Verify the cooking surface is level
- Open the oven door (if applicable), apply slight force to make sure unit will not tip over

Cooking 301: Definitions
- **Anti-tip bracket**: Safety device preventing a freestanding range from tipping forward
- **Automatic pot detection**: Technology that senses cookware placement
- **Dedicated circuit**: Electrical circuit used exclusively for one appliance
- **Induction cooking**: Cooking technology using electromagnetic fields to directly heat cookware
- **Power boost function**: Feature temporarily increasing power for tasks like rapid boiling

Cooking 301: Troubleshooting

Problem	Solutions
Unit won't power on	Check circuit breaker. Verify connections. Check the control lock.
Cookware not heating	Test cookware with a magnet. Center cookware in the cooking zone.
Circuit breaker trips	Verify proper wire size. Replace circuit breaker. Call a service technician.
Cooktop buzzes	Normal operation, especially at high power. Try different cookware.
Range not level	Adjust leveling legs; ensure floor is even; check anti-tip bracket placement

Cooking 301: Limitations
- Requires compatible cookware (ferromagnetic materials)
- Higher initial cost than other cooking appliances
- May require electrical upgrades
- May interfere with pacemakers

References and resources: <www.suspra.com/practice/energy/cooking-301.html>

Cooking 302: Convection Cooking

Install an energy-efficient electric convection oven

Use electricity efficiently to cook with convection ovens that use fans to circulate hot air, cooking food approximately 25% faster than conventional ovens and allowing lower temperature settings (typically 25°F below standard recipes). "Standard" convection just has a fan in the oven; "true" convection adds a heating element near the fan; and "dual" convection has two fans that circulate hot air with more even heat distribution. Proper installation ensures safety, efficiency, and optimal cooking results.

Cooking 302: Equipment, Materials and Cost
- Electric convection oven ($1,000-$5,000+)

Cooking 302: Steps
1. Select an appropriate convection oven
   - Look for ENERGY STAR certification
   - Consider European-style "true convection" for maximum efficiency
   - Measure space precisely: cabinet opening for built-ins or width for ranges
2. ***Hire an electrician unless you have the necessary electrical knowledge and skills***

3. Prepare for installation
   - If replacing gas, have professional cap the gas line
   - Verify electrical service can support the appliance
   - Turn off power to oven circuit at main panel; verify power is off with voltage tester
4. For freestanding range or oven installation
   - Connect power cord to range if not pre-installed
   - Plug in or hardwire according to instructions
   - Install anti-tip bracket (critical safety feature)
   - Level the range using adjustable legs
5. For built-in wall oven installation
   - Confirm cabinet cutout dimensions match specifications
   - Prepare electrical connection
   - Connect wires according to instructions or plug in
   - Slide oven into cabinet opening with helper
   - Secure to cabinet using provided screws
   - Check that oven is level
6. Complete installation
   - Restore power at circuit breaker
   - Test that oven powers on; verify convection fan operation
   - Run empty at 400°F for 30 minutes to burn off manufacturing oils

Cooking 302: Definitions

- **Convection**: Cooking method using a fan to circulate hot air for faster, more even results
- **Dedicated circuit**: Electrical circuit serving only one appliance
- **Hardwiring**: Connecting an appliance directly to a home's electrical system
- **True convection**: System with a heating element near the fan for more consistent heating

Cooking 302: Troubleshooting

Problem	Solutions
Oven doesn't fit	Measure before purchasing. Modify cabinet for minor discrepancies.
Outlet mismatch	Hire an electrician to install the correct outlet. Never modify plugs.
Door doesn't seal	Check for debris. Adjust hinges. Replace damaged gaskets.
Convection fan noisy	Ensure nothing is in the fan. Check the fan cover. Call a service technician.
Circuit breaker trips	Verify wire gauge. Replace circuit breaker. Hire an electrician.

Cooking 302: Limitations

- Professional installation recommended for inexperienced individuals
- Cabinet modifications may be necessary
- Older homes may need electrical service upgrades

References and resources: <www.suspra.com/practice/energy/cooking-302.html>

Heating & Cooling 101: Setting Thermostats

Set back thermostats

Setting back a thermostat means either manually changing the setpoint or, for a programmable thermostat, setting a schedule to decrease energy consumption, lower your utility bills, and reduce emissions associated with energy production. Lower the temperature in the winter when you are asleep or away; raise it in the summer when you are out of the house. For heating, aim to reduce the temperature by 10 degrees Fahrenheit (6 degrees Celsius). For cooling, raise the temperature similarly. Significantly reduce the workload on your heating and cooling systems, as your home loses heat more slowly in winter and gains heat more slowly in summer when the indoor temperature is closer to the outdoor temperature.

References and resources: <www.suspra.com/practice/energy/heating-cooling-101.html>

Heating & Cooling 201: Programming Thermostats

Install and program smart thermostats

Reduce energy usage by automatically adjusting your home's temperature based on your schedule with a programmable or smart thermostat. Basic programmable thermostats allow manual schedule setting, while smart thermostats offer remote control, learning capabilities, occupancy sensing, and energy usage reports. Most energy savings come from programming longer setback periods (8 hours or more) when you're away or sleeping.

Heating & Cooling 201: Equipment & Materials
- Programmable or smart thermostat
- Smartphone or computer (for smart thermostats)
- WiFi network information (for smart thermostats)

Heating & Cooling 201: Steps
1. Prepare for installation
    - Check compatibility with your system
    - Turn off power at circuit breaker
2. Remove old thermostat
    - Take photo of current wiring
    - Label each wire with masking tape
    - Disconnect wires and unscrew mounting plate
3. Install new mounting plate
    - Thread wires through center hole
    - Use level to position
    - Secure to wall with screws
4. Connect wires
    - Match labeled wires to corresponding terminals
    - Insert each wire and tighten connection
5. Attach thermostat to mounting plate
    - Push excess wires into wall
    - Snap or screw thermostat onto plate
6. Restore power and test
7. Set up and program following manufacturer's instructions
    - Set current day and time
    - Program for efficiency:
        - For heating: Set *lower* temperatures when away or sleeping

- For cooling: Set *higher* temperatures when away or sleeping

Heating & Cooling 201: Definitions
- **C wire**: Provides continuous power to the thermostat
- **Learning mode**: Feature that observes adjustments to create an automated schedule
- **Recovery mode**: Calculates when to begin heating/cooling to reach desired temperature
- **Setback/Setup**: Adjusting temperature down (for heating) or up (for cooling) to save energy

Heating & Cooling 201: Troubleshooting

Problem	Solutions
No power	Check circuit breaker. Verify wire connections. Get a C wire adapter.
System doesn't respond	Check mode setting. Verify wire connections.
Inaccurate readings	Move the thermostat away from sources of heat or drafts. Calibrate.
WiFi connection issues	Check the network. Reset settings. Reboot WiFi router. Update firmware.

Heating & Cooling 201: Limitations
- Standard models won't adjust to unexpected schedule changes
- Some older systems incompatible with smart thermostats
- Many smart thermostats require a C wire
- Learning features take weeks to optimize

References and resources: <www.suspra.com/practice/energy/thermostats-201.html>

Heating & Cooling 202: Circulating Air

Use wood stove fans to circulate warm air

Use wood stove fans to distribute warm air throughout your space, improving comfort and potentially reducing fuel consumption. Without circulation, hot air rises to the ceiling, creating stratification where the ceiling is hot while floor areas remain cold. Heat-powered fans operate using either thermoelectric or Stirling engine technology, requiring no external power. Electric fans move more air and can be positioned more flexibly but require electricity. For optimal circulation, create a continuous airflow loop that brings warm air to cold areas and cold air back to the heat source.

Heating & Cooling 202: Equipment & Materials
- Fan
  - Heat-powered wood stove fan (Stirling engine or thermoelectric)
  - Electric fan (box, table, or ceiling fan)
- Thermometer
- Heat-resistant blocks (for positioning)
- *Optional: Aluminum foil (for DIY heat reflector)*

Heating & Cooling 202: Steps
1. Assess your wood stove setup
   - Identify areas where heat is needed
   - Measure temperature differences between rooms
2. Choose appropriate fan solution

- Heat-powered fans: select size appropriate for room
- Electric fans: select fan with appropriate power
3. Position heat-powered fan correctly
    - Place on flat section of stove top (150-650°F / 65-340°C)
    - Position near back or side with adequate clearance
    - Point toward living area
    - Keep away from flue pipe
4. Position electric fans strategically
    - Doorway placement
        - at floor level pointing into colder room, or
        - at top pointing away from stove
    - Ceiling fans: run clockwise at low speed during heating season
    - Tabletop fans: create gentle airflow from warm to cold areas
5. Optional: Create a DIY heat reflector, conductor, or channel
    - Position curved shield of aluminum foil behind stove to reflect heat into room
    - Convection platform: place metal sheet across heat-resistant blocks by stove
    - Heat channel: create foil channel from stove to cooler area

Heating & Cooling 202: Definitions

- **Convection**: Air rising when heated and sinking when cooled
- **CFM**: Cubic Feet per Minute, measurement of airflow volume
- **Seebeck effect**: Conversion of temperature differences into electricity
- **Stratification**: Layering of different air temperatures, warmest at top

Heating & Cooling 202: Troubleshooting

Problem	Solutions
Heat-powered fan doesn't start	Check stove temperature (must be at least 150°F). Ensure flat placement. Clean heat conductor plate
Fan runs slowly	Reposition fan to a hotter area. Clean blades. Check for obstructions
Uneven heating	Add another fan. Rearrange furniture blocking airflow. Use a ceiling fan.
Fan makes noise	Allow to cool; check for loose parts. Oil moving parts.
Heat distribution	Use a box fan in doorways. Install vents above doorways.

Heating & Cooling 202: Limitations

- Heat-powered fans move relatively small air volumes
- Effectiveness limited by home layout
- Heat-powered fans require minimum stove temperature
- Most heat-powered fans have maximum temperature limits
- Electric fans require power and manual operation
- Effectiveness decreases in large or poorly insulated spaces

References and resources: <www.suspra.com/practice/energy/circulating-air-202.html>

Heating & Cooling 301: Sealing Ducts

Locate and seal air leaks in ducting

Seal connections, joints, and seams to reduce energy usage and improve comfort. Mastic sealant (water-based paste) creates a permanent, flexible seal that accommodates duct expansion and contraction. Metal foil tape (UL-181 rated) is suitable for bridging gaps. Standard cloth "duct tape" is NOT appropriate for sealing ducts.

Heating & Cooling 301: Equipment & Materials
- Mastic sealant (water-based, UL-181 rated)
- Metal foil tape (UL-181 rated, not regular duct tape)

Heating & Cooling 301: Steps
1. Assess your duct system
    - Identify duct types (sheet metal, flex duct, duct board)
    - Create simple diagram
    - Take photos of difficult-access areas
2. ***Hire a professional if you do not have the knowledge or skills to seal ducts***
3. Locate leaks in accessible ducts
    - Focus on high-priority areas:
        - Connections between main ducts and branches
        - Connections to registers
        - Connections to equipment
        - Seams between sections
    - Look for visible gaps, dust streaks, damaged areas
4. Prepare surfaces
    - Clean with damp cloth
    - Remove debris and old tape
    - Ensure surfaces are dry
5. Seal sheet metal ducts
    - For small holes (less than ¼ inch):
        - Apply mastic 1/16 to 1/8 inch thick
        - Extend 1 inch beyond seam
    - For larger gaps (¼ to ¾ inch):
        - Bridge with metal foil tape
        - Apply mastic over tape
6. Seal connections to boots and registers
    - Remove register covers
    - Apply mastic around connection
    - For flex ducts, secure inner liner with zip tie before sealing
7. Seal flex duct connections
    - Pull inner liner completely over fitting
    - Secure with zip tie
    - Apply mastic at connection
    - Seal outer vapor barrier with metal foil tape
8. Address duct board systems
    - Use metal foil tape for seams
    - Apply mastic to reinforce corners and joints
9. Test your work
    - After sealant dries, turn on fan-only mode
    - Check for whistling sounds or air movement

Sustainable Practices Handbook Energy Practices: Optimizing Energy Efficiency

- o   Feel for leakage around sealed connections

Heating & Cooling 301: Definitions
- **Boot**: Fitting connecting ductwork to floor, wall, or ceiling register
- **Duct board**: Rigid fiberglass boards with foil facing
- **Flex duct**: Flexible, insulated ductwork with inner liner, insulation, and outer vapor barrier
- **Mastic**: Thick, paste-like sealant designed for ductwork
- **UL-181**: Safety standard for duct closure systems

Heating & Cooling 301: Troubleshooting

Problem	Solutions
Mastic won't stick	Clean thoroughly. Ensure the surface is dry. Remove all dust and grease.
Sealant cracking	Surface may have too much movement; use reinforcing mesh with mastic
Cannot reach ducts	Use extension tools. Consider professional aerosol sealing.
Flexible duct damaged	Replace damaged sections rather than sealing.
Airflow reduced	Check filters. Adjust registers. Verify system balance.

Heating & Cooling 301: Limitations
- DIY duct sealing is limited to accessible areas
- Badly damaged ducts should be replaced, not sealed
- Very old systems may have multiple issues
- Homes with asbestos require professional assessment
- Sealing cannot fix undersized or poorly designed systems

Resources and references: <www.suspra.com/practice/energy/heating-cooling-301.html>

Heating & Cooling 302: Installing Wood Stoves

How to install an EPA-certified wood stove with dedicated makeup air

Burn wood efficiently and produce a minimum of pollution using a modern EPA-certified stove. The dedicated makeup air system is crucial, bringing in outside air for combustion, preventing dangerous negative pressure situations where carbon monoxide can be drawn back into living spaces. When wood burns, it goes through moisture evaporation, vaporization of wood gases, combustion of gases, and charcoal burning after volatile gases and tars have been vaporized. EPA-certified stoves optimize this process through controlled air introduction, insulated fireboxes, and secondary combustion systems. Consider heat distribution, wood storage, and handling needs when selecting a location. Use properly seasoned firewood (under 20% moisture) to reduce creosote buildup and get more heat from less wood.

Heating & Cooling 302: Equipment & Materials
- EPA-certified wood stove
- Manufacturer-approved stove pipe or chimney system and supports
- Heat-resistant floor protection (hearth pad)
- Combustion air kit (dedicated makeup air system)
- Carbon monoxide detector
- Non-combustible wall shield (if needed)

Sustainable Practices Handbook
Energy Practices: Optimizing Energy Efficiency

Heating & Cooling 302: Steps

1. Plan and prepare (1-3 months before)
   - Determine best location based on:
     - Central location for heat distribution
     - Proximity to combustibles
     - Practicality of makeup air installation
   - Check local building codes and permit requirements
   - Select appropriate EPA-certified stove
   - Purchase necessary materials
2. ***Hire a professional if you do not have the knowledge or skills to install a stove***
3. Obtain permits (2-4 weeks before)
   - Submit application with stove specs and installation details
   - Schedule required inspections
4. Prepare installation site
   - Install hearth pad meeting specifications:
     - Extend at least 18" in front of stove door
     - Extend at least 8" from sides and back
   - Install wall protection if needed
5. Install dedicated makeup air system
   - Determine location for outside air intake
   - Cut hole through exterior wall
   - Install vent hood with screen and damper
   - Run ductwork from exterior to stove
   - Seal connections and penetrations
   - Connect to stove's air intake
6. Install the stove
   - Position according to clearance requirements
   - Level the stove
   - Connect to makeup air
   - Install rear heat shield if required
7. Install chimney system
   - For interior installation:
     - Mark ceiling penetration using plumb bob
     - Install ceiling support box
     - Extend chimney through roof with proper flashing
     - Extend at least 3 feet above roof
     - Install chimney cap
   - For exterior installation:
     - Install wall pass-through
     - Install support brackets
     - Extend chimney upward
   - Ensure all components are secure and sealed
8. Verify clearances
   - Check all clearance requirements:
     - Sides, back, and above stove
     - Chimney clearance
     - Floor protection
9. Schedule inspection
10. Conduct break-in fire
    - Follow manufacturer's instructions
    - Start with small fires
    - Gradually increase size over several uses

Revision: 25.1.8

11. Install carbon monoxide detectors

Heating & Cooling 302: Definitions

- **Catalytic combustor**: Ceramic device allowing smoke to burn at lower temperatures
- **Clearance**: Required safe distance between stove components and combustible materials
- **Creosote**: Flammable tar-like substance that accumulates in chimneys
- **Dedicated makeup air**: Outside air ducted directly to stove for combustion
- **EPA-certified**: Stoves meeting emissions standards (2.0 grams of particulate matter per hour)
- **Negative pressure**: Indoor air pressure lower than outdoor, potentially causing backdrafting

Heating & Cooling 302: Troubleshooting

Problem	Solutions
Smoke entering room	Check chimney draft. Ensure makeup air functions. Look for blockages. Verify chimney height. Open window during startup.
Difficulty starting fire	Use properly seasoned wood (<20% moisture). Check makeup air. Ensure the chimney is unobstructed.
Low heat output	Use seasoned hardwood. Increase air supply during active burning.
Excessive creosote	Use only dry wood. Burn hot. Avoid smoldering. Clean chimney.
CO detector alarms	Ventilate immediately. Extinguish fire. Check for chimney blockage. Verify makeup air. Have professionally inspected.

Heating & Cooling 302: Limitations

- Wood stoves are subject to local building codes and regulations; banned in some areas
- Requires significant space for stove, clearances, and wood storage
- Limited heat distribution without additional circulation
- Regular maintenance required
- Initial cost can be substantial ($3,000-7,000+)
- Wood availability varies by region
- Even EPA-certified stoves produce some particulate matter
- Insurance rates may increase

References and resources: <www.suspra.com/practice/energy/heating-cooling-302.html>

Heating & Cooling 303: Fanning Rooms

Install and use energy-efficient ceiling fans in summer and winter

In summer, make room occupants feel cooler without changing air temperature by operating ceiling fans to create a wind chill effect. Raise your thermostat setting by 4-8°F without sacrificing comfort, saving 3-5% on cooling costs per degree. In winter, run a fan at low speed to push air against the ceiling and force warm air down along the walls into the living space, improving comfort.

Rooms under 75 square feet need 29-36" fans, rooms 75-175 square feet need 42-48" fans, and larger rooms need 52-60" fans. For optimal airflow, mount blades 8-9 feet above the floor and at least 10-12 inches below the ceiling.

Heating & Cooling 303: Equipment & Materials

- Energy-efficient ceiling fan with reversible motor
- Ceiling fan mounting bracket
- Support brace (if needed)

Heating & Cooling 303: Steps

1. Buy an energy-efficient fan
2. ***Hire a professional if you do not have the knowledge or skills to install a fan***
3. Plan your installation
   - Measure room to determine appropriate fan size
   - Ensure ceiling height is at least 8 feet
   - Locate ceiling joists
   - Turn off power and verify with tester
4. Install mounting bracket
   - Remove existing light fixture (if applicable)
   - Install ceiling-fan-rated electrical box if needed
   - Attach mounting bracket securely
5. Assemble the fan
6. Mount and wire the fan
   - Connect house wiring to fan wiring
   - Attach fan housing to bracket
7. Complete installation and test
   - Verify all connections
   - Turn power back on
   - Test at all speeds
   - Check for wobbling
8. Optimize for summer use
   - Set fan to blow air *down*
   - Use *medium* to *high* speeds
   - Turn off when room is unoccupied
9. Optimize for winter use
   - Reverse fan to blow air *up*
   - Use *low* speed to circulate warm air
   - In winter, ceiling fans should suck air up and push warm air down along walls
10. Establish maintenance routine
    - Clean blades seasonally
    - Check for loose screws quarterly
    - Oil motor if required

Heating & Cooling 303: Definitions

- **Blade pitch**: Angle of fan blades; higher pitch moves more air but requires more energy
- **CFM**: Cubic Feet per Minute; measurement of airflow
- **DC motor**: Direct current motor using less energy than AC motors
- **Downrod**: Metal pipe connecting motor to mounting bracket
- **Hugger fan**: Fan mounting flush with ceiling for low-ceiling rooms
- **Reversible motor**: Motor running in either direction for seasonal optimization

Heating & Cooling 303: Troubleshooting

Problem	Solutions
Fan wobbles	Verify blades are firmly attached; check for warping; secure mounting bracket; use balancing kit
Noisy operation	Tighten all connections; check blade holders; ensure light kit is secure
Fan doesn't turn	Check power at breaker; inspect wire connections; test pull chain
Little air movement	Verify correct rotation direction; ensure adequate blade pitch; check fan size for room
Light kit doesn't work	Check bulbs; verify wiring; ensure pull chain is "on"

Heating & Cooling 303: Limitations
- Fans don't change room temperature
- Not suitable for rooms with ceilings under 8 feet
- Limited effectiveness in very large spaces without multiple fans
- Requires electrical wiring and structural support
- Energy savings disappear if fans run in unoccupied rooms

References and resources: <www.suspra.com/practice/energy/heating-cooling-303.html>

Heating & Cooling 304: Fanning Home

Install and use a whole-house fan

Whole-house fans pull air from living spaces into the attic and outdoors, creating negative pressure that draws cooler outside air through open windows. A properly sized fan can exchange all air in your home in 15-30 minutes. These fans are most effective in regions with hot days and cool nights, using 10-25% of the electricity of air conditioning. Traditional ceiling-mounted models can be noisy (4-5 sones), while newer models operate much more quietly. Never operate a whole-house fan when using combustion appliances like fireplaces, as the negative pressure can cause dangerous backdrafting.

Heating & Cooling 304: Equipment & Materials
- Whole-house fan (ceiling-mounted or through-the-wall model)
- Weatherstripping and insulated fan cover for winter
- *Optional: Timer switch or smart controls*

Heating & Cooling 304: Steps
1. Choose fan location
   - Select central hallway near home's center for ceiling-mounted fans
   - Choose hallway on upper floor or attic gable for through-the-wall fans
   - Ensure location has attic space above or exterior wall access
2. Prepare for installation
   - Turn off electricity at the circuit breaker
   - Verify power is off using a voltage tester
   - Ensure adequate attic ventilation
3. Install the fan per manufacturer's instructions
4. Test

Sustainable Practices Handbook
Energy Practices: Optimizing Energy Efficiency

- Clear area around fan of debris
- Turn circuit breaker back on
- Test operation at all speeds
- Check for unusual noises or vibrations
- Install timer or smart controls
5. Create proper airflow
    - Open windows in rooms you want to cool
    - Keep interior doors open for optimal airflow
    - Operate fan when outdoor temperature is lower than indoor temperature
6. Maintain seasonally
    - Install insulated cover in winter
    - Remove cover in spring
    - Clean fan blades annually
    - Lubricate bearings as needed

Heating & Cooling 304: Definitions

- **CFM (Cubic Feet per Minute)**: Measurement of airflow volume
- **Backdrafting**: Dangerous condition where combustion gases are pulled back into living spaces
- **Negative pressure**: Condition when air is removed faster than it can naturally replace itself
- **NFVA (Net Free Vent Area)**: Actual area available for air to flow through attic vents
- **Sone**: Unit of perceived loudness, similar to decibels; normal conversation is about 4 sones

Heating & Cooling 304: Troubleshooting

Problem	Solutions
Fan won't turn on	Check circuit breaker, electrical connections, controller, and fan motor.
Little airflow	Ensure windows are open. Check for blocked attic vents. Clean fan blades.
Excessive noise	Tighten hardware. Check for debris on blades. Add rubber dampeners between fan and framing.
Cold air leaks in winter	Install insulated cover with a good seal. Add weatherstripping.
House doesn't cool effectively	Operate when outdoor temperature is at least 5°F cooler than indoors. Open windows in cooler areas.

Heating & Cooling 304: Limitations

- Not effective in hot, humid climates where nighttime temperatures remain high
- Limited usefulness in areas with high outdoor pollution or seasonal allergies
- Requires open windows, which can be a security concern
- Creates noise that may disturb sleep or activities
- Requires adequate attic space and ventilation
- Not suitable for use with combustion appliances unless specially designed

References and resources: <www.suspra.com/practice/energy/heating-cooling-304.html>

Heating & Cooling 305: Pumping Heat

Install and use heat pumps for heating and cooling

Heat pumps move heat rather than generate it, making them highly efficient. They extract heat from outside air or ground water (even in cold weather) and transfer it indoors during winter, then reverse the process for summer cooling. Modern systems provide up to five units of heating or cooling for every unit of electricity consumed. Air-to-air heat pumps are most common and affordable. Minisplits don't require ductwork and provide zoned conditioning. Ground-source (geothermal) systems offer highest efficiency but require excavation or drilling. When selecting a system, prioritize models with lower greenhouse warming potential (GWP) refrigerants to minimize environmental impact.

Heating & Cooling 305: Equipment & Materials

- Heat pump system (air-source, ground-source, or Suspra) and mounting brackets
- Electrical supplies (wire, conduit, circuit breakers)
- Refrigerant line set with insulation
- Condensate drain components
- *Optional: Smart thermostat*

Heating & Cooling 305: Steps

1. Get quotes from licensed professionals
   - Choose between air-to-air, air-to-water, or ground-source (groundwater) systems
   - Select unit appropriate for your climate
   - Look for systems with sustainable refrigerants
2. Install outdoor unit
3. Install indoor components
4. Connect refrigerant lines
5. Complete electrical connections
6. Set up drainage
   - Create proper condensate drainage pathway
   - Install secondary drain pan if required
   - Consider condensate pump if gravity drainage isn't possible
7. Test operation in both heating and cooling modes

Heating & Cooling 305: Definitions

- **BTU (British Thermal Unit)**: Standard measure of heating/cooling capacity (United States); the rest of the world uses watts (W)
- **COP (Coefficient of Performance)**: Ratio of useful heating/cooling provided to energy input
- **HSPF (Heating Seasonal Performance Factor)**: Heat pump heating efficiency measurement
- **SEER (Seasonal Energy Efficiency Ratio)**: Cooling efficiency measurement
- **Global Warming Potential (GWP)**: Measure of how much heat a greenhouse gas traps relative to CO_2

Heating & Cooling 305: Troubleshooting

Problem	Solutions
System short-cycles	Clean or replace air filters. Verify the thermostat location isn't near heat sources. Check refrigerant charge (professional).

Problem	Solutions
Insufficient heating in cold weather	Adjust fan speed settings. Check auxiliary heat settings. Consider a supplemental heat source.
Ice on outdoor unit	Ensure the defrost cycle works properly. Check refrigerant charge.
Water leaking from indoor unit	Verify condensate drain isn't clogged. Check the drain slope. Install condensate pump if needed.
Uneven temperatures	Adjust airflow distribution. Consider multiple indoor units. Check for disconnected ducts.

Heating & Cooling 305: Limitations
- Installation requires specialized HVAC knowledge
- Refrigerant handling requires EPA certification
- Extremely cold climates may require backup heat source
- Ground-source systems require significant property space or deep drilling
- Work best in homes with adequate air sealing and insulation

References and resources: <www.suspra.com/practice/energy/heating-cooling-305.html>

Heating & Cooling 306: Ventilating

Install and use a heat recovery or energy (enthalpy) recovery ventilator

Recover 70-95% of the heat energy that would otherwise be lost through ventilation by using a heat recovery ventilator (HRV) or energy (also called enthalpy) recovery ventilator (ERV) to provide fresh air while recovering energy from exhaust air. They simultaneously extract stale indoor air and bring in fresh outdoor air, passing both through a heat exchanger where energy transfers without the airstreams mixing. This significantly reduces the energy needed to condition incoming air. The key difference between HRVs and ERVs is that ERVs also transfer moisture between airstreams, helping maintain comfortable humidity levels. Heat-recovery ventilation is a best practice for healthy indoor air quality in high-efficiency homes with good air sealing and insulation.

Heating & Cooling 306: Equipment & Materials
- Heat recovery ventilator (HRV) or energy recovery ventilator (ERV) unit
- Insulated flexible and rigid metal ducting
- Exterior wall caps with screens and dampers
- Interior registers and grilles
- Condensate drain components

Heating & Cooling 306: Steps
1. Choose appropriate system
   - Select HRV for cold, dry climates or where indoor humidity needs removal
   - Select ERV for hot, humid climates or very cold climates with dry indoor air
   - Size unit based on home square footage and required air changes
2. Determine installation locations
   - Position main unit in accessible location with electrical access and condensate drainage
   - Place fresh air intake on north or east side, away from pollution sources
   - Locate exhaust away from windows, doors, and at least 6 feet from intake
3. Install exterior components

4. Mount the ventilator unit
5. Install ducting system
6. Connect electrical components
7. Balance the system
8. Test and maintain
    - Verify proper operation and airflow at all registers
    - Confirm condensate drain functions correctly
    - Set appropriate operating modes based on season
    - Replace filters every 3-6 months
    - Clean exterior vent screens annually
    - Inspect and clean heat exchange core every 2-3 years

Heating & Cooling 306: Definitions

- **Balancing**: Process of adjusting airflow rates to ensure equal supply and exhaust volumes
- **Condensate**: Water that forms when warm, humid air is cooled below its dew point
- **Frost protection**: Features that prevent the heat exchanger from freezing in cold weather
- **Heat exchanger core**: Component where heat (and moisture in an ERV) transfers between airstreams without mixing
- **Energy Recovery Ventilator (ERV)**: Similar to HRV but also transfers moisture between airstreams
- **Heat Recovery Ventilator (HRV)**: Exchanges stale indoor air with fresh outdoor air while transferring heat to reduce energy loss

Heating & Cooling 306: Troubleshooting

Problem	Solutions
Insufficient airflow	Clean filters and exterior vents. Check for crushed ductwork. Increase fan speed if necessary.
Excessive noise	Check for loose components. Install vibration isolators. Add acoustic insulation to ductwork.
Condensate leaks	Verify proper drain slope. Clean drain line. Ensure P-trap is properly installed.
Freezing in cold weather	Verify defrost cycle is functioning. Consider adding a pre-heater. Ensure the unit is in heated space.
Indoor air feels stale	Increase ventilation rate. Exhaust air from high-pollution areas.

Heating & Cooling 306: Limitations

- Existing buildings can be difficult to retrofit to add effective ventilation
- Professional installation recommended or required by building codes
- Higher initial cost than simpler ventilation solutions
- Requires regular maintenance including filter changes
- Ducting requires significant space in walls, ceilings, or attics

References and resources: <www.suspra.com/practice/energy/heating-cooling-306.html>

Heating & Cooling 401: Distributing Heat

Replace forced air with hydronic, electric, or advanced heat distribution

Achieve greater comfort, efficiency, and air quality by installing a better heat distribution system than forced air (blowing air through ducts). Hydronic systems use water as the heat transfer medium, moving more energy per volume of material circulated, because water has a much higher heat capacity than air. Radiant floor heating warms people and objects directly, providing superior comfort at lower thermostat settings. Electric distribution systems offer flexibility and zone control without extensive piping. Ductless mini-splits combine heating and cooling without requiring ductwork. Advanced systems like integrated ceiling panels or capillary tube mats operate at temperatures closer to room temperature, improving heat pump efficiency and response time.

Heating & Cooling 401: Equipment & Materials

- Building plans or layout diagrams
- Pipes and radiators (for hydronic systems)
- Wires and heating elements (for electric systems)
- Cost: $6-$20 per square foot of heated space

Heating & Cooling 401: Steps

1. Assess current system and needs
   - Conduct home energy assessment
   - Document current heating and cooling costs
   - Identify problem areas (cold spots, overheated areas)
   - Consider seasonal needs and climate conditions
2. Evaluate alternative distribution systems
   - **Hydronic systems**
     - Radiant floor heating
     - Modern panel radiators
     - Hydronic baseboard heaters
     - Fan coil units
   - **Electric systems**
     - Electric radiant floors or panels
     - Electric baseboard heaters
     - Suspra heat pumps
   - **Advanced systems**
     - Integrated ceiling panels
     - Capillary tube mats
     - Thermal mass systems
3. Work with a qualified HVAC contractor to design the system
   - Calculate proper sizing and distribution based on heat load calculation
   - Plan zoning strategy for room-by-room control
   - Select complementary heat source
   - Plan smart control system
4. Prepare for installation
   - Schedule during moderate weather if possible
   - Make arrangements for temporary heating and cooling
5. Install the system
6. Commission and optimize
   - Test all components and zones
   - Balance for even heat distribution
   - Calibrate thermostats and controls

Heating & Cooling 401: Definitions

- **BTU**: Unit of heat energy equal to energy needed to raise 1 pound of water by 1°F
- **Emitter**: Device that transfers heat from distribution system to living space
- **Heat load calculation**: Analysis determining heating requirements based on size, insulation, and climate
- **Hydronic**: Using water as heat transfer medium
- **Radiant heat**: Heat transferred directly from warm surface to people and objects
- **Thermal mass**: Materials that store significant heat energy
- **Zone control**: Ability to maintain different temperatures in different areas independently

Heating & Cooling 401: Troubleshooting

Problem	Solutions
Uneven heating or cooling	Balance system by adjusting flow rates. Check for air in hydronic lines. Verify zone valves function properly.
System noise	Check for air in lines, proper pump installation, and pipe sizing. Ensure proper mounting to prevent vibration.
Higher than expected energy costs	Verify proper system sizing. Check for unauthorized temperature adjustments. Inspect insulation and air sealing.
Slow response time	Check temperature settings. Improve insulation. Add portable systems.
Cold floors with underfloor radiant	Verify proper water temperature. Check for air in the system. Add insulation beneath heating elements.

Heating & Cooling 401: Limitations

- Higher initial costs compared to forced air systems
- Some systems require professional maintenance
- Radiant cooling requires careful design to avoid condensation
- Difficult to retrofit existing buildings
- Converting from forced air means losing built-in air filtration
- Some systems have slower response times
- Many systems require separate dehumidification in humid climates

References and resources: <www.suspra.com/practice/energy/heating-cooling-401.html>

Landscaping 301: Planting Shade Trees

Plant deciduous trees to provide noon and afternoon shade in summer

Plant deciduous trees to provide summer shade when needed and allow winter sun when beneficial. Plant on sun-facing and sun-setting sides for maximum energy savings. Trees shade windows, walls, and heat pump units, potentially reducing cooling costs by 15-50%. Select native species for better adaptation to local conditions and wildlife benefits.

Landscaping 301: Equipment & Materials

- Deciduous tree saplings appropriate for your climate zone

Landscaping 301: Steps

1. Plan optimal tree placement
   - Explore the south and west sides of your home
   - Mark locations 10-20 feet from home (based on mature tree size)
   - Position to shade windows, walls, and heat pump units
   - Check for utilities and local regulations
2. Select appropriate tree species
   - Choose deciduous trees native to your region
   - Consider mature height and spread
   - Select disease-resistant varieties for your hardiness zone
3. Prepare for planting
   - Call utility location services (811 in US)
   - Water container saplings thoroughly
4. Dig the planting hole
   - Make hole 2-3 times wider than root ball but only as deep as root ball height
   - Create sloping sides for easier root spread
5. Prepare the tree
   - Remove from container or burlap
   - Prune any damaged or circling roots
   - Position so trunk flare sits at or slightly above ground level
6. Plant the tree
   - Place in hole, ensuring it's straight
   - Backfill halfway with original soil
   - Press firmly and water thoroughly to remove air pockets
   - Finish backfilling to ground level
   - Create a slight basin around the tree to hold water so it soaks down to roots
7. Mulch and water
   - Apply 2-4 inches of mulch in a circle (3-4 feet diameter)
   - Keep mulch 3 inches away from trunk
   - Water deeply immediately after planting, then every 3 days for first 3 weeks
8. Stake (if necessary)
   - Stake top-heavy trees or in windy areas
   - Use 3 stakes outside the root ball
   - Remove stakes after one growing season
9. Nurture young tree
   - Water deeply weekly during first growing season
   - Gradually reduce watering over two years
   - Prune only to remove damaged branches for first 3 years

Landscaping 301: Definitions

- **Deciduous**: Trees that shed leaves annually
- **Evapotranspiration**: Process by which trees release water vapor, creating cooling
- **Root ball**: Mass of roots and soil in container-grown or burlap-wrapped tree
- **Trunk flare**: Area where trunk expands at tree base, should remain visible above ground

Landscaping 301: Troubleshooting

Problem	Solutions
Tree not thriving	Check soil moisture. Do a soil test. Ensure the species suits your climate.
Tree too close to house	Transplant young trees. Prune mature trees. Cut roots near the foundation.

Revision: 25.1.8

Problem	Solutions
Shade not on target	Transplant young trees. Add a second tree for better coverage.
Slow growth	Ensure adequate sunlight, water and nutrients. Plant fast-growing species.

Landscaping 301: Limitations

- Trees take years to mature and provide significant shade
- Space constraints may limit ideal placement

References and resources: <www.suspra.com/practice/energy/landscaping-301.html>

Landscaping 302: Planting Windbreaks

Plant evergreen trees and shrubs to provide windbreaks in winter

Plant windbreaks to decrease heating costs by 10-30% while creating more comfortable outdoor spaces. The ideal windbreak has 50-60% density—dense enough to reduce wind but permeable enough to prevent turbulence. Evergreen conifers make ideal windbreak plants because they maintain foliage year-round. Species diversity increases long-term success and resilience. Windbreaks also reduce noise, screen views, prevent snow drifting, and provide wildlife habitat.

Landscaping 302: Equipment & Materials

- Evergreen trees and shrubs appropriate for your region

Landscaping 302: Steps

1. Assess your site and needs
   - Identify prevailing winter wind direction (typically north/northwest in North America)
   - Determine areas needing protection
   - Measure available space
   - Note utilities and structures
2. Determine planting locations
   - Position perpendicular to prevailing winter winds
   - Place at a distance of 2-5 times the mature tree height from protected area
   - Plan for multiple rows when space allows (2-3 rows for residential settings)
   - Allow adequate spacing based on mature width (typically 6-15 feet between trees)
3. Follow steps 2 to 9 from Landscaping 301: Planting Shade Trees

Landscaping 302: Definitions

- **Evergreen**: Plants that maintain foliage year-round
- **Leeward**: The side sheltered from the wind (downwind)
- **Prevailing wind**: The predominant wind direction in a specific location
- **Windbreak**: A planting designed to reduce wind speed and provide protection
- **Windward**: The side facing the wind (upwind)

Landscaping 302: Troubleshooting

Problem	Solutions
Limited space	Plant a single dense row with ground-to-top foliage, use columnar varieties, or combine trees and shrubs

Problem	Solutions
Poor growth	Check soil moisture. Test soil. Inspect for pests or diseases.
Gaps forming	Interplant faster-growing species. Add shrubs in gaps.
Slow growth	Be patient—evergreens establish roots before showing top growth.
Soil drainage problems	Plant on raised berms. Select species tolerant of moist soil.

Landscaping 302: Limitations
- Evergreens do not thrive in all climates
- Maximum effectiveness develops as trees mature over 10-20 years
- Space requirements may be prohibitive for small lots
- Requires initial investment and establishment care
- May interfere with desirable views

References and resources: <www.suspra.com/practice/energy/landscaping-302.html>

Lighting 101: Installing LEDs

Install light-emitting diode (LED) lighting

Install LED lighting to use up to 90% less energy and many fewer bulbs over time. When selecting LEDs, consider brightness (measured in lumens, not watts), color temperature (2700-3000K for warm white, 3500-4100K for cool white, 5000-6500K for daylight), and whether they're dimmable.

Lighting 101: Equipment & Materials
- LED bulbs or fixtures

Lighting 101: Steps

A. Simple Bulb Replacement
1. Turn off power at the light switch
2. Allow existing bulb to cool, then remove
3. Check socket type and wattage requirements
4. Select appropriate LED replacement with matching base type
5. Install the new LED bulb
6. Turn power back on and test

B. Fixture Replacement
1. Turn off power at the circuit breaker
2. Verify power is off using a voltage tester
3. Remove existing fixture:
   - Remove shade, cover, or diffuser
   - Remove mounting screws
   - Pull fixture away to expose wiring
   - Label or take pictures of wires (if needed)
   - Disconnect wiring
4. Connect new LED fixture wiring:
   - Match wire colors (black to black, white to white, green/bare to green/bare)
5. Mount the fixture and restore power

C. Installing Recessed LED Lighting
1. For retrofit into existing housing:

- Remove existing bulb and trim
- Connect adapter to socket
- Attach LED module and push trim flush with ceiling
2. For new installation: hire an electrician unless you have electrical knowledge and skills

D. Installing LED Strip Lighting
1. Plan installation route
2. Clean mounting surface
3. Measure and cut LED strips at designated cutting points
4. Apply strips to surface
5. Connect to power supply following manufacturer instructions
6. Mount power supply in accessible location
7. Test operation

Lighting 101: Definitions

- **Color temperature**: Measure in Kelvin (K) of how warm or cool light appears
- **Lumens**: Measure of total light output
- **Retrofit kit**: LED components designed to replace conventional lighting in existing fixtures
- **Integrated LED**: Lighting where the LED is built into the fixture and not replaceable as a bulb

Lighting 101: Troubleshooting

Problem	Solutions
LED doesn't light up	Check power, seating in socket, try bulb in another fixture, or check for loose wires.
LED flickers	Ensure compatibility with the dimmer switch, check connections, or try different brands.
Smart LED not working	Check Wi-Fi signal strength. Reset bulb. Check network compatibility.
LED too dim	Verify correct lumen output. Check if the fixture is dimmed.

Lighting 101: Limitations

- Higher initial cost than incandescent bulbs
- Not all fixtures or dimmers are compatible with LED technology
- Color consistency can vary between manufacturers

References and resources: <www.suspra.com/practice/energy/lighting-101.html>

Lighting 201: Controlling Lighting

Install motion sensors to turn lighting off automatically

Install motion sensors to reduce lighting energy use by 30-80% by automatically turning off lights in unoccupied rooms. Occupancy sensors turn lights on automatically when motion is detected and off after inactivity. Vacancy sensors require manual activation but turn off automatically, providing greater energy savings. Most residential sensors use passive infrared (PIR) technology, detecting heat signatures from moving bodies.

Lighting 201: Equipment & Materials

- Motion sensor switch (occupancy or vacancy sensor)

Lighting 201: Steps

1. Turn off power to circuit at breaker box and verify with voltage tester
2. Remove wall plate and unscrew existing switch
3. Take photo of existing wiring for reference
4. Identify wiring configuration:
   - Single-pole: one black (hot) wire and one black/red (load) wire
   - Three-way: three wires plus ground
5. Disconnect wires from old switch
6. Connect motion sensor switch:
   - Connect black (hot) wire to "LINE" terminal
   - Connect black/red (load) wire to "LOAD" terminal
   - Connect green/bare (ground) wire to ground terminal
   - Connect white (neutral) wire if required
7. Mount sensor and attach wall plate
8. Restore power and allow sensor to calibrate
9. Adjust time delay, sensitivity level, and ambient light sensor if available

Lighting 201: Definitions

- **Line**: Incoming electrical power source
- **Load**: Electrical device controlled by the switch
- **Occupancy sensor**: Automatic on when motion is detected and off when not detected
- **Passive Infrared (PIR)**: Technology that detects heat signatures from moving bodies
- **Time delay**: Period sensor keeps lights on after last detected motion
- **Vacancy sensor**: Manual (not automatic) on; automatic off when no motion is detected

Lighting 201: Troubleshooting

Problem	Solutions
Lights don't turn on	Check power, wiring connections, bulbs, and sensor mode.
Room occupied; lights turn off	Increase time delay. Increase sensitivity. Reposition sensor.
Lights turn on randomly	Reduce sensitivity. Move the sensor away from vents or windows.
Lights flicker	Ensure light fixtures are compatible. Check wire connections.

Lighting 201: Limitations

- May not suit areas where people remain still for long periods
- Some sensors require a neutral wire, absent in older homes
- Pets may trigger sensors set at lower heights
- May not work with certain lighting types unless specifically rated
- Not recommended for controlling heat lamps, fans, or motor-driven devices

References and resources: <www.suspra.com/practice/energy/lighting-201.html>

Lighting 301: Dimming

Install automatic daylight dimming

Reduce energy consumption by installing automatic daylight dimming systems that decrease artificial lighting when natural daylight is available. These systems maintain consistent illumination throughout changing daylight conditions. They typically include photosensors, dimming controls, and dimmable fixtures. The most effective installations follow the "closed loop" approach, where sensors measure both natural and artificial light in the space.

Lighting 301: Equipment & Materials
- Daylight-responsive dimming controls or sensors
- Dimming-compatible LED light fixtures or bulbs
- *Optional: Light meter app on smartphone for testing*

Lighting 301: Steps
1. Assess space and lighting needs:
   - Identify areas where natural daylight enters
   - Determine which fixtures need daylight dimming
   - Map sensor placement for optimal detection
2. Select compatible components:
   - Choose dimming-compatible LED fixtures or bulbs
   - Select compatible daylight sensor system
   - Verify voltage requirements match your system
3. Turn off power and verify with voltage tester
4. Install daylight sensors and dimming controls:
   - Place where they accurately measure daylight
   - Mount and connect according to manufacturer instructions
5. Restore power and test basic function
6. Program and calibrate:
   - Set maximum and minimum light levels
   - Set response rate
   - Establish target illumination levels
7. Test system at different times of day and adjust as needed

Lighting 301: Definitions
- **Automatic daylight dimming**: Adjust artificial lighting in response to available natural light
- **Closed-loop control**: System where output of system itself is used to modify control signal
- **Open-loop control**: Control system that does not use feedback to modify control signal
- **Photosensor**: Device that detects light levels and converts them to electrical signals
- **Set point**: Target illumination level that the system aims to maintain

Lighting 301: Troubleshooting

Problem	Solutions
Lights flicker when dimming	Verify fixtures are dimming-compatible, check wiring, ensure control compatibility.
No daylight dimming	Check sensor placement, sensor operation, and wiring connections.
Lights dim too much	Adjust ramp rate settings. Widen the deadband setting. Recalibrate levels.
Occupants complain about light levels	Fine-tune set points. Provide manual override options. Adjust minimum levels.

Lighting 301: Limitations
- Requires compatible dimmable fixtures and bulbs

- Effectiveness depends on building architecture and window placement
- May not be cost-effective in spaces with limited natural daylight
- Some systems struggle with rapidly changing light conditions
- Users may override automatic controls if the system doesn't meet preferences

References and resources: <www.suspra.com/practice/energy/lighting-301.html>

Lighting 302: Piping Light

Install light pipes to provide passive daylight in interior rooms

Bring natural daylight into windowless interior spaces with light pipes (also called solar tubes or sun tunnels). Using highly reflective materials, they can transmit sunlight up to 30 feet from roof to interior. The system consists of a weatherproof exterior dome, a highly reflective tube, and an interior diffuser. A 10-inch diameter light pipe can typically light a 300 square foot room. Rigid tubes with highly reflective interiors provide the most efficient light transfer; flexible tubes are easier to install but less efficient.

Lighting 302: Equipment & Materials
- Light pipe kit (dome, flashing, reflective tubing, diffuser)
- Caulk and roofing sealant
- Insulation material

Lighting 302: Steps
1. Plan installation:
   - Identify interior rooms needing natural light
   - Check for obstructions in attic or ceiling cavity
   - Choose optimal location considering roof orientation and solar modules
   - Measure distance from ceiling to roof
   - Select appropriate light pipe type and size
2. Mark installation points:
   - Mark ceiling location and verify no joists or wiring between roof and ceiling
   - Mark corresponding roof location (use plumb bob and drill a small pilot hole)
3. Install roof components and tube per manufacturer's instructions
   - Cut ceiling opening first, then roof opening
   - Seal and insulate around tube
   - Install ceiling diffuser

Lighting 302: Definitions
- **Diffuser**: Interior component that spreads incoming light evenly
- **Dome**: Clear exterior component that captures daylight
- **Flashing**: Waterproof material that seals the roof penetration
- **Flexible tube**: Light pipe using accordion-like material with reflective coating
- **Light pipe**: Tubular system transferring daylight using reflection
- **Rigid tube**: Light pipe using solid sections with highly reflective interiors

Lighting 302: Troubleshooting

Problem	Solutions
Roof leaks	Check flashing. Apply additional sealant.
Condensation in tube	Add insulation or fan. Seal seams. Consider a double-dome system.

Problem	Solutions
Insufficient light	Clean dome. Check for obstacles. Verify the reflective surface is clean.
Hot spots or glare	Install a better diffuser.

Lighting 302: Limitations

- Light transmission decreases with tube length and number of bends
- Performance varies with weather conditions
- Roof penetrations carry risk of leakage
- Some roof types require special adapters
- Loses heat in winter, adds heat in summer

References and resources: <www.suspra.com/practice/energy/lighting-302.html>

Maintaining Efficiency 101: Cleaning Systems

Clean coils, ducts, and filters of furnaces, heat pumps, and refrigerators

Dust and debris accumulation acts as insulation on refrigerator and heat pump coils, hindering their ability to release or absorb heat effectively. This forces the appliance to work harder, using more energy and potentially shortening its lifespan. For furnaces and heat pumps, dirty ducts and filters restrict airflow, making the system strain to circulate air, again increasing energy use and reducing heating or cooling effectiveness. Cleaning is straightforward: for coils, gently vacuum or brush away dust; for ducts, professional cleaning is recommended every few years, but ensure vents are unobstructed; and for filters, replace disposable filters monthly or clean reusable ones according to the manufacturer's instructions. By ensuring these systems are clean, you allow them to operate as designed.

References and resources: <www.suspra.com/practice/energy/maintaining-101.html>

Maintaining Efficiency 201: Replacing Filters

Replace disposable filters per manufacturer recommendations

Regularly replace disposable filters in your heating, ventilation, and air conditioning systems, as well as in appliances like vacuum cleaners and clothes dryers, to optimize energy efficiency. Dirty filters restrict airflow, forcing your systems to work harder to circulate air. This increased strain leads to higher energy consumption and potentially premature system failure. By replacing filters according to manufacturer recommendations, you ensure optimal airflow, reduce energy waste, and extend the lifespan of your equipment.

References and resources: <www.suspra.com/practice/energy/maintaining-201.html>

Maintaining Efficiency 202: Insulating Ducts

Maintain insulation around ducts that go through unconditioned spaces

Maintain insulation around ducts to prevent condensation, which can lead to water damage and mold, and to mitigate energy loss when conditioned air travels through unconditioned spaces. Common insulation includes fiberglass duct wrap (R-4 to R-8), flexible foam, and reflective insulation. Always seal ducts before insulating; remove and replace insulation that shows signs of air blowing through it.

Maintaining Efficiency 202: Equipment & Materials
- Aluminum foil tape (not cloth duct tape)
- Duct insulation material
- Zip ties
- *Optional: Infrared thermometer, mastic sealant*

Maintaining Efficiency 202: Steps
1. Turn off heating and cooling system
2. Inspect ducts
   - Locate all ductwork in unconditioned spaces
   - Check for tears, gaps, water damage, fallen insulation
3. Take photos and measurements of damaged areas
4. Repair minor damage
   - Clean area, realign existing insulation
   - Secure with foil tape or zip ties
5. Replace severely damaged insulation per manufacturer's instructions
6. Verify insulation integrity
   - Ensure complete coverage with no gaps
   - Check all seams are sealed
   - Verify insulation isn't compressed

Maintaining Efficiency 202: Definitions
- **Conditioned space**: Areas intentionally heated or cooled
- **Foil tape**: Aluminum tape for sealing ductwork
- **Mastic sealant**: Paste-like substance for sealing duct seams
- **R-value**: Measure of thermal resistance; higher is better
- **Unconditioned space**: Areas not intentionally heated or cooled
- **Vapor barrier**: Material preventing water vapor passage

Maintaining Efficiency 202: Troubleshooting

Problem	Solutions
Insulation won't stay attached	Clean surface before applying tape. Use proper foil tape. Add zip ties if needed.
Moisture persists after insulating	Check vapor barrier installation. Ensure seams are sealed. Consider a higher R-value.
Mold present	Remove affected insulation. Fix moisture source.
Limited access to ducts	Use a mirror or smartphone to view hard-to-reach areas.
No matching insulation	Use an equal or higher R-value. Ensure proper sealing at transitions.

Maintaining 202: Limitations
- Some ducts may be inaccessible without opening walls
- Insulating alone won't fix leaky ducts or system balance problems
- Insulation requires intact vapor barrier to be effective
- Older homes may have asbestos materials requiring professional remediation

References and resources: <www.suspra.com/practice/energy/maintaining-202.html>

Maintaining Efficiency 203: Inspecting Burners

Inspect and clean all fuel-burning equipment every year

Regularly inspecting and cleaning the burners of your fuel-burning appliances—such as furnaces, boilers, and stoves—boosts energy efficiency. Over time, burners can accumulate soot and debris, which obstructs proper combustion. This inefficiency forces your appliance to work harder and consume more fuel to generate the same amount of heat or cooking power. By performing an annual inspection and cleaning, you ensure optimal fuel combustion, leading to lower energy consumption, reduced utility bills, and decreased emissions of pollutants.

References and resources: <www.suspra.com/practice/energy/maintaining-203.html>

Optimizing Appliances 201: Installing Smart Strips

Install smart power strips that automatically turn off devices

Smart power strips are designed to eliminate "vampire loads"—the electricity consumed by devices when they're in standby mode. First, identify the devices in a specific area (like your entertainment center or home office) that consistently draw power even when not in use. Plug these devices into the smart strip's designated outlets. The main device, typically a TV or computer, should be plugged into the "control" outlet. When the control device is turned off, the smart strip automatically cuts power to the other devices plugged into its switched outlets. This saves energy by preventing these devices from drawing unnecessary power. For example, when your computer is shut down, the printer, speakers, and monitor connected to the same smart strip will also power down. Look for smart strips with features like adjustable sensitivity and surge protection to maximize effectiveness and safety.

References and resources: <www.suspra.com/practice/energy/optimizing-appliances-201.html>

Optimizing Appliances 202: Upgrading Electronics

Upgrade televisions and computers with more efficient models

When replacing older electronics, prioritize models with high Energy Star ratings. These devices consume significantly less power during operation and standby modes. For televisions, look for LED or OLED screens, which are inherently more efficient than older LCD or plasma displays. For computers, consider laptops or desktops with power-saving features like automatic sleep modes and efficient processors. Beyond the initial purchase, properly dispose of old electronics through certified e-waste recycling programs to recover valuable materials and prevent environmental contamination.

References and resources: <www.suspra.com/practice/energy/optimizing-appliances-202.html>

Optimizing Fenestration 101: Closing Windows

Close windows when outside temperature or humidity is uncomfortable

Close windows when the outside temperature or humidity is uncomfortable. During hot summer days, keeping windows closed prevents warm air from entering your home, reducing the load on your air conditioning system. Similarly, during cold winter months, closed windows retain heat, minimizing the need for excessive heating. Pay attention to the relative humidity as well. High humidity levels can make indoor spaces feel muggy and uncomfortable, even at moderate temperatures. Closing windows during humid summer days prevents excess moisture from entering your home.

References and resources: <www.suspra.com/practice/energy/optimizing-fenestration-101.html>

Sustainable Practices Handbook Energy Practices: Optimizing Energy Efficiency

Optimizing Fenestration 102: Using Blinds

Open and close curtains or blinds to optimize the benefits of sunshine

During the winter, open blinds on sun-facing windows during sunny days to allow sunlight to naturally warm your home. Close blinds at night to retain the heat. In the summer, close blinds during the hottest part of the day, especially on east and west-facing windows, to block direct sunlight and reduce the need for air conditioning. This practice leverages natural resources to maintain a comfortable indoor temperature, reducing your reliance on artificial heating and cooling and lowering your energy use.

References and resources: <www.suspra.com/practice/energy/optimizing-fenestration-102.html>

Optimizing Fenestration 201: Installing Inserts

Install storm windows or insulating inserts to reduce air and energy flows

Create an insulating air space between the primary window and a window insert. Plastic film kits ($5-20) reduce heat loss by up to 55% but last only one season. Rigid panels ($40-250) reduce heat loss by 50-70% and can be removed seasonally. Exterior storm windows ($100-500) protect the primary window and last 20-30 years. Cellular shades ($30-150) can reduce heat loss by up to 40%. Most inserts pay for themselves through energy savings within five years.

Optimizing Fenestration 201: Equipment & Materials
- Measuring tape, level, pencil, and cleaning supplies
- Caulk and caulk gun
- Safety gloves and glasses
- Step ladder
- Hair dryer
- Materials for your chosen insert type:
  - Interior storm windows (kit or premade inserts)
  - Exterior storm windows (with mounting hardware)
  - Thermal inserts (panels, weatherstripping)
  - Cellular shades (with mounting brackets)

Optimizing Fenestration 201: Steps
1. Measure your windows carefully
   - For exterior storms: measure outside of window casing
   - For interior storms: measure inside of window frame
   - Record smallest measurements for width and height
2. Clean the window frame thoroughly
3. Check primary window for needed repairs; fix them first
4. Install your chosen insert type:
   - For plastic film interior storms:
     - Apply double-sided tape around frame
     - Attach film and shrink with hairdryer
   - For rigid panel interior storms:
     - Attach weatherstripping to frame or panel edges
     - Secure panel with clips or mounting system
   - For exterior storm windows:
     - Apply caulk around window casing
     - Position and center storm window
     - Secure with screws
     - Caulk edges (leave bottom with no caulk for drainage)

- For cellular shades:
  - Install mounting brackets
  - Snap headrail into brackets
5. Test installation and seal any remaining drafts

Optimizing Fenestration 201: Definitions
- **Air infiltration**: Uncontrolled air leakage through gaps
- **Fenestration**: Any opening in a building's envelope (windows, doors, skylights)
- **R-value**: Measure of thermal resistance; higher is better
- **Storm window**: Secondary window installed outside or inside the primary window
- **U-factor**: Measure of heat transfer; lower is better

Optimizing Fenestration 201: Troubleshooting

Problem	Solutions
Plastic film is wrinkled	Reinstall with more tension. Use a hairdryer starting from the center.
Condensation between windows	Ensure the primary window is sealed. Add moisture absorbers between the primary window and the insert. Increase room ventilation.
Insert doesn't fit	Double-check measurements. Order custom sizes for irregular windows.
Still feel draft	Check for gaps with a draft detector. Add weatherstripping where needed.
Difficulty removing	Clean mounting hardware. Consider magnetic mounting.

Optimizing Fenestration 201: Limitations
- May interfere with window coverings
- Plastic film inserts last only one season
- May not be suitable for very large or irregular windows
- Increased air sealing may require better ventilation
- Can't open windows when inserts are in

References and resources: <www.suspra.com/practice/energy/fenestration-201.html>

Optimizing Fenestration 202: Using Awnings

Install and use window shade or awnings to keep summer sun out

Block direct sunlight before it penetrates windows, using awnings to reduce solar heat gain by 65-77% on south-facing windows and 72-77% on west-facing windows. They use passive solar principles, blocking high summer sun while potentially allowing beneficial winter sun. Fixed awnings provide consistent shading in summer but allow winter sun through; retractable models offer flexibility; drop-arm awnings adjust to changing sun positions. Awnings typically pay for themselves in seven years through energy savings.

Optimizing Fenestration 202: Equipment & Materials
- Awning kit or materials (fabric, metal, or wood)

Optimizing Fenestration 202: Steps
1. Choose awning locations, windows where sun shines through

2. Measure and select appropriate awnings
   - Choose width that extends 6 inches beyond each side of the window
   - For sun-facing windows: cover about 45-60% of window height
   - For east or west-facing windows: cover about 65-75% of window height
3. *Hire a handyman if you doubt your ability to install an awning*
4. Prepare for installation
   - Mark stud locations for secure mounting
   - Ensure adequate clearance for opening and closing the awning
5. Attach the awning following instructions provided by the plans or by the manufacturer
6. Use retractable awnings seasonally
   - Extend before rooms heat up (mid-morning)
   - Retract during high winds
   - Remove in winter (if removable) to allow solar heat gain
7. Maintain your awnings
   - Clean twice a year
   - Check and tighten hardware before each season

Optimizing Fenestration 202: Definitions

- **Drop-arm awning**: Has adjustable arms to change the shade angle
- **Fenestration**: Any opening in a building's envelope
- **Fixed awning**: Permanent shade structure that cannot be adjusted
- **Projection**: Distance an awning extends from the wall
- **Retractable awning**: Can be extended or withdrawn using crank or motor

Optimizing Fenestration 202: Troubleshooting

Problem	Solutions
Still too much sun	Increase projection. Add side panels. Lower front edge. Use darker fabric.
Catches too much wind	Choose a retractable or drop-arm model. Use heavy-duty mounting.
Mechanism jams	Clean and lubricate moving parts. Check for debris. Ensure alignment.
Fabric holds water	Ensure proper tensioning. Add center supports. Increase pitch for runoff.
Mold or mildew	Clean, then dry in the sun. Change tension or fabric to shed water faster.

Optimizing Fenestration 202: Limitations

- May not suit all architectural styles; may require homeowner association approval
- Can be damaged by extreme weather
- Effectiveness varies by window orientation and climate
- May interfere with window cleaning or air conditioners

References and resources: <www.suspra.com/practice/energy/fenestration-202.html>

Optimizing Fenestration 203: Fixing Panes

Fix cracked panes in windows

Repair windows to preserve architectural character and maintain energy efficiency by blocking air leaks. Traditional single-pane windows use glass set in wooden frames secured with glazier points and glazing compound. The glazing compound creates a weather seal while accommodating different expansion rates between glass and frame. Standard replacement glass is typically 1/8" (3 mm) thick.

Optimizing Fenestration 203: Equipment & Materials
- Replacement window glass and window glazing compound (putty)
- Safety glasses, heavy-duty work gloves, dust mask
- Heat gun or hair dryer
- Putty knife (1" and 3")
- Glazier points or glazing clips
- Utility knife, small hammer, needle-nose pliers
- Glass cleaner and soft cloth
- *Optional: Glass cutter, measuring tape, steel ruler*

Optimizing Fenestration 203: Steps
1. *Hire a handyman if you doubt your ability to repair a windowpane*
2. Prepare safely
   - Wear safety equipment before handling glass
   - Place drop cloth under window
   - Gently tap broken glass inward to prevent outside falls
3. Remove broken pane
   - Heat old glazing putty until soft, then remove old putty with putty knife
   - Extract glazier points using pliers
   - Remove all glass fragments
   - Clean frame thoroughly
4. Measure and cut new glass
   - Measure opening width and height, then subtract 1/8" from both measurements
   - Have glass cut professionally or cut your own glass:
     - Score firmly once with glass cutter
     - Break along score line
5. Install new pane
   - Apply thin bed of glazing compound to rabbet
   - Place glass into frame, press onto glazing
   - Insert glazier points (2 per side) to hold glass in place
   - Apply rope of glazing compound around edges
   - Smooth with putty knife at 45-degree angle
   - Remove excess compound
6. Finish repair
   - Clean glass once glazing is dry to touch
   - Paint glazing compound after full curing; overlap paint onto glass by 1/16" for weather seal

Optimizing Fenestration 203: Definitions
- **Glazier points**: Small metal triangles securing glass within frame, that press into wood
- **Glazing compound**: Putty-like material sealing the gap between glass and frame
- **Rabbet**: Recessed ledge in window frame where glass sits
- **Score**: Shallow cut on glass creating a controlled breaking point
- **Single-pane window**: Window consisting of a single layer of glass

Optimizing Fenestration 203: Troubleshooting

Problem	Solutions
Glazing won't stick	Ensure the frame is clean and dry. Apply linseed oil to very dry wood first.
Glazing cracks	Applied too thickly. Remove and reapply thinner. Use fresh compound.
Glass breaks	Handle by edges. Use suction cups for larger panes. Clean window opening.
Setting glazing points	Wood may be too hard. Pre-drill tiny pilot holes or use smaller points.
Removing old putty	Apply more heat. Use a putty softener. Try an oscillating tool.

Optimizing Fenestration 203: Limitations
- Insulated units require specialized replacement
- Large panes may need professional installation
- Historic windows with special glass need specialized restoration
- Metal frames require different techniques
- Extreme weather affects glazing compound curing time

References and resources: <www.suspra.com/practice/energy/fenestration-203.html>

Optimizing Fenestration 301: Repairing Windows

Repair or replace windows with broken seals

Repair or replace windows with seal failures to prevent moisture problems and improve energy efficiency. Repair approaches (defogging) are less expensive but temporary, while replacement costs more but restores energy efficiency. Repairing sash and frame seals is always worthwhile. For the insulated glass unit (IGU) itself, replacement is generally the most sustainable long-term solution.

Optimizing Fenestration 301: Equipment & Materials
- Replacement insulated glass unit (IGU) or window defogging kit
- Weatherstripping and replacement gaskets (as needed)
- Caulk and caulk gun
- Microfiber cloths and isopropyl alcohol
- Heat gun (for removing old caulk)

Optimizing Fenestration 301: Steps
1. *Hire a handyman if you doubt your ability to repair or replace a window*
2. Assess window condition
    - Check for visible signs of seal failure: fogging, condensation between panes
    - Test for air leaks with a lit candle or incense (movement indicates leaks)
    - Determine if the problem is with the sash, frame, or insulated glass unit
3. For window sash or frame seal problems:
    - Remove loose caulk with utility knife and scraper
    - Clean surfaces with isopropyl alcohol and dry completely
    - Apply new caulk in a continuous bead along joints
    - Replace damaged weatherstripping
    - Allow caulk to cure (24-48 hours)
4. For insulated glass unit with broken seal:
    - *Option A: Attempt defogging (temporary solution)*

- Drill small vent holes (1/16" to 1/8") in outside pane (not inside pane)
- Use a window defogging kit or flush with isopropyl alcohol
- Insert desiccant materials to absorb moisture
- Seal vent holes with clear silicone
  - *Option B: Replace the insulated glass unit (permanent fix)*
    - Measure window dimensions precisely
    - Remove the window sash or access the IGU
    - Remove the failed IGU carefully
    - Install the new IGU with appropriate gaskets
    - Secure with original hardware

Optimizing Fenestration 301: Definitions

- **Condensation**: Water droplets that are formed when warm air contacts a cold surface
- **IGU (Insulated Glass Unit)**: Multiple panes of glass separated by a spacer
- **Seal failure**: Breakdown of the airtight seal around an IGU
- **Spacer**: Material between glass panes that maintains the gap

Optimizing Fenestration 301: Troubleshooting

Problem	Solutions
Condensation returns after defogging	Defogging is temporary. Consider IGU replacement. Maintain indoor humidity at 30-50%.
Caulk doesn't adhere	Remove failed caulk, clean thoroughly, dry completely, then reapply.
Window operation stiff	Trim excess caulk or sealant. Check alignment of sash in frame.
Moisture between panes	Enlarge vent holes or replace IGU.
New IGU doesn't fit	Double-check measurements. Adjust frame.

Optimizing Fenestration 301: Limitations

- Defogging doesn't restore original energy efficiency
- Some window designs don't allow for DIY IGU replacement
- DIY replacement may void warranties
- Custom or historical windows may require professional servicing

References and resources: <www.suspra.com/practice/energy/fenestration-301.html>

Optimizing Fenestration 302: Installing Windows

Install energy-efficient windows

Reduce energy consumption while improving comfort by installing energy-efficient windows. Windows account for 25-30% of residential heating and cooling energy use; high-performance windows can reduce this by 30-50%. The National Fenestration Rating Council (NFRC) label provides standardized performance ratings to compare products. Different climates have different requirements: cold climates need a low U-factor, while hot climates need a low Solar Heat Gain Coefficient (SHGC). Install windows properly—even the best window will perform poorly if installed incorrectly.

Optimizing Fenestration 302: Equipment & Materials

- Energy-efficient windows with NFRC labels
- Window flashing tape and weather-resistant barrier
- Shims and low-expansion spray foam insulation
- High-quality exterior caulk
- Helper (recommended for larger windows)

Optimizing Fenestration 302: Steps

1. Understand window efficiency ratings
   - Check NFRC label and ENERGY STAR certification
   - Select windows with low U-factor (0.30 or lower) and appropriate Solar Heat Gain Coefficient (SHGC) for your climate
2. Choose sustainable window materials
   - Consider frame options (fiberglass, wood, aluminum with thermal breaks)
   - Select appropriate glass (double/triple glazing with low-E coatings)
3. *Hire a contractor if you doubt your ability to install new windows*
4. Measure accurately
   - Measure at three points for both width and height
   - Account for shim space (1/4" to 1/2" on all sides)
   - Confirm window is square by measuring diagonals
5. Existing construction: Remove old window
   - Reuse interior trim if possible
   - Insulate around and repair rough opening (if necessary)
6. New construction: Prepare rough opening
7. Install the window per manufacturer's instructions
8. Insulate and seal

Optimizing Fenestration 302: Definitions

- **Low-E coating**: Microscopic metal layer on glass that reduces heat transfer
- **NFRC**: National Fenestration Rating Council, which rates window performance
- **Solar Heat Gain Coefficient (SHGC)**: Fraction of solar radiation admitted
- **Thermal break**: Low-conductivity material that reduces heat transfer in frames
- **U-factor**: Rate of heat transfer; lower numbers indicate better insulation

Optimizing Fenestration 302: Troubleshooting

Problem	Solutions
Window doesn't operate properly	Check for square installation. Adjust shims. Ensure the frame isn't twisted. Check fasteners.
Condensation in window	Indicates seal failure; requires warranty replacement.
Water leaks around window	Check exterior caulking. Verify flashing installation. Ensure proper drainage slope of sill.
Air leakage	Add caulk. Check weatherstripping. Apply additional foam to voids.
Difficult operation	Check for paint on tracks. Apply lubricant. Ensure the frame isn't warped.

Optimizing Fenestration 302: Limitations

- DIY installation may void manufacturer warranties

- Improper installation causes leaks and reduces performance
- Structural modifications require knowledge of load-bearing elements
- Building codes may require permits
- Large or special windows may require professional installation

References and resources: <www.suspra.com/practice/energy/fenestration-302.html>

Optimizing Fenestration 303: Installing Doors

Install energy-efficient doors

Install a high-quality door to reduce energy consumption, provide a feeling of security, and improve comfort. The most energy-efficient doors typically have fiberglass or steel shells with polyurethane foam cores. If your door includes windows, look for double or triple-pane glass with low-E coatings. Proper installation is crucial for energy savings—the door must be level, plumb, properly shimmed, securely fastened, and thoroughly sealed to prevent airflow around it.

Optimizing Fenestration 303: Equipment & Materials

- Energy-efficient exterior door (pre-hung recommended)
- Flashing tape
- Low-expansion spray foam insulation
- Shims (cedar or non-biodegradable plastic)
- Exterior-grade screws (typically 3-inch)
- Weather stripping and door sweep (if not included)
- Carpentry tools for advanced home improvement projects
- Helper (recommended for handling heavy doors)

Optimizing Fenestration 303: Steps

1. Select an energy-efficient door
    - Choose doors with ENERGY STAR certification
    - Check U-factor (aim for 0.30 or less)
    - Consider sustainable materials (fiberglass, FSC-certified wood)
2. Prepare and measure
    - Measure width in three places: top, middle, and bottom
    - Measure height in three places: left, center, and right
    - Check for square corners using diagonal measurements
    - Allow clearance per manufacturer's specifications
3. ***Hire a handyman if you doubt your ability to install a prehung door***
4. Replacing a door: Remove existing door
    - Remove and save interior trim if salvaging
    - Remove hinge pins and door slab
    - Unscrew door frame from rough opening
    - Clean opening and inspect for damage
5. Prepare the rough opening
    - Ensure opening is level, plumb, and square
    - Install flashing at the sill
    - Apply caulk along the sill
    - Ensure slight outward slope for drainage
6. Test fit the door
    - Place door and frame in rough opening without fastening
    - Check clearances and operation
    - Mark shim locations

7. Install the door and frame per manufacturer's instructions
8. Insulate and seal around the frame and door
   - Apply low-expansion spray foam between frame and wall
   - Allow foam to cure completely
   - Install weather stripping and door sweep
   - Apply exterior caulk around perimeter
9. Install trim and verify door operation
   - Install interior and exterior trim
   - Test door operation; verify weather stripping makes complete contact
   - Check latching and locking

Optimizing Fenestration 303: Definitions

- **Air infiltration rate**: Measure of air leakage through a door assembly
- **Door sweep**: Strip attached to bottom of door to seal gap at threshold
- **Low-E coating**: Microscopic metal layer on glass that reduces heat transfer
- **Pre-hung door**: Door pre-installed in its frame with hinges attached
- **U-factor**: Measure of heat transfer; lower values indicate better insulation
- **Weatherstripping**: Material applied to door edges to seal gaps

Optimizing Fenestration 303: Troubleshooting

Problem	Solutions
Doesn't close properly	Check the frame for equal diagonals. Adjust shims. Verify hinge seating.
Gaps around edges	Add or adjust weatherstripping. Check for warping. Adjust the strike plate.
Threshold leaks	Adjust threshold height. Replace door sweep. Apply caulk to the exterior.
Drafts around frame	Add foam insulation. Add caulking; apply backer rod to larger gaps.
Door hard to operate	Check the frame and hinges. Check for warping. Adjust the strike plate.

Optimizing Fenestration 303: Limitations

- High-performance doors are expensive
- DIY installation of large doors or in non-standard openings is challenging

References and resources: <www.suspra.com/practice/energy/fenestration-303.html>

Optimizing Vehicles 101: Inflating Tires

Keep tires inflated to the pressure on the door jamb or in the owner's manual

Check your vehicle's door jamb or owner's manual for the recommended tire pressure. In the United States, this is often measured in units of *pounds per square inch* (PSI); in Europe, in *bar*; and in other parts of the world in *Kilopascals* (kPa). Use a reliable tire pressure gauge to measure the current pressure, then inflate or deflate your tires accordingly. Use an electric air pump or a hand pump (bicycle pumps work fine) to inflate each tire. Properly inflated tires reduce rolling resistance, leading to better gas mileage and lower emissions. This also extends tire lifespan, reducing waste.

Tires naturally lose air pressure over time. In addition, you'll need to add air when outdoor temperatures drop and bleed air when temperatures rise, to compensate for the relative density of

Sustainable Practices Handbook Energy Practices: Optimizing Energy Efficiency

colder air. Regularly check your tire pressure, ideally monthly or before long trips, to ensure optimal performance and safety.

References and resources: <www.suspra.com/practice/energy/optimizing-vehicles-101.html>

Optimizing Vehicles 102: Cruising

Use cruise control to maximize fuel economy

When driving on highways or relatively flat roads, engage cruise control to maintain a consistent speed. This minimizes unnecessary acceleration and deceleration, which consume extra energy, and allows fuel-burning engines to operate more efficiently, reducing fuel consumption and emissions.

References and resources: <www.suspra.com/practice/energy/optimizing-vehicles-102.html>

Optimizing Vehicles 201: Using Racks

Use a trunk rack or hitch rack rather than a roof rack to improve fuel economy

Roof racks create substantial aerodynamic drag, increasing fuel consumption. Opt instead for a trunk-mounted rack or a hitch-mounted rack to minimize wind resistance, leading to better mileage. Trunk racks attach to the vehicle's trunk or rear hatch, while hitch racks connect to a receiver hitch installed on the vehicle's frame. By reducing drag, these racks help you conserve fuel. When not in use, remove the rack altogether to further enhance fuel economy.

References and resources: <www.suspra.com/practice/energy/optimizing-vehicles-201.html>

Optimizing Vehicles 301: Improving Racks

Choose an aerodynamic roof rack with a wind deflector

If you need a roof rack, upgrade to an aerodynamic roof rack equipped with a wind deflector. Standard roof racks create significant wind resistance, especially at highway speeds, leading to increased fuel consumption. Opt for a sleek, low-profile rack designed to minimize drag. A wind deflector, mounted at the front of the rack, redirects airflow over and around the cargo, further reducing resistance. When choosing a rack, consider models specifically tested and rated for aerodynamic performance. Installation is usually straightforward, but ensure the rack is securely attached and compatible with your vehicle's specifications.

References and resources: <www.suspra.com/practice/energy/optimizing-vehicles-301.html>

Plumbing 201: Insulating Pipes

Insulate hot water and heating pipes

Add pipe insulation to maintain water temperature, reduce energy use, and prevent freezing pipes. Foam sleeves are suitable for temperatures up to 180°F and provide R-3 to R-4 insulation value. Fiberglass wrap works for temperatures up to 450°F with slightly better insulation (R-4 to R-5). Rubber insulation offers excellent flexibility, moisture resistance, and temperature range (-70°F to 220°F). Prioritize insulating hot water pipes from your water heater, heating system pipes in unheated spaces, and cold water pipes in unheated areas.

Plumbing 201: Equipment & Materials
- Duct tape, zip ties, or insulation tape

- Pipe insulation materials (choose one):
  - Foam pipe sleeves (easiest for DIY)
  - Fiberglass pipe wrap with vapor barrier
  - Rubber pipe insulation (higher temperature applications)
  - Reflective insulation (foil-faced)

Plumbing 201: Steps

1. Measure pipe diameters and total length of pipe to be insulated
2. Turn off heating systems before working on heating pipes
3. Clean and dry pipes before installation
4. Install insulation per manufacturer's instructions
5. Insulate fittings and valves with small pieces of insulation or specialized jackets
6. Inspect all insulation for gaps and add fasteners where needed

Plumbing 201: Definitions

- **Closed-cell foam**: Insulation with sealed air pockets that resist moisture migration
- **Hydronic heating: Water-based heating system circulating hot water through pipes**
- **R-value**: Measure of thermal resistance; higher values indicate better insulation
- **Vapor barrier**: Material preventing water vapor from passing through insulation

Plumbing 201: Troubleshooting

Problem	Solutions
Insulation pops open	Use tape along the entire seam or cable ties every 12 inches.
Insulation too tight	Verify pipe diameter. Purchase the next size up.
Moisture under insulation	Ensure pipes are dry before installation; check for leaks.
Deteriorating outdoors	Use UV-resistant products. Add protective covering.
Difficulty insulating valves	Use removable insulation jackets designed for valves.
Pipes still freezing	Add thicker insulation or a second layer. Consider heat tape.

Plumbing 201: Limitations

- Not suitable for very high-temperature applications (above 200°F) without specialized products
- Requires regular inspection and maintenance, especially exterior applications
- Insulation effectiveness diminishes if compressed or wet
- Extreme cold may require additional measures like heat tape

References and resources: <www.suspra.com/practice/energy/plumbing-201.html>

Plumbing 301: Pumping Heat

Install an electric heat pump water heater

Use 60-70% less electricity than standard electric water heaters by extracting heat from the surrounding air with a heat pump water heater. Proper installation is critical. These units need adequate air space and perform best in temperatures above 50°F. Hybrid models offer multiple operating modes: Heat Pump/Efficiency Mode (most efficient), Hybrid Mode (for high demand), Electric/Standard Mode (least efficient), and Vacation Mode (lowers temperature to save energy).

Revision: 25.1.8

Plumbing 301: Equipment & Materials
- Heat pump water heater unit
- Flexible water supply lines or copper piping
- Electrical supplies (wire cutters/strippers, electrical tape, appropriate gauge wire)
- Pressure relief valve and discharge pipe
- Water heater pan with drain
- Drain valve
- Thermal expansion tank
- Thermostatic mixing valve
- Condensate drain line
- Water temperature gauge
- *Optional: Condensate pump*

Plumbing 301: Steps
1. Choose a heat pump water heater
    - Hybrid models require dedicated 240 volt circuit
    - Heat-pump only model can plug in to dedicated 120 volt outlet
    - Choose size of tank based on hot water needs
2. ***Hire a professional plumber and electrician if you are unsure of your skills***
3. Select an installation location
    - Ensure sufficient air space based on manufacturer recommendations
    - Ambient temperature range of 40-90°F
    - At least 7 feet clearance height
    - Floor drain for condensate (or condensate pump)
4. Prepare for installation
    - Turn off power to existing water heater
    - Shut off cold water supply
    - Drain existing water heater (if applicable)
    - Disconnect electrical connections and water lines
    - Place water heater pan under unit
5. Install heat pump water heater per manufacturer instructions
    - Install shutoff valve and expansion tank
    - Install thermostatic mixing valve on hot water outlet
    - Install temperature and pressure relief valve and discharge pipe
6. Connect water lines
7. Install condensate drain line
8. Make electrical connections
9. Complete installation and test
10. Set water heater to desired temperature (120°F recommended)

Plumbing 301: Definitions
- **Condensate**: Water collected as air contacts the cool evaporator coil
- **Expansion tank**: Tank accommodating expanded water volume when heating
- **First Hour Rating**: Gallons of hot water the heater can supply in an hour
- **T&P relief valve**: Safety device if temperature or pressure exceeds safe levels

Plumbing 301: Troubleshooting

Problem	Solutions
Inadequate hot water	Check mode setting. Increase temperature setting. Ensure proper sizing. Verify adequate clearance for airflow.
Unit runs constantly	Ensure the room is large enough. Check for air leaks. Clean air filter.
Loud operation	Level the heater. Check for objects against the fan. Tighten loose panels.
Water leaks	Check connections and the T&P valve. Inspect condensate drain for clogs.
No power	Check circuit breaker. Test outlet. Verify electrical connections.
Cold air issues	Redirect exhaust air using ducts. Relocate unit to beneficial space.

Plumbing 301: Limitations

- Requires air space and ventilation for proper operation
- Works less efficiently in cold spaces (below 50°F)
- Produces cool air that may be undesirable in cold areas
- Initial heating takes longer than conventional water heaters
- Higher upfront cost than standard electric water heaters
- Fan noise during operation
- Requires periodic maintenance of air filters
- Installation requires specialized plumbing and electrical knowledge
- Requires condensate drain

References and resources: <www.suspra.com/practice/energy/plumbing-301.html>

Refrigerating 101: Circulating Air

Ensure your refrigerator has good air circulation around it to allow hot air to escape

To maximize your refrigerator's efficiency and longevity, ensure proper air circulation around it by keeping the back and sides clear of obstructions. A minimum of two inches of clearance is generally recommended; check your refrigerator's manual for specific instructions. Poor air circulation forces your refrigerator to work harder, consuming more energy and potentially shortening its lifespan.

References and resources: <www.suspra.com/practice/energy/refrigerating-101.html>

Refrigerating 201: Shading Refrigerators

Shade refrigerators and freezers from sunlight

Shade your refrigerator and freezer from direct sunlight to reduce energy consumption. Direct sunlight heats the appliance's exterior, forcing it to work harder to maintain the desired internal temperature. Position your refrigerator away from windows that receive direct sunlight, if you can. If this isn't possible, use blinds, curtains, or reflective window film to block sunlight during peak hours. Or create physical shade by installing a shelf or screen above the refrigerator to prevent direct light from reaching the top and sides. For outdoor refrigerators, build or purchase a simple shade structure.

References and resources: <www.suspra.com/practice/energy/refrigerating-201.html>

Refrigerating 301: Upgrading

Install an energy-efficient refrigerator or freezer

Upgrade to a modern refrigerator to use less than half the electricity of models made before 2000. Check ENERGY STAR for requirements and ratings of energy-efficient models. Consider models that use refrigerants with lower greenhouse warming potential.

Refrigerating 301: Equipment & Materials

- Energy-efficient refrigerator (price depends on size and convenience features)

Refrigerating 301: Steps

1. Evaluate your current refrigerator
   - Measure energy consumption using a Kill-a-Watt or similar plug-in meter
2. Select an energy-efficient model that uses environmentally friendly refrigerant
3. Plan placement away from heat sources and direct sunlight
4. Install the refrigerator
   - Ensure unit is level
   - Verify door seals are tight
   - Connect water supply (if applicable)
   - Plug into grounded outlet
   - Set temperature (37-40°F for refrigerator, 0-5°F for freezer)

Refrigerating 301: Definitions

- **CEE tiers**: Efficiency classifications exceeding ENERGY STAR requirements
- **Energy Guide label**: Yellow label showing estimated annual energy consumption
- **ENERGY STAR**: EPA certification for energy efficient products
- **kWh (kilowatt-hour)**: Unit measuring electricity consumption
- **R-600a (isobutane)**: Environmentally friendly refrigerant

Refrigerating 301: Troubleshooting

Problem	Solutions
Not cooling	Verify power, clearance, temperature settings. Allow 24 hours to stabilize.
Excessive noise	Check leveling, wall clearance, packaging removal.
High energy use	Check door seals, placement, temperature settings, coil cleanliness.

Refrigerating 301: Limitations

- High upfront cost for premium models
- Efficiency ratings based on ideal conditions

References and resources: <www.suspra.com/practice/energy/refrigerating-301.html>

Sealing 101: Caulking

Use caulk and foam to seal air gaps to reduce unwanted airflow

Block air leakage to save 25-40% of heating and cooling energy use in a typical home. Caulk works best for smaller, non-moving joints while expanding foam is ideal for larger gaps. Apply when temperatures are between 40°F and 90°F for best results. Silicone caulk provides excellent water resistance for bathrooms and kitchens but isn't paintable. Acrylic latex caulk is paintable and good for interior trim. Polyurethane caulk is durable for exterior applications. Choose the right type of expanding foam: look for products specifically labeled for doors and windows when foaming around doors and windows.

Sealing 101: Equipment & Materials

- Caulk gun
- Caulk tubes (silicone for wet areas, acrylic latex for interior, polyurethane for exterior)
- Expanding foam sealant with applicator straw (for larger gaps)
- Putty knife and utility knife or caulk removal tool
- Clean rags or paper towels
- Isopropyl alcohol
- Spray bottle with water and drop of dish soap
- Safety glasses, gloves, and N95 respirator (when using expanding foam)
- *Optional: Caulk backing rod, heat gun, painter's tape*

Sealing 101: Steps

1. Identify air leaks
   - Feel for drafts with back of hand on cold days
   - Look for visible gaps around windows, doors, pipes, and outlets
   - Check where different building materials meet
2. Prepare the surface
   - Remove old caulk
   - Clean surface thoroughly and let dry
   - *Optional: Apply painter's tape along both sides of joint*
3. Choose appropriate sealant
   - For gaps under 1/4 inch: Use caulk
   - For gaps 1/4-3 inches: Use expanding foam
   - For gaps over 3/8 inch when using caulk: Insert backing rod first
4. Apply expanding foam
   - Shake can vigorously
   - Fill only 1/3 to 1/2 of depth (foam will expand)
   - Work from bottom to top
   - Avoid overfilling
   - Allow proper curing time per manufacturer's instructions (typically 24-72 hours)
   - Let expanding foam cure completely before trimming excess
5. Apply caulk
   - Cut tube nozzle at 45-degree angle
   - Pierce inner seal with nail or wire
   - Hold gun at 45-degree angle to joint
   - Apply steady pressure while moving consistently
   - Work in 2-3 foot sections
6. Finish the caulk within 5-10 minutes, before caulk skins over
   - Remove painter's tape immediately while caulk is wet
   - Use damp finger or finishing tool
   - Move in one continuous motion
7. Clean up according to caulk type (water or solvent)

Sealing 101: Definitions

- **Air infiltration**: Uncontrolled air leakage through cracks and gaps
- **Backing rod**: Foam material inserted into deep cracks before caulking
- **Bead**: Continuous line of caulk or sealant

- **Skinning over**: Process of caulk forming surface film while interior remains uncured
- **Tooling**: Shaping newly applied caulk for better adhesion and appearance

Sealing 101: Troubleshooting

Problem	Solutions
Caulk not adhering	Ensure the surface is clean and dry. Use appropriate caulk for the material.
Caulk shrinking	Use higher quality caulk. For deep cracks, use a backing rod first.
Bubbles in caulk bead	Cut tip openings larger. Apply with slower pressure. Tool immediately.
Messy application	Use painter's tape. Cut smaller tip openings. Practice on scrap first.
Foam over-expanding	Use "minimal expanding" foam. Fill only 1/3 of cavity depth.
Difficult to remove	Apply caulk remover. Use a heat gun on a low setting. Try a specialty tool.

Sealing 101: Limitations

- Doesn't repair significant defects
- Temperature limitations for application (typically 40°F-90°F)
- Expanding foam can damage window and door frames if wrong type used
- Takes 24-72 hours to fully cure
- Some sealants emit VOCs during application

References and resources: <www.suspra.com/practice/energy/sealing-101.html>

Sealing 201: Weatherstripping

Maintain window and door weatherstripping to prevent unwanted airflow

Create a barrier with weatherstripping to prevent air leakage around fenestration (doors and windows). V-strips work well for sliding surfaces, foam tape for compression areas, and door sweeps for gaps under doors. Most weatherstripping lasts 1-5 years depending on quality and conditions.

Sealing 201: Equipment & Materials

- Replacement weatherstripping
- Cleaning supplies (warm water, mild soap, soft cloth)
- Screwdriver or utility knife
- Measuring tape
- Scissors or tin snips
- *Optional: Hair dryer, mineral spirits, adhesive, finishing nails, brad nailer*

Sealing 201: Steps

1. Inspect existing weatherstripping
    - Check exterior doors and windows for gaps, cracks, or drafts
    - Look for damaged or missing weatherstripping
    - Test with lit candle, smoke stick, or tissue paper on windy days
2. Clean existing weatherstripping
    - Remove dirt with soft cloth and warm, soapy water
    - Dry thoroughly
3. Repair minor issues

- Reposition weatherstripping that has slipped
- Gently pull out compressed weatherstripping; use hair dryer on low to restore shape
4. Remove and replace failed weatherstripping
    - Measure length needed plus 10% extra
    - Purchase appropriate type:
        - V-strip for sides of double-hung windows or hinged doors
        - Adhesive foam tape for irregular cracks
        - Door sweeps for bottom of doors
        - Tubular rubber or silicone for door or window stops
        - Interlocking metal for thresholds
    - Remove fasteners with screwdriver
    - For adhesive types, use utility knife to loosen
    - Clean surface thoroughly
5. Install new weatherstripping
    - Cut to measured length
    - For self-adhesive types:
        - Remove backing incrementally
        - Press firmly along entire length
        - Avoid stretching material
    - For nail-on types:
        - Position and secure with nails or staples every 4-6 inches
    - For door sweeps:
        - Position to just contact threshold without excess drag
6. Test installation, adjust as needed
    - Close doors and windows to check fit and check for drafts
    - Ensure proper operation without excessive force
7. Check after extreme weather

Sealing 201: Definitions

- **Compression weatherstripping**: Forms seal by being compressed when closed
- **Door sweep**: Strip attached to bottom of door to seal gap
- **Tension seal (V-strip)**: V-shaped strip using tension for sealing
- **Threshold**: Floor surface beneath door that may include weatherstripping
- **Weatherstripping**: Materials sealing gaps between movable components

Sealing 201: Troubleshooting

Problem	Solutions
Difficult to close	Weatherstripping is too thick. Trim or replace with thinner material.
Falls off	Clean the surface thoroughly. Consider mechanically fastened types.
Gaps still present	Ensure proper contact along the entire length. Use a combination of types.
Squeaking noises	Apply talcum powder or dish soap. Avoid petroleum-based lubricants.
Bottom of door leaks	Adjust threshold or use adjustable door sweep.
Adhesive leaves residue	Use rubbing alcohol to clean before installing new weatherstripping.

Sealing 201: Limitations
- Cannot compensate for structural issues like warped doors or windows
- May interfere with operation of certain window styles
- Less effective on very irregular surfaces or gaps over 1/4 inch
- Adhesive types may not stick well in extreme temperatures
- Materials eventually degrade and require replacement

References and resources: <www.suspra.com/practice/energy/sealing-201.html>

Washing 101: Using Cold Water

Wash clothes in cold water using detergents containing cold-water enzymes

Switch your washing machine's temperature setting from hot or warm to cold. This practice reduces the energy needed to heat water. Modern detergents, especially those labeled for cold water, are formulated with enzymes that effectively clean clothes in colder temperatures. Most clothing can be cleaned effectively in cold water, and this method can also help prevent color fading and fabric shrinkage.

References and resources: <www.suspra.com/practice/energy/washing-101.html>

Washing 201: Upgrading Washing Machines

Install an energy-efficient washing machine with a high-speed spin cycle

Use a high-efficiency washer to clean clothes with 25-50% less water and energy than conventional models. Front-loaders typically offer higher spin speeds (1,000-1,600 RPM) than top-loaders (800-1,200 RPM). Each 100 RPM increase reduces drying time by approximately 4%. Take care to level, especially for high-speed spin cycles where slight imbalances can cause excessive vibration. On front-loading models, carefully dry after each cycle and leave the door open so the drum can dry out.

Washing 201: Equipment & Materials
- New energy-efficient washing machine with high-speed spin cycle
- Water inlet hoses and drain hose (usually provided with new machine)
- Drain hose clamp or bracket
- *Optional: Floor tray, anti-vibration pads*

Washing 201: Steps
1. Select an appropriate washing machine
   - Choose a machine with ENERGY STAR rating and spin speed of at least 1,000 RPM
   - Verify dimensions will fit your space
2. **Hire a licensed plumber if you doubt your ability to install a washing machine**
3. Prepare for installation
   - Make sure floor is relatively level and can handle weight and vibration
   - Have electrical and plumbing hook ups ready
   - Install floor tray (recommended)
   - Place anti-vibration pads (if needed)
4. Install the new washing machine per manufacturer instructions
5. Connect water supply: hand-tighten supply hoses, then use wrench to tighten 1/4 to 1/2 turn
6. Connect drain hose: form a U-shaped high loop to prevent siphoning
7. Plug machine into a grounded outlet and turn on water supply valves
8. Run short test cycle without clothes: verify proper filling, draining, and spinning
9. Make final adjustments, re-level if necessary

Washing 201: Definitions

- **RPM (Revolutions Per Minute):** Measure of spin speed; higher RPM indicates better water extraction
- **Shipping Bolts:** Rods that secure the drum during transport; must be removed before use
- **Standpipe:** Vertical pipe connected to drainage system for washer drain hose
- **Siphoning:** Unwanted backward flow of water from drain into washing machine

Washing 201: Troubleshooting

Problem	Solutions
Machine not level	Adjust leveling feet. For persistent problems, use anti-vibration pads.
Water leaks	Check and tighten connections. Apply new Teflon tape if needed.
Excessive vibration	Verify shipping bolts are removed. Ensure the machine is level on a solid floor. Install anti-vibration pads.
Water fills slowly	Check that supply valves are fully open. Clean inlet hose screens.
Machine doesn't drain	Check for kinks in the drain hose. Ensure proper drain height.

Washing 201: Limitations

- May require professional help for plumbing or electrical modifications
- High-efficiency machines cost more upfront
- Front-loaders require more maintenance to prevent mold issues
- Noise and vibration may be problematic in apartments or upper floors
- Some high-efficiency washers have longer cycle times

References and resources: <www.suspra.com/practice/energy/washing-201.html>

Washing 301: Drying Clothes

Install a ventless electric clothes dryer

Dry clothes without the need for external venting with a ventless dryer. Heat pump dryers are the most energy efficient, using 50-70% less energy than conventional vented dryers, but have longer drying times (1.5-2 hours). Standard condensing dryers are more affordable but less efficient, with faster cycles than heat pumps but slower than vented dryers. Both types collect water that must be drained or manually emptied from a reservoir, rather than blown out through an air vent.

Washing 301: Equipment & Materials

- Ventless electric clothes dryer (heat pump or condenser type)
- Drain hose (if not included) and clamp
- *Optional: Drain pan, anti-vibration pads*

Washing 301: Steps

1. Prepare for installation
   - Measure space to ensure proper fit
   - Verify electrical requirements (either 240 or 120 volts)
   - No air vents are necessary for ventless electric clothes dryers
2. Plan drainage system

Sustainable Practices Handbook Energy Practices: Optimizing Energy Efficiency

- o Choose where condensed water will drain:
    - Direct to plumbed drain
    - Into washing machine standpipe
    - Into utility sink or floor drain
    - Into included water reservoir (to be removed and emptied manually)
3. ***Hire a handyman if you doubt your ability to install a dryer***
4. Install the dryer and test operation per the manufacturer's instructions

Washing 301: Definitions

- **Condenser**: Component that removes moisture from air inside the dryer
- **Heat pump**: Device that transfers heat using a refrigeration cycle
- **Ventless dryer**: Clothes dryer that doesn't require an exterior exhaust vent
- **Water reservoir**: Container that collects condensed water

Washing 301: Troubleshooting

Problem	Solutions
Dryer doesn't power on	Check electrical connections and circuit breaker. Ensure the door is closed.
Takes too long to dry	Clean lint filter and condenser. Reduce load size. Spin clothes in a washer.
Water leaking	Check the drain hose for kinks or clogs. Verify connections are secure.
Excessive vibration	Ensure the dryer is level. Check that shipping materials are removed.
Water not draining	Check for blockages in the drain hose. Ensure continuous downward slope.

Washing 301: Limitations

- Typically smaller capacity than vented dryers
- Longer drying cycles (especially heat pump models)
- Higher purchase cost than vented models
- Heat released into room may be undesirable in hot weather

References and resources: <www.suspra.com/practice/energy/washing-301.html>

Conserving Energy

Cooking 201: Microwaving

Cook in a microwave instead of a conventional oven

Cook in microwave ovens to use 70-80% less energy than conventional ovens. Microwaves directly heat water molecules inside food rather than heating surrounding air, significantly reducing cooking time and energy use. Best suited for foods with high moisture content; preserves more nutrients than boiling due to shorter cooking times and less water use. Metal can cause sparks; do not place it in microwaves. For crisping or browning, cook food on a microwave crisper pan.

Cooking 201: Equipment & Materials
- Microwave oven
- Microwave-safe cookware (glass and ceramic)
- Microwave cover or splatter guard (silicone)
- Oven mitts or potholders
- *Optional: Food thermometer, microwave crisper pan*

Cooking 201: Steps
1. Clean your microwave before and after each use
2. Use glass and ceramic containers labeled "microwave-safe"; avoid metal and plastics
3. Prepare food for microwaving
   - Cut into uniform pieces; arrange in a single layer when possible
   - Pierce foods with skins to let out steam (and avoid explosions)
4. Adapt recipes
   - Cooking happens internally as water heats up; use a microwave crisper pan for browning
   - Reduce liquids by 25%; reduce cook times by 50-75%
   - Add 2 tablespoons water for vegetables; cover dishes in microwave to retain moisture
5. Set power level and cooking times
   - Experiment to find settings that give you good results
   - Start with high power setting and 50% of conventional cooking time
   - Stir food halfway through cooking when possible
6. Check for doneness: use a food thermometer for meat
7. Let food stand covered five minutes after removing from microwave (will continue cooking)

Cooking 201: Definitions
- **Microwave crisper pan**: A pan designed to concentrate heat in a microwave
- **Microwave-safe**: Materials tested for microwave use that won't melt or leach chemicals
- **Power levels**: Settings controlling percentage of time microwave generates energy
- **Standing time**: Period after microwaving when food continues cooking using residual heat
- **Wattage**: Measure of microwave cooking power (typically 700-1200 watts)

Cooking 201: Troubleshooting

Problem	Solutions
Uneven cooking	Cut food into equal pieces. Arrange thicker parts toward the outside. Stir halfway. Use lower power for a longer time.
Food drying out	Cover dish. Add 2 tablespoons of water. Use lower power for a longer time.

Problem	Solutions
Food exploding	Pierce foods with skins before cooking. Use a cover. Cook at lower power.
Overcooked meat	Cook at 50% power for less time. Use a thermometer for doneness.
Soggy breaded foods	Use microwave crisper pans. Finish briefly in a toaster oven for crispness.

Cooking 201: Limitations
- Requires a crisper pan to brown or crisp foods
- Large items or quantities may cook unevenly
- Not all cookware is microwave-safe
- Challenging to cook multiple dishes simultaneously

References and resources: <www.suspra.com/practice/energy/cooking-201.html>

Cooking 202: Pressure Cooking

Cook in a pressure cooker to save energy

Use a pressure cooker to reduce energy use by 50-75% and cut cooking times by up to 70%. The sealed environment raises water's boiling point to approximately 250°F (121°C), accelerating cooking while retaining moisture and nutrients.

Cooking 202: Equipment & Materials
- Pressure cooker (stovetop or electric)
- Heat-resistant cooking utensils
- Measuring cups and spoons
- Potholders or oven mitts

Cooking 202: Steps
1. Choose your pressure cooker
   - Stovetop or plug-in electric; 6-quart is versatile for most households
2. Understand basic components
   - Lid with locking mechanism, sealing gasket, pressure valve, pressure indicator
3. Prepare ingredients
   - Cut food uniformly; add appropriate liquid (generally 1-2 cups minimum)
4. Secure properly according to instructions
5. Set pressure and time
   - Stovetop: Use high heat until pressure is reached, then reduce heat
   - Electric: Select appropriate pressure setting (high 10-15 PSI or low 5-8 PSI)
   - Set cooking time (typically 1/3 to 1/2 of conventional cooking time)
6. Monitor cooking process: adjust heat as needed for stovetop models
7. Release pressure safely
   - Natural release: Turn off heat, let pressure decrease naturally (best for meats, beans)
   - Quick release: Carefully turn valve to release steam (best for vegetables)
8. Open lid safely
   - Ensure pressure indicator shows no pressure remains; open away from face
9. Clean and maintain: wash after cooling; store with lid inverted

Cooking 202: Definitions

- **PSI (Pounds per Square Inch)**: Unit of pressure; most pressure cookers operate at 10-15 PSI
- **Natural release**: Allowing pressure to decrease gradually by turning off heat
- **Quick release**: Manually opening pressure valve to release pressure rapidly
- **Sealing gasket**: Rubber ring creating airtight seal between pot and lid

Cooking 202: Troubleshooting

Problem	Solutions
Won't pressurize	Check sealing ring installation. Ensure enough liquid. Verify pressure valve position. Check the lid lock.
Food burning	Use minimum required liquid. Add oil to prevent sticking. Use trivet.
Steam leaking	Check the sealing ring. Ensure the lid is properly aligned.
Undercooked food	Increase cooking time. Check the sealing ring. Use natural release.

Cooking 202: Limitations

- Not ideal for foods requiring browning or crisping
- Limited visibility to monitor food during cooking
- Learning curve for timing various foods
- Not suitable for dishes requiring reduction or evaporation
- Some delicate foods can easily overcook

References and resources: <www.suspra.com/practice/energy/cooking-202.html>

Cooking 203: Cooking Outside

Cook outside during the summer to reduce your indoor cooling load

Reduce cooling needs and save energy by cooking outdoors during warm weather. Cooking generates significant heat and humidity indoors, requiring fans and air conditioning systems to remove it. High-temperature, long-duration cooking activities like baking, roasting, or simmering are particularly good candidates for outdoor cooking to save energy.

Cooking 203: Equipment & Materials

- Outdoor cooking apparatus (electric grill, portable induction cooktop, solar oven, camp stove)
- Weather-protected outdoor space
- Outdoor table or stable surface
- GFCI-protected outlet and extension cord rated for outdoor use (for electric appliances)
- Basic cooking tools
- Fire extinguisher
- *Optional: Portable kitchen storage bin*

Cooking 203: Steps

1. Assess outdoor cooking options
   - Evaluate available space, equipment, proximity to kitchen, local regulations
2. Plan outdoor-friendly meals and cooking sessions
   - Create weekly menu for foods that cook well outdoors; group cooking tasks
   - Create windbreaks if necessary; adjust cooking times for outdoor temperature

3. Store equipment properly: cover and protect when not in use

Cooking 203: Definitions
- **Cooling load**: Heat energy that must be removed from a space
- **GFCI outlet**: Ground Fault Circuit Interrupter outlet that protects against electric shock
- **Batch cooking**: Preparing multiple portions of food at once for several meals

Cooking 203: Troubleshooting

Problem	Solutions
Weather changes	Have a contingency plan for quickly moving cooking indoors. Use equipment that can be moved quickly.
Limited space	Use portable induction cooktops or small electric grills.
Transporting supplies	Use a dedicated bin for outdoor cooking supplies. Organize ingredients in advance.
Insects	Use food covers, mesh tents, citronella candles, or fans. Clean up promptly.
No outdoor outlet	Use a solar oven. Use a portable solar array and power station.

Cooking 203: Limitations
- Weather dependency makes outdoor cooking unpredictable
- Limited practicality in urban environments or apartments
- Seasonal utility (beneficial only during warm months)
- Requires more planning than conventional cooking
- Some recipes difficult to execute outdoors

References and resources: <www.suspra.com/practice/energy/cooking-203.html>

Cooking 204: Preparing Cold Meals

Prepare cold meals that don't require heat for cooking

Prepare cold meals to reduce energy demands of cooking while offering nutritional benefits, as some nutrients are preserved better without heating. For balanced nutrition, combine complementary plant proteins, include fermented foods for digestion, and incorporate varied colors and textures. Make dressings, chopped vegetables, and pre-cooked grains in advance to reduce daily preparation time.

Cooking 204: Equipment & Materials
- Basic kitchen tools and equipment
- *Optional: Food processor or blender*

Cooking 204: Steps
1. Keep a stock of shelf-stable ingredients, long-lasting vegetables, and flavor enhancers
2. Learn basic techniques
   - Build balanced salads with proper ingredient ratios
   - Create marinated dishes where acidic components "cook" ingredients
   - Use smashing, massaging, or fine chopping to soften vegetables
   - Prepare overnight soaking methods for oats and seeds

3. Follow the cold meal blueprint
   - Base: Leafy greens, pre-cooked grains, or sliced vegetables
   - Proteins: Beans, canned fish, nuts, seeds, tofu, or hard-boiled eggs
   - Vegetables and Fruits: Raw, pickled, or pre-roasted options
   - Fats: Olive oil, avocado, nuts, seeds, or cheese
   - Flavor boosters: Herbs, spices, vinegars, citrus juice

Cooking 204: Definitions
- **Cold meals**: Meals prepared without applying heat
- **Marination**: Soaking foods in seasoned, often acidic liquid to enhance flavor and alter texture
- **Massaging**: Working salt, acid, or oil into greens by hand to break down cell walls
- **Overnight soaking**: Softening foods by soaking in liquid for 8+ hours
- **Protein complements**: Combining plants to ensure all essential amino acids are present

Cooking 204: Troubleshooting

Problem	Solutions
Meals leave you hungry	Add nuts and seeds. Include more fiber-rich foods.
Limited fresh produce	Thaw frozen vegetables. Use canned goods. Sprout seeds.
Lack of flavor	Add fermented elements. Use strongly flavored ingredients.
Monotonous texture	Mix crunchy elements with chewy and creamy elements.
Packing meals	Layer ingredients in jars. Use divided containers. Pack with freezer packs.

Cooking 204: Limitations
- Some nutrients are more available and digestible when cooked; others less so
- Less satisfying in cold weather
- Requires more vigilance with food safety
- Greater reliance on seasonal availability

References and resources: <www.suspra.com/practice/energy/cooking-204.html>

Cooking 205: Preparing Multiple Meals

Plan and cook multiple meals in the oven at the same time

Plan multi-meal cooking (batch cooking) to reduce energy consumption by maximizing oven efficiency. Modern ovens use 2-5 kilowatt-hours of electricity per use. Convection ovens are ideal for this practice as fans circulate hot air for more even cooking, reducing cooking times by about 25% compared to conventional ovens.

Cooking 205: Equipment & Materials
- Energy-efficient oven
- Multiple oven-safe baking dishes and pans
- Aluminum foil or parchment paper
- Oven thermometer
- Oven mitts
- Food storage containers

Sustainable Practices Handbook   Energy Practices: Conserving Energy

Cooking 205: Steps
1. Plan compatible meals
   - Choose dishes with similar cooking temperatures (within 25°F/15°C)
   - Select recipes that cook well without frequent attention
2. Prepare oven and kitchen
   - Position racks optimally (one in top third, one in bottom third)
   - Preheat oven; place thermometer inside
3. Chop all vegetables at once; pre-measure ingredients for each meal
4. Arrange food optimally
   - Place dense, longer-cooking items on lower rack
   - Position delicate items on upper rack
   - Leave 1 inch between dishes and walls, 2 inches between dishes
5. Adjust cooking techniques
   - Set temperature to accommodate most dishes
   - Tent foods with foil that would normally cook at lower temperature
   - Place dishes needing higher heat higher in oven
6. Monitor and rotate
   - Check internal temperatures periodically; keep door closed as much as possible
   - Rotate dishes halfway if needed
7. Remove each dish as it finishes; cool slightly before packaging; label containers

Cooking 205: Definitions
- **Batch cooking**: Preparing multiple meals at once to be eaten over several days
- **Convection oven**: Oven using fans to circulate hot air for more even cooking
- **Temperature gradient**: Variation in temperature from one part of the oven to another
- **Tenting**: Covering food with foil to prevent over-browning while allowing air circulation

Cooking 205: Troubleshooting

Problem	Solutions
Uneven cooking rates	Cover faster-cooking foods with foil. Place faster items on lower racks. Add faster-cooking items later.
Uneven browning	Rotate dishes halfway through. Use convection if available. Use a baking stone for heat distribution.
Too much moisture	Leave more space between dishes. Partially vent high-moisture foods.
Flavor transfer	Cover aromatic dishes. Separate strongly flavored foods.
Poor fit in oven	Use cookware with different heights. Choose rectangular dishes, not round.

Cooking 205: Limitations
- Not all dishes can cook at the same temperature
- Flavor transfer between dishes possible
- Requires more advance planning
- Limited ability to actively cook (stir, baste)
- Conventional ovens may have hot spots
- Some delicate dishes perform poorly when sharing oven space

References and resources: <www.suspra.com/practice/energy/cooking-205.html>

Revision: 25.1.8

Cooking 303: Solar Cooking

Use a solar cooker

Directly harness sunlight to cook without fuel. **Box cookers** (250-350°F) work like slow cookers for baking and simmering; **panel cookers** (200-300°F) are lightweight and portable; **parabolic cookers** (up to 500°F) concentrate intense heat for frying and boiling. Cooking times vary: vegetables (1-1.5 hours), grains (1-2 hours), meats (2-4 hours), beans (3-5 hours). Unlike conventional methods, solar cooking rarely overcooks food and preserves nutrients better.

Cooking 303: Equipment & Materials
- Solar cooker (box, panel, or parabolic style)
- Dark, thin-walled cooking pots with tight-fitting lids
- Oven mitts, UV-blocking sunglasses
- Food thermometer, timer

Cooking 303: Steps
1. Select a level surface with full sunlight for 3 hours, protected from strong winds
2. Set up your solar cooker
   - Follow the manufacturer's instructions for your specific type (box, panel, or parabolic)
   - Position directly facing the sun: shadow should be directly behind cooker
3. Prepare food for cooking
   - Cut into smaller, uniform pieces; soak dense foods like beans beforehand
   - Put in dark, thin-walled pots with tight lids (sunlight will heat up pots)
4. Load the cooker
   - Place the pots in the center or at focal point
   - Wear UV-blocking sunglasses when cooking with parabolic cookers
5. Monitor temperature
   - Use food thermometer to check internal temperatures; aim for safe cooking temperatures
6. Reorient as needed
   - Adjust position every 30 minutes to track the sun for longer cooking times
7. Remove food safely
   - Use oven mitts; be cautious of steam when opening lids
   - Be extremely careful with parabolic cookers
8. Clean reflective surfaces with soft cloth; store in dry location

Cooking 303: Definitions
- **Box cooker**: Insulated container with transparent lid and reflective panels that traps heat
- **Focal point**: Spot where light rays converge in a parabolic cooker
- **Panel cooker**: Design using flat reflective panels to concentrate sunlight onto cooking vessel
- **Parabolic cooker**: Curved reflective device concentrating sunlight to a focal point
- **Solar window**: Optimal time for solar cooking (typically 10AM-2PM)

Cooking 303: Troubleshooting

Problem	Solutions
Slow cooking	Ensure proper orientation. Use darker, thinner pots. Cut food smaller. Add a heat-resistant oven bag around the pot.
Wind issues	Place weights on base. Use anchors to secure. Position in sheltered location.

Problem	Solutions
Intermittent clouds	Use an insulated box cooker. Place the pot in a heat-resistant bag. Plan longer cooking time.
Burnt food (parabolic)	Check food frequently. Place the pot slightly off the focal point. Use double pots or heat diffusers.
Can't track sun	Use the stick shadow method for alignment.

Cooking 303: Limitations

- Requires direct sunlight; not effective in strong winds, overcast conditions, or at night
- Longer cooking times than conventional methods
- Requires frequent adjustment to track the sun
- Smaller capacity than conventional stoves
- High-temperature cooking only possible with parabolic models
- Reduced effectiveness in extreme latitudes, especially winter

References and resources: <www.suspra.com/practice/energy/cooking-303.html>

Driving 101: Driving Slower

Drive slower to improve fuel economy

Drag is proportional to the square of velocity, which means your vehicle experiences much more drag the faster you go. Going from 15 miles per hour to 60 mph creates 16 times more drag; going to 75 mph creates 25 times more drag. The more drag, the worse your fuel economy.

References and resources: <www.suspra.com/practice/energy/driving-101.html>

Driving 102: Driving Gently

Accelerate slower and brake more gently to improve fuel economy

More gradual acceleration and braking use less energy.

References and resources: <www.suspra.com/practice/energy/driving-102.html>

Driving 103: Offloading Weight

Offload unnecessary items before driving to improve fuel economy

Remove all unnecessary items from vehicles. The less weight in vehicles, the better the fuel economy.

References and resources: <www.suspra.com/practice/energy/driving-103.html>

Driving 104: Rolling Up Windows

Keep windows rolled up at highway speeds to reduce drag and improve fuel economy

Closing windows improves aerodynamics and fuel economy, especially when driving at highway speeds. Keeping windows closed and recirculating air when running the air conditioning uses less energy than rolling down windows, because recirculated air usually is cooler and less humid than outdoor air, requiring less energy to keep at a comfortable temperature and humidity level.

References and resources: <www.suspra.com/practice/energy/driving-104.html>

Driving 201: Transporting Items

Transport items inside your vehicle rather than on a rack

Items on racks can reduce aerodynamics and fuel economy, especially when driving at highway speeds. Items fully inside the vehicle or in an enclosed roof carrier do not affect aerodynamics.

References and resources: <www.suspra.com/practice/energy/driving-201.html>

Driving 301: Removing Racks

Remove racks when not needed

Remove racks from your roof and hitch to improve aerodynamics and fuel economy.

References and resources: <www.suspra.com/practice/energy/driving-301.html>

Driving 302: Minimizing Cabin Heat

Minimize the use of cabin heat when driving a fully electric vehicle

Bundle up so you don't need to turn up the heat as much when you drive. Turn on your heated steering wheel or heated seats to stay warm. These are slightly more efficient than blowing warm air.

References and resources: <www.suspra.com/practice/energy/driving-302.html>

Economizing 105: Unplugging Appliances

Unplug appliances so they don't draw power in standby mode

Eliminate "vampire loads" by unplugging appliances when not in use. Or, put them on a power strip to protect them from surges and make it easy to completely cut power to them by switching off the strip.

References and resources: <www.suspra.com/practice/energy/economizing-105.html>

Economizing 106: Drinking Cold Beverages

Drink more cold beverages and fewer hot beverages

Drink more cold beverages, especially tap water. It takes less energy to keep drinks cold than to make hot drinks. An efficient full-size refrigerator (25 cubic feet) can keep hundreds of 12-ounce cans cold using about 1.5 kWh per day; brewing one pot of coffee and keeping it warm consumes about 0.25 kWh. Storing items in your refrigerator actually makes it slightly more efficient because keeping more items in the refrigerator means less cold air seeps out each time you open the door.

References and resources: <www.suspra.com/practice/energy/economizing-106.html>

Sustainable Practices Handbook Energy Practices: Conserving Energy

Economizing 107: Watching Shows

Watch shows on smaller devices rather than large televisions

Watch movies on smartphones using less than 2 watts; large televisions consume 200 watts.

References and resources: <www.suspra.com/practice/energy/economizing-107.html>

Economizing 108: Listening

Listen to music on headphones rather than using speakers

Listen to music over headphones on a smartphone using less than 2 watts; room speakers consume between 15 and 150 watts, depending on volume.

References and resources: <www.suspra.com/practice/energy/economizing-108.html>

Economizing 109: Reading

Walk to your local library to check out and read printed books from their collection

Read printed books using daylight; no electricity is required.

References and resources: <www.suspra.com/practice/energy/economizing-109.html>

Economizing 110: Showering Cold

Take colder showers to use less hot water

The closer to ground temperature and shorter the shower, the less energy required to heat water for it.

References and resources: <www.suspra.com/practice/energy/economizing-110.html>

Economizing 202: Using Elbow Grease

Use outdoor equipment that does not require fuel or electricity

Rakes, shovels, and hand saws do not require fuel or electricity.

References and resources: <www.suspra.com/practice/energy/economizing-202.html>

Economizing 301: Sweeping

Choose flooring you can sweep instead of vacuum

Reduce energy consumption and maintenance costs by installing hard flooring that can be swept or dust mopped rather than vacuumed, especially in entryways. Options like hardwood, bamboo, cork, and tile eliminate the need for vacuum cleaners that use 500-1500 watts of power. Select smooth surfaces without grooves or deep textures that trap dust and debris. Consider both initial cost and longevity—quality hardwood can last four decades or more compared to carpet's 5-15 years.

Economizing 301: Equipment & Materials
- Wood, tile, or other hard flooring material
- Basic carpentry tools

Economizing 301: Steps

1. ***Hire a handyman if you doubt your ability to install flooring***
2. Measure rooms for new flooring
3. Choose flooring that is easy to sweep clean and made from sustainable materials
   - Hardwood, bamboo, cork, tile, stone, concrete, linoleum
   - Avoid deep grooves, texturing, and large grout lines
   - Look for
     - Recycled or recyclable materials
     - Locally-sourced options
     - Zero-VOC materials, finishes, and adhesives
4. Install per manufacturer's instructions

Economizing 301: Definitions

- **Dust mop**: Cleaning tool with flat head and microfiber or cotton material that traps dust
- **FSC-certified**: Wood products from responsibly managed forests
- **Linoleum**: Natural flooring from linseed oil, cork dust, wood flour, and renewable ingredients
- **Low-VOC/Zero-VOC**: Products with reduced or no volatile organic compounds

Economizing 301: Troubleshooting

Problem	Solutions
Budget constraints	Consider engineered flooring. Look for factory-finished options. Phase project by prioritizing high-traffic areas first.
Cold hard surfaces	Use area rugs strategically. Consider radiant floor heating. Choose naturally warmer materials like cork.
Flooring is noisy	Install proper underlayment for sound absorption. Use area rugs.

Economizing 301: Limitations

- Hard flooring typically has higher initial costs than carpet
- Hard surfaces can increase noise transfer in multi-level homes
- Some materials require specific cleaning products

References and resources: <www.suspra.com/practice/energy/economizing-301.html>

Heating & Cooling 102: Adjusting Thermostats

Adjust thermostats lower all winter and higher all summer to save energy

Embrace a slightly wider comfort range by permanently adjusting your thermostat settings. Aim for a lower temperature in winter (e.g., 68°F or 20°C) and a higher temperature in summer (e.g., 78°F or 26°C). This approach isn't about temporary setbacks, but about adapting to a more energy-conscious lifestyle. By accepting a minor degree of discomfort, you significantly reduce the workload on your heating and cooling systems. This translates to lower energy consumption. Consistent, permanent adjustments are more effective than sporadic changes, as they optimize your home's energy usage over the long term. Pair this practice with other energy-saving habits, such as dressing appropriately for the season and using fans for supplemental cooling, to maximize your impact.

References and resources: <www.suspra.com/practice/energy/heating-cooling-102.html>

Lighting 102: Turning Off

Turn off lights when you leave a room if you'll be gone for more than a minute

Switching off lights saves energy, but the energy savings for very brief intervals may be outweighed by the wear and tear on mechanical switches, which eventually fail.

References and resources: <www.suspra.com/practice/energy/lighting-102.html>

Lighting 103: Leaving Off

Leave off lights when daylight is sufficient

Not turning on lights when daylight is sufficient saves energy and prolongs the life of mechanical switches. Use a smartphone light meter app to determine when daylight is sufficient.

References and resources: <www.suspra.com/practice/energy/lighting-103.html>

Lighting 202: Reducing Power

Install less powerful lighting to save energy

Save energy by removing light bulbs or fixtures and installing lower-wattage replacements. Watts measure power consumption; lumens measure light output; lux measure lumens per square meter. For general living areas, 100-200 lux is adequate, while task areas may need 300-500 lux. Use a light meter app on your smartphone to see where your home is over-lit compared to actual needs.

Lighting 202: Equipment & Materials

- Lower-wattage LED bulbs (5-9 watts for general use) or new LED light fixtures
- *Optional: Lumen meter or smartphone light meter app, socket covers for unused sockets*

Lighting 202: Steps

1. Assess where you could replace bulbs or fixtures with lower-wattage lighting
2. Reduce total wattage in multi-bulb fixtures
   - Remove one or more bulbs or replace all bulbs with lower-wattage alternatives
   - *Optional: Install socket covers on unused sockets*
3. Choose lower-wattage LED replacements with appropriate lumens
   - Living areas: 450-800 lumens
   - Kitchens and workspaces: 450-1600 lumens
   - Bedrooms: 450-800 lumens
4. *Hire a licensed electrician if you doubt your ability to replace a lighting fixture*
5. Install lower-wattage fixtures
   - Turn off power to fixture
   - Remove old fixture
   - Install new fixture that uses less wattage

Lighting 202: Definitions

- **Color temperature**: Measured in Kelvin (K), indicates whether light appears warm (yellow/orange, lower K) or cool (blue/white, higher K)
- **Efficacy**: How efficiently a light source produces visible light (lumens per watt)
- **Lumen**: Unit of measurement for amount of light produced
- **Lux**: Metric unit of light intensity (one lumen per square meter)
- **Watt**: Unit of measurement for electrical power consumption

Sustainable Practices Handbook
Energy Practices: Conserving Energy

Lighting 202: Troubleshooting

Problem	Solutions
Room feels too dark	Try higher lumen output. Clean windows to maximize natural light.
Flicker with dimmers	Replace old dimmers switches. Use dimmable LED bulbs.
Inconsistent light levels	Distribute bulbs evenly in multi-bulb fixtures. Choose wider beam angles.

Lighting 202: Limitations
- Very low light levels may create safety hazards

References and resources: <www.suspra.com/practice/energy/lighting-202.html>

Lighting 203: Task Lighting

Use task lighting rather than ambient lighting to save energy

Reduce lighting energy consumption by 40-60% while improving visibility by installing task lighting that focuses light exactly where needed rather than illuminating an entire room. A well-positioned 8-watt LED desk lamp can replace a 12-watt overhead light. Task lighting also eliminates shadows created by overhead lighting and creates a more comfortable visual environment. When selecting task lights, prioritize adjustability in both positioning and brightness.

Lighting 203: Equipment & Materials
- LED task lights (desk lamps, reading lights, under-cabinet lights)

Lighting 203: Steps
1. Analyze your lighting needs
   - Identify specific areas needing focused light
   - Determine appropriate brightness for each task
2. Select appropriate task lighting
   - For reading and desk work: Choose adjustable lamps with 400-600 lumens
   - For kitchen counters: Select under-cabinet LED strips or puck lights (200-300 lumens per foot)
   - For detailed work: Choose lamps with magnification and 600-800 lumens
3. Position task lights correctly
   - Place reading lamps over your shoulder to avoid glare
   - Position desk lamps to illuminate work surface without shadows
   - Mount under-cabinet lights toward front edge
   - Keep task lights 12-18 inches from work surfaces
4. Reduce ambient lighting
   - Remove excess bulbs from multi-bulb fixtures
   - Replace remaining ambient lighting with lower-wattage options
5. Create lighting zones
   - Group lighting so individual areas can be lit separately
   - Add switches or smart plugs
6. Establish new lighting habits
   - Turn on only the task light needed for current activity
   - Turn off ambient lighting when task lighting is sufficient
   - Adjust brightness to minimum needed

- Turn off task lights when not in use

Lighting 203: Definitions
- **Ambient lighting**: General illumination for an entire room
- **Lumens**: Measurement of total light output; higher numbers indicate brighter light
- **Lux**: Lumens per square meter (300-500 lux typically required for tasks)
- **Task lighting**: Focused lighting for a specific activity area

Lighting 203: Troubleshooting

Problem	Solutions
Task light creates glare	Reposition light to avoid screen reflection. Use directional shades.
Light is too harsh	Add diffusers. Select warmer color temperatures. Use dimmable lights.
Not enough light	Move light closer to the work surface. Choose higher lumen output.

Lighting 203: Limitations
- Some tasks require both ambient and task lighting
- Hardwired installations may require professional services
- Household members must develop new habits to maximize savings

References and resources: <www.suspra.com/practice/energy/lighting-203.html>

Optimizing Fenestration 103: Opening Windows

Open windows in summer to catch cross breezes instead of running fans

Allow natural pressure differences to bring in fresh air and exhaust stale air by opening windows on two different sides of a building and providing an unobstructed path for air to flow between them.

References and resources: <www.suspra.com/practice/energy/optimizing-fenestration-103.html>

Plumbing 202: Lowering Temperatures

Lower the temperature of domestic hot water for showers, sinks, and washing

Most water heaters are set to 140°F (60°C), but 120°F (49°C) is generally sufficient for household needs, reducing the risk of scalding and saving energy. To adjust your water heater, locate the thermostat dial (often near the bottom of the tank) and turn it to the desired setting. If you have a newer model, it might have a digital display. For tankless water heaters, consult the manufacturer's instructions. By reducing the temperature, you'll use less energy to heat water.

References and resources: <www.suspra.com/practice/energy/plumbing-202.html>

Plumbing 302: Scheduling Hot Water

Put your water heat on a timer and schedule your use of hot water

Install a water heater timer to cut power during programmed periods when hot water is unlikely to be used, reducing standby heat loss—the energy wasted maintaining hot water temperature. Greatest savings occur in homes with predictable usage, long periods without hot water needs, and water heaters in unconditioned spaces. Energy savings typically range from 5-12% of water heating costs, with investment usually paying for itself within a year.

Plumbing 302: Equipment & Materials
- Water heater timer (mechanical or digital, $20-$60)

Plumbing 302: Steps
1. *Hire a handyman if you doubt your ability to install a water heater timer*
2. Assess your household hot water usage
   - Track when hot water is used
   - Create a schedule that clusters usage into specific time blocks
3. Select an appropriate timer
   - Mechanical timers ($20-$40): Limited programming but cheaper
   - Digital timers ($40-$60): Multiple on/off cycles and programming options
4. Install the timer per manufacturer's instructions
5. Program the timer based on usage
   - Set timer to heat water 30-60 minutes before scheduled use
   - Program to turn off during long periods of non-use
   - Include buffer time after expected use
6. Create a written schedule for household
7. Fine-tune for maximum savings
   - Monitor energy usage
   - Adjust for seasonal changes

Plumbing 302: Definitions
- **Buffer time**: Additional heating time after expected usage
- **Digital programmable timer**: Electronic timer with multiple daily settings
- **Mechanical timer**: Uses physical pins to create on/off cycles
- **Recovery time**: Period required to reheat water after use
- **Standby heat loss**: Energy wasted maintaining water temperature when not in use

Plumbing 302: Troubleshooting

Problem	Solutions
Hot water runs out	Extend heating periods. Boost water temperature setting.
Timer doesn't work	Check electrical connections. Verify power to the timer.
Household resists	Start with a generous schedule. Be flexible about special needs.
Hard to see savings	Compare energy bills before and after. Monitor hot water circuit.

Plumbing 302: Limitations
- Not suitable for tankless water heaters
- Less effective for unpredictable usage patterns
- Some gas water heaters require specialized timers
- May require schedule adjustments for guests or special events
- Timer failure could result in no hot water

References and resources: <www.suspra.com/practice/energy/plumbing-302.html>

Refrigerating 202: Operating Just One

Operate a single refrigerator instead of multiple ones.

Consolidate items into a single refrigerator rather than keeping two refrigerators running.

References and resources: <www.suspra.com/practice/energy/refrigerating-202.html>

Refrigerating 203: Raising Temperatures

Raise the temperature of your refrigerator without spoiling food too quickly

Raise refrigerator and freezer temperatures to the highest safe settings (staying below 40°F/4.4°C for refrigerators) to reduce energy consumption by 2-9% while maintaining food safety. Each degree Fahrenheit you raise the temperature saves approximately 2-3% of the refrigerator's energy use. Temperature zones vary inside refrigerators, with the back wall and bottom shelves typically coldest and door compartments warmest.

Refrigerating 203: Equipment & Materials
- Two refrigerator thermometers
- Notebook for tracking
- *Optional: Digital temperature logger*

Refrigerating 203: Steps
1. Measure current temperatures in refrigerator and freezer
   - Place thermometer in middle shelf of refrigerator
   - Place second thermometer in freezer or move first one after recording
   - Wait 24 hours before reading; record baseline temperatures
2. Set optimal temperature targets
   - Standard refrigerator: 35-38°F (1.7-3.3°C); Energy-efficient: 38-40°F (3.3-4.4°C)
   - Standard freezer: 0°F (-18°C); Energy-efficient freezer: 0-5°F (-18 to -15°C)
3. Adjust refrigerator temperature
   - Raise temperature 1 degree at a time
   - Wait 24 hours between adjustments
   - Measure and record new temperature
4. Adjust freezer temperature (if separate control)
   - Follow same gradual process as refrigerator
5. Organize refrigerator for efficiency
   - Place perishable items on lower shelves (coldest area)
   - Store condiments in door shelves (warmest area)
   - Keep fruits and vegetables in designated drawers
   - Leave space between items for air circulation
6. Monitor food for spoilage
   - Check perishables daily for first week; look for changes in color, texture, or odor
   - Note changes in shelf life
   - Adjust temperatures if needed

Refrigerating 203: Definitions
- **Danger Zone**: Temperatures between 40-140°F (4.4-60°C) where bacteria multiply rapidly
- **Temperature buffer**: Margin to accommodate door openings and ambient temperature
- **Temperature gradient**: Variation in temperature between different areas of the refrigerator

Refrigerating 203: Troubleshooting

Problem	Solutions
Food spoiling faster	Lower temperature. Check door seals. Spread food out.
Temperatures vary	Check for blocked vents. Ensure adequate space between items.

Refrigerating 203: Limitations

- Results vary based on refrigerator age, model, and condition
- Older refrigerators may have poor temperature control
- Ambient room temperature affects performance
- Some foods are more sensitive to temperature changes

References and resources: <www.suspra.com/practice/energy/refrigerating-203.html>

Refrigerating 302: Moving Refrigerators

Move your refrigerator so it isn't next to any heat sources, such as an oven

Your refrigerator works harder and uses more energy when it's located next to a heat source like an oven, dishwasher, or direct sunlight. By simply relocating your refrigerator, you can significantly improve its efficiency. Position the refrigerator away from these heat sources, ensuring there's adequate ventilation around it. This simple move allows the refrigerator to maintain its internal temperature with less effort, reducing energy consumption. Aim for at least a few inches of clearance on all sides.

References and resources: <www.suspra.com/practice/energy/refrigerating-302.html>

Refrigerating 303: Downsizing Refrigerators

Install a smaller refrigerator that uses less power

Save energy with a new, smaller refrigerator to replace an older, larger model. Refrigerators typically account for 7-15% of a home's electricity use. Modern refrigerators are substantially more efficient than older models, and smaller refrigerators use less energy than larger models.

Refrigerating 303: Equipment & Materials

- Smaller energy-efficient refrigerator

Refrigerating 303: Steps

1. Carefully evaluate actual refrigeration needs
   - Analyze how much space you actually use
   - Identify items that could be stored differently
   - Determine minimum capacity needs
2. Research energy-efficient smaller refrigerators
   - Look for ENERGY STAR certified models
   - Compare annual energy consumption (kWh/year)
3. Remove old refrigerator and install new refrigerator

Refrigerating 303: Definitions

- **Annual energy consumption**: Electricity a refrigerator uses in a year (kWh)
- **ENERGY STAR**: Certification for appliances meeting strict energy efficiency guidelines

Revision: 25.1.8

Refrigerating 303: Troubleshooting

Problem	Solutions
No energy savings	Check temperature settings. Ensure proper ventilation. Verify door seals.
Food doesn't fit well	Use stackable containers. Adjust shopping habits.

Refrigerating 303: Limitations
- Less cold storage for perishables and frozen food

References and resources: <www.suspra.com/practice/energy/refrigerating-303.html>

Refrigerating 401: Digging a Root Cellar

Dig a root cellar to store food

Build a root cellar to use the earth's constant below-ground temperature (typically 50-60°F at 10 feet deep) and use ventilation and evaporation to maintain humidity and temperatures suitable for storing food. Root cellars work through several principles: earth's constant temperature, cool air sinking, warm air rising, and the cooling effect of evaporation. Different designs (hillside, underground room, basement section, buried container) offer various advantages depending on your land and needs.

Refrigerating 401: Equipment & Materials
- Land with suitable soil for a root cellar, or section of a basement
- Drainage materials (gravel, perforated pipe)
- Ventilation pipes (4-6" PVC or metal)
- Vapor barrier (6-mil polyethylene) and insulation for below-grade installation
- Wood for shelving and door frame
- Door with weatherstripping
- Thermometer and hygrometer
- *Optional: Concrete for floor and walls*

Refrigerating 401: Steps
1. ***Hire a contractor if you doubt your ability to create a root cellar***
2. Plan and design your root cellar
   - Size based on cold storage needs (25-100 square feet)
   - Choose location with proper drainage
   - Select type: hillside, underground room, basement section, or buried container
   - Check building codes and obtain permits
   - Call 811 to mark utilities before digging
3. Follow these steps if digging a new root cellar into the ground or a hillside.
4. Test soil conditions
   - Dig test holes for bedrock, water table, or unstable soil
   - Perform percolation test to assess drainage
5. Excavate the root cellar
   - Dig to minimum depth of 4 feet (below frost line)
   - Create slightly sloped floor toward drainage point
6. Establish drainage system
   - Install perimeter drain with buried perforated pipe around outside base
   - Create gravel floor with slight slope to drain point
   - Consider a sump pump if water table is high or soil drains poorly

7. Construct walls and ceiling
   - For earthen walls: compact soil and apply lime wash
   - For reinforced walls: install concrete, stone, or block
   - Create ceiling with pressure-treated beams and cover with waterproof membrane
8. Insulate appropriately
   - Cold climates: insulate ceiling and upper walls, leave lower walls uninsulated
   - Hot climates: insulate all walls
   - Install vapor barrier on warm side of insulation
     - Interior in cold climates
     - Exterior in warm climates
9. Install ventilation system
   - Create two vents for air circulation (intake and exhaust)
   - Position intake vent lower and exhaust vent higher
   - Extend vent pipes 12-24 inches above ground
   - Install screened caps to prevent pest entry
10. Build entrance
    - Install well-sealed door with weather stripping
    - Consider double-door system for better temperature control
11. Create storage systems
    - Install wooden shelving (cedar is rot-resistant)
    - Keep shelves 1-2 inches from walls for air circulation
    - Include different height sections for various crops
12. Monitor and adjust
    - Install thermometer and hygrometer
    - Maintain 32-40°F and 85-95% humidity
    - Make seasonal adjustments to ventilation

Refrigerating 401: Definitions

- **Frost line**: Maximum depth to which ground freezes in winter
- **Passive ventilation**: Airflow system operating without electricity
- **Percolation test**: Assessment of how quickly water drains through soil
- **Thermal mass**: Materials that absorb and store heat energy
- **Vapor barrier**: Material that restricts moisture movement

Refrigerating 401: Troubleshooting

Problem	Solutions
Water seepage	Improve external drainage. Add perimeter drainage. Regrade land.
Too cold in winter	Reduce ventilation during extreme cold. Add thermal mass (buckets of water). Increase insulation on ceiling and door.
Too warm	Increase ventilation, especially at night. Add more soil over top. Create a cooling tunnel underground for incoming air.
Humidity too low	Decrease ventilation. Bring in more water.
Humidity too high	Increase ventilation. Add moisture-absorbing materials.
Pests	Seal all cracks. Add fine mesh screens to vents. Set traps.

Sustainable Practices Handbook Energy Practices: Conserving Energy

Refrigerating 401: Limitations

- Requires significant physical labor
- Not suitable for areas with high water tables or frequent flooding
- Difficult in urban settings with space limitations
- Challenging in areas with bedrock near surface
- Limited temperature control compared to powered refrigeration
- Requires regular monitoring and seasonal adjustments

References and resources: <www.suspra.com/practice/energy/refrigerating-401.html>

Synchronizing 401: Using Solar Power

Synchronize electricity usage with solar power generation

To maximize the benefits of solar energy, synchronize your electricity usage with periods of peak solar generation. This means scheduling energy-intensive tasks, such as running dishwashers, washing machines, and charging electric vehicles, during the sunniest parts of the day. For example, if you have a solar panel system, monitor your energy production using a smart meter or monitoring app. Then, adjust your appliance usage to coincide with peak production times. This reduces reliance on grid electricity and increases self-consumption of solar power. Consider using smart home devices or timers to automate these processes. Many smart thermostats, for instance, can be programmed to pre-cool your home during midday when solar production is highest, reducing the need for evening air conditioning. This practice not only lowers your electricity bill but also reduces the overall carbon footprint by utilizing clean, renewable energy when it is most abundant.

References and resources: <www.suspra.com/practice/energy/synchronizing-401.html>

Synchronizing 402: Getting Sleep

Set your sleep schedule to make maximum use of sunlight

The simple practice of setting your sleep schedule so you are awake and able to make maximum use of natural daylight has transformative effects. (Daylight saving was introduced in Germany in 1916 during World War I as an energy-saving measure, and was adopted by the United States in 1942 during World War II for the same reason.) When you set your alarm clock by the sun, you will naturally be able to:

- Reduce the need for artificial lighting.
- Synchronize your power demand to match solar power production.
- Travel more safely by walking or cycling.
- Turn down heating sooner overnight during winter.

References and resources: <www.suspra.com/practice/energy/synchronizing-402.html>

Washing 302: Hanging Laundry

Hang clothes to dry rather than use a gas or electric clothes dryer

Hang laundry to dry to save energy while extending clothing life. Air-dried clothes suffer less dryer wear and tear. Indoor drying adds beneficial moisture to dry indoor air during winter.

Washing 302: Equipment & Materials

- Clothespins or clips
- For outdoor drying: clothesline (rope, wire, or retractable)

- For indoor drying: folding drying rack, over-the-door rack, or retractable indoor clothesline

Washing 302: Steps

1. Use a high-speed spin cycle in your washing machine
2. Set up your drying area and hang laundry to dry
   - For outdoor lines: best choice is a sunny, breezy location
   - For indoor racks: place in well-ventilated area
3. Check for dryness
   - Items are dry when they feel room temperature with no damp spots
   - Check seams and waistbands, which dry more slowly

Washing 302: Definitions

- **Clothesline**: Rope, cord, wire, or plastic line for hanging laundry
- **Drying rack**: Freestanding frame with horizontal rods for indoor drying
- **Line-drying**: Practice of hanging wet laundry to dry naturally

Washing 302: Troubleshooting

Problem	Solutions
Stiff clothes	Use less detergent. Add vinegar to the rinse cycle. Snap items vigorously.
Slow indoor drying	Increase air circulation with a fan. Position near heat sources.
Fading colors	Hang colorful items inside-out. Dry in shade. Remove as soon as dry.
Wrinkled clothes	Smooth out wrinkles before hanging. Use hangers for shirts.
Items blowing off line	Use multiple clothespins per item. Pin at opposite corners.

Washing 302: Limitations

- Requires more time than using a dryer
- Weather-dependent for outdoor drying
- May be restricted by homeowners associations
- May increase indoor humidity in already damp environments
- Some fabrics become stiffer than when machine-dried

References and resources: <www.suspra.com/practice/energy/washing-302.html>

Electrifying

Cooking 304: Cooking with Electricity

Upgrade to a 100% electric cooking system

Reduce energy consumption and prevent pollution by upgrading to 100% electric cooking appliances. Most full-size electric range and oven combinations require a dedicated 240 volt 50 amp circuit, which may require upgrading your utility service and electrical panel. For power outage concerns, consider a wood stove or a small emergency propane stove solely for emergencies.

Cooking 304: Equipment, Materials & Costs
- Adequate electrical service (200 amps) and electrical panel (40 slots)
- $50-$150 for an electric pressure cooker
- $100-200 for plug-in induction cook plates
- $200-$3,000 for microwave ovens
- $1,000-$8,000+ for an induction range and convection oven

Cooking 304: Steps
1. Research electric cooking appliances
   - Induction cooktops and ranges
   - Electric convection ovens
   - Electric pressure cookers, rice cookers, slow cookers
   - Electric grills and specialty devices
   - Microwave ovens
2. Create a transition plan
   - Prioritize which appliances to replace first
   - Choose between built-in or countertop options
   - Plan for interim solutions if needed
3. Consult professionals
   - Electrician to evaluate home's electrical service and circuits
   - Contractor for kitchen renovations if needed
   - Salesperson for appliances
4. Upgrade electrical service and panel (if necessary)
5. Select and purchase electric appliances
6. Remove fuel-burning appliances
7. Install new electric appliances
8. Learn new cooking techniques

Cooking 304: Definitions
- **Amperage (Amp):** Measurement of electrical current; most homes have 100-200 amp service
- **Voltage:** Electrical potential; standard outlets provide 120V while electric ranges use 240V

Cooking 304: Troubleshooting

Problem	Solutions
Limited electrical capacity	Upgrade electrical panel. Install load management systems. Use multiple smaller appliances instead of one large one.

Problem	Solutions
Difficulty adjusting to electric cooking	Practice with various temperature settings. Use quality cookware with thick bases for better heat distribution.
Power outages affecting cooking	Install a battery backup system. Keep a portable power station for small appliances. Plan cold meal options.

Cooking 304: Limitations
- Electrical upgrades can be expensive in older homes
- Some buildings have restrictions on electrical modifications
- Rental properties may not allow permanent changes
- Power outages affect electric cooking without backup

References and resources: <www.suspra.com/practice/energy/cooking-304.html>

Driving 303: Driving with Electricity

Replace all fuel-burning vehicles with fully electric ones

Prevent pollution and drive a vehicle that is three to four times more energy-efficient than fuel-burning vehicles. EVs have higher upfront costs but lower operating expenses. Modern EVs typically offer 200-400 miles of range from a full battery. Most modern EV batteries retain 80% capacity after 10 years or 100,000 miles. Home charging meets 80-90% of most owners' needs. Level 1 charging (120V) provides 3-5 miles of range per hour, while Level 2 (240V) delivers 15-40 miles per hour.

Driving 303: Equipment, Materials & Costs
- Electric passenger vehicle ($30,000-$100,000+)
- Parking space with access to electricity
- *Optional: Level 2 charging equipment (240 volt)*

Driving 303: Steps
1. Assess your vehicle needs (travel distances, passengers, cargo, towing)
2. Research available electric vehicles
   - Go for test drives
   - Compare new, used, and lease options
   - Review warranty terms, especially for battery
3. Plan for charging infrastructure
   - Charging while parked or charging at public charging stations
   - For apartments, discuss options with management
4. Purchase or lease vehicle
5. Set up home charging (if applicable)
   - Start with Level 1 (existing 120 volt outlet)
   - Install Level 2 240 volt outlet or Level 2 charger if necessary
   - Charge at off-peak times if possible and register for special EV electricity rates if available
6. Learn efficient driving
   - Practice regenerative braking
   - Understand climate control's effect on range
   - Precondition cabin temperature while plugged in
7. Plan for longer trips
   - Research compatible charging networks

- Set up charging network apps
- Plan routes around charging stations
- Allow time for charging stops

Driving 303: Definitions

- **Battery electric vehicle (BEV)**: Vehicle powered exclusively by electricity stored in a battery
- **Charging levels**:
  - **Level 1**: Standard 120V outlet charging (1.3-2.4 kW)
  - **Level 2**: 240V charging system (3.3-19.2 kW)
  - **DC Fast Charging**: High-powered stations (50-350 kW) for rapid charging
- **kWh (kilowatt-hour)**: Unit of energy for battery capacity
- **Preconditioning**: Warming or cooling the vehicle while connected to a charger
- **Regenerative braking**: System capturing energy during braking to recharge the battery

Driving 303: Troubleshooting

Problem	Solutions
Range less than advertised	Adjust climate controls. Reduce highway speeds. Maintain proper tire pressure. Precondition while plugged in.
Home electrical panel limitations	Start with Level 1 charging. Investigate load-sharing systems. Use public charging to supplement.
Charging station issues on trips	Plan routes with multiple apps. Have backup locations. Maintain a range buffer. Join multiple networks.
Winter range reduction	Precondition while plugged in. Use seat heaters instead of cabin heating.
Apartment charging limitations	Request installation from property management. Use workplace charging or public charging stations.

Driving 303: Limitations

- Not all vehicle categories have electric options yet
- Long-distance travel requires more planning
- Cold weather can reduce range by 20-40%
- Rural areas have limited public charging
- Apartment dwellers face charging challenges
- High upfront costs despite lower operating expenses
- Battery degradation affects long-term value

References and resources: <www.suspra.com/practice/movement/driving-303.html>

Heating & Cooling 307: Heating Air with Electricity

Upgrade to a 100% electric space heating system

Upgrade to 100% electric space heating to reduce energy consumption and prevent pollution. Heat pumps are the most energy-efficient electric heating option, providing 2-4 units of heat energy for each unit of electricity consumed. Modern cold-climate heat pumps work efficiently even when outdoor temperatures drop to -13°F (-25°C). Ductless mini-splits offer flexibility for homes without existing ductwork. Your home's electrical service may need upgrading from 100A to 200A or even 400A, especially if you're electrifying other systems. Numerous incentives are available to offset costs.

Sustainable Practices Handbook
Energy Practices: Electrifying

Heating & Cooling 307: Equipment & Materials

- 200 or 400 amp electric service and electrical panel (40 or 80 slots)
- Utility bills for past 12 months
- Floor plan of your home
- Energy recovery or heat recovery ventilator ($1,500-$4,500)
- Electric baseboard heating ($2.50-$10 per square foot)
- Electric radiant panels ($8-$15 per square foot)
- Electric boiler ($1,500-$9,000)
- Suspra air-to-air heat pump ($4,000-$15,000+)
- Ground-source heat pump ($10,000-$50,000+)

Heating & Cooling 307: Steps

1. *Hire a professional if you doubt your ability to plan a heating system upgrade*
2. Do a Manual J residential load calculation for your home
3. Improve air sealing and insulation to reduce heating and cooling loads (if necessary)
4. Install an ERV or an HRV to provide fresh air (if necessary)
5. Determine your electrical capacity
   - Check service panel rating and available spaces for circuit breakers
   - Consult an electrician about potential service upgrades
6. Research electric heating options
   - Air-to-air heat pumps (ducted or ductless mini-splits)
   - Air-to-water heat pumps (hydronic distribution)
   - Ground source (geothermal) water-to-water or water-to-air heat pumps
   - Electric resistance options as backup or supplemental heat
7. Obtain three quotes from qualified HVAC contractors
8. Select your system and contractor
9. Upgrade your electrical service and panel (if needed)
10. Remove existing fuel-burning equipment and chimneys (if applicable)
11. Install heating distribution system and heating and cooling equipment
12. If you live in a cold climate, consider a wood stove as a backup heat source
13. Plan for solar array and battery backup

Heating & Cooling 307: Definitions

- **Air source heat pump (ASHP)**: System that transfers heat between indoor and outdoor air
- **COP (Coefficient of Performance)**: Ratio of useful heating provided relative to energy input
- **Heat pump**: Device that moves heat from a cold space to a warm space using a refrigeration cycle
- **Load calculation**: Determine heating requirements (Manual J is the standard method)
- **Manual J calculation**: Standard method for determining residential heating and cooling load
- **Minisplit**: Ductless heat pump system with an outdoor unit connected to indoor air handlers

Heating & Cooling 307: Troubleshooting

Problem	Solutions
Inadequate electrical service	Upgrade service.
Cold climate performance concerns	Select cold-climate rated heat pumps. Consider a wood stove as backup heating for extreme conditions.
Limited space for equipment	Consider mini-splits or packaged units.

Revision: 25.1.8

Problem	Solutions
High upfront costs	Borrow. Apply for rebates and incentives.

Heating & Cooling 307: Limitations
- Higher initial costs than fossil fuel systems
- Some homes require substantial electrical service upgrades
- Converting hydronic (radiator) systems is more complex than forced air
- Cold climate performance may require backup heating in extreme conditions

References and resources: <www.suspra.com/practice/energy/heating-cooling-307.html>

Heating & Cooling 402: Organizing a Buying Group

Organize a buying group in your neighborhood for heat pumps

Help more people install heat pumps in your neighborhood with a buying group of 5-20 households who coordinate heat pump purchases and installations. Aim for discounts of 10-25% compared to individual purchases, as contractors reduce customer acquisition costs and optimize installation scheduling. Focus on air-to-air heat pumps, which are a mature technology. Time installations during spring and fall for better pricing and less disruptive installations.

Heating & Cooling 402: Equipment & Materials
- Meeting space (physical or virtual)
- Website or social media group

Heating & Cooling 402: Steps
1. Research heat pumps and local installers
   - Learn about heat pump types and manufacturers
   - Identify qualified local HVAC contractors
   - Research available rebates and incentives
2. Gauge community interest
   - Talk to neighbors about their heating needs
   - Create a simple survey
   - Host an informal gathering
   - Establish a minimum number of participants (5-10 homes)
3. Create an organizing committee of 3-5 committed neighbors
4. Develop a communication system
   - Create an email list or social media group
   - Set up a simple website or shared document on a cloud service
5. Reach out to contractors
   - Develop a request for proposals (RFP)
   - Contact multiple qualified contractors
     - Ask about volume discounts
     - Request information about experience and warranties
6. Host an educational meeting
   - Invite interested neighbors
   - Share information about heat pumps and the buying process
   - Address questions and concerns
7. Arrange for contractors to assess interested homes
8. Solicit and compare proposals

Sustainable Practices Handbook Energy Practices: Electrifying

- - - Request detailed proposals from 3 contractors
    - Create a comparison sheet
    - Host a meeting to review proposals
    - Select 1-2 final contractors
9. Negotiate volume discounts and warranties
10. Finalize group commitment
11. Coordinate installations
    - Designate a point person for troubleshooting
    - Create a shared calendar to track installations
12. Follow up
    - Host a post-installation gathering
    - Share energy savings data
    - Consider expanding to other energy improvements

Heating & Cooling 402: Definitions

- **Air-to-air heat pump**: System that transfers heat between outdoor and indoor air
- **Cold climate heat pump**: Designed to operate efficiently in below-freezing temperatures

Heating & Cooling 402: Troubleshooting

Problem	Solutions
Not enough interest	Expand your geographic area, partner with environmental organizations
Contractors unwilling	Approach more contractors. Increase group size. Partner with programs.
Homes too different	Standardize equipment brands while customizing capacity.
People drop out	Collect a refundable deposit. Establish clear commitment protocols.

Heating & Cooling 402: Limitations

- Requires significant volunteer time to organize
- Success depends on finding cooperative contractors
- Group decision-making can be slower than individual purchases
- Not suited for emergency replacements when heating systems fail

References and resources: <www.suspra.com/practice/energy/heating-cooling-402.html>

Landscaping 201: Borrowing Electric Equipment

Borrow or rent electric outdoor power equipment rather than fuel-burning equipment

When you borrow or rent a lawnmower, leaf blower, string trimmer ("weed whacker"), chain saw, or other outdoor power equipment, choose an electric model rather than a fuel-burning one.

References and resources: <www.suspra.com/practice/energy/landscaping-201.html>

Landscaping 202: Buying Electric Equipment

Buy electric outdoor power equipment

If you need to own a leaf blower, lawn mower, chain saw, chipper, weed wacker, hedge trimmer, snow blower, or other outdoor power equipment, buy an electric one. Manufacturers offer both corded and cordless electric equipment. Corded models are more sustainable but less convenient than models that use a battery. For corded equipment, you'll need an outdoor-rated extension cord. An extension cord reel is handy to manage the cord. Batteries have not yet been standardized, so if you do choose a cordless model, consider the range of tools available that can share a battery and charger.

References and resources: <www.suspra.com/practice/energy/landscaping-202.html>

Lending 401: Lending Out Electric Tools

Create a library of things to lend out electric tools

Establish a tool library in your community to enable shared access to occasionally-used tools, reducing the total number of items manufactured while increasing community access to quality equipment. Battery management is crucial for cordless tools; emphasize electrical safety with regular testing for proper grounding and insulation. Track usage to identify which tools are most valuable to your community and which might need replacement.

Lending 401: Equipment & Materials
- Electric tools to lend
- Tool maintenance supplies
- Secure storage space with shelving
- Inventory management system (logbook or digital)
- Labeling system
- User agreements and liability waivers, checkout and return forms
- *Optional: Battery chargers, insurance policy, security system*

Lending 401: Steps
1. Plan your tool library: scale, goals, and legal structure
2. Secure resources: storage space, budget, legal organization, volunteers
3. Collect electric tools
   - Request tool donations from individuals and businesses
   - Apply for grants to purchase high-demand tools
   - Prioritize energy-efficient, durable models
4. Set up inventory management and maintenance schedule
5. Decide hours of operation and lending policies
   - Create membership requirements and liability waivers
   - Establish borrowing periods
   - Develop fee structures and damage policies
6. Implement safety protocols
   - Create safety guidelines for each tool
   - Develop tool inspection process
   - Include basic training requirements for specialized tools
7. Design checkout and return procedures and protocols, including cleaning requirements
8. Promote your tool library at community meetings; partner with local organizations
9. Train users and volunteers
10. Operate program and evaluate

Lending 401: Definitions
- **Liability waiver**: Legal agreement that borrowers won't sue the tool library for injuries

Lending 401: Troubleshooting

Problem	Solutions
Tools damaged	Implement pre- and post-lending inspections. Require deposits.
Battery management	Implement "return charged" policy. Keep spare batteries.
Liability concerns	Obtain insurance, create clear liability waivers, require safety training
Tools not returned	Require deposits. Charge late fees. Revoke memberships.

Lending 401: Limitations

- Requires dedicated storage space with appropriate security
- Needs consistent volunteer or staff time for management
- Tool maintenance requires specific knowledge
- Maintenance costs increase as tools age and usage increases

References and resources: <www.suspra.com/practice/energy/lending-401.html>

Plumbing 303: Heating Water with Electricity

Upgrade to a 100% electric water heating system

Use electricity to heat domestic water for showers, sinks, and appliances to prevent pollution and save energy. Heat pump water heaters extract heat from surrounding air and transfer it to water, making them 2-4 times more efficient than electric resistance models, and much more efficient than fuel-burning heaters. They're rated by Uniform Energy Factor (UEF), with most units ranging from 2.0 to 4.0, and work best in spaces that maintain temperatures above 40°F year-round. Tankless electric units eliminate standby losses but require high power draw (20-30kW). Traditional electric resistance water heaters draw less power (5 kW) but cost more to operate, with UEF ratings of 0.9 to 0.95. All electric heaters can be powered by solar electricity; they complement batteries for energy storage.

Plumbing 303: Equipment & Materials

- Electric water heater
  - Heat pump water heater
  - Electric on-demand (tankless) water heater
  - Electric resistance water heater
- Electrical panel with sufficient capacity

Plumbing 303: Steps

1. Plan your installation
   - Assess your household's hot water needs
   - Measure available space for new water heater
   - Verify electrical service capacity
   - Check local building codes and permit requirements
   - Choose between heat pump, resistance, or tankless
2. Select appropriate water heater
   - For heat pump water heaters:
     - Choose appropriate tank size (typically 50-80 gallons)
     - Verify installation location has 700-1,000 cubic feet of air space
     - Ensure location maintains temperatures between 40-90°F

- For tankless water heaters:
  - Calculate required flow rate and temperature rise based on groundwater temperature
  - Determine necessary kilowatt rating
3. ***Hire a licensed plumber and electrician (unless you can do the work yourself)***
4. Obtain necessary permits
5. Upgrade electrical service and panel (if necessary)
6. Have a licensed gas technician cap gas line to old water heater (if necessary)
7. Install new electric water heater per manufacturer's instructions
   - For heat pump units, install condensate drain line and ensure adequate airflow
8. Verify or install new dedicated electrical circuit
   - Verify proper grounding, wire gauge, and circuit breaker
9. Commission water heater
10. Optimize system
    - Set temperature (typically 120°F) and operating mode (for heat pump water heaters)
    - Insulate hot water pipes
    - Schedule time hot water will be available (if appropriate)
11. Maintain system annually
    - Flush tank to remove sediment
    - Test pressure relief valve
    - For heat pump units, clean air filter

Plumbing 303: Definitions

- **Condensate**: Water formed when moisture in air condenses on the cold evaporator coil
- **Heat pump**: Device that transfers heat using mechanical energy
- **Recovery rate**: Amount of water a heater can heat to a specified temperature in a given time
- **Standby loss:** Energy wasted keeping water hot when it is not needed
- **Uniform Energy Factor (UEF)**: Efficiency rating for water heaters; higher is better

Plumbing 303: Troubleshooting

Problem	Solutions
Insufficient hot water	Check for sediment buildup. Verify unit sizing. Increase temperature.
Excessive noise	Ensure the unit is level. Check for objects in the fan.
Condensate overflow	Clean out the condensate line. Ensure proper slope. Use a pump.
Circuit tripping	Verify correct circuit sizing. Check for loose connections.

Plumbing 303: Limitations

- Heat pump water heaters require adequate air volume and temperature
- Heat pump units are larger than conventional water heaters
- Tankless electric water heaters require very high electrical capacity
- Recovery rates for heat pump water heaters are typically slower than gas models
- Heat pump water heaters make more noise than conventional water heaters

References and resources: <www.suspra.com/practice/energy/plumbing-303.html>

Solarizing

Charging 101: Using Solar Chargers

Use solar chargers for cell phones and small devices

Convert sunlight to electricity to charge your small devices, such as smartphones and headphones. Charge the integrated battery in a portable solar charger using its built-in solar module or a separate solar module connected with a USB cable. A separate solar module without a battery is a better choice, because modules can withstand the elements better than batteries. You can use a separate solar module to shade your solar charger, extending the life of its battery. Later, connect your device to the solar charger to transfer stored electricity from the charger's battery to your device's battery. Most batteries can now handle hundreds of full charge and discharge cycles before losing significant capacity.

Charging 101: Equipment & Materials

- Small devices to charge via USB cable (smartphone, tablet, headphones)
- Portable solar charger with integrated battery and USB ports
- USB charging cable for your device
- Separate solar module with USB output (recommended)

Charging 101: Steps

1. Purchase a solar charger with integrated battery storage
2. *Optional: purchase a separate solar module with USB output*
3. Position solar charger or solar module in direct sunlight to charge integrated battery
4. Use energy stored in solar charger to charge your device

Charging 101: Definitions

- **Battery bank/Power bank**: Portable battery that stores energy for later use
- **Port:** A slot where a cable can plug in
- **Solar charger:** A device that combines a solar module and a battery to store electricity
- **Solar module:** A device that converts sunlight to electricity (also called a "panel")
- **Universal Serial Bus (USB):** A cable standard that allows interconnecting devices

Charging 101: Troubleshooting

Problem	Solutions
Device not charging or charging slowly	Ensure modules are in direct sunlight and properly angled. Clean modules. Check cable connections. Try a different cable.
Solar charging stops when clouds pass	Normal behavior. Wait for the sun to reappear.
Battery percentage doesn't increase	Try better sun positioning. Use a USB digital meter to verify power flow. Check cable connections. Try a different cable.
Solar charger very hot	Some warming is normal. Shade under a separate solar module.

Charging 101: Limitations

- Solar charging is slower than charging from a wall outlet
- Weather and seasons affect performance

- Not suitable for high-power devices
- Requires direct sunlight; doesn't work at night or indoors
- Needs repositioning throughout the day

References and resources: <www.suspra.com/practice/energy/charging-101.html>

Choosing Solar 101: Choosing "Green" Electricity

Choose a "green" electricity supplier

Pay for green electricity to support renewable power without installing your own system. In deregulated markets, you select a supplier while your local utility delivers the electricity. In regulated markets, utilities may offer "green pricing" programs. Direct renewable supply means the supplier generates or purchases renewable electricity; renewable energy certificate (REC) programs match your usage with renewable generation elsewhere.

Choosing Solar 101: Equipment & Materials

- Your current electricity bill

Choosing Solar 101: Steps

1. Understand "green" electricity options
   - Switch to a renewable electricity supplier
   - Buy Renewable Energy Certificates (RECs)
   - Join a community solar program
   - Pay into a renewable electricity fund managed by a utility
2. Evaluate the green electricity options available to you
   - Compare renewable energy mix (solar, wind, hydro, biomass, geothermal)
   - Check for third-party certifications
   - Examine contract terms and pricing
   - Verify green claims
3. Choose and enroll in a green electricity plan
4. Monitor your electricity bills monthly to confirm continued enrollment

Choosing Solar 101: Definitions

- **Deregulated electricity market**: Consumers can choose their electricity supplier
- **Fixed-rate plan**: Electricity plan with constant price for the contract duration
- **Kilowatt-hour (kWh)**: Standard unit of electricity consumption
- **Megawatt-hour (MWh)**: 1,000 kWh
- **Renewable Energy Certificate (REC)**: Represents 1 megawatt-hour of renewable electricity

Choosing Solar 101: Troubleshooting

Problem	Solutions
No green electricity options available	Check for utility green pricing programs. Subscribe to community solar. Purchase RECs.
Verifying green claims	Get third-party certifications. Request disclosure documents.
Higher costs	Compare multiple suppliers. Reduce electricity consumption.
Confusing contracts	Request clear explanations. Prompt AI to explain.

Problem	Solutions
No change on bill	Contact the supplier and your utility to verify enrollment.

Choosing Solar 101: Limitations
- Not available in all areas, particularly regulated electricity markets
- Physical electricity still comes from local grid mix
- Contract terms may limit flexibility to switch providers
- Quality and environmental impact vary significantly between programs

References and resources: <www.suspra.com/practice/energy/choosing-solar-101.html>

Choosing Solar 102: Subscribing to Solar

Subscribe to a solar farm for electricity

Subscribe to a community solar farm to support solar energy without installing equipment on your property. Electricity from the solar arrays on the farm goes into the grid; you receive credits on your utility bill proportional to your share's production. As a subscriber, pay a monthly fee for the electricity the farm produces. Check contract terms regarding length of commitment and termination fees, if any.

Choosing Solar 102: Equipment & Materials
- Your electricity bills for past 12 months

Choosing Solar 102: Steps
1. Check availability of community solar farms in your area
   - Search online for "community solar" plus your location
   - Contact your utility company to understand billing
2. Compare available options and choose one
3. Monitor your subscription

Choosing Solar 102: Definitions
- **Allocation:** Your portion of the community solar farm's output
- **Bill credit:** Monetary credit applied to your utility bill
- **Community solar:** Solar system providing financial benefits to multiple subscribers
- **Escalator:** Clause increasing subscription rate by fixed percentage yearly
- **Virtual net metering:** System allowing credits from remote solar to apply to subscriber's bill

Choosing Solar 102: Troubleshooting

Problem	Solutions
No community solar available	Check nearby utility territories. Express interest to local organizations. Consider buying green electricity.
Bill credits lower than expected	Verify allocation matches contract. Check weather conditions. Ensure utility is correctly applying credits.
Moving to a new location	Within the same utility territory: transfer subscription. Otherwise, review the contract for transfer or termination options.

Problem	Solutions
Credits not appearing on bill	Confirm utility account information is correct. Check for initial credit delay (often 2-3 billing cycles).
Savings unclear	Keep a spreadsheet of bill credits versus subscription costs.

Choosing Solar 102: Limitations
- Not available everywhere
- Contract terms can be long (10-25 years) with termination fees
- Production varies seasonally and with weather
- Moving outside service territory complicates subscriptions

References and resources: <www.suspra.com/practice/energy/choosing-solar-102.html>

Installing Solar 201: Building a Solar Shed

Build a solar shed or greenhouse for storing and charging electric tools

Build a solar shed to combine storage functionality with renewable power generation for electric tools and lighting. Harness sunshine to charge batteries, eliminating the need for grid power. The heart of the system is a power bank which combines a charge controller, fuse, battery management system, and battery cells. An inverter is unnecessary (although many power banks include one) unless you'd like a 120 volt or 240 volt alternating current outlet for plug loads. Orient the solar modules to maximize energy collection; store electricity in batteries to have power when needed. Size the powerbank for your specific needs, secure it with weather-tight construction, and ensure safe electrical connections.

Installing Solar 201: Equipment & Materials
- Pre-built shed, or shed plans and materials
- Solar modules and mounting system (to attach modules to roof)
- Electrical wiring, disconnects, MC4 connectors, grounding equipment
- Integrated power bank or separate charge controller, fuse, and battery
- Basic construction tools: saw, drill, level, measuring tape, ladder
- *Optional: Inverter for alternating current loads, concrete blocks for foundation, weather barrier, siding, door, windows*

Installing Solar 201: Steps
1. Select sunny location with no shade during peak hours (10am-2pm)
2. Select a shed kit or design your own shed (typically 8×8 to 10×12 feet)
   - Design roof for optimal solar collection (25-45° angle)
   - Plan number of solar modules in array and voltage of array
   - Plan interior layout for tool storage and battery charging stations
3. Prepare foundation
   - Level site, establish corner points, and ensure roof points toward sun at noon
   - Install concrete blocks or build pressure-treated wood base frame (optional)
4. Deliver pre-built shed or build shed on site per plans
5. Mount solar modules (solar array) on roof
   - Install mounting system
   - Secure modules to mounting system
6. Install electrical components
   - Establish grounding

Sustainable Practices Handbook — Energy Practices: Solarizing

- Install combiner box (if necessary) and a disconnect (to stop power flow from array)
- Run solar wire from array to a disconnect near a power bank (charge controller and battery)
- Install power bank and inverter (optional) in ventilated area

7. Wire the system
   - Use an integrated power bank or create your own power bank
     - Connect battery to charge controller; put fuse on positive wire
   - Connect modules into a solar array; connect array to power bank
   - *Optional: Install inverter, circuit breakers, and receptacles for alternating current loads*
8. Charge the power bank batteries when sun shines on solar array
9. Use stored electricity
   - Plug in direct current loads (such as battery chargers) to the power bank
   - *Optional: plug in alternating current loads to receptacles powered by inverter*

Installing Solar 201: Definitions

- **Charge controller:** Regulates voltage and current flow in an electrical system
- **Inverter:** Converts direct current to alternating current
- **MC4 connectors:** Standard weatherproof connectors for solar wiring
- **Power bank:** A charge controller, fuse, battery management system, and battery cells
- **Solar module:** Solar cells enclosed in a rectangular frame with wires attached

Installing Solar 201: Troubleshooting

Problem	Solutions
No power	Clean array. Check for shading. Verify connections.
Battery loses charge	Test battery voltage. Clean terminals. Check controller settings.
Inverter shuts off	Check for overload. Ensure adequate ventilation. Verify battery voltage.
Winter performance	Insulate battery compartment. Keep batteries charged. Adjust array angle.

Installing Solar 201: Limitations

- Power generation varies with weather and seasons
- System performance depends on proper orientation and sunlight
- Battery performance diminishes in extreme temperatures

References and resources: <www.suspra.com/practice/energy/installing-solar-201.html>

Installing Solar 202: Lighting

Install solar-powered outdoor lighting

Deploy solar-powered outdoor lighting to provide nighttime illumination using daytime sunlight. LED technology combined with solar modules and batteries makes these standalone systems reliable year-round in most climates. Place solar modules to receive maximum direct sunlight. Seasonal adjustments may be necessary to capture solar energy in regions with significant seasonal variations.

Installing Solar 202: Equipment & Materials

- Solar light fixtures (path lights, spotlights, string lights, security lights)

Installing Solar 202: Steps

1. Plan your lighting layout
   - Space path lights 6-8 feet apart; position motion sensors appropriately
   - Ensure solar modules will receive at least six hours of direct sunlight daily
2. Select and install outdoor-rated solar lights per manufacturer's instructions
3. Test and monitor your installation:
   - Charge batteries by putting solar modules in full sun
   - Cover light sensor to simulate darkness
   - After a week, check that lights are still working at night

Installing Solar 202: Definitions

- **Lumens:** Measurement of brightness; higher values indicate brighter lights
- **Light sensor:** Component that activates the light when ambient light levels drop
- **PIR sensor:** Passive Infrared sensor used in motion-detecting lights
- **Watts:** Measure of power, used to indicate how quickly modules can recharge batteries

Installing Solar 202: Troubleshooting

Problem	Solutions
Lights don't turn on	Verify switch position. Clean solar module. Check battery connections.
Lights dim quickly	Reposition module for better sun exposure. Replace batteries.
Moisture inside fixture	Check seals. Apply silicone sealant if needed.
Dim lights in winter	Reposition for better winter sun exposure. Replace batteries.

Installing Solar 202: Limitations

- Performance depends on adequate sunlight
- Light brightness and duration lower than wired fixtures
- Cold temperatures reduce battery efficiency
- Batteries will fail long before solar modules and LED chips
- Not suitable for areas requiring consistent, bright illumination all night long

References and resources: <www.suspra.com/practice/energy/installing-solar-202.html>

Installing Solar 203: Pumping Water

Install solar-powered water pumps

Use solar energy to move water without grid electricity by installing a solar pump. Systems range from simple direct-solar setups that only run during sunlight hours to sophisticated battery-based systems for continuous operation. Direct systems connect solar panels directly to a DC pump and are most efficient but only operate during daylight. Systems with inverters allow use of AC pumps, but are less efficient. Battery-based systems store electricity to enable continuous pumping.

Installing Solar 203: Equipment & Materials

- Water pump (with high-efficiency direct current motor recommended)
- Plumbing supplies (pipe, fittings, Teflon tape)
- Solar module (25W-500W depending on application)
- Mounting hardware for solar module

Sustainable Practices Handbook — Energy Practices: Solarizing

- Wiring and electrical components (solar wire, MC4 connectors)
- Basic home improvement tools
- *Optional: Pump controller, float switch*
- *Power bank or charge controller, fuse, and battery*
- *Inverter*

Installing Solar 203: Steps

1. Plan your system
   - Determine water needs (gallons per day, flow rate, time of flow)
   - Estimate vertical lift, horizontal distance, and friction loss in piping
   - Choose between direct DC pumping or AC pump with inverter
   - Choose between intermittent pumping or continuous pumping
2. Select appropriate components
   - Choose pump type based on your water source and needs
   - Size solar array based on pump power requirements
   - Select a compatible power bank or inverter (for continuous pumping)
3. Prepare installation sites
   - Choose location with maximum sun exposure for solar array
   - Prepare stable mounting location for pumps
   - Choose sheltered location with easy access for power bank and inverter (if used)
4. Install pump controller or inverter (if used)
   - Mount in protected location away from water and direct sunlight
   - Enclose in weatherproof container with proper ventilation
5. Install the mounting system and attach solar module
6. Install the pump on surface or submersed, connected to plumbing
   - Install foot valve or check valve for surface pumps
7. Complete electrical connections
   - If using power bank (for continuous pumping)
     - First connect pump to power bank or inverter; test operation
     - Then connect solar array to power bank; verify power flow
   - If not using power bank (for intermittent pumping)
     - Connect solar array to DC pump; verify sunlight on array starts pump
   - Install float switch (if using); verify that it stops pump
8. Ensure all connections, both electrical and plumbing, are secure and watertight

Installing Solar 203: Definitions

- **Charge controller:** Device that controls voltage and current in an electrical system
- **Flow rate:** Volume of water moved per unit of time (gallons per minute)
- **Float switch:** Device that automatically turns a pump on or off based on water level
- **Friction loss:** Reduction in water pressure caused by water flowing through pipes and fittings
- **Pump controller:** Device that optimizes power to the pump based on available sunlight
- **Total Dynamic Head (TDH):** The total equivalent height water is pumped, including vertical distance, pipe friction, and pressure

Installing Solar 203: Troubleshooting

Problem	Solutions
Pump doesn't run	Check electrical connections. Test voltage. Ensure modules aren't shaded.
Water doesn't flow	Check priming. Look for air leaks, proper submersion, or clogs.

Revision: 25.1.8

Problem	Solutions
Reduced water output	Clean modules. Check for pipe restrictions. Test for air leaks.
Pump cycles rapidly	Adjust controller settings. Check for leaks. Verify float switch operation.

Installing Solar 203: Limitations

- Performance depends on available sunlight
- Direct solar systems cannot operate at night
- Deep wells require specialized high-head pumps
- Battery-based systems add significant cost and maintenance

References and resources: <www.suspra.com/practice/energy/installing-solar-203.html>

Installing Solar 204: Running Fans

Install solar-powered attic fans

Install a solar attic fan to remove hot air from your attic. Best for homes where attics are used for storage, they operate on sunlight without electricity costs and during power outages. Proper installation requires sealing the attic from the rest of the house (so the fan does not suck cooled, dehumidified air out of the house), ensuring soffit vents are adequate, and creating a watertight seal around the fan on the roof while maintaining optimal solar module orientation. The fan effectiveness depends on proper sizing (one standard fan per 1,200 square feet) and adequate intake ventilation through soffit vents.

References and resources: <www.suspra.com/practice/energy/installing-solar-204.html>

Installing Solar 301: Heating Water

Install solar thermal systems to heat water

Capture sunlight to heat water for domestic use. Active systems use pumps and controllers to circulate fluid between collectors and storage tanks; passive systems rely on natural convection (cold fluids sink, so putting the storage tank above the collectors naturally circulates water). Actively pumping an antifreeze solution through a heat exchanger makes pressurized closed-loop systems suitable for cold climates. Another strategy is to circulate water and use drain back to prevent pipes freezing and interrupting circulation of the heating fluid through the collectors. Household systems typically include 40-80 gallons of storage and 50-80 square feet of collector area for a family of four. New solar thermal hot water systems are very uncommon now in cold climates; most installers have switched to heat pump hot water heaters and solar photovoltaic modules, which are more reliable, useful, and durable.

Installing Solar 301: Equipment & Materials

- Solar collector panels (flat plate or evacuated tube)
- Mounting hardware to hold panels
- Storage tank with heat exchanger
- Circulation pump and controller with temperature sensors
- Heat transfer fluid (propylene glycol for closed-loop systems)
- Expansion tank and pressure relief valve
- Copper pipe, insulation, and plumbing fittings
- Tools for plumbing home improvement projects

Sustainable Practices Handbook

Installing Solar 301: Steps

1. Conduct site and needs assessment
   - Size system based on household hot water needs
   - Check roof structural integrity and available space
   - Determine optimal collector location (south-facing with 10-45° tilt)
   - Determine storage tank placement inside and pipe routing
2. Obtain necessary permits (plumbing and electrical)
3. Select appropriate system type
   - For freeze-prone climates:
     - Closed-loop system with antifreeze
     - Drain-back system with water
   - For mild climates: Direct water heating systems
4. Install mounting hardware on roof
5. Secure solar collectors to mounting hardware
6. Install storage tank and heat exchanger
7. Install pump station and controls
   - Mount circulation pump and controller near storage tank
   - Install expansion tank and pressure relief valves
   - Connect temperature sensors to controller
8. Run plumbing connections
   - Install supply and return lines between collectors and storage tank
   - Install valves and temperature sensors
   - Insulate all pipes
9. Fill and pressure test the system
10. Complete electrical connections per manufacturer's specifications
11. Commission the system
    - Verify proper pump operation
    - Check controller operation
    - Test pressure relief valve

Installing Solar 301: Definitions

- **Active solar system**: System using pumps and controllers to circulate heat transfer fluid
- **Closed-loop system**: System where antifreeze circulates through collectors and heat exchanger without mixing with potable water
- **Flat plate collector**: Solar collector with dark absorber plate under transparent covering
- **Evacuated tube collector**: Solar collector using glass tubes with vacuum insulation for higher efficiency
- **Heat exchanger**: Device transferring heat between fluids without mixing them

Installing Solar 301: Troubleshooting

Problem	Solutions
Not heating water	Check the controller, pump, and sensors. Ensure no trapped air.
Runs continuously	Check temperature sensors and controller settings.
Leaking connections	Turn off system, release pressure, and repair connections.
Freezing in collectors	Check antifreeze concentration. Verify freeze protection mode.
Excessive pressure	Check expansion tank pressure and relief valve operation.

Revision: 25.1.8

Sustainable Practices Handbook   Energy Practices: Solarizing

Installing Solar 301: Limitations

- Requires adequate solar exposure (at least four hours of direct sunlight daily)
- Performance varies with weather and seasons
- Requires sufficient roof space with proper orientation
- May require structural reinforcement for older roofs
- Professional installation recommended

References and resources: <www.suspra.com/practice/energy/installing-solar-301.html>

Installing Solar 302: Generating Electricity

Install solar photovoltaic systems to generate electricity

Generate electricity directly from sunlight with a photovoltaic solar array. Batteries and solar modules operate on direct current; to alternate current to be compatible with international power grids, install an inverter. Systems can be grid-tied without battery storage (most common), grid-tied with battery storage, or off-grid (requires batteries). As of 2025, systems convert between 15% and 22% of received solar energy to electricity, with losses from module efficiency, temperature effects, inversion, and wiring. Well-designed systems reliably operate for 30 years with minimal maintenance.

Installing Solar 302: Equipment & Materials

- Mounting system (roof, awning, balcony, or ground)
- Solar photovoltaic (PV) modules
- Electrical wire, conduit, junction boxes, and disconnects
- Charge controller
- Tools for electrical and roofing home improvement projects
- *Optional: Inverter(s) (string, microinverters, or power optimizers)*
- *Electrical panel with breaker space*
- *Battery (recommended)*

Installing Solar 302: Steps

1. Plan and design the system
   - Size solar array based on how much electricity you want to generate
   - Decide whether to interconnect with utility grid power
   - Decide whether to store electricity in a battery
   - Decide where to mount array: roof, awning, balcony, or ground
   - Create electrical single-line diagram for permits and utility review
2. Obtain necessary permits; file interconnection request with utility (if interconnecting)
3. ***Hire a professional solar contractor if you doubt your ability to install solar yourself***
4. Install mounting system
   - Roof: replace roofing (if necessary) before installing solar mounting hardware
   - Awning or balcony: attach brackets to wall or railing
   - Ground:
     - Use ground screws (recommended) or pour concrete footings (not recommended)
     - Build racking and mounting system on foundation
5. Attach solar modules to mounting system
   - Attach microinverters or power optimizers to rails first (if using)
6. Install power bank or inverter and make electrical connections
   - Run conduit, wiring, and equipment grounding; make all electrical connections
   - Install disconnects
   - For systems serving AC loads:

Sustainable Practices Handbook — Energy Practices: Solarizing

- Install inverter(s) and land power on a circuit breaker in an electrical panel
  - For systems with energy storage:
    - Install power bank (charge controller and battery)
    - Connect DC loads to power bank
7. Commission the system and verify proper operation
8. Get final inspection
   - Schedule inspection with local authority having jurisdiction
   - For grid-tied systems, arrange utility review and get permission to operate

Installing Solar 302: Definitions

- **Anti-islanding protection**: Safety feature preventing solar inverters from energizing the grid during outages
- **Grid-tied system**: Solar system connected to utility grid, allowing power export
- **Inverter**: Device converting DC electricity to AC electricity
- **Microinverter**: Small inverter attached to individual panels (as opposed to a string inverter)
- **Racking**: Mounting structure for solar panels

Installing Solar 302: Troubleshooting

Problem	Solutions
Inverter won't start	Check connections, voltage, and grounding. Call the manufacturer.
Low power production	Clean modules; check for shading. Test array voltages.
Inverter overheating	Ensure proper ventilation. Clean cooling fins. Shade from direct sun.
Electrical tripping	Verify wire size. Check for ground faults. Ensure weatherproof connections.

Installing Solar 302: Limitations

- Some jurisdictions require licensed electricians to install solar arrays
- Local codes may restrict system size or placement
- Stand-alone systems without storage cannot operate during grid power outages
- Utilities may deny interconnection requests

References and resources: <www.suspra.com/practice/energy/installing-solar-302.html>

Installing Solar 401: Storing Electricity

Install batteries to store electricity

Maintain electrical power even during grid outages by installing a battery. If you have a solar array that generates electricity, you can charge your power bank directly without an inverter (DC-coupled). If you prefer to charge your power bank with grid power, get one with a rectifier and inverter built in (AC-coupled). As of 2025, manufacturers are using lithium-ion cell chemistries (particularly LFP) for their high energy density, long cycle life, and declining costs. Systems are typically sized from 5-15 kW of power with 10-30 kWh of energy storage, and can be programmed for self-consumption of solar electricity, time-of-use optimization, backup power, or grid services (preventing power outages).

Installing Solar 401: Equipment & Materials

- Battery storage system (i.e., power bank)
- Cables, connectors, disconnect switches

- *Optional: Inverter, electrical panel for battery backup circuits, automatic or manual transfer switch (if grid connected)*

Installing Solar 401: Steps

1. Plan your battery energy storage system
   - Determine electricity needs based on equipment to power
   - Identify critical loads for backup power
2. ***Hire a licensed electrician if you doubt your ability to install a power bank***
3. Research and select the power bank system to buy
   - Chemistry of battery cells (LFP is becoming most common)
   - Power (kW) and energy storage (kWh) capacity
   - Charge from utility power (AC) or a solar array (DC)
   - Battery cell cycle life and system warranty
   - Inverter included or not; if included, type of inverter
4. Select installation location meeting requirements for temperature, ventilation, and access
5. If putting whole building on battery backup, install an automatic transfer switch
6. If backing up only some circuits:
   - Determine whether you can simply plug loads into power bank
   - If not, install a new electrical panel and a manual transfer switch
7. Install power bank per manufacturer's instructions
8. Commission and program system operation
   - Set battery parameters for charging and discharging
   - Set reserve percentage
9. Test the system
   - Verify proper voltage at all connection points
   - For grid-connected systems: Test transfer to battery power and return to grid power
   - Check monitoring system functionality (usually a smartphone app)
10. Schedule inspection

Installing Solar 401: Definitions

- **AC-coupled**: System where batteries connect to the AC side through their own inverter
- **DC-coupled**: System where batteries connect on the DC side, not requiring an inverter
- **Battery management system (BMS)**: Electronic system monitoring battery health and safety
- **Critical loads panel**: Electrical subpanel containing circuits for backup power
- **Depth of discharge (DoD)**: Percentage of total battery capacity used before recharging
- **State of charge (SoC)**: Current level of charge relative to capacity

Installing Solar 401: Troubleshooting

Problem	Solutions
Not charging from solar	Check connections. Verify settings. Check for error codes.
Batteries not discharging	Check minimum state of charge settings. Inspect connections.
Switches to grid unexpectedly	Check battery state of charge. Verify loads aren't exceeding capacity.
Backup function not working	Check transfer switch connections. Verify sufficient battery charge.
Batteries overheating	Improve ventilation. Check clearances. Verify charging parameters.

Sustainable Practices Handbook — Energy Practices: Solarizing

Installing Solar 401: Limitations
- High upfront costs (although prices are falling)
- Battery performance affected by temperature extremes
- Battery capacity degrades over time (20-30% over 10 years for lithium)
- Permitting processes vary by jurisdiction
- Limited energy storage compared to fossil fuels

References and resources: <www.suspra.com/practice/energy/installing-solar-401.html>

Investing in Solar 401: Farming Electricity

Invest in a community solar farm

Invest in solar energy without installing equipment on your own properties. Privately owned community solar farms typically range from 100 kilowatts to 5 megawatts and serve multiple community members through ownership shares or subscriptions. Financial returns come from electricity sales, bill credits, or renewable energy certificates. Different models suit different investors: subscription models offer simplicity with minimal upfront cost, share purchases provide steady returns with moderate risk, and new project development involves higher risk but potentially higher yields. Some community solar farms include battery energy storage systems, so electricity can be provided to the grid when it is most valuable rather than when the sun happens to be shining.

Investing in Solar 401: Equipment & Materials
- 5-25 acres of land near a public road and three-phase power
- Solar modules, wire, connectors, and inverters
- Ground mount structures
- Solar development company

Investing in Solar 401: Steps
1. Understand community solar farms
   - Solar arrays deliver electricity to the distribution system of a public utility
   - A meter records the amount of electricity each array delivers to the grid
   - Contracts specify how the owners of the solar farm are paid for this power
   - Local laws and regulations determine the contractual terms allowed
2. Decide your investment strategy
   - Develop a new project and retain or sell an ownership share
   - Buy an ownership share in an existing project
   - Buy shares of a solar development company that develops many projects
3. Research opportunities and make investment
4. For new projects
   - Hire a solar development company to manage project
   - Select and acquire land (typically a 25-year lease)
   - Find offtakers (who will pay for the electricity the solar farm generates)
   - Design project, obtain permits, then secure utility interconnection agreement
   - Finance, construct, and commission project
   - Collect payments from offtakers for the electricity the project generates
   - Sell Renewable Energy Credits and other monetizations enabled by legislation

Investing in Solar 401: Definitions
- **Bill credits:** Monetary credits applied to electricity bills based on solar production
- **Capacity factor:** Ratio of actual energy produced to theoretical maximum (15-25% for solar)
- **Community solar:** Shared solar systems providing benefits to multiple community members

- **Interconnection**: Process allowing a solar system to connect to the electrical grid
- **Power Purchase Agreement (PPA)**: Contract between electricity producer and purchaser
- **Virtual net metering**: Allows electricity from one array to be credited to multiple customers

Investing in Solar 401: Troubleshooting

Problem	Solutions
Capital requirements	Join with other small investors to reach minimum thresholds.
Finding local projects	Contact solar developers. Form a solar investment group.
Limited returns	Invest wisely as part of a diversified portfolio strategy.
Interconnection delays	Begin utility discussions early. Budget conservatively.

Investing in Solar 401: Limitations
- Regulatory frameworks vary widely and change frequently
- Returns depend heavily on local electricity rates and policies
- Many projects have minimum investment thresholds ($5,000+)
- Geographic limitations on participation exist in many regions
- Long-term contracts (10-25 years) limit flexibility

References and resources: <www.suspra.com/practice/energy/investing-401.html>

Organizing Solar 401: Purchasing Solar

Organize a group purchase of solar PV for your neighborhood

Reduce solar purchase costs by 15-30% compared to individual installations by leveraging collective bargaining power. When installers work with multiple homes in the same area during the same time period, they achieve efficiencies in marketing, site assessment, permitting, and installation. Successful programs typically use tiered pricing where per-watt costs decrease as more participants join, creating incentives for group members to recruit neighbors.

Organizing Solar 401: Equipment & Materials
- Meeting space (physical or virtual)
- Basic knowledge of solar PV systems

Organizing Solar 401: Steps
1. Assess feasibility and build interest (2-3 months)
   - Research local solar regulations and interconnection policies
   - Identify available incentives, rebates, and tax credits
   - Survey neighborhood to gauge interest
   - Organize informational meeting
   - Form core team of 3-5 committed individuals
2. Develop group structure (1 month)
   - Decide on organization structure (committee, nonprofit, co-op)
   - Create mission statement and clear goals
   - Define geographic boundaries for participation
   - Establish communication channels and decision-making processes
3. Build technical specifications (1-2 months)

- Research appropriate solar technology options
- Develop standardized system specifications
- Create household questionnaire (roof age, electrical panel, energy usage)
- Organize roof assessments for interested households
4. Create Request for Proposal (1 month)
5. Solicit and evaluate proposals (1-2 months)
    - Research qualified installation companies
    - Send RFP to at least 5-7 installers
    - Host bidders' conference to answer questions
    - Evaluate proposals using predefined criteria
    - Check references and invite top 2-3 installers to present
6. Select installer and finalize participation (1 month)
    - Select winning installer based on evaluation
    - Negotiate final terms including volume discount tiers
    - Create participation agreement for homeowners
    - Hold information sessions with selected installer
    - Collect commitments from homeowners
7. Facilitate installation process (3-6 months)
    - Create schedule for site assessments and installations
    - Assist with paperwork (permits, incentives, interconnection)
    - Establish point person for questions
    - Monitor installations for quality and timeline adherence
8. Complete project (1 month)
    - Organize final inspections and system activations
    - Collect participant feedback
    - Document savings, capacity installed, and lessons learned
    - Share experience with other neighborhoods

Organizing Solar 401: Definitions

- **Bulk purchasing**: Coordinated buying to achieve economies of scale
- **Interconnection agreement**: Contract allowing solar system connection to the grid
- **Kilowatt (kW)**: Unit of power (typical residential systems: 4-12 kW)
- **Net metering**: Policy providing credit for excess electricity sent to grid
- **Request for Proposal (RFP)**: Formal solicitation document requesting bids
- **Volume discount**: Price reduction for purchasing large quantities

Organizing Solar 401: Troubleshooting

Problem	Solutions
Limited initial interest	Start with a small core group. Host a solar open house.
Varying conditions	Develop 2-3 standard system packages. Allow some customization.
Installer issues	Include timelines and standards in contracts. Establish regular check-ins.
Dropouts	Collect refundable deposits. Maintain regular communications.
Interconnections	Select installers with local experience. Invite local politicians to join.
HOA restrictions	Engage HOA board early. Provide low-profile installation examples.

Organizing Solar 401: Limitations

- Requires 8-12 months from initiation to completion
- Core team must commit substantial volunteer time
- Many homes are not good solar sites (aging roofs, heavy shading, etc.)
- Local policy significantly affects project economics
- Utility interconnection policies are critical factors

References and resources: <www.suspra.com/practice/energy/organizing-401.html>

Organizing Solar 402: Distributing Solar

Build a direct current microgrid to distribute solar for a campus or neighborhood

Build a direct current microgrid to distribute the electricity that solar panels generate and batteries store, eliminating conversion losses between DC and AC. Improve reliability, efficiency, and simplicity compared to systems with inverters. DC microgrids operate independently of the local power grid, supporting critical loads and providing resilience for connected buildings. They can start small and scale incrementally as more equipment in a building and more buildings join the network.

Organizing Solar 402: Equipment & Materials

- Solar arrays and mounting systems
- Energy storage systems (i.e., power banks)
- Power distribution cables, conduit, connectors, disconnects, and electrical panels
- *Optional: Inverters*

Organizing Solar 402: Steps

1. Assemble a qualified team of engineers, electricians, and solar installers
2. Assess needs and site conditions
   - Conduct energy audit of participating buildings
   - Identify critical and non-critical electrical loads
   - Evaluate which critical loads can operate on DC power
   - Identify solar array installation sites and power bank locations
3. Design the DC microgrid
   - Calculate required solar generation and energy storage capacity
   - Determine DC voltage standards (low voltage and high voltage)
   - Design distribution network with appropriate cable sizing
   - Prepare a single-line electrical diagram
4. Secure permits and approvals
   - Submit electrical plans to local building department
   - Secure necessary variances, permits, and easements for distribution infrastructure
5. Procure materials and select contractors
6. Install mounting systems and solar arrays
7. Install power banks
8. Construct DC distribution network to interconnect solar arrays and power banks
9. Use DC power in buildings
   - Connect DC loads (LED lighting, computers, etc.) directly to power banks where possible
   - Install DC-DC converters where needed to change voltages
   - Install DC-AC inverters where AC loads must be maintained
10. Commission the system
11. Have system inspected by authority having jurisdiction

Organizing Solar 402: Definitions

- **Bus**: Electrical conductor serving as common connection for multiple circuits
- **Charge controller**: Device regulating voltage and current in an electrical system
- **DC-DC converter**: Device that changes one DC voltage level to another
- **Direct current (DC)**: The type of electricity that batteries and solar modules use
- **Islanding**: When a local generator continues powering a location despite utility power loss
- **Microgrid**: Localized group of electricity sources and loads that can operate autonomously

Organizing Solar 402: Troubleshooting

Problem	Solutions
Battery system underperforming	Check for cell imbalances. Verify temperature control. Review charging parameters.
Voltage drop	Increase conductor size. Install DC-DC converters as voltage boosters.
Regulatory barriers	Engage early with authorities. Provide detailed safety documentation.
System overload	Shed non-critical loads. Add storage capacity. Install smart controllers.
Intermittent failures	Check for loose connections and corrosion. Verify grounding.

Organizing Solar 402: Limitations

- Requires specialized expertise not found in conventional electrical contractors
- Limited availability of DC-native appliances and equipment
- Complex regulatory approval process
- Higher upfront costs compared to individual building systems
- Less standardization in components compared to AC systems
- May require significant modifications to existing building electrical systems
- Works best with buildings in close proximity with no public roads between them
- Potential challenges with code compliance in many jurisdictions

References and resources: <www.suspra.com/practice/energy/organizing-402.html>

Goods (Materials) Practices

Buying Less, page 381	
Goals	**Indicators**
• Reduce material consumption	• Budget spent on goods • Volume of solid waste

Choosing Green Goods, page 395	
Goals	**Indicators**
• Prevent pollution • Reduce eutrophication • Promote a circular economy	• Types of materials and substances being purchased

Maintaining and Reusing, page 409	
Goals	**Indicators**
• Reduce consumption of materials	• Budget spent on goods • Volume of solid waste

Managing Waste Wisely, page 419	
Goals	**Indicators**
• Return materials to productive use	• Percentage of waste landfilled or incinerated

Buying Less

Borrowing 101: Borrowing Tools

Borrow tools from a library of things or from family, friends, or neighbors

Instead of purchasing tools you'll only use occasionally, explore borrowing options. Check if your community has a "library of things"—these organizations lend out various items, including tools, for a small fee or membership. Alternatively, reach out to family, friends, or neighbors. Before purchasing a tool, ask yourself if you genuinely need to own it, or if borrowing would suffice.

References and resources: <www.suspra.com/practice/goods/borrowing-101.html>

Borrowing 102: Renting

Rent rather than buy things you'll only need for a few days or weeks

Rent items instead of purchasing them to reduce the demand for new goods. Consider renting tools for home repairs, party supplies for events, or specialized sports equipment. Before buying something you'll only use occasionally, search online for rental services in your area. Many local hardware stores, event rental companies, and online platforms offer a wide variety of items for rent. Maximize the use of durable goods and avoid the clutter and potential disposal issues associated with owning infrequently used items. Try out higher-quality items before committing to a purchase to make wiser and well-informed future purchases.

References and resources: <www.suspra.com/practice/goods/borrowing-102.html>

Choosing Less 101: Giving Experiences

Give experiences or gift certificates rather than physical items

Instead of purchasing material gifts, consider giving experiences or gift certificates. This could include tickets to a concert, a cooking class, a spa day, a guided tour, or a gift certificate to a local restaurant. Focus on creating memories and shared moments rather than accumulating more possessions. Gift certificates allow the recipient to choose an experience that aligns with their interests, reducing the chance of unwanted or unused items.

References and resources: <www.suspra.com/practice/goods/choosing-less-101.html>

Choosing Less 102: Buying Quality

Buy quality items that are durable and repairable

Invest in items made from durable materials with a focus on longevity and repairability. Look for products with warranties or guarantees that reflect the manufacturer's confidence in their quality. Consider materials like solid wood, stainless steel, or recycled plastics for household items. Before purchasing, ask yourself if the item can be easily repaired or if replacement parts are readily available. Prioritize purchasing from companies that offer repair services or provide detailed repair instructions.

References and resources: <www.suspra.com/practice/goods/choosing-less-102.html>

Sustainable Practices Handbook   Goods Practices: Buying Less

Crafting 301: Making Items

Make household items from natural materials

Connect to traditional crafts and reduce use of synthetic materials by making household items from natural materials. Wood is versatile and durable; clay creates permanent vessels when fired properly; plant fibers can be woven into countless functional items; gourds form natural containers; and stone offers unparalleled durability. Start with simple projects and develop skills over time.

Crafting 301: Equipment & Materials

- Natural materials
- Basic hand tools
- *Optional: Sewing supplies, power tools, kiln, traditional woodworking tools*

Crafting 301: Steps

1. Identify practical applications of natural crafting
   - Kitchen: Wooden spoons and bowls, clay vessels, reed baskets
   - Storage: Woven baskets, wooden boxes, clay jars
   - Furniture: Stools, benches, shelving from local wood
   - Garden: Trellises, dibbers, harvesting baskets
2. Prepare to craft
   - Inventory local availability of natural materials (wood, clay, plants, stones, etc.)
   - Acquire tools: saws, pruners, banding wheels, needles, etc.
   - Allocate storage space for materials and projects
3. Harvest, clean, and store natural material for projects
   - Take only what you need, minimize damage to living plants, get permission from landowners
   - Brush, soak, and dry in the sun to remove dirt, insects, fungus, bacteria, etc.
   - Process, cure, or treat materials as necessary for use and long-term storage
   - Date and label storage bins; keep a spreadsheet for inventory management
4. Learn and practice sustainable crafting techniques
   - Read books, take classes, attend workshops, find mentors
   - Make practical items for your own household and to give to others
   - Schedule time for projects

Crafting 301: Definitions

- **Natural**: Materials that occur naturally without human intervention

Crafting 301: Troubleshooting

Problem	Solutions
Wood splits	Dry more slowly. Seal end grain with wax. Store away from direct heat.
Clay items crack	Ensure even thickness. Dry very slowly. Wedge thoroughly.
Wooden utensils develop fuzzy texture	Sand again with progressively finer sandpaper. Apply additional oil finish.
Plant fibers break	Soak fibers longer. Select younger materials.
Finishes remain sticky	Apply thinner coats. Ensure proper curing between coats.

Problem	Solutions
Gourds develop mold	Ensure gourds are completely dry. Treat with vinegar.

Crafting 301: Limitations
- Requires significant time and skill compared to purchasing ready-made items
- Durability varies by materials and techniques
- Some items need regular maintenance
- Available materials may be limited by region

References and resources: <www.suspra.com/practice/goods/crafting-301.html>

Economizing 110: Resisting Impulses

Resist impulse purchases and cultivate intentional consumption

Avoid impulse buying. Digital commerce amplifies mindless consumption through 24/7 shopping access, one-click purchasing, and targeted advertising. Combine awareness of your personal triggers with practical systems for mindful purchasing.

Economizing 110: Equipment & Materials
- *Optional: Spending tracker app, browser extension to block shopping sites*

Economizing 110: Steps
1. Track purchases carefully for two weeks; note impulse buys and identify triggers
2. Create a values-based spending framework
   - List core values and financial goals
   - Establish criteria for "need" versus "want" and policies for different purchase types
3. Implement waiting periods before purchasing "wants"
   - 24-hour rule for small "wants" (under $50)
   - 72-hour rule for medium "wants" ($50-200)
   - 30-day rule for large "wants" (over $200)
   - Create a prioritized "want list" to rank items during waiting periods
4. Develop shopping protocols
   - Research products thoroughly before buying
   - Create shopping lists before entering stores or websites
   - Set specific spending limits for each shopping trip
   - Eat before grocery shopping
5. Restructure your shopping environment
   - Unsubscribe from retailer emails and texts; delete shopping apps
   - Remove saved payment information from websites
   - Use browser extensions to block shopping sites
6. Practice mindful shopping techniques
   - Step away from tempting items for at least 10 minutes
   - Calculate the "hours worked" cost of potential purchases

Economizing 110: Definitions
- **Impulse purchase**: Unplanned decision to buy something, made just before purchase
- **Intentional consumption**: Mindful approach to consumption based on needs and values
- **Scarcity marketing**: Tactics creating sense of urgency ("limited time offer")
- **Value-based spending**: Aligning purchases with core values and life goals

Economizing 110: Troubleshooting

Problem	Solutions
Still making impulse purchases	Switch to cash-only and brick-and-mortar stores for problem categories. Leave credit cards at home. Shop with an accountability partner.
Online shopping	Install website blocking extensions. Delete stored payment information. Use a separate email for shopping so offers don't appear in regular email.
Feeling deprived	Plan treats in your budget. Practice gratitude for items you already own.
Irresistible sales	Ask if you'd buy at full price. Create a limited "sales purchase" fund.
Emotional coping	Develop other stress-relief activities. Go outside for a walk. Watch nature.

Economizing 110: Limitations
- Changing ingrained habits takes time and persistence
- Marketing tactics continuously evolve to bypass consumer defenses
- Complete elimination of impulse purchases isn't realistic
- Social and cultural pressures toward consumption remain powerful

References and resources: <www.suspra.com/practice/goods/economizing-110.html>

Economizing 111: Adjusting Frequency

Track and adjust washing and cleaning frequency

Clean to the extent necessary for health and hygiene, when items are actually soiled, rather than on a rigid schedule. Many people wash clothing, linens, and surfaces more frequently than required, consuming excessive water, energy, and cleaning products while causing unnecessary wear. For example, jeans can be worn five times before washing (unless visibly soiled), saving approximately 700 gallons of water per year compared to washing them after every use.

Economizing 111: Equipment & Materials
- *Optional: Whiteboard, "wear it again" hooks*

Economizing 111: Steps
1. Perform a baseline assessment: track current cleaning frequencies for one month
2. Research appropriate cleaning frequencies
3. Create condition tests for each category of cleaning, rather than cleaning on a schedule
   - Clothing and sheets: Wash when visibly soiled, odorous, or after heavy sweating
   - Towels: Hang to dry completely between uses, wash when odorous
   - Floors: Clean when visibly dirty rather than on schedule
   - Vehicles: Spot clean to remove sap and bird poop; rinse off salt on undercarriage
4. Implement systems to minimize need for cleaning and track frequency
   - Have a doormat and boot tray at exterior doors; take off shoes at entry ways
   - Create designated "wear again" location for clothing
   - Train pets to avoid some areas of house
   - Place calendar or tracking sheet in relevant locations
   - Mark cleaning activities with dates
5. Experiment and adjust

- Start with small changes from baseline
- Extend time between washes incrementally
- Evaluate results after each extension
- Record observations about cleanliness and comfort

Economizing 111: Definitions

- **Baseline assessment**: Initial measurement of current cleaning frequencies
- **Condition test**: Evaluating items based on actual state rather than time-based schedules
- **Frequency adjustment**: Systematic modification of cleaning task frequency
- **Overcleaning**: Washing more frequently than necessary for health and comfort
- **Spot cleaning**: Treating only soiled areas rather than washing entire items

Economizing 111: Troubleshooting

Problem	Solutions
Household members resist changes	Start with small adjustments. Share information about benefits. Involve everyone in tracking savings.
Uncertain about frequencies	Consult health guidelines. Experiment incrementally. Use condition rather than time as the primary guide.
Odors	Dry thoroughly between uses. Air outdoors. Clean more frequently.
Social concerns	Spot clean for visible marks. Wear freshly cleaned clothes in public.
"Wear again" clothing	Designate hooks or an open shelf for worn items. Allow air circulation.

Economizing 111: Limitations

- Health conditions may require more frequent cleaning
- Households with young children or pets have less flexibility
- Some textiles require frequency-based cleaning
- Cultural expectations create social pressure for frequent cleaning
- Shared living situations require negotiation of standards

References and resources: <www.suspra.com/practice/goods/economizing-111.html>

Economizing 204: Buying in Bulk

Buy concentrated solutions and in bulk to buy less unnecessary packaging

Buy in bulk and choose concentrated products to reduce packaging waste. The practice works best for non-perishable items and consistently used products. For limited storage space, focus on concentrated products that offer significant packaging reduction relative to storage requirements. Cleaning supplies, laundry detergents, and shelf-stable foods are excellent candidates. Pay attention to dilution instructions for concentrated products to ensure proper usage.

Economizing 204: Equipment & Materials

- Reusable containers (jars, bottles, tubs)
- Cloth or mesh bags for dry goods
- Funnel for transferring liquids
- Labels and marker for dating purchases

- Storage space in pantry, cabinets, or shelving
- Kitchen scale for weighing bulk items
- Measuring cups for portioning
- *Optional: Vacuum sealer, smartphone for price comparison, wheeled cart*

Economizing 204: Steps

1. Assess your household needs and storage capacity
   - Identify regularly used products
   - Inventory available storage space
   - Consider climate control and pest prevention needs
2. Research bulk buying options
   - Traditional grocery store bulk sections
   - Warehouse clubs (Costco, Sam's Club)
   - Food co-ops with bulk sections
   - Zero-waste or refill shops
   - Online bulk retailers
   - Buying clubs or community supported agriculture
3. Prepare reusable containers
   - Clean and thoroughly dry containers
   - Weigh empty containers and label with "tare" weight
   - Pack cloth bags for dry goods
4. Practice smart shopping techniques
   - Compare unit prices rather than package prices
   - Consider product shelf life before purchasing large quantities
   - Look for concentrated formulas for cleaning products
5. Store bulk purchases properly
   - Transfer food to airtight containers promptly
   - Label with purchase date and expiration information
   - Store dry goods in cool, dry places away from sunlight
   - Use FIFO method (First In, First Out)
   - Divide large packages for freezing if needed
6. Manage concentrated products
   - Read dilution instructions carefully
   - Mark dilution ratios on containers
   - Use measuring tools for proper dilution
   - Prepare only needed amounts of diluted product

Economizing 204: Definitions

- **Bulk buying**: Purchasing larger quantities to reduce packaging and cost per unit
- **Concentrated products**: Items formulated with less water or filler, requiring dilution
- **Dilution ratio**: Proportion of product to water needed for usable solution
- **FIFO (First In, First Out)**: System where oldest items are used first
- **Refill shop**: Store where customers bring containers to fill with bulk products
- **Tare weight**: Weight of empty container, subtracted to determine product weight
- **Unit price**: Cost per standard measurement used to compare value across sizes

Economizing 204: Troubleshooting

Problem	Solutions
Limited storage space	Focus on concentrated products. Use vertical storage solutions. Store items under beds or in closets using sealed containers.

Problem	Solutions
Products expiring before use	Purchase smaller quantities or split with others. Properly store to extend shelf life. Track consumption rates.
Difficulty transporting heavy items	Use delivery services. Bring a wheeled cart. Cycle with a trailer. Shop with a friend. Break shopping into multiple smaller trips.
Concentrated product mixing errors	Use dedicated measuring tools. Label containers with dilution instructions. Make smaller batches initially.
Higher upfront costs	Start with high-use items where savings are greatest. Calculate long-term savings. Look for sales on bulk items.
Pest problems with stored foods	Use airtight containers. Add bay leaves to dry goods storage. Store in cool, dry areas. Inspect regularly.

Economizing 204: Limitations

- Not all products available in bulk or concentrated forms
- Requires storage space that may be limited in small homes
- Initial costs are higher despite long-term savings
- Some products have limited shelf life
- Concentrated products require measuring to dilute to useable products
- Transportation of bulk items challenging without a vehicle

References and resources: <www.suspra.com/practice/goods/economizing-204.html>

Economizing 205: Managing Menstruation

Choose washable menstrual products

Switch to washable menstrual products, such as cloth pads or menstrual cups. Research different types of washable products to find what suits your needs and lifestyle. Cloth pads come in various sizes and absorbencies, while menstrual cups offer a reusable, internal option. Once you've chosen a product, follow the manufacturer's instructions for use and care. Proper cleaning involves rinsing with cold water, washing with mild soap, and air drying. By replacing disposable pads and tampons, you'll reduce landfill waste and the resources required to produce single-use items.

References and resources: <www.suspra.com/practice/goods/economizing-205.html>

Joining 201: Buy Nothing

Join your local Buy Nothing group or use the Buy Nothing app

Join a local Buy Nothing group or use the Buy Nothing app to reduce consumption, foster community, and support the principle of giving and receiving freely within a local network. Start by searching for a nearby Buy Nothing group on Facebook or downloading the Buy Nothing app. Once joined, you can post items you wish to give away, request items you need, or offer and seek skills and services.

References and resources: <www.suspra.com/practice/goods/joining-201.html>

Joining 202: Freecycle Network

Join your local Freecycle Network

The Freecycle Network is a global movement of people who are giving and receiving items for free in their own towns. To participate, simply visit Freecycle.org to create an account, find your local group, and request membership. Once accepted, you can post items to give away or request items you need.

References and resources: <www.suspra.com/practice/goods/joining-202.html>

Lending 301: Lending Tools

Lend your tools to family, friends, and neighbors so they don't have to buy

Balance generosity with protecting your investment when lending your tools to family, friends, and neighbors. Prevent tool loss with a consistent tracking system and maintain good relationships with borrowers with clear expectations. Consider your relationship with the borrower when deciding lending terms—close family might have different access than acquaintances. For inexperienced users, provide a quick tutorial on proper tool use to prevent damage and ensure safety.

Lending 301: Equipment & Materials

- Tools to lend
- Inventory system (spreadsheet, notebook, or lending app)
- Labels or permanent marker for marking tools
- Camera or smartphone
- *Optional: Condition assessment checklist, lending agreement*

Lending 301: Steps

1. Create an inventory of lendable tools
   - Mark all tools with your name
   - Document current condition; photograph each tool for reference
2. Create a tracking system: tool, borrower, borrow date, return date, condition
3. Set clear guidelines
   - Decide which tools you'll lend and to whom
   - Establish maximum lending periods
   - Set expectations for cleaning before return
   - Create a policy for damage or loss
4. Document each loan
   - Record borrower's name and contact information
   - Note lending date and expected return date
   - Take photos of valuable tools before lending
   - Consider written agreements for expensive items
5. Set calendar reminders for return dates; send friendly reminders before due dates
6. Maintain your tools
   - Clean and inspect tools after return
   - Perform necessary maintenance
   - Return tools to proper storage

Lending 301: Troubleshooting

Problem	Solutions
Late returns	Send a friendly reminder. Offer to pick up the tool if convenient.

Problem	Solutions
Damaged tool	Minor damage: discuss repairs. Serious damage, request replacement.
Missing tool	Check your tracking system. If not recorded, contact likely borrowers.
Multiple requests	Create a simple reservation system.

Lending 301: Limitations
- Some tools are too dangerous or valuable to lend
- Works best in stable communities where people know each other
- Not ideal for tools you need frequently
- Potential liability concerns with dangerous tools

References and resources: <www.suspra.com/practice/goods/lending-301.html>

Organizing 302: Organizing Possessions

Organize your possessions so you know what you already have

Organize items to extend their lifespans through proper storage, make sharing resources easier, and identify patterns in consumption habits. When possessions are disorganized, we often buy duplicates and miss opportunities to use what we already own. Create systems that work with your natural habits. Prioritize organizing categories of possessions where you often make unnecessary purchases.

Organizing 302: Equipment & Materials
- Sorting containers (boxes, bins, baskets)
- Labels and marker
- Notebook or app for inventory
- Camera or smartphone
- *Optional: Storage containers, shelving, drawer dividers*

Organizing 302: Steps
1. Create a plan
   - Divide the project into manageable sections
   - Schedule specific times for each section
   - Plan what to do with unwanted items
2. Gather items by category
   - Choose one category to begin (clothing, tools, kitchen items)
   - Collect all items in that category from throughout your home
   - Place in a central sorting area
3. Sort and categorize
   - Create logical groupings based on how you use items
   - Remove duplicates and unnecessary items
   - Identify items for repair or repurposing
   - Set aside items no longer needed
4. Create a simple inventory
   - Use a spreadsheet, photo inventory, or basic list
   - Include item locations
   - Note maintenance requirements for valuable items
5. Organize by frequency of use

- Place frequent-use items in accessible locations
- Store seasonal items in less accessible spaces
- Keep similar items together to prevent duplicates
6. Label storage areas clearly
    - Create specific labels for containers and shelves
    - Use consistent labeling throughout your home
    - Consider pictures for households with children
7. Establish a "check first" habit
    - Check inventory before making purchases
    - Create a system for updating when items are used
    - Share the system with household members
8. Maintain the system
    - Schedule quarterly or seasonal reviews
    - Update inventory when acquiring or removing items

Organizing 302: Definitions

- **5-minute daily reset**: Taking 5 minutes to move items to landing zones, storage, or disposal
- **Categorization**: Grouping similar items based on type, function, or use
- **Landing zone**: A designated area to put all items before storing them in their place
- **Resource visibility**: Degree to which items are visible and accessible in storage

Organizing 302: Troubleshooting

Problem	Solutions
Feeling overwhelmed	Start with a small area like a drawer. Focus on one category at a time. Schedule short organizing sessions.
Family not helping	Involve everyone in creating the system. Use visual cues. Keep it simple.
Deciding what to keep	"Used in the past year?" "Would I buy this today?" Set category limits.
Clutter	Identify problem areas. Create "landing zones." 5-minute daily resets.

Organizing 302: Limitations

- Requires time and energy; habits are hard to break
- Shared living spaces require compromise

References and resources: <www.suspra.com/practice/goods/organizing-302.html>

Organizing 401: Creating a Library of Things

Create a library of things

Reduce consumption by enabling community access to shared resources like tools, equipment, and household items that are used infrequently. A "library of things" (LoT) promotes sustainability by decreasing the total number of items manufactured while increasing access to high-quality tools and equipment. Most households use tools like drills for only a few minutes per year, making them ideal for sharing. Develop clear policies addressing membership criteria, item checkout duration, late returns, and maintenance responsibility. Operate using one of three models: 1) volunteer-run community initiative, 2) addition to existing public libraries, or 3) a social enterprise with combined volunteer and paid staff. The average setup period is 6-12 months. Tool libraries typically serve 20-30 people daily with inventories ranging from 500-5,000 items. Studies show each shared tool replaces 20-40 private

Sustainable Practices Handbook — Goods Practices: Buying Less

purchases. Beyond environmental benefits, LoTs foster community connections, skill-sharing, and resource equity.

Organizing 401: Equipment & Materials
- Organizational space (garage, community center, storefront)
- Inventory management system
- Storage shelving and bins
- Basic tools and equipment to start the collection
- Computer with internet access
- Checkout system (software or paper-based)
- *Optional: funding source or grant, insurance policy, volunteer management system*

Organizing 401: Steps
1. Research and plan (2-3 months)
   - Study existing models and best practices
   - Define your community's needs through surveys
   - Create a mission statement and operational plan
   - Explore partnerships with existing community organizations
2. Establish organizational structure (1-2 months)
   - Choose legal structure (nonprofit, cooperative, or informal)
   - Build a core team with diverse skills
   - Create policies for membership, lending, and liability
   - Develop budget and funding strategy
3. Secure location and resources (1-3 months)
   - Find appropriate space with accessibility and storage
   - Establish initial funding through grants, donations, or membership fees
   - Acquire insurance coverage
   - Set up inventory management system
4. Build initial inventory (2-3 months)
   - Host community donation drives
   - Target high-demand, durable items
   - Establish relationships with local businesses for donations
   - Develop intake procedures for inspecting and cataloging items
5. Implement operational systems (1-2 months)
   - Create membership structure and agreements
   - Develop checkout and return procedures
   - Train volunteers and staff
   - Establish maintenance and repair processes
6. Launch and promote (1 month)
   - Hold grand opening event
   - Conduct demonstrations and workshops
   - Implement marketing and outreach plan
   - Establish community partnerships
7. Monitor and improve (ongoing)
   - Track usage patterns and member feedback
   - Adapt inventory based on demand
   - Recruit additional volunteers
   - Evaluate and refine policies and procedures

Organizing 401: Definitions
- **Cooperative**: Organization jointly owned and democratically controlled by its members

- **Fiscal sponsorship**: Arrangement where an established nonprofit extends legal and tax-exempt status to a new initiative
- **Item lifecycle management**: Process for maintaining, repairing, and eventually retiring items from circulation
- **Liability waiver**: Document signed by borrowers acknowledging risks and taking responsibility
- **Library of Things (LoT)**: Lending collection of non-book items like tools, kitchen equipment, and recreational items
- **Tool Library**: Specialized LoT focused on lending tools and equipment

Organizing 401: Troubleshooting

Problem	Solutions
Low initial donations	Partner with local businesses for donated items. Apply for grants. Focus on quality over quantity.
Space limitations	Implement a reservation system. Focus on smaller, high-demand items. Partner with other organizations for storage.
Item damage or loss	Create clear liability policies. Collect deposits. Develop maintenance training for members.
Volunteer burnout	Create smaller, defined volunteer roles. Implement scheduled rotations. Develop tiered membership with service requirements.
Insufficient funding	Institute modest user fees. Create sponsorship programs for local businesses. Apply for sustainability grants.
Low awareness	Partner with existing community organizations. Host skill-building workshops. Attend community events with mobile displays.

Organizing 401: Limitations

- Requires significant volunteer time for organization and maintenance
- Initial setup costs can be substantial
- Finding appropriate accessible space is challenging in many communities
- Insurance and liability concerns require careful consideration
- Some items require regular maintenance and repair
- Not all items are suitable for sharing (consumables, very personal items)
- May face competition from commercial tool rental businesses

References and resources: <www.suspra.com/practice/goods/organizing-401.html>

Volunteering 402: Leading Your Freecycle Network

Lead your local Freecycle Network

The Freecycle Network operates on a simple premise: members post unwanted items; others claim them for free pickup. This peer-to-peer gifting system reduces waste while building community connections. Provide active, consistent moderation to ensure all listings meet guidelines (free, legal, appropriate), resolve occasional disputes, and maintain group momentum.

Volunteering 402: Equipment & Materials
- Computer and reliable Internet access
- Email account
- Time (10-15 hours/week initially, 5-10 hours ongoing)

Volunteering 402: Steps
1. Learn Freecycle fundamentals: everything free, legal, and appropriate
   - Study official guidelines and policies
   - Join active groups to observe best practices
2. Establish your group
   - Check if a group already exists in your area
   - Apply through the official Freecycle website
   - Define geographic boundaries
   - Create clear group rules
3. Build a moderation team: recruit 2-4 co-moderators to share responsibilities
4. Launch effectively
   - Announce through local channels
   - Create informative welcome message
   - Personally welcome initial members
   - Post example offerings
5. Implement effective moderation
   - Review membership requests daily
   - Address inappropriate content promptly
   - Develop a system for handling violations
6. Grow membership
   - Partner with local environmental organizations
   - Contact local media
   - Distribute flyers in community locations
   - Encourage members to invite others
7. Maintain engagement
   - Share success stories
   - Recognize active members
   - Gather feedback through surveys
8. Handle challenges
   - Create protocols for dispute resolution
   - Document rule violations and actions
   - Maintain confidentiality
9. Expand impact
   - Organize occasional in-person events
   - Connect with other Freecycle group leaders
   - Mentor new moderators in nearby communities

Volunteering 402: Definitions
- **Curb alerts**: Notifications about items left at the curb for anyone to take
- **Freecycle Network**: Nonprofit organization promoting gift-giving to reuse goods
- **ISO (In Search Of)**: Posts from members looking for specific items
- **OFFER**: Standard prefix for posts offering an item
- **PENDING**: Status of an item promised but not yet picked up
- **TAKEN**: Status of an item gifted and received

Volunteering 402: Troubleshooting

Problem	Solutions
Low activity	Create "seed" posts to demonstrate use. Reach out to community organizations. Share success stories.
Rule violations	Clarify rules with examples. Create a quick guide for new members. Implement a "three strikes" policy.
Moderator burnout	Recruit additional moderators. Create a rotation schedule. Automate repetitive tasks when possible.
Member disputes	Develop a clear resolution protocol. Remain neutral. Document communications. Reference official policies.

Volunteering 402: Limitations

- Requires significant time commitment
- Digital platform excludes those without Internet access
- Successful exchanges depend on members having transportation

References and resources: <www.suspra.com/practice/goods/volunteering-402.html>

Choosing Green Goods

Avoiding Materials 101: Deplastifying

Avoid using single-use disposable plastic items

There isn't a word for "avoiding the use of plastic," so we've made one up: "desplastifying." Avoid single-use plastics. Begin with high-volume items like shopping bags, beverage containers, food packaging, and take away cutlery. Aim first for significant reduction, rather than complete elimination.

Avoiding Materials 101: Equipment & Materials
- Reusable shopping bags and produce bags
- Stainless steel, glass, or silicone food containers
- Reusable water bottles and coffee mugs
- Stainless steel or bamboo utensils
- Cloth napkins and dish towels
- Silicone food covers
- Glass jars

Avoiding Materials 101: Steps
1. Audit your plastic use
    - Keep all single-use plastic waste for one week in a separate bag
    - Sort and identify the most common plastic items in your waste
    - Prioritize finding alternatives for your most frequently used plastic items
2. Replace disposable bags
    - Keep reusable shopping bags in your car, purse, or backpack
    - Use cloth or mesh produce bags instead of plastic produce bags
3. Eliminate disposable plastic drinkware
    - Fill a reusable bottle from the tap instead of buying bottled water
    - Bring your own coffee mug to cafes
    - Request beverages without plastic straws or bring a reusable straw
4. Replace food packaging and storage
    - Shop at bulk food stores using your own containers
    - Use silicone covers instead of plastic wrap
    - Store leftovers in glass, ceramic, or stainless steel containers
5. Avoid plastic in personal care
    - Switch to bar soap, shampoo, and conditioner instead of liquid in plastic bottles
    - Choose personal care products packaged in glass, metal, or paper
6. Replace disposable items in the kitchen
    - Replace plastic wrap with containers with lids
    - Choose wood, bamboo, or stainless steel cooking utensils
7. Shop strategically
    - Make a shopping list to avoid impulse purchases of plastic-packaged items
    - Choose loose produce instead of pre-packaged; bring a produce bag
    - Buy from local farmers' markets where less packaging is used

Avoiding Materials 101: Definitions
- **Single-use plastics**: Plastic items intended to be used once before being discarded

Avoiding Materials 101: Troubleshooting

Problem	Solutions
Forgetting bags	Keep bags in your vehicle and by the door. Add "bags" to your shopping list.
Plastic at local stores	Try different stores for different items. Shop at farmers markets or co-ops.
Higher costs	Start with lower-cost swaps. Use savings from drinking tap water.
Family resists	Start with personal changes. Involve family in making choices.

Avoiding Materials 101: Limitations

- Some plastic use is unavoidable, particularly for medical applications
- Plastic-free alternatives sometimes have higher upfront costs
- Comprehensive deplastifying requires access to specialty shops

References and resources: <www.suspra.com/practice/goods/avoiding-materials-101.html>

Avoiding Materials 201: Avoiding Mercury

Avoid products containing mercury, such as fluorescent lighting

Avoid mercury, a neurotoxin that can damage the brain, kidneys, and developing fetuses. Fluorescent lighting contains mercury vapor that releases when bulbs break. Old thermostats, switches, and batteries contain mercury because it expands to fill voids and conducts electricity. If you have a mercury spill, do not vacuum up pieces. Instead, wear gloves, use stiff paper to gather bits, a damp paper towel or sticky tape to blot, and put it in a sealed glass jar labeled "Household Hazardous Waste: Mercury."

Avoiding Materials 201: Equipment & Materials

- Jar, tape and newspaper (for cleanup in case of breakage)
- Glass containers for temporary storage

Avoiding Materials 201: Steps

1. Inventory your current mercury sources
   - Fluorescent lighting (tube lights, CFLs)
   - Thermostats, thermometers, very old batteries
2. Create a mercury spill kit for emergencies
   - Paperboard or cardboard, sticky tape, damp paper towels, and glass jars
3. Prioritize replacements that pose the highest risk (damaged items or bulbs in high-traffic areas)
4. Research mercury-free alternatives
   - For lighting, select LED bulbs
   - For thermostats and thermometers, choose digital or alcohol-based options
5. Replace items safely
   - Handle fluorescent bulbs carefully; remove by holding and twisting their base, not the glass
   - Place old bulbs in original packaging or wrap in paper to prevent breakage
6. Store removed items properly
   - Never throw mercury-containing items in regular trash
   - Create and label a designated, secure area for storing household hazardous waste
7. Dispose of mercury items properly
   - Check if local hardware stores offer recycling; drop off items there if possible
   - Visit your local household hazardous waste facility or attend a collection event

Avoiding Materials 201: Definitions

- **CFLs (Compact Fluorescent Lamps)**: Energy-efficient bulbs containing mercury vapor
- **LED (Light Emitting Diode)**: More efficient lighting technology without mercury
- **Mercury**: A toxic heavy metal element that is liquid at room temperature

Avoiding Materials 201: Troubleshooting

Problem	Solutions
Accidentally broke a fluorescent bulb	Open windows for 5-10 minutes. Don't vacuum. Use stiff paper to collect pieces and powder, then sticky tape for remaining particles. Seal materials in a glass jar for hazardous waste disposal.
Local recycling won't accept mercury items	Check with county environmental services. Contact local hardware stores that often have lamp recycling programs.

Avoiding Materials 201: Limitations

- Local hazardous waste disposal options vary widely by location

References and resources: <www.suspra.com/practice/goods/avoiding-materials-201.html>

Avoiding Materials 301: Avoiding VOCs

Avoid products containing high amounts of volatile organic compounds

Reduce air pollution from volatile organic compounds (VOCs), which evaporate easily at room temperature. Building materials (particularly composite wood products containing formaldehyde), household products (cleaning agents, personal care products), and activities (cooking, burning candles or incense) are the three main sources.

Avoiding Materials 301: Steps

1. Identify VOC sources in your home
   - Identify high-risk categories: paints, sealants, adhesives, carpeting, composite wood products, cleaning products, air fresheners
   - Check labels for ingredients like formaldehyde, benzene, toluene, xylene, and ethylene glycol
   - Use your nose to detect "new car" smell
2. Develop a replacement strategy
   - Prioritize replacement based on VOC concentrations and proximity to living spaces
   - Create an action plan for replacing items during normal maintenance cycles
   - Research product certifications like GreenGuard, Green Seal, or SCS Indoor Advantage
3. Select low-VOC building materials
   - Choose solid wood over particle board, MDF, or plywood when possible
   - Select zero-VOC paints
   - Use water-based polyurethane finishes instead of oil-based options
   - Select formaldehyde-free insulation
   - Choose hard flooring (tile, solid wood, concrete) over vinyl or new carpeting
   - Select products labeled CARB Phase 2 Compliant or NAF (No Added Formaldehyde)
4. Select low-VOC household products
   - Choose sustainable cleaning products
   - Eliminate air fresheners, scented candles, and incense
   - Choose fragrance-free personal care products
   - Select water-based art supplies rather than solvent-based options

- Store automotive products, paints, and solvents in a detached garage or shed

Avoiding Materials 301: Definitions
- **Formaldehyde**: A VOC commonly used in adhesives in composite wood products
- **Off-gassing/Outgassing**: The release of VOCs from solid materials into the air
- **TVOC (Total Volatile Organic Compounds)**: The sum of all VOCs present in the air
- **VOCs (Volatile Organic Compounds)**: Carbon-containing chemicals that evaporate into gases at room temperature
- **Zero-VOC**: Products containing extremely low levels (usually less than 5 g/L for paints)

Avoiding Materials 301: Troubleshooting

Problem	Solutions
High VOC levels	Check for overlooked sources (stored chemicals, attached garage, recent deliveries). Increase ventilation. Consider professional testing.
New furniture	Place furniture in a well-ventilated area for a week before bringing it indoors. Use fans to increase air circulation.
Renovation project	Schedule during moderate weather for maximum ventilation. Seal off work areas from living spaces. Relocate during and immediately after the project.
Budget constraints	Prioritize bedroom and frequently used living spaces.
VOC levels spike	Use a dehumidifier to maintain indoor humidity below 60%. Increase ventilation during early morning when outdoor air is coolest.

Avoiding Materials 301: Limitations
- Complete VOC elimination is practically impossible in modern homes
- Low-VOC alternatives may have higher upfront costs
- Consumer-grade VOC meters measure total VOCs but cannot identify specific compounds
- Some "VOC-free" products may contain exempt compounds that still impact health

References and resources: <www.suspra.com/practice/goods/avoiding-materials-301.html>

Avoiding Materials 302: Avoiding All Plastic

Avoid products made from plastic

First eliminate all single-use plastics (bags, bottles, packaging), which constitute about 40% of all plastic production, then work to replace durable plastic items with ones made from other materials. Follow the hierarchy: refuse what you don't need, reduce what you do need, reuse what you have, repurpose before recycling, and recycle as a last resort.

Substitute Equipment & Materials to Avoid Plastic
- Reusable shopping bags and produce bags
- Glass or stainless steel food storage containers
- Metal or wooden utensils
- Reusable water bottle, stainless steel or glass
- Reusable coffee cup
- Bar soap and shampoo bars

- Mason jars for bulk shopping
- Silicone food wraps
- Natural fiber cleaning brushes
- Cloth napkins and towels

Avoiding Materials 302: Steps

1. Assess your current plastic use
    - Collect all plastic waste for one week, sort into categories
    - Identify the biggest sources of plastic in your household
2. Create a strategic replacement plan
    - Research plastic-free alternatives for each item you own
    - Prioritize replacing disposable plastics before durable plastic items
3. Change shopping habits
    - Research local stores with bulk sections or refill stations
    - Shop at farmers markets, bulk stores, and package-free shops
    - Bring reusable shopping and produce bags on every shopping trip
    - Choose products in glass, metal, or paper packaging
    - Buy larger quantities to reduce packaging waste
4. Transform your kitchen
    - Replace plastic food storage with glass, stainless steel, or ceramic containers
    - Use silicone covers instead of plastic wrap
    - Use wooden or cork cutting boards
    - Use cloth instead of plastic food bags for sandwiches and snacks
    - Replace plastic cooking utensils with wood, bamboo, or metal ones
5. Revamp your bathroom
    - Switch to bar soap, shampoo, and conditioner
    - Choose plastic-free toothpaste tablets or powder
    - Use bamboo toothbrushes and compostable dental floss
    - Use metal safety razors with replaceable blades
    - Select toilet paper wrapped in paper rather than plastic
6. Rethink cleaning supplies
    - Make your own cleaning solutions using vinegar, baking soda, and castile soap
    - Purchase cleaning supplies in bulk with refillable containers
    - Use natural fiber brushes, mops, and brooms
    - Choose wooden or metal cleaning tools with natural fiber bristles
7. Address clothing and laundry
    - Choose natural fibers (cotton, wool, linen, hemp)
    - Buy laundry detergent in cardboard boxes
8. Manage on-the-go situations
    - Carry a zero-waste kit (reusable utensils, container, napkin, water bottle)
    - Request "no plastic" when ordering takeout or at restaurants
    - Bring your own containers for restaurant leftovers

Avoiding Materials 302: Definitions

- **Microplastics:** Tiny plastic particles less than 5mm in size
- **Single-use plastic:** Plastic items designed to be used once and then discarded
- **Synthetic fibers:** Man-made fibers like polyester, nylon, and acrylic that are forms of plastic

Avoiding Materials 302: Troubleshooting

Problem	Solutions
Overwhelmed	Start with the kitchen or bathroom. Replace items as they run out.
Expense	Prioritize the most frequently used items first.
Family resists	Start with personal changes. Find alternatives that are equally convenient.
No alternatives	Consider whether the item is truly necessary.
Too time-consuming	Batch trips to specialty stores. Develop routines and systems.

Avoiding Materials 302: Limitations

- Complete elimination of plastic is virtually impossible in modern society
- Plastic alternatives have their own environmental impacts
- Regional availability of plastic-free options varies significantly
- Medical needs may necessitate certain plastic products
- Cost of alternatives can be prohibitive for some households
- Food safety regulations often require plastic packaging for certain items

References and resources: <www.suspra.com/practice/goods/avoiding-materials-302.html>

Cleaning 104: Using Microfiber

Clean with microfiber cloths

Reduce waste by replacing hundreds of disposable products and minimizing chemical use with microfiber cloths, which clean effectively through millions of tiny fibers that create a large surface area with a slight positive electric charge to attract dust and dirt. Their split fibers and wedge-shaped channels trap debris until washed. Wash microfiber cloths in specialized laundry bags that catch microplastics; seal microplastic lint in a container and send to a landfill to prevent pollution.

Cleaning 104: Equipment & Materials

- Microfiber cleaning cloths
- Mild, eco-friendly laundry detergent
- Laundry bag designed to catch microfiber particles

Cleaning 104: Steps

1. Set up your microfiber cleaning system
   - Purchase 20 microfiber cloths in different colors
   - Establish a color-coding system for different cleaning tasks
2. Prepare cloths for use
   - Wash new microfiber cloths before first use to remove manufacturing residues
     - Wash separately from other laundry in warm water (100-105°F/38-40°C)
     - Use mild detergent with no fabric softener
     - Put in a microfiber-catching laundry bag to prevent microplastic pollution
     - Air dry, don't iron
   - Ensure cloths are completely dry before first use
3. Use microfiber for daily cleaning
   - For dry dusting: Use dry microfiber cloths to trap dust

- For wet cleaning: Lightly dampen cloth with water (not soaking wet)
   - Fold cloth into quarters to create eight usable surfaces
   - Refold to expose clean sections as needed
4. Clean without chemicals
   - For windows and glass: Use a damp microfiber cloth followed by a dry one
   - For kitchen surfaces: Use hot water with microfiber to sanitize
   - For bathroom surfaces: Use dedicated bathroom cloths
5. Wash microfiber cloths properly
   - Rinse with water and dry thoroughly after each use
   - When you notice diminished cleaning performance, wash with detergent (see step two)
6. Replace when effectiveness diminishes (typically after 300-500 washes)

Cleaning 104: Definitions

- **GSM**: Grams per square meter; measurement of microfiber density (higher numbers indicate better quality)
- **Guppyfriend**: A washing bag designed to capture microfibers during laundering
- **Microfiber**: Synthetic fibers made from polyester and polyamide less than 1 denier in thickness
- **Microplastics**: Tiny plastic particles less than 5mm in size

Cleaning 104: Troubleshooting

Problem	Solutions
Streaks on glass	Use slightly damp, clean cloth followed by a completely dry one.
Cloths smell	Rinse and dry thoroughly after use. Wash with mild detergent.
Reduced effectiveness	Wash cloth with detergent. Avoid fabric softeners. Replace cloth.
Lint left behind	Pre-wash new cloths. Wash microfiber separately.

Cleaning 104: Limitations

- Oily messes require soap or detergent
- Requires proper laundering to prevent microplastic pollution
- Synthetic material isn't biodegradable
- Not suitable for hazardous messes requiring disposable materials

References and resources: <www.suspra.com/practice/goods/cleaning-104.html>

Clothing 301: Choosing Natural Fibers

Buy durable clothing made from natural fibers

Wear natural fiber clothing that is biodegradable and often more durable than synthetics. Cotton is versatile and breathable; linen excels in hot weather; hemp is extremely durable; wool provides natural temperature regulation; and silk offers lightweight strength.

Clothing 301: Steps

1. Identify natural fiber options
   - Plant-based: cotton, linen, hemp, jute
   - Animal-based: wool, silk, alpaca, mohair
   - Semi-synthetic: modal, lyocell, Tencel™

2. Read garment labels properly
   - Check fiber content labels
   - Look for 100% natural fiber or high percentage natural fiber blends
   - Be aware of misleading terminology (e.g., "bamboo" is usually rayon)
3. Research brands committed to natural fibers
   - Look for transparent supply chains
   - Read customer reviews about durability
4. Identify relevant certifications
   - Plant-based: GOTS, OCS, BCI
   - Animal-based: RWS, ZQ Merino, Peace Silk
   - General: OEKO-TEX® Standard 100, Cradle to Cradle
5. Follow fiber-specific care instructions

Clothing 301: Definitions

- **Biodegradable**: Materials that can decompose naturally
- **Blend**: Fabric made from two or more different fiber types
- **Staple length**: Length of individual fiber strands; longer staples create stronger fabrics

Clothing 301: Troubleshooting

Problem	Solutions
Too expensive	Look for sales and second-hand options. Calculate cost-per-wear.
Few options	Check specialty brands. Consider high-quality blends.
Shrinkage	Buy pre-shrunk fabrics. Buy a size up. Follow care instructions precisely.
Wrinkles	Accept natural textures. Use a steamer. Consider blends.

Clothing 301: Limitations

- Most natural fibers require specific care
- May be more expensive initially
- Some performance needs are difficult to achieve with 100% natural fibers
- Natural fibers often have seasonal limitations

References and resources: <www.suspra.com/practice/goods/clothing-301.html>

Clothing 302: Avoiding PFAS

Avoid clothing treated with PFAS for stain resistance or water repellency

Avoid PFAS chemicals that are added to clothing for water, stain, and oil resistance, particularly in outdoor gear and workwear. As "forever chemicals," they persist in the environment. Modern alternatives include non-fluorinated durable water repellent (DWR) treatments and naturally water-resistant materials like waxed cotton and densely woven fabrics.

Clothing 302: Steps

1. Understand what PFAS are in clothing
   - Identify common applications (water-repellent outerwear, stain-resistant workwear)
   - Learn terminology for PFAS finishes ("durable water repellent", "stain guard")
   - Recognize high-risk product categories

Sustainable Practices Handbook — Goods Practices: Choosing Green Goods

2. Check your existing wardrobe
   - Review outdoor gear, uniforms, and formal wear
   - Check labels for "stain-resistant," "water-repellent," or "Teflon"
   - Create an inventory of items likely containing PFAS
   - Prioritize replacements based on frequency of use
3. Research PFAS-free alternatives
   - Search for brands committed to PFAS-free manufacturing
   - Look for third-party certifications (OEKO-TEX, bluesign®)
   - Research natural alternatives (waxed cotton, tightly woven wool)
   - Identify companies using non-fluorinated water-repellent treatments
4. Decode marketing claims
   - Learn to distinguish legitimate PFAS-free claims from greenwashing
   - Understand terms like "PFC-free" and "fluorine-free"
   - Be skeptical of vague terms like "eco-friendly"
   - Contact manufacturers when information is unclear
   - Ask about specific durable water-repellent (DWR) treatments
5. Shop strategically
   - Prioritize natural, untreated fabrics
   - Choose mechanically water-resistant fabrics
6. Maintain clothing without PFAS
   - Apply natural water-repellent treatments
   - Follow proper care instructions; wash to remove stains

Clothing 302: Definitions

- **DWR**: Durable Water Repellent; a coating applied to fabrics for water resistance
- **Greenwashing**: Marketing that deceptively promotes products as environmentally friendly
- **PFAS**: Per- and polyfluoroalkyl substances; chemicals used for water and stain resistance
- **PFC**: Perfluorinated compounds; an older term often used for PFAS chemicals

Clothing 302: Troubleshooting

Problem	Solutions
Not sure about PFAS	Contact the manufacturer directly. Look for third-party certifications.
Need water resistance	Choose non-fluorinated DWR treatments. Buy tightly woven fabrics.
Too expensive	Replace high-use items first. Buy secondhand.
Limited selection	Ask for PFAS-free options to increase demand. Shop online.

Clothing 302: Limitations

- Difficult to confirm PFAS content without testing
- Non-PFAS water repellents may not perform as well in extreme conditions
- Some specialized applications have limited alternatives
- Natural alternatives may require more maintenance

References and resources: <www.suspra.com/practice/goods/clothing-302.html>

Revision: 25.1.8

Cooking 201: Avoiding PFAS

Cook with stainless steel or cast iron to avoid non-stick coatings that contain PFAS

Choose stainless steel and cast iron for superior durability and cooking performance (especially searing), without PFAS non-stick coatings. Stainless steel provides excellent versatility. Cast iron offers exceptional heat retention and develops a naturally non-stick surface through seasoning. Though they require different techniques than non-stick pans, these materials can last for generations.

Cooking 201: Equipment & Materials
- Stainless steel, cast iron, or carbon steel pots and pans
- Cooking oils
- Wooden, silicone, or stainless steel utensils

Cooking 201: Steps
1. Assess and replace your cookware
    - Identify cookware with PFAS (non-stick pans with Teflon® or similar coatings)
    - Replace with stainless steel for boiling, steaming, and general cooking
    - Replace with cast iron for high-heat cooking, baking, and oven use
2. Prepare and maintain stainless steel cookware
    - Heat pan thoroughly before adding oil
    - Test readiness with water drops—they should bead and dance
    - Add oil once hot and wait until it shimmers
    - Clean with warm soapy water or baking soda paste
3. Prepare and maintain cast iron cookware
    - For new pans: wash, dry, apply thin oil layer, bake at 450°F for one hour
    - Build seasoning through regular use
    - Clean with hot water and stiff brush (no soap for established pans)
    - For stubborn food, scrub with coarse salt and oil
    - Dry completely and apply thin oil layer before storing
4. Adapt cooking techniques
    - Preheat pans properly
    - Use sufficient oil to prevent sticking
    - Allow food to cook undisturbed until it naturally releases
    - Avoid overcrowding pans
    - For delicate foods, ensure proper preheating and use adequate oil
5. Use appropriate utensils and baking aids
    - Use wooden, silicone, or stainless steel utensils; avoid metal utensils on seasoned cast iron
    - Use parchment paper or silicone mats for baking

Cooking 201: Definitions
- **Heat retention**: Ability of material to stay hot after heat source is removed
- **PFAS**: Per- and polyfluoroalkyl substances used in non-stick cookware
- **Reactive cookware**: Reactive cookware can interact with acidic foods
- **Seasoning**: Polymerized oil layer on cast iron that provides non-stick properties

Cooking 201: Troubleshooting

Problem	Solutions
Food sticks (stainless)	Preheat before adding oil. Use enough oil. Allow food to release naturally.

Problem	Solutions
Food sticks (cast iron)	Preheat before adding oil. Re-season. Use more oil.
Cast iron develops rust	Dry completely. Apply light oil coating. Scrub with steel wool; re-season.
Uneven cooking	Use a heat diffuser for stainless steel. Preheat cast iron thoroughly.

Cooking 201: Limitations

- Learning curve for proper techniques
- Stainless steel doesn't retain heat as well as cast iron
- Cast iron is heavy and requires specific maintenance
- Cast iron is reactive; may affect flavor or color of acidic dishes

References and resources: <www.suspra.com/practice/food/cooking-201.html>

Furnishing 301: Avoiding PFAS

Avoid furniture treated with PFAS for stain resistance or water repellency

Buy furniture made from natural materials, without synthetic PFAS chemicals added for stain and water resistance. Wool naturally repels stains, while cotton, hemp, and linen can be cleaned with simple soap and water. Verify PFAS-free claims by checking certifications and contacting manufacturers directly. Choose quality pieces with washable covers.

Furnishing 301: Equipment & Materials

- Furniture without stain-resistant and water-resistant PFAS chemical coatings

Furnishing 301: Steps

1. Identify PFAS in furniture
   - Look for terms indicating PFAS: stain-resistant, water-resistant, Teflon™, Scotchgard™, GoreTex™
   - Watch for marketing phrases like "won't absorb spills" or "liquids bead up"
2. Select non-upholstered furniture when possible
   - Opt for solid wood, metal frames, or glass-topped surfaces
3. For upholstery, choose safer materials
   - Natural, untreated fibers: organic cotton, hemp, linen, wool, canvas
   - Leather with vegetable tanning
   - Untreated synthetics
4. Check for certifications
   - Look for: OEKO-TEX® Standard 100, GOTS, GREENGUARD Gold, Declare Label, MADE SAFE®
   - Verify explicit PFAS-free claims
5. Consider secondhand options
   - Look for pre-1970s vintage furniture
   - Choose solid wood pieces that can be refinished
6. Contact manufacturers directly
   - Ask about PFAS policies and testing protocols
   - Request information about alternative treatments
7. Apply alternative protections
   - Use washable, removable slipcovers
   - Apply beeswax for wood or natural oils for leather

- Use plant-based fabric protectors

Furnishing 301: Definitions
- **PFAS**: Per- and polyfluoroalkyl substances; chemicals used for stain and water resistance
- **Performance fabrics**: Textiles engineered to resist stains and water, often using PFAS
- **OEKO-TEX® Standard 100**: Certification testing textiles for harmful substances
- **GOTS**: Global Organic Textile Standard certification
- **Vegetable tanning**: Leather treatment using plant-based tannins rather than chemicals

Furnishing 301: Troubleshooting

Problem	Solutions
Higher cost	Prioritize key pieces, consider secondhand furniture, use washable covers.
Need stain protection	Use washable covers. Apply non-PFAS protectors.

Furnishing 301: Limitations
- Complete PFAS avoidance is difficult as these chemicals are widespread
- Consumer-level testing for PFAS is not readily accessible
- Many certifications don't test for all PFAS chemicals

References and resources: <www.suspra.com/practice/goods/furnishing-301.html>

Selecting Materials 201: Choosing Recyclables

Buy products made from fully compostable or recyclable materials

Buy compostable or recyclable materials to support a circular economy where resources are continuously reused. Glass and metals can be recycled indefinitely without quality loss. Paper products can typically go through seven recycling cycles before fibers become too short. Wood products, unless pressure untreated, can be composted. Plastics are different: while some are technically recyclable, actual recycling rates remain low, and many can only be "downcycled" into lower-quality products.

Selecting Materials 201: Steps
1. Learn which materials can be recycled and composted
   - Metals (aluminum, steel, copper) can be recycled indefinitely
   - Glass can be recycled indefinitely with no quality loss
   - Paper and cardboard can typically be recycled 5-7 times
   - Natural materials (like wood) can be composted, unless treated with preservatives
   - Of plastics, only #1 (PET) and #2 (HDPE) are commonly recycled
2. Research your local recycling infrastructure
3. Prioritize materials based on:
   - Recyclability (how many times it can be recycled)
   - Local recycling infrastructure availability
   - Product durability and lifespan
   - Renewable resource content
   - Transportation impact (weight and shipping distance)
4. Verify that packaging labeled "recyclable" is accepted locally
5. Consider the percentage of recycled content already in the packaging
6. Select household goods with end-of-life in mind
   - For kitchenware, choose glass, stainless steel, or ceramic options

Sustainable Practices Handbook — Goods Practices: Choosing Green Goods

- For storage, select metal, glass, or solid wood containers
- For cleaning tools, choose those with replaceable parts
- For consumables, look for products in recyclable containers
- Avoid items combining multiple materials that can't be separated
7. Choose recyclable or compostable furniture
    - Choose solid wood over particle board, medium-density fiberboard, or plastic
    - Select metal frames that can be recycled at end of life
    - Consider natural materials like bamboo, rattan, or sustainably harvested wood
    - Look for furniture with replaceable parts or modular design
    - Check for certification labels (FSC for wood, Global Recycled Standard)
8. Select recyclable building materials
    - Choose natural stone, ceramic, or glass for durable surfaces
    - Select metal fixtures, hardware, and structural elements
    - Use reclaimed or FSC-certified wood products
    - Consider cork, linoleum, or hardwood for flooring
    - Avoid composite materials that can't be separated at end of life
9. Verify claims before purchasing
    - Check for specific information about material composition
    - Research manufacturer recycling programs
    - Verify percentage of recycled content (pre- and post-consumer)
    - Look for third-party certifications

Selecting Materials 201: Definitions

- **Circular economy**: Economic system eliminating waste through continual reuse and recycling
- **Composite materials**: Two or more constituent materials that are difficult to separate
- **Downcycling**: Converting waste into new materials of lesser quality and reduced functionality
- **Post-consumer content**: Material used by consumers, diverted from waste, then recycled
- **Virgin materials**: Materials not previously used, containing no recycled content

Selecting Materials 201: Troubleshooting

Problem	Solutions
Limited recycling	Focus on durability and reusability instead.
Mixed materials	Prioritize items with recyclable main components.
Local facilities don't accept certain materials	Don't buy those materials. Store materials until recycling facilities become available.

Selecting Materials 201: Limitations

- Local recycling infrastructure varies widely
- Some product categories have few fully recyclable options
- Composite materials often have performance benefits
- Recycling symbols indicate technical recyclability but don't guarantee actual recycling

References and resources: <www.suspra.com/practice/goods/selecting-materials-201.html>

Selecting Materials 301: Choosing RoHS

Buy products that comply with the Restriction on Hazardous Substances

Buy RoHS-compliant products to reduce toxic material release during use and disposal, making electronic waste less harmful. The Restriction of Hazardous Substances directive restricts hazardous materials in products, starting with electronics but expanding to influence manufacturing globally. RoHS compliance may appear as a logo or in specifications: look for the word "RoHS" along with a checkmark. While originally a directive of the European Union, many manufacturers produce RoHS-compliant products for the global market.

Selecting Materials 301: Definitions

- **RoHS**: Restriction of Hazardous Substances directive
- **RoHS 2**: The 2011 recast (2011/65/EU) expanding scope and requirements
- **RoHS 3**: The 2015 amendment adding four phthalates to restricted substances
- **CE marking**: European conformity mark often accompanying RoHS compliance
- **Declaration of Conformity**: Document confirming a product meets requirements
- **Phthalates**: Plasticizers restricted under RoHS 3

Selecting Materials 301: Troubleshooting

Problem	Solutions
No RoHS marking	Check specifications online. Contact the manufacturer directly.
Unsure if RoHS applies	When in doubt, choose RoHS-compliant versions.
Inconsistent labeling	Focus on compliance statements rather than specific logo design.

Selecting Materials 301: Limitations

- RoHS compliance alone doesn't guarantee a product is completely non-toxic
- Verification is difficult without specialized testing
- Standards vary somewhat between regions
- Some product categories have exemptions due to technical limitations
- Doesn't address all environmental concerns like energy efficiency
- Regulations evolve, meaning older "compliant" products may not meet current standards

References and resources: <www.suspra.com/practice/goods/selecting-materials-301.html>

Maintaining and Reusing

Choosing Goods 101: Choosing Reusables

Choose reusable goods

Identify common disposable items in your daily routine, such as plastic water bottles, coffee cups, grocery bags, and food storage containers. Replace them with durable, reusable versions made from materials like stainless steel, glass, silicone, or cloth. For example, carry a reusable water bottle and coffee cup, use cloth grocery bags, and store food in glass containers. This reduces the demand for single-use plastics and other disposable materials, minimizing waste and resource depletion.

References and resources: <www.suspra.com/practice/goods/choosing-101.html>

Choosing Goods 102: Choosing Rechargeables

Choose rechargeable batteries rather than disposable ones

Use rechargeable batteries 500-1,000 times before replacement; avoid disposable batteries. Battery cells use different chemistry for their cathodes; nickel-metal halide (NiMH) and lithium ion are two types of chemistries used in small rechargeable batteries. Disposable alkaline batteries cells start with a 1.5 voltage; battery voltage decreases as they discharge. Battery capacity (how long they can provide electricity) is measured in milliampere-hours (mAh). NiMH batteries (1.2 volts) work well in most devices even though they have a slightly lower starting voltage. All batteries discharge over time, even if not connected to a load. Low Self-Discharge NiMH batteries hold charge for months, making them ideal for all applications. Be aware that some lithium batteries are disposable and some are rechargeable; make sure to buy rechargeable ones. Remove batteries from devices and store them separately whenever possible.

Choosing Goods 102: Equipment & Materials
- Rechargeable batteries (AA, AAA, AAAA, C, D, 9V or built in)
- Battery charger compatible with your battery type
- Devices that use batteries
- *Optional: Battery tester, battery storage case, label maker or marker*

Choosing Goods 102: Steps
1. Assess which battery types you use most frequently
    - Check devices to identify battery types needed
    - Note which devices drain batteries quickly
2. Research rechargeable battery options
    - Choose NiMH or *rechargeable* lithium (not *disposable* lithium) batteries
    - Check capacity (mAh) - higher numbers mean longer runtime
    - Consider "low self-discharge" batteries for infrequently used devices
3. Select an appropriate battery charger
    - Choose a charger compatible with your battery types
    - Look for chargers with individual charging channels
    - Consider "smart chargers" that prevent overcharging–this is an important safety feature
4. Buy enough rechargeable batteries so devices aren't idle while batteries are charging
5. Follow manufacturer's instructions for initial charging and recharging
6. Manage old rechargeable batteries properly
    - Do not send to landfill
    - Take batteries to electronics retailers or hazardous waste facilities so materials are recycled

Choosing Goods 102: Definitions

- **Capacity:** Energy a battery can store, measured in milliampere-hours (mAh)
- **Low Self-Discharge (LSD):** Rechargeable batteries that retain charge for long periods
- **mAh (Milliampere-hour):** Unit measuring battery capacity; higher numbers indicate longer running time
- **NiMH (Nickel-Metal Hydride):** Common type of rechargeable battery
- **Self-discharge:** Natural loss of charge in batteries when not in use
- **Smart charger:** Battery charger that prevents overcharging

Choosing Goods 102: Troubleshooting

Problem	Solutions
Won't hold charge	Use a quality charger. Try the recondition cycle. Check battery age.
Short runtime	Check mAh rating; higher capacity lasts longer.
Device doesn't work	Some devices may need 1.5V (alkaline) instead of 1.2V (NiMH).
Charger doesn't work	Check connections and battery insertion. Try different batteries.
Charging overheats	Disconnect immediately. Test battery after cooling. Use a different charger.
Unknown charge level	Use a battery tester or charger with indicators.

Choosing 102: Limitations

- Higher initial investment than disposables
- 1.2 V output may not work in some older devices designed for 1.5 V
- Requires planning to ensure charged batteries are available
- Requires bringing charger when traveling

References and resources: <www.suspra.com/practice/goods/choosing-102.html>

Maintaining 101: Keeping Manuals

Read and keep maintenance manuals for reference

Read user manuals and keep a copy for reference. On the manual, write down model numbers, purchase dates, and details about where you bought the item; attach receipts if you keep them. File paper manuals in a storage cabinet or desk drawer or use a smartphone or scanner to take a picture of them and store manuals electronically. Organize electronic copies of owner and repair manuals in folders by location of the item, such as kitchen, bathroom, garage, basement, etc. Rename files with a clear description of the item, followed by the type of manual. Take a moment when you first purchase an item to read through all the manuals that came with it. Be sure to track down a troubleshooting or repair manual, so that you have it on hand if you need it. For larger appliances, get a copy of the installation manual to keep on file. If the manual recommends a cleaning or maintenance schedule, enter those dates into your household calendar as a recurring event.

References and resources: <www.suspra.com/practice/goods/maintaining-101.html>

Organizing 402: Starting a Reuse Program

Organize a reuse program at your local school or community organization

Start a reuse program to keep valuable resources in circulation rather than disposing of them after a single use. Focus on high-volume items with substantial environmental impact that can be collected, cleaned, and redistributed, such as takeaway containers at a school. Develop rigorous cleaning protocols that meet local health department requirements. Make participation easy with simple systems and clear instructions. Integrate with existing procedures to minimize disruption; measure impacts to reinforce the program's value.

Organizing 402: Equipment & Materials
- Collection bins (durable, clearly labeled) and storage space
- Cleaning facilities and supplies
- Tracking system (spreadsheet or database)
- Signage and educational materials
- Transportation for collecting and distributing items
- *Optional: Scales for measuring waste diversion, label maker for program items*

Organizing 402: Steps
1. Form a planning team of at least three committed individuals
2. Conduct a waste audit
3. Develop your program's goals and scope
4. Pitch the idea to decision makers and secure organizational support
5. Plan your logistics carefully
6. Establish partnerships, especially with your local health department
7. Develop program policies and procedures
8. Set up your physical infrastructure
   - Install labeled collection bins in strategic locations
   - Set up cleaning stations
   - Create clear signage at all collection points
9. Develop training materials and train institutional participants
10. Launch your program with a pilot phase and kickoff event
11. Track key metrics and work to improve
12. Expand and promote success

Organizing 402: Definitions
- **Closed-loop system**: Process where materials are reused within the originating organization
- **Contamination**: Inappropriate items in the reuse stream requiring disposal
- **Sanitization**: Process of reducing microorganisms to safe levels
- **Waste audit**: Systematic analysis of waste stream to identify types and quantities

Organizing 402: Troubleshooting

Problem	Solutions
Low participation	Improve signage and education. Make collection points more visible.
Contamination	Add clear visuals to signage. Station volunteers at collection points.
Cleaning capacity	Adjust collection schedule. Recruit additional volunteers.

Problem	Solutions
Storage limitations	Use vertical storage. Reduce program scope.
Health concerns	Have the health department inspect and approve protocols.
High costs	Seek sponsorships. Improve efficiency.

Organizing 402: Limitations
- Requires ongoing coordination and oversight
- Some items cannot be safely or practically reused
- Health regulations may limit certain types of reuse
- Initial setup costs can be substantial
- Space requirements for collection, cleaning, and storage
- Significant staff or volunteer time commitment
- Some participants may resist behavioral changes

References and resources: <www.suspra.com/practice/goods/organizing-402.html>

Reusing 101: Reusing Containers

Reuse containers and bags

Get in the habit of washing out containers and bags so you can reuse them. Consider this practice as part of a closed loop: your main goal is to reduce the volume of material flowing through your household or organization. For example, rather than throwing out plastic take out containers, rinse them and stack them in your kitchen. Use them when packing a lunch or bring them along in a "take out kit" next time you eat out at the same establishment.

Glass jars from pasta sauce, salsa, and pickles make excellent storage for homemade soups, leftovers, and bulk pantry items like rice and beans. Coffee canisters work well for storing dry goods or as scoops for pet food. Yogurt containers can hold small household items like screws and nails in the garage or art supplies in a craft room. Mesh produce bags from oranges or potatoes can become scrubbers for cleaning jobs.

Rinse plastic bags and stand them upside down over wooden spoons or utensil handles to dry (or buy a special-purpose wooden bag dryer stand with many spokes to hold bags), then fold and store them for reuse. Larger plastic bags from bread or produce can be turned inside out, wiped clean, and reused as lunch bags or for storing partially used vegetables in the refrigerator.

Create a simple system to make reusing easier: designate a drying station near your sink with a dish rack specifically for containers and lids. Once dry, sort containers by size; if they can nest, stack them and lids separately to save space. Store bags in an empty tissue box for organized easy access. Label a cabinet or drawer as your "reusables station" so everyone in the household knows where to find and return containers. Before shopping, grab a few containers and bags from your station to avoid accumulating new ones. This system turns what might seem like extra work into a seamless sustainable habit that saves money and reduces waste.

References and resources: <www.suspra.com/practice/goods/reusing-101.html>

Reusing 102: Reusing Jars

Reuse glass jars for drinking glasses

Glass jars from food products like pasta sauce, pickles, jelly, and nut butters can be transformed into stylish, durable drinking glasses with just a little effort. Some brands, like Classico pasta sauce, come in mason jars, an especially good choice for repurposing into drinking glasses. Start by removing labels completely—soak jars in warm soapy water, then use a mixture of baking soda and cooking oil to remove stubborn adhesive. Thoroughly wash inside and out, paying special attention to the threads where the lid screws on. Sort your collection by size, using smaller jars for juice or wine and larger ones for water or iced tea. These repurposed jars not only reduce waste but add rustic charm to your table setting. Store them upside down in your cabinet to prevent dust accumulation. Use silicone sleeves for hot beverages or better grip.

References and resources: <www.suspra.com/practice/goods/reusing-102.html>

Reusing 103: Accepting Used Items

Accept gifts of used items from friends and family

When friends and family offer used clothing, furniture, or household items, accept them. This practice extends the lifespan of existing goods, diverting them from landfills and reducing the need for new production. Before accepting, assess the item's condition and determine whether a little cleaning or minor repairs can make it usable. By accepting hand-me-downs, you actively participate in a circular economy, where resources are shared and reused.

References and resources: <www.suspra.com/practice/goods/reusing-103.html>

Reusing 104: Thrifting

Shop at second-hand stores and yard sales

Thrifting, or shopping at second-hand stores and yard sales, is a practical way to extend the lifespan of goods and reduce the demand for new production. Start by identifying items you need, from clothing and furniture to books and electronics. Research local thrift stores, consignment shops, and yard sales in your area. By choosing pre-owned items, you decrease the need for new manufacturing, which reduces resource consumption, energy use, and waste. Thrifting also supports local economies and reduces the environmental impact associated with transporting new goods.

References and resources: <www.suspra.com/practice/goods/reusing-104.html>

Repairing 201: Fixing Clothing

Repair torn clothing and broken zippers

Repair clothing to extend garment life and reduce waste. Use the correct technique for the fabric—woven fabrics need simple stitching, knits require methods that maintain stretch, and denim benefits from reinforced repairs. Make repairs strong enough to withstand washing and regular wear.

Repairing 201: Equipment & Materials
- Sewing needles (assorted sizes)
- Thread in various colors to match clothing
- Sewing scissors or fabric shears
- Pins or safety pins

- Thimble
- Fabric scraps or patches
- Iron and ironing board
- Sewing gauge or ruler
- Chalk or fabric marker
- For zippers: replacement zippers, seam ripper
- *Optional: Sewing machine, darning mushroom, fusible interfacing, fabric glue, zipper pliers*

Repairing 201: Steps

For straight tears in woven fabrics:
1. Clean the garment before repair
2. Turn inside out and pin torn edges together
3. Thread needle with matching thread and tie a knot
4. Start ½ inch before tear, use small running stitch along the tear line
5. Continue ½ inch past end and secure with small stitches

For a reinforced repair:
1. Turn garment inside out
2. Cut interfacing or matching fabric slightly larger than the tear
3. Position patch under tear
4. Apply interfacing or pin fabric in position
5. Sew around patch edges with whip stitch
6. Turn right side out and stitch tear closed

To patch a hole:
1. Cut patch from similar fabric, ½ inch larger than hole on all sides
2. For hidden patch: turn inside out, pin patch, secure with whip stitch
3. For visible patch: position patch on outside, use decorative stitch

For knit repairs:
1. Position over darning mushroom
2. Work horizontal rows across hole, catching intact stitches
3. Turn 90 degrees and work vertically to weave new fabric

For fixing zippers:
1. For separated zipper: move slider to bottom, squeeze with pliers to tighten
2. For stuck zipper: remove obstruction, apply lubricant
3. For missing teeth: sew new stop above last good teeth
4. To replace zipper: remove old zipper with seam ripper, pin and sew new zipper

Repairing 201: Definitions

- **Blanket stitch**: Decorative stitch creating right angles along fabric edge
- **Darning**: Technique to repair holes by weaving new threads
- **Fusible interfacing**: Heat-activated fabric backing
- **Running stitch**: Basic stitch passing needle in/out in straight line
- **Seam ripper**: Tool with forked end for removing stitches
- **Whip stitch**: Stitch that wraps around fabric edge
- **Zipper tape**: Fabric portion of zipper
- **Zipper slider**: Moving part that joins or separates teeth

Repairing 201: Troubleshooting

Problem	Solutions
Visible repair	Use exact matching thread; make smaller stitches; work from inside.

Problem	Solutions
Stitches pull out	Reinforce beginning or end with backstitches; use stronger thread.
Thread breaks	Use appropriate thread weight; check for needle rough spots.
Fabric puckers	Use pins; work on a flat surface; reduce tension; press when done.
Zipper off track	Feed tape back into the slider; sew a new stop if missing.
Zipper won't stay closed	Tighten the slider with pliers; add hook and eye above the zipper.
Knit doesn't stretch	Use stretchable darning technique; choose elastic thread.
Patch edges fray	Finish with zigzag stitch; apply fray check liquid.

Repairing 201: Limitations
- Delicate fabrics may require professional repair
- Worn fabric may not hold stitches well
- Heavy-duty zippers may need specialized tools
- Stretch fabrics are difficult to repair invisibly
- Waterproof garments may lose protection
- High-stress areas need frequent reinforcement

References and resources: <www.suspra.com/practice/goods/repairing-201.html>

Repairing 301: Fixing Appliances

Repair efficient appliances and replace inefficient ones

Balance factors when deciding between repairing and replacing a broken appliance. Use the "50% rule" as a guideline: replace if repairs exceed half the cost of a new, efficient model. Consider efficiency gains and remaining lifespan. Many failures result from poor maintenance or simple part issues that are easy to fix, such as refrigerator fan motors, washing machine drain pumps, or oven heating elements. Modern electronic control boards are sometimes available as a plug-in replacement part. Buy refurbished parts from reputable vendors that offer warranties. Search online by model number or by part number, which you can often find printed near the electrical plate.

Repairing 301: Equipment & Materials
- Appliance-specific tools as needed
- Basic tool kit (screwdrivers, pliers, wrenches, multimeter)
- Safety equipment (gloves, safety glasses)
- Cleaning supplies
- Replacement parts
- Appliance manuals
- *Optional: Smart device for guides, camera, energy usage meter, notepad, flashlight*

Repairing 301: Steps
1. **Do not repair fuel-burning appliances; replace them with electric appliances**
2. Decide whether to repair or replace:
   - Inspect for hazardous materials (mercury, lead, asbestos, etc.)
   - Determine appliance age and availability of spare parts

- o Measure or estimate energy consumption, compare to new appliances
- o Estimate repair costs, compare to replacement cost
3. Replace hazardous or inefficient appliances:
   - o Discard responsibly, recycle materials
   - o Research energy-efficient, durable, and repairable alternatives
4. Diagnose problem
5. Make repairs
6. Test operation

Repairing 301: Definitions

- **Annual energy consumption**: Electricity used in a year (kWh)
- **Control board**: Electronic "brain" managing appliance functions
- **Embodied energy**: Total energy consumed throughout product lifecycle
- **Energy Star**: Certification for energy-efficient appliances
- **Multimeter**: Device measuring voltage, resistance, and current
- **Payback period**: Time for energy savings to equal upgrade cost
- **Total cost of ownership**: Purchase price plus lifetime operating costs

Repairing 301: Troubleshooting

Problem	Solutions
Won't power on	Check cord, outlet, breaker, internal fuses, power switch.
Repair didn't fix issue	Verify diagnosis; check for multiple failing components.
Can't find parts	Consider a universal part. Manufacture your own part.
Declining efficiency	Clean coils and filters; check seals and ventilation; ensure proper leveling.
Repair vs. replace	Check reliability data; research if issue is common; consider timing.

Repairing 301: Limitations

- Some repairs require specialized tools or expertise
- DIY repairs may void warranties
- Advanced diagnostics may need proprietary tools
- Sealed systems usually require professional repair
- Parts for older models may be limited, requiring making your own

References and resources: <www.suspra.com/practice/goods/repairing-301.html>

Repairing 401: Leading a Team

Lead a repair team for your local library of things

Lead a repair team to transform the "use and discard" model into a circular system where items remain in service longer. Keep the items in a "library of things" in circulation, extend product lifespans, and preserve repair knowledge. Document repairs thoroughly to create a resource for future projects. Consider environmental factors in repair decisions. Nurture the social dimension: build community resilience and preserve practical skills through team engagement.

Repairing 401: Equipment & Materials

- Dedicated repair space with proper lighting and ventilation
- Basic tool collection and safety equipment
- Inventory management system and shared calendar
- Documentation equipment (camera, laptop)
- Liability waivers and documentation forms
- *Optional: Reference library, diagnostic tools, Internet access*

Repairing 401: Steps

1. Recruit a core team of at least three volunteers
2. Establish protocols:
   - Draft liability protection documents
   - Have a "safety glasses on" area that is strictly enforced
   - Work only on manually operated or electric items, not fuel-burning ones
   - Develop intake procedures
   - Create triage system to assess repair difficulty and viability
3. Manage parts and tools:
   - Create "parts harvesting" protocol for unrepairable items
   - Build relationships with suppliers
   - Implement shared database of common parts
4. Implement tracking:
   - Create standardized repair logs and a check-in/check-out system
   - Establish maximum repair timelines
5. Train your team:
   - Create a mentoring system to welcome and support new volunteers
   - Schedule skill-sharing sessions
   - Maintain library of repair guides
   - Develop relationships with professionals for training
   - Organize workshops on specialized techniques
6. Manage environmental impact:
   - Create responsible disposal system, recycling as much as possible
   - Source environmentally preferable parts
   - Replace, rather than repair, inefficient or hazardous appliances
7. Handle challenges:
   - Develop protocol and dedicated storage area for potentially hazardous items
   - Explain liability limits for botched repairs
8. Continuously improve

Repairing 401: Definitions

- **Parts harvesting**: Salvaging components from unrepairable items
- **Repair log**: Documentation of repair process and outcomes
- **Triage**: Evaluating repairs for urgency, complexity, and resources

Repairing 401: Troubleshooting

Problem	Solutions
Volunteer availability	Implement scheduling system; create flexible roles; cross-train members.
Sourcing parts	Develop multiple supplier relationships. Harvest parts. Make parts.
Repairs taking too long	Set time limits; implement triage; establish escalation procedures.

Sustainable Practices Handbook — Goods Practices: Maintaining and Reusing

Problem	Solutions
Liability concerns	Create appropriate waivers; test repairs thoroughly; document procedures.
Team disagreements	Establish decision protocols. Vote if no consensus can be reached.
Safety concerns	Develop protocols for hazardous items. Provide training and equipment.
Team burnout	Celebrate successes; create social events; rotate responsibilities.

Repairing 401: Limitations

- Some devices designed to prevent repair
- Manufacturer support varies widely
- Safety certifications may be voided
- Limited budgets for parts and tools
- Environmental benefits must be weighed against shipping impacts
- Volunteer teams may have knowledge gaps
- Diagnostic equipment can be prohibitively expensive
- Specialized facilities impractical for community settings

References and resources: <www.suspra.com/practice/goods/repairing-401.html>

Managing Waste Wisely

Composting 001: Safety

Stay safe while composting

- Wear gloves or wash hands after handling organic waste
- Wear dust protection (N95 mask) when handling dry materials
- Use proper lifting technique when moving large amounts of materials
- Keep your tetanus vaccination current within 10 years

References and resources: <www.suspra.com/practice/goods/composting-001.html>

Composting 002: Collecting Kitchen Waste

Collect kitchen waste for composting

Collecting kitchen scraps is a fundamental building block for many composting practices. You can use a mixing bowl if you'll empty it right away; a dedicated compost pail can be emptied after a few days. Metal compost pails are the most sustainable, being durable, easy to clean, and fully recyclable. A good compost pail has a tight-fitting lid that allows air flow and may have a filter to prevent odors and deter fruit flies. Depending on what you eat and how you compost, you will keep some or all organic matter out of your garbage. Putting a paper bag or shredded junk mail into the compost pail before adding kitchen scraps will help keep waste from getting stuck to the bottom and sides, making it easier to clean.

Composting 002: Equipment & Materials
- Container for collecting scraps
- Knife and Cutting board
- *Optional: Compost pail (1-2 gallon) with tight-fitting lid, compost pail filter, sink basket, paper bags, basic kitchen scale (1g precision)*

Composting 002: Steps
1. Observe composting safety practices
2. Place container, such as your compost pail, near kitchen sink
3. *Optional: place sink basket in sink to collect scraps before putting them in compost pail*
4. *Optional: place a paper bag or a layer of shredded junk mail inside empty compost pail to make cleaning easier*
5. Use knife and cutting board to cut large scraps into 2-inch pieces to speed decomposition
6. Put scraps in container; if using a compost pail, put lid on tightly
7. *Optional: weigh compost pail when full and record data in your solid waste log*
8. Empty container when full (where to empty depends on how you compost)
9. Clean container to prevent odors and pests
10. *Optional: replace compost pail filters as necessary to prevent odors and pests*

Composting 002: Definitions
- **Compost pail:** a metal, plastic, or ceramic container for collecting kitchen scraps
- **Decomposition:** breaking down organic matter into simpler substances by microorganisms, fungi, and other decomposers
- **Kitchen scraps:** organic matter including waste produced preparing meals and uneaten food
- **Organic matter:** material that comes from living organisms, containing carbon
- **Sink basket:** a metal basket or filter placed in the corner of a sink, handy for scraping off plates and keeping small items placed in the sink from going down the drain

Composting 002: Troubleshooting

Problem	Solutions
Odors	Clean your compost pail or replace the filter.
Fruit flies	Clean your compost pail or replace the filter. Place dishes of vinegar with a dash of dish soap to catch flies.
Waste sticks to bottom and sides of pail	Place a paper bag in the pail before adding waste. Place a layer of shredded junk mail in the pail before adding waste.
Not sure what to collect	Based on how you compost, create a YES and NO list to put on your pail.

Composting 002: Limitations
- Collecting kitchen scraps only prepares you to compost; next, you will need to decide how to compost what you collect.
- Fruit flies can be difficult to prevent entirely if you eat fresh fruit.

References and resources: <www.suspra.com/practice/goods/composting-002.html>

Composting 003: Collecting Household Waste

Collect compostable household waste for composting

Collecting compostable household waste outside of the kitchen is a fundamental building block for many composting practices. The highest volume of this waste is paper and cardboard, but it also includes natural fibers, leather, and wood. Use paper bags or wastepaper bins to collect this waste separately from plastic and other non-compostable waste. Keep compostable organic matter out of your garbage that you send to a landfill or incinerator.

Composting 003: Equipment & Materials
- Containers, such as paper bags or wastepaper bins, for collecting compostable waste

Composting 003: Steps
1. Observe composting safety practices
2. Place containers in bathrooms, bedrooms, and offices
3. *Optional: label bins for compostable waste with a green square, bins for landfill waste with a red diamond*
4. Empty container when full (where to empty depends on how you compost)

Composting 003: Definitions
- Compostable: items that are made entirely of organic matter without preservatives
- Organic matter: material that comes from living organisms, containing carbon

Composting 003: Troubleshooting

Problem	Solutions
Not sure what to collect	Paper that soaks up water is compostable. Modern soy-based inks are compostable.

Composting 003: Limitations

- Collecting compostable household waste only prepares you to compost; next, you will need to decide how to compost what you collect.
- Many household items are a combination of paper and plastic; only the paper in these items will compost, the plastic will not.

References and resources: <www.suspra.com/practice/goods/composting-003.html>

Composting 004: Collecting Leaves

Collect and store leaves for composting

Collecting leaves is a fundamental building block for many composting practices. Collect leaves in the fall and use them all year. Shredding reduces storage volume and quickens composting. Storing dry leaves provides a ready source of "browns" (material relatively low in nitrogen and high in carbon) to mix with "greens" from your kitchen to maintain optimal conditions for odor-free composting.

Composting 004: Equipment & Materials

- Rake
- *Optional: Electric leaf blower, tarp, wheelbarrow, electric string trimmer, electric lawn mower, garbage can, paper leaf bags or large plastic garbage bags*

Composting 004: Steps

1. Observe composting safety practices
2. Rake or blow leaves into a pile
3. *Optional: place leaves on a tarp or in a wheelbarrow so you can move them in batches*
4. *Optional: put leaves in a garbage can and use a string trimmer to shred them*
5. *Optional: put leaves in a pile and use a lawn mower to shred them*
6. *Optional: store shredded leaves under a tarp or in bags under cover so they dry out*

Composting 004: Definitions

- String trimmer: a handheld power tool that uses a spinning monofilament to cut groundcover; also known as a "weed wacker"

Composting 003: Troubleshooting

Problem	Solutions
Too many leaves	Shred to reduce volume. Use some as mulch.
Leaves are diseased	Compost separately from healthy leaves; sun dry finished compost. Compost in a "hot" pile.

Composting 004: Limitations

- Collecting leaves only prepares you to compost; next, you will need to decide how to compost.
- Leaves are only available if you have trees on your property.

References and resources: <www.suspra.com/practice/goods/composting-004.html>

Composting 101: Using a Single Pile

Compost yard waste, such as leaves and grass clippings, in a single outdoor pile

Let nature take its course: all organic material eventually decomposes. Cut or shred material into smaller pieces, consolidate material into one pile, and provide water for the organisms that do the decomposing to speed up the process. Use a compost thermometer to determine if composting is happening; measuring temperature inside the pile that is higher than ground temperature next to the pile indicates that composting organisms are active. Alternate "browns" (dry leaves, etc.) with "greens" (fresh grass clippings, etc.) and mix material to produce better results more quickly. At the end of the composting process, a much smaller amount of dark humus material will remain.

Composting 101: Equipment & Materials

- Yard waste such as leaves, grass clippings, branches, etc.
- *Optional: Rake, pruners, tarp, wheelbarrow, electric string trimmer, electric lawn mower, pitchfork, wire fencing, compost thermometer*

Composting 101: Steps

1. Observe composting safety practices
2. Move yard waste into one pile directly in contact with soil
3. *Optional: Use pruners, a string trimmer, or a lawn mower to cut or shred material into pieces*
4. *Optional: Construct a frame using wire fencing, use a garbage can with the bottom cut off, or buy an "Earth Machine"-type composter to contain the pile*
5. Water the pile as you add layers, so all material is completely soaked
6. *Optional: Turn over material in the pile every few weeks*
7. *Optional: Water pile to speed up decomposition*

Composting 101: Definitions

- Aerobic: in the presence of oxygen molecules (O_2)
- Browns: organic matter that has a low nitrogen to carbon ratio and low moisture content
- Compost thermometer: a metal probe with thermometer, used to measure temperature in a pile
- Composting: decomposing in a controlled manner using aerobic organisms
- Decomposition: breaking down organic matter into simpler substances by microorganisms, fungi, and other decomposers
- Greens: organic matter that has a high in nitrogen to carbon ratio and high moisture content
- Humus: dark, rich material that forms in soil when organic matter decomposes
- Organic matter: material that comes from living organisms, containing carbon

Composting 101: Troubleshooting

Problem	Solutions
Pile doesn't break down	Add water. Cut up or shred material in the pile. Add more greens. Wait.
Pile smells bad.	Turn pile. Add more browns.

Composting 101: Limitations

- Woody pieces take much longer to decompose.
- An uncovered pile is unsuitable for composting kitchen scraps due to the risk of pests.

References and resources: <www.suspra.com/practice/goods/composting-101.html>

Composting 102: Burying Organic Waste

Compost organic waste, such as kitchen scraps, used tissues, hair or bones, by burying it

Bury organic waste to use the natural soil ecosystem to break down materials while enriching the surrounding soil. Sometimes called "trench composting" or "dig and drop composting," this simple form of composting requires minimal equipment and maintenance. A rich ecosystem of bacteria, fungi, invertebrates, and other decomposers break down organic matter underground, releasing nutrients directly into the soil where plants can access them. The burial method also helps retain moisture and prevents odors that might attract pests.

This method is particularly suitable for people who:
- Don't have the space or time for a traditional compost pile
- Have only small amounts of compostable material, especially kitchen waste
- Want to enrich soil in specific areas of their garden
- Need to compost problematic materials (like meat scraps, bones, or oily foods)

Dig trenches between rows of plants or in fallow areas, not disturbing the roots of established trees or bushes. In forests, dig test holes to find areas with relatively few roots. In areas with high water tables, dig test holes and make sure they don't fill with water. Buried organic matter will decompose (unless buried below the water table) over several months, enriching the soil for future plantings.

Composting 102: Equipment & Materials
- Garden shovel or trowel
- Bucket or container for collecting organic waste
- Garden gloves
- *Optional: Marker or small stakes to mark burial spots, garden journal or map*

Steps
1. Observe composting safety practices
2. Collect kitchen waste or collect household waste
3. Choose a suitable location in your yard or garden where:
   - The soil is workable (not too rocky or compacted)
   - You won't disturb existing plant roots
   - You won't be planting vegetables within four months (for food safety)
   - Water doesn't pool after rain and holes don't spontaneously fill with water
4. Dig a hole approximately 8-12 inches (20-30 cm) deep
5. Place your organic waste in the hole, filling it no more than 2/3 full
6. Cover the waste with at least 6-8 inches (15-20 cm) of soil, mounding it to allow for settling
7. *Optional: Mark the location with a small stake or marker*
8. *Optional: Record the location and date in a garden journal*
9. Allow the buried waste to decompose for four months before planting in that spot
10. For your next burial, choose a different location at least 12 inches (30 cm) away

Composting 102: Definitions
- **Decompose/Decomposition**: The process of breaking down organic materials into simpler substances by microorganisms and other decomposers
- **Organic matter**: Material derived from living organisms containing carbon compounds
- **Trench composting**: A variation where a longer trench is dug and filled and covered over time
- **Water table**: The level of water underground; a hole below the water table will fill with water

Composting 102: Troubleshooting

Problem	Solutions
Animals dig up the buried waste	Bury waste deeper (at least 8 inches/20 cm). Cover with a heavy stone temporarily. Add a layer of twigs on top to discourage digging.
Waste isn't decomposing	Ensure the waste isn't buried below the water table. Add some garden soil before covering to introduce more microbes.
Unpleasant odors	Cover with more soil (at least 8 inches/20 cm). Avoid burying large amounts of meat or dairy. Mix in some dry leaves or shredded paper.
The burial site is sinking	This is normal as materials decompose. Add more soil to maintain ground level; mound soil slightly when burying to account for settling.
Not enough space for burying	Use smaller, deeper holes. Rotate through your garden systematically. Use other composting methods, like vermicomposting.

Composting 102: Limitations

- Not suitable for large volumes of waste unless you have significant land area
- Buried waste takes longer to decompose than in active compost piles (3-6 months minimum)
- Certain materials (large branches, woody materials) will decompose very slowly when buried
- Not recommended for use in areas where the water table is high, or flooding is common
- Not ideal for urban areas with limited garden space
- Temporary reduction in nitrogen availability to nearby plants as decomposition occurs

References and resources: <www.suspra.com/practice/goods/composting-102.html>

Composting 201: Curbside Composting

Compost using a curbside composting service

Use a curbside composting service, if one is available near you.

- **Municipal programs**: Run by local governments, often included with regular waste service
- **Private subscription services**: Fee-based services in areas without municipal programs

Perfect for people who want to compost but lack the space, time, or ability to manage a home composting system, these programs collect compostable materials and process them at industrial-scale facilities that can handle meat, dairy, and compostable packaging. Industrial composting facilities maintain high temperatures to break down materials quickly and kill pathogens that might survive in lower-temperature home systems. Many facilities use advanced techniques like forced aeration and regular turning to create finished compost in weeks rather than months.

The primary environmental benefits of curbside composting include:
- Reducing methane emissions from landfills
- Creating valuable soil amendments for agriculture and landscaping
- Conserving landfill space
- Reducing the need for chemical fertilizers

Keep synthetic chemicals out of the composting process by eliminating non-stick cookware from your kitchen; all coatings eventually wear off and contaminate the food you eat and food scraps that have come in contact with those surfaces. Microwave in glass bakeware or use oil and metal cookware.

Composting 201: Equipment & Materials

- Curbside compost bin provided by your municipality or service
- Kitchen compost container for collecting scraps (1-2 gallon capacity)
- *Optional: Compostable bin liners, small kitchen scale to record data, compost pail with activated carbon filter, freezer storage container for odorous scraps, newspaper or brown paper bags to wrap wet food scraps, service pickup schedule, calendar*

Composting 201: Steps

1. Observe composting safety practices
2. Research and sign up for a curbside composting service available in your area
3. Set up your in-home collection system and collect compostable materials
4. Empty your in-home compost container into your curbside bin (often a 5-gallon bucket)
5. Place your curbside bin at the designated pickup location on collection day
6. After collection, rinse or clean your curbside bin as needed
7. *Optional: In your solid waste log, track the weight of materials you compost*

Composting 201: Definitions

- **Curbside composting**: Service that picks up organic waste from residential properties
- **Compostable**: Materials that will break down safely and completely in a composting system
- **Compostable bags**: Certified to break down completely in industrial composting facilities
- **Industrial composting**: Large-scale composting operations

Composting 201: Troubleshooting

Problem	Solutions
Odors in kitchen container	Empty more frequently. Use a container with a tight-fitting lid and carbon filter. Freeze scraps until collection day. Sprinkle baking soda in your container. Wrap wet food scraps in newspaper or a paper bag.
Fruit flies	Empty containers more frequently, especially in warm weather. Keep container lids closed. Clean containers thoroughly after emptying. Store containers in the refrigerator or freezer between additions.
Uncertainty about acceptable materials	Check your service provider's website or app. Keep a list of accepted materials near your compost container.
Missed pickups	Set calendar reminders. Check the service provider's holiday schedule. Sign up for pickup reminders if offered by your service.
Animals getting into bin	Ensure the bin lid is securely closed. Use a bin with a locking mechanism. Store the bin in a secure area until collection day.

Composting 201: Limitations

- Not all areas offer curbside composting services
- Programs vary widely in what materials they accept
- Industrial composting causes transportation emissions
- Some "compostable" products may not fully decompose even in industrial facilities
- Contamination with non-compostable materials can reduce the quality of finished compost

References and resources: <www.suspra.com/practice/goods/composting-201.html>

Composting 202: Municipal Composting

Compost using a drop-off municipal composting facility

Transform organic waste into humus that can be used in public parks, sold to farmers, or given back to residents by using a municipal composting facility. These facilities often accept meat, dairy, and diseased plants, serving people who want to compost but lack space, time, or ability to maintain a home composting system. Advantages of municipal composting include:

- **Higher processing capacity**: Industrial facilities can reach and sustain higher temperatures than home systems, allowing for more complete decomposition and pathogen elimination.
- **Broader range of acceptable materials**: Many facilities accept meat, dairy, compostable serviceware, and other items that are challenging for home composting.
- **Reduced home maintenance**: You don't need to maintain your own compost pile.

Create a circular system where your waste becomes a resource rather than a problem. Municipalities may test and give finished compost back to residents for free or at a discount, allowing you to build healthy soil and add nutrients to your own yard or garden.

Composting 202: Equipment & Materials
- Container for collecting kitchen scraps (compost pail or bucket with lid)
- Reusable container, bin, or compostable bags for transporting waste
- Vehicle to transport compostable materials (car, bike with trailer, etc.)
- Rake or shovel (for yard waste)
- *Optional: Paper for collecting and wrapping food scraps, dedicated bin for storing yard waste before transport, gloves, tarp for collecting and transporting large amounts of yard waste*

Steps
1. Observe composting safety practices
2. Find a municipal composting facility near you and learn the facility's specific guidelines
3. Collect compostable materials
4. Prepare materials for transport:
    - Remove any non-compostable contaminants (plastic, etc.)
    - Transfer kitchen waste to a sealed container (5-gallon buckets are a good option)
    - Bundle yard waste in manageable portions (wrap in a tarp)
5. Transport materials to the municipal facility
6. *Optional: Record your contribution in your waste management log*
7. Clean your collection containers thoroughly after each drop-off to prevent odors and pests

Definitions
- **Biodegradable**: Materials that break down naturally but may require specific conditions or longer timeframes than a composting facility provides
- **Compostable**: Materials that will fully break down in an industrial composting facility
- **Contamination**: Non-compostable materials that can ruin a batch of compost
- **Feedstock**: Raw materials accepted by the composting facility
- **Municipal composting**: Large-scale composting operations run by local governments or contracted waste management companies
- **Tipping fee**: A charge assessed for dropping off materials at a composting facility

Troubleshooting

Problem	Solutions
Facility doesn't accept certain materials	Keep these items separate. Explore alternative disposal methods such as home composting or specialized collection services.
Odors during transportation	Use sealed containers. Double-bag food scraps in paper bags. Sprinkle baking soda in transport containers.
Inconvenient drop-off hours	Freeze food scraps until you can make a trip. Coordinate with neighbors to take turns making drop-offs.
Leaking or messy transportation	Line containers with paper or leaves. Use tight-fitting lids. Place the transport container in a plastic bin or tray.
No municipal facility in your area	Call your local elected officials. Form a community composting initiative. Subscribe to a private composting service.
Unable to transport materials regularly	Freeze food scraps to reduce odor and pest issues between trips. Find a neighbor who uses the facility; offer to combine trips.

Limitations

- Not available in all communities
- Requires transportation, which has an environmental impact
- Drop-off hours may be limited to certain days and times
- May require sorting materials differently than for home composting
- Some facilities charge tipping fees
- Residential access may be limited to residents of specific municipalities
- No direct access to the finished compost unless the facility offers a giveback program

References and resources: <www.suspra.com/practice/goods/composting-202.html>

Composting 203: Using Three Bins

Compost yard waste and kitchen scraps using a three-bin outdoor system

Keep organic material out of landfills, processing yard and kitchen waste into rich, garden-ready compost every few months. Build a three-bin system to manage the composting process efficiently through different stages: collecting fresh materials, actively decomposing, and curing finished compost.

The system promotes aerobic decomposition, where microorganisms break down organic matter in the presence of oxygen. Continuously add new materials while removing finished compost. Water the compost to keep microbes alive. Turn the compost to introduce fresh oxygen, which speeds decomposition and helps raise temperatures to kill weed seeds and pathogens. For optimal composting:

- Maintain a good carbon-to-nitrogen ratio (roughly 3:1 browns to greens)
- Keep compost moist but not soggy
- Turn regularly to introduce oxygen
- Monitor temperature in the active bin; 130-150°F indicates vigorous microbial activity
- Locate bins in a partially shaded area to prevent excessive drying

Composting 203: Equipment & Materials

- Lumber for bin construction (untreated wood or cedar recommended)
    - 12 posts (4x4 inches, 3-4 feet long)
    - Planks for sides (1x6 inches, quantity depends on bin size)
    - *Optional: use shipping pallets instead of building your own sides*
- Hardware
    - Screws or nails
    - *Optional: Hinges for lids, wire mesh (hardware cloth, 1/4 to 1/2 inch)*
- Basic hand tools and yard tools, garden gloves, dust mask
- Composting materials
    - "Browns" (carbon-rich materials): dry leaves, straw, shredded newspaper, cardboard
    - "Greens" (nitrogen-rich materials): kitchen scraps, fresh grass clippings, plant trimmings
- *Optional: Garden fork or pitchfork, compost thermometer (for monitoring composting conditions), garden hose with spray nozzle, wheelbarrow or garden cart, tarp (for covering bins)*

Composting 203: Steps

1. Observe composting safety practices
2. Select an outdoor location for your three-bin system
    - Choose a level area with good drainage
    - Ensure easy access for adding materials and turning compost
    - Consider proximity to garden and kitchen
    - *Optional: Choose a shaded location to prevent compost from drying out*
3. Determine dimensions of each bin (typically 3-4 feet wide, 3-4 feet deep, and 3-4 feet high)
4. Construct the bins
    - Option A: Build three adjacent bins
        - Dig post holes at corners and between bins
        - Set corner posts in ground, ensure they're level and sturdy
        - Attach side planks to posts, leaving 1-2 inch gaps between planks for airflow
        - For the front of each bin, make removable slats or a hinged door for easy access
    - Option B: Use pallets
        - Arrange three pallets in a square (minus one side for access)
        - Secure corners with wire, screws, or rope
        - Create three such units side by side
5. *Optional: Line the side and bottom of bins with wire mesh to deter rodents*
6. Understand the system
    - Bin 1: Add fresh materials to this "collection" bin
    - Bin 2: Help materials break down in the "active composting" bin
    - Bin 3: Allow finished compost to mature in the "curing" bin
7. Add materials to Bin 1
    - Chop or shred larger materials to speed decomposition
    - Layer browns and greens in approximately 3 browns to 1 green ratio
    - Water layers as you add them (should be damp like a wrung-out sponge)
8. When Bin 1 is full (usually after 1-3 months):
    - Transfer contents to Bin 2 by turning and mixing thoroughly
    - This aeration accelerates the decomposition process
9. Continue adding fresh materials to Bin 1
10. Monitor Bin 2
    - Turn materials every one or two weeks for faster decomposition
    - Add water to keep moisture level similar to a wrung-out sponge
    - *Optional: Check that contents heat up (130-150°F in center indicates active composting)*
11. When Bin 2 shows signs of being mostly broken down (dark, crumbly, earthy smell):

- Move contents to Bin 3 for final curing
- At this point, Bin 1 may be full again and ready to move to Bin 2
12. Allow compost in Bin 3 to cure for one or two months
    - Turn occasionally during this time
    - Finished compost is dark, crumbly, and has an earthy smell
13. Harvest finished compost from Bin 3
14. Repeat the cycle as Bin 1 continues to fill

Composting 203: Definitions

- **Aerobic decomposition:** Breaking down organic matter in the presence of oxygen
- **Browns:** Carbon-rich materials that provide energy to decomposer organisms
- **Compost thermometer:** A long probe thermometer to reach into compost piles
- **Curing:** Final stage of composting; broken-down materials mature into usable compost
- **Greens:** Nitrogen-rich materials that allow decomposer organisms to build proteins
- **Hot composting:** Reaching temperatures of 130-150°F, killing pathogens and weed seeds
- **Turning:** Mixing and aerating compost to introduce oxygen and speed decomposition

Troubleshooting

Problem	Solutions
Not heating up	Add more greens. Make larger piles. Check moisture level; add water if too dry. Turn the pile to introduce oxygen.
Compost smells bad (like ammonia)	Too much nitrogen. Add more browns like dry leaves, straw, or shredded paper. Turn the pile to introduce more oxygen.
Compost smells bad (like rotten eggs)	Pile is too wet or compacted. Add dry browns and turn thoroughly to introduce oxygen. Ensure adequate drainage at bottom of bins.
Compost is too wet	Add dry brown materials. Turn piles more frequently. Consider covering bins during heavy rain.
Compost is too dry	Add water while turning piles. Aim for a moisture level of a wrung-out sponge. Consider adding a cover to prevent excessive evaporation.
Pests (rodents, flies) in compost	Avoid adding meat, dairy, oils, or fatty foods. Cover greens with browns. Secure bins with hardware cloth. Turn piles to discourage nesting.
Compost is breaking down very slowly	Chop or shred materials into smaller pieces. Check moisture levels. Turn more frequently. Balance greens and browns better. Add material.

Limitations

- Initial setup requires carpentry skills and materials
- Requires more space than single-bin or tumbler systems
- May not be suitable for very small urban yards
- Involves moderate physical labor for turning and moving compost between bins
- Requires ongoing management and monitoring for optimal results
- May attract pests if not properly maintained
- Not ideal for composting meat, dairy, or oily foods
- Takes up to nine months for complete composting cycle, depending on conditions

References and resources: <www.suspra.com/practice/goods/composting-203.html>

Composting 204: Using a Kitchen Appliance

Compost using an electronic kitchen appliance

Reduce food waste volume up to 90% and produce a nutrient-rich soil amendment that can be used immediately. Electric kitchen composters provide a quick, convenient way to process food waste, especially for apartment dwellers or those with limited outdoor space. Outdoor composting can take months, whereas electric kitchen composters accelerate the breakdown process through heat, aeration, and sometimes grinding mechanisms. The resulting material is often drier and more concentrated than traditional compost but works well for houseplants, container gardens, or outdoor garden beds.

Most electric composters combine heat, agitation, and aeration to speed up the composting process. Some models primarily dehydrate and physically break down material, while others use microorganisms and enzymes for decomposition. The resulting product varies, ranging from a dry, coffee ground-like material to a more traditional compost texture. Electric composters can often handle small meat scraps, dairy, and cooked foods. Check your specific model's guidelines, as capabilities vary.

Electric composters typically emit little to no odor during operation when used properly, making them suitable for indoor use. Most units have carbon filters to mitigate smells. Clean and maintain as specified by the manufacturer to enjoy odor-free operation.

Composting 204: Equipment & Materials
- Electric kitchen composter
- Available power outlet or portable power bank
- Carbon additives (included with most composters or available for purchase)
- *Optional: Kitchen waste bin for collecting scraps, kitchen scale to measure materials composted, small container for storing finished compost*

Composting 204: Steps
1. Observe composting safety practices
2. Set up your composter in a convenient location with electric power and good ventilation
3. Read the manufacturer's instructions, as specific operation varies by model
4. Collect kitchen scraps
5. Add scraps to the composter according to the manufacturer's guidelines
   - Some units require chopping larger items into smaller pieces
   - Most units have maximum fill lines that should not be exceeded
6. Add carbon additives if recommended by your composter's manufacturer
7. Start the composting cycle (4-24 hours) according to your device's instructions
8. Allow the unit to complete its cycle (most units have automatic shut-off features)
9. Remove the processed compost according to the manufacturer's instructions
   - Some units have removable bins, others require scooping out the finished material
10. Use the finished product as a soil amendment
11. Clean the unit and reset for the next batch according to the manufacturer's instructions

Composting 204: Definitions
- **Carbon additives**: Materials high in carbon added to balance nitrogen-rich food waste; in electric composters, these are often specially formulated pellets or sawdust mixtures
- **Composting cycle**: The period during which the electric composter processes food waste
- **Electric kitchen composter**: A countertop or under-counter appliance that accelerates the decomposition of food waste through heat, grinding, aeration, or a combination of methods
- **Finished compost**: The end product of the composting process; in electric composters, this is typically a dry, nutrient-rich material that can be used as a soil amendment
- **Soil amendment**: a substance that improves the properties of soil

Composting 204: Troubleshooting

Problem	Solutions
Composter emits unpleasant odors	Don't overload with food scraps. Clean thoroughly. Replace carbon filters. Add carbon additives. Provide ventilation around the unit.
Finished compost is too wet	Add more carbon additives. Drain liquid from food scraps before processing. Run an additional drying cycle.
Unit won't start or stops mid-cycle	Check the plug and outlet. Consult the manual for troubleshooting specific to your model. Contact the manufacturer.
Compost isn't breaking down properly	Review compostables list. Cut scraps into smaller pieces. Check operating temperature. Clean vents. Unblock stirring mechanisms.
Noise during operation	Some noise is normal. Check for loose components or foreign objects that might be causing vibration or obstruction.
Pests attracted to the unit	Ensure the unit is properly sealed during operation. Clean the exterior. Store finished compost in sealed containers.

Composting 204: Limitations

- Initial cost investment ranges from $300 to $1,000 depending on the model and capacity
- Requires electricity to operate, adding to energy consumption
- Limited capacity compared to outdoor composting systems (typically processes two to five liters of food waste per cycle)
- Some models may have limitations on what types of food waste can be processed
- Carbon filters need regular replacement (typically every 3 to 6 months) to maintain odor control
- Some models can be noisy during operation
- Finished product may differ from traditional compost in texture and appearance
- May require specialized carbon additives that need to be purchased regularly

References and resources: <www.suspra.com/practice/goods/composting-204.html>

Composting 301: Fermenting First

Ferment waste using the bokashi method before composting it

Use beneficial microorganisms (primarily bacteria and yeasts) to ferment organic matter without producing foul odors. Unlike aerobic ("with air") composting, bokashi is an anaerobic (closed container "without air") fermentation process that originated in Japan. Its primary advantages are:

- It accepts ALL food waste including meat, dairy, and oils (items that can attract pests in outdoor composting systems)
- It's faster than traditional composting (two to four weeks versus months)
- It can be done indoors in a small space with no odors when sealed properly
- It retains more nutrients than traditional composting
- It creates a liquid fertilizer (bokashi tea) as a beneficial byproduct

While bokashi isn't technically composting but fermentation, it's an excellent first step that prepares organic matter for more rapid decomposition in soil or a traditional compost pile. Fermented materials become highly bioavailable to soil organisms, improving soil health and plant growth.

Revision: 25.1.8

The bokashi process creates an acidic environment (pH around 3.5) preserving food waste rather than decomposing it. This acidic pre-compost material neutralizes quickly once buried in soil. The microbes added through the bokashi bran help accelerate the further breakdown of the waste once it's exposed to oxygen. For apartment dwellers or those with limited outdoor space, bokashi provides a viable solution for processing food waste sustainably without odor issues or attracting pests.

Composting 301: Equipment & Materials

- Bokashi bucket with tight-fitting lid and spigot (or two 5-gallon buckets with lids, one with a spigot installed at the bottom)
- Bokashi bran (wheat bran inoculated with effective microorganisms)
- Plate, disk, or plastic sheet that fits inside the bokashi bucket to press down waste
- Spray bottle
- 1 tablespoon measuring spoon
- Regular compost bin or soil burial location
- *Optional: Kitchen scale to track waste amounts*

Composting 301: Steps

1. Observe composting safety practices
2. Set up your bokashi bucket in a convenient indoor location (under sink, in pantry, etc.)
3. Add a layer of bokashi bran (approximately 1-2 tablespoons) to the bottom of the empty bucket
4. Add a one or two inch layer of food scraps to the bucket
5. Sprinkle one tablespoon of bokashi bran evenly over the food scraps
6. Press down firmly on the food scraps using a plate or plastic disk to remove air pockets
7. Cover with the tight-fitting lid
8. Drain liquid from the spigot every two or three days (this is bokashi tea)
9. Dilute bokashi tea 1:100 with water and use as a fertilizer, or pour down drains as a cleaner
10. Repeat steps 4-8 each time you add scraps until the bucket is full
11. When full, seal the bucket and let ferment in a warm location for 10 to 14 days
12. After fermentation is complete, either:
    - Bury the fermented waste in a garden bed (8-12 inches deep)
    - Add to a regular compost pile
    - Mix with soil in a separate container and let sit for two to four weeks

Composting 301: Definitions

- **Anaerobic**: A process that occurs without oxygen
- **Bokashi**: Japanese term meaning "fermented organic matter"
- **Bokashi bran**: Wheat bran, rice bran, or sawdust inoculated with effective microorganisms
- **Bokashi tea**: Liquid from fermenting materials, rich in nutrients and microorganisms
- **Effective microorganisms (EM)**: A specific blend of microbes that aid in fermentation
- **Fermentation**: Microorganisms convert organic compounds into simpler substances in the absence of oxygen
- **pH**: Measure of acidity or alkalinity; bokashi creates an acidic environment with pH of 3.5

Composting 301: Troubleshooting

Problem	Solutions
Foul odor from bokashi bucket	Make sure the lids are sealed properly. Add more bokashi bran. Drain liquid. Press down to remove air pockets.
Mold in the bucket	White or blue-white mold is normal. Black, green, or blue mold are problems; add more bokashi bran and press materials down better.

Problem	Solutions
Not enough bokashi tea being produced	Some materials (dry bread or grains) produce less liquid; add fruits and vegetables or green plant waste.
Bokashi materials not breaking down after burial	Soil may be too cold. Bury in warmer weather. Add to a hot compost pile. Ensure burial location has active soil biology.
Pests (fruit flies, etc.) getting into bucket	Check the lid. Close the bucket immediately after adding waste. Keep a small bowl of vinegar near the bucket to attract flies away.
Bokashi tea smells very foul	This is normal. Dilute before use (100 parts water to 1 part tea).

Composting 301: Limitations

- Requires specialized bokashi bran (you can make your own)
- Not a complete composting solution; requires a second step (burial or traditional composting)
- Takes up some kitchen space
- The acidic fermented material will harm plants if used directly; process further for safety
- Not ideal for large volumes of yard waste like leaves and branches

References and resources: <www.suspra.com/practice/goods/composting-301.html>

Composting 302: Using a Tumbler

Compost in an enclosed tumbler

Use a convenient, enclosed compost tumbler to deter pests, contain odors, and accelerate decomposition. Rotate your tumbler to mix materials thoroughly and introduce oxygen throughout the pile, without the need to turn the pile with a pitchfork or shovel. Frequently turn your tumbler to accelerate the composting process, potentially producing finished compost in as little as three weeks under optimal conditions (though eight weeks is more typical). The enclosed design helps retain heat and moisture, making composting possible year-round in many climates.

Fill your tumbler to the right capacity—not too empty (which limits heating) and not too full (which limits tumbling effectiveness). Start with a batch that fills about one-third to one-half of the tumbler and allows room for turning while providing enough mass for heating.

For best results, maintain a ratio of approximately three parts carbon-rich "browns" (dried leaves, paper, cardboard, wood chips) to one part nitrogen-rich "greens" (food scraps, fresh grass clippings, coffee grounds). If your compost smells bad or isn't heating up, adjust this ratio.

Composting 302: Equipment & Materials

- Compost tumbler
- "Browns": Carbon materials (shredded paper, dried leaves, or cardboard)
- "Greens": Nitrogen materials (green grass clippings, vegetable scraps)
- Water source (hose or watering can)
- *Optional: Compost activator/starter, thermometer designed for composting, small container for collecting kitchen scraps, pruning shears or scissors for cutting large pieces*

Composting 302: Steps

1. Observe composting safety practices
2. Set up your tumbler in a location that:

- Receives partial sun (some sun helps maintain heat)
- Has a level surface
- Is accessible for turning and harvesting
3. Collect a good balance of "browns" (carbon-rich materials) and "greens" (nitrogen-rich materials) to fill at least one-third of your tumbler
4. Add materials to the tumbler, mixing browns and greens
5. Add water as you go to achieve the moisture level of a wrung-out sponge
6. *Optional: Add a handful of finished compost or commercial compost starter to introduce beneficial microorganisms*
7. Close the tumbler securely
8. Turn the tumbler five complete rotations every two days
9. *Optional: Check internal temperature with a compost thermometer; 120-150°F (49-65°C) indicates active composting*
10. Continue adding materials as they become available, maintaining the brown-to-green ratio
11. When the tumbler is nearly full, stop adding new materials and continue turning regularly
12. Allow materials to decompose (can take from 3 to 8 weeks depending on conditions)
13. Harvest finished compost when it appears dark and crumbly with an earthy smell
14. *Optional: If some larger pieces remain incompletely composted, sift them out and return them to the tumbler for the next batch*

Composting 302: Definitions

- **Aeration**: Introducing air into the compost pile, necessary for aerobic decomposition
- **Browns**: Carbon-rich materials that provide structure and energy to composting organisms
- **Compost activator/starter**: Microorganisms that help jump-start the composting process
- **Compost tumbler**: An enclosed container designed to rotate and mix composting materials
- **Greens**: Nitrogen-rich materials that allow composting organisms to make proteins
- **Thermophilic**: Heat-loving microorganisms that thrive above 120°F

Troubleshooting

Problem	Solutions
Compost is too wet	Add more dry browns (leaves, shredded paper). Leave the tumbler open in dry weather.
Compost is too dry	Add water. Add more greens.
Bad odor (rotten eggs)	Too wet or compacted. Add browns, turn more frequently, ensure drainage holes aren't blocked.
Bad odor (ammonia)	Too much nitrogen. Add more browns, turn more frequently.
Not heating up	Insufficient volume, too dry, or wrong green-to-brown ratio. Add more materials, check moisture, or adjust ratio.
Difficult to turn	Tumbler is too full. Remove some material or wait for contents to shrink as decomposition progresses.
Pests attracted to tumbler	Ensure the tumbler is securely closed. Bury fresh food scraps in the center of existing materials. Avoid adding meat, dairy, or oils.

Problem	Solutions
Slow decomposition	Add water. Add more materials. Add more greens. Turn more frequently. Add an activator. Move the tumbler to a sunnier location. Wait for warmer weather.

Limitations

- Limited capacity compared to larger composting systems
- Can be difficult to turn when completely full
- May not reach high enough temperatures in cold climates during winter
- Quality tumblers can be a significant investment compared to simple bin or pile systems
- Not suitable for large volumes of yard waste
- Some designs do not allow continuous addition of materials

References and resources: <www.suspra.com/practice/goods/composting-301.html>

Composting 303: Using a Buried Chamber

Compost pet waste and other material in a partially-buried chamber

Use buried chamber composting systems to handle materials that are typically challenging to compost in traditional systems, particularly pet waste and food scraps that might attract pests in open compost piles. These systems use a combination of anaerobic (without oxygen) and aerobic (with oxygen) decomposition processes to break down waste materials. The two main types of buried chamber systems serve slightly different purposes:

Green Cone systems are primarily designed for food waste disposal. These digesters feature a double-wall construction with an inner and outer cone. The outer cone is partially buried and allows the sun to heat the chamber, accelerating decomposition. The inner cone allows waste to break down and slowly release nutrients directly into the surrounding soil. Green Cones can process large amounts of food waste without requiring emptying, as the decomposed material filters directly into the soil.

Doggie Dooley systems are specifically designed for pet waste disposal. These are essentially mini-septic tanks that use bacterial action to break down pet waste. They're particularly useful for households with multiple pets where waste accumulation is significant. Some models require occasional emptying while others allow waste to percolate into the surrounding soil.

Both systems rely on beneficial bacteria and other microorganisms to break down the waste material. The decomposition process is accelerated by warmth, moisture, and the addition of compost activators or accelerators that contain bacterial cultures. In warm weather, waste can decompose within weeks, while in colder conditions, the process may slow significantly or even temporarily halt. Unlike traditional composting systems, buried chambers don't require the careful balancing of carbon-rich "browns" and nitrogen-rich "greens," though adding some carbon materials like shredded paper can help with odor control and decomposition.

The main advantage of these systems is their ability to safely dispose of materials that would otherwise go to landfills, reducing methane emissions and returning nutrients to the soil. They also provide a hygienic way to handle pet waste that minimizes health risks to humans and animals.

Composting 303: Safety Considerations

- Always wash hands thoroughly after handling pet waste or adding materials to the system
- Keep the lid secured to prevent access by children or animals
- Never use resulting compost on edible gardens or crops

Sustainable Practices Handbook — Goods Practices: Managing Waste Wisely

- For pet waste systems, locate away from vegetable gardens and water sources
- Wear gloves when handling the system or waste materials
- Don't use the system for disposable diapers, cat litter, or non-biodegradable materials
- Be aware that these systems may not fully eliminate pathogens, especially in cold weather

Composting 303: Equipment & Materials

- Buried chamber system (Green Cone, Doggie Dooley, or similar)
- Shovel, pickaxe or mattock (for hard soil)
- Compostable pet waste bags or newspaper
- Bucket with lid for temporary waste collection
- Water
- *Optional: Compost thermometer, hose with spray nozzle, compost accelerator/activator or septic starter, gravel or small rocks (for drainage in poorly draining soils), cardboard, wood chips, or straw (for carbon-rich materials), wood ash or garden lime (to control odor), power drill (if modifications are needed), hardware cloth (to deter pests)*

Composting 303: Steps

1. Choose location and system
   - Choose a location that receives sunlight (to promote microbial activity)
   - Ensure the location is well-drained and not in a low spot that collects water
   - Select a spot at least 10 feet from any vegetable garden and 3 feet from property lines
   - Keep system away from wells, streams, or other water sources (at least 100 feet)
   - Choose a location with easy access for adding waste materials
2. Prepare the site
   - Dig a hole according to manufacturer's instructions (typically 18-24 inches deep)
   - For poor-draining soils, add 2-3 inches of gravel at the bottom for drainage
   - For very wet areas, consider excavating a larger area and adding drainage material
3. Install the system per the manufacturer's instructions
4. Activate the system
   - Add a compost accelerator, activator, or septic starter according to package instructions
   - Add two gallons of water to moisten the system and activate microbes
   - For DIY systems, add a shovelful of garden soil to introduce microorganisms
5. Use the system
   - For pet waste:
     - Collect pet waste in biodegradable bags or newspaper
     - Open the lid and add waste to the chamber
     - Optionally sprinkle a small amount of accelerator after adding waste
     - Keep lid closed when not in use
   - For food waste:
     - Add fruit and vegetable scraps, eggshells, coffee grounds, and tea bags
     - Avoid adding meat, dairy, oils, or large amounts of citrus
     - Chop or break down larger items for faster decomposition
     - Keep lid closed when not in use
6. Maintain the system
   - Add water periodically to maintain moisture, especially during dry periods
   - Add compost accelerator monthly according to manufacturer's instructions
   - During cold weather, expect slower decomposition
   - If odor develops, add a small amount of garden lime or wood ash
   - Monitor fill levels and ensure proper drainage
7. Managing the finished material
   - For Green Cone and similar systems:
     - Material naturally filters into surrounding soil

Sustainable Practices Handbook — Goods Practices: Managing Waste Wisely

- No removal or harvesting required
  - For Doggie Dooley and similar tank systems:
    - After two years, check if system is near full capacity
    - If needed, install a new system in a different location
    - Allow the full system to continue decomposing for an additional year
    - Use resulting material only for ornamental gardens, never food crops

Composting 303: Definitions

- **Aerobic decomposition:** Breakdown by microorganisms that require oxygen
- **Anaerobic decomposition:** Breakdown by microorganisms that don't require oxygen
- **Compost accelerator/activator:** Products containing beneficial bacteria and/or enzymes that speed up the composting process
- **Hardware cloth:** Wire mesh useful for deterring animals like raccoons, skunks, and rats
- **Leachate:** Liquid that drains from decomposing material, containing nutrients and potentially pathogens
- **Pathogen:** Disease-causing microorganisms that may be present in pet waste or spoiled foods
- **Percolation:** The process of liquid slowly filtering through soil

Composting 303: Troubleshooting

Problem	Solutions
System has strong odors	Add garden lime or wood ash to neutralize odors. Add carbon materials like shredded paper or leaves. Check that the system isn't waterlogged.
Waste isn't decomposing	Check if the system is too dry and add water if needed. Add compost activator or accelerator. Ensure the system receives adequate sunlight.
System is attracting flies or pests	Add soil or browns on top of fresh waste. Install hardware cloth around the buried portion if rodents are a problem.
System is waterlogged	Add gravel beneath and around the system. Relocate the system to higher ground. Add holes to the buried portion for better drainage.
Contents are freezing in winter	Accept slower decomposition during cold months. Insulate the above-ground portion with straw bales in extremely cold climates.
System is full	For Green Cone type systems, wait. For Doggie Dooley types, install a new system; allow the full one to finish decomposing for a year.

Limitations

- Not suitable for large volumes of waste in small yards
- Performance decreases significantly in cold weather
- Not suitable for meat, dairy, bones, or large amounts of oily foods
- Cannot be used for cat litter, even "flushable" varieties of litter
- Requires consistent moisture management
- Contents from pet waste systems cannot be used on food crops
- May be prohibited in some locations, especially in watershed protection areas
- Requires soil with adequate drainage capability
- May not fully eliminate pathogens, especially in cold conditions
- Not suitable for compostable packaging, which require higher temperatures to break down

References and resources: <www.suspra.com/practice/goods/composting-301.html>

Composting 304: Using Worms

Compost using worms (vermicomposting)

Transform kitchen waste into a nutrient-rich soil amendment with worms, harnessing their digestive systems to break down organic matter quickly and produce castings (worm poop) that are exceptionally rich in beneficial microbes and plant nutrients. Red wigglers (*Eisenia fetida*) thrive in the organic-rich environments of a worm bin, reproduce quickly, and can process approximately half their body weight in food scraps each day. European nightcrawlers (*Eisenia hortensis*) are another good option, especially if you plan to use some worms for fishing as well.

Vermicomposting can be done outdoors during warm weather or indoors year-round. Maintain consistent moisture in your worm bin and adequate air flow around your bin. Plastic storage bins or wooden boxes work well; specialized commercial worm bins with stacking trays can simplify the harvesting process. Regardless of bin type, provide drainage to prevent excessive moisture that can create anaerobic conditions and kill worms. A properly maintained worm bin should not produce unpleasant odors, making it suitable for kitchens, basements, or garages.

Vermicompost contains higher concentrations of beneficial microorganisms, enzymes, and plant growth hormones than other types of compost. It also tends to have more readily available nutrients and better soil-building properties. Liquid from a worm bin ("worm tea") is a valuable fertilizer. Dilute 1 part tea to 10 parts water to use directly on plants.

Composting 304: Equipment & Materials
- Worm bin container (plastic tote, wooden box, or commercial worm bin)
- Red wiggler worms (*Eisenia fetida*) or European nightcrawlers (*Eisenia hortensis*)
- Bedding material (shredded newspaper, cardboard, coir, or aged compost)
- Spray bottle with water
- Kitchen scraps
- Small trowel or garden fork
- *Optional: Thermometer, small scale to measure material composted, fine mesh screen (for harvesting), tarp or large plastic sheet (for harvesting)*

Composting 304: Steps
1. Observe composting safety practices
2. Prepare the worm bin
   - Drill 8 to 12 small drainage holes (1/8 to 1/4 inch) in the bottom of your container
   - For plastic bins, add 10-20 small air holes (1/16 inch) along the upper sides
   - Place a tray underneath to catch any liquid (worm tea)
   - Position the bin in a location with temperature between 55 and 77°F (13 and 25°C)
3. Prepare the bedding
   - Tear or shred newspaper/cardboard into 1-inch strips
   - Soak the bedding material in water until damp but not soggy
   - Squeeze out excess water (bedding should feel like a wrung-out sponge)
   - Fill the bin 3/4 full with the damp bedding material
   - Mix in a cup of soil or aged compost to introduce microorganisms
4. Add the worms
   - Add one pound of worms per square foot of surface area
   - Gently spread worms on top of the bedding
   - Leave bin uncovered with a light on for first day to encourage worms to burrow down
5. Begin feeding
   - Wait two days before adding first food scraps
   - Bury small amounts of kitchen scraps (1 cup) in one corner of the bin

- Cover food with 2 inches of bedding
- Rotate feeding areas throughout the bin for subsequent feedings
6. Maintain the bin
    - Feed worms approximately 1/2 pound of scraps per pound of worms per week
    - Keep bedding as moist as a wrung-out sponge (spray with water if necessary)
    - Cover newly added food with fresh bedding
    - Add fresh bedding material every three months or when bin appears to be filling up
7. Harvest the compost (after six months)
    - Choose a method:
        - **Light method:** Dump contents on tarp in bright light and make small piles. Worms will move to the bottom, allowing you to remove vermicompost from the top.
        - **Side-to-side method:** Push contents to one side of the bin and add fresh bedding and food to the empty side. Worms will migrate to the fresh side over three weeks.
        - **Screen method:** Dump bin contents onto mesh screen over a tarp and sift, allowing finished compost to fall through while worms remain on top.
8. Use the finished vermicompost
    - Apply as top dressing for houseplants (1/4 inch layer)
    - Mix into potting soil (1 part vermicompost to 4 parts potting soil)
    - Brew into "worm tea" by steeping in water (1 cup vermicompost per gallon of water)

Composting 304: Definitions

- **Bedding:** Material that provides the living environment for worms, typically high-carbon materials like shredded paper or cardboard that retain moisture and provide air space
- **Castings:** Worm excrement; the finished product of vermicomposting, rich in beneficial microorganisms and plant nutrients
- **Coir:** Coconut fiber, a sustainable alternative to peat moss used as worm bedding
- **Red wigglers:** *Eisenia fetida*, the most common species used for vermicomposting due to their ability to thrive in organic waste and reproduce quickly
- **Vermicompost:** The end product of the breakdown of organic matter by worms, consisting of worm castings, decomposed organic waste, and beneficial microorganisms
- **Worm tea:** Liquid from a worm bin, rich in microorganisms and soluble plant nutrients

Composting 304: Troubleshooting

Problem	Solutions
Foul odor from bin	Bin is too wet or anaerobic. Add dry bedding, ensure proper drainage, and avoid overfeeding. Check that air holes aren't blocked.
Worms trying to escape	Check moisture, temperature, or presence of foods worms dislike (citrus, onions, garlic). Shade the bin from direct sunlight.
Fruit flies or other insects	Cover food scraps with at least 2 inches of bedding. Freeze scraps before adding to kill fly eggs. Cover with fine mesh. Reduce feeding temporarily.
Mold growing in bin	Some mold is normal. Excessive mold suggests overfeeding or too much moisture. Reduce feeding rate. Add dry bedding.
Worms dying	Check temperature (should be 55 to 77°F), moisture level (should be like a wrung-out sponge), and potential toxins in food. Start a second bin.
Slow processing of food	Check bin temperature. Chop food into smaller pieces. Give the worm population time to grow (takes several months).

Problem	Solutions
Too wet or bin leaking	Add more dry bedding. Ensure the bin has adequate drainage holes. Place a tray underneath to catch excess moisture.
Too dry	Mist with water from a spray bottle. Add moist (but not soaking) food scraps.

Limitations

- Cannot process large volumes of waste quickly without a large worm population
- Temperature sensitivity limits outdoor use in extreme climates
- Not suitable for meat, dairy, oils, citrus, or onion family scraps
- Requires more monitoring and management than traditional compost piles
- Harvesting the finished vermicompost can be labor-intensive
- Initial cost of worms can be higher than starting a traditional compost pile
- Not ideal for yard waste like branches or large amounts of leaves

References and resources: <www.suspra.com/practice/goods/composting-304.html>

Composting 305: Using Flies

Compost using black soldier flies

Transform food waste into nutrient-rich compost using insect larvae rather than primarily relying on microorganisms. Black soldier fly (*Hermetia illucens*) composting is particularly effective for processing high-nitrogen materials, including meat and dairy.

The life cycle of black soldier flies makes them ideal for composting. Adult black soldier flies live only five to eight days, don't eat, don't bite, and aren't considered pests. The female lays about 500 eggs near decomposing material. The eggs hatch into larvae that consume organic matter voraciously—they can eat twice their body weight daily. In three weeks, larvae grow from tiny hatchlings to approximately 1 inch long. When larvae are ready to pupate, they naturally migrate upward and out of the composting material, making collection relatively easy if you design your system with this behavior in mind.

The products of BSF composting include:

1. Nutrient-rich compost
2. Protein-rich larvae that can be used as feed for chickens, fish, or other animals
3. Liquid fertilizer (leachate) that can be diluted 1 part leachate to 9 parts water for use on plants

BSF composting offers several advantages over traditional composting:

- Processes food waste much faster (days instead of months)
- Significantly reduces volume (up to 95% reduction)
- Can safely process meat, dairy, and oily foods
- Requires less space and turning than traditional compost
- Produces minimal odor when managed properly
- Creates protein-rich larvae in addition to compost and leachate

The system works best in warmer climates or during warm seasons, as black soldier flies are most active at temperatures between 65 and 85°F (18 to 29°C). In colder climates, the system can be moved indoors during winter or supplemented with purchased larvae to maintain the colony.

Composting 305: Equipment & Materials

- Composting bin with lid (plastic tote, wooden box, or specialized black soldier fly bin)
- Black soldier fly (*Hermetia illucens*) starter larvae or eggs
- Drill (for making ventilation and drainage holes)
- Mesh screen (1-2 mm openings)
- Container for collecting leachate
- Small ramp inside bin for adult flies to exit
- Food scraps (vegetables, fruit, grains, small amounts of meat or dairy)
- Garden soil or finished compost (as starter material)
- Spray bottle with water
- *Optional: Harvesting containers for larvae, thermometer, pitchfork or turning tool, small LED light to attract adult flies*

Composting 305: Steps

1. Observe composting safety practices
2. Choose location for your black soldier fly (BSF) composting bin
   - Select a warm, partially shaded area (65 to 85°F or 18 to 29°C)
   - Place it where some odor won't be problematic
   - Ensure accessibility for adding scraps and harvesting compost
3. Prepare the composting bin
   - Drill 16 small drainage holes (1/4") in the bottom
   - Drill 1/4" ventilation holes around the upper sides
   - Cover drainage holes with fine mesh to prevent larvae escape
   - Place bin on blocks above a tray to catch leachate
4. Prepare the bedding
   - Add three inches of moistened soil or finished compost
   - Mix in some shredded cardboard or coco coir
   - Spray with water until damp but not soaking (similar to a wrung-out sponge)
5. Add food waste
   - Start with two pounds of kitchen scraps
   - Chop larger pieces into 2" or smaller pieces
   - Mix into the top layer of bedding and cover with a thin layer of dry bedding material
6. Attract or introduce black soldier flies
   - Option 1: Add purchased BSF larvae or eggs
   - Option 2: Place bin outdoors in warmer months where flies naturally occur
   - Option 3: Add some material from an existing BSF system
7. Maintain proper conditions
   - Keep moisture levels appropriate (65-70%)
   - Maintain temperature between 65 and 85°F (18 to 29°C)
   - Add food scraps regularly but avoid overfeeding
   - If material becomes too wet, add dry bedding
   - If too dry, mist with water
8. Continue adding food waste
   - Add new food scraps every other day
   - Bury scraps under a thin layer of bedding to reduce odors and deter pests
   - Avoid overfeeding; wait until most previous scraps are consumed
9. Harvest compost and larvae
   - After three months, stop adding food to the active side of bin
   - Mature larvae will self-harvest by crawling up ramps
   - *Optional: Collect migrating larvae in collection containers*
   - *Optional: Use larvae as animal feed or fishing bait*
   - Allow remaining material to cure for four weeks

Sustainable Practices Handbook Goods Practices: Managing Waste Wisely

- o Remove finished compost from bottom of bin
10. Start a new cycle
    - o Leave some larvae and eggs in the bin to process new waste
    - o If system is properly maintained, the colony will be self-sustaining

Composting 305: Definitions

- **Black soldier fly (BSF)**: *Hermetia illucens*, a non-pest fly species whose larvae efficiently consume organic waste
- **BSF larvae**: The immature form of black soldier flies; voracious eaters of organic matter
- **Leachate**: Liquid from the composting material; can be used as liquid fertilizer when diluted
- **Pupation**: The transformation stage between larva and adult fly
- **Self-harvesting**: The natural behavior of mature BSF larvae to crawl out before pupation

Troubleshooting

Problem	Solutions
Few or no flies appearing	Check the temperature (may be too cold). Add purchased larvae. Ensure the bin is in a location accessible to wild BSF. Add a small amount of fish or meat to attract flies. Use LED light near system to attract adults
Foul odors	System is likely too wet or overfed. Add dry bedding material. Reduce feeding rate. Ensure proper drainage. Mix contents to increase aeration.
Other insects or pests invading	Ensure the lid is secure. Reduce feeding rate. Bury food waste more thoroughly. Check for gaps in the container. Add protective screens.
Larvae dying	Check moisture (should be like a wrung-out sponge). Verify temperature range. Ventilate. Reduce the amount of acidic materials like citrus peels.
Too much leachate	Add more dry bedding. Reduce watering. Ensure proper drainage.
Larvae escaping	Install better barriers around edges. Improve the self-harvesting ramp design. Check for cracks or holes.
Slow decomposition	Raise temperature. Add more larvae. Chop food into smaller pieces. Add more diversity of food waste.
White mold appearing	Normal in BSF systems. Reduce moisture. Improve ventilation.

Limitations

- Not suitable for individuals uncomfortable with handling insect larvae
- May attract unwanted wildlife if not properly secured
- Requires temperatures between 65 to 85°F (18 to 29°C) to function optimally; significantly slows or stops below 60°F
- May need to purchase starter larvae in regions where BSF aren't native or during cold seasons
- Not as accepted as traditional composting methods; may be banned in some settings
- Requires more active management than traditional composting
- Less effective at processing large amounts of carbon-rich materials like leaves and branches
- Higher initial setup cost than simple compost piles

References and resources: <www.suspra.com/practice/goods/composting-305.html>

Sustainable Practices Handbook — Goods Practices: Managing Waste Wisely

Discarding 101: Landfilling

Landfill plastic and other synthetic waste materials

Most plastic waste isn't actually recyclable, even when placed in recycling bins. The recycling symbols (numbers 1-7) on plastic items indicate the type of resin used, not recyclability. In most communities, only plastics labeled #1 (PET) and #2 (HDPE) are consistently recycled, while plastics #3-7 are rarely recycled due to economic and technical limitations. Many items that technically could be recycled are not accepted by local programs due to contamination, small size, or lack of market demand.

Furthermore, many plastic products are composed of multiple types of plastic or other materials that cannot be separated in the recycling process. When these mixed-material items enter recycling streams, they can contaminate entire batches of otherwise recyclable materials.

Until significant changes occur in plastic production and recycling infrastructure, landfilling many types of plastic waste remains a necessary practice. While not ideal from an environmental perspective, modern landfills are engineered to contain waste safely, with liners to prevent leaching into groundwater and systems to capture methane gas emissions. Thoroughly rinsing plastic containers reduces the amount of organic material entering landfills that produce methane.

When discarding plastic waste in landfills, ensure it's properly contained to prevent it from becoming litter. Remember that the most effective waste management strategy is to reduce consumption of single-use plastics and other non-recyclable materials in the first place.

References and resources: <www.suspra.com/practice/goods/discarding-101.html>

Discarding 201: Removing Junk

Hire a junk removal company

When decluttering or renovating, large items and significant amounts of waste can be overwhelming. Hire a junk removal company to keep solid waste out of landfills through proper sorting, recycling, and donation. To begin, research local junk removal services, prioritizing those with transparent recycling and donation policies. Before scheduling, inventory your items to ensure an accurate quote. During pickup, clearly label items for donation or recycling, and ask the company for a detailed report on where your waste is processed. For example, many junk removal companies will donate usable furniture and household items to local charities, and recycle metal, wood, and electronics.

References and resources: <www.suspra.com/practice/goods/discarding-201.html>

Donating 101: Sharing Used Items

Share used items with friends and family

Instead of throwing away clothing, toys, or household items that are still in good condition, share them with friends, family, or neighbors. This practice reduces waste by extending the lifespan of goods and lessens the demand for new production, which consumes resources and emits greenhouse gases. Start by organizing items you no longer need and reaching out to people who might benefit. For clothing, consider hosting a swap or creating a shared online album. For children's items, coordinate with playgroups or parent networks. This simple act minimizes landfill waste and fosters a sense of community. Sharing hand-me-downs contributes to the "Goods" pathway by promoting reuse and reducing the need to buy new items.

References and resources: <www.suspra.com/practice/goods/donating-101.html>

Revision: 25.1.8

Sustainable Practices Handbook — Goods Practices: Managing Waste Wisely

Donating 102: Reselling or Donating

Resell or donate items you no longer need

Resell or donate items in working condition to extend products' useful lives, conserve resources and keep materials out of landfills. First try reselling to ascertain whether the item has any value. Inquire with a charity before assuming they would accept a donation of a physical item. Do your charity a favor and sell your item and then donate the money to them. Most organizations have policies about which types of physical goods they can accept; money is almost always preferred. If you are unable to sell the item or find a charity interested in accepting it, then try posting on a Buy Nothing or Freecycle group.

Before making donations, clean all items thoroughly, make any quick fixes you can, find all parts and components, make sure items are in fact usable as is or with a simple repair, and package them in their original packaging or a suitable container along with any manuals (if applicable). For electronic items that may contain personal data, find out how to remove all information from the device before giving it away to protect yourself from fraud.

References and resources: <www.suspra.com/practice/goods/donating-102.html>

Organizing Waste 101: Sorting Into Five Streams

Sort your solid waste into five streams: reuse, compost, recycle, divert, and landfill

Direct each waste type to its proper destination with a five-stream color-coded sorting system. Prepare labels for each type of bin with distinctive shapes and colors:

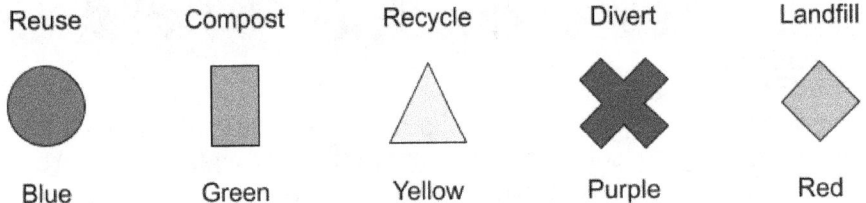

Reuse	Compost	Recycle	Divert	Landfill
Blue	Green	Yellow	Purple	Red

In "blue circle bins," set aside items for reuse, such as glass milk jars, to be returned to a retailer or for your own reuse, as well as items to resell or donate. Establish a convenient reuse center in your household or organization for locally reusable items, such as boxes and shipping materials, take-away containers, glass jars, scratch paper that is blank on one side, etc. and for larger items that you plan to resell or donate. In "green box bins," collect all organic waste, including all food scraps, used tissues, and soiled paper products that can be composted. In "yellow triangle" bins, put metal, glass, cardboard, and–if your community allows–#1 PET or #2 HDPE rigid plastic that can be recycled. In "purple X" bins, divert hazardous materials that require special handling. In "red diamond" bins, put your remaining trash, mostly plastics that would be sorted out of single-stream recycling and sent to a landfill or incinerator anyway.

After setting up five types of labeled bins, observe which kinds of garbage cause confusion. Prepare labels to provide clear guidance. For example, "Stinky stuff in here!" for compost. Collect for composting all organic waste that rots and smells bad. Landfill trash should only contain synthetic materials like plastic wrappers; rinse out and dry wrappers before placing them in the landfill bin. Trash that produces foul odors in your landfill bin will cause environmental problems in a landfill.

Organizing 101: Equipment & Materials

- Five containers for sorting waste (reuse, compost, recycling, landfill, and divert)

- Labels for each container
- *Optional: Reference sheet listing what goes in each stream*

Organizing 101: Steps

1. Create several collecting stations with clearly labeled bins for each type of waste
2. Observe how people use the bins, then create labels to clarify what goes in each one
3. Create one combining station to receive waste streams from collecting stations
4. Establish a convenient reuse center for locally reusable items, to encourage reuse
5. Set up a hazardous waste storage area
    - Label clearly, and keep secure from children and pets
    - Have plastic tubs with lids for things like paint cans and expired medications
    - Have metal containers for batteries; put tape on battery terminals to prevent shorting
6. Manage your waste on a regular schedule

Organizing 101: Definitions

- **Compostable**: Materials that break down into nutrient-rich soil amendment
- **Contamination**: When items from one waste stream mix with another
- **Divert stream**: Special handling for hazardous items
- **Hazardous waste**: Materials requiring special disposal
- **Single stream**: One bin to collect all types of recycling (metal, glass, paper, plastics)
- **Waste stream**: Category of waste based on how it should be processed

Organizing 101: Troubleshooting

Problem	Solutions
Compost bin odors	Empty containers more frequently. Use a tight-fitting lid. Wrap wet food scraps in newspaper or brown paper bags. Sprinkle baking soda on food scraps. Freeze compost between additions.
Family members not following system	Conduct a family training session. Assign waste management as a chore.
Lack of space	Install pull-out bins. Use smaller containers; empty frequently.
Uncertainty about which stream	Create a detailed reference guide. When in doubt, compost paper products with food residue.

Organizing 101: Limitations

- Space constraints in small apartments
- Some multifamily buildings lack areas for waste sorting

References and resources: <www.suspra.com/practice/goods/organizing-101.html>

Organizing Waste 102: Storing Hazardous Waste

Create a household hazardous waste collection area for storing hazards until safe disposal

Properly store household hazardous waste to protect health, safety, and the environment until disposal. The four guidelines are 1) security (keeping materials away from children and pets), 2) containment (preventing leaks), 3) compatibility (preventing dangerous chemical reactions), and 4) accessibility (finding items when needed). Use secondary containment—placing already contained hazardous materials inside another container—to protect against leaks. Store hazardous waste only temporarily; at least once a year, send all accumulated waste to the proper facility to reduce risk.

Organizing 102: Equipment & Materials
- Storage shelving with raised edges (metal preferred)
- Chemical-resistant containers with secure lids
- Secondary containment bins or trays
- Absorbent materials (cat litter or commercial spill pads)
- Waterproof labels and permanent marker
- Childproof cabinet locks or padlock
- Work gloves (chemical-resistant nitrile or neoprene)
- Safety glasses and first aid kit
- Baking soda (for neutralizing small acid spills)
- *Optional: Commercial spill kit*

Organizing 102: Steps
1. Select an appropriate storage location not accessible to children or pets
   - Choose a cool, dry, well-ventilated area away from living spaces
   - Locate away from heat sources, flames, and direct sunlight
2. Prepare the storage area
   - Post "Hazardous Waste" sign and emergency contact information
   - Keep a fire extinguisher and spill control materials nearby
   - Ensure adequate ventilation in case of spill
   - Install shelving units with raised edges to contain spills
   - Install locking mechanisms on cabinets
3. Keep incompatible materials separated by category
   - Flammable and combustible (paints, solvents, gasoline)
   - Corrosive (acids, bases, drain cleaners)
   - Toxic (pesticides, herbicides)
   - Oxidizers (pool chemicals, hydrogen peroxide)
   - Electronic waste and batteries
   - Keep acids separate from bases
   - Keep flammables away from oxidizers
   - Use secondary containment trays under each category
4. Prepare storage containers
   - Keep materials in original containers when possible
   - Ensure all containers are tightly sealed
   - Label all containers with contents, date, and hazard type
5. Store different types properly
   - **Paints and solvents**: Keep lids tight to prevent drying and fumes
   - **Oils and liquid fuels**: Use secondary containment, keep away from ignition sources
   - **Pesticides**: Store in original containers, away from food products
   - **Toxic cleaners**: Keep acids separate from bases
   - **Batteries**: Tape terminals of rechargeable and lithium batteries
   - **Light bulbs with mercury**: Add packing peanuts, etc. to bin to prevent breakage
6. Keep an up-to-date list of material type, quantities, and planned disposal method
   - Inspect every three months for leaks or damage
   - At least once a year, take waste to the appropriate facility to prevent accumulation

Organizing 102: Definitions
- **Corrosive**: Materials that can damage other substances through chemical action

Sustainable Practices Handbook — Goods Practices: Managing Waste Wisely

- **Flammable**: Substances that easily ignite and burn
- **Hazardous waste**: Discarded materials harmful to human health or environment
- **Incompatible materials**: Substances that can react dangerously when mixed
- **Oxidizer**: Chemical compounds that promote combustion of other materials
- **Secondary containment**: Backup system to prevent leaks from reaching the environment

Organizing 102: Troubleshooting

Problem	Solutions
Limited storage space	Prioritize the most hazardous. Schedule frequent trips to facilities.
Strong odors	Check for leaks or unsealed containers. Take outside to inspect.
Containers deteriorating	Transfer contents to new containers. Avoid prolonged storage.
Children accessing storage	Use childproof locks or padlocks. Store in elevated locations. Use multiple security layers.
Unclear what materials are hazardous	Check product labels for signal words like "Danger," "Warning," "Caution," "Corrosive."

Organizing 102: Limitations

- Some materials degrade even in optimal storage conditions
- Space constraints may limit thorough separation of incompatible materials

References and resources: <www.suspra.com/practice/goods/organizing-102.html>

Organizing Waste 401: Neighborhood Composting

Organize a neighborhood composting program

Divert organic waste from landfills, reduce methane emissions, build healthy soil, and strengthen community bonds by creating a neighborhood composting program. Choose between supporting individual household composting versus creating centralized or cluster systems based on your neighborhood's characteristics. Individual systems have lower regulatory hurdles and provide immediate benefits to participants. Cluster systems work well for homes with limited yard space. Centralized community composting can handle larger volumes but requires more coordination. Or utilize a hybrid approach: start by supporting individual systems while developing centralized capacity.

Organizing 401: Equipment & Materials

- Core team of at least three people
- Venue for workshops and meetings
- Demonstration composting systems
- Educational materials about composting
- *Optional: Social media or website for the program*

Organizing 401: Steps

1. Assess neighborhood conditions, including local regulations and composting options
2. Form a core team of at least three people or partner with an existing organization
3. Design your program
   - Determine primary approach:

Sustainable Practices Handbook
Goods Practices: Managing Waste Wisely

- Individual household systems with education and support
- Cluster approach with shared systems between nearby homes
- Centralized collection with community composting site
- Hybrid model incorporating multiple approaches

4. Secure necessary resources: funding, educational materials, space
5. Launch awareness and education campaign
6. Implement your composting program
   - For individual household systems:
     - Organize bulk purchasing of bins or materials
     - Create a buddy system pairing new composters with experienced ones
   - For centralized systems:
     - Secure and prepare the site(s)
     - Create clear signage for drop-off procedures
     - Establish a maintenance schedule with volunteer rotation
7. Manage ongoing operations; expand if successful

Organizing 401: Definitions

- **Centralized composting**: Materials from multiple households are composted at a shared site
- **Cluster composting**: Shared system used by a small group of neighboring households
- **Compost champion**: Volunteer with composting experience who helps others
- **Individual systems**: Systems operated by single households on their own property

Organizing 401: Troubleshooting

Problem	Solutions
Low participation rates	Survey to identify specific barriers. Offer multiple entry points with varying commitment levels. Use testimonials from successful composters.
Concerns about odors and pests	Provide educational materials about proper practices. Offer troubleshooting home visits. Showcase well-managed systems.
Homeowners association resistance	Research property value benefits. Propose a pilot with strict aesthetic guidelines. Develop specific composting guidelines for HOA approval.
Contamination in communal compost	Improve signage with clear visuals. Station volunteers at drop-off points initially. Implement training requirements.
Seasonal challenges	Develop seasonal composting guides. Host quarterly workshops addressing upcoming challenges.
Volunteer burnout	Create rotating leadership positions. Develop clear role descriptions with time limits. Build documentation for new volunteers.

Organizing 401: Limitations

- May face regulatory barriers in some municipalities
- Requires consistent volunteer engagement
- Centralized sites require suitable locations and potentially permits
- Program coordination requires significant time investment

References and resources: <www.suspra.com/practice/goods/organizing-waste-401.html>

| Sustainable Practices Handbook | Goods Practices: Managing Waste Wisely |

Organizing Waste 402: Collecting Hazardous Waste

Organize a household hazardous waste collection event

Organize a local household hazardous waste (HHW) collection event to provide neighbors with a responsible disposal option while raising awareness about hazardous products. HHW includes products containing chemicals that can catch fire, react, explode, or are corrosive or toxic. Make safety your primary concern; work with local authorities and hazardous waste professionals. For a neighborhood-scale event, limit the quantities you'll accept from each household (e.g., 5 gallons of paint, 10 electronics items). Share information about less-toxic alternatives and waste reduction.

Organizing 402: Equipment & Materials

- A core team of at least three people
- Collection containers for different waste types
- Folding tables
- Personal protective equipment (PPE): chemical-resistant gloves, safety glasses, chemical-proof aprons, N95 masks
- First aid kit
- Spill containment materials (absorbent pads, kitty litter)
- Hand sanitizer and cleaning supplies
- *Optional: Canopy tent for shelter, clipboards for record-keeping, traffic cones and safety vests, portable fire extinguisher*

Organizing 402: Steps

1. Form core organizing team (2-3 months before)
2. Research and plan (2-3 months before)
3. Build partnerships (1-2 months before)
4. Recruit and train volunteers (3-4 weeks before)
5. Promote event (1 month before)
6. Setup and collect waste (Day of event)
7. Hand off waste, or transport safely for disposal, and obtain documentation of proper disposal
8. Clean up and share results with your community

Organizing 402: Definitions

- **Corrosive**: Substances that can wear away surfaces; strong acids or bases
- **Flammable**: Substances that easily ignite and burn rapidly
- **Household Hazardous Waste**: Products containing hazardous substances
- **PPE (Personal Protective Equipment)**: Safety gear protecting the wearer from hazards
- **Universal Waste**: Specific regulated waste streams including batteries, pesticides, mercury-containing equipment, and light bulbs

Organizing 402: Troubleshooting

Problem	Solutions
Low community participation	Increase promotion through multiple channels. Choose a more convenient time or location. Piggyback on another community event.
Too much waste collected	Limit quantities per household in advance. Schedule a follow-up event. Prepare a contingency plan with additional transportation.

Revision: 25.1.8

Problem	Solutions
Unaccepted items brought	Clearly communicate acceptance criteria beforehand. Prepare handouts with alternative disposal locations.
Inadequate volunteer coverage	Create shifts to prevent volunteer fatigue. Have backup volunteers on call. Adjust event scale to match volunteer availability.
Spills or accidents	Keep spill containment materials readily available. Train all volunteers on basic spill response. Have emergency contacts posted.
Funding shortfalls	Seek local business sponsorships. Apply for community environmental grants. Request voluntary donations from participants.

Organizing 402: Limitations

- Requires significant planning and resources
- Some hazardous wastes need specialized handling beyond volunteer capabilities
- Transportation regulations may limit what you can legally transport
- Disposal costs can be substantial
- Legal liability concerns may require expensive insurance

References and resources: <www.suspra.com/practice/goods/organizing-waste-402.html>

Organizing Waste 403: Having a "Green" Neighborhood Yard Sale

Organize a "green" neighborhood yard sale and waste management event

Combine a traditional community yard sale with environmentally responsible waste removal services, to divert usable goods from landfills while providing an opportunity for community education about waste management. Achieve 70-90% diversion rates from landfills by staggering the yard sale and waste collection components, with the yard sale occurring first to maximize reuse, followed by responsible disposal options for remaining items.

Build community connections around sustainability, normalize reuse practices, provide proper channels for difficult-to-dispose items, and create opportunities for environmental education. Help participants save money through both sales income and avoided disposal costs.

For maximum impact, frame the event as a community sustainability celebration rather than just a disposal opportunity. Emphasize the hierarchy of reduce, reuse, repair, and recycle. Include educational elements such as repair demonstrations, composting workshops, or upcycling ideas alongside the sales and collection activities.

Organizing 403: Equipment & Materials

- Organizing team of at least three people
- Meeting space (physical or virtual)
- Signage and promotion materials
- Sorting bins and containers for different waste streams
- *Optional: Portable canopies or tents, scale for weighing diverted items, digital camera for documentation, truck or trailer for hauling*

Organizing 403: Steps

1. Form a planning committee of at least three people (3-4 months before event)

2. Secure necessary permissions and partnerships (2-3 months before)
3. Develop comprehensive waste plan (2 months before)
4. Establish yard sale guidelines (2 months before)
5. Build community engagement (2 months before)
6. Recruit and train volunteers (1-2 months before)
7. Prepare logistics (1 month before)
8. Conduct the event (event day, with a backup day for inclement weather)
9. Process remaining materials (day of/day after)
10. Evaluate and share results (1-2 weeks after)

Organizing 403: Definitions

- **Diversion rate**: Percentage of waste kept out of landfills
- **E-waste**: Electronic waste requiring specialized recycling (computers, TVs, small appliances)
- **Household hazardous waste**: Hazardous substances requiring special disposal
- **Material recovery facility**: Facility that separates and prepares recyclable materials
- **Repair café**: Community event where volunteer experts help fix broken items
- **Waste coach**: Volunteer who educates participants about proper sorting
- **Waste stream**: Flow of waste materials from point of generation to final disposal
- **Zero waste**: Eliminate waste through redesign, reduction, reuse, and recovery

Organizing 403: Troubleshooting

Problem	Solutions
Insufficient volunteer participation	Start recruitment earlier. Offer shorter shifts. Partner with service groups, schools, or faith communities. Provide free food.
Improper waste sorting	Position trained waste coaches at each station. Create clear, visual signage. Provide sorting demonstrations. Implement pre-sorting inspection.
Too many unsold items	Arrange donation pickup at the event's end. Create a "free" section for the last hour. Set up an online exchange for remaining items.
Weather complications	Secure indoor backup location. Have tarps and coverings ready. Set a rain date. Rent canopies or use garage spaces.
Hazardous waste handling concerns	Partner with certified handlers. Provide proper containment materials. Train volunteers on safety protocols. Consult local environmental agencies.
Traffic and parking issues	Create designated parking areas. Implement one-way traffic flow. Schedule staggered drop-off times. Arrange satellite parking with shuttles.

Organizing 403: Limitations

- Requires significant planning time (3-4 months minimum)
- Success depends on dedicated volunteer team
- Weather can significantly impact outdoor events
- Some waste types require professional handling
- Space needs can be substantial for larger communities
- Many municipalities have restrictions on certain waste collections
- Costs for proper waste handling must be covered
- Liability concerns must be addressed for certain materials

References and resources: <www.suspra.com/practice/goods/organizing-waste-403.html>

| Sustainable Practices Handbook | Goods Practices: Managing Waste Wisely |

Recycling 101: Recycling Metal, Cardboard, and Glass

Recycle metal, clean cardboard, and glass

To effectively recycle metal, cardboard, and glass, start by understanding your local recycling guidelines, which you can typically find on your city's website or through your waste management provider. First, rinse out metal and glass containers to remove food residue; this prevents contamination of other recyclables. Clean cardboard should be flattened to save space, and remove any non-cardboard elements like tape or plastic labels. For metal, this includes aluminum cans, steel food cans, and clean foil. For cardboard, focus on corrugated cardboard boxes and clean paperboard, like cereal boxes. For glass, recycle bottles and jars, but avoid broken glass, which can often be a contaminant. By properly sorting and preparing these materials, you significantly reduce landfill waste and conserve resources, as recycled materials require less energy to process than raw materials.

References and resources: <www.suspra.com/practice/goods/recycling-101.html>

Recycling 202: Recycling Electronics and Batteries

Recycle electronic devices and batteries

Recycle electronics and batteries (e-waste) to recover valuable metals like copper, gold, silver, palladium, and platinum and prevent environmental contamination from hazardous substances such as polychlorinated biphenyls, lead, mercury, and cadmium. Understand the risks posed by different types of e-waste—old cathode ray tube televisions and computer monitors contain lead, while batteries pose fire risks if damaged. Choose certified recyclers (e-Stewards or R2) to ensure environmental responsibility and data security.

Managing 202: Equipment & Materials

- Containers for sorting electronics and batteries
- Masking or electrical tape for battery terminals
- Boxes or bins for transport
- *Optional: Protective gloves, anti-static bags*

Managing 202: Steps

1. Prepare electronics
   - Back up important data
   - Perform factory reset to remove personal information
   - Remove batteries, memory cards, and SIM cards
   - Keep accessories with the device
2. Prepare batteries
   - Sort by type: alkaline, rechargeable, lithium-ion, button cell, lead-acid
   - Cover terminals of lithium, lithium-ion, and 9-volt batteries with tape
   - Store damaged batteries in a fireproof container away from flammables
   - Keep in a dry, cool location until recycling
3. Research local options
   - Check municipal waste management websites
   - Search for certified e-waste recyclers
   - Contact electronics retailers about take-back programs
   - Look for community e-waste collection events
4. Choose appropriate method
   - **Batteries:** Store drop-offs, auto parts stores (lead-acid), Call2Recycle locations
   - **Small electronics:** Retailer drop-offs, mail-back programs, hazardous waste facilities
   - **Large electronics:** Curbside pickup, municipal centers, certified recyclers

5. Transport safely
   - Pack securely to prevent damage; secure items so they won't shift during transport
   - Keep battery types separated
   - Transport damaged lithium batteries with extreme caution (they can explode)

Managing 202: Definitions

- **CRT (Cathode Ray Tube)**: Old-style monitors containing significant amounts of lead
- **E-waste**: Discarded electrical or electronic devices
- **Extended Producer Responsibility (EPR)**: Policy requiring manufacturers to manage the entire lifecycle of their products
- **Lithium-ion battery**: Rechargeable battery commonly used in portable electronics
- **WEEE**: European term for e-waste and related regulations

Managing 202: Troubleshooting

Problem	Solutions
No local recycling options	Use manufacturer mail-back programs. Save for regional collection events. Use retailer take-back programs.
Swollen or damaged batteries	Place in a fireproof container with cat litter or sand. Take to hazardous waste disposal. Never place swollen batteries in landfill trash.
Devices with sensitive data	Use secure data wiping software. Remove and destroy hard drives if necessary. Use certified recyclers with data destruction services.
Unsure if recyclable	Contact your local waste authority or the manufacturer.
Limited transportation	Look for mail-in programs. Request pickup services. Organize neighborhood collection to share transportation.

Managing 202: Limitations

- Electronics recycling infrastructure varies by location
- Not all components can be recycled
- Battery recycling systems aren't yet standardized
- Proprietary designs make some devices difficult to disassemble
- Some items may have recycling fees

References and resources: <www.suspra.com/practice/goods/recycling-202.html>

Habitat Practices

Sheltering Well, page 455

Goals	Indicators
• Choose and provide sheltered habitat with fewer negative and more positive environmental impacts	• Shelter choices and certifications

Renovating Wisely, page 463

Goals	Indicators
• Increase number of people land sustains • Increase water and energy efficiency • Prevent pollution • Close the loop by using recycled materials	• Occupancy rate of renovated buildings • Materials used during renovation • Certifications and performance ratings of renovated buildings

Protecting Nature, page 490

Goals	Indicators
• Protect and promote biodiversity • Prevent pollution	• Conservation budget • Amount of land growing wild • Pesticide and fertilizer applications

Sheltering Well

Building 403: Building Homes

Build single-family housing with fewer negative and more positive environmental impacts

Whether you envision living in a conventional stick-built house, a prefabricated home, a converted shipping container, a yurt, an earthship, a skoolie, or an alternative dwelling, use your resources wisely to create more sustainable housing.

Phase 1: Establish Your Vision

- Define your priorities
    - Set your environmental performance goals
    - Consider your lifestyle needs
    - Recognize your budget realities: borrow money or use savings
- Right-size your home
    - Consider all housing types: tiny homes, skoolies, yurts, earthships, prefabricated modular homes, shipping container conversions, straw bale or cob construction, and conventional wooden frame ("stick-built") structures or a deep renovation of an existing structure
    - Minimize your footprint
    - Anticipate future adaptations

Phase 2: Select Your Location

- Evaluate land
    - Consider the climate
    - Assess solar access
    - Note natural features
    - Assess connections to infrastructure (utilities, public transportation, walkability, etc.)
    - Review zoning and regulations
- Plan your site
    - Orient your building for sunlight, ventilation, and views
    - Preserve native vegetation
    - Manage water

Phase 3: Assemble Your Team

- Hire key team members (depending on scale of project)
    - Choose an architect or lead designer
    - Retain consultants for specialized knowledge
    - Hire a builder and subcontractors: plumber, electrician, HVAC technician, etc.
- Collaborate and iterate
    - Establish your budget and performance goals
    - Use a design-build process to iterate through plans

Phase 4: Develop Your Design

- Decide the shell
    - Optimize use of passive solar energy
    - Minimize heat flow with air sealing and insulation
- Integrate systems
    - Go all electric and solar

- o   Ventilate with energy recovery
- Select materials
  - o   Minimize embodied carbon
  - o   Build with healthy, durable, and natural materials that are locally plentiful

Phase 5: Construct and Verify

- Provide oversight
- Inspect, certify, and document

References and resources: <www.suspra.com/practice/habitat/building-403.html>

Building 404: Building Offices

Build commercial offices with fewer negative and more positive environmental impacts

Hire an architect or lead designer and a builder. Work with them to choose a green building system, build to that standard, and obtain certification. Choose one of the following:

- BREEAM (Building Research Establishment Environmental Assessment Method)
- CASBEE (Comprehensive Assessment System for Built Environment Efficiency)
- DGNB (Deutsche Gesellschaft für Nachhaltiges Bauen)
- EDGE (Excellence in Design for Greater Efficiencies)
- Green Globes Building Certification
- Green Mark (Building and Construction Authority of Singapore)
- Green Star (Green Building Council of Australia, also available in New Zealand and South Africa)
- LBC (Living Building Challenge)
- LEED (Leadership in Energy and Environmental Design)
- WELL Building Standard

References and resources: <www.suspra.com/practice/habitat/building-404.html>

Building 405: Building Apartments

Build apartments with fewer negative and more positive environmental impacts

To build greener apartments, follow the same general procedure as building greener commercial offices: hire an architect or lead designer and a builder, choose a green building system, build to that standard, and obtain certification. Choose one of the following green building standards for multifamily residential structures:

- Any of the standards listed for Building 404: Building Offices
- NGBS (National Green Building Standard)

References and resources: <www.suspra.com/practice/habitat/building-405.html>

Choosing Shelter 101: Living in a Walkable Neighborhood

Live in a walkable neighborhood

Live in a walkable neighborhood to make efficient use of the built environment, reducing the need for sprawling infrastructure. When apartment or house hunting, use tools like Walk Score, Google Maps' walking directions, or apps like AllTrails to evaluate distances to daily destinations. Visit neighborhoods at different times to personally experience walking conditions, including sidewalk quality, street lighting, crosswalks, and traffic patterns. To find housing in walkable areas, work with real estate agents who specialize in urban or walkable communities, use housing search filters for walkability on sites like Apartments.com or Zillow, and consider trade-offs like higher costs for smaller spaces, as walkable neighborhoods often command premium prices due to their desirability and convenience.

References and resources: <www.suspra.com/practice/habitat/choosing-shelter-101.html>

Choosing Shelter 102: Apartment Living

Live in an apartment

Live in an apartment to reduce your environmental footprint compared to a single-family home. Apartments share walls, floors, and ceilings, maximizing the beneficial use of building materials and minimizing energy loss for heating and cooling. Furthermore, many apartment buildings are multi-story, increasing population density per acre of land devoted to housing.

Establish a good relationship with your property manager or landlord, as they'll be your point of contact for maintenance issues rather than handling repairs yourself. Adapt to shared spaces by learning building etiquette—keeping noise reasonable, respecting common areas, and following recycling procedures. Consider vertical storage solutions and multi-purpose furniture to maximize your space; be prepared to downsize your possessions if you are moving from a single-family home. Take time to meet neighbors, as the community aspect of apartment living can be one of its greatest benefits.

References and resources: <www.suspra.com/practice/habitat/choosing-shelter-102.html>

Choosing Shelter 201: High-Performance Housing

Select high-performance housing

Choose high-performance housing to reduce utility costs and improve comfort. Look for homes or apartments with recognized certifications.

- ENERGY STAR certified homes are rated on a scale of 1 to 100 for energy efficiency, with a score of 75 or higher indicating a top-performing, energy-efficient home.
- The Home Energy Rating System (HERS) Index measures energy efficiency on a scale of 0-150, where lower scores indicate better performance (a score of 100 represents a baseline home).
- LEED (Leadership in Energy and Environmental Design) certification evaluates homes on a broader sustainability scale with four levels: Certified, Silver, Gold, and Platinum, considering factors beyond energy such as water usage, materials, and site design.
- Passive House certification represents the most stringent energy performance standard.

When touring properties, ask for documentation of these ratings, utility bills for existing homes, or energy models for new construction. Consider hiring a home energy auditor to assess unlabeled properties, and evaluate the home's envelope (insulation, windows, air sealing), mechanical systems efficiency, renewable energy features, and water conservation measures.

References and resources: <www.suspra.com/practice/habitat/choosing-shelter-202.html>

Choosing Shelter 301: Downsizing

Downsize your living space

Move to a smaller living space to use less energy for heating and cooling, discourage unnecessary purchases, and preserve more natural areas by taking advantage of a residential setting that enables higher-density living. Sell, donate, or discard possessions that you cannot take with you. Thoughtfully assess your needs versus wants; take a creative approach to space optimization. Start by categorizing your possessions as essential, occasionally useful, or rarely used, then eliminate duplicates and items you haven't used in over a year. Invest in multi-functional furniture like storage ottomans, Murphy beds, or extendable dining tables that adapt to different needs. Maximize vertical space with tall shelving units and wall-mounted storage to maintain floor space for living.

References and resources: <www.suspra.com/practice/habitat/choosing-shelter-301.html>

Developing Shelter 401: Cohousing

Develop a cohousing community with sustainability at its core

Develop a sustainability-focused cohousing community to share resources and infrastructure. Cluster housing with common facilities like kitchens, dining areas, and laundry rooms to reduce each resident's ecological footprint. Allow for more efficient use of energy through district heating systems, community-scale solar microgrids, and reduced materials consumption.

Incorporate sustainable design principles from the ground up—including passive solar orientation, highly insulated building envelopes, water-conserving fixtures, and native landscaping. Encourage sustainable practices like carpooling, tool sharing, and community gardening while providing social benefits that make sustainable living more enjoyable and accessible. Provide ways for residents to share vehicles. Build within walking distance to essential services like grocery stores and medical providers.

Cohousing communities typically consist of 15-40 private homes clustered around shared space. The development process requires substantial member involvement. Development timelines typically extend 3-7 years from initial group formation to move-in.

Developing 401: Equipment, Materials and Costs

- Core group of committed individuals (5 minimum)
- Legal entity (typically a limited liability company) to manage development process
- Professional services budget ($50,000-$200,000+)
- Project development budget ($2-15 million)
- Land or existing building(s)

Developing 401: Cohousing Steps

1. Form core group and establish vision (6-12 months)
   - Gather interested individuals to develop shared vision, values, and goals
   - Establish legal structure
   - Develop preliminary budget
2. Select and acquire site (6-18 months)
   - Determine location criteria
   - Find land for new construction or existing buildings for retrofitting
   - Raise funds; acquire site
3. Assemble professional team (2-4 months)
   - Project manager (lead developer), architect, and builder (general contractor)
   - Sustainability consultants
   - Accountant and lawyer
4. Design community (6-12 months)
5. Plan finances and recruit members (ongoing)
6. Obtain permits and approvals (3-12 months)
   - Submit zoning applications
   - Apply for building permits
   - Present at public hearings if required

- Secure environmental permits
- Obtain financing commitments
7. Construct or renovate (12-24 months)
8. Move in and develop community (3-6 months)
    - Create governance structure
    - Establish operational committees
9. Operate and evolve (ongoing)
    - Hold regular community meetings
    - Continuously improve governance

Developing 401: Definitions

- **Cohousing:** Intentional community of private homes clustered around shared space
- **Common house:** Shared building containing facilities used by all residents
- **Consensus:** Decision-making process seeking solutions acceptable to all participants
- **Design charrette:** Intensive planning session where stakeholders craft solutions
- **Participatory design:** Approach involving all stakeholders in the design process
- **Intentional community:** Planned residential community with shared vision and resources

Developing 401: Troubleshooting

Problem	Solutions
Group process stalls	Hire facilitator; improve decision-making processes; revisit shared values.
Financing difficulties	Reduce project scale. Consider hybrid ownership.
Permitting or zoning	Engage municipal staff early; provide case studies; request variances.
Cost escalation	Implement value engineering; phase construction; adjust unit mix.

Developing 401: Cohousing Limitations

- Lengthy development timeline (3-7 years)
- Substantial time commitment from future residents; shared governance demands
- Higher initial costs than conventional housing
- Legal and financial complexity
- Difficulty securing conventional financing
- Zoning challenges for unconventional layouts
- Finding suitable sites in desired locations

References and resources: <www.suspra.com/practice/habitat/developing-401.html>

Inspecting Shelter 201: Rating Performance

Rate the performance of buildings

Assess your building's performance by reviewing utility bills or hiring professionals. For a quick baseline rating, gather all electricity, fuel, water and utility bills for a one-year period. Add up the total amount of energy and water consumed and divide by the square footage of your building to calculate the energy use intensity and water use intensity. You can compare these numbers to published values for buildings in your climate zone to get a sense of your relative performance.

Hire a home inspector ($300-$500) to perform a general assessment during home purchases. For a comprehensive evaluation, hire a certified energy auditor ($250-$700) who conducts blower door tests to measure air leakage, infrared thermography to identify insulation gaps, and combustion safety testing for heating systems. Look for auditors certified by the Building Performance Institute (BPI) or holding Home Energy Rater (HERS) credentials–these professionals follow standardized procedures and can provide precise performance scores like the HERS Index. The most advanced option is a professional rater who can issue formal certifications like ENERGY STAR or LEED, typically charging $500-$1,500 depending on property size and certification complexity.

Get an energy audit to identify projects to save energy, address comfort issues (drafts, temperature imbalances), and improve indoor air quality. To find qualified professionals, contact your electric utility (many offer discounted or free audits), search the BPI or RESNET (Residential Energy Services Network) directories for certified professionals in your area, or ask local green building organizations for recommendations. Request sample reports and references before hiring to ensure you receive actionable recommendations rather than just sales pitches for specific products.

References and resources: <www.suspra.com/practice/habitat/inspecting-shelter-201.html>

Sharing Shelter 101: Living With Roommates

Share living space with other people

Share living space with roommates to decrease the overall demand for resources like energy, water, and materials. Promote the efficient use of existing housing stock, preventing the need for new construction. A single-family home shared by three or four individuals reduces the energy needed for heating, cooling, and lighting per person. Further, shared spaces naturally lead to shared resources, like appliances and furniture, reducing overall consumption. Coordinate grocery shopping and meal preparation with roommates to minimize food waste and promote the purchase of bulk items, reducing packaging. Live with roommates to foster a sense of community and shared responsibility, encouraging sustainable habits that extend beyond the home.

References and resources: <www.suspra.com/practice/habitat/sharing-shelter-101.html>

Sharing Shelter 301: Renting Out Rooms

Rent out rooms in your home

Rent out rooms in your home to increase your home's occupancy rate–a key sustainability indicator that measures how many people your land sustains. Reduce per-person energy and water consumption, with occupants sharing heating, cooling, appliances, and common areas. Overcome privacy concerns, safety considerations, or uncertainty about becoming a landlord by creating a separate entrance, establishing clear house rules and boundaries in a written agreement, and implementing a thorough vetting process including background checks.

Check local regulations regarding zoning and rental permits, as some municipalities restrict room rentals or require inspections. Start by renting to people within your extended network–friends or friends of friends. Once you're comfortable being a landlord, use room-rental platforms that allow detailed profiles and references to find suitable tenants.

References and resources: <www.suspra.com/practice/habitat/sharing-shelter-301.html>

Sharing Habitat 401: Accessory Dwelling

Build an accessory dwelling unit

Build an accessory dwelling unit (ADU) to provide additional housing on a single-family lot. Begin with thorough research into local regulations, which vary dramatically between jurisdictions.

Choose a smaller footprint (300-400 square feet) plan with a simple layout to minimize construction costs while maximizing energy efficiency. Prioritize superinsulation with recycled or natural materials like cellulose or wool insulation. Incorporate passive solar design by orienting windows for winter heat gain and summer shading. Power essential loads with a solar module and power bank, starting small with the option to expand later. Harvest rainwater from the roof for toilets and gardens. For structures built on site, use reclaimed wood, windows, doors, and fixtures from architectural salvage stores. For heating and cooling, use an air-to-air mini-split heat pump.

Sharing Habitat 401: Equipment, Materials and Costs

- Property deed and zoning information
- Budget for construction ($50,000-$300,000)
- General contractor (unless self-building)

Sharing Habitat 401: Steps

1. Research local regulations, including setbacks and permits required
2. Develop your project plan and establish your budget
3. Design your ADU: work with architect/designer or select pre-approved plans
4. Secure financing
5. Obtain permits
6. Prepare site and construct foundation
   - Mark utility lines
   - Install erosion controls
   - Grade site, excavate, and install footings and foundation
   - Install drainage systems
7. Build exterior of structure
8. Install utilities
   - Connect to existing electric utility or use solar power
   - Connect to sewer or septic, or use a composting or incinerating toilet
9. Finish interior and install fixtures and appliances
10. Complete exterior and landscaping
11. Pass inspections

Sharing Habitat 401: Definitions

- **Accessory Dwelling Unit (ADU):** Secon self-contained housing unit on a single-family lot
- **Certificate of Occupancy:** Official document certifying a building is safe for occupancy
- **Detached ADU:** Standalone structure separate from main house
- **Junior ADU (JADU):** Smaller ADU created within an existing structure
- **Setback:** Required minimum distance between structure and property lines

Sharing Habitat 401: Troubleshooting

Problem	Solutions
Zoning restrictions	Get a variance. Build an in-law apartment instead.

Sustainable Practices Handbook
Habitat Practices: Sheltering Well

Problem	Solutions
Neighbor opposition	Engage neighbors early. Address specific concerns. Obtain permits.
Water issues	Ensure proper grading. Install appropriate drainage systems.

Sharing Habitat 401: Limitations
- High upfront costs
- Construction disrupts property use
- Property taxes and insurance may increase
- Local regulations may restrict development
- Not all properties have suitable space
- Return on investment takes time
- Utility upgrades may be required

References and resources: <www.suspra.com/practice/habitat/sharing-habitat-401.html>

Sustainable Practices Handbook Habitat Practices: Renovating Wisely

Renovating Wisely

Abating 201: Replacing Fluorescent Lighting

Replace fluorescent lighting that contains mercury

Remove and recycle fluorescent lighting to mitigate the risk of mercury poisoning; replace with LED lighting to increase energy efficiency. Each fluorescent tube contains 3-5 mg of mercury, a neurotoxin that poses health and environmental risks. LED replacements use 40-60% less energy, last 2-3 times longer, contain no mercury, and provide better lighting quality with less maintenance.

Abating 201: Equipment & Materials

- Multimeter (voltage tester)
- LED replacement tubes or fixtures
- Secure storage area for fluorescent tubes until they can be recycled
- In case you break a fluorescent tube:
    - Duct tape (for securing broken tubes if necessary)
    - Damp paper towels (for cleaning up broken tubes)
    - Glass jar with lid (for containing broken tube pieces if necessary)

Abating 201: Steps

1. Choose your replacement approach
    - Replace just the lamp ("tube" or "light bulb"); keep the rest of the fixture
    - Replace the whole fixture
2. Get ready
    - Turn off power to the lighting fixture; verify power is off using a voltage tester
    - Place drop cloth under work area
    - Prepare a storage container for removed fluorescent tubes
3. Remove existing fluorescent lamps or entire fixture
    - If a tube breaks: leave room 5-10 minutes, return with gloves and facemask, carefully collect pieces with damp paper towels and put them in glass jars
4. Install LED lamp or new LED fixture
5. Properly dispose of fluorescent tubes
    - Never throw in regular trash (they contain mercury)
    - Take to local hazardous waste collection

Abating 201: Definitions

- **Ballast**: Device that regulates current to fluorescent tubes
- **Color temperature**: Color appearance of light, measured in Kelvins (K)
- **Type A LED tubes**: Work with existing fluorescent ballasts
- **Type B LED tubes**: Bypass the ballast and connect directly to line voltage
- **Type C LED tubes**: Require an external LED driver

Abating 201: Troubleshooting

Problem	Solutions
LED tubes don't work	Check ballast compatibility, tube orientation, and power supply.
LED tubes flicker	The ballast may be failing; consider Type B tubes or replace ballast.

Revision: 25.1.8 www.suspra.com

Problem	Solutions
Broken fluorescent	Leave room 5-10 minutes; collect bits wearing gloves; use damp paper towels for cleanup; store pieces in glass jars; manage hazardous waste.
No matching lamps	Standard tube lengths are 2, 3, 4, and 8 feet. Replace the entire fixture.

Abating 201: Limitations
- Some dimming systems incompatible with LED replacements
- Type B installations require electrical knowledge
- May require permits in some jurisdictions

References and resources: <www.suspra.com/practice/habitat/abating-201.html>

Abating 202: Replacing Mercury Thermostats

Replace thermostats that contain mercury

Remove old mercury thermostats that contain 3-5 grams of mercury in glass "tilt switches" that control heating and cooling systems. Old manual rotary dial thermostats in particular are likely to contain mercury. Replace with a thermostat that has a RoHS (restriction on hazardous substances) certification mark. Store your old thermostat as household hazardous waste; take it to a collection event or facility.

Thermostats typically control a low-voltage 24 volt electrical circuit, with a relay to send this signal to your heating and cooling system. However, some electrical heating systems have high-voltage thermostats which pose more risk of personal harm when replacing. Know basic electrical science to understand and troubleshoot thermostat wiring.

Abating 202: Equipment & Materials
- Multimeter (voltage tester)
- New programmable or smart thermostat
- Container for the old thermostat

Abating 202: Steps
1. *Hire a contractor if you are not comfortable replacing a thermostat*
2. Purchase a compatible replacement thermostat
3. Follow manufacturer's instructions to remove old thermostat and install new one
    - Before removing old thermostat
        - Take photos of wiring configuration
        - Label each wire with its terminal connection
4. Handle old thermostat properly
    - Place entire thermostat in a container
    - Mark "Household hazardous waste: mercury"
    - Take to a collection event or facility

Abating 202: Definitions
- **Mercury**: Toxic heavy metal that is liquid at room temperature
- **Tilt switch**: Switch using mercury to complete/break electrical circuit when tilted
- **R-wire**: Power wire (usually red)
- **W-wire**: Controls heating (usually white)
- **Y-wire**: Controls cooling (usually yellow)

Sustainable Practices Handbook

Habitat Practices: Renovating Wisely

- **G-wire**: Controls fan (usually green)
- **C-wire**: Common wire providing continuous power (usually blue/black)

Abating 202: Troubleshooting

Problem	Solutions
System doesn't turn on	Check power, wire connections, and R-wire jumper placement.
Heating and cooling reversed	Check O/B wire connection for heat pump systems.
Blank display	Check batteries or C-wire connection.
Mercury spill	Evacuate area, ventilate, don't vacuum, contact health department.

Abating 202: Limitations

- Complex HVAC systems may require professional installation
- Older systems without C-wire have limited options for smart thermostats
- Rental properties may require landlord permission
- Some wall repair may be necessary for different footprint thermostats

References and resources: <www.suspra.com/practice/habitat/abating-202.html>

Abating 203: Encapsulating Lead Paint

Remove or encapsulate surfaces covered in lead paint

Remove or encapsulate (i.e., paint over) lead paint to mitigate the serious health risks it poses, particularly to children under six, pregnant women, and pets. Avoid creating lead dust that can be ingested or inhaled; this can cause permanent learning disabilities and other health problems. Homes built before 1978 likely contain lead paint; any home built before 1950 almost certainly contains it. Encapsulation is less expensive and creates less hazardous waste than removal but isn't permanent. Remove lead paint from deteriorating surfaces or those subject to impact, friction, or moisture.

Abating 203: Equipment & Materials

- Lead test kit (EPA-recognized)
- EPA-approved lead encapsulant product
- Plastic sheeting (6-mil thickness)
- HEPA vacuum
- Respirator rated for lead dust (N100, P100, or R100)
- Disposable coveralls, shoe covers, gloves, and safety goggles
- Paint brushes, rollers, or sprayers
- Clean-up supplies; plastic trash bags (heavy-duty)

Abating 203: Steps

1. Test for lead paint or hire a professional to test for you
   - Buy an EPA-recognized lead test kit and follow the instructions
   - Test multiple areas
2. Prepare work area
   - Remove furniture and possessions; cover floors with plastic sheeting
   - Cover vents and turn off HVAC; seal off area from other parts of home

Revision: 25.1.8

- Set up a cleaning station
3. Prepare surfaces (for encapsulation)
    - Wear all protective equipment
    - Clean surfaces thoroughly
    - Repair damaged areas; remove loose paint using wet methods
    - Allow surface to dry
4. Apply encapsulant by following manufacturer's instructions
5. For paint removal (if encapsulation isn't appropriate)
    - Use chemical strippers, low-temperature heat guns, or wet sanding
    - Keep surfaces wet to minimize dust
    - Collect debris immediately
    - Never dry sand or use open flames
6. Clean up
    - Clean from top to bottom
    - HEPA vacuum all surfaces; wet mop hard surfaces
    - Place all cleanup materials in sealed plastic bags; send to landfill
    - Shower immediately after

Abating 203: Definitions

- **Abatement**: Permanent elimination of lead-based paint hazards
- **Encapsulant**: Coating forming a barrier between lead paint and environment
- **Enclosure**: Covering lead surfaces with a solid barrier
- **HEPA filter**: Captures 99.97% of particles 0.3 microns or larger
- **Lead-safe**: Practices minimizing creation or spread of lead dust
- **RRP Rule**: EPA's Renovation, Repair, and Painting Rule requiring certification

Abating 203: Troubleshooting

Problem	Solutions
Encapsulant adhering	Ensure the surface is clean and dry. Prime first.
Encapsulant peeling	Remove failed encapsulant; prepare surface better; reapply.
Inconclusive results	Test a different area. Hire a professional.

Abating 203: Limitations

- DIY testing may miss lead paint under newer layers
- Encapsulation requires ongoing monitoring
- DIY removal creates significant health risks
- Improper mitigation methods can create more hazards

References and resources: <www.suspra.com/practice/habitat/abating-203.html>

Abating 204: Removing Contaminated Soil

Remove soil contaminated with lead paint or other hazards

Remove contaminated soil to mitigate environmental risks. Inspect for petroleum products from leaking containers or underground storage tanks, pesticides, preserved wood pressure treated with arsenic, and lead paint that has flaked off buildings, especially in the "drip zone" near foundations. For low to moderate contamination, cover with landscape fabric and clean soil. For extensive contamination, hire a certified remediation contractor.

Contact your local health department or environmental agency for testing recommendations or hire an environmental consultant who specializes in residential soil testing. If you want to remove contaminated soil yourself, contact your local waste management authority to determine the best local facility to receive it.

Abating 204: Equipment & Materials
- Soil test kit or professional testing service
- Hand tools (shovels, trowels, rake) and wheelbarrow or garden cart
- Heavy-duty contractor trash bags
- Clean replacement soil or mulch

Abating 204: Steps
1. Test soil to determine contamination type and extent
2. Plan your approach based on contamination levels
3. Remove contaminated soil and replace with clean soil
4. Dispose of contaminated soil properly

Abating 204: Definitions
- **Contaminated soil**: Soil containing substances at concentrations posing health risks
- **Drip zone**: Area 2-3 feet from a building's foundation where contaminants typically fall
- **ppm (parts per million)**: Measurement of concentration; EPA considers >400 ppm lead hazardous in children's play areas
- **Remediation**: Process of removing or reducing environmental contamination
- **Soil barrier**: Material used to separate contaminated soil from clean replacement soil

Abating 204: Troubleshooting

Problem	Solutions
Disposing of soil	Contact local authorities. Hire a certified professional.
Getting all soil	Remove accessible soil; encapsulate the rest.

Abating 204: Limitations
- DIY removal not appropriate for large areas or severe contamination
- Difficult to completely remove soil around foundations and utilities
- Disposal options vary by location
- Effectiveness depends on accurate identification of contamination extent
- Not suitable for deep contamination
- May require permits in some areas

References and resources: <www.suspra.com/practice/habitat/abating-204.html>

Abating 205: Blocking Vapor

Install vapor barriers in basements to mitigate moisture problems

Block moisture in your basement to maintain your home's structural integrity and mitigate mold growth. Seal your basement to eliminate damp conditions that damage possessions, rot wood, and make heating and cooling systems work harder. Start by identifying moisture sources. Slope soil away from your foundation, install functional gutters with extended downspouts, and seal any visible foundation cracks with hydraulic cement. Inside, thoroughly clean basement walls, then apply waterproof paint or sealant. Install a vapor barrier on your basement floor if necessary. For ongoing protection, operate a dehumidifier to maintain appropriate humidity levels.

Call professionals when:

- You have standing water or severe flooding issues
- Multiple approaches haven't resolved persistent moisture problems
- You notice structural foundation issues (significant cracks or bowing walls)
- You're planning to finish a previously damp basement
- The moisture issues coincide with plumbing or sewer problems
- You suspect toxic mold has developed that requires remediation

Professional waterproofing might include installing interior or exterior drainage systems, sump pumps with battery backups, or applying specialized foundation membranes—solutions that require expertise and specialized equipment for proper installation.

Abating 205: Equipment & Materials
- Moisture meter for testing
- Caulk gun and vapor barrier sealant
- Vapor barrier options:
  - 6-mil or 10-mil polyethylene sheeting
  - Vapor barrier paint or primer
  - Dimpled membrane systems
  - Spray foam insulation kits

Abating 205: Steps
1. Assess moisture conditions
2. Address existing moisture problems first; run a dehumidifier
3. Choose appropriate vapor barrier solution
4. Prepare surfaces
5. Install vapor barrier
6. Seal all edges and penetrations

Abating 205: Definitions
- **Capillary action**: Liquid flow against gravity through tiny spaces
- **Condensation**: Conversion of water vapor to liquid on cooler surfaces
- **Perm rating**: Measure of water vapor permeability; lower numbers indicate better resistance
- **Vapor barrier**: Material that restricts water vapor passage (perm rating ≤0.1)
- **Vapor retarder**: Material that restricts but doesn't block water vapor (perm rating 0.1-1.0)

Abating 205: Troubleshooting

Problem	Solutions
Moisture remains	Check for gaps. Verify exterior drainage. Run a dehumidifier.
Barrier pulls away	Use mechanical fasteners. Clean surface. Use a dimpled system.
Mold appears	Remove barriers. Clean and remediate. Reinstall with better sealing.

Problem	Solutions
Punctures or tears	Repair with vapor barrier tape. Patch larger tears with same material.
Barrier adhesive	Ensure walls are clean and dry. Use mechanical fasteners.

Abating 205: Limitations
- Vapor barriers alone cannot solve active water leaks
- Installation in finished basements requires removing wall materials
- Improper installation can create moisture traps
- Not appropriate for historic masonry requiring breathability

References and resources: <www.suspra.com/practice/habitat/abating-205.html>

Abating 301: Abating Asbestos

Abate asbestos hazards

Abate asbestos in your home or building to keep everyone safe. Widely used in building materials until the late 1970s, asbestos releases microscopic fibers that can cause asbestosis, lung cancer, and mesothelioma. Manage asbestos in place for intact materials (i.e., try not to disturb it), encapsulate it to prevent fiber release, or remove it. Hire a professional; improper handling causes harm.

Abating 301: Equipment & Materials
- Asbestos home test kit (for preliminary identification)
- Licensed asbestos abatement contractor

Abating 301: Steps
1. Identify potential asbestos materials common in pre-1980 homes:
   - Pipe and boiler insulation
   - 9" x 9" vinyl floor tiles
   - Textured ceilings
   - Roofing and siding
   - Vermiculite insulation
   - Document location and condition; don't disturb suspected materials
2. Choose appropriate response
   - Good condition: Monitor or encapsulate
   - Slight damage: Professional repair or encapsulation
   - Significant damage: Professional removal
   - Friable materials: Professional assessment and removal
3. Hire a licensed asbestos abatement professional (recommended for most situations)
4. During professional abatement (what to expect)
   - Complete area sealing
   - HEPA air filtration
   - Material wetting
   - Proper material containment
   - Air quality testing

Abating 301: Definitions
- **Abatement**: Process of removing or minimizing exposure to asbestos
- **ACM**: Asbestos-Containing Material (more than 1% asbestos)

- **Encapsulation**: Treatment with sealants to prevent fiber release
- **Friable**: Material easily crumbled by hand when dry
- **HEPA filter**: Captures 99.97% of particles ≥0.3 microns
- **Negative air pressure**: System ensuring air flows into (not out of) work area

Abating 301: Troubleshooting

Problem	Solutions
Uncertain material	Assume asbestos until proven otherwise. Hire a professional to test.
Material damaged	Stop work immediately; seal area; wet debris; contact professional/
Expense	Encapsulate. Move.
Elevated fiber levels	Don't reoccupy. Repeat testing. Conduct additional abatement.

Abating 301: Limitations

- Home testing kits have limited accuracy
- DIY encapsulation is temporary
- Homeowners cannot legally perform abatement in most jurisdictions
- Some materials extremely difficult to abate without reconstruction
- Encapsulated asbestos must still be disclosed when selling
- Improper abatement creates greater risks than leaving materials undisturbed
- Complete abatement may be impractical in older homes with extensive asbestos

References and resources: <www.suspra.com/practice/habitat/abating-301.html>

Constructing 201: Selecting Lumber

Select lumber from locally available tree species

Use local lumber to connect your projects to the regional environment while reducing transportation impacts. Recognize that lumber from smaller mills often isn't graded to commercial standards, requiring personal assessment. Choose specific boards with characteristics suited to your particular project. Talk with local contractors to find out which hardware stores have qualified salespeople who can best answer your questions about lumber origin, so you can support mills in your neck of the woods.

Constructing 201: Steps

1. Research locally available tree species
    - Identify native species in your region
    - Research which species match your project needs
    - Contact your state forestry department for information
2. Locate sources for local lumber
    - Talk with local contractors about where they buy lumber
    - Check with arborists about salvaged urban trees
3. Inspect lumber quality before purchasing

Constructing 201: Definitions

- **Board foot**: Unit of measurement equal to 1 foot square by 1 inch thick (144 cubic inches)
- **Hardwood**: Wood from deciduous trees, generally denser than softwoods
- **Kiln-dried**: Lumber dried in a controlled environment to reduce moisture content

- **Plain-sawn**: Lumber cut tangential to growth rings, creating "cathedral" patterns
- **Quarter-sawn**: Lumber cut with growth rings perpendicular to the face, increasing stability
- **Softwood**: Wood from coniferous trees, generally less dense than hardwoods

Constructing 201: Troubleshooting

Problem	Solutions
Limited selection of local species	Adapt your design to available materials. Mix species for different components.
Higher cost than big-box lumber	Use higher-grade local wood for visible components only. Consider the value of quality and sustainability.
Moisture content	Allow longer acclimation time. Consider using a local kiln drying service.
Dimensions	Plane to consistent dimensions. Design with the variability in mind.
Identifying species	Ask the sawyer. Use wood identification apps. Consult local experts.

Constructing 201: Limitations

- Local species may lack properties needed for specialized applications
- Smaller sawmills may have irregular supplies
- Local lumber often comes in random widths rather than standardized dimensions

References and resources: <www.suspra.com/practice/habitat/constructing-201.html>

Constructing 202: Screwing Foundations

Use metal ground screws or helical posts rather than poured concrete footings

Eliminate the need for concrete and create minimal soil disturbance by using metal ground screws and helical posts as foundations to transfer structural loads to stable soil. They can be completely removed if needed, bear loads immediately after installation, and work in most weather conditions. Screws and helices are suitable for decks, sheds, solar panel mounts, fencing, and walkways. Most systems include adjustable tops for fine-tuning height, particularly useful on uneven sites.

Constructing 202: Definitions
- **Bearing capacity**: Maximum load a foundation can support without failure
- **Embedment depth**: Depth to which a ground screw is installed
- **Frost heave**: Lifting of soil during freezing conditions
- **Ground screw**: Smaller version of helical pile for lighter structures
- **Helical post or pile**: Foundation system with helical plates welded to a central shaft

Constructing 202: Troubleshooting

Problem	Solutions
Ground screw won't penetrate	Check for rocks or roots. Move location slightly. Create a pilot hole with an auger. Use a more aggressive cutting edge.
Hitting rock layer	Try a different location. Visualize with ground penetrating radar.

Problem	Solutions
Different heights	Use the adjustment mechanism. Extract and reinstall.
Screw feels loose	Continue until reaching stable soil. Use a model with larger helical plates.
Structure not level	Use height adjustment features. Add shims at connection points.

Constructing 202: Limitations
- May not suit extremely heavy structures
- Limited effectiveness in very rocky soil or near bedrock
- Not always recognized in all building codes for permanent structures
- May require specialized installation equipment for larger models
- Not suitable for certain soil types (quicksand, loose gravel)

References and resources: <www.suspra.com/practice/habitat/constructing-202.html>

Constructing 203: Fenestrating with Fiberglass

Choose fiberglass rather than vinyl window frames

When replacing or installing new windows, opt for fiberglass frames instead of vinyl. Fiberglass offers superior durability and energy efficiency, contributing to a more sustainable home. Unlike vinyl, which can warp and degrade over time, fiberglass is resistant to temperature fluctuations, ensuring a longer lifespan and reduced need for replacement. This durability translates to less waste and lower resource consumption. Furthermore, fiberglass frames provide excellent thermal insulation, minimizing heat transfer and reducing the need for excessive heating or cooling. This improves energy efficiency and lowers your carbon footprint. Look for fiberglass windows with high-performance glazing and proper installation to maximize these benefits. Consider brands like Pella or Andersen, which offer fiberglass window lines.

References and resources: <www.suspra.com/practice/habitat/constructing-203.html>

Constructing 301: Reclaiming Lumber

Build with reclaimed lumber

Adapt your woodworking approach to use reclaimed lumber, reducing forestry pressure on remaining forests. Reclaimed wood may be harder and more brittle than new lumber. Expect variations in dimensions, moisture content, and condition even within boards from the same structure. Older wood, particularly from old-growth forests, typically features tighter growth rings, indicating denser, stronger wood than modern timber.

Constructing 301: Equipment & Materials
- Wood reclaimed from existing structures or furniture

Constructing 301: Steps
1. Evaluate wood before salvage
    - Check for insect damage, rot, or mold
    - Test painted surfaces for lead
    - Identify wood species
2. Salvage carefully

- Remove nails and hardware as you go
- Label pieces and sort by size, species, and condition
3. Transport and store properly
    - Stack with spacers between layers for airflow
    - Store in a dry, covered area
    - Keep wood elevated off the ground
4. Process the lumber
    - Remove all metal; use a metal detector to find hidden nails
    - Remove lead paint first
    - Mill, plane, and sand
5. Build with reclaimed lumber
    - Pre-drill holes to prevent splitting
    - Use screws rather than nails

Constructing 301: Definitions

- **Acclimate**: Allow wood to adjust to the temperature and humidity before working with it
- **Frass**: Powdery refuse produced by boring insects
- **Growth rings**: Concentric circles visible in wood cross-sections
- **Moisture content**: Percentage of water weight in wood compared to its dry weight
- **Old-growth**: Trees from forests that developed naturally over long periods

Constructing 301: Troubleshooting

Problem	Solutions
Excessive mold or fungi	Brush off outdoors wearing a respirator. Clean with bleach.
Hidden nails	Scan with a metal detector. Use sacrificial blades for initial sizing cuts.
Wood splits	Pre-drill holes.
Thickness varies	Plane to consistent thickness. Design to accommodate varied thicknesses.
Lead paint	Remove with a stripper and scrape wet. Never sand lead paint.

Constructing 301: Limitations

- Requires more time investment than using new lumber
- Finding specific dimensions or quantities can be challenging
- Quality and condition vary significantly
- May contain contaminants like lead paint or chemical treatments
- Harder and potentially more brittle than new lumber
- Removing nails and hardware is time-consuming

References and resources: <www.suspra.com/practice/habitat/constructing-301.html>

Constructing 302: Recycling Plastic

Build with recycled plastic composites

Build with recycled plastic composites to close the recycling loop and reduce demand for new materials. Wood-Plastic Composites (WPC) combine recycled plastic with wood fiber, offering wood appearance with enhanced durability. Recycled Plastic Lumber (RPL) is made primarily from recycled plastic with minimal wood content. These materials expand and contract more with temperature changes, are typically heavier, have less rigidity, and create fine dust when cut. Use them for decking, fencing, outdoor furniture, landscaping features, and docks.

Constructing 302: Definitions
- **Capstock**: Outer protective layer on some composite materials
- **Recycled Plastic Lumber (RPL)**: Construction material made primarily from recycled plastic
- **Thermal expansion**: Tendency of materials to change size with temperature changes
- **Wood-Plastic Composite (WPC)**: Material made from wood fibers combined with recycled plastic resin

Constructing 302: Troubleshooting

Problem	Solutions
Material splitting	Pre-drill holes. Use screws designed for composite materials.
Expansion gaps	Follow manufacturer spacing guidelines.
Staining	Clean with soap and water. Avoid bleach.
Cut edges look different	Sand cut edges. Use touch-up paint. Use factory ends for visible cuts.
Boards sagging	Reduce joist spacing manufacturer specifications. Add additional supports.

Constructing 302: Limitations
- Higher initial cost than pressure-treated wood
- Heavier than natural wood
- Less rigid, requiring closer support spacing
- Cannot be easily painted or stained
- Generates fine dust when cut
- Not suitable for primary structural components
- Heat absorption can make some products hot in direct sunlight

References and resources: <www.suspra.com/practice/habitat/constructing-302.html>

Constructing 303: Siding with Cement

Build with fiber cement siding that contains recycled content

Choose fiber cement siding with recycled content for durability; the product lasts for 50 years or more and resists fires and insects. Put recycled wood fibers, post-consumer paper, fly ash, slag cement, and recycled glass aggregate to beneficial use. When cutting, always follow proper dust management procedures due to silica content, which is a lung irritant.

Constructing 303: Equipment & Materials
- Fiber cement siding panels with recycled content
- Circular saw with fiber cement blade or shears
- NIOSH N95 respirator mask
- Safety glasses and hearing protection

Constructing 303: Definitions

- **Fiber cement siding**: Exterior cladding made from cement, sand, cellulose fibers, and additives
- **Fly ash**: Coal power plant byproduct used to replace portion of cement
- **Moisture barrier and house wrap**: Water-resistant material installed between sheathing and siding
- **Flashing**: Material used to direct water away from critical areas
- **Post-consumer recycled content**: Materials reclaimed from consumer waste streams
- **Post-industrial recycled content**: Manufacturing waste recycled back into production

Constructing 303: Troubleshooting

Problem	Solutions
Panels cracking	Pre-drill holes near edges. Keep nails 3/8 inch from edges.
Water intrusion	Verify moisture barrier. Check flashing. Check clearance at bottom edge.
White powder	Clean with mild detergent. Ensure moisture barriers and ventilation.
Difficulty cutting	Use proper tools. Cut face down. Support panels during cutting.

Constructing 303: Limitations

- Higher initial cost than vinyl or wood siding
- Heavier than alternatives, requiring more labor
- Requires special cutting tools and dust management
- Professional installation may be required for warranty
- Transportation impacts significant if not locally sourced

References and resources: <www.suspra.com/practice/habitat/constructing-303.html>

Constructing 304: Metal Roofing

Upgrade asphalt shingle roofing to metal roofing that simplifies adding solar

Install metal roofing that lasts 70 years, better matching the 30-year lifespan of solar modules, eliminating the need to remove and reinstall solar arrays for roof replacement. Standing seam metal roofing is ideal for solar integration because it allows mounting without roof penetrations. Exposed fastener (corrugated) metal roofing also works but typically requires penetrating mounts.

Constructing 304: Definitions

- **Closure strips**: Foam or metal pieces that fill gaps in corrugated or ribbed panels
- **Concealed fastener roofing**: Fasteners are hidden beneath overlapping panels
- **Exposed fastener roofing**: Metal roofing attached with screws or nails through the material
- **Ice and water shield**: Self-adhering waterproof membrane for vulnerable areas
- **Standing seam**: Metal roofing with raised seams, vertical legs above the panel's flat area
- **Underlayment**: Water-resistant barrier between roof deck and metal panels

Constructing 304: Troubleshooting

Problem	Solutions
Cost exceeds budget	Phase installation. Use exposed fastener systems which cost less.
Noise concerns	Install proper sound-dampening underlayment. Add attic insulation.
Fire rating	Choose Class A fire-rated options.
Ice chunks sliding off	Install snow guards in snowy regions.

Constructing 304: Limitations

- Initial cost higher than asphalt shingles

References and resources: <www.suspra.com/practice/habitat/constructing-304.html>

Constructing 401: Building with Straw

Construct walls from straw bales

Use an agricultural byproduct to create highly insulated straw bale walls with R-values of 30-50. Load-bearing straw bale walls are simpler to build but can't support as much weight as post-and-beam framing with straw-bale infilling, which allows for more design flexibility and better weather protection during construction. Keep straw moisture content below 20% at all times. Finish with natural plaster to protect the straw while allowing walls to "breathe."

Constructing 401: Equipment & Materials

- Straw bales (typically 3-string, approximately 18" x 24" x 36-48")
- Work gloves and dust masks
- Hammer and pry bar
- Utility knife or Japanese saw
- Gravel, crushed stone, or rigid foam for foundation base
- Concrete foundation or concrete-filled block foundation
- Moisture barrier (6-mil polyethylene sheet)
- Steel rebar or bamboo pins (4-5 feet long)
- 2x4 or 2x6 lumber for plates and framing
- Galvanized nails or screws
- String and line level
- Sledgehammer or mallet
- Wooden stakes or rebar for bracing
- Chainsaw or electric knife for trimming bales
- Pre-built window and door frames

Constructing 401: Steps

1. Choose construction method:
   - Load-bearing: Bales support roof load (simpler, good for dry climates)
   - Post-and-beam: Structural frame with bale infill (better for wet climates)
2. Create raised foundation:
   - Construct foundation at least 12-18" above ground level
   - Include drainage features to direct water away
   - Install capillary break below base plate

- Secure treated wooden base plates to foundation
3. Prepare first course of bales:
  - Install moisture barrier on base plate
  - Place bales with cut ends facing up and down
  - For load-bearing, pin first course to base plate
  - For post-and-beam, secure wire mesh to frame
4. Stack additional courses:
  - Stagger bales like bricks to offset joints
  - Use rebar or bamboo pins between courses
  - Use string line to ensure walls remain plumb
  - Compress bales after every two courses
  - Add bracing as needed
5. Create door and window openings:
  - Install pre-built frames
  - Add temporary bracing above openings for load-bearing walls
  - Secure frames to adjacent bales
  - Pack gaps with loose straw
6. Install top plate:
  - Compress entire wall before securing
  - For load-bearing walls, connect top plate to foundation
  - For post-and-beam, attach to structural frame
7. Prepare for plastering:
  - Trim uneven sections
  - Install electrical conduit if needed
  - Test wall moisture content (keep below 20%)
  - Apply natural plaster or stucco in multiple coats

Constructing 401: Definitions

- **Capillary break**: Material preventing moisture from wicking up from ground
- **Load-bearing construction**: Straw bales themselves support roof weight
- **Post-and-beam construction**: Structural frame supports roof with bales as insulation
- **R-value**: Measure of thermal resistance; higher numbers indicate better insulation
- **Thermal mass**: Ability of material to absorb, store, and release heat

Constructing 401: Troubleshooting

Problem	Solutions
Bales too wet	Reject damp bales. Dry bales completely. Replace severely wet bales.
Uneven walls	Brace temporarily. Compress bales. Use string lines to maintain plumb.
Gaps between bales	Fill with loose straw. Retie bales. Use custom-cut pieces.
Difficulty pinning bales	Pre-drill holes with metal rod. Hammer pins at a slight angle.
Rodent infestations	Fill all gaps. Install metal mesh at foundation. Apply plaster promptly.
Settling	Build with adequate compression. Allow settling before final plastering.
Building codes	Provide engineering documentation. Consult an engineer.

Constructing 401: Limitations

- Requires protecting bales from moisture
- May face building code challenges
- Requires careful integration of utilities
- Limited availability of experienced contractors
- More difficult to modify or renovate once built
- Load-bearing method has limitations on building height

References and resources: <www.suspra.com/practice/habitat/constructing-401.html>

Constructing 402: Building with Earth

Construct floors and walls from rammed earth

Use dirt (rammed earth) to create solid structural elements with excellent thermal mass properties. Prepare a soil mix of 70% sand or aggregate and 30% clay or silt. Too much clay causes cracking; too little creates weakness. Determining proper moisture content with the "drop test": squeeze soil into a ball and drop from shoulder height–it should break into a few large pieces.

Constructing 402: Equipment & Materials

- Soil with appropriate composition (70% sand/gravel, 30% clay/silt)
- Clean water
- Formwork (wooden or metal forms)
- Tampers (manual hand tampers or pneumatic/electric)
- Moisture meter or simple field test equipment
- Shovels and rakes
- Wheelbarrow or small cement mixer
- Buckets and measuring containers
- Screening equipment (1/4" to 1/2" mesh)
- Level and plumb bob
- Protective gear (gloves, glasses, dust mask)
- Spray bottle for moisture control
- Tarpaulins for curing and protection
- *Optional: 5-10% stabilizer (Portland Cement or lime)*

Constructing 402: Steps

1. Prepare site and materials:
   - Check local building codes and obtain permits
   - Test soil composition (ideal mix: 70% sand/aggregate, 30% clay/silt)
   - Use jar test: mix soil with water, shake, let settle 24 hours
   - Screen soil to remove particles larger than 3/4"
   - Create test blocks to verify performance
2. Build formwork:
   - Construct sturdy, reusable forms using plywood and 2x4s
   - Ensure forms can withstand ramming pressure
   - Apply form release agent to interior surfaces
   - Install any electrical conduit or box cutouts before ramming
3. Mix and ram walls (traditional method):
   - Mix soil to optimal moisture content (should form ball when squeezed)
   - Place 4-6 inch loose layers into forms
   - Compress each layer with tampers until "ping" sound is heard
   - Scarify surface between layers for better bonding

- Continue adding layers until desired height
4. For floors:
    - Prepare base of gravel or crushed stone (4-6 inches)
    - Install moisture barrier if appropriate for climate
    - Place soil mix in 4-inch layers and compact thoroughly
    - Add stabilizer to final layer for improved durability
5. Finish and cure:
    - Remove forms carefully after initial set (24-48 hours)
    - Patch any voids immediately
    - Cover walls with tarps to slow drying in hot, dry climates
    - Mist walls periodically during first week
    - Allow walls to cure 2-4 weeks before applying loads

Constructing 402: Definitions

- **Aggregate**: Coarse particles in soil mix, typically sand and small gravel
- **Drop test**: Field test for proper moisture content
- **Formwork**: Temporary molds built to contain rammed earth during compaction
- **Pneumatic tamper**: Air-powered compaction tool
- **Stabilized rammed earth**: Soil mixture with additives like cement or lime
- **Thermal mass**: Ability to absorb, store, and release heat energy

Constructing 402: Troubleshooting

Problem	Solutions
Soil too clayey	Add coarse sand to achieve the proper ratio. Test small batches.
Formwork bulging	Add additional bracing. Reduce layer thickness. Check ties and spreaders.
Cracks during drying	Check moisture content. Cover with tarps to slow drying. Mist occasionally.
Mixture too dry/wet	Add water gradually or add dry soil mix as needed.
Compaction	Use consistent layer thickness. Tamp with overlapping strokes.
Layers not bonding	Scarify each compacted layer before adding next. Keep layers moist.

Constructing 402: Limitations

- Labor-intensive; requires significant physical effort
- Construction time longer than conventional methods
- Limited structural capabilities without reinforcement
- Requires good quality control of soil composition
- Limited number of experienced contractors
- May require special permitting or engineering approval
- Difficult to modify after construction

References and resources: <www.suspra.com/practice/habitat/constructing-402.html>

Constructing 403: Building with Adobe

Construct walls from adobe

Use sun-dried earth bricks to create structures with excellent thermal mass and low embodied energy. Traditional adobe uses hand-formed or molded bricks with clay mortar and earth plaster finishes. Modern adaptations include stabilized adobe, compressed earth blocks, reinforcement systems, and integration with conventional foundation and roofing. Adobe walls naturally regulate temperature and humidity through thermal mass and vapor permeability.

Constructing 403: Equipment & Materials

- Soil with appropriate clay content (20-30%)
- Sand (if needed to adjust soil composition)
- Straw or natural fiber (4-6 inches long)
- Screens for sifting soil (1/4" mesh)
- Water
- Rectangular wooden forms (typically 10" × 14" × 4"), levels and string line
- Shovel and hoe, wheelbarrow or mixing tub
- Work gloves and dust mask
- Trowels and mason's hammer
- *Optional: Stabilizers (asphalt emulsion, lime, cement)*

Constructing 403: Steps

1. Test and prepare soil:
   - Perform jar test: Fill quart jar 1/4 with soil, add water, shake, let settle 24 hours
   - Ideal adobe soil contains 20-30% clay, 70-80% sand/silt
   - Conduct ball test: Form moistened soil into 2" ball, let dry, check for cracking
   - Sift soil through 1/4" screen to remove debris
   - Adjust composition if needed
2. Make adobe bricks:
   - Mix 3 parts soil, 1 part straw, and water to oatmeal-like consistency
   - Wet wooden forms to prevent sticking
   - Pack mixture firmly into forms, pressing into corners
   - Smooth top surface and remove forms immediately
   - Allow bricks to dry 3-7 days until firm enough to handle
   - Turn bricks onto edge for even drying
   - Continue curing 2-4 weeks, protecting from rain
3. Prepare for construction:
   - Ensure foundation extends at least 8" above ground
   - Waterproof top of foundation
   - Install moisture barrier if required
   - Mark wall layout
   - Prepare mortar (3 parts sand to 1 part clay or lime)
4. Build walls:
   - Dampen foundation lightly
   - Apply 1" thick mortar bed
   - Place corner bricks first, then fill between using string line
   - Tap bricks into place with trowel handle
   - Keep courses level and plumb
   - Stagger vertical joints (minimum 4" overlap)
   - Build 3-4 courses per day to allow mortar to set
5. Create openings and reinforcement:

- Install lintels over door and window openings
- Extend lintels at least 12" beyond each side of opening
- Add reinforcement (wire mesh, bamboo) every 2-3 courses
- Install bond beam at wall top for roof attachment
6. Finish the walls:
    - Allow walls to cure 2-4 weeks before applying finish
    - Apply earth, lime, or cement-lime plaster in multiple thin coats
    - Allow proper drying time between coats

Constructing 403: Definitions

- **Adobe**: Sun-dried bricks made of earth, water, and fibrous material
- **Bond beam**: Continuous horizontal reinforcement at the top of a wall
- **Compressed Earth Blocks (CEBs)**: Machine-pressed blocks for more uniform, denser bricks
- **Lintel**: Horizontal support above door and window openings
- **Stabilizers**: Materials added to increase water resistance and durability
- **Thermal mass**: Ability to absorb, store, and release heat

Constructing 403: Troubleshooting

Problem	Solutions
Adobe mix too wet/dry	Add dry soil mixture or water gradually. Test by forming a ball.
Bricks crack	Add more straw. Protect from direct sun while drying. Use stabilizer.
Uneven brick sizes	Fill forms completely and pack firmly. Use consistent technique.
Bricks stick to forms	Wet forms before each use or line with sand. Remove forms swiftly.
Mortar dries too fast	Work in smaller sections. Keep mortar covered. Dampen bricks first.
Wall not plumb	Use level frequently. Check plumb at corners. Correct issues immediately.
Erosion of finished wall	Apply plaster. Ensure adequate roof overhangs. Install proper drainage.

Constructing 403: Limitations

- Labor-intensive and time-consuming
- Not suitable for regions with frequent heavy rainfall without substantial roof overhangs
- Requires appropriate soil with proper clay content
- May be restricted by local building codes
- Needs regular maintenance, including reapplication of plaster every 5-10 years
- Construction season limited by weather conditions
- Limited number of experienced contractors in many regions

References and resources: <www.suspra.com/practice/habitat/constructing-403.html>

Insulating 301: Avoiding Fiberglass

Avoid fiberglass when insulating

Insulate with cellulose, rock wool, or cotton. Fiberglass batt insulation, while common, is less likely to be installed effectively than other types. The primary reason is that without proper air sealing, fiberglass allows air to flow through it, acting as an air filter rather than an insulator. Over time, fiberglass becomes the perfect breeding ground for mold as organic particles accumulate and moist air flows through. Cellulose, made from recycled paper, naturally blocks airflow, offers excellent thermal performance, and is treated for fire resistance. Rock wool, produced from volcanic rock, is naturally fire-resistant and offers superior sound insulation. Cotton insulation, derived from recycled denim, is another eco-friendly option that is naturally mold-resistant. When choosing, consider the R-value (thermal resistance) appropriate for your climate and the ease of installation.

Properly installing any insulating material ensures better energy efficiency and reduces the risk of mold growth. For existing fiberglass, pay close attention to air sealing to ensure better performance as an insulating material.

References and resources: <www.suspra.com/practice/habitat/insulating-301.html>

Maintaining 102: Cleaning Fans and Ducts

Clean kitchen and bathroom exhaust fans and ducting

Clean ducts and exhaust fans regularly to maintain ventilation efficiency and control odors, moisture problems, and fire hazards. Bathroom fans collect dust and lint while kitchen exhausts accumulate grease. Clean bathroom fans and ducts every 6-12 months and kitchen filters every 1-3 months.

Maintaining 102: Equipment & Materials

- Vacuum with brush attachment
- Microfiber cloths, small brush or old toothbrush
- Spray bottle with mild dish soap solution
- *Optional: Compressed air, vent brush*

Maintaining 102: Steps

1. Turn off power to the exhaust fan at the circuit breaker for safety.
2. For bathroom exhaust:
    - Remove fan cover (pull down or unscrew)
    - Vacuum dust from cover and housing; vacuum duct (as far as you can reach)
    - Clean fan blades with brush avoiding motor
    - Check damper moves freely
    - Inspect visible ductwork with flashlight; use cloth or brush to clean
    - Reassemble once dry
3. For kitchen range hood:
    - Remove grease filters; soak in hot soapy water for 10-15 minutes
    - Scrub gently to remove grease
    - Clean hood interior with damp cloth
    - Inspect visible ductwork for grease buildup; use cloth or brush to clean
    - Reinstall dry filters
4. Restore power and test operation.

Maintaining 102: Definitions

- **Backdraft damper:** Flap preventing outside air from flowing back in
- **Grease filter:** Removable mesh in range hoods capturing grease particles
- **Vent termination:** Exterior endpoint of the duct system

Sustainable Practices Handbook
Habitat Practices: Renovating Wisely

Maintaining 102: Troubleshooting

Problem	Solutions
Little air movement	Check exterior vent and damper for blockage.
Unusual noise	Check for loose parts or improperly secured cover.
Grease filters still dirty	Soak longer in hotter water with stronger degreaser.
Mold around fan	Clean with bleach. Run fans for 20-30 minutes after showering.

Maintaining 102: Limitations

- Deep duct cleaning requires specialized equipment
- May need professional service for multi-story or complex ductwork
- Older homes may have asbestos-containing materials

References and resources: <www.suspra.com/practice/habitat/maintaining-102.html>

Maintaining 103: Controlling Humidity

Keep indoor humidity below 60% to mitigate mold and mildew

Keep your home in the ideal indoor relative humidity range of 30-50%, with 60% as the maximum safe limit. Excess humidity promotes mold, mildew, and dust mites, while very low humidity causes respiratory issues and damages wood.

Maintaining 103: Equipment & Materials

- Hygrometer (humidity meter)
- Dehumidifier
- Humidifier
- Weatherstripping
- Exhaust fans
- Caulk or sealant
- *Optional: Moisture barriers, ceiling fans*

Maintaining 103: Steps

1. Measure humidity levels in different areas of your home
   - Aim for 30-50% relative humidity (never exceeding 60%)
   - Record measurements to identify problem areas
2. Identify moisture sources
   - Check for leaks in plumbing, roof, and foundation
   - Note poor ventilation areas
   - List daily activities that generate moisture
3. For high humidity (above 50%):
   - Use exhaust fans in bathrooms and kitchens
   - Run air conditioners during humid weather
   - Use dehumidifiers in problem areas
   - Fix any leaks immediately
   - Improve drainage around foundation
4. For low humidity (below 30%):
   - Use a humidifier

- Leave bathroom door open when showering
- Add indoor plants
- Air-dry clothes indoors
5. Improve ventilation
   - Open windows when outdoor humidity is lower than indoors
   - Use ceiling fans for air circulation
   - Ensure clean HVAC filters
6. Establish daily habits
   - Run bathroom fans 20-30 minutes after showering
   - Use kitchen exhaust when cooking
   - Keep furniture slightly away from exterior walls

Maintaining 103: Definitions

- **Condensation**: Conversion of water vapor to liquid on cold surfaces
- **Dehumidifier**: Appliance removing moisture from air
- **Humidifier**: Appliance adding moisture to air
- **Hygrometer**: Device measuring humidity levels
- **Relative humidity (RH)**: Water vapor in air as a percentage of maximum capacity at that temperature

Maintaining 103: Troubleshooting

Problem	Solutions
Humidity remains high	Check dehumidifier size. Close doors and windows. Look for leaks.
Window condensation	Add insulation. Use storm windows. Increase ventilation.
Mold reappears	Address underlying humidity issues. Improve ventilation
Home too dry in winter	Use a humidifier. Lower thermostat. Grow herbs and houseplants.
Basement damp	Improve drainage. Install vapor barriers. Use a dehumidifier.

Maintaining 103: Limitations

- Climate conditions may make ideal levels difficult without significant energy use
- Older homes with poor insulation present greater challenges
- Humidifiers require regular cleaning to prevent mold growth
- Multi-unit buildings may be affected by neighboring units

References and resources: <www.suspra.com/practice/habitat/maintaining-103.html>

Maintaining 201: Fixing Roof Leaks

Fix roof leaks

Find and fix roof leaks before they cause big problems. Water often travels along rafters or structures before becoming visible inside, so the interior damage may not be directly below the entry point. Upgrade to a metal roof to fix roof dams and other problems associated with asphalt roofing.

Maintaining 201: Steps

1. Prioritize safety

- Work only in dry, calm weather
- Use properly secured ladder and safety harness
- Have a helper on the ground
2. Locate the leak
3. Implement a temporary fix
4. Make permanent repairs based on the issue
5. Test your repair with a hose on the roof
6. Maintain roof to prevent future leaks
   - Clear gutters regularly
   - Remove debris from roof surface
   - Schedule annual inspections

Maintaining 201: Definitions

- **Flashing**: Metal or impervious material at joints preventing water entry
- **Ice dam**: Ridge of ice at roof edge forcing water under shingles
- **Ridge**: Highest point where two roof planes meet
- **Roof deck**: Structural surface over framing to which roofing materials attach
- **Valley**: Internal angle formed by intersecting roof planes
- **Vent boots**: Prefabricated flashing with rubber collars sealing around vent pipes

Maintaining 201: Troubleshooting

Problem	Solutions
Leak persists	Expand the search area.
Multiple leaks	Replace the roof.
Cannot safely access	Install a temporary tarp from accessible areas. Hire a professional.
Mold has developed	Address both the leak and mold. Ensure the area dries completely.
Condensation	Check attic ventilation and insulation.

Maintaining 201: Limitations

- May void warranties if not done by authorized contractors
- Building codes may require permits for extensive work
- Steep roofs (greater than 6:12 pitch) require professional equipment

References and resources: <www.suspra.com/practice/habitat/maintaining-201.html>

Maintaining 202: Installing Gutters

Install gutters or roofline drainage to direct water away from buildings

Install proper gutter systems to prevent foundation problems, basement flooding, and landscape erosion by channeling roof water away from your building. Choose aluminum (good balance of cost and durability), steel (very durable but heavier), or copper (premium but expensive). Select a 6-inch gutter to prepare for the heavier and more intense rainfalls that climate change is causing.

Maintaining 202: Equipment & Materials

- Gutters and downspouts, end caps, hangers/brackets, outlet tubes, fasteners, sealant

Maintaining 202: Steps

1. Plan your system
   - Measure roof perimeter
   - Identify downspout locations (typically at corners)
2. Prepare the fascia board
   - Inspect for rot; repair if necessary
   - Mark rafter positions for securing hangers
3. Establish proper slope
   - Slope toward downspouts at 1/4 inch per 10 feet
   - Snap chalk line along fascia for height guide
   - For buildings over 40 feet, slope from middle toward both ends
4. Install gutters
   - Start at a corner or high point
   - Attach end caps with sealant
   - Install outlet tubes at downspout locations
   - Mount hangers according to manufacturer instructions
   - Place gutter sections and secure
   - Join sections with connectors and sealant
5. Install downspouts
   - Cut to required length; ensure water directs at least 5 feet from foundation
   - Attach elbows to direct water away from foundation
   - Secure to building with brackets

Maintaining 202: Definitions

- **Downspout**: Vertical pipe carrying water from gutter to ground
- **Fascia board**: Vertical edge connected to rafter ends where gutters attach
- **K-style gutter**: Common profile resembling letter K when viewed from side
- **Half-round gutter**: Semi-circular profile often used on historic homes
- **Splash block**: Pad placed under downspout to direct water away from foundation

Maintaining 202: Troubleshooting

Problem	Solutions
Overflowing gutters	Check slope and gutter size. Clean debris. Add downspouts.
Leaking at joints	Apply sealant. Ensure proper overlap. Replace damaged sections.
Gutters pulling away	Add hangers. Secure to rafters, not just fascia. Repair damaged fascia.
Water pooling	Extend downspouts. Install splash blocks. Check the ground slope.
Gutters sagging	Add additional hangers. Verify the proper slope is maintained.

Maintaining 202: Limitations

- Installation on two-story buildings may require professional help
- Seamless gutters require specialized equipment
- Some roofing warranties void with improper installation

References and resources: <www.suspra.com/practice/habitat/maintaining-202.html>

Maintaining 301: Installing Batteries

Install battery backup to maintain power during grid outages

Install batteries to maintain electricity during grid outages. Portable power banks based on lithium-ion battery cells require minimal maintenance and can keep critical loads like a refrigerator or emergency lighting operational for a few days. For longer durations, install larger batteries. Integrate with solar for the longest run-time–a large enough solar array and battery system will provide perpetual power.

Install a critical load backup subpanel to backup just a few circuits; install a whole-house battery system and automatic transfer switch to power all circuits. Whole-house battery systems are actually easier to install, but more expensive because they require more battery cells and more powerful inverters.

Maintaining 301: Equipment & Materials

- Battery storage system (LFP or other chemistry)
- Battery inverter or hybrid inverter
- Automatic transfer switch (for whole-house systems)
- Critical load panel (for partial home backup)

Maintaining 301: Steps

1. **Hire a licensed electrician unless you are qualified to do the work yourself**
2. Plan your system
   - Assess energy needs during outages and calculate required runtime
   - Determine battery location and verify structural support
3. Obtain permits and approvals
4. Prepare installation location
5. Install electrical components
6. Install batteries
7. Integrate system and commission

Maintaining 301: Definitions

- **Automatic Transfer Switch**: Device that switches between power sources
- **Battery Management System**: Electronic system monitoring battery pack health
- **Critical Load Panel**: Subpanel for essential circuits receiving backup power
- **Depth of Discharge**: Percentage of battery capacity used relative to total
- **Hybrid Inverter**: Converts DC power from solar panels and batteries into AC power

Maintaining 301: Troubleshooting

Problem	Solutions
Battery doesn't work	Check charge level. Verify transfer switch operation. Reset system.
Battery drains quickly	Reduce loads. Check for phantom loads. Verify battery charge.
Battery not charging	Check charging settings. Verify grid connection. Check connections.
Battery overheating	Provide more ventilation. Reduce charge and discharge rates.

Maintaining 301: Limitations

- Batteries are expensive
- Battery performance deteriorates over time (20-30% capacity loss over 10-15 years)

- Temperature extremes affect performance

References and resources: <www.suspra.com/practice/habitat/maintaining-301.html>

Painting 201: Avoiding Toxins

Paint with non-toxic, zero-VOC coatings

Many conventional paints release volatile organic compounds (VOCs) that harm human health and the environment. To reduce your impact, switch to "zero-VOC" or "low-VOC" paints. Look for certifications such as Cradle to Cradle, EPA Safer Choice, or Green Seal, which indicate that the product meets stringent environmental and health standards. Before purchasing, check the product's material safety data sheet (MSDS) for a detailed list of ingredients.

References and resources: <www.suspra.com/practice/habitat/painting-201.html>

Plumbing 304: Protecting Pipes

Move plumbing runs to avoid frozen pipes

Move plumbing runs to interior spaces to prevent frozen pipes. Interior walls maintain higher temperatures, protecting pipes even during extreme cold. Well-planned relocations also often deliver hot water faster to fixtures, increasing efficiency. Consider proper slope for drainage, accessibility for future repairs, and maintaining adequate water pressure through the new route. PEX tubing is ideal for relocation projects due to its flexibility, requiring fewer joints and access points.

References and resources: <www.suspra.com/practice/habitat/plumbing-304.html>

Sharing Shelter 401: Creating an In-Law Apartment

Convert rooms in your home to an in-law apartment to rent

Create an in-law apartment (also called accessory dwelling units or secondary suites) to provide additional housing in your community utilizing existing space in your home.

- Basement conversions require addressing moisture, adequate exits, and sufficient ceiling height. They benefit from natural temperature regulation but may lack natural light.
- Garage conversions offer separate entry and straightforward electrical upgrades but need significant insulation improvements.
- First-floor conversions provide immediate livability but require careful planning for privacy.

Universal design principles—such as wider doorways and zero-step entrances—make the space usable by people of all ages and abilities, increasing long-term value.

Sharing Shelter 401: Steps

1. Evaluate your space
2. Research local regulations
3. Create a sustainable design and develop a budget
4. Secure necessary approvals
5. Hire a contractor or do the work to create a separate entrance and required rooms
   - Build or modify bathroom with ventilation
   - Install kitchen facilities
6. Install or upgrade utilities
7. Finish the space
8. Complete final inspections

Sharing Shelter 401: Definitions

- **Accessory Dwelling Unit (ADU)**: Secondary housing unit on a single-family residential lot
- **Certificate of Occupancy**: Document stating a building meets codes and is suitable for occupancy
- **Egress window**: Emergency exit window meeting specific size requirements
- **Fair Housing Laws**: Regulations prohibiting discrimination in housing
- **Universal Design**: Design approach creating spaces accessible to all ages and abilities
- **Zoning**: Municipal regulations controlling land use and building function

Sharing Shelter 401: Troubleshooting

Problem	Solutions
Ceiling height	Get a variance. Remove dropped ceilings. Lower basement floor.
Natural light	Install larger windows. Use glass block for privacy. Add solar tubes.
Moisture issues	Install exterior drainage and waterproofing. Use dehumidifiers. Apply waterproof sealants. Install a sump pump.
Electrical capacity	Upgrade service. Get more efficient appliances.
Noise transfer	Install insulation. Install solid-core doors. Add sound dampening.

Sharing Shelter 401: Limitations

- Local regulations may prohibit or restrict in-law apartments
- Construction costs can be substantial
- Close proximity to tenants creates privacy challenges
- Landlord responsibilities include legal obligations
- Units must meet current building codes
- Managing tenant issues requires time and skills

References and resources: <www.suspra.com/practice/habitat/sharing-shelter-401.html>

Protecting Nature

Landscaping 203: Planting Natives

Plant native species in your yard

Give native plants a place to thrive–they have evolved in your region over thousands of years, developing relationships with local wildlife, soil microbes, and climate conditions. They typically require less water, fertilizer, and maintenance once established. Plan for plant communities that naturally occur together rather than individual specimens. Create a unique sense of place while providing essential habitat for local wildlife.

Landscaping 203: Equipment & Materials

- Native plants suitable for your region
- *Optional: plant labels, garden journal, pH testing kit, soil knife, garden stakes and string*

Landscaping 203: Steps

1. Research native plants for your region
   - Identify your hardiness zone, soil type, and microclimate conditions
   - Choose plants that provide year-round interest and support wildlife
2. Source native plants
   - Use local native plant nurseries or native plant sales
   - Avoid purchasing wild-harvested plants
3. Create a planting plan
   - Map existing yard conditions (sunny, shady, wet, dry areas)
   - Group plants with similar water and light requirements
   - Plan for mature size to avoid overcrowding
4. Prepare the planting area
   - Remove unwanted vegetation
   - Loosen compacted soil with a garden fork; add compost
5. Plant during appropriate season
   - Cool climates: early spring or fall
   - Warm climates: fall or early winter
   - Desert climates: early fall or late winter
6. Plant properly
   - Dig holes twice as wide as the root ball but same depth
   - Loosen circling roots if root-bound
   - Ensure top of root ball is level with soil surface
   - Backfill with existing soil
   - Water thoroughly immediately after planting
   - Apply 2-3 inches of mulch, keeping it away from stems
7. Care for new plantings
   - Water deeply but infrequently to encourage deep roots
   - Monitor for signs of stress; provide more water if necessary
   - Remove competing weeds while plants establish
8. Maintain your native plant garden
   - Allow leaf litter to remain as natural mulch
   - Leave seed heads for winter interest and wildlife food

Landscaping 203: Definitions

- **Ecological community**: Interacting plant and animal species that naturally occur together

- **Hardiness zone**: Geographic areas defined by average annual minimum winter temperatures
- **Microclimate**: Small-scale variations in climate conditions within a yard
- **Native plant**: Plant species that evolved in a particular region without human introduction
- **Nativar**: Cultivated variety of a native plant selected for specific traits
- **Root-bound**: Condition where plant roots have grown densely in a container

Landscaping 203: Troubleshooting

Problem	Solutions
Plants not thriving	Check microclimate. Replace plants that die. Choose different varieties.
Plants look "messy"	Group plants in drifts for visual impact. Add defined edges.
Neighbors complain	Create a "tidy frame" (mow around nature). Install educational signage.
Not enough water	Water deeply when planting. Create watering basins around new plantings.
Animals eating plants	Fence. Choose less palatable species for wildlife-heavy areas.

Landscaping 203: Limitations

- Native plants may be harder to find than non-native ornamentals
- Gardens take several years to reach maturity and full visual impact
- Neighbors or HOAs may resist "wild" appearances
- Some aggressive native plants may require management

References and resources: <www.suspra.com/practice/habitat/landscaping-203.html>

Landscaping 204: Managing Pests

Manage pests with an integrated plan that minimizes synthetic pesticide use

Integrate multiple strategies to control pests while minimizing larger environmental harms. Consider your entire ecosystem; use chemical pesticides only as a last resort. Understand pest life cycles and ecology; time interventions for maximum impact with minimum effort. Prevent disease whenever possible—healthy plants naturally resist many pest problems. When controls are needed, start with the least invasive methods.

Landscaping 204: Equipment & Materials

- Magnifying glass or smartphone with macro lens
- Garden journal or pest monitoring log
- Field guides for pest identification
- Yellow sticky traps
- Beneficial insect habitat materials
- Row covers or insect netting
- Garden pruners and gloves
- Sprayer for non-toxic solutions
- *Optional: Camera, soil testing kit, specimen containers*

Landscaping 204: Steps

1. Learn Integrated Pest Management (IPM) principles
   - Focus on prevention through ecosystem management; aim for management, not elimination

- Follow control hierarchy: prevention, mechanical, biological, then chemical as last resort
2. Identify pests correctly
    - Determine if the organism is actually causing damage
    - Photograph unknown pests and use guides for identification
    - Research pest life cycle and natural predators
    - Document pest populations in your garden journal
3. Implement preventive measures
    - Select pest-resistant plant varieties
    - Space plants properly for adequate airflow
    - Establish beneficial insect habitats
    - Install physical barriers for vulnerable plants
    - Practice crop rotation for vegetable gardens
4. Monitor pest populations regularly
    - Inspect plants weekly during growing season; check sticky traps and record findings
    - Set thresholds for action based on plant tolerance
5. Apply controls progressively
    - **Level 1**: Manual removal (hand-pick, prune, water spray)
    - **Level 2**: Physical controls (adjust irrigation, add barriers)
    - **Level 3**: Biological controls (beneficial insects, nematodes)
    - **Level 4**: Minimal-risk chemical pesticides (neem oil, insecticidal soaps)
    - **Level 5**: Highly toxic synthetic chemical pesticides (last resort, targeted application)
6. Evaluate and adjust your approach based on outcomes
7. Practice year-round IPM
    - Perform end-of-season cleanup
    - Plan crop rotations
    - Create a calendar of preventive actions

Landscaping 204: Definitions

- **Action threshold**: Point at which pest control action must be taken
- **Beneficial insects**: Organisms that prey on pests or contribute to ecosystem health
- **Biological control**: Using living organisms to suppress pest populations
- **Broad-spectrum pesticide**: Chemicals that kill a wide range of organisms
- **Horticultural oil**: Refined petroleum or plant-based oils that smother pests
- **Insecticidal soap**: Potassium salts of fatty acids that control soft-bodied insects
- **Integrated Pest Management (IPM)**: Ecosystem-based strategy using multiple techniques
- **Mechanical control**: Physically removing pests or creating barriers

Landscaping 204: Troubleshooting

Problem	Solutions
Cannot identify a pest	Take clear photos; consult extension service. Use online tools.
Few beneficial insects	Increase habitat diversity. Leave untreated refuge areas.
Pest problems recur	Improve soil health. Increase biodiversity. Remove susceptible plants.
Few natural predators	Provide enough prey and water sources. Reduce broad-spectrum controls.
Treatments ineffective	Identify pests. Improve timing. Cover completely. Combine methods.

Landscaping 204: Limitations

- Requires more knowledge than conventional pesticide approaches
- May not provide immediate results compared to synthetic chemicals
- Environmental conditions may limit effectiveness of certain controls
- Requires consistent monitoring and record-keeping
- Some severe pest situations may still require synthetic intervention

References and resources: <www.suspra.com/practice/habitat/landscaping-204.html>

Landscaping 303: Going Organic

Landscape with organic methods, avoiding all synthetic fertilizers and pesticides

Work with nature to build healthy soil that supports vigorous plants naturally resistant to pests and diseases. Patiently transition from synthetic methods—soil previously treated with chemicals may take three years to recover biodiversity. Rely on biodiversity, prevention, soil health, and water conservation. While requiring more initial investment, long-term benefits include lower maintenance costs, reduced water usage, and safer spaces for children, pets, and wildlife.

Landscaping 303: Equipment & Materials

- Soil testing kit
- Organic compost, soil amendments, and fertilizers
- Organic pest management supplies (neem oil, insecticidal soap)
- Natural weed management tools (hoe, flame weeder, mulch)
- Pruning tools and garden gloves
- Garden fork and spade
- Watering equipment (soaker hoses, drip irrigation)
- *Optional: Biological controls, tarp for weed solarization*

Landscaping 303: Steps

1. Assess your current landscape
   - Analyze site conditions (sun/shade, drainage, soil quality)
   - Test soil to determine pH and nutrient levels
   - Document recurring pest and weed issues
2. Develop an organic landscape plan
   - Choose native plants suited to your specific conditions
   - Plan for biodiversity to reduce pest problems
   - Design efficient irrigation zones based on plant needs
3. Build healthy soil
   - Remove persistent weeds using manual methods
   - Add organic matter to improve soil structure; inoculate with beneficial microorganisms
   - Apply amendments based on soil test results
4. Plant properly
   - Plant during appropriate seasons for your climate
   - Space plants properly for air circulation
   - Use proper planting hole techniques
   - Apply mycorrhizal fungi to roots when planting
5. Establish organic maintenance practices
   - Install water-efficient irrigation; collect and store rainwater
   - Water deeply but infrequently
   - Maintain 2-3 inches of organic mulch to retain moisture and suppress weeds
6. Feed plants naturally

- Apply compost as top dressing annually
- Use compost tea for growing season feeding
- Apply specific amendments for flowering plants
- Utilize cover crops in vegetable areas
7. Manage pests and diseases organically
    - Choose resistant varieties
    - Create habitat for beneficial insects
    - Monitor regularly for early detection
    - Apply controls progressively: mechanical, biological, then botanical
8. Control weeds without chemicals
    - Use mulch and corn gluten meal to suppress weed growth
    - Remove weeds manually when small; flame weed hard surfaces
    - Plant cover crops

Landscaping 303: Definitions

- **Beneficial insects**: Insects that prey on garden pests or provide pollination
- **Biological controls**: Living organisms used to control pests
- **Compost tea**: Liquid extract of compost containing beneficial microorganisms
- **Cover crops**: Fast-growing plants sown to cover bare soil and add organic matter
- **Foliar feeding**: Spraying nutrients (such as compost tea) on plant leaves
- **Hydrozoning**: Grouping plants by water requirements
- **Mycorrhizal fungi**: Beneficial fungi that enhance plant root nutrient uptake
- **Sheet mulching**: Layered mulching technique that smothers weeds and builds soil
- **Soil food web**: Community of organisms living in soil that contribute to plant health
- **Solarization**: Using sun's energy to heat soil under plastic, killing weed seeds

Landscaping 303: Troubleshooting

Problem	Solutions
Nutrient deficiencies	Check soil pH. Amend soil. Apply foliar feeding.
Persistent pests	Identify pests. Increase plant diversity. Add insectary plants.
Weeds	Mulch to 3-4 inches. Use corn gluten. Weed more frequently.
Compacted soil	Add organic material. Use cover crops with deep taproots. Limit foot traffic.
Patchy lawn	Overseed. Raise mowing height. Core aerate and top-dress with compost.
Fungal diseases	Improve air circulation. Water only on sunny mornings. Apply compost tea.

Landscaping 303: Limitations

- Organic methods show results more slowly than synthetic alternatives
- Requires more knowledge of ecological principles
- May involve more time for monitoring and manual interventions
- Some pests may be more challenging to control organically
- Transitioning from synthetic-dependent landscapes requires adjustment period
- Neighbors' conventional practices may affect your landscape

References and resources: <www.suspra.com/practice/habitat/landscaping-303.html>

Learning 105: Identifying Hazards

Identify environmental hazards in and around your home and yard

Identify hazards around your home and yard to create safer, more sustainable home habitat.

Urban properties often contend with legacy industrial contamination, lead paint in older buildings, air pollution from traffic, and limited green space.

Suburban properties frequently face challenges from lawn chemicals, habitat fragmentation, and stormwater management issues.

Rural properties may encounter agricultural chemical exposure, well water contamination, septic system issues, and erosion.

Document locations and quantities to establish a baseline so you can track improvements over time. Conduct an initial assessment yourself; bring in professionals if you have areas of concern.

Do it yourself:
- Identify peeling paint, water damage, or mold
- Assess chemical storage and household hazardous waste
- Identify invasive plants or poor drainage areas
- Test water with home test kits (for pH, chlorine, hardness)
- Test for lead paint with commercially available kits
- Screen for radon

Hire a professional:
- Confirm presence of radon, lead, asbestos, or other toxic materials
- Test well water quality
- Identify structural issues in your house or building
- Assess subsurface soil contamination (especially leaking underground storage tanks)

Learning 101: Definitions
- **Asbestos**: A mineral in building materials that can cause health problems when fibers are released
- **Invasive species**: Non-native plants or animals harmful to environment
- **Lead**: Toxic metal formerly used in paint and plumbing
- **Radon**: Naturally occurring radioactive gas that can accumulate in buildings

Learning 105: Troubleshooting

Problem	Solutions
Uncertain about hazardous materials	Use test kits for initial screening. Assume older materials (pre-1978 for lead paint, pre-1980s for asbestos) contain hazards until professionally tested.
Can't access all areas	Document inaccessible areas on your map. Use pole-mounted camera.
Property boundary	Consult property records. Focus on areas clearly within your property first.
Results inconclusive	Retest using different methods. Hire a professional.
Plants identification	Take photos; use identification apps; consult extension offices.

Problem	Solutions
Overwhelmed	Start with high-risk areas near living spaces or water.

Learning 105: Limitations
- Visual inspection cannot identify all hazards
- Home test kits are less accurate than professional testing
- Seasonal variations may hide certain issues
- Some hazards only appear during specific weather conditions

References and resources: <www.suspra.com/practice/habitat/learning-105.html>

Managing 101: Keeping Cats Indoors

Keep cats indoors so birds and other animals can live in your neighborhood

Keeping cats indoors significantly reduces their impact on local wildlife, particularly bird populations. This simple practice directly contributes to biodiversity conservation within your neighborhood. Begin by creating an enriching indoor environment for your cat. Provide ample vertical space with cat trees or shelves, engage them with interactive toys, and ensure regular playtime. Consider leash training for supervised outdoor excursions if your cat craves outdoor experiences. By keeping your cat indoors, you protect vulnerable wildlife from predation, allowing local ecosystems to thrive.

References and resources: <www.suspra.com/practice/habitat/managing-101.html>

Managing 102: Keeping Dogs on Leash

Keep dogs on leash when hiking in areas where sensitive species live

When dogs are allowed to roam freely, they can disturb or even harm wildlife, disrupt nesting sites, and chase animals, causing stress and potential injury. This is especially critical in habitats where endangered or vulnerable species reside. By keeping your dog on a leash, you minimize these risks and allow wildlife to thrive undisturbed. Additionally, leashes prevent dogs from wandering into dangerous areas or encountering hazards like poisonous plants or steep cliffs. Before hiking, research the area to understand any leash laws or specific wildlife concerns. Always carry a leash and ensure it is securely attached to your dog.

References and resources: <www.suspra.com/practice/habitat/managing-102.html>

Managing 303: Placing an Easement

Put your land under conservation easement

To protect conservation values while you retain ownership, place your land under conservation easement, a voluntary legal agreement that permanently limits land uses. The process typically takes 6-18 months to complete. Different easement types include agricultural, forest, wildlife habitat, scenic, and watershed protection. Financial benefits may include income tax deductions, reduced property taxes, and estate tax benefits. Transaction costs typically range from $20,000-$60,000, though some land trusts can help cover these expenses.

Managing 303: Equipment & Materials
- An easement holder: a land trust or conservation organization
- Land ownership documentation (deed, title insurance, survey)

- Property maps and boundary descriptions
- Documentation of conservation values (photos, surveys)
- Financial records (property tax statements, mortgage documents)
- Access to legal counsel specializing in conservation law
- Access to financial and tax advisors with conservation easement experience

Managing 303: Steps

1. Assess your land's conservation value
   - Identify significant natural, scenic, historic, or agricultural features
   - Document wildlife habitats, waterways, rare species, or productive farmland
   - Take photographs throughout different seasons
2. Clarify your conservation and personal goals
   - Define what you want to protect and why
   - Determine which land uses to continue or prohibit
   - Consider your financial needs and tax situation
3. Research conservation easement options
4. Select an easement holder
5. Negotiate easement terms
6. Hire legal and financial professionals to establish the easement

Managing 303: Definitions

- **Baseline documentation report**: Inventory of property features when easement is recorded
- **Conservation easement**: Legal agreement permanently limiting land uses
- **Development rights**: Rights to build structures or develop land
- **Easement holder**: Organization that holds and enforces the conservation easement
- **Land trust**: Nonprofit organization working to conserve land through acquisition or easements
- **Mortgage subordination**: Agreement making mortgage interest subordinate to easement
- **Perpetuity**: Forever; easements bind all future owners
- **Stewardship endowment**: Funds for long-term monitoring and enforcement

Managing 303: Troubleshooting

Problem	Solutions
Can't find an easement holder	Enhance conservation values. Contact government agencies.
High transaction costs	Explore grants.
Mortgage lender won't subordinate	Refinancing with a different lender. Pay down the mortgage.
Family disagreements	Consider less restrictive terms for certain portions.
Documentation	Hire professional ecologists or historians. Use historical aerial photos.
Concerns about future	Reserve some rights. Include limited development zones.

Managing 303: Limitations

- Conservation easements are permanent and difficult to change
- Transaction costs can be substantial ($20,000-$60,000+)
- Not all properties have sufficient conservation values

- Tax benefits require meeting specific legal standards
- Easement restrictions may reduce property value
- Future owners will be bound by terms you negotiate
- Ongoing monitoring creates perpetual relationship with easement holder

References and resources: <www.suspra.com/practice/habitat/managing-303.html>

Removing 401: Removing Roads

Remove roads on your land

Remove roads and paved trails to provide larger intact habitat tracts and restore natural water flow across your land. Completely remove all road materials to produce the best ecological outcomes, though even partial removal with proper drainage and vegetation restoration yields significant benefits. Tailor your specific approach to your site conditions, soil type, and climate.

Removing 401: Equipment & Materials
- Heavy equipment (for extensive roads and bridges)
- Hand tools (for driveways and small areas of pavement)

Removing 401: Steps
1. Plan and assess the site; create a removal and restoration plan
2. Prepare for removal: secure permits and install erosion control measures
3. Remove surface materials
4. Remove road base and sub-base
5. Restore natural drainage patterns
6. Address soil compaction
7. Restore vegetation

Removing 401: Definitions
- **Base course**: Layer of crushed stone beneath road surface providing structural support
- **Compaction**: Increased soil density that reduces water infiltration and root penetration
- **Culvert**: Structure allowing water to flow under a road
- **Geotextile fabric**: Permeable material used to separate road layers or provide stability

Removing 401: Troubleshooting

Problem	Solutions
Utilities discovered	Stop work immediately. Contact utility companies.
Severe soil compaction	Add organic matter. Use deep ripping. Plant deep-rooted species.
Erosion	Install erosion controls. Create check dams.
Invasive plants	Weed. Increase native planting density. Apply mulch.

Removing 401: Limitations
- Requires significant resources and equipment
- Complete ecological recovery takes years or decades
- Permits may restrict timing or methods
- Heavy equipment may cause temporary site disturbance

- Some compaction effects may persist for decades

References and resources: <www.suspra.com/practice/habitat/removing-401.html>

Removing 402: Removing Buildings

Remove unnecessary buildings on your land

Remove unnecessary buildings to create wildlife habitat, improve soil health, and enhance ecosystem services. Prioritize deconstruction over demolition. Plan to recover 50-90% of materials for reuse or recycling, drastically reducing landfill waste.

Removing 402: Equipment & Materials
- Permits (if required)
- Demolition tools (pry bars, hammers, saws)
- Material testing kits for hazardous materials
- Dumpsters to sort materials for recovery and reuse
- Temporary fencing and caution tape
- *Optional: heavy machinery (excavator, backhoe)*

Removing 402: Steps
1. Assess the building and create a plan: deconstruction or demolition
2. Secure necessary permits and approvals
3. Test for hazardous materials
4. Prepare the site
   - Set up fencing and signage
   - Establish access routes
   - Position dumpsters for sorting materials
5. Salvage reusable materials (deconstruction)
   - Remove fixtures, appliances, and furniture first
   - Dismantle trim, doors, windows, and other components
   - Remove flooring, wall coverings, and ceiling materials
   - Label and store salvaged materials properly
6. Demolish the structure (if deconstruction isn't feasible)
7. Remove foundation and subsurface elements
8. Restore the site
9. Handle deconstructed or demolished materials properly

Removing 402: Definitions
- **Deconstruction**: Systematic disassembly of a building to maximize material recovery
- **Demolition**: Tearing down a building with minimal material recovery
- **Hazardous materials**: Substances that pose health risks, such as asbestos and lead paint
- **Salvage**: Recovery of usable building materials for reuse

Removing 402: Troubleshooting

Problem	Solutions
Hazardous materials	Stop work. Contact specialists for testing and abatement.
Structural instability	Get professional advice. Consider mechanical demolition if unsafe.

Problem	Solutions
Removing foundation	Rent specialized equipment or hire professionals.
Wildlife nesting	Consult wildlife specialists. Schedule work when not being used for nesting.

Removing 402: Limitations
- Complete deconstruction not feasible for all building types
- Hazardous materials increase removal costs
- Heavy machinery can cause soil compaction
- Permits may be time-consuming and expensive
- Buildings with historical significance may have legal protections

References and resources: <www.suspra.com/practice/habitat/removing-402.html>

Supporting 101: Conserving Land

Donate money to land trusts and other organizations that conserve natural land

Land trusts and organizations dedicated to land conservation acquire and manage land to protect it from development and allow natural processes to occur. Research land trusts operating in your region or areas with high conservation value. Consider organizations like The Nature Conservancy or local land trusts that focus on specific ecosystems. Determine a donation amount that aligns with your budget and values. Regular, smaller donations from a large base of donors help these organizations operate by providing a source of income they can depend on.

References and resources: <www.suspra.com/practice/habitat/supporting-101.html>

Supporting 102: Voting for Nature

Vote for parks and wilderness areas

Research candidates and ballot measures that prioritize environmental protection. Look for those supporting funding for parks, land conservation, and policies that restrict development in sensitive ecological zones. Attend town hall meetings or review candidate websites to understand their stances on these issues. Protecting natural spaces is crucial for biodiversity, clean air and water, and community well-being. Use your vote to support the creation and maintenance of parks and wilderness areas.

References and resources: <www.suspra.com/practice/habitat/supporting-102.html>

Supporting 201: Registering Your Biodiversity

Register your native plantings on the Homegrown National Park Biodiversity Map

Plant native species and register your property on the Homegrown National Park Biodiversity Map to connect your individual efforts to a larger conservation movement. Add your property to a growing network of habitat "steppingstones" that help wildlife navigate through fragmented landscapes. Even small plantings are worth registering—container gardens, boulevard strips, or small beds all provide crucial habitat when connected across landscapes.

Supporting 201: Steps
1. Document your native plant garden
   - Take clear photos of your native plant areas

- List the native plant species you have planted
- Calculate the approximate area (square feet or acres)
2. Visit the Homegrown National Park website at <HomegrownNationalPark.org>
3. Follow the instructions posted there

Supporting 201: Definitions

- **Biodiversity**: Variety of life in a habitat, including species and ecosystem diversity
- **Homegrown National Park**: Initiative to encourage landowners to plant native species
- **Native plants**: Plant species evolved in a specific region with relationships to local wildlife
- **Steppingstones**: Smaller habitat areas allowing wildlife movement between larger areas
- **Wildlife corridor**: Connected habitat areas allowing animals to move safely

Supporting 201: Troubleshooting

Problem	Solutions
Plant identification	Use native plant databases. Consult local native plant societies.
Mapping plant areas	Estimate using online mapping tools or simple length × width calculations.

Supporting 201: Limitations

- Primarily focuses on the United States
- Requires Internet access and basic digital skills
- Shows approximate locations rather than exact boundaries
- Relies on self-reporting, which may lead to data inconsistencies
- Doesn't provide legal protection or conservation status

References and resources: <www.suspra.com/practice/habitat/supporting-201.html>

Supporting 202: Certifying Your Habitat

Certify your yard or garden as National Wildlife Federation Certified Wildlife Habitat

Certify your yard or garden as National Wildlife Federation Certified Wildlife Habitat to contribute to community-level conservation efforts. The certification process guides you through creating a genuine wildlife sanctuary with each element serving a specific ecological purpose: food sustains wildlife through different seasons; water is critical for drinking and bathing; cover protects animals from predators and weather; and nesting sites ensure reproduction.

Supporting 202: Equipment & Materials

- Land that can be certified

Supporting 202: Steps

1. Provide food sources: trees, shrubs, flowers
2. Create water sources: a bird bath, pond, water garden, or rain garden
3. Establish cover for wildlife: brush piles, rock piles, mature trees, or dense shrubs
4. Create places for wildlife to raise young
   - Plant dense shrubs, host plants for caterpillars
   - Install nesting boxes or include dead trees
5. Practice sustainable gardening
6. Complete the certification application by visiting <www.nwf.org/certify>

Sustainable Practices Handbook   Habitat Practices: Protecting Nature

Supporting 202: Troubleshooting

Problem	Solutions
Limited space	Do vertical gardening with native vines. Use container gardens.
HOA restrictions	Choose neat plantings. Explain wildlife benefits to the HOA board.
Wildlife isn't visiting	Be patient—habitat development takes time. Add features.

Supporting 202: Limitations

- Small urban lots may attract limited wildlife diversity
- Full habitat development may take several seasons to mature

References and resources: <www.suspra.com/practice/habitat/supporting-202.html>

Improving Practices

Improve your sustainability proficiency using a six-step continual improvement process.

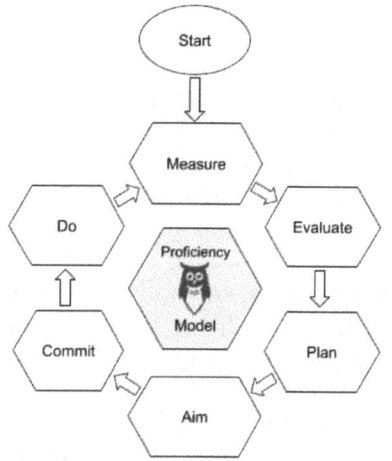

1. **Measure** sustainability indicators.
2. **Evaluate** current practices and opportunities to improve.
3. **Plan** projects to reach milestones.
4. **Aim** for success by setting specific, measurable, achievable, relevant, and time-bound milestones.
5. **Commit** to achieving milestones.
6. **Do** the work to improve practices.

How to Measure Results

- **Logbooks**
  Keep logbooks, either electronically or on paper, to record field measurements or estimates.

- **Financial Records**
  Financial records contain many sustainability indicators, including the amount spent on food, fuel, and other consumption. Create line items on profit and loss statements to report values for specific sustainability indicators, such as the amount of fossil fuel purchased.

- **Utility Bills**
  Utility bills are an especially convenient type of financial record. They usually record not just money spent but also the precise amount of electricity, fuel, or water consumed.

How to Evaluate Practices

- **Suspra Website**
  Visit <www.suspra.com> to calculate a Quick-Start, Regular, or Detailed Suspra Score.

How to Plan

Avoid wasting effort and money on dead-end detours on your way to your next sustainability milestone. Create a *sustainability plan* to describe a *project* that will improve *practices* over a *period of time* to protect our planet's ability to sustain human life. Start with your ends in mind along all seven pathways and work back from there. Choose the *destination milestones* you intend your home, organization, or community to reach, and the *pathways* people will take to reach *interim milestones* in between.

- **Time: Planning Horizon**
  - When is the *baseline* for comparison (i.e., what is the start date for the project)?
    Set goals to improve practices compared to a baseline.

- - How long will the project take (i.e., what is the end date)?
    Transcend the short-term thinking that dominates most decision-making in modern society; encourage people to work toward lifetime and legacy goals. Thirty years is the useful life of a solar module, the warranty on most roofing materials, the most common home mortgage term in the United States, and three-quarters of the average working life of a person, so you probably already have experience planning over that time period.

- **Context: Property and People**
  Is this plan for a household, an organization, or a community? What land, buildings, and equipment are part of this plan? Who needs to be involved in creating and approving this plan? You can start planning alone and on your own, but at some point your plan will involve other people and property that will persist after your time on Earth. Get your whole team on board.

- **Milestones: Seven Pathways**
  How will you reach your goals? You've already evaluated your practices, so you know where you currently are on each of the seven pathways. Working backward from your destination milestones to your current milestones, what are the best ways to connect them?

Keep in mind *all seven* pathways to sustainability to make wiser decisions. For example, when planning a "green" home in the country, choosing the "greenest" materials for kitchen cabinets and counters is fun, but what about the fact that living in the kitchen will require driving a car every time groceries need to be purchased? If you consider pathways to sustainable energy, movement, and habitat, as well as sustainable goods (materials), you may choose to build your home on different land, closer to town, where people can enjoy living and have more beneficial environmental impacts.

How to Aim (Set Goals)

Choose the *best next steps*. Once your whole team understands the project plan, set specific, measurable, achievable, relevant, and time-bound (*SMART*) goals that fit into that plan.

- **Specific:** Who will change which practices, and how will they do that?
- **Measurable:** Which sustainability indicators will you measure to evaluate results?
- **Achievable:** How can these practices be changed?
- **Relevant:** How will changing these practices improve sustainability indicators?
- **Time-Bound:** When will these practices be changed?

How to Commit

After you know exactly who will change which practices and how they will do that, make a commitment.

- *Accept* the plan and aims.
- *Assemble* and *authorize* the team.
- *Allocate* the time and budget necessary.

Write down your commitments and have all stakeholders sign the commitments they agree to make.

How to Do

Put your plan into action. See the Practice Guides section of this handbook for details.

Financing Projects

Learn the basic principles of investing, borrowing, and lending so you can make the best use of your financial resources to practice sustainability.

Project Financial Analysis

This section considers the most common scenario requiring financial analysis: you are making an investment in a project that lowers ongoing operating and maintenance expenses.

Primary motivation for project	Investment analysis to use
Reduce operating costs rather than earn a return	Savings Simple payback
Earn a return on investment	Return on investment Net present value

Savings

$$\begin{array}{r}\text{Operating and Maintenance Expenses of Old Equipment}\\ -\ \text{Operating and Maintenance Expenses of New Equipment}\\ \hline \text{Savings}\end{array}$$

Savings are also called "avoided costs."

Simple Payback

$$Simple\ Payback = \frac{Project\ Cost}{Savings\ per\ Period}$$

Example: A project that costs $1,000 that saves $250 per year has a payback of four years.

Return on Investment

$$Return\ on\ Investment = \frac{Value\ of\ All\ Savings}{Project\ Cost}$$

A simple return on investment calculation does not take into account the time value of money. For that, use a more sophisticated way to calculate the value of all savings.

Net Present Value

The standard way to calculate the total value of an investment over time is to discount future cash flows (savings) back to their present value and then subtract the initial investment. This puts a higher value on cash available now and a declining value on cash available in the future. The higher the discount rate, the lower the net present value of an investment.

$$\text{Net Present Value} = \sum_{Period=Start}^{End} \left(\frac{\text{Savings per Period}}{(1 + \text{Discount Rate})^{Period}}\right) - \text{Project Cost}$$

Example: $1,000 invested that saves $250 per year for 10 years in an economy with 4.5% interest rates has a net present value of $978. This same investment in an economy with a 5% rate has a lower net present value of $930; and in an economy with a 25% rate has a negative net present value of -$107.

Year	1	2	3	4	5	6	7	8	9	10	Total	Invested	NPV
Cash Flow	$250	$250	$250	$250	$250	$250	$250	$250	$250	$250	**$2,500**	$1,000	
Discounted													
0.0%	$250	$250	$250	$250	$250	$250	$250	$250	$250	$250	**$2,500**	$1,000	$1,500
4.5%	$239	$229	$219	$210	$201	$192	$184	$176	$168	$161	**$1,978**	$1,000	$978
5.0%	$238	$227	$216	$206	$196	$187	$178	$169	$161	$153	**$1,930**	$1,000	$930
25.0%	$200	$160	$128	$102	$82	$66	$52	$42	$34	$27	**$893**	$1,000	-$107

Internal Rate of Return

Calculate internal rate of return to compare projects, the higher the better, or compare against the rate of return you can earn in interest or in the stock market. The internal rate of return is the discount rate that solves this equation (i.e., net present value is zero):

$$\sum_{Period=Start}^{End} \left(\frac{\text{Savings per Period}}{(1 + \text{Internal Rate of Return})^{Period}}\right) = \text{Project Cost}$$

Modified Internal Rate of Return

Modify the internal rate of return to account for reinvestment of positive cash flows from savings per period and the financing cost of negative cash flows from the project cost. Do this with a spreadsheet function, because manual calculation is tedious.

$$MIRR = \sqrt[n]{\frac{FVCF}{PVCF}} - 1$$

- FVCF = future value of positive cash flows discounted at the reinvestment rate
- PVCF = present value of negative cash flows discounted at the financing rate
- n = number of periods

Levelized Cost of Energy

Calculate the levelized cost of energy for investments in projects such as solar arrays.

$$LCOE = \frac{\text{Capital Cost} + \sum_{1}^{n} C_n + \text{Decommissioning Costs}}{\sum_{1}^{n} E_n}$$

where C = operating and maintenance costs, E = energy produced, n = number of periods

Borrowing and Lending

Borrow money to do projects sooner than you could if you waited until you had cash in the bank. If you have savings that you can risk, either direct your bank or financial advisor to lend it to sustainable projects or lend directly to borrowers you trust. Because a loan carries a risk of default (i.e. not being paid back), lenders require borrowers to pay interest on the principal (the amount loaned). Interest rates are typically expressed as a percentage of the outstanding balance per year. The lower the interest rate, the more you can afford to borrow.

Example: If you borrow $1,000 at an annual percentage rate (APR) of 5%, at the end of a year you will owe the lender $1,050 ($1,000 in principal + $50 in interest). If your project generates $50 in savings per year, you likely can afford the project because your savings will cover the interest payments.

Simple Interest

Simple interest is calculated on just the principal amount of the loan.

Example: A loan of $1,000 with simple interest of 5% APR will accrue $50 in interest the first year ($1,000 × 5%), $50 the second year ($1,000 × 5%), etc.

Compound Interest

Compound interest accrues on the principal amount plus the accumulated interest. Even if the APR stays the same, the amount of interest due per year will increase.

Example: A loan of $1,000 with compound interest of 5% APR will accrue $50 in interest the first year ($1,000 × 5%), but $52.50 in interest the second ($1,050 × 5%), etc.

Mortgages

A mortgage is a loan with a real estate security as collateral. A "security" is an ownership right, such as a deed to land. A "real estate security" gives a person a right to use land or a building. Collateral is a security that a lender holds with the right to take it if the borrower defaults (fails to pay) on a loan.

Example: A borrower takes out a mortgage on their home. The bank loans money to the borrower. If the borrower fails to repay the mortgage, the bank can take the home.

Math

Look up mathematical definitions and symbols right here instead of getting lost in technical jargon. This reference material helps you identify knowledge gaps that might otherwise lead to poor decisions. Rather than needing to memorize all this information, having it organized in one place gives you confidence to engage more deeply with sustainability science and practice.

Numbers by Magnitude

US Name	Decimal	1×10^x	Metric	Related Names
Septillionth	0.000 000 000 000 000 000 000 001	-24	yocto	
Sextillionth	0.000 000 000 000 000 000 001	-21	zepto	
Quintillionth	0.000 000 000 000 000 001	-18	atto	
Quadrillionth	0.000 000 000 000 001	-15	femto	
Trillionth	0.000 000 000 001	-12	pico	Parts per trillion (ppt)
Billionth	0.000 000 001	-9	nano	Parts per billion (ppb)
Millionth	0.000 001	-6	micro	Parts per million (ppm)
Hundred Thousandth	0.000 01	-5		
Ten Thousandth	0.000 1	-4		Basis point (bip)
Thousandth	0.001	-3	milli	milliwatt (mW)
Hundredth	0.01	-2	centi	Percent (%)
Tenth	0.1	-1	deci	
One	1	0		
Ten	10	1	deca	Order of magnitude
Hundred	100	2	hecto	hectare (100 m²)
Thousand	1,000	3	kilo	kilowatt (kW)
Ten Thousand	10,000	4		
Hundred Thousand	100,000	5		
Million	1,000,000	6	Mega	Megawatt (MW)
Billion	1,000,000,000	9	Giga	Gigawatt (GW)
Trillion	1,000,000,000,000	12	Tera	Terawatt (TW)
Quadrillion	1,000,000,000,000,000	15	Peta	Petawatt (PW)
Quintillion	1,000,000,000,000,000,000	18	Exa	Exawatt (EW)
Sextillion	1,000,000,000,000,000,000,000	21	Zetta	
Septillion	1,000,000,000,000,000,000,000,000	24	Yotta	

Notable Numbers

Name	Decimal	Scientific	Description
Phi (φ)	~1.61803	~1.61×10^0	golden ratio, a+b/a = a/b = 1 + $\sqrt{5}$ / 2
e	~2.71828	~2.72×10^0	limit of $(1 + 1/n)^n$
Pi (π)	~3.1415926535	~3.14×10^0	circle circumference divided by diameter
Mole or Avogadro's #		6.022×10^{23}	1 mole of matter = atomic weight in grams

Mathematical Symbols

Symbol	Meaning	Example	Read As
=	Equal to	a = b	"a equals b"
≠	Not equal to	a ≠ b	"a is not equal to b"
≈	Approximately equal	a ≈ 3.14	"a is approximately equal to 3.14"
<	Less than	a < b	"a is less than b"
>	Greater than	a > b	"a is greater than b"
≤	Less than or equal to	a ≤ b	"a is less than or equal to b"
≥	Greater than or equal to	a ≥ b	"a is greater than or equal to b"
+	Addition	a + b	"a plus b"
-	Subtraction	a - b	"a minus b"
× or · or *	Multiplication	a×b or a·b or a*b or ab	"a times b"
÷ or / or —	Division	a ÷ b or a/b or $\frac{a}{b}$	"a divided by b"
^ or ² or ³	Exponent	a^b or a² or a³	"a raised to the power of b" or "a squared" or "a cubed"
√	Square root	√a	"the square root of a"
Σ	Summation	$\sum_{i=1}^{n} a_i$	"the sum of a from i equals 1 to n"
Δ	Change in value	Δt	"delta t" or "change in t"

Science

This handbook is a comprehensive reference to support your sustainability journey. While the practice guides show you "how to do" specific actions, this science reference section gives you the foundational knowledge to understand "why" these practices matter. When you encounter new terminology while reading scientific articles, researching options, or discussing sustainability with experts, you can quickly look up definitions and concepts right here instead of getting lost in technical jargon. This reference material helps you identify knowledge gaps that might otherwise lead to poor decisions. By understanding basic scientific principles, technological options, and mathematical concepts, you'll be better equipped to evaluate claims, adapt practices to your specific situation, and make truly wise choices for sustainability.

Units and Definitions

International System of Units (SI)

Name	Symbol	Measures	Definition
second	s	time	9,192,631,770 (~9.19×10^9) transitions of Cs-133 ground state
meter	m	distance	how far light travels in 1/299,792,458 (~3.34×10^{-9}) seconds
gram	g	mass	1/1,000 (1×10^{-3}) of the international prototype kg in 2018
elementary charge	e	charge	the electric charge carried by one proton or electron
coulomb	C	charge	~6.241509×10^{18} e
newton	N	force	accelerate 1 kg m / s²
joule	J	energy	work done by 1 N m
watt	W	power	1 J / s
volt	V	force	1 J / C
ampere	A	current	1 C / s
ohm	Ω	resistance	1 V / A
kelvin	K	temperature	change of thermal energy by 1.380649×10^{-23} J
celsius	°C	temperature	K - 273.15
mole	mol	amount	number of atoms in 12 g of carbon, ~6.023×10^{23}
candela	cd	radiation	amount of visible light in one steradian from a source that emits radiation of frequency 5.4×10^{18} Hz with a radiant intensity of ~1.46×10^{-3} watts per steradian
liter	L	volume	1/1,000 (1×10^{-3}) of a cubic meter

Sustainable Practices Handbook

Science

Physical Constants

Name	Decimal	Scientific	Description
g	9.8 m/s²	9.80×10^0 ms^{-2}	gravity at Earth's surface
c	~299,792,458 m/s	~3.00×10^8 ms^{-1}	speed of light in a vacuum
	334 J/g		Latent heat of fusion for water at 0°C
	2,260 J/g		Latent heat of vaporization for water at 100°C

Time

Name	Value	Units	Seconds	Description
Millisecond	0.001	seconds	0.001	1/1,000th of a second
Second	1	seconds	1	
Minute	60	seconds	60	
Hour	60	minutes	3,600	
Sidereal Day	23.93	hours	~86,164	One rotation of Earth relative to fixed stars
Day	24	hours	86,400	One rotation of Earth relative to our sun
Week	7	days	604,800	
Month	28	days	2,419,200	February (except leap years)
Month	29	days	2,505,600	February (leap years)
Month	30	days	2,592,000	April, June, September, November
Month	31	days	2,678,400	Other months
Standard Year	365	days	31,536,000	Calendar year
Sidereal Year	365.256	days	31,558,118	One orbit of Earth around our sun
Leap Year	366	days	31,622,400	
Decade	10	years	315,581,184	
Century	100	years	3,155,811,840	
Millennium	1,000	years	31,558,118,400	

Temperature

Condition	Celsius (°C)	Kelvin (K)	Fahrenheit (°F)
Absolute zero	-273.15	0	-459.67
Coldest surface temperature recorded on Earth	-89.2	184	-128.6
Laboratory freezers for long-term storage	-80.0	193	-112

Condition	Celsius (°C)	Kelvin (K)	Fahrenheit (°F)
Mercury freezes	-38.8	234	-37.9
Home freezers (FDA recommendation)	-17.8	255	0
Water freezes (standard conditions)	0	273	32
Home refrigerators (FDA recommendation)	4.4	278	40
Food "danger zone" (bacteria grow rapidly)	4.4 to 60	277 to 333	40 to 140
Average surface temperature of Earth	15.0	288	59
Room temperature	20.0	293	68
Body temperature (healthy human)	37.0	310	98.6
Domestic hot water (DOE recommendation)	49.0	322	120
Thermophilic composting range (optimal)	49 to 60	322 to 333	120 to 140
Hot composting (pathogens destroyed)	55.0	328	131
Hottest surface temperature recorded on Earth	56.7	329.9	134.1
Water sanitized (bacteria killed)	71.0	344	160
Water boils (standard conditions)	100.0	373.0	212
Paper spontaneously ignites	218 to 246	491 to 519	424 to 475
Gasoline spontaneously ignites	247 to 280	520 to 553	477 to 536
Lead melts	327.5	600.7	621.5
Ethanol spontaneously ignites	365.0	638	689
Hydrogen spontaneously ignites	535.0	808	995
Methane spontaneously ignites	537.0	810	999

Energy Units

Name	Joules	Notes
Joule	1.000	Able to accelerate 2 kg from rest to 1 m / s
Gram calorie	4.184	
Milliamp hour (mAh)*	4.320	As used on some 1.2V NiMH batteries
Kilojoule (kJ)	1,000	

Name	Joules	Notes
British Thermal Unit (BTU)	1,055.060	Able to raise 1 pound of water 1 °F
Watt hour	3,600	
Kilocalorie	4,184	Food calorie in the United States
Amp hour (Ah)*	43,200	As used on some 12V lead acid batteries
Megajoule (MJ)	1,000,000	
Kilowatt Hour (kWh)	3,600,000	
Therm (US)	105,480,000	As used in the United States
Therm (UK)	105,505,585	As used in the United Kingdom
Therm (EC)	105,506,000	As used in the European Community
Gigajoule (GJ)	1,000,000,000	

Milliamp hours and amp hours are technically a measure of coulombs (charge) in batteries but are functionally used to specify energy capacity because each battery cell type has a known voltage.

Power Units

Name	Watts	Notes
Milliwatt	0.001	
Ft-lb / min	0.023	
BTU/hr	0.293	
Watt	1	1 J / s
Mechanical horsepower	745.7	
Kilowatt	1,000	
Ton of refrigeration	3,516.85	Cooling power of 2,000 pounds of ice
Megawatt	1,000,000	
Gigawatt	1,000,000,000	

| Sustainable Practices Handbook | Science |

Physics

Look up physics concepts and definitions right here to better understand scientific articles.

Forces of Our Universe

- **Strong Nuclear Force**: Binds protons and neutrons in atomic nuclei
- **Weak Nuclear Force**: Responsible for radioactive decay and nuclear fusion in stars
- **Gravity**: Attraction between objects with mass; weakest but longest-range force
- **Electromagnetic Force**: Interaction between electrically charged particles; responsible for electricity, magnetism, and chemical bonds
  - Electric charges create electric fields
  - Moving electric charges create magnetic fields
  - Changing magnetic fields induce electric currents
  - Electromagnetic waves (light, radio, etc.) propagate through space without requiring a medium

Atoms and Mass

- **Matter:** Substance which occupies space and possesses mass
- **Velocity:** The rate of change of matter's position with respect to time, which emerges from the interaction between matter and the four fundamental forces of our universe
- **Mass:** A measure of the amount of matter in an object, which resists changes to its velocity
- **Atom**: The basic unit of matter, consisting of a nucleus surrounded by an electron cloud
- **Proton**: Positively charged particle in the nucleus of an atom
- **Neutron**: Neutral particle (no charge) in the nucleus of an atom
- **Electron**: Negatively charged particle that orbits the nucleus of an atom
- **Element**: Substance made up of atoms with the same number of protons
- **Electric Charge**:
  - Fundamental property measured in coulombs: $|\sim 1.6022 \times 10^{-19}|$ C
  - Electrons have negative charge; protons have positive charge
  - Like charges repel; opposite charges attract; charge cannot be created or destroyed

States of Matter

- **Solid**:
  - Definite shape and volume; minimal compressibility
  - Particles arranged in fixed, orderly patterns (crystalline structure)
  - Particles vibrate but remain in fixed positions
- **Liquid**:
  - Definite volume but takes the shape of its container; low compressibility
  - Particles close together but free to move past one another
  - Flows and can be poured
- **Gas**:
  - No definite shape or volume (expands to fill container); highly compressible
  - Particles widely separated with minimal attractive forces
  - Particles move rapidly in random directions
  - Diffuses readily
- **Plasma**:
  - Substance containing roughly equal numbers of positively and negatively charged ions
  - Typically exists at extremely high temperatures
  - No definite shape or volume
  - Electrically conductive and responds to electromagnetic fields

Phase Transitions

- **Phase Transitions**: Transitions between solid, liquid, and gas states
  - Requires addition or removal of heat (latent heat)
  - Occurs at specific temperatures at a given pressure
  - Critical in refrigeration and heating systems
- **Melting or Freezing**: Transition between solid and liquid states
  - Melting point: temperature at which a solid becomes a liquid at standard pressure
  - Requires addition of energy (heat) for melting
  - Releases energy during freezing
  - Occurs at constant temperature for pure substances
- **Evaporation or Condensation**: Transition between liquid and gas states
  - Boiling point: temperature at which a liquid becomes a gas at standard pressure
  - Evaporation can occur below boiling point at liquid surface
  - Requires significant energy for evaporation (latent heat of vaporization)
  - Releases energy during condensation
- **Sublimation or Deposition**: Direct transition between solid and gas states
  - Bypasses the liquid phase
- **Ionization or Recombination**: Transition between gas and plasma states
  - Requires extreme energy to strip electrons from atoms (ionization)
  - Releases energy when electrons recombine with ions
- **Phase Diagrams**: Visual representations showing states of matter under different temperature and pressure conditions
  - Triple point: unique combination where solid, liquid, and gas phases coexist
  - Critical point: conditions beyond which distinct liquid and gas phases do not exist
- **Ideal Gas Law**: The state of an amount of gas is determined by its pressure, volume, and temperature

$$pV = nRT$$

where p = pressure, V = volume, n = moles of gas, R = gas constant, T = temperature

Energy Concepts

- **Force**: Influence, measured in newtons (N), that can accelerate an object (change its velocity)
- **Work**: Force applied over a distance
- **Energy**: The capacity to do work, measured in joules (J)
- **Power**: Rate of energy transfer, measured in watts (W = J/s)
- **Conservation of Energy**: Energy cannot be created or destroyed, only converted from one form to another
- **Potential Energy**: Stored energy due to position or state
- **Kinetic Energy**: Energy of motion
- **Newton's second law**: Momentum is equal to the product of an object's mass and velocity

$$F = ma$$

where F = force, m = mass, and a = acceleration

Electricity

- **Voltage**: Electric potential difference, measured in volts (V), that drives current
  - Higher voltage means stronger electric force
  - Provided by batteries, generators, or power supplies
  - Measured with voltmeters connected in parallel to the powered circuit being measured
- **Resistance**: Opposition to current flow, measured in ohms (Ω)
  - Depends on material, length, cross-sectional area, and temperature

- Conductors have low resistance (metals)
- Insulators have high resistance (rubber, plastic)
- Measured with ohmmeters connected in series with the power source disconnected
- **Electric Current**: Flow of electric charge, measured in amperes (A), Coulombs per second
  - Conventional current flows from positive to negative
  - Electron flow is from negative to positive
  - Direct current (DC) flows in one direction
  - Alternating current (AC) periodically reverses direction
  - Measured with ammeters connected in series in a powered circuit, clamp meters around one conductor to detect magnetic induction, or indirectly by measuring voltage and using Ohm's law
- **Conductors vs. Insulators**:
  - Conductors (e.g., metals) have free electrons that can move easily among atoms
  - Insulators (e.g., plastics) have electrons tightly bound to atoms
  - Semiconductors have properties between conductors and insulators
- **Kirchhoff's Current Law**: The current entering a node equals the current leaving the node
- **Kirchhoff's Voltage Law**: The sum of voltage drops around a circuit loop is equal to zero
- **Ohm's Law**: The current flowing through a conductor is directly proportional the voltage, and inversely proportional to the resistance

$$V = IR$$
where V = voltage, I = current, and R = resistance

Heat

- **Temperature**: Measure of the average kinetic energy of particles in a substance, measured in degrees Celsius (°C) or Kelvin (K)
- **Heat**: Energy that transfers from hotter to cooler objects due to temperature difference
- **Conduction**: Heat transfer through direct contact between substances
  - Measured using thermal conductivity (W/mK) in materials
  - Tested with devices like heat flow meters or guarded hot plate apparatus
- **Convection**: Heat transfer through the movement of fluids (liquids or gases)
  - Natural convection: fluid movement caused by density differences due to temperature
  - Forced convection: fluid movement caused by external means (fans, pumps)
  - Measured using convection coefficients (W/m²K)
- **Radiation**: Heat transfer through electromagnetic waves that require no medium
  - All objects emit thermal radiation based on their temperature
  - Emissivity determines how efficiently a surface emits radiation (0-1 scale)
  - Measured using radiometers, pyrometers, or infrared cameras
- **Latent Heat**: Energy absorbed or released during phase change without temperature change
  - Latent heat of fusion: energy for solid-to-liquid transition
  - Latent heat of vaporization: energy for liquid-to-gas transition
  - Measured in joules per kilogram (J/kg)

Thermodynamics

- **Entropy**: Measure of disorder or randomness in a system
- **First Law**: Energy is conserved in all processes
- **Second Law**: Entropy in closed systems always increases; heat flows naturally from hot to cold
- **Efficiency**: always less than 100% due to the Second Law

$$\frac{Useful\ output\ energy}{Input\ energy} < 1$$

Chemistry

Look up chemistry concepts and definitions right here to better understand scientific articles.

Fundamental Principles

- **Elements**: Substances that cannot be broken down into simpler substances by chemical means
- **Compounds**: Substances formed by chemically bonded elements
- **Molecule**: Group of atoms bonded together, representing the smallest unit of a compound
- **Mole:** A unit of amount of a substance
  - One mole of any substance contains Avogadro's number (6.022×10^{23}) of particles
  - One mole of a substance has a mass equal to its atomic or molecular weight in grams
  - Used to convert between mass and number of particles
  - Essential for balancing chemical equations and stoichiometry calculations (the relationship between the relative quantities of substances taking part in a reaction or forming a compound)
  - *One mole of carbon is 12.01 grams; one mole of water (H_2O) is 18.02 grams*

Chemical Formulas and Notation

- **Chemical Symbol**: A one or two-letter abbreviation for an element
  - First letter is always capitalized, second letter (if present) is lowercase
  - *H (hydrogen), O (oxygen), Na (sodium), Cl (chlorine), Fe (iron)*
- **Chemical Formula**: Shows the types and numbers of atoms in a molecule or compound
  - Subscript numbers indicate the number of atoms (H_2O has two hydrogen and one oxygen atom)
  - No subscript means there is one atom (O in H_2O)
- **Structural Formula**: Shows how atoms are arranged and bonded in a molecule
  - *H-O-H for water, showing bonds between atoms*
- **Ion Notation**:
  - Superscript numbers and signs show electrical charge
  - *H^+ is a hydrogen ion (proton), missing one electron, with a +1 charge*
  - *OH^- is a hydroxide ion with a -1 charge, gained one extra electron*
  - *Ca^{2+} is a calcium ion with a +2 charge (lost two electrons)*
- **Ionic Compound Formulas**: Show the ratio of positive to negative ions
  - Parentheses group atoms together when more than one polyatomic ion is present
  - *NaCl (table salt) has one sodium ion (Na^+) and one chloride ion (Cl^-)*
  - *$Ca(OH)_2$ (calcium hydroxide) has one calcium ion (Ca^{2+}) and two hydroxide ions (OH^-)*
- **Chemical Equation**: Represents a chemical reaction
  - Shows reactants (left side), products (right side), and their quantities
  - Numbers in front of formulas (coefficients) show the relative number of molecules or moles
  - *$2H_2 + O_2 \rightarrow 2H_2O$ (two hydrogen plus one oxygen yields two water molecules)*
- **Common Notations**:
  - (s) = solid, (l) = liquid, (g) = gas, (aq) = aqueous (dissolved in water)
  - $\rightarrow$ indicates direction of reaction (one-way)
  - $\rightleftharpoons$ indicates a reversible reaction (goes both ways)
  - Δ above arrow indicates heat is applied
  - *$H_2O(l) \rightarrow H_2O(g)$ (liquid water becoming water vapor)*

Chemical Bonds and Reactions

- **Chemical Bond**: Attractive force that holds atoms together in molecules or compounds
  - **Ionic Bond**: Bond formed by the transfer of electrons between atoms, creating oppositely charged ions that attract each other

- **Covalent Bond**: Bond formed by the sharing of electrons between atoms
- **Hydrogen Bond**: Weak attraction between a hydrogen atom bonded to an electronegative atom and another electronegative atom
- **Why Elements Combine**:
  - Elements combine to achieve a more stable electron configuration
  - Most atoms seek to fill their outer electron shell with eight electrons
- **Chemical Reactions**: Substances change by breaking and forming chemical bonds
  - **Reactants**: Starting materials in a chemical reaction
  - **Products**: Substances formed by a chemical reaction
  - **Activation Energy**: Minimum energy required for a reaction to occur
  - **Catalyst**: Substance that increases reaction rate without being consumed
  - **Inhibitor**: Substance that decreases reaction rate
- **Exothermic Reaction:** Reaction that releases energy (usually as heat) to the surroundings
  - Energy released when new bonds form exceeds energy required to break bonds
  - Results in temperature increase of surroundings
  - Energy diagram shows products at lower energy level than reactants
  - *combustion, neutralization reactions, respiration*
- **Endothermic Reaction:** Reaction that absorbs energy (usually as heat) from the surroundings
  - Energy required to break bonds exceeds energy released when new bonds form
  - Results in temperature decrease of surroundings
  - Energy diagram shows products at higher energy level than reactants
  - *photosynthesis, cooking an egg, melting ice*

Ions and Electrochemistry

- **Ion**: Compound with an unequal number of protons and electrons
  - **Cation**: Positively charged ion (lost electrons)
  - **Anion**: Negatively charged ion (gained electrons)
- **Electrolyte**: Substance that produces ions when dissolved in water; conducts electricity
- **Electrochemical Cell**: Device that converts between electrical and chemical energy
  - **Anode**: Electrode where oxidation occurs (electrons are lost)
  - **Cathode**: Electrode where reduction occurs (electrons are gained)
  - **Electrolyte**: Medium that allows ion movement between electrodes
- **Battery Types**:
  - **Primary Batteries**: Non-rechargeable (alkaline, zinc-carbon)
  - **Secondary Batteries**: Rechargeable (lithium-ion, lead-acid, nickel-metal hydride)
  - **Flow Batteries**: Store energy in liquid electrolyte solutions (for large-scale storage)

Gradients and Energy Flow

- **Concentration Gradient**: Difference in concentration of a substance between two areas
  - Molecules naturally move from areas of high concentration to low concentration (diffusion)
- **Electrical Gradient**: Difference in electrical charge across a barrier
- **pH Gradient**: Difference in hydrogen ion concentration
- **Electrochemical Gradient**: Combination of concentration and electrical gradients
- **Energy Gradient**: Difference in potential energy between systems
  - Energy naturally flows from high potential to low potential

pH and Acid-Base Chemistry

- **pH**: Measure of hydrogen ion concentration (0-14 scale; 7 is neutral)
  - **Acidic**: pH < 7, higher concentration of hydrogen ions (H^+)
  - **Neutral**: pH = 7, equal amounts of hydrogen (H^+) and hydroxide (OH^-) ions

- o **Basic/Alkaline**: pH > 7, higher concentration of hydroxide ions (OH⁻)
- **Acids**: Substances that donate hydrogen ions (H⁺) in solution
  - o Strong acids (like hydrochloric acid, HCl) completely dissociate in water
  - o Weak acids (like acetic acid in vinegar) partially dissociate in water
- **Bases**: Substances that accept hydrogen ions or donate hydroxide ions (OH⁻)
  - o Strong bases (like sodium hydroxide, NaOH) completely dissociate in water
  - o Weak bases (like baking soda) partially dissociate in water
- **Neutralization**: Reaction between an acid and a base to form water and a salt
- **Buffers**: Systems that resist pH changes when acids or bases are added

Cleaning Chemistry

- **Soaps and Detergents**:
  - o Contain molecules with hydrophilic (water-loving) and hydrophobic (water-repelling) ends
  - o Surround oil and grease particles, allowing them to be washed away with water
- **Acidic Cleaners**:
  - o Effective for removing mineral deposits, limescale, and rust
  - o Work by dissolving alkaline substances through neutralization
  - o *vinegar, citric acid solutions*
- **Alkaline Cleaners**:
  - o Effective for removing grease, oil, and protein-based stains
  - o Work by breaking down fats through saponification
  - o *baking soda, ammonia, trisodium phosphate (TSP)*
- **Oxidizing Cleaners**:
  - o Break down stains through oxidation reactions
  - o Effective on organic stains like mold, mildew, and biological residues
  - o *hydrogen peroxide, bleach*
- **Enzymatic Cleaners**:
  - o Contain proteins that catalyze breakdown of specific substances
  - o Often used in laundry detergents and drain cleaners
  - o *protease (breaks down proteins), lipase (breaks down fats)*

Organic Chemistry

- **Organic Chemistry**: Study of carbon-containing compounds
- **Hydrocarbons**: Compounds containing only carbon and hydrogen
  - o **Alkanes**: Single bonds only (methane, ethane, propane)
  - o **Alkenes**: Contain at least one carbon-carbon double bond
  - o **Alkynes**: Contain at least one carbon-carbon triple bond
  - o **Aromatic**: Contain ring structures with delocalized electrons (like benzene)
- **Functional Groups**: Specific arrangements that give characteristic properties
  - o **Alcohols** (-OH): Found in ethanol, methanol, isopropyl alcohol
  - o **Carboxylic Acids** (-COOH): Found in vinegar (acetic acid), citric acid
  - o **Amines** (-NH$_2$): Found in amino acids, proteins
  - o **Esters** (-COO-): Responsible for many fruit fragrances, used in biodiesel
- **Polymers**: Large molecules made of repeating structural units
  - o **Natural Polymers**: Cellulose, starch, proteins, deoxyribonucleic acid (DNA)
  - o **Synthetic Polymers**: Plastics, synthetic fibers, adhesives
- **Biodegradation**: Breakdown of organic compounds by microorganisms
  - o Complex synthetic compounds are often less biodegradable

Combustion Chemistry

- **Combustion**: Rapid chemical reaction between a fuel and an oxidizer (usually oxygen) that produces heat and light
- **Requirements for Combustion**:
  - Fuel (something that can burn)
  - Oxygen (or another oxidizer)
  - Heat (ignition source)
  - Chain reaction (self-sustaining process)
- **Complete Combustion**: Sufficient oxygen to produce only carbon dioxide and water
  - Maximum energy released; minimal pollution (except CO_2)
  - CH_4 (methane) $+ 2O_2 \rightarrow CO_2 + 2H_2O +$ heat
- **Incomplete Combustion**: When insufficient oxygen is available
  - Produces carbon monoxide (CO), soot (carbon particles), and other pollutants
  - Less efficient energy conversion; greater pollution
  - $2CH_4 + 3O_2 \rightarrow 2CO + 4H_2O +$ heat
- **Combustion Pollutants**:
  - **Carbon Dioxide (CO_2)**: Greenhouse gas; inevitable product of hydrocarbon combustion
  - **Carbon Monoxide (CO)**: Toxic gas produced from incomplete combustion
  - **Nitrogen Oxides (NO_x)**: Formed when nitrogen in air reacts at high temperatures
  - **Sulfur Dioxide (SO_2)**: Produced when fuels containing sulfur are burned
  - **Particulate Matter**: Tiny solid or liquid particles suspended in air
  - **Volatile Organic Compounds (VOCs)**: Unburned hydrocarbons
- **Fuel Destruction in Combustion**:
  - Atoms rearrange to form new compounds (primarily CO_2 and H_2O)
  - Original fuel molecules cannot be recovered (irreversible process)
- **Carbon Cycle Disruption**:
  - Combustion converts carbon stored over millions of years into atmospheric CO_2
  - Natural carbon sequestration processes (photosynthesis, ocean absorption) operate too slowly to offset rapid combustion

Sustainable Chemistry Applications

- **Green Chemistry**: Design of chemical products and processes that reduce or eliminate hazardous substances
  - Principles include waste prevention, atom economy, safer solvents, and energy efficiency
- **Biodegradable Materials**: Substances that can be broken down by natural processes
  - Rate of biodegradation depends on chemical structure, environmental conditions
- **Water Treatment Chemistry**:
  - **Coagulation and Flocculation**: Using chemicals to make particles clump for removal
  - **Disinfection**: Using chemicals (chlorine, ozone) or UV light to kill pathogens
  - **pH Adjustment**: Adding acids or bases to optimize water treatment processes
- **Battery Chemistry**: Essential for renewable energy storage
  - **Lithium-ion**: High energy density, used in electronics and electric vehicles
  - **Lead-acid**: Reliable and recyclable, used in conventional vehicles
  - **Flow batteries**: Promising for grid-scale storage with longer lifespans
- **Solar Panel Chemistry**:
  - Photovoltaic cells convert sunlight to electricity through semiconductor materials
  - Different materials (silicon, cadmium telluride, copper indium gallium selenide) offer different efficiencies and environmental profiles

Environmental Chemistry

- **Bioaccumulation**: Increasing concentration of substances in organisms higher in food chains
- **Carbon Cycle**: Movement of carbon through atmosphere, organisms, soil, and water
- **Greenhouse Gases**: CO_2, CH_4 (methane), N_2O (nitrous oxide), etc.
- **Nitrogen Cycle**: Movement of nitrogen through air, soil, and living things
- **Persistent Organic Pollutants (POPs)**: Chemicals that resist environmental degradation
    - Examples: PCBs, certain pesticides, flame retardants
    - Can bioaccumulate in living organisms and cause health problems
- **VOCs (Volatile Organic Compounds)**: Carbon-based chemicals that evaporate at room temperature; many are harmful to health

Earth Sciences

Look up Earth science concepts and definitions right here to better understand scientific articles.

Fundamental Principles of Earth Science (Geology)
- **Geology**: Study of Earth's physical structure, substances, history, and processes that shape it
- **Earth's structure**: Concentric layers from interior to surface
  - Core (inner solid and outer liquid) → Mantle → Crust → Atmosphere
  - Continental crust (20-70 km thick) vs. oceanic crust (5-10 km thick)
- **Geological time**: Earth is approximately 4.6 billion years old
  - Geological time scale divided into eons, eras, periods, and epochs
  - *Human civilization represents 0.0001% of Earth's history*
- **Rock cycle**: Continuous transformation of rocks through Earth processes
  - Igneous (from cooling magma/lava) → Weathering/erosion → Sedimentary (from deposition and compaction) → Metamorphic (from heat and pressure) → Melting → Igneous
  - Understanding local rock cycle stage helps predict site conditions
- **Weathering**: Physical and chemical breakdown of rock
  - Physical weathering: Mechanical breaking without changing composition
  - Chemical weathering: Decomposition of minerals through chemical reactions
  - Rate of weathering varies by climate, with faster weathering in warm, wet regions

Soil Science
- **Soil**: Complex mixture of minerals, organic matter, water, air, and organisms
- **Soil formation factors**:
  - Parent material (underlying bedrock or deposited material)
  - Climate (temperature and precipitation patterns)
  - Organisms (vegetation, microbes, animals)
  - Topography (slope, aspect, elevation)
  - Time (development period)
  - Human activity (increasingly recognized as a sixth factor)
- **Soil horizons**: Distinct layers in soil profile
  - **O** (organic): Surface layer of decomposing organic matter
  - **A** (topsoil): Dark layer rich in organic matter and biological activity
  - **B** (subsoil): Accumulation of minerals leached from above
  - **C** (parent material): Weathered parent rock
  - **R** (bedrock): Unaltered parent rock
  - *Most plant roots are concentrated in top 15-30 cm (A horizon)*
- **Soil texture**: Proportion of sand, silt, and clay particles
  - **Sand**: 0.05-2.0 mm, gritty, drains quickly, low nutrient retention
  - **Silt**: 0.002-0.05 mm, smooth when wet, moderate drainage/retention
  - **Clay**: <0.002 mm, sticky when wet, drains slowly, high nutrient retention
  - **Loam**: Balanced mixture of sand, silt, and clay; ideal for most plants
- **Soil structure**: Arrangement of soil particles into aggregates
  - Good structure improves water infiltration, root penetration, and aeration
  - Damaged by compaction, over-tilling, chemical imbalances
- **Local soil types**: Important to understand for sustainable site development
  - *Most residential areas in U.S. have USDA soil surveys available free online*
  - Specific soil types have different management requirements and capabilities

Hydrogeology

- **Groundwater**: Water stored in underground aquifers
  - Major source of drinking water for many regions
  - Replenished through infiltration of surface water (recharge)
- **Water table**: Upper boundary of groundwater; depth varies seasonally
  - High water table (near surface): May cause basement flooding, septic issues
  - Low water table (deep): May require deeper wells, affect vegetation
- **Aquifers**: Underground layers of water-bearing permeable rock or sediment
  - **Unconfined aquifers**: Directly recharged from surface water infiltration
  - **Confined aquifers**: Trapped between impermeable layers; under pressure
  - **Perched aquifers**: Small, isolated water bodies above main water table
- **Porosity**: Percentage of void space within rock or soil
  - Affects water storage capacity (higher porosity = more storage)
  - *Sandstone: 5-30% porosity; Fractured granite: <1% porosity*
- **Permeability**: Ability of material to transmit fluids
  - Affects groundwater flow rates and well productivity
  - Critical for drainage system design and rainwater management
- **Infiltration rate**: Speed at which water enters soil
  - Influenced by soil texture, structure, moisture content, vegetation
  - *Sandy soils: 20-30 mm/hour; Clay soils: 1-5 mm/hour*
- **Site water balance**: Relationship between precipitation, runoff, infiltration, and evapotranspiration
  - Essential for sustainable water management planning
  - Influenced by geology, soil, vegetation, and impervious surfaces

Landscape Processes

- **Topography**: Three-dimensional surface features of land
  - Described by elevation, slope, aspect, and landforms
- **Drainage patterns**: Configuration of surface stream networks
  - **Dendritic**: Tree-like pattern in uniform materials
  - **Parallel**: On steep slopes or with linear geological controls
  - **Radial**: Streams flowing outward from central high point
  - **Trellis**: Rectangular pattern following geological structures
  - *Understanding local drainage patterns helps prevent flooding issues*
- **Watersheds**: Land areas that drain to a specific water body
  - Property may be part of multiple nested watersheds
  - Local watershed conditions affect stormwater dynamics
  - Property management impacts downstream water quality
- **Slope stability**: Resistance of inclined land to movement
  - **Factors affecting stability**: Slope angle, soil type, water content, vegetation
  - **Failure types**: Slides, flows, falls, creep
  - Critical consideration for building placement and landscape modifications
- **Erosion**: Removal and transport of soil or rock by water, wind, ice, or gravity
  - **Sheet erosion**: Uniform removal of thin layers across a surface
  - **Rill erosion**: Formation of small channels
  - **Gully erosion**: Formation of larger channels that cannot be removed by tilling
  - **Mass wasting**: Large-scale movement of soil and rock
  - *One inch of topsoil can take 500+ years to form but be lost in a single storm*
- **Sedimentation**: Deposition of eroded materials
  - Can clog drainage systems, smother vegetation, and degrade water quality
  - Managed through erosion control and sediment capture strategies

Natural Hazards Assessment

- **Flood potential**: Risk of excess water inundating normally dry land
  - Influenced by elevation, proximity to water bodies, local drainage
  - Assessed through flood zone maps (FEMA in U.S.)
  - *Properties in 100-year floodplains have 26% chance of flooding during 30-year mortgage*
- **Seismic risk**: Potential for earthquake damage
  - Varies by proximity to fault lines and underlying geology
  - Amplified by unconsolidated soils, fill areas, and high water tables
  - *Soft soils can amplify earthquake shaking by 2-5 times*
- **Land subsidence**: Gradual settling or sudden sinking of ground
  - **Causes**: Groundwater withdrawal, limestone dissolution, underground mining, thawing permafrost
- **Expansive soils**: Soils containing clay minerals that swell when wet
  - Can exert pressure of 15,000+ pounds per square foot on foundations
  - Identified by deep cracks in dry soil, sticky consistency when wet
  - *Causes more structural damage than floods, earthquakes, and hurricanes combined in the U.S.*
- **Radon potential**: Risk of radioactive gas accumulation
  - Produced by decay of uranium in certain types of bedrock (granite, shale, phosphate)
  - Enters buildings through foundation cracks, joints, and openings
  - Levels vary dramatically even between adjacent properties
  - *Second leading cause of lung cancer in the U.S.*

Site Geology Assessment

- **Bedrock characteristics**: Physical properties of underlying rock
  - **Depth to bedrock**: Affects excavation, foundation design, drainage
  - **Rock type**: Determines stability, drainage characteristics, nutrient availability
  - **Fracture patterns**: Influence groundwater movement, excavation difficulty
- **Fill areas**: Locations where natural materials have been augmented
  - Often less stable than natural soil; may compress unevenly
  - Identified by mixed soil layers, foreign objects, abrupt boundaries
- **Seasonal ground changes**: Annual cycles of soil moisture and volume
  - **Frost heave**: Upward swelling of soil during freezing
  - **Seasonal shrink-swell**: Volume changes with moisture fluctuations
  - *Depth of frost penetration varies from 0 cm in southern regions to 200+ cm in northern areas*
- **Site-specific geological challenges**:
  - **Karst terrain**: Areas with sinkholes, caves, and irregular bedrock surface
  - **Hydric soils**: Permanently or seasonally saturated soils
  - **Shallow bedrock**: Rock within typical excavation depths
  - **Hardpan layers**: Dense, nearly impermeable soil layers

Material Resources and Properties

- **Construction aggregates**: Gravel, sand, and crushed stone
  - *Transportation typically doubles aggregate cost at 20-30 miles from source*
- **Building stone**: Dimension stone used for construction and landscaping
  - **Granite**: Igneous rock; very durable, low maintenance
  - **Limestone**: Sedimentary rock; easily cut but vulnerable to acid rain
  - **Sandstone**: Sedimentary rock; variable durability based on cementing material
  - **Slate**: Metamorphic rock; excellent for roofing and paving
  - **Marble**: Metamorphic limestone; attractive but prone to weathering
- **Clay**: Fine-grained soil used for brick, pottery, and natural building

- o Found in most regions, often in river valleys and ancient lake beds
- **Sand**: Granular material used in concrete, mortar, and filtration
  - o *Construction-grade sand shortages becoming common in many regions*
- **Locally derived materials**: Reduced environmental impact compared to imported materials

Sustainable Earthworks

- **Cut and fill balance**: Matching excavated soil volume with fill needs
- **Soil management during construction**:
  - o **Topsoil preservation**: Strip, store, and reuse valuable upper soil layer
  - o **Soil compaction prevention**: Define access routes, use proper equipment
  - o **Erosion control**: Install silt fences, cover exposed soil, maintain vegetation
- **Earth-sheltered design**: Using earth mass for thermal regulation
  - o Reduces heating and cooling needs by utilizing stable ground temperature
  - o *At depth of 6-8 feet, soil temperature approximately equals annual average air temperature*
- **Earthen building materials**: Use less processing energy compared to conventional materials
  - o **Rammed earth**: Compressed soil mixture in formwork
  - o **Cob**: Hand-formed mixture of clay, sand, and straw
  - o **Adobe**: Sun-dried bricks of clay and organic material
  - o **Compressed earth blocks**: Mechanically compressed soil blocks
- **Geothermal heating and cooling**: Utilizing stable ground temperatures
  - o **Ground source heat pumps**: Exchange heat with soil through buried loops
  - o **Earth tubes**: Passive air conditioning by drawing air through underground pipes

Applied Geology for Property Management

- **Drainage system design**: Managing water movement based on geology
  - o **Surface grading**: Directing runoff away from structures
  - o **Swales and berms**: Earthworks that slow and direct water flow
  - o **French drains**: Gravel-filled trenches with perforated pipes
  - o **Dry wells**: Underground structures for infiltration
- **Foundation approaches**: Adapting to geological conditions
  - o **Slab-on-grade**: Suitable for stable, well-drained soils
  - o **Crawl space**: Provides buffer from wet or unstable soils
  - o **Full basement**: Requires well-drained soils, low water table
  - o **Pier foundation**: Adapts to varied terrain and unstable soils
  - o **Helical piers**: For weak soils requiring deep support
- **Retaining walls**: Structures that hold back soil on slopes
  - o *Failure usually results from inadequate drainage behind wall*
- **Rain gardens and bioswales**: Natural drainage solutions
  - o Design based on soil infiltration rate and seasonal water table
  - o Plant selection matched to hydrological conditions
- **Permeable paving**: Alternative to impervious surfaces

Water Resource Management

- **Well siting and design**: Locating groundwater sources
  - o *Typical residential well yields 5-20 gallons per minute*
- **Spring development**: Capturing naturally emerging groundwater
  - o *Spring flow often varies seasonally based on recharge patterns*
- **Rainwater harvesting**: Capturing precipitation for later use
  - o *One inch of rain on 1,000 square feet yields approximately 600 gallons*
- **Groundwater recharge**: Returning water to aquifers

- Methods include infiltration basins, permeable paving, and dry wells
  - Effectiveness depends on soil permeability and depth to water table
- **Impervious surface management**: Reducing runoff from developed areas
  - Goal of maintaining pre-development hydrology
  - Techniques include green roofs, permeable paving, and infiltration systems

Site-Specific Considerations

- **Microclimate effects**: How geology influences local conditions
  - **Thermal mass**: Rock and soil storing and releasing heat
  - **Cold air drainage**: Cool air flowing downslope into valleys
  - **Solar exposure**: Varies by slope aspect (south-facing warmer in northern hemisphere)
  - *South-facing slopes in temperate climates receive up to 50% more solar radiation*
- **Vegetation-geology relationships**: How plants indicate underlying conditions
  - Certain plants serve as indicators of soil type, depth, and moisture
- **Resilient design**: Adapting to geological constraints rather than fighting them
  - Work with natural landforms and drainage patterns
  - Choose appropriate plantings for soil conditions
  - Site structures with awareness of geological hazards

Advanced Concepts

- **Ecosystem services of geological features**:
  - **Aquifer recharge areas**: Locations where surface water replenishes groundwater
  - **Natural water filtration**: Soil and rock removing contaminants from water
  - **Carbon sequestration**: Carbon storage in soil and sediments
  - **Climate regulation**: Geological features moderating local temperatures
- **Climate change impacts on geological processes**:
  - **Increased erosion**: From more intense precipitation events
  - **Groundwater changes**: Altered recharge patterns and water tables
  - **Coastal impacts**: Sea level rise affecting shoreline properties
  - **Expanded frost-free zones**: Changing foundation requirements
- **Regenerative land management**: Practices that build soil and restore geological function
  - **Keyline design**: Water management system following natural contours
  - **Restoration agriculture**: Farming methods that mimic natural ecosystems
  - **Stream restoration**: Returning waterways to stable, functional conditions

Key Concepts for Assessment

- **Geological site analysis process**:
  - Research existing geological data (maps, surveys, histories)
  - Observe site features (outcrops, slopes, drainage patterns)
  - Test soil characteristics (texture, structure, pH)
  - Assess water movement (surface and subsurface)
  - Identify potential hazards and constraints
  - Develop appropriate design responses
- **Simple field tests**:
  - **Soil texture**: Ribbon test (rolling moistened soil between fingers)
  - **Infiltration**: Percolation test (timing water drainage in test hole)
  - **Soil pH**: Simple test kits or meters
  - **Slope measurement**: Clinometer or smartphone app
  - **Soil depth**: Probe rod or auger

Biology

Look up biology concepts and definitions right here to better understand scientific articles.

Fundamental Principles of Biology

- **Study of Life**: Characterized by organization, energy use, response to environment, growth, reproduction, and adaptation
- **Biological organization**: Hierarchical arrangement from molecules to the biosphere
  - Molecules → Cells → Tissues → Organs → Organ systems → Organisms → Populations → Communities → Ecosystems → Biosphere
- **Homeostasis**: Maintenance of relatively stable internal conditions despite external changes
- **Energy flow**: Capture, transformation, and transfer of energy through living systems
- **Evolution**: Change in heritable traits of populations over successive generations
  - Provides unifying framework for understanding biological diversity and adaptation

Molecular Biology

- **Amino acids:** The building blocks of proteins
  - Organic compounds that contain both amino and carboxylic acid functional groups
  - Essential amino acids: Ones that human cells cannot make; must be obtained in the diet
- **DNA** (Deoxyribonucleic Acid): Genetic material containing hereditary information
  - Double helix structure composed of nucleotides
  - Nucleotides contain deoxyribose sugar, phosphate group, and nitrogenous base
  - Four nitrogenous bases: Adenine (A), Thymine (T), Guanine (G), Cytosine (C)
  - Complementary base pairing: A-T and G-C
  - *Human genomes contain approximately 3 billion base pairs*
- **RNA** (Ribonucleic Acid): Single-stranded nucleic acid involved in protein synthesis
  - Contains ribose sugar instead of deoxyribose
  - Uses uracil (U) instead of thymine (T)
  - Types include: messenger RNA (mRNA), transfer RNA (tRNA), ribosomal RNA (rRNA)
- **Proteins**: Complex molecules composed of amino acids that perform most cellular functions
  - Structure determined by amino acid sequence (primary structure)
  - Functions include: catalysis (enzymes), transport, structure, signaling, defense
- **Central Dogma**: Information flow from DNA to RNA to protein
  - **Transcription**: DNA → RNA (occurs in nucleus)
  - **Translation**: RNA → Protein (occurs at ribosomes)
- **Enzymes**: Protein catalysts that increase reaction rates without being consumed
  - Lower activation energy required for reactions
  - Often named with suffix "-ase" (e.g., DNA polymerase, lactase)
  - Activity affected by temperature, pH, substrate concentration, inhibitors

Cellular Biology

- **Cell**: Basic structural and functional unit of all organisms
  - Cell theory: All living things composed of cells; cells come from pre-existing cells
  - *Human body contains approximately 25-40 trillion human cells*
- **Cell types**:
  - **Prokaryotic cells**: No membrane-bound nucleus or organelles (bacteria, archaea)
    - Typically 0.1-5 µm in diameter
    - Single circular chromosome plus plasmids
    - Reproduce through binary fission

- o **Eukaryotic cells**: Membrane-bound nucleus and organelles (animals, plants, fungi, protists)
    - Typically 10-100 μm in diameter (20-100 times larger than prokaryotic cells)
    - Multiple linear chromosomes
    - Reproduce through mitosis or meiosis
- **Cell membrane**: Phospholipid bilayer with embedded proteins
  - Selectively permeable barrier
  - Fluid mosaic model: proteins can move within membrane
  - Functions in cell communication, transport, and structural integrity
- **Transport mechanisms**:
  - **Passive transport**: No energy required (diffusion, osmosis, facilitated diffusion)
  - **Active transport**: Requires energy (pumps, endocytosis, exocytosis)
- **Eukaryotic organelles**: Functional structures within cells
  - **Nucleus**: Contains genetic material
  - **Mitochondria**: Energy production through cellular respiration
    - Have their own DNA (mitochondrial DNA)
    - Endosymbiotic theory: May have originated from engulfed ancient bacteria
  - **Chloroplasts**: Photosynthesis in plant and algal cells
    - Have their own DNA
    - May also have originated from bacteria through endosymbiosis
  - **Endoplasmic reticulum**: Protein and lipid synthesis
  - **Golgi apparatus**: Modification, sorting, and packaging of proteins
  - **Lysosomes**: Contain digestive enzymes for breaking down materials
  - **Peroxisomes**: Oxidative enzymes for breaking down toxic substances
  - **Ribosomes**: Protein synthesis
- **Cell division**:
  - **Mitosis**: Division of somatic cells; produces genetically identical daughter cells
    - Phases: Prophase, Metaphase, Anaphase, Telophase, Cytokinesis
  - **Meiosis**: Division resulting in gametes (sex cells); reduces chromosome number by half
    - Involves two rounds of division
    - Creates genetic diversity through crossing over and independent assortment
  - **Cell cycle**: G1 (growth) → S (DNA synthesis) → G2 (preparation) → M (mitosis)
    - Regulated by cyclins and cyclin-dependent kinases
    - *Human cells divide approximately 50-70 times before reaching replicative senescence*

Genetics

- **Genes**: Segments of DNA that code for specific proteins or RNA molecules
  - *Human genomes contain approximately 20,000-25,000 protein-coding genes*
- **Genome**: Entire set of DNS instructions found in a cell
- **Genotype**: Genetic makeup of an organism
- **Phenotype**: Observable characteristics resulting from genotype and environment
- **Genetic variation**: Diversity in genetic material among individuals
  - Created through mutation, recombination, and gene flow
  - *About 0.1% of DNA differs between any two humans*
- **Chromosomes**: Structures containing DNA and associated proteins
  - Human somatic cells have 46 chromosomes (23 pairs)
  - Human gametes have 23 chromosomes (haploid)
- **Allele**: Variant form of a gene
  - **Dominant**: Expressed when present in one or both copies
  - **Recessive**: Expressed only when present in both copies
  - **Codominant**: Both alleles expressed simultaneously
- **Mendelian inheritance**:

- **Law of segregation**: Allele pairs separate during gamete formation
  - **Law of independent assortment**: Genes on different chromosomes assort independently
- **Non-Mendelian inheritance**:
  - **Incomplete dominance**: Heterozygote shows intermediate phenotype
  - **Codominance**: Both alleles fully expressed in heterozygote
  - **Multiple alleles**: More than two possible alleles in population
  - **Polygenic traits**: Influenced by multiple genes
  - **Pleiotropy**: One gene affects multiple traits
- **Mutations**: Changes in DNA sequence
  - **Types**: Point mutations, insertions, deletions, duplications, translocations
  - **Effects**: Neutral, harmful, or beneficial
  - **Sources**: Replication errors, radiation, chemicals, viruses
  - *Mutation rate in humans approximately 1 in 100 million per base pair per generation*
- **Genetic engineering**:
  - **Recombinant DNA technology**: Combining DNA from different sources
  - **CRISPR-Cas9**: Precise genome editing tool
  - **Genetically Modified Organisms (GMOs)**: Organisms with artificially modified genes
  - **Applications**: Medicine, agriculture, research, industrial production

Evolution and Biodiversity

- **Natural selection**: Process by which organisms survive, reproduce, and transmit genes
  - Requires variation, heritability, differential reproduction
  - Leads to adaptation: traits that increase fitness in specific environments
- **Mechanisms of evolution**:
  - **Natural selection**: Differential survival and reproduction based on traits
  - **Genetic drift**: Random changes in allele frequencies, especially in small populations
  - **Gene flow**: Exchange of genetic material between populations through migration
  - **Mutation**: Ultimate source of genetic variation
  - **Non-random mating**: Selection of mates based on phenotype
- **Speciation**: Formation of new species
  - **Allopatric speciation**: Populations separated by geographic barriers
  - **Sympatric speciation**: Populations diverge without geographic separation
  - **Parapatric speciation**: Divergence across environmental gradients
- **Biodiversity**: Variety of life forms on Earth
  - **Genetic diversity**: Variation within species
  - **Species diversity**: Variety of species in ecosystem
  - **Ecosystem diversity**: Variety of ecosystems in region
  - **Functional diversity**: Diversity of ecological roles
  - *Current extinction rates estimated at 100-1000 times background rate*
- **Taxonomic classification**:
  - Hierarchical system: Domain → Kingdom → Phylum → Class → Order → Family → Genus → Species
  - Three domains: Bacteria, Archaea, Eukarya
  - Scientific naming uses binomial nomenclature (genus + species name)

Plant Biology

- **Photosynthesis**: Process converting light energy to chemical energy stored in glucose
  - Equation: $6CO_2 + 6H_2O + \text{light energy} \rightarrow C_6H_{12}O_6 + 6O_2$
  - **Light-dependent reactions**: Capture light energy, produce ATP and NADPH
  - **Calvin cycle**: Uses ATP and NADPH to fix carbon into sugar

- Occurs in chloroplasts containing chlorophyll
- **C3 plants**: First product is 3-carbon molecule; most common pathway
- **C4 plants**: First product is 4-carbon molecule; adaptation to hot, dry conditions
- **CAM plants**: Open stomata at night to reduce water loss (succulents, cacti)
- **Plant structure**:
  - **Roots**: Absorb water and minerals, anchor plant
    - **Root hairs**: Increase surface area for absorption
    - **Mycorrhizae**: Symbiotic relationships with fungi
    - **Root nodules**: House nitrogen-fixing bacteria in legumes
  - **Stems**: Support, transport water and nutrients
    - **Xylem**: Transports water and minerals up from roots
    - **Phloem**: Transports sugars throughout plant
  - **Leaves**: Primary photosynthetic organs
    - **Stomata**: Pores regulated by guard cells for gas exchange
    - **Mesophyll**: Internal tissue where most photosynthesis occurs
    - **Cuticle**: Waxy layer preventing water loss
- **Transpiration**: Water loss through stomata
  - Creates "pull" that helps move water up from roots
  - Cools plant through evaporation
  - *A large tree can transpire over 100 gallons of water per day*
- **Plant reproduction**:
  - **Sexual reproduction**:
    - **Flowers**: Reproductive structures of angiosperms
    - **Pollination**: Transfer of pollen (male) to stigma (female)
    - **Double fertilization**: Forms zygote and endosperm
    - **Seeds**: Embryonic plants with stored nutrients
    - **Fruits**: Mature ovaries containing seeds
  - **Asexual reproduction**:
    - **Vegetative propagation**: New plants from stems, roots, or leaves
    - **Runners/stolons**: Horizontal stems producing new plants
- **Plant responses**:
  - **Tropisms**: Directional growth responses to stimuli
    - **Phototropism**: Response to light
    - **Gravitropism**: Response to gravity
    - **Thigmotropism**: Response to touch
  - **Photoperiodism**: Response to day and night length
    - Controls flowering in many species

Animal Biology

- **Animal characteristics**:
  - Multicellular eukaryotes
  - Heterotrophic (cannot produce their own food)
  - Usually motile and respond rapidly to stimuli
- **Animal diversity**:
  - **Invertebrates**: Animals without backbones
    - Comprise about 95-99% of animal species
    - *Include arthropods, mollusks, annelids, cnidarians, etc.*
  - **Vertebrates**: Animals with backbones
    - *Fish, amphibians, reptiles, birds, mammals*
- **Animal physiology**:
  - **Digestive system**: Breaks down food into absorbable nutrients

- - **Circulatory system**: Transports materials throughout body
  - **Respiratory system**: Gas exchange (oxygen in, carbon dioxide out)
  - **Excretory system**: Removes metabolic wastes
  - **Nervous system**: Rapid communication via electrical signals
  - **Endocrine system**: Chemical communication via hormones
  - **Immune system**: Defends against pathogens
  - **Reproductive system**: Produces offspring
- **Animal reproduction**:
  - **Sexual reproduction**: Combines genetic material from two parents
    - **Fertilization**: Union of egg and sperm
    - **Development**: Process of growth from zygote to adult
  - **Asexual reproduction**: Offspring genetically identical to single parent
    - **Budding**: New individual grows from parent's body
    - **Fragmentation**: Pieces of parent develop into new individuals
- **Animal behavior**:
  - **Innate behavior**: Present without learning (instinct)
  - **Learned behavior**: Acquired through experience
  - **Social behavior**: Interactions between members of same species

Microbiology

- **Microorganisms**: Microscopic organisms including bacteria, archaea, fungi, protists, and viruses
  - *One gram of soil may contain billions of microbes from thousands of species*
- **Bacteria**:
  - Prokaryotic single-celled organisms
  - Cell walls contain peptidoglycan
  - Reproduce asexually through binary fission
  - Some form endospores that resist harsh conditions
  - Incredibly diverse metabolically
- **Archaea**:
  - Prokaryotic single-celled organisms distinct from bacteria
  - Often found in extreme environments (extremophiles)
  - Cell walls lack peptidoglycan
  - Some produce methane (methanogens)
- **Fungi**:
  - Eukaryotic organisms with cell walls containing chitin
  - Absorb nutrients after external digestion
  - Reproduce via spores
  - *Include yeasts, molds, and mushrooms*
- **Protists**:
  - Diverse eukaryotic organisms not classified as plants, fungi, or animals
  - *Include algae, amoebas, paramecia*
- **Viruses**:
  - Non-cellular infectious agents
  - Consist of genetic material (DNA or RNA) enclosed in protein coat
  - Replicate only inside host cells
  - Some considered on boundary between living and nonliving
- **Microbial metabolism**:
  - **Aerobic respiration**: Uses oxygen as final electron acceptor
  - **Anaerobic respiration**: Uses other compounds as electron acceptors
  - **Fermentation**: Partial oxidation without external electron acceptors
  - **Photosynthesis**: Light energy conversion (cyanobacteria, algae)

- ○ **Chemolithotrophy**: Energy from inorganic compounds
- **Beneficial microbial processes**:
  - ○ **Nutrient cycling**: Breaking down organic matter, fixing nitrogen
  - ○ **Fermentation**: Food preservation and production
  - ○ **Composting**: Decomposition of organic waste
  - ○ **Bioremediation**: Cleaning environmental pollutants
  - ○ *Certain fungi can break down petroleum, pesticides, and other pollutants*

Soil Biology

- **Soil**: Complex ecosystem composed of minerals, organic matter, water, air, and organisms
- **Soil formation**:
  - ○ **Weathering**: Physical and chemical breakdown of parent material
  - ○ **Biological activity**: Incorporation of organic matter
  - ○ **Time**: Formation of 1 cm soil typically takes 100-1000 years
  - ○ **Horizons**: Distinct layers in soil profile (O, A, B, C, R)
- **Soil organisms**:
  - ○ **Microorganisms**: Bacteria, fungi, archaea, protozoa
  - ○ **Mesofauna**: Nematodes, arthropods, enchytraeids
  - ○ **Macrofauna**: Earthworms, termites, ants
  - ○ *A single handful of healthy soil contains more organisms than humans on Earth*
- **Soil organic matter** (SOM):
  - ○ Carbon-containing material derived from organisms
  - ○ **Humus**: Stable organic compounds resistant to decomposition
  - ○ *Increasing SOM by 1% can increase water holding capacity by 27,000 gallons per acre*
- **Mycorrhizal fungi**:
  - ○ Symbiotic relationships between fungi and plant roots
  - ○ **Ectomycorrhizae**: Fungi form sheath around root
  - ○ **Endomycorrhizae/arbuscular mycorrhizae**: Fungi penetrate root cells
  - ○ Increase nutrient uptake, water access, pathogen protection
  - ○ *Up to 90% of terrestrial plants form mycorrhizal relationships*
- **Nitrogen fixation**:
  - ○ Conversion of atmospheric nitrogen (N_2) into ammonia (NH_3)
  - ○ Performed by certain bacteria and archaea
  - ○ **Symbiotic nitrogen fixation**: Bacteria living within plant roots (e.g., Rhizobium in legumes)
  - ○ *One hectare of legumes can fix 100-300 kg of nitrogen annually*

Ecology

- **Ecology**: Study of interactions between organisms and their environment
- **Levels of ecological organization**:
  - ○ **Population**: Group of same species in same area
  - ○ **Community**: Multiple populations interacting in same area
  - ○ **Ecosystem**: Community of organisms plus abiotic environment
  - ○ **Biome**: Large region with similar climate and characteristic communities
  - ○ **Biosphere**: All ecosystems on Earth
- **Ecosystem components**:
  - ○ **Abiotic factors**: Non-living components (temperature, water, soil, light)
  - ○ **Biotic factors**: Living components (plants, animals, microbes)
- **Trophic levels**:
  - ○ **Producers** (autotrophs): Create their own food through photosynthesis or chemosynthesis
  - ○ **Consumers** (heterotrophs): Obtain energy by consuming other organisms

Sustainable Practices Handbook — Science

- - **Primary consumers** (herbivores): Eat producers
  - **Secondary consumers**: Eat primary consumers
  - **Tertiary consumers**: Eat secondary consumers
  - **Omnivores**: Eat both producers and consumers
  - **Decomposers**: Break down dead organic matter
- **Energy flow**:
  - **Primary production**: Amount of solar energy converted to chemical energy by producers
    - **Gross primary production (GPP)**: Total energy fixed
    - **Net primary production (NPP)**: GPP minus energy used in cellular respiration
    - *Tropical rainforests have highest NPP of terrestrial ecosystems (1000-3500 g/m²/year)*
  - Only about 10% of energy transfers between trophic levels (ecological efficiency)
  - Energy pyramid shows decrease in available energy at higher trophic levels
- **Biogeochemical cycles**:
  - **Carbon cycle**: Movement through photosynthesis, respiration, decomposition
    - *Human activities add approximately 35 billion tons of CO_2 to atmosphere annually*
  - **Nitrogen cycle**: Fixation, nitrification, denitrification, ammonification
    - *Human activities now fix more nitrogen than natural processes*
  - **Phosphorus cycle**: Weathering, uptake, decomposition, sedimentation
  - **Water cycle**: Evaporation, transpiration, condensation, precipitation
- **Ecological relationships**:
  - **Competition**: Struggle for limited resources
  - **Predation**: One organism consumes another
  - **Parasitism**: One organism benefits, other harmed
  - **Mutualism**: Both organisms benefit
  - **Commensalism**: One organism benefits, other unaffected
- **Population ecology**:
  - **Population growth**: Change in population size over time
    - **Exponential growth**: Unrestricted growth (J-curve)
    - **Logistic growth**: Growth limited by carrying capacity (S-curve)
  - **Carrying capacity**: Maximum population size environment can sustain
  - **Limiting factors**: Resources that restrict population growth
    - **Density-dependent factors**: Effects increase with population density
    - **Density-independent factors**: Effects unrelated to population density
- **Community ecology**:
  - **Ecological succession**: Process of community change over time
    - **Primary succession**: Development on newly exposed surfaces
    - **Secondary succession**: Recovery after disturbance where soil remains
    - Primary succession can take hundreds to thousands of years
  - **Keystone species**: Species with disproportionate effects on community
  - **Ecological niche**: Sum of species' use of resources and its ecological role
  - **Biodiversity**: Variety of species in community
    - Higher biodiversity generally increases ecosystem stability and resilience

Conservation Biology

- **Conservation biology**: Science addressing biodiversity loss and ecosystem protection
- **Biodiversity conservation**:
  - **Species conservation**: Protecting individual species from extinction
  - **Habitat conservation**: Protecting places where species live
  - **Ex-situ conservation**: Preservation outside natural habitats (zoos, seed banks)
  - **In-situ conservation**: Preservation within natural habitats
  - *Only about 15% of Earth's land and 7% of oceans are protected areas*

- **Threats to biodiversity**:
  - **Habitat loss and fragmentation**: Primary threat to biodiversity
  - **Overexploitation**: Harvesting species faster than they can reproduce
  - **Invasive species**: Non-native species causing ecological or economic harm
  - **Pollution**: Contamination that harms organisms or ecosystems
  - **Climate change**: Altering habitats faster than species can adapt
  - **Disease**: Emerging pathogens threatening vulnerable populations
- **Conservation strategies**:
  - **Protected areas**: Legally protected land and water
  - **Ecological restoration**: Assisting recovery of degraded ecosystems
  - **Captive breeding**: Breeding endangered species in controlled environments
  - **Reintroduction**: Returning species to areas where they were extirpated
  - **Habitat corridors**: Connecting fragmented habitats to allow movement
  - *Corridors connecting habitat patches can increase species movement by 50%*
- **Conservation tools**:
  - **IUCN Red List**: Global inventory of species' conservation status
  - **GIS (Geographic Information System)**: Spatial analysis for conservation planning
  - **Population viability analysis**: Assessing extinction risk
  - **Environmental impact assessment**: Evaluating potential environmental effects

Applied Ecology for Sustainability

- **Ecological restoration**:
  - Process of assisting recovery of degraded ecosystems
  - **Passive restoration**: Removing stressors to allow natural recovery
  - **Active restoration**: Direct intervention to accelerate recovery
  - *Restoration of one hectare of degraded land can sequester 3-26 tons of carbon*
- **Agroecology**:
  - Application of ecological concepts to sustainable food production
  - **Polycultures**: Growing multiple crops in same area
  - **Crop rotation**: Sequence of different crops in same field
  - **Cover cropping**: Planting non-harvested crops to protect and improve soil
  - **Integrated pest management**: Comprehensive approach to pest control
  - *Diverse cropping systems can reduce pest damage by 50% compared to monocultures*
- **Permaculture**:
  - Design system for sustainable human settlements
  - **Food forests**: Multi-layer polycultures mimicking forest structure
  - Based on principles like working with nature, obtaining yield, reducing waste
  - *Food forests can produce up to 10 times more food per unit area than conventional agriculture*
- **Urban ecology**:
  - Study of organisms and environment in urban settings
  - **Urban heat island effect**: Higher temperatures in cities than surrounding areas
  - **Green infrastructure**: Natural systems providing ecosystem services
  - *Urban trees can reduce ambient temperature by 2-8°C*
- **Biomimicry**:
  - Innovation inspired by nature
  - Studying how organisms solve problems and applying solutions to human challenges
  - *Velcro (inspired by burdock seeds) and self-cleaning surfaces (inspired by lotus leaves)*
- **Regenerative design**:
  - Creating systems that restore rather than deplete
  - **Regenerative agriculture**: Farming practices that improve soil and ecosystem health
  - *Can increase soil carbon by 0.5-2 tons per hectare annually*

Ecosystem Services

- **Ecosystem services**: Benefits humans receive from functioning ecosystems
  - **Provisioning services**: Material goods (food, water, timber, medicines)
  - **Regulating services**: Process benefits (climate regulation, flood control, pollination)
  - **Cultural services**: Non-material benefits (recreation, spiritual values, aesthetics)
  - **Supporting services**: Underlying processes (nutrient cycling, soil formation)
- **Pollination**:
  - Transfer of pollen between flowers enabling plant reproduction
  - *About 75% of food crops depend partly on animal pollination*
- **Water filtration and purification**:
  - Wetlands and forests filter contaminants from water
- **Carbon sequestration**:
  - Removal and storage of carbon from atmosphere
  - Forests, soils, and oceans are major carbon sinks
  - *One hectare of forest can sequester 3-15 tons of carbon annually*
- **Soil formation**:
  - Creation of soil through weathering and biological activity
  - *Natural formation of 1 cm of topsoil can take 100-1,000 years*
- **Nutrient cycling**:
  - Movement and transformation of nutrients through ecosystem
  - Decomposers return nutrients to soil for plant uptake

Economics

Look up economics concepts and definitions right here to better understand technical articles.

Fundamental Principles of Economics

- **Economics**: Study of how societies allocate scarce resources to satisfy wants and needs
- **Scarcity**: Resource availability limited relative to wants
- **Opportunity cost**: Value of next best alternative foregone when making a choice
    - *Installing a $20,000 solar array means foregoing other uses of that money*
- **Marginal analysis**: Evaluating costs and benefits of one additional unit
- **Economic systems**:
    - **Market economy**: Resource allocation through private ownership and markets
    - **Command economy**: Central authority makes resource allocation decisions
    - **Mixed economy**: Combination of market forces and government intervention
    - *Modern economies are mixed with varying degrees of government involvement*

Microeconomics

- **Supply and demand**: Framework explaining price determination in competitive markets
    - **Supply curve**: Relationship between price and quantity suppliers will produce
    - **Demand curve**: Relationship between price and quantity consumers will purchase
    - **Equilibrium price**: Where supply equals demand
    - *Higher demand for solar panels without increased production capacity leads to higher prices*
- **Elasticity**: Measurement of responsiveness of quantity to price changes
    - **Elastic demand**: Percentage change in quantity > percentage change in price
    - **Inelastic demand**: Percentage change in quantity < percentage change in price
    - *Gasoline has relatively inelastic demand; small price increases don't reduce consumption*
- **Market structures**:
    - **Perfect competition**: Many sellers, identical products, price takers
    - **Monopolistic competition**: Many sellers, differentiated products
    - **Oligopoly**: Few large sellers dominating market
    - **Monopoly**: Single seller controlling market
    - *Utility companies often operate as regulated monopolies in specific service areas*
- **Market failure**: When free markets don't allocate resources efficiently
    - **Externalities**: Costs or benefits affecting third parties
        - **Negative externality**: External cost (e.g., pollution)
        - **Positive externality**: External benefit (e.g., education, pollination)
    - **Public goods**: Non-excludable and non-rivalrous (e.g., clean air)
    - **Common-pool resources**: Non-excludable but rivalrous (e.g., fishing grounds)
    - **Information asymmetry**: Unequal access to relevant information

Macroeconomics

- **Gross Domestic Product (GDP)**: Total value of goods and services produced within a country
    - **Real GDP**: Adjusted for inflation
    - **Nominal GDP**: Not adjusted for inflation
    - *U.S. GDP was approximately $27 trillion in 2023*
- **Economic growth**: Percentage increase in real GDP over time
    - **Intensive growth**: Increasing productivity with same resources
    - **Extensive growth**: Increasing total resources used
- **Business cycle**: Recurring pattern of expansion and contraction

- **Expansion**: Increased economic activity, falling unemployment
- **Peak**: Economy reaches maximum output
- **Contraction or recession**: Decreased economic activity, rising unemployment
- **Trough**: Economy reaches lowest point before recovery
- **Inflation**: General increase in prices over time
  - **Deflation**: General decrease in prices
  - **Consumer Price Index (CPI)**: Measures average price changes for consumer goods
  - **Producer Price Index (PPI)**: Measures average price changes received by producers
- **Unemployment**:
  - **Frictional**: Temporary unemployment during job transitions
  - **Structural**: Mismatch between worker skills and available jobs
  - **Cyclical**: Related to business cycle downturns
  - **Natural rate**: Level of unemployment when economy at full capacity
- **Fiscal policy**: Government use of taxation and spending to influence economy
  - **Expansionary**: Increased spending or reduced taxes to stimulate economy
  - **Contractionary**: Decreased spending or increased taxes to cool economy
- **Monetary policy**: Central bank actions to influence money supply and interest rates
  - **Expansionary**: Lower interest rates to stimulate borrowing and spending
  - **Contractionary**: Higher interest rates to reduce borrowing and spending

Government Interventions

- **Subsidies**: Government payments to reduce costs or increase production
  - **Direct subsidies**: Cash payments to producers or consumers
  - **Indirect subsidies**: Tax breaks, low-interest loans, insurance
  - **Effect**: Lower prices and increased production
- **Taxes**: Government charges on economic activity
  - **Purpose**: Generate revenue, discourage consumption, address externalities
  - **Pigouvian tax**: Tax on goods producing negative externalities
  - **Carbon tax**: Tax on carbon emissions to internalize environmental costs
- **Price controls**:
  - **Price ceilings**: Maximum legal prices (e.g., rent control)
  - **Price floors**: Minimum legal prices (e.g., minimum wage)
- **Regulations**:
  - **Command-and-control**: Direct regulations mandating specific actions
  - **Market-based**: Creating incentives through market mechanisms
  - **Performance standards**: Setting goals without specifying methods
- **Tariffs**: Taxes on imported goods
  - **Purpose**: Protect domestic industries, raise revenue, address "unfair" trade
  - **Effect**: Higher prices for consumers, reduced international trade
  - **Types**: Ad valorem (percentage of value), specific (fixed amount per unit)
- **Quotas**: Limits on quantity of imported goods
  - **Effect**: Similar to tariffs but directly limiting quantity
  - **Tariff-rate quota**: Lower tariff for imports under quota, higher above
- **Trade agreements**: Arrangements between countries to reduce trade barriers
  - **Free trade agreement**: Eliminates tariffs between participating countries
  - **Customs union**: Free trade agreement plus common external tariff
  - **Common market**: Customs union plus free movement of factors of production

Financial Concepts

- **Time value of money**: Concept that money available now is worth more than same amount later

- Present value: Current worth of future sum of money
  - Future value: Worth of current sum at a future date
  - Discounting: Process of determining present value of future cash flows
  - *$1,000 today is worth more than $1,000 received in one year*
- **Interest rates**:
  - **Simple interest**: Paid only on principal
  - **Compound interest**: Paid on principal and accumulated interest
  - **Nominal rate**: Stated interest rate without accounting for compounding
  - **Effective annual rate (EAR)**: Actual annual rate accounting for compounding
  - *5% compounded monthly has an EAR of 5.12%*
- **Risk and return**:
  - **Risk premium**: Additional return expected for taking additional risk
  - **Diversification**: Spreading investments to reduce risk
  - **Systematic risk**: Market-wide risk that cannot be eliminated through diversification
  - **Unsystematic risk**: Firm-specific risk that can be reduced through diversification
- **Capital budgeting**: Process of evaluating and selecting long-term investments
  - **Capital**: Long-term assets used in production
  - **Fixed capital**: Physical assets (buildings, equipment)
  - **Working capital**: Current assets minus current liabilities
- **Financing options**:
  - **Debt financing**: Borrowing money to be repaid with interest
  - **Equity financing**: Selling ownership shares in exchange for capital
  - **Internal financing**: Using retained earnings for investment
  - *Green bonds are debt instruments specifically for environmental projects*

Environmental Economics

- **Environmental valuation**: Assigning monetary values to environmental goods and services
  - **Use value**: Direct benefits from using resource
  - **Non-use value**: Value without direct use (existence value, option value)
  - **Contingent valuation**: Survey methods to determine willingness to pay
  - **Hedonic pricing**: Inferring values from related market transactions
- **Environmental Kuznets Curve**: Hypothesis that environmental degradation first rises, then falls with economic development
  - **Turning point**: Level of income where environmental quality begins to improve
  - **Criticism**: Applies to some pollutants but not all environmental impacts
- **Natural capital**: Environmental assets providing resource inputs and ecosystem services
  - **Depreciation**: Depletion or degradation of natural capital
  - **Strong sustainability**: Natural capital cannot be substituted with manufactured capital
  - **Weak sustainability**: Natural capital can be substituted with manufactured capital
- **Green accounting**: Incorporating environmental costs and benefits into economic accounts
  - **Gross Domestic Product (GDP)**: Doesn't account for environmental degradation
  - **Genuine Progress Indicator (GPI)**: Adjusts GDP for environmental and social factors
  - **System of Environmental Economic Accounting (SEEA)**: UN framework for environmental accounting
- **Circular economy**: Economic system minimizing waste and maximizing resource reuse
  - **Linear economy**: Take-make-dispose model
  - **Principles**: Design out waste, keep products and materials in use, regenerate natural systems

Behavioral Economics

- **Bounded rationality**: Limited cognitive capacity affects decision-making

- People use heuristics (mental shortcuts) rather than complex calculations
  - *Homeowners may choose appliances with lower upfront costs despite higher lifetime costs*
- **Loss aversion**: Losses hurt more psychologically than equivalent gains feel good
  - **Endowment effect**: Valuing things more highly once owned
  - **Status quo bias**: Preference for current state over change
  - *Framing efficiency as avoiding losses rather than generating savings increases adoption*
- **Present bias**: Tendency to overvalue immediate benefits and costs compared to future ones
  - Leads to procrastination and underinvestment in long-term benefits
  - *Explains underinvestment in energy efficiency despite positive returns*
- **Social norms**: Behavior influenced by what others do
  - **Descriptive norms**: What people typically do
  - **Injunctive norms**: What people should do
  - *Showing households their energy use compared to neighbors can reduce consumption*
- **Choice architecture**: Designing how choices are presented to influence decisions
  - **Default options**: Pre-selected options that apply if no active choice made
  - **Simplification**: Making complex decisions more manageable
  - *Making green energy the default option increases renewable energy adoption*

Sustainable Business Models

- **Triple bottom line**: Framework measuring performance on economic, social, and environmental dimensions
  - **People**: Social impact
  - **Planet**: Environmental impact
  - **Profit**: Economic performance
- **Sustainability business strategies**:
  - **Eco-efficiency**: Reducing resource use and pollution while maintaining output
  - **Circular business models**: Designing waste out of system
  - **Product-service systems**: Selling service rather than product
  - **Industrial symbiosis**: Waste from one process becomes input for another
- **Corporate social responsibility (CSR)**: Business practices benefiting society
  - **Strategic CSR**: Aligning social and environmental initiatives with business strategy
- **ESG (Environmental, Social, Governance)**: Framework for evaluating sustainability
  - **Environmental**: Resource use, pollution, climate impact
  - **Social**: Labor practices, community relations, product responsibility
  - **Governance**: Corporate ethics, transparency, board structure
- **Green marketing**:
  - **Greenwashing**: Misleading claims about environmental benefits
  - **Ecolabels**: Certified environmental performance (Energy Star, USDA Organic)

Energy Economics

- **Energy markets**:
  - **Wholesale electricity markets**: Power generators sell to utilities
  - **Retail electricity markets**: Utilities sell to end consumers
  - **Capacity markets**: Payments to ensure sufficient generation capacity
- **Energy pricing**:
  - **Time-of-use pricing**: Different rates based on time of day
  - **Peak demand pricing**: Higher rates during highest demand periods
  - **Feed-in tariffs**: Guaranteed prices for renewable energy sold to grid
  - **Net metering**: Credit for electricity sent to grid from distributed generation
- **Grid parity**: When alternative energy costs equal or less than traditional sources

- o **Socket parity**: Equal to retail electricity prices
- o **Generation parity**: Equal to wholesale electricity prices
- **Energy efficiency economics**:
  - o **Energy efficiency gap**: Underinvestment in cost-effective efficiency measures
  - o **Rebound effect**: Increased efficiency leads to increased use, partially offsetting savings
  - o **Split incentives**: When benefits accrue to different party than who pays costs

Public Finance for Sustainability

- **Green fiscal policy**: Revenue and spending measures promoting environmental objectives
  - o **Environmental taxes**: Levies on environmentally harmful activities
  - o **Tax incentives**: Reduced tax liability for sustainable activities
  - o **Green bonds**: Fixed-income securities funding environmental projects
- **Carbon pricing mechanisms**:
  - o **Carbon tax**: Direct tax on carbon emissions
  - o **Cap-and-trade**: System setting overall emission limit with tradable permits
  - o **Carbon offsets**: Credits for emission reductions used to compensate for emissions elsewhere
- **Public investment**:
  - o **Green infrastructure**: Public investment in low-carbon, resilient infrastructure
  - o **Research and development**: Government funding for sustainable technology innovation
  - o **Technology deployment**: Programs supporting market adoption of sustainable technologies
- **Public-private partnerships**: Collaboration between government and private sector
  - o **Shared risks and rewards**: Government provides guarantees; private does work
  - o **Performance contracting**: Private company paid from resulting savings

Technology

This section describes important technologies that can dramatically reduce our environmental impact while maintaining or improving our quality of life. Batteries, cleaning solutions, electric motors, heat pumps, insulation, solar photovoltaics, and windows represent areas where knowledge is crucial and technological advances are rapidly changing what's possible in sustainable living. Rather than simply telling you which products to buy, these sections explain fundamental concepts and terminology so you can make informed decisions about proven, new, and emerging technologies.

Batteries

Batteries and solar photovoltaic arrays enable the transition away from fossil fuel to clean energy.

Basic Battery Science

Batteries store and release electricity through electrochemical reactions. A battery consists of one or more cells, each containing seven key components:

1. **Cathode** (positive electrode): Accepts electrons during discharge
2. **Anode** (negative electrode): Releases electrons during discharge
3. **Electrolyte**: Medium that permits ion flow between electrodes
4. **Electrical Separator**: Prevents electrons from flowing directly between electrodes
5. **Current Collectors:** Provide a path for electrons to flow out of the battery cell
6. **Terminals:** Allow an electrical circuit to be connected to the battery cell
7. **Insulating Case:** Contains ions and electrons inside the battery cell

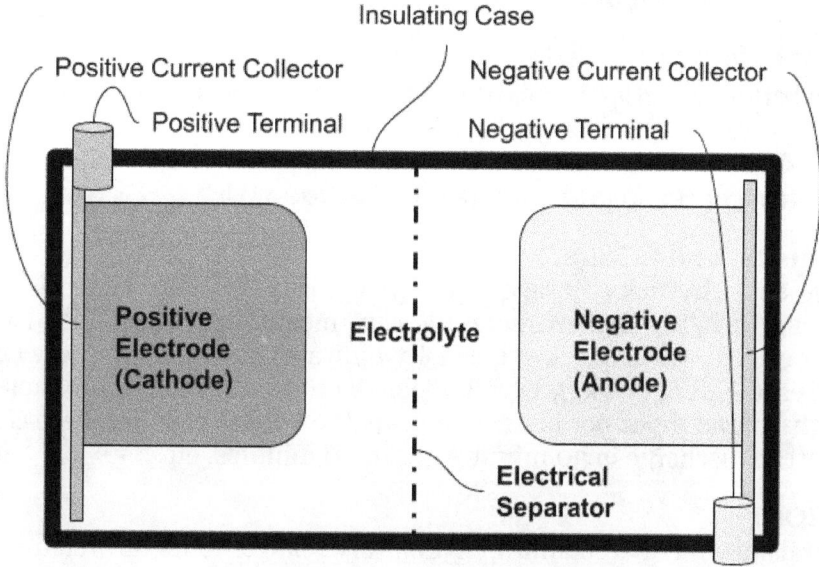

Components of a Battery Cell

During charging (in rechargeable batteries) or manufacture (of primary batteries), an external electrical force strips electrons from the positive electrode and stores them in the negative electrode. During discharge, a simultaneous set of spontaneous chemical reactions occur: *reduction* at the cathode, pulling electrons through an external circuit to power devices, and *oxidation* at the anode, releasing electrons. Once all of the electrons that have been stored in the negative electrode have been released, the flow of current through the external circuit stops. The type of chemical reactions that will occur in a battery cell depends on the molecules in its electrodes and electrolyte.

- **Primary batteries** (disposable): Designed for single use, with irreversible chemical reactions
  - *Alkaline, zinc-carbon, lithium primary cells*
- **Secondary batteries** (rechargeable): Designed for recharging, with reversible chemical reactions
  - *Lithium-ion, sodium-ion, nickel-metal hydride (NiMH), lead-acid*

Key Battery Performance Metrics

Performance metrics depend primarily on the materials in the positive electrode (cathode) of the cell.

Voltage

The electrical potential difference between the positive and negative terminal is measured in volts (V).
- **Nominal voltage**: The average operating voltage during discharge
- **Open-circuit voltage**: The voltage when no current is flowing
- **Cut-off voltage**: The minimum allowable voltage during discharge

Cathode Material	Lithium-ion	PbO_2 Lead-acid	MnO_2 Alkaline	NiMH and NiCd
Nominal Voltage	3.2 - 3.7 V	2.0 V	1.5 V	1.2 V

Charge (Ampere) Capacity

The amount of electric charge a battery can store and deliver is measured in ampere-hours (Ah) or milliampere-hours (mAh).
- 1 Ah = 1,000 mAh
- *Typical smartphone: 3,000-5,000 mAh (3-5 Ah)*

Energy (Watt-Hour) Storage Capacity

The total electricity a battery can store is measured in watt-hours (Wh) or kWh and calculated by:
- Energy (Wh) = Voltage (V) × Charge Capacity (Ah)
- 1 kWh = 1,000 Wh
- *Typical EV battery pack: 50,000-100,000 Wh (50-100 kWh)*

Energy, Power Density, and C-Rate

Energy density represents electricity storage capacity by mass (Wh/kg), which is also called "specific energy," or by volume (Wh/L). Higher energy density means lighter, smaller batteries—crucial for portable devices and electric vehicles. Power density indicates how quickly energy can be transferred, measured in watts per kilogram (W/kg), which depends on the C-rate of the battery cell. C-rate is the complete charge or discharge times per hour: 1C means the battery can discharge completely in 1 hour, 2C means the battery can discharge in 30 minutes, 3C in 20 minutes, etc.

State of Charge (SOC)

The percentage of available energy remaining in a battery relative to its fully charged state is called the state of charge. This cannot be directly measured, but it can be inferred by measuring the voltage between positive and negative terminals and by allowing current to flow and measuring the change in voltage that results. Voltage declines as stored charge depletes (chemical reactions occur).

Depth of Discharge (DOD)

The percentage of capacity removed from a fully charged battery.

Self-Discharge Rate

Rate at which a battery loses charge (ions move between electrodes and chemical reactions occur) when not in use. Self-discharge accelerates at higher temperatures and in older batteries.

Cycle Life
The number of charge-discharge cycles before capacity falls below a specified percentage (typically 80%) of original capacity. Deeper discharges, higher temperatures, faster charge and discharge rates, and charging to maximum voltage all typically reduce cycle life.

Cathode Material	Lithium-ion	NiMH	Lead-acid	Supercapacitors
Specific Energy (Wh/kg)	100-300	60-120	30-50	
Energy Density (Wh/L)	300-700	180-220	20-50	
Power Density (W/kg)	300-1,500	450-550	180	2,000-10,000
Charge C-Rate	1-10C or higher	1C	0.05-0.2C	
Discharge C-Rate	10C	2-10C	0.05-0.2C	
Self Discharge per Month	2-3%	20-30%	5-15%	
Cycle Life	2,000-5,000+	500-2,000	200-300	

Temperature Performance
Batteries perform differently across temperature ranges:
- Low temperatures: Reduced capacity, slower chemical reactions
- High temperatures: Faster reactions but accelerated degradation
- Optimal range: Typically 15-25°C (59-77°F)

Internal Resistance
The opposition to ionic current flow within the battery, measured in ohms (Ω).
- Increases as batteries age
- Higher in cold temperatures
- Causes voltage drop under load
- Results in power loss as heat

Calendar Aging
Degradation that occurs over time regardless of use. Higher temperatures and storing batteries at a high state of charge accelerates aging for most types (although lead acid batteries like to stay fully charged).

Lithium-Ion Battery Chemistry
Non-toxic lithium-ion cells are now prevalent; toxic lead-acid batteries are losing market share.
1. During **charging**, positive lithium ions are forced from the positive electrode to the negative electrode, attracting electrons to what will be the anode during discharging.
2. During **discharging**, positive lithium ions spontaneously move from the anode to the cathode, creating an electrical potential that pulls electrons from the anode through the external circuit.

Lithium hexafluorophosphate in carbonate solvents, polyolefin film, and graphite carbon are most commonly used for the electrolyte, separator, and negative anode, respectively, in lithium-ion battery cells. Several different types of lithium-ion chemistries are used for the positive electrode (cathode).

- **Lithium Iron Phosphate (LFP):** $LiFePO_4$, contains no nickel or cobalt

- **Nickel Manganese Cobalt Oxide (NMC):**
  - NMC 111: equal parts Ni, Mn, Co
  - NMC 532, 622, 811: higher nickel content for increased energy density
  - NMC 9½½: 90% nickel, 5% manganese, 5% cobalt
- **Nickel Cobalt Aluminum Oxide (NCA), Lithium Titanate (LTO), Lithium Manganese Oxide (LMO)**
  - Less common lithium-ion electrode formulations for niche applications

Chemistry	LFP Lithium-Ion	NMC Lithium-Ion
Toxic	No	Yes
Thermal Stability	Better	Worse
Cycle Life	5,000+	2,000+
Cost	Lower	Higher
Energy Density	160 Wh/kg	300 Wh/kg
Cell Voltage	3.2 V	3.6 V
Deep Discharge Tolerance	Better	Worse

Anode Materials

Most lithium-ion batteries use graphite negative electrodes (anodes) with some recent innovations:

- **Graphite (C)**: Traditional anode material, good stability
- **Silicon-graphite (Si-C) composites**: Higher capacity but challenges with expansion
- **Lithium titanate ($Li_4Ti_5O_{12}$)**: Lower energy density but superior safety and cycle life
- **Silicon-dominant**: Emerging technology with significantly higher capacity

Electrolyte Innovations

Electrolytes significantly impact battery performance and safety:

- **Liquid electrolytes**: Standard in most batteries (lithium salts in organic solvents)
- **Gel electrolytes**: Higher safety, slightly lower performance
- **Solid-state electrolytes**: Promising technology offering safety and energy density improvements

Other Battery Chemistries

- **Alkaline:** A type of primary (non-rechargeable) cell where the electrolyte has a pH above 7
- **Lead-Acid:** An old rechargeable battery technology, still used in some automotive starting, lighting, and ignition (SLI) applications and uninterruptible power supplies (UPS)
- **Nickel-Metal Hydride (NiMH):** Used in older hybrid vehicles and applications where energy density is not important
- **Nickel-Cadmium (NiCd):** No longer competitive; should be handled as household hazardous waste due to toxicity
- **Sodium-Ion Batteries:** An emerging technology using abundant sodium instead of lithium

Emerging Technologies
- **Solid-state batteries**: Replace liquid electrolytes with solid materials
- **Lithium-sulfur**: Potentially much higher energy density
- **Lithium-air**: Theoretical energy density approaching gasoline
- **Sodium-sulfur**: High-temperature technology for grid storage
- **Aluminum-ion**: Uses abundant materials with potentially fast charging
- **Zinc-air**: High energy density using atmospheric oxygen

Battery Management Systems (BMS)
Modern batteries have sophisticated management systems to ensure safety and longevity.
1. **Cell balancing**: Ensures all cells in a pack maintain similar voltage levels
2. **Thermal management**: Monitors and regulates temperature
3. **State of charge (SOC) estimation**: Tracks remaining capacity
4. **State of health (SOH) monitoring**: Assesses battery degradation
5. **Protection**: Prevents overcharge, over-discharge, overcurrent, and overtemperature
6. **Communication**: Interfaces with device or charger

Battery Charging
Most lithium-ion batteries charge in two consecutive phases:
1. **Constant Current (CC)**: Maintain a steady current, increase voltage until reaching target voltage
2. **Constant Voltage (CV)**: Maintain voltage, decrease current until cell fully charged

Overcharging a battery or charging it too fast increases voltage and in extreme cases will cause a battery to catch fire and explode. Always monitor voltage carefully when charging batteries.

Battery Safety
While older battery technologies could emit explosive hydrogen gas even in normal charging conditions and therefore required ventilation for safety, modern battery cells are designed not to emit gas. Battery cases are now sealed, designed to contain hydrogen gas, and can withstand some variations in pressure as hydrogen ions are created and reabsorbed during charging cycles. Nonetheless, the fact that batteries store electricity means that there is always some risk of fire if that electricity is released suddenly or if the batteries are severely overcharged. In addition, some electrolytes are flammable, creating a fire hazard if the electrical separator inside the battery fails and electrical current flows directly between electrodes inside the cell. Batteries have many safety devices:

- **Current interrupt devices (CID)**: Physical disconnection during overpressure
- **Positive temperature coefficient (PTC) devices**: Limit current when overheated
- **Vent mechanisms**: Release pressure safely
- **Thermal fuses**: Cut connection when temperature exceeds safe limits

Best Safety Practices
- Charge and store batteries in fire-proof areas
- Avoid extreme temperatures
- Use manufacturer-recommended chargers
- Prevent physical damage to batteries
- Avoid complete discharge or prolonged full charge
- Be cautious with counterfeit or low-quality batteries

Cleaning: Soaps, Solvents and Disinfectants

Basic Cleaning Science

Cleaning removes unwanted substances ("soil") from surfaces. At the molecular level, this is primarily a battle between adhesive forces (keeping soil stuck to surfaces) and the cleaning solution's ability to overcome these forces.

The core challenge in cleaning stems from a fundamental principle: like dissolves like. Water (a polar molecule, i.e. one with a positively charged pole and a negatively charged pole) effectively dissolves water-soluble (polar hydrophilic) substances but struggles with oils and greases (non-polar hydrophobic). Soaps and detergents bridge this molecular divide; solvents work within it.

Soap Chemistry

Soaps are salts of fatty acids, typically produced through saponification—a reaction between fat or oil and a strong base (like sodium hydroxide). The resulting molecules have a dual nature:

- A hydrophilic "head" (carboxylate group) that interacts with water
- A hydrophobic "tail" (hydrocarbon chain) that interacts with oils and greases

This dual structure allows soaps to act as surfactants (surface active agents), reducing the surface tension of water and forming connections between water and oily substances.

Synthetic Detergent Chemistry

Synthetic detergents emerged in the early 1900s as alternatives to soap. Like soaps, they have amphipathic structures, but instead of carboxylate groups, they typically feature sulfonate or sulfate groups as their hydrophilic heads.

Common synthetic surfactants include:
- Anionic surfactants (negative charge): Linear alkylbenzene sulfonates (LAS), alkyl sulfates
- Nonionic surfactants (no charge): Alcohol ethoxylates, alkylphenol ethoxylates
- Cationic surfactants (positive charge): Quaternary ammonium compounds
- Amphoteric surfactants (charge depends on pH): Betaines, phosphatidylcholine

Synthetic detergents offer several advantages over traditional soaps:
- Function effectively in hard water (don't form insoluble scum with calcium or magnesium ions)
- Can be engineered for specific applications and conditions
- Work better in acidic conditions
- Can be formulated for cold water washing

Micelle Formation

Both soaps and detergents clean through micelle formation. When their concentration reaches the critical micelle concentration (CMC), the molecules arrange themselves into spherical structures:
1. The hydrophilic heads face outward toward the water
2. The hydrophobic tails cluster inward, creating an oil-friendly environment

When micelles encounter oils or greases:
1. The hydrophobic tails interact with and penetrate the oil
2. The oil is gradually pulled into the center of the micelle
3. The entire soil-containing micelle becomes suspended in water (emulsified)
4. Water movement carries away the suspended soils

Physical Actions in Cleaning

Beyond chemistry, physical factors enhance cleaning:
- **Mechanical action**: Agitation (rubbing, scrubbing, machine movement) helps dislodge soils
- **Temperature**: Heat generally accelerates chemical reactions and softens greases
- **Time**: Longer exposure to cleaning solutions allows better penetration and soil loosening

Enzymes in Detergents

Enzymes are biological catalysts (proteins) that accelerate specific chemical reactions, breaking down complex molecules into smaller, more soluble components.

Major Detergent Enzymes

1. **Proteases**
   - Target protein-based stains (blood, egg, grass, body soils)
   - Break peptide bonds in proteins, fragmenting them into smaller, water-soluble peptides and amino acids
   - *Subtilisin, Savinase, Esperase*
2. **Amylases**
   - Target starch-based stains (pasta, potatoes, gravy, chocolate)
   - Hydrolyze starch molecules into smaller, soluble sugars
   - *Termamyl, Duramyl*
3. **Lipases**
   - Target fat or oil stains (cooking oils, butter, cosmetics)
   - Break down triglycerides into glycerol and fatty acids
   - *Lipolase, Lipex*
4. **Cellulases**
   - Target cellulose fibers to remove trapped dirt and restore fabric appearance
   - Break down cellulose microfibrils that form on cotton during wear
   - *Carezyme, Celluclean*
5. **Mannanases**
   - Target food stains containing mannans (ice cream, chocolate, tomato sauce)
   - Hydrolyze mannan-containing polysaccharides
   - *Mannaway*
6. **Pectinases**
   - Target fruit and vegetable stains
   - Break down pectin, a complex polysaccharide in plant cell walls
   - *Pectaway*

Cold-Water Enzymes

Specially engineered enzymes work effectively at low temperatures:
1. Have modified protein structures to maintain activity and stability at low temperatures
2. Feature broader active site regions to accommodate substrates that move more slowly in cold water
3. Often include protein stabilizers to prevent denaturation
4. May be encapsulated to protect them from other detergent ingredients

Benefits of these cold-water enzymes include:
- Energy savings from reduced hot water usage
- Protection of temperature-sensitive fabrics
- Reduced color fading and fabric wear

Detergent Additives

Modern detergents include numerous components beyond surfactants and enzymes. Active ingredients (that help clean) include:
- **Enzyme stabilizers**: Protect enzymes from denaturation
- **Chelating agents:** Combine with metal ions to prevent interference with surfactants
  - *Phosphates, EDTA (ethylenediaminetetraacetic acid), citric acid, sodium gluconate*
- **Builders**: An alternative to chelating agents to combat water hardness (metal ions in water)
  - *Sodium carbonate, sodium metasilicate, sodium hydroxide*
- **Anti-redeposition agents**: Prevent removed soil from settling back on fabric

Useful ingredients (that provide other functional benefits besides cleaning):
- **Corrosion inhibitors**: Protect washing machine parts
- **Foam regulators**: Control amount of suds
- **Preservatives**: Prevent microbial growth

Marketing and sales ingredients (designed to entice consumers to buy a specific product):
- **Colorants**: Add visual appeal to product
- **Fragrances**: Provide pleasant scent
- **Optical brighteners**: Make fabrics appear whiter by converting UV light to visible blue light

Solvents

Solvents chemically dissolve or disperse substances, breaking down molecular bonds. Non-polar solvents (like oil) dissolve non-polar substances (like grease), while polar solvents (like water) dissolve polar substances (like sugars and other carbohydrates).
- *Isopropyl alcohol, glycerin, propylene glycol*

Disinfectants

Soaps and detergents primarily remove soils physically through solubilization and emulsification, while disinfectants chemically destroy or inactivate microorganisms.

Disinfectant Mechanisms

1. **Protein denaturation**: Disrupt protein structure, causing microbial proteins to lose function
   - *Alcohols, phenols*
2. **Membrane disruption**: Damage cell membranes, causing leakage of cellular contents
   - *Quaternary ammonium compounds, chlorhexidine*
3. **Oxidation**: Oxidize cellular components, causing irreversible damage to proteins and DNA
   - *Bleach, hydrogen peroxide, peracetic acid*
4. **Alkylation**: Form chemical bonds with proteins and nucleic acids, preventing proper function
   - *Glutaraldehyde, formaldehyde*

Antimicrobial Soap

Regular soap physically removes microbes from surfaces but doesn't necessarily kill them. Antimicrobial soaps contain additional active ingredients (like triclosan or benzalkonium chloride) designed to kill microorganisms.

Synergistic Effects

Detergents and disinfectants can work together:
- Detergents remove soils that might otherwise shield microorganisms
- Disinfectants then have direct contact with microbes on clean surfaces

Soiling Classification Matrix

Soiling Type	Chemical Nature	Water Solubility	Example Substances	Optimal Removal Agent
Particulate	Inorganic	Variable	Dust, clay, silt	Surfactants, mechanical action
Oily/Greasy	Hydrophobic	Insoluble	Mineral oils, sebum	Surfactants, solvents
Protein-based	Polypeptides	Variable	Blood, egg, milk	Proteases, alkaline detergents
Carbohydrate	Polysaccharides	Variable	Starches, sugars	Amylases, water
Tannin/Pigment	Polyphenols	Moderate	Coffee, tea, wine	Oxidizing agents, surfactants
Mineral	Inorganic salts	Variable	Limescale, rust	Acids, chelating agents

Environmental Considerations

- **Alcohol ethoxylates**: Generally good biodegradability
- **Cold-water formulations**: Lower energy requirements for effective results
- **Enzymes**: Enzymes are biodegradable proteins
- **Linear alkylbenzene sulfonates (LAS)**: Slower biodegradation than soap
- **Phosphates**: Highly effective chelating agents but can cause algal blooms
- **Traditional soaps**: Generally biodegradable but can contribute to eutrophication

Electric Motors

Electric motors convert electrical energy into mechanical energy through electromagnetic interactions. Along with batteries and solar photovoltaics, they enable the transition from fossil fuels to clean energy.

Basic Electric Motor Physics

Electric current flowing through a conductor induces a magnetic field. If you point your thumb in the direction of the current, your fingers curl in the direction of the magnetic field. This is the basic principle behind all electric motors. The primary components of an electric motor include:
- **Stator:** The stationary part (often containing electromagnets or permanent magnets)
- **Rotor:** The rotating part attached to the output shaft
- **Commutator or Controller:** Manages the flow of electricity
- **Bearings:** Support the rotating shaft
- **Housing:** Protects internal components

Major Electric Motor Types

Direct Current (DC) Motors

- Brushed DC Motors: 70-80% efficient due to friction and arcing
  - Utilize physical brushes and a commutator to switch current direction
  - Simple, inexpensive, easy to control
  - Require maintenance due to brush wear
- Brushless DC Motors: 85-90% efficient
  - Use electronic controllers instead of physical brushes
  - Longer lifespan, less maintenance
  - More complex control systems; better speed control and torque characteristics

Alternating Current (AC) Motors

- Induction Motors (Asynchronous): 80-90% efficient
  - Rotor turns slightly slower than the stator's magnetic field (slip)
  - Robust, reliable, and relatively inexpensive
  - Difficult to control precisely without inverter drives
- Synchronous Motors: 90-95% efficient
  - Rotor turns at the same rate as the magnetic field
  - Excellent speed control
  - More complex construction
- Permanent Magnet Synchronous Motors (PMSM): 90-98% efficient
  - Use permanent magnets in the rotor
  - Excellent torque-to-weight ratio
  - Higher cost due to rare earth magnets

Key Performance Metrics

- **Efficiency:** The ratio of output mechanical power to input electrical power, expressed as a percentage; higher efficiency means less input energy is wasted as heat
- **Voltage Rating:** The designed operating voltage of the motor
- **Current Draw:** The electrical current consumed during operation
  - Locked Rotor Amps (LRA): the current drawn by a motor when starting; LRA is significantly higher than running load amps, typically 5-8 times higher for many motor types

- ○ Running Load Amps (RLA) or Full-Load Amps (LFA): the current drawn by a motor during normal operation under the specified load conditions; used to size wires and breakers
- **Power Rating**: The maximum power output capability, measured in watts (W)
- **Torque**: The rotational force produced by the motor, measured in newton-meters (Nm).
  - ○ Starting Torque (Locked Rotor Torque): The torque an electric motor produces when initially energized at standstill (zero speed) to overcome the inertia of the load and start rotation
  - ○ Rated Torque (Continuous Torque): The torque level that the motor can continuously deliver at its rated speed under specified operating conditions without exceeding its thermal limits
  - ○ Maximum Torque (Peak Torque): The highest torque the motor can deliver for short periods without stalling or suffering damage; maximum torque is typically well above rated torque
- **Speed**: The rotational velocity, measured in revolutions per minute (RPM)
- **Power Factor**: For AC motors, how effectively the motor converts apparent power to real power
- **Temperature Rise**: How much the motor heats up during operation
- **Duty Cycle**: The operating cycle the motor is designed for (continuous, intermittent, etc.)
- **Lifespan and Reliability**: Measured in operating hours and mean time between failures (MTBF)
- **Size and Weight**: Physical dimensions and mass, important for space-constrained applications
  - ○ Power Density: Power output per unit volume, measured in watts per liter (W/L or kW/L)
  - ○ Specific Power: Power output per unit mass, measured in watts per gram (W/g or kW/kg)
- **Noise Level**: Acoustic output during operation, measured in decibels (dB)

Motor Control

Modern motor systems rely heavily on power electronics to achieve high efficiency and precise control. Because direct current can be inverted to alternative current, and alternating current rectified to direct current, both AC and DC motors may be used with any electricity source, including grid power or solar power. In many applications, especially variable speed drives, power undergoes multiple conversions:
- Rectify: Convert AC to DC
  - ○ Produces DC with some ripple voltage
- Filter and Increase ("Boost") or Decrease ("Buck") Voltage
  - ○ Capacitors smooth the DC voltage
  - ○ DC-DC conversion achieves optimal voltage levels
- Invert: Convert DC back to AC
  - ○ Rapidly switch DC to create desired frequency and shape of AC curve
  - ○ Modern inverters operate at switching frequencies of 4-20 kHz

Variable Frequency Drives (VFDs) combine rectification and inversion to provide precise motor control:
- Enable efficient operation across a wide range of speeds
- Provide soft-start capabilities to reduce mechanical stress
- Allow for precise torque and speed control
- Reduce energy consumption in variable-load applications
- Can achieve 95-98% electrical efficiency

Applications

Electric motors are used in heat pumps to replace fuel-burning furnaces and in electric vehicles to replace fuel-burning engines. Electric motors are also used in speakers to produce sound waves, in fans and pumps to move air and water, and in most electric appliances.

Heat Pumps

Heat pumps transfer thermal energy from a *heat source* to a *heat sink* against the natural direction of heat flow. Despite their name, heat pumps can provide both heating and cooling.

Vapor compression heat pumps (the most common technology), circulate refrigerant fluids that absorb and release heat when they change phase between liquid and gas states, using four main components:
1. **Evaporator**: Absorbs heat from outside air, ground, or water, causing the refrigerant to evaporate
2. **Compressor**: Pressurizes the refrigerant vapor, raising its temperature
3. **Condenser**: Releases heat causing the refrigerant to condense
4. **Expansion Valve**: Reduces pressure of the refrigerant, cooling it before the evaporator

Either fans blow air or pumps move liquid across the evaporator and condenser coils.

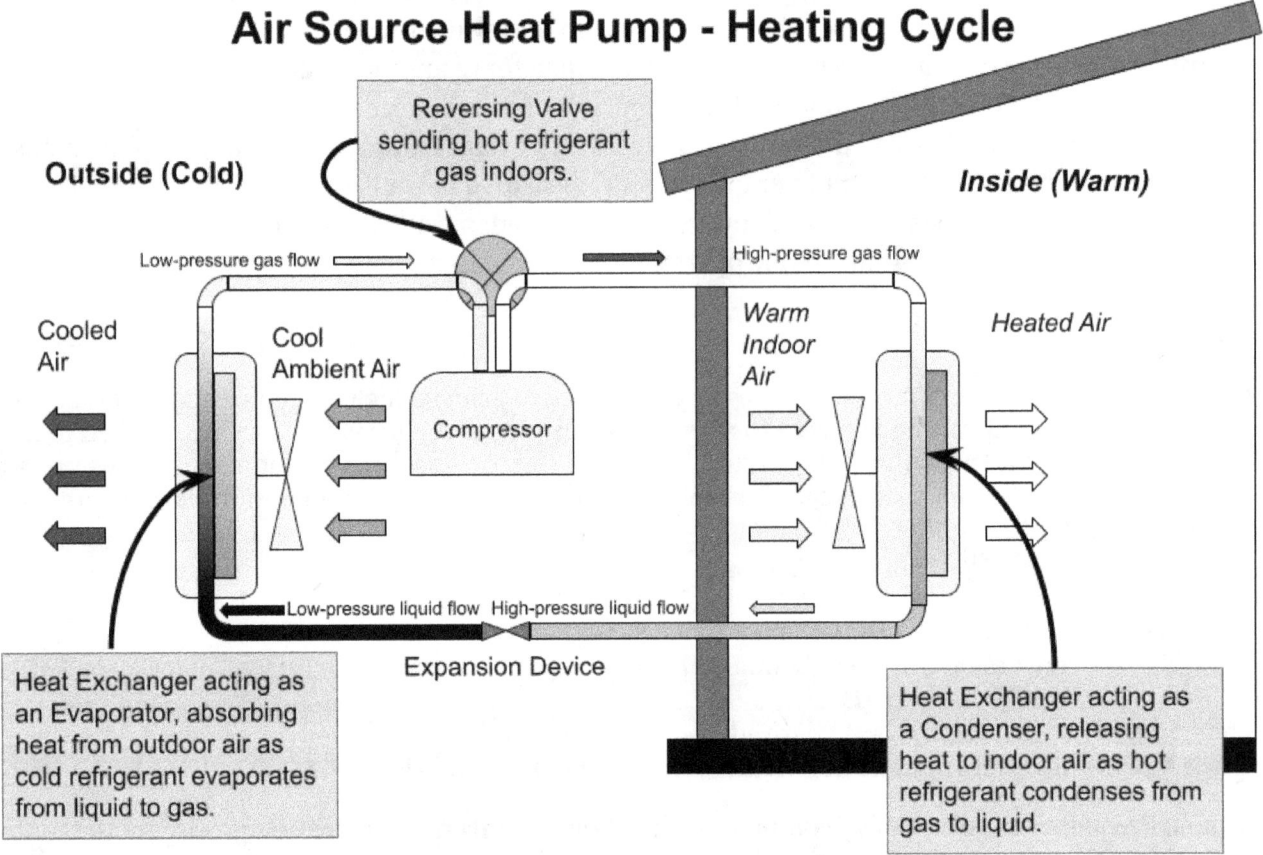

Thermodynamic Principles

The Second Law of Thermodynamics states that heat naturally flows from warm to cold. To reverse this flow, a compressor must provide energy input. Efficiency is measured by coefficient of performance:

$$COP = \frac{H_{Out}}{E_{In}}$$

where COP is coefficient of performance, H_{Out} is useful heat output, and E_{In} is energy input

Modern heat pumps typically deliver 3-5 units of heat energy per unit of electrical energy consumed, heating much more efficiently than electrical resistance or combustion heating systems.

Key Terms
- **Condensate:** Water vapor extracted from air that forms on the evaporator
- **SEER (Seasonal Energy Efficiency Ratio):** Cooling efficiency over a typical season
- **HSPF (Heating Seasonal Performance Factor):** Heating efficiency over a typical season
- **Refrigerant charge:** Amount of refrigerant in the system

Air-to-Air Heat Pump

Use outdoor air as the heat source (in heating mode) or the heat sink (in cooling mode).
- Outdoor unit: evaporator/condenser coil, fan, and compressor
- Indoor unit: evaporator/condenser coil, fan, control module
- Refrigerant lines connect the units: gas line, liquid line
- Thermostat and control systems (typically a remote control)

Operating Characteristics:
- Efficiency decreases as outdoor temperature drops, especially below 30°F (-1°C)
- Requires defrost cycles when operating in cold, humid conditions
- Typical COP ranges from 2-4, depending on outdoor temperature

Variants:
- **Ducted systems**: Distribute conditioned air through ductwork
- **Ductless mini-splits**: Direct room-by-room conditioning with wall-mounted indoor units
- **Multi-zone systems**: Single outdoor unit serving multiple indoor units
- **Variable refrigerant flow (VRF)**: Advanced systems with precise capacity control

Air-to-Water Heat Pump

Use air as the heat source and a hydronic system (water or glycol mixture) as the heat sink for radiant floor, hydronic baseboard, or fan coil space heating, or domestic hot water. These systems are compatible with existing plumbing and heating distribution systems, can achieve higher delivery temperatures than air-to-air systems, and provide both space heating and hot water.

Ground-Source Heat Pump

Also called geothermal heat pumps, these systems use groundwater as their heat source or sink.
- **Closed Loops:** Circulate water or refrigerant in a closed loop, exchanging heat with groundwater
  - **Horizontal**: Pipes buried in trenches 4-6 feet deep, requiring substantial land area
  - **Vertical**: Pipes installed in boreholes 100-400 feet deep, suitable for limited land area
  - **Pond**: Coils submerged in water bodies
- **Open Loops**: Use groundwater directly, require suitable water quality and disposal

Characteristics:
- Higher installation cost than air-source heat pumps, but lower operating costs
- Consistent performance regardless of outdoor air temperature or weather
- Typical COP of 3-5
- Longer lifespan than air-source systems (20+ years)

Absorption Heat Pump

Unlike mechanical compression heat pumps, these systems use a thermal compression process driven by heat rather than electricity.
- Uses ammonia-water or lithium bromide-water as working fluid pairs
- Heat source (natural gas, propane, solar thermal) drives the absorption process
- No mechanical compressor needed
- **Application:** Areas with limited electrical capacity, abundant waste heat, solar thermal integration

Refrigerants

In vapor compression heat pumps, refrigerants transport heat. Refrigerants that have chlorine destroy the ozone layer and are being phased out under the Montreal Protocol, an international treaty. Refrigerants that don't contain chlorine but that have a high global warming potential are being phased down under the Kigali Amendment to the Montreal Protocol.

- **Ozone Depletion Potential (ODP)**: Ability to destroy stratospheric ozone relative to CFC-11 (assigned a value of 1.0)
- **Global Warming Potential (GWP)**: Ability to trap heat in the atmosphere relative to CO_2 (assigned a value of 1.0) over a period of time
- **Artificial Refrigerants**: synthetic substances developed to replace natural refrigerants
  - **Chlorofluorocarbons (CFCs):** phased out due to their high ozone depletion potential
  - **Hydrochlorofluorocarbon (HCFC):** developed to replace CFCs
  - **Hydrofluorocarbon (HFC):** developed to replace CFCs and HCFCs
  - **Hydrofluoroolefin (HFO):** developed to replace HCFCs and HFCs
- **Natural Refrigerants:** substances that occur naturally in the environment

Refrigerant	Type	ODP	GWP (100 yr)	Status as of 2025
R-22	HCFC	0.055	1,810	Being phased out under the Montreal Protocol
R-410A	HFC blend of R-32 and R-125	0	2,088	Being phased down under the Kigali Amendment to the Montreal Protocol
R-134a	HFC	0	1,430	Being phased down under the Kigali Amendment
R-32	HFC	0	675	Subject to phasedown under the Kigali Amendment
R-454B	HFC/HFO blend of R-32 and R-1234yf	0	466	Growing adoption
R-744 (CO_2)	Natural	0	1	Increasing use
R-1234yf	HFO	0	<1	Widely used in new automotive air conditioning systems
R-290 (propane)	Natural	0	3	Growing for small systems; flammability is a concern

Other Heat Pump Technologies without Refrigerants

- **Thermoelectric** technology uses electricity and semiconductors for cooling (the Peltier effect).
- **Magnetocaloric** heating and cooling changes magnetic fields to pump heat.
- **Thermoacoustic** heating and cooling uses high-amplitude sound waves to pump heat.
- **Adsorption cooling** uses adsorbents that capture and release refrigerant gases.
- **Vortex tubes** split compressed air into hot and cold streams.

Insulation

Basic Insulation Science

Insulation slows the natural flow of energy from hot to cold, which occurs through three mechanisms:

1. **Conduction**: Direct energy transfer through solid materials
2. **Convection**: Energy transfer through movement of molecules of air or liquid
3. **Radiation**: Energy transfer through electromagnetism

Effective insulation addresses all three mechanisms by:

- Using materials with low thermal conductivity
- Preventing moisture migration and trapping air in small pockets
- Installing reflective surfaces to redirect radiation

Key Performance Metrics

- **R-value**: Measures resistance to heat flow; higher values indicate better insulation
    - Expressed in $m^2 \cdot K/W$ (metric) or $ft^2 \cdot °F \cdot h/BTU$ (imperial)
    - R-values are additive (R-19 + R-11 = R-30)
- **U-value**: Measure of heat flow rate; lower values indicate better insulation
    - $U = 1/R$ (reciprocal of R-value)
- **Thermal conductivity (k-value)**: Lower values indicate better insulation properties
- **Thermal mass**: Ability to absorb and store heat energy
- **Vapor permeance**: Measured in "perms"; indicates moisture transmission rate
- **Air permeability**: Indicates resistance to air infiltration

Fibrous Insulation

The key to effective installation is using a vapor barrier in addition to fibrous insulation. Place this vapor barrier on the *warm* side (interior side in cold climates, exterior in hot and humid climates) to prevent moisture from passing through and condensing within your insulation. Use polyethylene plastic sheets, kraft paper backing on fiberglass insulation, or specialized vapor barrier paints.

- **Fiberglass**: Fine glass fibers arranged in a wool-like structure, trapping many small air pockets
    - Composition: 70-75% post-consumer recycled glass, silica sand, limestone, and soda ash
    - Forms: Batts, rolls, loose-fill
    - Manufacturing process: Melting glass at ~2,500°F and spinning into fibers
- **Mineral Wool**: Also called rock wool or slag wool, derived from molten rock or slag; similar basic structure as fiberglass
    - Composition: Basalt rock, slag (byproduct of steel production)
    - Forms: Batts, loose-fill
    - Manufacturing process: Melting rock or slag at ~3,000°F and spinning into fibers
- **Cellulose**: Made primarily from recycled paper products, treated with fire retardants
    - Composition: 85% post-consumer recycled paper, borate or ammonium sulfate fire retardants
    - Forms: Loose-fill, wet-spray
    - Manufacturing process: Shredding paper and treating with fire retardants

Foam Insulation

Foam insulation includes rigid boards and liquid sprays that harden to become rigid. Open cell foam contains cells that are broken, allowing some air movement and vapor diffusion and providing excellent sound dampening. Closed cell foam contains unbroken cells filled with a gas (blowing agent); it blocks the flow of air and moisture but does not dampen sound as well as open cell foam. A cell in foam refers to a tiny bubble formed when the liquid components of foam are mixed together and react chemically.

Keys to effective spray foaming are cleaning and drying surfaces, applying when ambient temperatures are within recommendations, allowing for expansion, applying uniformly (especially gaps), and allowing it to cure fully before covering. Chemicals in spray foam can be hazardous.

- **Expanded Polystyrene (EPS)**: Rigid closed-cell foam board made from polystyrene beads
  - Composition: Polystyrene polymer
  - Forms: Rigid boards, molded shapes
  - Manufacturing process: Expanding polystyrene beads with pentane and steam
- **Extruded Polystyrene (XPS)**: Melted polystyrene forced through a die to make closed-cell foam
  - Composition: Polystyrene polymer with HFC blowing agents
  - Forms: Rigid boards
  - Manufacturing process: Extrusion of polystyrene resin with blowing agents
- **Polyisocyanurate (Polyiso)**: Thermoset plastic with closed-cell structure
  - Composition: Polyisocyanurate polymer
  - Forms: Rigid boards, often foil-faced to provide a radiative barrier
  - Manufacturing process: Reaction of isocyanates with polyols and blowing agents
- **Spray Polyurethane Foam (SPF)**: Applied as a liquid that expands and hardens in place as an open-cell or closed-cell foam
  - Composition: Polyurethane polymer created by mixing isocyanates and polyols
  - Forms: Open-cell (0.5 lb/ft^3) or closed-cell (2.0 lb/ft^3) depending on mixture
  - Manufacturing process: On-site mixing and application

Reflective Insulation and Radiant Barriers

Thin sheets with highly reflective surfaces that reduce radiant heat transfer.

- Composition: Aluminum foil
- Forms: Foil-faced rigid materials or plastic films, multiple layers separated by plastic bubbles
- Manufacturing process: Aluminum applied to surface by lamination, vacuum metallization, or sputter coating

Insulation Type	R-value per inch	Blowing Agent	Moisture Resistance	Maximum Temperature	Recyclability
Fiberglass	2.2-4.3	None	Poor-Medium	538°C	Low
Mineral Wool	3.0-4.0	None	Good	1,000°C	Medium
Cellulose	3.2-3.8	None	Poor	149°C	Low
EPS	3.6-4.2	Pentane/HFOs	Good	75°C	Low
XPS	4.5-5.0	HFCs/HFOs	Excellent	74°C	Low
Polyiso	5.6-7.5	Pentane/HFOs	Good	177°C	None
Open-cell SPF	3.5-3.9	Water	Poor	82°C	None
Closed-cell SPF	6.0-7.0	HFCs/HFOs	Excellent	82°C	None

Solar Photovoltaics

Solar photovoltaic (PV) technology directly converts sunlight into electricity.

Basic Photovoltaic Science

Semiconductors with a built-in electric field:
1. Absorb photons: Suitable photons (certain frequencies of light) reach a semiconductor material
2. Excite electrons: Photons transfer their energy to electrons, freeing them from their atomic bonds
3. Separate charge: A built-in electric field forces the freed electrons to move in one direction
4. Generate current: A complete circuit allows electric current to flow

To build in an electric field, a semiconducting material (such as silicon) is "doped" with impurities:
- P-type layer (positive charge carriers): Dopants are elements missing electrons
- N-type layer (negative charge carriers): Dopants are elements with extra electrons

The boundary between these layers ("P-N junction") creates a permanent electric field. On their own (without photons bothering them), electrons tend to concentrate on the P-type side of the P-N junction. When a photon excites an electron, that creates a "hole" that another electron can fill before the excited electron can return to it. The more photons bombarding the material, creating free electrons and holes, the bigger the electron stampede from the P-type to the N-type layer.

Each combination of semiconducting material and dopants has some maximum amount of electromotive force, measured in volts, based on the strength of the electric field of the P-N junction. In light, photovoltaic materials generate direct current electricity that flows through a conductor from the positive terminal connected to the P-type layer to the negative terminal connected to the N-type layer.

From Cells to Arrays

- **Solar cell**: Basic photovoltaic unit, typically producing 0.5-0.6V
- **Solar module**: Multiple cells electrically connected together (60, 72, or more)
- **Solar array**: Multiple modules connected electrically to achieve desired voltage and current

Series and Parallel Electrical Circuits

- Connect modules in series to increase voltage.
- Connect modules in parallel to increase current.

Solar Cell Types

- **Monocrystalline silicon** (mono-Si or single-crystal silicon)
  - Made from single crystal silicon ingots
  - Recognizable by their uniform dark color and rounded edges
  - Higher efficiency (20-24%) and longer lifespan
- **Polycrystalline silicon** (poly-Si or multi-crystalline silicon)
  - Made from multiple silicon crystals melted together
  - Recognizable by their speckled blue appearance and square edges
  - Lower efficiency (15-18%) and shorter lifespan but more affordable
- **Amorphous silicon** (a-Si)
  - Non-crystalline form of silicon deposited as a thin film; uses significantly less silicon material
  - Lower efficiency (6-12%) but flexible and lightweight
  - Less affected by high temperatures

- **Cadmium telluride** (CdTe)
  - Thin film containing toxic cadmium, creating recycling challenges
  - Moderate efficiency (14-18%)
- **Copper indium gallium selenide** (CIGS)
  - Flexible thin film
  - Higher efficiency among thin films (15-20%)
- **Perovskite solar cells**
  - Rapidly improving efficiency (now exceeding 25% in lab settings)
  - Potential for low-cost manufacturing
  - Currently facing stability and durability challenges
- **Multi-junction cells**
  - Uses multiple semiconductor layers to capture different wavelengths
  - Very high efficiency (up to 47% in lab settings)
  - Primarily used in space applications due to high cost
- **Bifacial solar cells**
  - Capture light from both sides of the panel
  - Can increase energy generation by 5-30% depending on installation

Key Module Performance Specifications

- **Standard Test Conditions (STC)**: Laboratory test parameters
  - Irradiance: 1000 W/m²
  - Cell temperature: 25°C
  - Air mass: 1.5 (spectrum of light after traveling through 1.5 times Earth's atmosphere)
- **Temperature coefficient**: Rate at which performance parameters change with temperature
  - Typically -0.3% to -0.5% per °C for power output in silicon modules
- **Module efficiency**: Percentage of sunlight energy converted to electricity
- **Peak power**: Maximum current times voltage under STC, measured in watts (W)
- **Power tolerance**: Range of possible power output deviation from rated peak power (e.g., +/-3%)
- **Voltage at maximum power (Vmp)**: Voltage at which the module produces maximum power
- **Current at maximum power (Imp)**: Current at which the module produces maximum power
- **Open-circuit voltage (Voc)**: Maximum voltage produced when no current is flowing
- **Short-circuit current (Isc)**: Maximum current when the module terminals are shorted

Solar Module Performance

The current-voltage (I-V) curve graphically represents a PV module's electrical output from short circuit (zero voltage, maximum current, zero power) to maximum power point (optimal voltage, optimal current, maximum power) to open circuit (maximum voltage, zero current, zero power). To obtain maximum power from a solar module, vary the resistance of the attached circuit to adjust the amount of current flowing through it. How much electricity a module generates depends on many factors:

- **Solar irradiance**: More sunshine equals more power; output roughly proportional to irradiance
- **Temperature**: Higher temperatures decrease voltage and power output
- **Shading**: Even partial shading can significantly reduce output
- **Soiling**: Dust, dirt, snow, and other debris block sunlight
- **Degradation**: Performance decreases gradually over time (typically 0.5-1% annually)
- **Angle of incidence**: Maximum output occurs when sunlight hits the panel perpendicularly

Sustainable Practices Handbook — Technology

System Integration

Solar electricity can be used directly to power DC loads or charge batteries, or inverted to AC power.

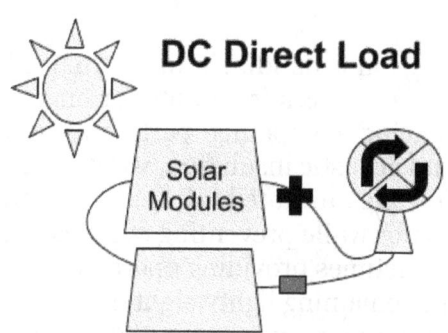

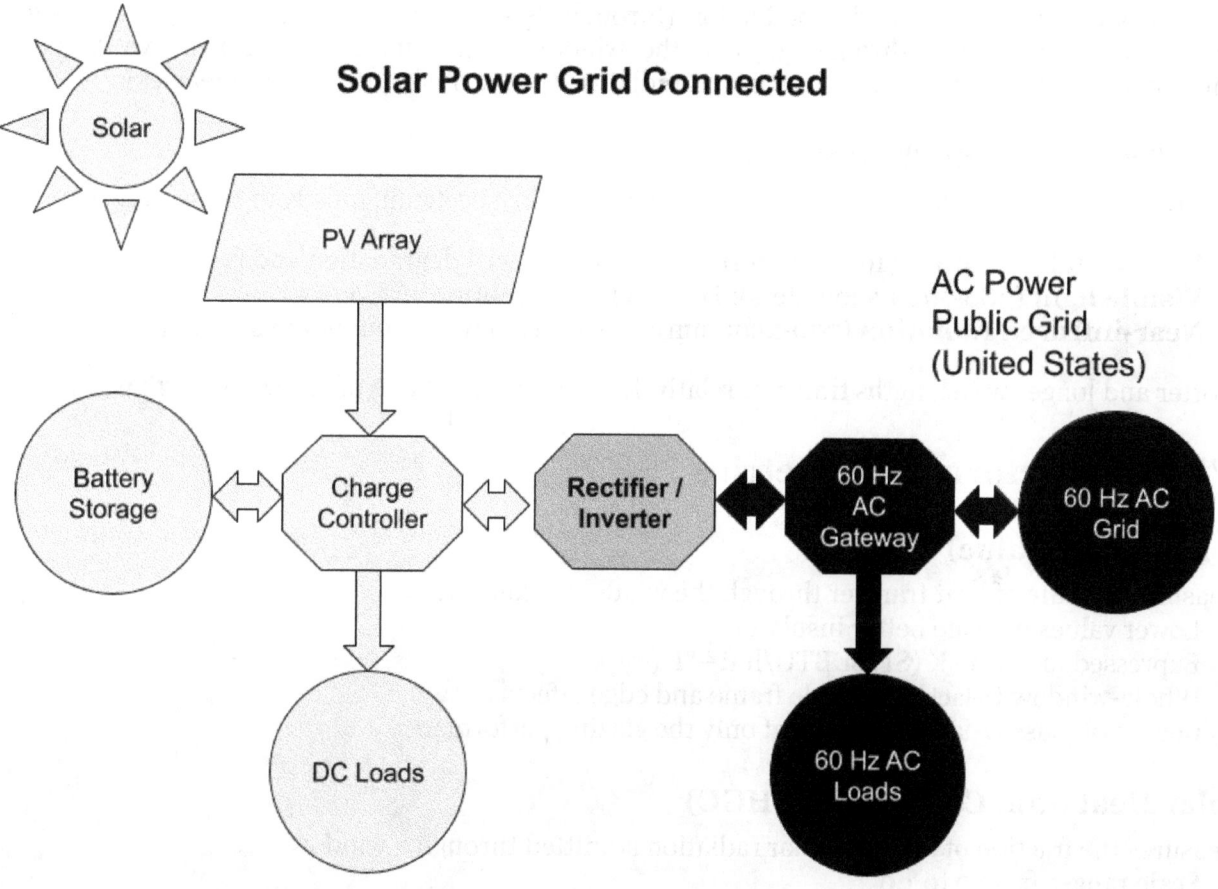

Windows

Basic Window Science

Windows are fenestration (openings in a building's walls) that admit light and allow ventilation, yet must also separate conditioned indoor spaces from outdoor environments. The fundamental technical challenge with windows is balancing competing performance requirements. While walls can be optimized primarily for thermal and acoustic insulation, windows must
- Transmit visible light while blocking unwanted infrared and ultraviolet radiation
- Allow for heat gain in cold climates while preventing overheating in warm climates
- Maintain airtight seals while sometimes providing operable ventilation
- Provide acoustic isolation while remaining lightweight enough for operation
- Resist condensation while maintaining surface temperatures close to room temperature

Heat Transfer Through Windows

Heat flows through windows via conduction (through its solid frame, spacers, and glass), convection (via air movement, both through gaps in the window's construction and convective loops inside multiple panes and on window surfaces), and radiation (primarily in infrared frequencies).

Light Transmission Physics

Windows interact with electromagnetic radiation across the spectrum, mostly in these ranges:

- **Ultraviolet radiation** (100-380 nm): Can cause material degradation and fading
- **Visible light** (380-700 nanometers): Desired for daylighting and views
- **Near-infrared radiation** (700-2500 nm): Desirable in winter but not in summer

Shorter and longer wavelengths transmit relatively negligible amounts of energy through windows.

Window Performance Metrics

U-Factor (U-Value)

Measures the rate of heat transfer through the window assembly:
- Lower values indicate better insulation
- Expressed in $W/m^2 \cdot K$ (SI) or $BTU/h \cdot ft^2 \cdot °F$ (imperial)
- Whole-window U-factors include frame and edge effects
- Center-of-glass U-factors represent only the glazing performance

Solar Heat Gain Coefficient (SHGC)

Measures the fraction of incident solar radiation admitted through a window:
- Scale ranges from 0 to 1.0
- Higher values indicate more solar heat transmission
- Climate-specific optimal values:
  - Cold climates: Higher SHGC preferred (>0.5)
  - Hot climates: Lower SHGC preferred (<0.3)
  - Mixed climates: Orientation-specific values optimal
    - High SHGC windows in northern and southern exposures for winter heating
    - Low SHGC windows in east and west exposures for summer cooling

Visible Transmittance (VT)

Measures the percentage of visible light passing through:
- Scale ranges from 0 to 1.0
- Higher values provide more natural daylight
- Modern high-performance glazing can maintain high VT (0.6-0.7) while controlling heat gain

Light-to-Solar Gain Ratio (LSG)

The ratio of visible transmittance to solar heat gain coefficient:
- Higher values (>1.25) indicate spectrally selective performance
- Premium windows achieve LSG ratios of 1.8-2.0+

Condensation Resistance

Measures a window's ability to resist the formation of condensation:
- Scale ranges from 1-100 (higher is better)
- Determined by interior surface temperatures at standardized conditions

Air Leakage

Measures air infiltration through window assembly:
- Expressed in cubic feet per minute per square foot (cfm/ft²)
- Lower values indicate better sealing performance
- High-performance windows achieve rates below 0.1 cfm/ft²

Window Components

A window system consists of several key components:
1. **Glazing**: Glass or transparent material that forms the primary barrier ("pane")
2. **Frame**: Structural support that holds the glazing and attaches to the building
3. **Spacers**: In multi-pane windows, maintain separation between glass layers
4. **Sealants**: Prevent air and water infiltration at joints
5. **Hardware**: Mechanisms for operation (hinges, locks, handles) in operable windows
6. **Weather-stripping**: Flexible materials that seal gaps in operable windows

Glazing

- **Insulated Glazing Unit (IGU)**: Two or more panes separated by a sealed space
- **Gas fill**: The space between panes is filled with a gas to reduce heat transfer
  - Air: The baseline option, inexpensive but less insulating than noble gases
  - Argon: Improves thermal performance by about 30% over air
  - Krypton: 65% more insulating than argon
  - Xenon: 38% more insulating than krypton
  - IGUs generally have a service life of 15-20 years before significant leakage occurs
- **Low-Emissivity (Low-E) Coatings**: Microscopically thin metal or metallic oxide layers applied to glass surfaces that selectively filter infrared radiation while allowing visible light to pass through

Frames

Frames can be made of wood, fiberglass, composites, aluminum or polyvinyl chloride (PVC). Fiberglass generally offers the best insulating value because it is dimensionally stable and durable, with an expansion rate similar to the glass used in glazing.

Sustainability Concepts

The United Nations defines sustainability as "meeting the needs of the present without compromising the ability of future generations to meet their own needs." Sustainability has environmental, economic, social, and legal dimensions. This handbook focuses exclusively on the core challenge of practical environmental sustainability: to *prevent* or *reduce* global risks to human well-being.

We can *adapt* to some planetary changes, but unmitigated extreme environmental changes will kill us. The Stockholm Resilience Centre, based on the work of Johan Rockström, publicizes international scientific research that quantifies "a set of nine planetary boundaries within which humanity can continue to develop and thrive for generations to come."

Planetary Boundaries

1. Climate Change	• Burning fossil fuel changes our global climate. • By reducing carbon pollution, we can **mitigate** how fast and how much more our global climate will change.
2. Ocean Acidification	• Burning fossil fuel acidifies our ocean. • By reducing carbon pollution, we can **mitigate** how fast and how much more our ocean will acidify.
3. Stratospheric Ozone Depletion	• Venting some kinds of refrigerants and propellants depletes stratospheric ozone. • By reducing chlorine and bromine emissions, we can **restore and protect** our ozone layer.
4. Loss of Biosphere Integrity	• Destroying natural habitats causes species extinction. • By allowing and encouraging plants, fungi, and animals to grow and reproduce naturally, we can **protect** Earth's biodiversity.
5. Deforestation	• Killing trees harms global ecosystems. • By killing fewer trees, we can **protect** global ecosystems.
6. Atmospheric Aerosols	• Burning fuel dumps aerosols into our atmosphere. • By using clean energy, we can **restore and protect** clean air.
7. Novel Substance Pollution	• Releasing new substances (chemicals and plastics) pollutes our planet. • By reducing our use of novel substances, we can mitigate future pollution. • By collecting and recycling materials into safer products, we can **restore and protect** a healthful environment.
8. Freshwater Depletion	• Overusing water depletes freshwater resources. • By reducing our water use, we can **prevent** freshwater shortages.
9. Excess Nutrients	• Dumping excess nitrogen and phosphorus harms aquatic ecosystems. • By reducing nitrogen and phosphorus discharges, we can **restore and protect** healthy aquatic ecosystems.

United Nations Sustainable Development Goals

In 2015, all United Nations members adopted the 2030 Agenda for Sustainable Development, committing the world to 17 Sustainable Development Goals:

1. No Poverty
2. Zero Hunger
3. Good Health and Well-Being
4. Quality Education
5. Gender Equality
6. Clean Water and Sanitation
7. Affordable and Clean Energy
8. Decent Work and Economic Growth
9. Industry, Innovation and Infrastructure
10. Reduced Inequalities
11. Sustainable Cities and Communities
12. Responsible Consumption and Production
13. Climate Action
14. Life Below Water
15. Life On Land
16. Peace and Justice, Strong Institutions
17. Partnerships for the Goals

Global Environmental Issues

Activists and journalists often group global environmental issues into nine categories:

1. ***Human-caused climate change*** (also called ***global warming***) occurs because human activities have unnaturally increased concentrations of greenhouse gases such as carbon dioxide and methane in Earth's atmosphere. These gases persist for decades or centuries, trapping excess heat near the surface of our planet.

2. ***Ocean acidification*** is happening due to burning fossil fuel which raises levels of carbon dioxide, methane, and other pollution in Earth's atmosphere. From air, these gasses dissolve into water, where they form acids.

3. ***Deforestation*** is happening mostly to create pasture for livestock, primarily cattle. Loss of forests leads to soil erosion, changes in rainfall patterns, and loss of biodiversity.

4. ***Extinctions*** occur mainly due to climate change, ocean acidification, deforestation, introduced diseases, and competition from non-native species. The loss of species permanently changes ecosystems and often lowers their productivity.

5. ***Hazardous pollution*** is happening for many reasons, including burning fossil fuel for energy and using hazardous compounds in products. Pollution harms people and other forms of life.

6. ***Freshwater scarcity*** is happening largely due to withdrawals for animal agriculture and inadequate infrastructure. Lack of water makes it harder to grow food.

7. ***Soil depletion*** is caused by unsustainable agricultural practices. A lack of fertile topsoil makes it harder to grow food.

8. ***Poverty*** is happening mostly because wealth is being concentrated rather than redistributed. Poverty stunts human development and can lead to violence.

9. ***Resource limits*** exist; their effects depend on our level of technology and infrastructure. If we fail to improve our technology and infrastructure quickly enough, our population will grow beyond our resource limits, leading to greater poverty, misery, and death.

Sustainability Scoring Systems

The Suspra Score is an evolved version of the *ecological footprint* idea. Many other systems exist.

Ecological Footprint

Mathis Wackernagel and William Rees developed The **Ecological Footprint** concept in 1990 to measure how much nature we have and how much nature we use. On the supply side, biocapacity measures the ability of the Earth's surface to provide resources and absorb waste. On the demand side, our Ecological Footprint adds up all the biologically productive surface area of the Earth required to produce the resources we consume and absorb the waste we produce, especially our carbon emissions.

Carbon Footprint

A carbon footprint measures the amount of gas with global warming potential, expressed in units of carbon dioxide equivalent, released into the atmosphere as a result of activities over a period of time. Greenhouse Gas Protocol, developed by the World Resources Institute and the World Business Council for Sustainable Development, categorizes emissions as scope 1 direct emissions, scope 2 indirect emissions from electricity consumed, and scope 3 indirect emissions from other entities that provide goods or services. Greenhouse gasses are a concern because they persist in our atmosphere and warm our planet over many years.

Green Building Standards

See Practice Guide Certifying 301: Certifying Your Sustainability on page 76.

IPAT Equation (Limits to Growth)

In 1972, Paul Ehrlich and John Holdren proposed the **IPAT equation** to model the world's total environmental impact (I) as a function of population size (P) times affluence (A) times technology (T).

$$I = PAT$$

If P, the world's population, continues to grow (as projected), we can still quickly reduce our total environmental impact by improving practices to conserve resources to reduce A, our *affluence* factor, and to implement more sustainable technology to reduce T, our *technology* factor.

Glossary

New words can yield new sensitivity, for vocabulary filters experience, shapes perception, and guides understanding.

– *William R. Catton, Jr.*
  OVERSHOOT: The Ecological Basis of Revolutionary Change

Acidification: a reduction in pH
Ocean water is becoming less basic and more acidic, primarily as a result of absorbing carbon dioxide from the atmosphere, which makes it more difficult for shellfish, coral, and calcareous plankton to grow calcium carbonate shells.

Aerosol loading: adding particles, such as smoke, soot, dust, to the atmosphere

Ambient air: air at its natural temperature, not actively heated or cooled

Anthropogenic climate change: changes to long-term weather patterns due to human activity

Bioaccumulate: to pervade the environment and be found in greater concentrations in biological tissues over time and at higher trophic levels in the food web

Biodegradable: materials that naturally decompose to safe and inert substances

Carbon dioxide: a *greenhouse gas* that is accumulating in our atmosphere primarily as a result of burning fossil fuel
Besides warming our planet, more carbon dioxide in our atmosphere causes *acidification* of rivers, lakes, and oceans.

Carbon footprint: the amount of *greenhouse gasses* emitted as a result of activities over a period of time, expressed in units of *global warming potential* with carbon dioxide as the base unit
GHG Protocol defines three scopes: 1) direct emissions, 2) indirect emissions from electricity, and 3) indirect "upstream" and "downstream" emissions as a result of all other activities.

Carbon pollution: carbon pollution is carbon monoxide and carbon dioxide emitted into the atmosphere by burning carbohydrates (such as wood) or hydrocarbons (fossil fuel)
Burning carbohydrates or hydrocarbons produces both carbon monoxide, which is immediately dangerous to human life or health at 1,200 parts per million, and carbon dioxide, which is immediately dangerous to human life or health at 40,000 parts per million and contributes to both global warming and ocean acidification. Carbon monoxide is oxidized to carbon dioxide within a few years; carbon dioxide persists in air for centuries.

Carcinogenic: causing cancer

Circular economy: an economic system designed to eliminate waste and continually reuse resources
Materials are kept in use through reuse, repair, remanufacturing, and recycling, minimizing resource inputs and waste generation. Unlike the traditional linear "take-make-discard" model, a circular economy keeps products and materials in productive cycles for as long as possible.

Composting: using oxygen-breathing microbes, fungi, and other organisms to decompose organic waste into a nutrient-rich soil amendment

Conservation: a reduction in the consumption of a resource; may lower living standards

Decomposition: breaking down organic matter into simpler substances by microorganisms, fungi, and other decomposers

Digesting: using anaerobic microbes in air-tight vessels sealed off from atmospheric oxygen to decompose organic waste into biogas (mostly methane, carbon dioxide, and water)
Biogas can be directly burned for electricity or scrubbed of carbon dioxide and other impurities to produce methane that meets standards for distribution in natural gas pipelines.

Diminishing (non-renewable) resource: a resource, such as petroleum, that does not replenish naturally; as this type of resource is consumed, the amount remaining diminishes

Downcycling: taking a waste material and recycling it in a way that produces a less valuable material than the virgin material
Recycled plastic waste is most often downcycled rather than recycled.

Ecological footprint: a measure of the biologically productive surface area of the Earth required to produce resources and absorb waste

Efficiency: reducing consumption of a resource without lowering living standards

Egregiously unsustainable: practices that have much worse environmental impacts than close substitutes, such as eating domesticated beef compared to wild-caught venison

Energy: the ability to change temperature, accelerate mass, compute calculations, and convert one form of energy to another
The scientific unit of energy is the *joule*, but a common unit is the *kilowatt hour*: the energy of one thousand *watts* of *power* expended for one hour.

Environmental impacts: changes to natural processes as a result of human activities

Energy productivity: a measure of how effectively energy resources are being used to create value
The closely related term, energy efficiency, emphasizes the technical aspects of reducing energy input for the same amount of work output. Reducing energy waste through technological improvements and system optimization can increase both energy efficiency and energy productivity.

Enzymes: biodegradable proteins that remove stains and odors by catalyzing reactions to break down molecules to pieces that are more easily removed by surfactants and detergents

Eutrophication: an increase in the concentration of plant nutrients in water
If excessive, this can lead to algae blooms and die-offs that deplete oxygen and kill aquatic animals.

EV: an electric vehicle, either a battery electric vehicle (BEV) or a plug-in hybrid electric vehicle (PHEV)

Forever chemicals: synthetic substances that do not decompose naturally and therefore tend to persist and bioaccumulate

Global warming potential: how much heat a type of gas traps in our atmosphere, expressed in relation to the global warming potential of carbon dioxide

Green building: designing and constructing buildings in ways that minimize negative environmental impacts while maximizing resource efficiency
Green building uses sustainable materials and methods, reduces energy and water consumption, and creates healthy indoor environments. Common green building standards include LEED (Leadership in Energy and Environmental Design), Living Building Challenge, and Passivhaus.

Greenhouse gasses: gasses that trap heat in our atmosphere, warming Earth's surface

Habitable land: Earth's solid surface area that is not covered by water, glaciers, deserts and other barren land; land that humans can inhabit

Incandescent lighting: lighting that produces light by heating a metal filament until it glows, converting only about 5% of input energy to visible light while the rest becomes heat

Integrated pest management: monitoring for, identifying, observing, and controlling pests using interventions that have the least environmental harm

Hazardous: activities or substances that can cause harm, especially hazardous waste

Jevons paradox (or Jevons effect): increasing the efficiency of resource use can lead to greater consumption rather than conservation of the resource due to induced demand
For example, improving energy efficiency lowers energy costs which induces demand for energy. Taking efficiency measures may counter-intuitively result in more energy being consumed.

Joule: a unit of energy equal to the work done when a force of one newton moves an object one meter, or when one watt of power is applied for one second

kWh: kilowatt hour, the energy of a thousand watts of power for one hour

Life-cycle analysis: a systematic assessment of the "cradle-to-cradle" environmental impacts associated with a product, service, or system, including extracting raw materials, manufacturing, distributing, using, and disposing of or recycling finished goods and supplies

Microplastics: small pieces of plastic debris less than 5,000 microns in size (the size of a pencil eraser or smaller)

Mutagenic: causing genetic mutations

MWh: megawatt hour, the energy of a million watts of power for one hour

Natural: processes that occur without human intervention

Nominal dollars: prices *not* adjusted for inflation

Organic matter: material that comes from living organisms, containing carbon

Parsimony: the inverse of the rate of resource consumption; expressed as time per unit
The units of parsimony depend on the resource. *Energy parsimony* is measured in seconds per joule (or minutes per kWh). It is the inverse of *power* (which is measured in joules per second).

Pescatarian diet: a diet that includes vegetables, fruits, grains, legumes, nuts, seeds, and aquatic animals including fish and shellfish, but excludes other animals
A pescatarian diet may or may not include eggs and dairy products. The prefix "pesca-" derives from "piscis," the Latin word for fish. See also, *vegan diet, vegetarian diet*

Permeable surfaces: ground coverings that allow water to pass through to underlying soil

PFAS: per- and polyfluoroalkyl substances that are *forever chemicals* of concern

Planetary boundaries: "safe limits for human pressure on the nine critical processes which together maintain a stable and resilient Earth," as defined by the Stockholm Resilience Centre
Environmental scientists in 2009 at the Stockholm Resilience Centre and Australian National University developed a science-based framework to quantify how far human activities can push Earth systems before triggering catastrophic changes.

Power: energy per time
 The unit of power is the watt, one joule per second.

Pumped hydropower: an energy storage system that uses two water reservoirs at different elevations, pumping water to the higher reservoir when excess electricity is available and releasing it through turbines to the lower reservoir to generate electricity when needed

Photovoltaic (PV): producing electricity from light

Real dollars: *nominal dollars* adjusted for inflation
 Pricing in real dollars allows meaningful comparisons of consumption between time periods.

Recyclable: materials that can be recycled
 Reasonable people disagree about what is recyclable, especially plastics. For waste plastic to achieve the same material properties as virgin plastic, the polymer must be completely broken down to the monomer, all contaminants must be removed, and the polymer must be reassembled from the monomer, which is not practical to do. Instead, plastic waste is *downcycled* or *wish-cycled*.

Recycling: collecting and processing waste material so that it can be reused for an equivalent purpose

Regenerative: farming methods that ensure land remains agriculturally productive in perpetuity

Renewable: a resource, especially energy, that replenishes naturally

Resource: a material, energy source, or natural system that can be used to meet human needs
 Resources can be renewable (naturally replenishing within human timescales) or diminishing (non-renewable, with finite available quantities).

Restorative process: a process by which a natural environment returns to a healthy, self-sustaining state by rebuilding soil health, water quality, biodiversity, or other ecological functions
 Restorative processes go beyond merely reducing negative impacts to actively improving environmental conditions, such as regenerative agriculture practices that build soil fertility.

Safe share: each person's share of consumption and pollution that stays within planetary boundaries; calculated by taking safe limits at a planetary scale and dividing by the number of people on Earth

Sequestered carbon: carbon that is chemically in a solid state, such as coal, rather than in a gaseous state, such as carbon dioxide
 Burning fossil fuel releases carbon from a sequestered state. *Sequestration* is chemically reacting carbon dioxide or carbon monoxide gas with another substance to produce a solid product that becomes part of a living organism or part of the Earth's crust.

Solar year: approximately 365.25 days; Earth's annual orbit time around the sun
 Leap years occur every fourth year because the Earth's annual orbit time is approximately 365 and one quarter days.

Suspra App: a web app for practical sustainability, published by Sustainable Practice

Suspra Certification Exam: a test of knowledge across a full range of practical sustainability topics

Suspra Score: a score that quantifies the sustainability of practices along seven pathways
 A *negative* Suspra Score indicates that practices have impacts that exceed planetary boundaries, so they are *unsustainable*; a *positive* score indicates that practices are *sustainable*.

Sustainability: the ability to meet current needs in ways that allow our posterity to meet their needs

Sustainability indicators: measurements of the rate and type of resource use and pollution emissions in a system
 These measurements for a home or organization indicate whether the environmental impacts of practices are within or exceed the ability of natural systems to regenerate and persist.

Teratogenic: causing birth defects

Trophic level: the functional distance from the primary energy source of an ecosystem
 Sunlight is primary energy. Plants that use sunlight directly are at the first trophic level; herbivores are at a higher trophic level; and carnivores on up to apex predators are at the highest trophic level.

Toxic: substances that are especially hazardous to humans or other life
 Toxins can be poisonous, radioactive, explosive, *carcinogenic* (causing cancer), *mutagenic* (causing genetic mutations), or *teratogenic* (causing birth defects).

Upcycling: taking a waste material and recycling or reusing it in a way that produces a more valuable product than the virgin material
 An example is upcycling old sails into expensive bags.

Vegan diet: eating everything except animal-derived food products
 Vegans avoid eating meat, fish, poultry, dairy, and eggs. *Entovegans* eat insects but no other animal food products. Some vegans avoid eating honey because bees produce it.

Vegetarian diet: eating everything except animals
 Animals include mammals, reptiles, amphibians, birds, and fish. Some vegetarians also avoid eating multicellular invertebrates like insects, but eat substances that insects produce, such as honey. A *lacto-ovo vegetarian diet* is a plant-based diet that includes eggs and dairy and mushrooms, but excludes meat, fish, and poultry. See also, *vegan diet*, *pescatarian diet*

Watt: a unit of power equal to one joule of energy per second
 Power is the rate at which energy is transferred or work is done.

Wish-cycling: putting items in a recycling bin even though they won't actually be recycled
 Wish-cycling soothes the guilt of over-consumption or buying disposable products for convenience. Plastic waste is often wish-cycled.

Xeriscape: a landscaping approach that minimizes water usage
 The term combines "xeros" (Greek for "dry") with "landscape."

Index

A - B

Accessory Dwelling Units, 461
Action
    Advanced Practices, 74
    Intermediate Practices, 74
    Quick-Start Practices, 73
    Transformative Practices, 75
Active Transportation
    see Cycling
    see Walking
Aerators, 222
Affordability, 2
Air Travel, Minimizing, 261
Antimicrobial Soap, 548
Apartment Living, 457
Appliances
    Dishwashers, 228
    Kitchen Composting, 430
    Refrigerators, 325
    Repairing, 415
    Smart Strips, 312
    Unplugging, 341
    Upgrading, 312
    Ventless Dryers, 331
    Washing Machines, 230, 330
Artificial Intelligence, Prompting, 55
Asbestos, 469
Awnings, see *Fenestration*
Backyard Habitat, 501
Baths, *see Showers*
Batteries, 541
    Battery Management Systems (BMS), 545
    Charging, 545
    Installing, 373, 487
    Lithium-Ion, 543
    Other Chemistries, 544
    Rechargeable, 409
    Safety, 545
Bicycles, *see Cycling*

Biodiversity, Registering, 500
Biology, Fundamental Principles, 527
    Animal Biology, 530
    Cellular Biology, 527
    Conservation Biology, 533
    Ecology, 532
    Evolution and Biodiversity, 529
    Genetics, 528
    Microbiology, 531
    Molecular Biology, 527
    Plant Biology, 529
    Soil Biology, 532
Blinds, see *Fenestration*
Borrowing and Lending, 507
    Electric Tools, Lending 360
    Tools, Borrowing 381
    Tools, Lending, 388
Bottled Water, Avoiding, 176
Bridges, Building, 254
Building
    Adobe, 480
    ADUs, 461
    Apartments, 456
    Cementitious Siding, 474
    Foundations, 471
    Homes, 455
    In-Law Apartments, 488
    Lumber, Reclaiming, 472
    Lumber, Selecting, 470
    Offices, 456
    Performance Ratings, 459
    Rammed Earth, 478
    Straw Bale, 476
Buildings, Removing, 499
Burners, Inspecting, 312
Businesses, Starting, 120
Buying
    Buying Less, 383
    in Bulk, 385
    Quality, 381
Buy Nothing Groups, 387

C - D

Canning, *see Food, Preserving*
Carbon Footprint, 564
Car-Free Living, 268
Carpooling, 261
Cats, Keeping Indoors, 496
Caulking, *see Sealing*
Certifications, Developing, 123
Chemistry, Fundamental Principles, 517
Chickens, 206
Chimneys, Removing, 280
Chocolate, 189
Cleaning, 245 to 249
    Electrolyzed Water, 249
    Microfiber, 400
    Soap, 246
    Steaming, 247
Clothing
    Natural Fiber, 401
    Repairing, 413
Coffee, 190
Cohousing, 458
Cold-Water Enzymes, 547
Committing, 504
    Committing to Improve, 78
Community Kitchens, 170
Composting
    Buried Chambers, 435
    Burying, 423
    Collecting Household Waste, 420
    Collecting Kitchen Waste, 419
    Collecting Leaves, 421
    Curbside, 424
    Fermenting First, 431
    Kitchen Appliance, 430
    Municipal, 426
    Neighborhood, 447
    Safety, 419
    Single Pile, 422
    Three Bins, 427
    Tumblers, 433
    with Flies, 440

    with Worms, 438
Contaminated Soil, 466
Cooking
    Cold Meals, 336
    Convection, 286
    Induction, 285
    Microwave Ovens, 333
    Multiple Meals, 337
    Outside, 335
    Pressure Cookers, 334
    Solar Cooking, 339
    with Electricity, 354
Crafting, 382
Cycling, 266
    Cycling, E-Bikes, 276
Dairy
    Plant-based Substitutes, 187 to 188
Detergents, 546
    Additives, 548
    Enzymes, 547
    Phosphates, 247
    Soiling Classification, 549
Dishwashers, *see Appliances*
Disinfectants, 548
Dogs, on Leash, 496
Donating and Reselling, 443 to 444
Doors, see *Fenestration*
Downsizing, 457
Drinking, Cold Beverages, 341
Driving Efficiently, 340 to 341
Drying Food, *see Food, Preserving*
Ducts
    Cleaning, 482
    Insulating, 310
    Sealing, 291

E - F

Earth Science, Fundamental Principles, 522
Earthworks, 525
Easements, 496
Eating
    Leftovers, 143

    Portion Sizes, 141
E-Bikes, *see Cycling, E-Bikes*
Ecological Footprint, 564
Economics, Fundamental Principles, 536
    Behavioral Economics, 538
    Environmental Economics, 538
    Government Interventions, 537
    Public Finance, 540
    Sustainable Business, 539
Ecosystem Services, 535
Eggs, *see Chickens*
Electricity, 515
Electric Motors, 550
    AC Motors, 550
    Control, 551
    DC Motors, 550
Electrolyzed Water, 249
Energy Concepts, 515
    Energy Economics, 539
Energy Economizing, 341 to 342
Energy Recovery Ventilator, *see Ventilation*
Energy Units, 512
Engine Starts, Minimizing, 261
Evaluating Practices, 503
EVs, *see Vehicles*
Fans
    Ceiling, 294
    Cleaning, 482
    Solar, 370
    Whole Home, 296
    Wood Stove, 289
Farms
    Supporting Local, 137
    Supporting Organic, 190
Fencing, 256
Fenestration
    Awnings, 314
    Blinds, 313
    Doors, Installing, 320
    Windows, Closing, 312
    Windows, Installing, 318
    Windows, Opening, 346
    Windows, Repairing, 315 to 317

    Window Inserts, 313
Fermenting, *see Food, Preserving*
Fiberglass Fenestration, 472
Filters, Replacing, 310
Financial Analysis, 505
    Compound Interest, 507
    Financial Concepts, 537
    Internal Rate of Return, 506
    Levelized Cost of Energy, 506
    Modified Internal Rate of Return, 506
    Mortgages, 507
    Net Present Value, 505
    Return on Investment, 505
    Savings, 505
    Simple Interest, 507
    Simple Payback, 505
Food
    Buying, 128 to 139
    Distributing, 155
    Growing, 191 to 212
    In Season, 139
    Labeling, 172
    Organizing Donations, 152
    Preserving, 166
    Safety, 174
    Storing, 159 to 170
    Unsustainable Ingredients, 176
Freecycle Network
    Joining, 388
    Leading, 392
Freezing Food, *see Food, Preserving*
Fruits and Nuts, Growing, 199

G - H - I - J - K

Garden, Growing, 202
Geology, *see Earth Science*
Giving Experiences, 381
Global Environmental Issues, 563
Goals, *see Planning*
Goals, Setting, 504
Goods and Supplies
    Reusables, 409

Government, Seeking Office, 126
Green Building Standards, 564
Green Electricity, 364
Green Roofs, *see Roofing, Green*
Grid-Tied Solar, *see Solar, Electricity*
Growing Food, *see Food, Growing*
Gutters, 485
Hanging Laundry to Dry, 352
Hazardous Waste, *see Waste, Hazardous*
Hazards, Identifying, 495
Heat, 516
Heating & Cooling
    Heat Distribution, 301
    with Electricity, 356
Heat Pumps, 552
    Absorption, 553
    Air-to-Air, 553
    Air-to-Water, 553
    Buying Group, 358
    Ground-Source, 553
    Hot Water, 323
    Installing, 298
    Other Technologies, 554
Heat Recovery Ventilator, *see Ventilation*
Herbs, Growing, 197
Hot Water
    Electric, 361
    Heat Pumps, 323
    Lowering Temperature, 346
    Recirculation, 233
    Scheduling, 346
    Solar, 370
Household Hazardous Waste, *see Waste, Hazardous*
Housing, High Performance, 457
Humidity, 483
Insulating, 279
    Fiberglass, 481
    Pipes, 322
Insulation, 555
    Fibrous Insulation, 555
    Foam Insulation, 555
    Reflective and Radiant Barriers, 556

International System of Units (SI), 510
IPAT Equation (Limits to Growth), 564
Irrigation, 226
Jobs, Environmental, 119
Junk Removal, 443
Knowledge
    Learning, 56 to 65
    Sharing, 87 to 106
    Verifying, 66 to 68

L - M

Land Conservation, 500
Landfilling, 443
Landscaping
    Electric Equipment, 359
    Native Plants, 490
    Organic, 493
    Shade Trees, 302
    Windbreaks, 304
Leading
    Repair Teams, 416
Lead Paint, 465
Learning, *see Knowledge*
LEDs, *see Lighting*
Legislation, Proposing, 125
Legumes, 178
Lending
    see Borrowing and Lending
    see Financial Analysis
Library of Things, 390
Light Emitting Diodes, *see Lighting*
Lighting
    Controls, 306
    Dimming, 307
    Fluorescent, 463
    Installing LEDs, 305
    Light Pipes, 309
    Reducing Power, 344
Lighting, Solar, 367
Lighting, Task Lighting, 345
Lighting, Turning Off, 344
Light-to-Solar Gain Ratio (LSG), 561

Light Transmission, 560
Lithium-Ion, *see Batteries*
Litter, Picking Up, 257
Local Farms, *see Farms*
Maintenance, System, 310
Manuals, Keeping, 410
Maple Syrup, Making, 209
Materials
    Recyclable, 406
    RoHS, 408
Math, 508
    Mathematical Symbols, 509
    Numbers, by Magnitude, 508
    Numbers, Notable, 509
Meal Planning, 151
    Organizing Recipes, 150
Measuring Results, 503
    Tracking Metrics, 80 to 85
Meat-Free Mondays, 184
Medical Waste, *see Waste, Medical*
Menstrual Products, 387
Mercury, Avoiding, 396
Mercury Thermostats, 464
Microfiber Cloths, *see Cleaning*
Microgreens, Growing, 194
Microgrid, *see Solar, DC Microgrid*
Milk, *see Dairy*

N - O - P - Q - R

Nutrition, Understanding, 184
Offgrid Solar, *see Solar, DC Microgrid*
Organic Label, *see USDA Organic*
Painting, 488
Palm Oil, 189
Per- and polyfluoroalkyl substances (PFAS)
    in Clothing, 402
    in Cookware, 404
    in Furniture, 405
Permaculture, 212
Permeable Paving, 252
Pest Management, 491
pH and Acid-Base Chemistry, 518

Photovoltaic (PV), *see Solar*
Physical Constants, 511
Physics, Fundamental Principles, 514
Planetary Boundaries, 562
Planning Projects, 503
    Goals, Setting, 79
    Plans, Detailed, 80
    Plans, Simple, 79
Plant-based Meals, 182 to 188
Plastic
    Avoiding, 398
    Deplastifying, 395
    Recycling, 473
Plumbing, Protecting Pipes, 488
Politics, *see Government*
Possessions, Organizing, 389
Power Units, 513
Power Strips, *see Appliances, Smart Strips*
Rain Gardens, 250
Recycling
    Electronics and Batteries, 452
    Metal, Cardboard, and Glass, 452
    Plastic, 473
Refrigerants, 554
Refrigeration, 325
    Economizing, 348 to 349
Renting Items, 381
Restaurants, Creating, 185
Restriction on Hazardous Substances (RoHS), *see Materials*
Reusing
    Accepting Items, 413
    Containers, 412
    Jars, 413
    Organizing a Program, 411
    Thrifting, 413
Ride Sharing, 276
Riparian Buffer Zones, 257
Roads, Removing, 498
Roofing
    Cool, 283
    Green, 254
    Leaks, 484

Metal, 475
Roommates, 460
Root Cellar, 350

- S -

Seafood
- Certified, 177
- Endangered, 176
- Farmed, 181
- Shark, 181

Sealing
- Caulking, 326
- Weatherstripping, 328

Shade Trees, see *Landscaping*
Sharing, see *Knowledge*
Shopping Online, 261
Showers
- Navy Showers, 236
- Showerheads, 222
- Taking Showers, 236

Soap,
- see *Cleaning*
- see *Detergents*

Soil Science, 522
Solar
- Battery Storage, 373
- Chargers, 363
- Community Solar Farm, 365
- Cooking, 339
- DC Microgrid, 378
- Electricity, 372
- Fans, 370
- Group Purchasing, 376
- Hot Water, 370
- Investing, 375
- Lighting, 367
- Passive, 281
- Solar Shed, 366
- Water Pumps, 368

Solar Photovoltaics, 557
- Series and Parallel Electrical Circuits, 557
- Solar Cell Types, 557
- System Integration, 559

Solar Tubes, see *Lighting, Light Pipes*
Solid Waste, see *Waste*
Solvents, 548
Soup Stock, Making, 147
Sprouting Seeds, 191
Sun Tunnels, see *Lighting, Light Pipes*
Suspra Indicators, see *Sustainability Indicators*
Sustainability
- Certifying, 76
- Coaching, 109, 113 and 115
- Defining, 1
- Practicing, 2

Sustainability Committees, 112
Sustainability Indicators
- of Community Practices, 54
- of Energy Practices, 278
- of Food Practices, 127
- of Goods Practices, 380
- of Movement Practices, 260
- of Water Practices, 216
- of Habitat Practices, 454
- Suspra Indicators, 10

Sustainability Scoring Systems, 564
Synchronizing
- Sleep Schedule, 352
- Solar Power, 352

T - U - V

Take-away Containers, 146
Taking Action, see *Action*
Telecommuting
- Employing Workers, 263
- Working From Home, 262

Temperature, 511
Tenants, 460
Thermodynamics, 516
Thermostats
- Adjusting, 343
- Programming, 288
- Setting, 288

Thrifting, see *Reusing*

Time, 511
Toilets
- Composting Toilets, 240
- Displacing Tank Water, 234
- Flush Toilets, 223
- Flushing, 235
- Incinerating Toilets, 242
- Waterless Urinals, 238

Tracking, *see Measuring Results*
Transit, 270
Ugly Food, 128
United Nations Sustainable Development Goals, 563
USDA Organic, 189
Vapor Barriers, 467
Vegan, *see Plant-based Meals*
Vegetarian, *see Plant-based Meals*
Vehicles
- Buying an EV, 274
- Cruise Control, 322
- Electric, 355
- Inflating Tires, 321
- Plug-In Hybrids, 274
- Racks, 322
- Renting Electric, 274

Ventilation, 299
Verifying, *see Knowledge*
Vermicomposting, *see Composting with Worms*
Volatile Organic Compounds (VOCs), Avoiding, 397
Volunteering, 107 to 115
Voting, 118, 500

W - X - Y - Z

Walking, 271 to 272
- Walkable Neighborhood, 456

Washing
- in Cold Water, 330
- Less Frequently, 384

Washing Machines, *see Appliances*
Waste
- Five Streams, 444
- Hazardous Waste, Collecting, 449
- Hazardous Waste, Storing, 445
- Medical and Hazardous Waste, 257

Water Leaks, Detecting and Fixing, 217 to 219
Water Resource Management, 525
Water Use, Economizing, 221, 235 to 236
Weatherstripping, *see Sealing*
Wild Game, 178
- Venison, 177

Windbreaks, *see Landscaping*
Window Inserts, *see Fenestration*
Windows, *see also Fenestration*
- Air Leakage, 561
- Condensation Resistance, 561
- Frames, 561
- Glazing, 561
- Heat Transfer, 560
- Solar Heat Gain Coefficient (SHGC), 560
- U-Factor (U-Value), 560
- Visible Transmittance (VT), 561

Wood Stoves, 292
- Fans, 289

Workplace Suggestions, 119
Xeriscaping, 236
Yard Sale, Neighborhood, 450

What did we miss?
SustainablePractice.Life/feedback

Edition: *2025*
Major Revision: *1*
Minor Revision: *8*

*A **new edition** will be published each year.*

***Major revisions** correct factual errors, add new material, or remove outdated material.*

www.ingramcontent.com/pod-product-compliance
Lightning Source LLC
Chambersburg PA
CBHW080538030426
42337CB00024B/4792